HANDBOOK OF PSYCHOLOGICAL ASSESSMENT

HANDBOOK OF PSYCHOLOGICAL ASSESSMENT

SECOND EDITION

Gary Groth-Marnat

A Wiley-Interscience Publication

John Wiley & Sons

New York • Chichester • Brisbane • Toronto • Singapore

Library of Congress Cataloging-in-Publication Data

Groth-Marnat, Gary
    Handbook of psychological assessment/Gary Groth-Marnat. -- 2nd
  ed.
       p.   cm. -- (Wiley series on personality processes)
  Includes bibliographical references.
  ISBN 0-471-51034-3
  1. Psychological tests.   2. Personality assessment.   I. Title.
  II. Series.
  BF176.G76   1990
  150'.28'7--dc20   90-30640
                                                CIP

Printed in the United States of America
90 91 10 9

To Julie

CONTENTS

PREFACE

The first edition of the *Handbook of Psychological Assessment* was developed as a teaching and reference source for the most frequently used assessment instruments. It described and provided guidelines for the typical assessment procedure beginning with issues related to the role of the clinician and ending with the psychological report. A major portion of the first edition presented material on interpreting the seven most frequently used psychological tests. The presentation was made in a manner that would provide information on interpreting test scores, as well as provide ways to integrate these scores with other information and with the overall context and purpose of assessment.

The overall rationale and motivation behind writing the first edition is still present and has been incorporated into the second edition. However, much has changed within the field of assessment during the past six years. The more noteworthy of these changes include new editions of the MMPI and CPI, extensive research on the WAIS-R, greatly increased popularity of computer-based test interpretations, greater importance of structured clinical interviews, a current review of projective drawings, an emphasis on integrating behavioral and traditional forms of assessment, and an increased emphasis on neuropsychological assessment. All of the above areas have been accompanied by extensive literature. These changes and the accompanying literature have helped guide the development of this second edition.

In addition to noting changes within the field of assessment, I have also undergone changes in thinking and approaching the process of assessment. Many of these changes have been encouraged by discussions with colleagues and, in particular, by reviews of the first edition. Levinson refers to the midlife transition as a "flawed success," and certainly the phrase is appropriate for the first edition of a book. I thank my colleagues for the support and success of the first edition, but I also clearly see how it could have been improved.

My personal reflections and continued professional development, along with changes in the field of assessment, have resulted in a number of changes and additions to this second edition. General changes in emphasis include a more rigorous empirical evaluation of assessment strategies, greater emphasis on neuropsychological assessment, reference to a much wider range of instruments, extensive updating, the inclusion of a greater number of approaches and instruments, and a greater emphasis on both empirical guidelines as well as the processes involved in clinical decision making. The result has been the inclusion of a number of different specific chapters, sections, and subsections. These include an expansion of the first chapter into two chapters as well as chapters on the assessment interview and behavioral assessment. Specific new sections/subsections include patterns of test usage, incremental validity, clinical judgment, selecting psychological tests, computer-assisted interpretation, structured interviewing, specific strategies of behavioral assessment, incorporation of the Lack's system of Bender scoring, and the inclusion of material on the Beck Depression Inventory, Fear Survey Schedule, and the Rathus Assertiveness Schedule. My hope is that all of the above changes will not only satisfy my reviewers, but, more importantly, provide practitioners and students with a much more comprehensive, indepth, and useful guide for assessing persons.

The first edition of the *Handbook of Psychological Assessment* attempted to avoid a rigid "single sign" or "cookbook" approach to assessment. It did so by stressing the integration of test data into a wide context through considerations of the referral question and additional sources of data. This approach has been maintained and re-emphasized in the second edition. However, it also highlights an underlying philosophy for both the first and second editions. Psychological assessment is a dual process involving both a solid grounding in empirical research, and an appreciation of the inner integrative process of the clinician. It is both art and science. Often these two approaches or orientations are antagonistic to one another (the iconoclastic academic versus the enthusiastic clinician). Within the present text, empirical research has been presented in an up-to-date and, I hope, objective and rigorous manner. A thorough evaluation of each approach to assessment has been made, combined with data and encouragement to use cutoff scores and multiple regression equations when available and appropriate. Assessment is also given credence as an art. It involves clinical judgment, an understanding of the person within a wide context, rapport building, and the use of intuitive integrative processes. The empirical and artistic approaches both have inherent limitations and assets, yet both are necessary. A purely empirical approach can be too rigid, narrowly focused, and divorced from the real world of the client and practitioner. On the other hand, clinical judgment is subject to bias and runs the risk of proliferating unvalidated interpretations that are made based on a "fuzzy" clinical "lore." It is my hope that the *Handbook of Psychological Assessment* will give credence to and integrate the best of both of these traditions without bringing them into unnecessary conflict.

All of the above changes are underscored by, if anything, an increased need for a book such as the *Handbook of Psychological Assessment*. Psychology students are increasingly expected to learn and function within a wider range of nonassessment related roles requiring a wide range of skills. These expectations mean students will need to develop assessment skills in as efficient yet effective a manner as possible. It is becoming increasingly more difficult for training programs to justify teaching an entire semester course on a specific subarea of assessment. They do so at the risk of eliminating, or at least reducing, training in other vital areas. Even if there is a greater emphasis on computer-based interpretations, students and practitioners still need to know general information regarding assessment as a strategy, details regarding each test, and basic knowledge on how to interpret the test. My hope is that this second edition of the *Handbook of Psychological Assessment* will prove to be up to date, efficient, effective, and sufficiently comprehensive.

Numerous colleagues helped with the development of the first edition. I would again like to thank each of them for their invaluable assistance. In particular I would like to again thank Dorothy/Gita Morena for her contributions. Specifically, these included writing a relatively smooth draft of the projective drawing chapter and relatively smooth drafts of material on the Wechsler subtests, administration and interpretation guidelines for children on the Bender, and the validity and clinical scales on the MMPI. I also greatly appreciate her help in developing many of the initial ideas surrounding the book and proofreading drafts of the earlier chapters.

The second edition has likewise involved much appreciated help from many colleagues. The following persons reviewed different chapters and provided invaluable suggestions:

Richard Butman (Wheaton College)
Val Clarke (Deakin University)
Boris Crassini (Deakin University)

Gordon Curran (Warrnambool Institute)
Rona Fields (Private practice)
Alan Hudson (La Trobe University)
Robert King (Victorian Health Commission)
Tony Loquet (Warrnambool Institute)
Paul Oas (Private practice)
Mel Schwartz (Private practice)
Rick Thomas (University of San Diego)
John Toumbouru (Warrnambool Institute)

In addition, the support staff members at Warrnambool Institute were extremely useful. These included Collin Wallace in interlibrary loans for his relentless pursuit of countless books and journal articles, and John Pinson for his help in many literature searches. The typing assistance from Pam Johnston and Wendy Jacobs was amazingly accurate, efficient, and will no doubt place them in the top echelons of any international decoding operations for their ability to actually translate the handwritten portions of the manuscript. Any acknowledgments would be incomplete without appreciation to Herb Reich at John Wiley & Sons for his patience ("Trust me Herb, the manuscript will be in the mail soon"), support, and useful suggestions. In addition, my thanks go to the team at John Wiley & Sons who have been extremely helpful and a pleasure to work with. These include Judith McCarthy, Nana Prior, Ruth Greif, Thomas D'Adamo, and Ron Pronk. Finally, I need to thank all my friends and colleagues who were able to put up with my complaining about a project that began as a creative labor of love and ending up as a tyrant that owned and controlled my every thought and movement seven days a week. This second edition would not have been possible without help from all of the above persons.

Chapter 1

INTRODUCTION

The general purpose of the *Handbook of Psychological Assessment* is to provide a reference and instructional guide for professionals and students who are conducting psychological assessments. As a reference book, it can aid in the development of a large number and variety of interpretive hypotheses. It can also serve to point out obscure signs that are only infrequently encountered during evaluations but may still be crucial in developing a complete description of the client. As an instructional text, it provides the student with the basic tools relevant for conducting an integrated psychological assessment.

One significant and overriding emphasis in this book is its focus on assessing areas that are of practical use in evaluating individuals within a clinical context. It is applied in its orientation, and, for the most part, theoretical discussions have been kept to a minimum. Many books written on psychological testing, as well as courses organized around these books, focus primarily on test theory and provide a brief overview of a large number of tests. In contrast, the intent of this book is to focus on the actual processes that practitioners go through during assessment. This begins with such issues as role clarification and evaluation of the referral question and ends with the actual preparation of the report itself. Even though some material on test theory is included, its purpose is to review those areas that are most relevant for evaluating tests prior to including them in a battery.

One of the crucial skills that readers of this text will hopefully develop, or at least have enhanced, is a realistic appreciation of the assets and limitations of assessment. This includes an appraisal of both psychological assessment as a general strategy, as well as an awareness of the assets and limitations of specific instruments and procedures. One of the primary limitations that seems to occur with assessment lies in handling assessment data incorrectly. Specifically, the test data is not integrated within the context of other sources of information (behavioral observations, history, other test scores) and the results are not presented in a way that aids in solving the unique problems clients or referral sources are confronting. In order to counter these limitations, the text continually provides guidelines for practitioners to both integrate their data and present the data in as useful a manner as possible. The text is thus not so much a book on test interpretation (although this is an important component) but on test integration within the wider context of assessment. The result should be to aid in creating psychological reports that are accurate, effective, concise, and highly valued by the persons who receive them.

ORGANIZATION OF THE HANDBOOK

The central organizational consideration for the *Handbook of Psychological Assessment* is that it follow the same sequence practitioners follow when performing an evaluation. They are initially concerned with clarifying their roles, insuring that they understand all the implications of the referral question, deciding which procedures would be most appropriate for the assessment, and reminding themselves of the potential problems associated with clinical judgment (see Chapters 1 and 2). They also need to understand the context in which they will be conducting the assessment. This understanding includes developing an appreciation for the issues, concerns, terminology, and likely roles that persons from these contexts will be involved in. Practitioners also need to be clear regarding the different guidelines and cautions for assessment and the ways in which the above factors might influence their selection of procedures (see Chapter 2).

Once practitioners have fully understood the preliminary issues discussed in Chapters 1 and 2, they then must select different strategies of assessment. The three major strategies are interviewing, observing behavior, and psychological testing. An interview is likely to occur during the initial phases of assessment, and is also essential in interpreting either test scores or in understanding behavioral observations (see Chapter 3). The assessment of actual behaviors might also be undertaken as a means of assessment (see Chapter 4). Behavioral assessment might be either an end in itself or an adjunct to testing. It might involve a variety of strategies including the measurement of overt behaviors, cognitions, alterations in physiology, or relevant measures from self-report inventories.

The middle part of the book (Chapters 5 through 11) provides a general overview of the seven most frequently used tests. Each of these chapters begins with an introduction to the test in the form of a discussion of its history and development, current evaluation, and procedures for administration. The main portions of these chapters provide a guide toward interpretation, which includes such areas as a discussion of the meaning of different scales, significant relations between scales, frequent trends that may be encountered, and the meaning of unusually high or low scores. When appropriate, additional subsections have been included. For example, the chapter on the Wechsler scales (Chapter 5) includes a discussion of the nature of intelligence because it is especially crucial for a clinician to understand the theoretical construct of "intelligence" prior to attempting an interpretation of I.Q. scores. Likewise, the chapter on the Thematic Apperception Test (Chapter 10) includes a summary of Murray's theory of personality because a knowledge of his concepts is also an important prerequisite for adequately understanding and interpreting the test.

The decision on whether to include various tests was based primarily on their frequency of use as tools for assessment. These include the Minnesota Multiphasic Personality Inventory, Wechsler intelligence scales, Bender Visual Motor Gestalt Test, Rorschach, Thematic Apperception Test, and the Draw-A-Person and House-Tree-Person (Lubin, Larson, Matarazzo, & Seever, 1985; Piotrowski & Keller, 1989; Piotrowski, Sherry, & Keller, 1985; Wade & Baker, 1977). The Wechsler Adult Intelligence Scale-Revised (WAIS-R) and the Wechsler Intelligence Scale for Children-Revised (WISC-R) were chosen for inclusion instead of the Stanford-Binet because the WAIS-R and WISC-R are not only useful in providing cognitive assessments, but are also more helpful in evaluating personality and providing useful clinical information. The California Personality Inventory (CPI) was selected because of its excellent technical development (Anastasi, 1982, 1988; Baucom, 1985), numerous research studies based on it, and the finding that, except for the MMPI, it is the most frequently used objective personality inventory (Piotrowski & Keller, 1984). The above seven tests (Chapters 5 through 11) represent the core assessment devices used by most practitioners.

The final step a clinician must take is to integrate the data into a psychological report. Chapter 12 provides general guidelines for report writing, a report format, and four sample reports. The sample reports are representative of the four more common types of reports (psychiatric, legal, academic, personality) from the four most frequently encountered referral settings (medical setting, legal context, educational context, psychological clinic). It is therefore hoped that the above chapter sequence will be logical to follow and that the knowledge provided within them will be useful, concise, and practical.

ROLE OF THE CLINICIAN

The central role of clinicians conducting assessments should be to answer specific questions and aid in making relevant decisions. To fulfill this role, clinicians must be able to integrate a wide range of data and bring into focus diverse areas of knowledge. Thus, they are not merely administering and scoring tests. A useful distinction to highlight this point is the contrast that Maloney and Ward (1976) have made between a psychometrist and a clinician conducting psychological assessment. Psychometrists tend to use tests merely to obtain data, and their task is often perceived as emphasizing the clerical and technical aspects of testing. Their approach is primarily data oriented, and the end product is often a series of traits or ability descriptions. These descriptions are typically unrelated to the person's overall context and do not address unique problems the person may be facing. In contrast, psychological assessment attempts to evaluate an individual in a problem situation so that the information derived from the assessment can somehow help with the problem. Tests are only one method of gathering data, and the test scores are not end products, but merely means of generating hypotheses. Psychological assessment, then, places data in a wide perspective, with its main focus being problem solving and decision making.

The distinction between psychometric testing and psychological assessment can be better understood—and the ideal role of the clinician more clearly defined—by briefly elaborating on the historical and methodological reasons for the development of the psychometric approach. When psychological tests were originally developed, there was an early and noteworthy success of group measurements of intelligence. This was especially true in military and industrial settings where individual interviewing and case histories were too expensive and time consuming for general use. The data-oriented intelligence tests were considered to be advantageous because they appeared "objective" and thus seemed to reduce possible interviewer bias. More important, they were quite successful in producing a relatively high number of true positives when used for classification purposes. Their predictions were generally accurate and usable. However, this created the early expectation that all assessments could be performed using the same method and would provide a similar level of accuracy and usefulness. Later assessment strategies often tried to imitate the methods of earlier intelligence tests for such variables as personality and psychiatric diagnosis.

A further development consistent with the psychometric approach was the strategy of using a "test battery." It was reasoned that, if a single test could produce accurate descriptions of an ability or trait, then a series of tests could be administered to create a "total picture" of the person. The goal, then, was to develop a global, yet definitive, description for the person—using purely objective methods. This goal encouraged the idea that the tool (psychological test) was the best process for achieving the goal, rather than being merely one technique in the overall assessment procedure. Behind this approach were the concepts of individual differences and "trait" psychology. These assume that one of the best ways to describe the differences among individuals is to measure their strengths and weaknesses with respect to various traits. Thus, the clearest approach to the study of personality involved developing a relevant taxonomy of traits and then creating tests to measure these traits. Again, there was an emphasis on the tools as primary, with a deemphasis on the input of the clinician. The result of these trends was a bias toward administration and clerical skills. Within this context, the psychometrist requires little, if any, clinical expertise other than administering, scoring, and interpreting tests. According to the above view, the most preferred tests would be those that are machine scored, true-false or multiple choice, and that are constructed so that the normed scores—rather than the psychometrist—provide the interpretation.

The objective psychometric approach is most appropriately applicable to ability tests such as those measuring intelligence or mechanical skills. However, its usefulness decreases when attempting to assess personality traits such as dependence, authoritarianism, or anxiety. Personality variables are far more complex and therefore need to be validated within the context of history, behavioral observations, and interpersonal relationships. For example, a T score of 75 on the MMPI scale 9 (mania) takes on an entirely different meaning for a highly functioning physician than for an individual with a poor history of work and interpersonal relationships. When the purely objective psychometric approach is used for the evaluation of problems in living (neurosis, psychosis, etc.), its usefulness is questionable.

Psychological assessment is most useful in the understanding and evaluation of personality and especially of problems in living. These issues involve a particular problem situation having to do with a specific individual. The central role of the clinician performing psychological assessment is that of an expert in human behavior who must deal with complex processes and understand test scores within the context of a person's life. The clinician must have knowledge concerning problem areas and, on the basis of this knowledge, be able to form a general idea regarding behaviors to observe and areas in which to collect relevant data. This involves an awareness and appreciation of multiple causation, interactional influences, and multiple relationships. As Woody (1980) has stated, "Clinical assessment is individually oriented, but it always considers social existence; the objective is usually to help the person solve problems."

In addition to an awareness of the role suggested by psychological assessment, clinicians should possess other specific areas of knowledge. These include personality theory, abnormal psychology, and the psychology of adjustment, as well as a knowledge of test construction and of basic statistics. Furthermore, clinicians should know the main interpretive hypotheses in psychological testing and be able to identify, sift through, and evaluate a series of hypotheses to determine which are most relevant and accurate. For each assessment device, it is also important that clinicians understand conceptually what it is they are trying to test. Thus, rather than merely knowing the labels and definitions for various types of anxiety or thought disorders, clinicians should also have in-depth operational criteria for them. For example, the concept of intelligence, as represented by the I.Q. score, can sometimes appear misleadingly straightforward. However, intelligence test scores can be complex, involving a variety of different cognitive abilities, the influence of cultural factors, varying performance under different conditions, and issues related to the nature of intelligence. Unless clinicians are familiar with these areas, they are not adequately prepared to handle I.Q. data. A problem encountered in many training programs is that, although students will frequently have a knowledge of abnormal psychology, personality theory, and test construction, they are usually insufficiently trained in ways to integrate these knowledge areas into the interpretation of test results. Instead, their training focuses on developing competency in administration and scoring, rather than on knowledge relating to what it is they are testing.

The role stressed in this book is consistent with the approach of psychological assessment in that the clinician not only should be knowledgeable about traditional content areas in psychology and the nature of what is being tested, but also should be able to integrate the test data into a relevant description of the person. This description, although focusing on the individual, should take into account the complexity of his or her social environment, personal history, and behavioral observations. Yet, the end goal is not merely to describe the person, but rather to develop relevant answers to specific questions, aid in problem solving, and facilitate decision making.

PATTERNS OF TEST USAGE IN CLINICAL ASSESSMENT

During the 1940s and 1950s, the single most important activity professional psychologists were likely to engage in was psychological testing. In contrast, the past 20 years have seen psychologists become involved in a far wider diversity of activities. Lubin et al. (1984, 1985) found that the average time spent performing assessment across five treatment settings was 44% in 1959, 28% in 1969, and only 22% in 1982. The average time spent in 1982 performing assessments in the five different settings ranged from 14% in counseling centers to 31% in psychiatric hospitals (Lubin et al., 1984, 1985). This decrease is due in part to the widening role of psychologists. Whereas in the 1940s and 1950s a practicing psychologist was almost synonymous with a tester, professional psychologists currently are increasingly involved with such areas as administration, consultation, organizational development, and direct treatment in a wide number of areas (Bamgbose, Smith, Jesse, & Groth-Marnat, 1980; Groth-Marnat, 1988). Decline in testing has also been attributed to disillusionment with the testing process due to criticisms regarding the reliability and validity of most assessment devices (Ziskin & Faust, 1988). In addition, psychological assessment has come to include a wide variety of activities beyond merely the administration and interpretation of traditional tests. These include conducting structured and unstructured interviews, behavioral observations in natural settings, observations of interpersonal interactions, neuropsychological assessment, and behavioral assessment.

The relative popularity of different traditional psychological tests has been surveyed since 1935. These have been within a wide variety of settings including academic institutions, psychiatric hospitals, counseling centers, veterans administration centers, institutions for the developmentally disabled, private practice, and various APA memberships and professional organizations. A 1982 survey found that a composite rating of tests used across five professional settings indicated that the ten most frequently used tests were, in rank order, the MMPI, WAIS, Bender Visual Motor Gestalt Test, Rorschach, WISC, Sentence Completion Test (all kinds), TAT, Draw-A-Person, Rotter Sentence Completion Test, and House-Tree-Person Test (Lubin et al., 1985). The above pattern has remained relatively stable since 1969. The actual test usage will obviously vary considerably from setting to setting. Schools and centers for the intellectually disabled will emphasize tests of intellectual abilities such as the WISC-R, counseling centers might be more likely to use vocational interest inventories, and psychiatric settings would emphasize tests assessing level of pathology such as the MMPI.

One clear change in testing practices has been a relative decrease in the status of projective techniques. Criticisms have been wide ranging but have centered on overly complex scoring systems, subjectivity of scoring, poor predictive utility, and inadequate or even nonexistent validity (Munter, 1975; Cleveland, 1976; Ziskin & Faust, 1988). Further criticisms include the extensive time required to effectively learn the techniques, greater cost effectiveness and greater empirical validity of many objective tests (MMPI, CPI, etc.), and their heavy reliance on psychoanalytic theory. These criticisms have usually occurred from within the academic community where they are used less and less for research purposes (Reynolds & Sundberg, 1976). Despite these criticisms, the standard projective tests have not decreased in relative popularity; the Rorschach, TAT, House-Tree-Person, and Draw-A-Person are still among the ten most frequently used clinical assessment techniques (Lubin et al., 1984, 1985; Piotrowski, 1984, Piotrowski & Keller, 1989). Tests such as the Rorschach continue to be used even though other better instruments have been developed such as the Holtzman (Holtzman, 1988; Holtzman & Schwartz, 1983). The continued strong use of projectives within clinical settings might be attributed to lack of time available for practitioners to learn new techniques, expectations that students in internships know how to use them (Piotrowski & Keller, 1984; Durand, Blanchard, & Mindell, 1988), unavailability of other practical alternatives, and the fact that clinical experience is usually given more weight by practitioners than empirical evidence. This suggests distance between the quantitative, theoretical world of the academic and the practical, problem-oriented world of the practitioner. In fact, assessment practices in professional settings seem to have little relationship to the number of research studies done on assessment tools, attitudes by academic faculty (Piotrowski, 1984; Reynolds & Sundberg, 1976), or the psychometric quality of the test (Reynolds, 1979). Interestingly, even one-third of all behavior therapists, who have traditionally kept closer links to empirical research, report using standard projective devices such as the TAT, Rorschach, and Human Figure Drawings (Piotrowski & Keller, 1984).

The earliest form of assessment was through clinical interview. The first clinicians such as Freud, Jung, and Adler used unstructured interaction to obtain information regarding history, diagnosis, or underlying structure of personality. Later clinicians taught interviewing by providing outlines of the types of areas that should be discussed. During the 1960s and 1970s, much criticism was directed toward interviewing to the extent that many psychologists began to perceive interviews as unreliable and lacking empirical validation. Tests, in many ways, were designed to counter the subjectivity and bias that occurs in interview techniques alone. More recently, a wide variety of structured interview techniques have been gaining popularity and have often been found to be reliable and valid indicators of a client's level of functioning. Structured interviews such as the Diagnostic Interview Schedule (DIS; Robins, Helzer, Croughan, & Ratcliff, 1981), Structured Clinical Interview for the DSM-III (SCID; Spitzer & Williams, 1983), and Renard Diagnostic Interview (Helzer, Robins, Croughan, & Welner, 1981) are often given preference over psychological tests. However, these interviews are very different from the traditional unstructured approaches. They have the advantage of being psychometrically sound even though they might lack important elements of rapport, idiographic richness, and flexibility that characterize less structured interactions.

A further trend in recent years has been the development of neuropsychological assessment. The discipline is a synthesis between behavioral neurology and psychometrics and was created from a need to answer such questions as the nature of a person's organic deficits, severity of deficits, localization, and differentiating between functional versus organic impairment. The pathognomonic sign approach and the psychometric approaches are two clear traditions that have developed within the discipline. Clinicians relying primarily on a pathognomonic sign approach are more likely to interpret specific behaviors such as perseverations or weaknesses on one side of the body, which are highly indicative of the presence and nature of organic impairments. These clinicians tend to rely on the tradition of assessment associated with Luria (1973) and design interviews and tests based on a flexible method where they test possible hypotheses for different types of impairment. In contrast, the more quantitative tradition represented by Reitan and his colleagues (Reitan & Davison, 1974), is more likely to rely on critical cutoff scores, which distinguish between normal and brain-damaged persons. For example, Reitan and Wolfson (1985) recommended using an "impairment index," which is the proportion of brain-sensitive tests that fall into the brain-damaged range. In actual practice, most clinical neuropsychologists are more likely to use a combination of the psychometric and pathognomonic sign approaches. The two major neuropsychological test batteries currently used in the United States are the Luria-Nebraska batteries (Golden, Hammeke, & Purisch, 1980) and the Halstead Reitan Neuropsychological Test Battery (Reitan & Wolfson, 1985). A typical neuropsychological battery might include tests specifically designed to assess organic impairment and also tests such as MMPI, WAIS-R, WISC-R, Bender Gestalt, and Wechsler Memory Scales-Revised. As a result, extensive research over the past ten to fifteen years has been directed toward developing a greater understanding of how the older and more traditional tests relate to different types and levels of cerebral dysfunction.

During the 1960s and 1970s, behavior therapy was increasingly used and accepted. Initially, behavior therapists were concerned with an idiographic approach to the functional analysis of behavior. As their techniques became more sophisticated, formalized methods of behavioral assessment began to arise. These techniques arose in part from dissatisfaction with DSM-II methods of diagnosis as well as from a need to have assessment relate more directly to treatment and treatment outcomes. There was also a desire to be more accountable for documenting behavior change over time. For example, if behaviors related to anxiety in certain situations decreased after therapy, then the therapist should be able to clearly demonstrate that the treatment had been successful. Behavioral assessment could involve measurements of movements (behavioral checklists, behavioral analysis), physiological responses (GSR, EMG) or self-reports (self-monitoring, Beck Depression Inventory, assertiveness scales). Whereas the early behavioral assessment techniques showed little concern with the psychometric properties of their instruments, there has been an increasing push to have them meet adequate levels of reliability and validity (i.e. Lowe, 1985). Despite the many formalized techniques of behavioral assessment, many behavior therapists feel that an unstructured idiographic approach is most appropriate. Furthermore, many behavior therapists still feel that it is important for practitioners to be competent with standard objective and projective instruments (Piotrowski & Keller, 1984).

Traditional means of assessment, then, have decreased due to an overall increase in other activities of psychologists and an expansion in what is meant by "assessment." Currently, a psychologist doing assessment might include such techniques as interviewing, administering and interpreting traditional psychological tests (MMPI, WAIS-R, etc.), naturalistic observations, neuropsychological assessment, and behavioral assessment. In addition, professional psychologists might be required to assess new areas that were not given much emphasis before the 1980s. These include assessing personality disorders (borderline personality, narcissism), stress and coping (life changes, burnout, existing coping resources), psychological health, adaptation to new cultures, and the changes associated with increasing modernization (Dana, 1984). Additional areas might include family system interactions, relation between a person and his or her environment (social climate, social supports), cognitive processes related to behavior disorders, and personal control (self-efficacy). All these require clinicians to be continually aware of new and more specific assessment devices and to maintain flexibility in the approaches they take.

EVALUATING PSYCHOLOGICAL TESTS

Prior to using a psychological test, clinicians should investigate and understand the theoretical orientation of the test, practical considerations, the appropriateness of the standardization sample, and the adequacy of its reliability and validity. Often, helpful reviews that relate to these issues can be found in current and past editions of the *Mental Measurements Yearbook* (Conoley & Kramer, 1989; Mitchell, 1985), *Tests in Print* (Buros, 1974), *Test Critiques* (Keyser & Sweetland, 1985), or *Tests: A Comprehensive Reference for Assessment in Psychology, Education, and Business* (Sweetland & Keyser, 1983). Test users will also need to carefully review the manual accompanying the test. Table 1–1 outlines the more important questions that should be answered. The issues outlined in this table will be discussed further. The discussion is consistent with the practical orientation of this text in that it focuses on problems that clinicians using psychological tests are likely to confront. It is not intended to provide a comprehensive coverage of test theory and construction; if a more detailed treatment is required, the reader is referred to one of the many texts on psychological testing (e.g. Anastasi, 1988; Kaplan & Sacuzzo, 1989).

Table 1–1. Issues to address when evaluating a psychological test

Theoretical Orientation
 1. Do you adequately understand the theoretical construct the test is supposed to be measuring?
 2. Do the test items correspond to the theoretical description of the constructs?

Practical Considerations
 1. If reading is required by the examinee, does his or her ability match the level required by the test?
 2. How appropriate is the length of the test?
 3. Does the examiner require additional training? If so, how can this be acquired?

Standardization
 1. Is the population to be tested similar to the population the test was standardized on?
 2. Was the size of the standardization sample adequate?
 3. Have specialized subgroup norms been developed?
 4. Do the instructions permit standardized administration?

Reliability
 1. Are reliability estimates sufficiently high (generally around .90 for clinical decision making and around .70 for research purposes)?
 2. What implications do the relative stability of the trait, the method of estimating reliability, and the test format have on reliability?

Validity
 1. What were the criteria and procedures used to validate the test?
 2. Has the test been constructed in a manner that will produce accurate measurements?
 3. Will the test produce accurate measurements within the context and purpose for which you would like to use it?

Theoretical Orientation

Before a clinician can effectively evaluate whether a test is appropriate, it is first important to understand the theoretical orientation of the test. Clinicians should research the construct that the test is supposed to measure and then examine the manner in which the test approaches this construct. This information can usually be found in the test manual. However, if for any reason the information in the manual is insufficient, additional information should be sought elsewhere. Clinicians can frequently obtain useful information regarding the trait by assessing the individual test items. Usually, an individual analysis of the items, which can help the potential test user to evaluate whether or not these items appear relevant to the trait being measured, can be found in the manual.

Practical Considerations

A number of practical issues exist that relate more to the context and manner in which the test will be used than to the construction of the test. First, tests vary in terms of the level of education that examinees must have in order to understand them adequately. This level may be especially important in relation to any reading that is demanded of the examinee. The examinee must be able to read, comprehend, and respond appropriately to the test. Second, some tests are too long, which can lead to a loss of rapport with, or extensive frustration on the part of, the examinee. Sometimes this problem can be reduced by administering short forms of the test, provided these short forms have been properly developed and are treated with appropriate caution. Finally, clinicians have to assess the extent to which they will need training to administer and interpret the instrument. If further training is necessary, then a plan must be developed for acquiring this training.

Standardization

Another central issue relates to the adequacy of norms. Each test has norms that reflect the distribution of scores by a specific standardization sample. The basis upon which individual test scores have meaning relates directly to the similarity between that individual being tested and the standardization sample. If a similarity exists between the group or individual being tested and the standardization sample, then adequate comparisons can be made. For example, if the test was standardized on college students between the ages of 18 to 22, then useful comparisons can be made for college students within that age bracket (if one assumes that the test is otherwise sufficiently reliable and valid). The more dissimilar the person is from this standardization group (e.g. over 70 years of age with low educational achievement), the less useful the test is in evaluating him or her. The examiner may need to consult the literature to determine whether research that followed the publication of the test manual has developed norms for different groups. This is particularly important for tests such as the MMPI and the Rorschach where norms for younger populations have been published.

Three major questions that relate to the adequacy of norms must be answered. The first is whether or not the standardization group is representative of the population on which the examiner would like to use the test. The test manual should include sufficient information to determine the representativeness of the standardization sample. If this information is not sufficient or is in any way incomplete, then the degree of confidence with which the test can be used is greatly reduced. The ideal and current practice is to use stratified random sampling. However, this can be an extremely costly and time-consuming procedure, and, as a result, many tests are quite deficient in this respect. The second question is whether the size of the standardization group is large enough. If the group is too small, the results may not give stable estimates because too much random fluctuation might exist within the group. Finally, a good test will have specialized subgroup norms as well as broad national norms. Knowledge relating to subgroup norms will give examiners greater flexibility and confidence if they are using the test with similar subgroup populations. This is particularly important when subgroups produce significantly different sets of scores from the normal standardization group. These subgroups can be based on such factors as sex, geographic location, age, level of education, socioeconomic status, or urban versus rural environment. Knowledge of each of these subgroup norms allows for a more appropriate and meaningful interpretation of scores.

Standardization can also refer to administration procedures. A well-constructed test should have instructions that permit the examiner to give the test in a similar structured manner as other examiners and to also maintain this standardized administration between one testing session and the next. Research has demonstrated that varying the instructions between one administration and the next can alter the types and quality of responses the examinee makes, thereby tainting the reliability of the test. Standardization of administration should refer not only to the instructions, but also to insuring adequate lighting, quiet, no interruptions, and good rapport.

Reliability

The reliability of a test refers to its degree of stability, consistency, predictability, and accuracy. In other words, it addresses the extent to which scores obtained by a person will be the same if the person is reexamined by the same test on different occasions. Underlying the concept of reliability is the possible range of error, or "error of measurement," of a single score. This is an estimate of the range of possible random fluctuation that can be expected in an individual's score. However, it should be stressed that a certain degree of error or "noise" will always be present in the system, resulting from such factors as a misreading of the items, poor administration procedures, or the changing mood of the client. If there is a large degree of random fluctuation, the examiner cannot place a great deal of confidence in an individual's scores. The goal of a test constructor is to reduce, as much as possible, the degree of measurement error, or random fluctuation. If this is achieved, the difference between one score and another is more likely to be due to some true difference in the characteristic being measured rather than some chance fluctuation.

Two main issues relate to the degree of error in a test. The first is the inevitable, natural variation in human performance. Usually the variability is less for measurements of ability than for those of personality. Whereas ability variables (intelligence, mechanical aptitude, etc.) show gradual changes resulting from growth and development, many personality traits are much more highly dependent on factors such as mood. This is particularly true in the case of a characteristic like anxiety. The practical significance of this in evaluating a test is that certain factors outside the test itself can serve to reduce the reliability that the test can realistically be expected to achieve. Thus, an examiner should generally expect higher reliabilities for an intelligence test than for a test measuring a personality variable like anxiety. It is the examiner's responsibility to know the nature of that which is being measured, especially with regard to the degree of variability to be expected in the measured trait.

The second important issue relating to reliability is that psychological testing methods are necessarily imprecise. Within the fields of the "hard" sciences, direct measurements can be made—such as the concentration of a chemical solution, the relative weight of one organism compared to another, or the strength of radiation. In contrast to this are many constructs in psychology where measurements are often made indirectly. For instance, "intelligence" cannot be perceived directly; rather, it must be inferred by measuring behavior that has been defined as being intelligent. Variability relating to these inferences is likely to produce a certain degree of error due to the lack of precision in defining and observing inner psychological constructs. Variability in measurement will also be found simply because people have true (not due to test error) fluctuations in performance between one testing session and the next. Whereas it is impossible to control for the natural variability in human performance, adequate test construction can attempt to reduce the degree of imprecision that is a function of the test itself. Both natural human variability and test imprecision make the task of measurement extremely difficult. Although some error in testing is inevitable, the goal of test construction is to keep testing errors within reasonably accepted limits. A "high" correlation is generally .80 or more, but the variable being measured will also change the expected strength of the correlation. Likewise, the method of determining reliability will alter the relative strength of the correlation. Ideally, clinicians should hope for correlations of .90 or higher in tests that will be used to make decisions about individuals, whereas a correlation of .70 or more is generally adequate for research purposes.

The purpose of reliability is to estimate the degree to which the test varies due to error. There are four primary methods of obtaining reliability: Reliability can refer to the extent to which the test produces consistent results upon retesting (test-retest), the relative accuracy of a test at a given time (alternate forms), the internal consistency of the items (split half) and the degree of agreement between two examiners (interscorer). Another way to summarize this is that reliability can be time to time (test-retest), form to form (alternate forms), item to item (split half), or scorer to scorer (interscorer). Although these are the main types of reliability, there is a fifth type—the Kuder-Richardson—which, like the split half, is a measurement of the internal consistency of the test items. However, this method is considered appropriate only for tests that are relatively pure measures of a single variable, and is not covered in this book.

Test-Retest Reliability   Test-retest reliability is determined by administering the test and then giving a repeat administration on a second occasion. The reliability coefficient is determined by correlating the scores obtained by the same person on the two different administrations. The degree of correlation between the two scores indicates the extent to which the test scores can be generalized from one situation to the next. If the correlations are high, then the results are less likely to be due to random fluctuations in the condition of the examinee or the testing environment. Thus, when the test is being used in actual practice, the examiner can be relatively confident that differences in scores are the result of an actual change in the trait being measured rather than random fluctuation.

A number of factors must be considered in assessing the appropriateness of test-retest reliability. One is that the interval between administrations can affect reliability. Thus, a test manual should clearly specify the interval as well as any significant life changes that the examinees may have experienced—such as counseling, career changes, or psychotherapy. For example, tests of preschool intelligence often give reasonably high correlations if the second administration is within several months of the first one. However, correlations with later childhood or adult I.Q. results are generally low due to innumerable intervening life experiences. One of the major difficulties with test-retest reliability is the effect that practice and memory may have on performance, which can produce improvement between one administration and the next. This is a particular problem for speeded and memory tests such as those found on the Digit Symbol and Arithmetic subtests of the WAIS-R. Additional sources of variation may be the result of random, short-term fluctuations in the examinee, or of variations in the testing conditions. In general, test-retest reliability is the preferred method only if the variable being measured is relatively stable. If the variable is a highly changeable one, such as anxiety, then this method is usually not adequate.

Alternate Forms   The alternate forms method avoids many of the problems encountered with test-retest reliability. The logic behind alternate forms is that, if the trait is measured several times on the same individual by using parallel forms of the test, then the different measurements should produce similar results. The degree of similarity between the scores represents the reliability coefficient of the test. As in the test-retest method, the interval between administrations should always be included in the manual as well as a description of any significant intervening life experiences. If the second administration is given immediately after the first, then the resulting reliability is more a measure of the correlation between forms and not across occasions. Correlations determined by tests given with a wide interval, such as two months or more, provide a measure of both the relation between forms and the degree of temporal stability.

The alternate forms method eliminates many carry-over effects, such as the recall of previous responses the examinee has made to specific items. However, there is still likely to be some carry-over effect in that the examinee can learn to adapt to the overall style of the test even when the specific item content between one test and another is unfamiliar. This is most likely to occur when the test involves some sort of problem solving strategy in which the same principle in solving one problem can be used to solve the next one. An examinee, for example, may learn to use mnemonic aids to increase his or her performance on an alternate form of the WAIS-R Digit Symbol.

Perhaps the primary difficulty with alternate forms lies in determining whether the two forms are actually equivalent. For example, if one test is more difficult than its alternate form, then the difference in scores may represent actual differences in the two tests rather than differences due to the unreliability of the measure. Since the test constructor is attempting to obtain a measure of the reliability of the test itself and not of the difference between the two tests, this could serve to confound and lower the reliability coefficient. Alternate forms should be independently constructed tests that both use the same specifications—including the same number of items, type of content, format, and manner of administration.

A final difficulty is encountered primarily when there is a delay between one administration and the next. With such a delay, the examinee may perform differently due to short-term fluctuations—such as mood, stress level, or the relative quality of the previous night's sleep. Thus, an examinee's abilities may vary somewhat from one examination to another, thereby affecting test results. Despite these problems, alternate forms reliability has the advantage of, if not eliminating, at least reducing many of the carry-over effects found with the test-retest method. A further advantage is that the availability of alternate test forms can be useful for purposes other than determining reliability. These uses may include assessing the effects of a treatment program or monitoring a patient's changes over a period of time by administering the different forms on separate occasions.

Split Half Reliability   The split half method is the best technique for determining reliability for a trait in which there is a high degree of fluctuation. This is because the test is given only once, then the items are split in half, and the two halves are correlated. Since there is only one administration, it is not possible for the effects of time to intervene as they might with the test-retest method. Thus, the split half method gives a measure of the internal consistency of the test items rather than the temporal stability of different administrations of the same test. To determine split half reliability, the test is often split on the basis of odd and even items. This method of splitting is usually adequate for most tests. Dividing the test into a first half and second half can be effective in some cases, but is often inappropriate due to the cumulative effects of warming up, fatigue, and boredom—all of which can result in different levels of performance on the first half of the test compared to the second.

As is true with the other methods of obtaining reliability, the split half method has its limitations. When a test is split in half, there are fewer items on each half, which results in wider variability because the individual responses cannot stabilize as easily around a mean. As a general principle, the longer a test is, the more reliable it will be because the larger the number of items, the easier it is for the majority of items to compensate for minor alterations in responding to a few of the other items. As with the alternate forms method, differences in content may exist between one half and another.

Interscorer Reliability   In some tests, scoring is based partially on the judgment of the examiner. Since judgment may vary between one scorer and the next, it may be important to assess the extent to which reliability might be affected. This is especially true for projectives and even some ability tests where hard scorers may produce somewhat different results than easy scorers. This variance in interscorer reliability may apply for global judgments based on such test scores as brain damaged versus normal, or for small details of scoring such as whether a person has given a shading versus a texture response on the Rorschach. The basic strategy used to determine interscorer reliability is to obtain a series of responses from a single client and to have these responses scored by two different individuals. A variation is to have two different examiners test the same client using the same test and then to determine how close their scores or ratings of the person are. The two sets of scores can then be correlated to determine a reliability coefficient. Any test that requires even partial subjectivity in scoring should provide information on interscorer reliability.

The best form of reliability is dependent on both the nature of the variable being measured and the purposes for which the test will be used. If the trait or ability being measured is highly stable, the test-retest method is preferable, whereas split half is more appropriate for characteristics that are highly subject to fluctuations. When using a test to make predictions, the test-retest method is preferable since it gives an estimate of the dependability of the test from one administration to the next. This is particularly true if, when determining reliability, an increased time interval existed between the two administrations. If, on the other hand, the examinee is concerned with the internal consistency and accuracy of a test for a single, one-time measure, then either the split half or the test-retest method on the same day would be best.

Another consideration in evaluating the acceptable range of reliability is the format of the test. Longer tests will usually have higher reliabilities than shorter ones. Also, the format of the responses will affect reliability. For example, a true-false format is likely to have a lower reliability than multiple choice because each true-false item has a 50% possibility of the answer being correct due to chance. In contrast, each question in a multiple choice format having five possible choices has only a 20% possibility of being correct due to chance. A final consideration is that tests with various subtests or subscales should report the reliability for the overall test as well as for each of the subtests. In general, the overall test score will have a significantly higher reliability than its subtests. In estimating the confidence with which test scores can be interpreted, the examiner should take into account the lower reliabilities of the subtests. For example, a Full Scale I.Q. score on the WAIS-R can be interpreted with more confidence than the specific subscale scores.

Most test manuals include a statistical index of the amount of error that can be expected for test scores, which is referred to as the standard error of measurement (SEM). The logic behind the standard error of measurement is that test scores consist of both "truth" and error. Thus, there will always be noise or error in the system, and the standard error of measurement provides a range to indicate how extensive that error is likely to be. The range of error depends on the test reliability so that the higher the reliability, the narrower the range of error. The standard error of measurement is a standard deviation score so that, for example, a standard error of measurement of 5 on an intelligence test would indicate that an individual's score has a 68% chance of being within ± 5 I.Q. points from the estimated true score. This is because the SEM of 5 represents a "band" extending from -1 to +1 standard deviations above and below the mean. Likewise there would be a 95% chance that the individual's score would fall within a range of ± 10 points from the estimated true score. From a theoretical perspective, the standard error of measurement is a statistical index of how a person's repeated scores on a specific test would fall around a normal distribution. Thus, it is a statement of the relation-ship among a person's obtained score, his or her theoretically "true" score, and the test reliability. Since it is an empirical statement of the probable range of scores, the standard error of measurement has more practical usefulness than a knowledge of the test reliability. This band of error is also referred to as a "confidence interval."

The acceptable range of reliability is difficult to identify and depends partially on the nature of the variable being measured. In general, unstable aspects (states) of the person produce lower reliabilities than stable ones (traits). Thus, in evaluating a test, the examiner should expect higher reliabilities on stable traits or abilities than on changeable states. For example, a person's general fund of vocabulary words is highly stable and will therefore produce high reliabilities. In contrast is a person's level of anxiety, which is often highly changeable. This means examiners should not expect nearly as high reliabilities for anxiety as for an ability measure such as vocabulary. A further consideration, which is also related to the stability of the trait or ability, is the method of reliability that is used. Alternate forms are considered to give the lowest estimate of the actual reliability of a test, while split half provide the highest estimate. Another important way to estimate the adequacy of reliability is by comparing the reliability derived on other similar tests. The examiner can then develop a sense of what the expected levels of reliability should be, thereby giving him- or herself a baseline by which to make comparisons. In the example of anxiety, a clinician may not know what is an acceptable level of reliability. A general estimate can be made by comparing the reliability of the test under consideration with other tests measuring the same or a similar variable. The most important thing to keep in mind is that lower levels of reliability usually suggest that less confidence can be placed in the interpretations and predictions based on the test data. However, clinical practitioners are less likely to be concerned with low statistical reliability if there is some basis for believing the test is a valid measure of the current state the client is in at the time of testing. The main consideration is that the sign or test score does not mean one thing at one time and something different at another.

Validity

The most crucial issue in test construction is validity. Whereas reliability addresses issues of accuracy and consistency, validity assesses what the test is to be accurate about. A test that is valid for clinical assessment should measure what it is intended to measure and should also produce information useful to clinicians. A psychological test cannot be said to be valid in any abstract or absolute sense, but more practically, must be valid within a particular context and for a specific group of people. Although a test can be reliable without being valid, the opposite is not true. In other words, a necessary prerequisite for validity is that the test must first have achieved an adequate level of reliability. Thus, a valid test is one that accurately measures the variable it is intended to measure. For example, a test might be developed comprised of questions regarding a person's musical preference and erroneously state that it is a test of creativity. The test might be reliable in the sense that if it is given to the same person on different occasions, it will produce similar results each time. However, it would not be reliable in that an investigation might indicate that it does not correlate with other more valid measurements of creativity.

Establishing the validity of a test can be extremely difficult, primarily because psychological variables are usually abstract concepts such as intelligence, anxiety, and personality. These concepts have no tangible reality, so their existence must be inferred through indirect means. In constructing a test, a test designer must follow two necessary, initial steps. First, the construct must be theoretically evaluated and described; second, specific operations (test questions) must be developed to measure it. Even when these steps are closely and conscientiously followed, it is sometimes difficult to determine what the test really measures. For example, I.Q. tests are good predictors of academic success, but there are many questions as to whether they adequately measure the concept of intelligence as it is theoretically described. Another hypothetical test that, based on its item content, might seem to measure what is described as "musical aptitude," may in reality be highly correlated with verbal abilities. Thus, it may be more a measure of verbal abilities than of musical aptitude.

Any estimate of validity is concerned with relationships between the test and some external independently observed event. The *Standards for Educational and Psychological Testing* (AERA, APA, NCME, 1985) list the three main methods of establishing validity as content-related, criterion-related, and construct-related.

Content Validity During the initial construction phase of any test, the developers must first be concerned with its content validity. This refers to the subject matter of the test items and is achieved by making the appropriate selection of these items. During the initial item selection, the constructors must carefully consider the skills or knowledge area of the variable they would like to measure. The items are then generated based on this conceptualization of the variable. At some point it might be decided that the item content overrepresents, underrepresents, or excludes specific areas, and alterations in the items might be made accordingly. If experts on subject matter are used to determine the items, then the number of these experts and their qualifications should be included in the test manual. The instructions given to them and the extent of agreement between judges should also be provided. A good test will cover not just the subject matter of that which is being measured, but also specific additional variables as well. For example, factual knowledge may be one criterion, but of additional importance is the application of that knowledge and the ability to analyze data. Thus, a test with high content validity must cover all major aspects of the content area and must do so in the correct proportion.

A concept somewhat related to content validity is face validity. However, these terms should not be considered synonymous since content validity pertains to judgments made by experts while face validity has to do with judgments made by the test users. The central issue in face validity is test rapport. Thus, a group of potential mechanics who are being tested for basic skills in arithmetic should have word problems that relate to machines rather than to business transactions. Face validity, then, is present if the test "looks good" to the persons taking it, to policymakers who decide to include it in their programs, and to other untrained personnel. Despite the potential importance of face validity in regard to test-taking attitudes, disappointingly few formal studies on face validity are performed and/or reported in test manuals (Nevo, 1985; Nevo & Sfez, 1985).

One key factor in content validity is its heavy reliance on the personal judgment of the test designers. As an initial step, content issues are necessary, but as an end in itself, content validity is the least preferred method due to the subjectivity involved. In some cases, content validity can be adequate, such as in the development of achievement and occupational tests. This is because subject- or job-related criteria can be specified with a fairly high degree of accuracy. However, for aptitude and personality tests, content validity is usually inappropriate because the variables are both more complex and more abstract. These types of tests require more empirical verification through other validity procedures.

Criterion validity   A second major approach to determining validity is criterion validity, which has also been called empirical or predictive validity. Criterion validity is determined by comparing test scores with some sort of performance on an outside measure. The outside measure should have a theoretical relation to the variable that the test is supposed to measure. For example, an intelligence test might be correlated with grade point average, an aptitude test with independent job ratings, or general maladjustment scores with other tests measuring similar dimensions. The relation between the two measurements is usually expressed as a correlation coefficient.

Criterion-related validity is most frequently divided into either concurrent or predictive validity. Concurrent validity refers to measurements taken at the same, or approximately the same, time as the test. For example, an intelligence test might be administered at the same time as assessments of a group's level of academic achievement. Predictive validity is used to refer to outside measurements that were taken some time after the test scores were derived. Thus, predictive validity might be evaluated by correlating the intelligence test scores with measures of academic achievement a year after the initial testing. Concurrent validation is often used as a substitute for predictive validation because it is simpler, less expensive, and not as time consuming. However, the main consideration in deciding whether concurrent or predictive validation is preferable depends on how the test will be used. Predictive validity is most appropriate for tests used for selection and classification of personnel. This may include hiring job applicants, placing military personnel in specific occupational training programs, screening out individuals who are likely to develop emotional disorders, or identifying which category of psychiatric populations would be most likely to benefit from specific treatment approaches. These situations all require that the measurement device provide a prediction of some future outcome. In contrast, concurrent validation is preferable if an assessment of the client's current status is required, rather than a prediction of what might occur to the client at some future time. The distinction can be summarized by asking, "Is Mr. Jones maladjusted?" (concurrent validity) rather than "Is Mr. Jones likely to become maladjusted at some future time?" (predictive validity).

An important consideration is the degree to which a specific test can be applied to a unique work-related environment. In other words, can the test under consideration provide accurate assessments and predictions for the specific environment in which the examinee is working? To answer this question adequately, the examiner must refer to the manual and assess the similarity between the criteria used to establish the test's validity and the situation to which he or she would like to apply the test. For example, can an aptitude test that has adequate criterion validity in the prediction of high school grade point average also be used to predict academic achievement for a population of college students? If the examiner has questions regarding the relative applicability of the test, he or she may need to undertake a series of specific tasks. The first is to identify clearly the skills that are required for adequate performance in the situation involved. For example, the criteria for a successful teacher may include such attributes as verbal fluency, flexibility, and good public speaking skills. The examiner then must determine the degree to which each of these skills contributes to the quality of one's performance as a teacher. Next, the examiner has to assess the extent to which the test under consideration measures each of these skills. The final step is to evaluate the extent to which the attribute that the test measures is relevant to the skills the examiner needs to predict. Based on these evaluations, the examiner can estimate the confidence that he or she will place in the predictions developed from the test. This approach is sometimes referred to as synthetic validity since examiners must integrate or synthesize the criteria reported in the test manual with the variables they will be working within their clinical or organizational setting.

The strength of criterion validity will depend in part on the type of variable being measured. Usually, intellectual or aptitude tests give relatively higher validity coefficients than personality tests because there are generally a greater number of variables influencing personality than intelligence. As the number of variables that influence the trait being measured increases, it becomes progressively more difficult to account for them. When a large number of variables are not accounted for, the trait can be affected in unpredictable ways. This can create a much wider degree of fluctuation in the test scores, thereby lowering the validity coefficient. Thus, when evaluating a personality test, the examiner should not expect as high a validity coefficient as for intellectual or aptitude tests. A helpful guide is to look at the validities found in similar tests and compare them with the test being considered. For example, if an examiner wants to estimate the range of validity to be expected for the extraversion scale on the Myers Briggs Type Indicator, he or she might compare it with the validities for similar scales found in the California Personality Inventory and Eysenck's Personality Questionnaire. The relative level of validity, then, will depend both on the quality of the construction of the test as well as on the variable being studied.

An important consideration is the extent to which the test accounts for the trait being measured or the behavior being predicted. Take, for example, the typical correlation found between intelligence tests and grade point average, which usually ranges from .40 to .70. Since no one would say that grade point average is entirely the result of intelligence, the relative extent to which intelligence determines grade point average has to be estimated. This can be calculated by squaring the correlation coefficient and changing it into a percentage. Thus, if the correlation of .70 was squared, it would come out to 49%, indicating that 49% of academic achievement can be accounted for by I.Q. as measured by the intelligence test. The remaining 51% may include such factors as motivation, quality of instruction, and past educational experience. The problem facing the examiner is to determine whether 49% of the variance is sufficiently useful for the intended purposes of the test. This ultimately depends on the personal judgment of the examiner.

The main problem confronting criterion validity lies in finding an agreed upon, definable, acceptable, and feasible outside criterion. Whereas for an intelligence test the grade point average might be an acceptable criterion, it is far more difficult to specify adequate criteria for most personality tests. Even with so-called intelligence tests, many researchers argue that it is more appropriate to consider them tests of "scholastic aptitude" rather than of "intelligence." Yet another difficulty with criterion validity is the possibility that the criterion measure will be inadvertently biased. This is referred to as "criterion contamination" and occurs when knowledge of the test results influences an individual's later performance. For example, a supervisor in an organization may act differently toward a worker whom he or she knows has been tested and placed in a certain category. This situation may set up negative or positive expectations for the worker, which could influence his or her level of performance. The result is likely to artificially alter the level of the validity coefficients. To work around these difficulties, especially in regard to personality tests, a third major method must be used to determine validity.

Construct Validity   The method of construct validity was developed in part to correct the inadequacies and difficulties encountered with content and criterion approaches. Content validity relies too much on subjective judgment, while criterion validity is too restrictive in working with content areas and has a further difficulty in that there is often a lack of agreement in deciding upon adequate outside criteria. The basic approach of construct validity is to assess the extent to which the test measures a theoretical construct or trait. This assessment involves three general steps. Initially the test constructor must make a careful analysis of the trait. This is followed by a consideration of the ways in which the trait should relate to other variables. Finally, the test designer needs to test whether or not these hypothesized relationships actually exist. For example, a test measuring dominance should have a high correlation with the individual accepting leadership roles and a low or negative correlation with measures of submissiveness. Likewise, a test measuring anxiety should have a high positive correlation with individuals who are measured during an anxiety-provoking situation, such as an experiment involving some sort of physical pain. As these hypothesized relationships are verified by research studies, the degree of confidence that can be placed in a test increases.

There is no single, best approach for determining construct validity; rather, a variety of different possibilities exist. For example, if some abilities are expected to increase with age, then correlations can be made between a population's test scores and age. This may be appropriate for such variables as intelligence or motor coordination, but it would not be applicable for most personality measurements. Even in the measurement of intelligence or motor coordination, this approach may not be appropriate beyond the age of maturity. Another method for determining construct validity is to measure the effects of experimental or treatment interventions. Thus, a post-test measurement may be taken following a period of instruction to see if the intervention affected the test scores in relation to a previous pretest measure. For example, after an examinee completes a course in arithmetic, it would be predicted that scores on a test of arithmetical ability would increase. Often, correlations can be made with other tests that supposedly measure a similar variable. However, if the new test correlates too highly with already existing tests, this may represent needless duplication—unless the new test incorporates some additional advantage such as a shortened format, ease of administration, or superior predictive validity. Factor analysis is of particular relevance to construct validation because it can be used to identify and assess the relative strength of different psychological traits. Factor analysis can also be used in the design of a test to identify the primary factor or factors measured by a series of different tests. Thus, it can be used to simplify one or more tests by reducing the number of categories to a few common factors or traits. The "factorial" validity of a test is the relative "weight" or "loading" that a specific factor has on the test. For example, if spatial organization has a weight of .72 on a picture arrangement type of test, then the factorial validity is .72.

Another method used in construct validity is to estimate the degree of internal consistency by correlating specific subtests with the test's total score. For example, if a subtest on an intelligence test does not correlate adequately with the overall or Full Scale I.Q., then it should be either eliminated or altered in a way that will increase the correlation. A final method for obtaining construct validity is for a test to converge or correlate highly with variables that are theoretically similar to it. The test should not only show this "convergent validity" but should also have "discriminate validity," in which it would demonstrate low or negative correlations with variables that are dissimilar to it. Thus, scores on reading comprehension should show high positive correlations with performance in a literature class and low correlations with performance in a class involving mathematical computation.

Related to discriminant and convergent validity is the degree of sensitivity and specificity an assessment device demonstrates in identifying different categories. Sensitivity refers to the percentage of "true" positives that the instrument has identified, whereas specificity is the relative percentage of "true" negatives. For example, a structured clinical interview might be quite sensitive in that it would accurately identify 90% of schizophrenics in an admitting ward of a hospital. However, it may not be sufficiently specific in that 30% of schizophrenics would be incorrectly classified as either normal or having some other diagnosis. The difficulty in determining sensitivity and specificity lies in developing an agreed upon, objectively accurate outside criteria for such categories as psychiatric diagnosis, intelligence, or personality traits.

As is indicated by the variety of approaches discussed, no single, quick, efficient method exists for determining construct validity. It is similar to testing a series of hypotheses where the results of the studies determine the meanings that can be attached to later test scores (Hogan & Nicholson, 1988). Almost any type of data can be used, including material from the content and criterion approaches. The greater the amount of supporting data, the greater is the level of confidence with which the test can be used. In many ways, construct validity represents the strongest and most sophisticated approach to test construction. Hogan and Nicholson (1988) argue that all types of validity should be considered as subcategories of construct validity. It involves theoretical knowledge of the trait or ability being measured, knowledge of other related variables, hypothesis testing, and statements regarding the relationship of the test variable to a network of other variables that have been investigated. Thus, construct validation is a never-ending process in which new relationships always can be verified and investigated.

VALIDITY IN CLINICAL PRACTICE

Although a test may have been found to have a high level of validity during its construction, it does not necessarily follow that the test will also be valid within a specific situation with a particular client. A test can never be valid in any absolute sense because, in practice, numerous variables might affect the test results. A serious issue, then, is the degree of validity generalization that is made. In part, this generalization will depend on the similarity between the population used during various stages of test construction and the population and situation that it is being used for in practice. Validity in clinical practice also depends on the extent to which tests can work together to improve each other's accuracy. Some tests thus show "incremental validity" in that they improve accuracy in increments as increasing numbers of sources of data are used. Incremental validity, then, refers to the ability of tests to produce information above what is already known. Another important consideration is the ability of the clinician to generate hypotheses, test these hypotheses, and blend the data derived from hypothesis testing into a coherent, integrated picture of the person. Maloney and Ward (1976) refer to this latter approach to validity as "conceptual validity" since it involves creating a conceptually coherent description of the person.

Incremental Validity

For a test to be considered useful and efficient, it must be able to produce accurate results above and beyond the results that could be obtained with greater ease and less expense. If equally accurate clinical descriptions could be obtained through such basic information as biographical data and knowing the referral question, then there would be no need for psychological tests. Incremental validity also needs to be evaluated in relation to cost effectiveness. A psychological test might indeed demonstrate incremental validity by increasing the relative proportions of accurate diagnoses, or "hit rates," by 2%. However, practitioners need to question whether this small increase in accuracy is worth the extra time involved in administering and interpreting the test. Clinicians might direct their time more productively toward direct treatment.

In the 1950s, one of the theoretical defenses for tests having low reliabilities and validities was that, when used in combination, their accuracy could be improved. In other words, results from a series of different tests could provide checks and balances to correct for inaccurate interpretations. A typical strategy used to empirically test for this was to first obtain biographical data, make interpretations/decisions based on this data, and then test its accuracy based upon some outside criterion. Next, a test such as the MMPI could be given; then, the interpretations and decisions based on it could likewise be assessed for accuracy. Finally clinicians could be given both sets of data to assess any improvements in the accuracies of interpretation/decisions between either of the first two conditions and the combined information.

It would seem logical that the greater the number of tests used, the greater would be the overall validity of the assessment battery. However, research on psychological tests used in clinical practice has often demonstrated that they have poor incremental validity. An older but representative study by Kostlan (1954) on male psychiatric outpatients compared the utility of a case history, Rorschach, MMPI, and a sentence completion test. Twenty experienced clinicians interpreted different combinations of the above sources of test data. Their conclusions were combined against criterion judges who used a lengthy checklist of personality descriptions. The conclusions were that, for most of the data, the clinicians were no more accurate than if they had used only age, occupation, education, marital status, and a basic description of the referral question. The exception was that the most accurate descriptions were based on a combination of social history and the MMPI. In contrast, psychological tests have sometimes clearly demonstrated their incremental validity. For example, Schwartz and Wiedel (1981) demonstrated that neurological residents gave more accurate diagnoses when an MMPI was used in combination with history, EEG, and physical exam. This was probably due not so much to a specific MMPI "neurological profile," but rather that the MMPI increased diagnostic accuracy by enabling the residents to rule out other possible diagnoses.

Often clinical psychologists will attempt to make a series of behavioral predictions based on complex psychological tests. Although these predictions may show varying levels of accuracy, a simpler and more effective means of achieving this information might be to simply ask the clients to predict their own behaviors. People have consistently been found to not only be quite accurate at predicting their own behavior (Bem & Funder, 1978; Bandura, 1977), but their self-assessments are typically much better than the predictions derived from formal psychological reports. Thus clinicians should continually ask themselves whether they can obtain relevant information in a simpler, less expensive manner. Certainly, psychological tests are worthwhile, but more importantly they should be used with discretion and with an awareness of the alternatives that might be available.

Garb (1984), in a review of studies on incremental validity, has provided a number of general conclusions. He consistently found that the addition of an MMPI led to increases in validity although the increases were quite small when the MMPI was added to extensive data. The addition of projective tests to a test battery did not generally increase incremental validity. Lanyon and Goodstein (1982) have added that case histories are generally preferable to psychological test data. Furthermore, a single test in combination with case history data is generally as effective as a large number of tests with case history data. The MMPI alone was generally found to be preferable to a battery containing the MMPI, Rorschach, and Sentence Completion.

In defense of the poor incremental validity of many of the traditional clinical tests are weaknesses and unanswered questions relating to the above research. First, few studies have looked at statistically derived predictions and interpretations based on optimal multiple cutoff scores or multiple regression equations. However, more recent research, particularly on such tests as the MMPI and CPI, has emphasized this approach. For example, combined weightings on such variables as specific CPI scores, Scholastic Aptitude Test (SAT) scores, grade point average (GPA), and I.Q. can be combined to predict success in specific programs. Further research using this approach may yield greater incremental validity for a wide number of assessment techniques. Second, few studies on incremental validity have investigated the ways in which different tests might show greater incremental validity in specific situations for specific populations. Instead, most research has focused on the validity of global personality descriptions, perhaps without tying these descriptions to the unique circumstances or contexts persons might be involved in. Finally, since most previous studies have focused on global personality descriptions, certain tests will demonstrate greater incremental validity when predicting highly specific traits and behaviors.

Conceptual Validity

A further method for determining validity, and one that is highly relevant to clinical practice, is conceptual validity (Maloney & Ward, 1976). In contrast to the traditional methods (content validity, etc.), which are primarily concerned with evaluating the theoretical constructs within the test itself, conceptual validity focuses on individuals with their unique histories and behaviors. It is a means of evaluating and integrating test data so that the clinician's conclusions make accurate statements about the examinee (Vance & Guarnaccia, 1989). There are similarities with construct validity in that construct validity also tries to test specific hypothesized relationships between constructs. Conceptual validity is likewise concerned with testing constructs, but in this case the constructs relate to the individual rather than to the test itself.

In determining conceptual validity, the examiner generally begins with individuals for whom no constructs have been developed. The next phase is to observe, collect data, and form a large number of hypotheses. If these hypotheses are confirmed through consistent trends in the test data, behavioral observations, history, and additional data sources, then the hypotheses can be considered to represent valid constructs regarding the person. The focus is on an individual in his or her specific situation, and the data are derived from a variety of sources. The conceptual validity of the constructs is based on the logicalness and internal consistency of the data. Unlike construct validity, which begins with previously developed constructs, conceptual validity produces constructs as its end product. Its aim is for these constructs to provide valid sources of information that can be used to help solve the unique problems that an individual may be facing.

CLINICAL JUDGMENT

Any human interaction involves mutual and continually changing perceptions. Clinical judgment is a special instance of perception in which the clinician attempts to use whatever sources are available to create accurate descriptions of the client. These sources may include test data, case history, medical records, personal journals, and verbal and nonverbal observations of behavior. Relevant issues and processes involved in clinical judgment include data gathering, data synthesis, the relative accuracy of clinical versus statistical/actuarial descriptions, and judgment in determining what to include in a psychological report. This sequence also parallels the process clinicians go through when assessing a client.

Data Gathering and Synthesis

Most of the research related to the strengths and weaknesses of data gathering and synthesis has focused on the assessment interview (see Chapter 3). However, many of the issues and problems related to clinical judgment during interviewing also have implications for the gathering and synthesis of test data. One of the most essential elements in gathering data from any source is the development of an optimum level of rapport. Rapport increases the likeli-hood that clients will give their optimum level of performance. If rapport is not sufficiently developed, it is increasingly likely that the data obtained from the person will be inaccurate.

Another important issue is that the interview itself is typically guided by the client's responses and the clinician's reaction to these responses. A client's responses might be nonrepresentative of the person due to such factors as a transient condition (stressful day, poor night's sleep, etc.) or conscious/unconscious faking. The client's responses also need to be interpreted by the clinician. These interpretations can be influenced by a combination of personality theory, research data, and the clinician's professional and personal experience. The clinician typically develops hypotheses based on a client's responses and combines his or her observations with his or her theoretical understanding of the issue. These hypotheses can be further investigated and tested by interview questions and test data, which can result in confirmation, alteration, or elimination of the hypotheses. Thus, bias can potentially enter into this process from a number of different directions, including the types of questions asked, initial impressions, level of rapport, or theoretical perspective.

Much of the initial data regarding a client is typically collected through unstructured or semistructured interviews. Unstructured approaches in gathering and interpreting data provide flexibility, focus on the uniqueness of the person, and are ideographically rich. In contrast, an important disadvantage of unstructured approaches is that a clinician, like most other persons, can be influenced by a number of personal and cultural biases. For example, clinicians might develop incorrect hypotheses based on first impressions (primacy effect). They might end up seeking erroneous confirmation of incorrect hypotheses by "soliciting" expected responses rather than objectively "probing" for possible disconfirmation. Thus clinicians might be unduly influenced by their preferred theory of personality, halo effects, self-fulfilling prophecies, expectations, and cultural stereotypes. These areas of potential sources of error have led to numerous questions regarding the dependability of clinical judgment.

Accuracy of Clinical Judgments

Once the data has been collected and organized, clinicians then need to make final judgments regarding the client's state. Determining the relative accuracy of these judgments is crucial. One possible source of inaccuracy is that clinicians frequently do not take into account the "base rate," or the rate at which a particular behavior, trait, or diagnosis occurs in the general population. For example, an intake section of a psychiatric hospital might evaluate a population of whom 50% could be considered to be schizophrenic. A clinician who would randomly diagnosis patients as either schizophrenic or nonschizophrenic would be correct 50% of the time. Thus, even a 60% correct diagnosis of schizophrenia would only exceed the base rate (or chance occurrence) by 10%. It is also rare for clinicians to receive feedback regarding either the accuracy of their diagnoses or other frequently used judgments such as behavioral predictions, personality traits, or the relative success of their recommendations (Garb, 1989). Thus it is possible for inaccurate strategies for arriving at conclusions to be continued with little likelihood of being corrected.

Research on person perception accuracy indicates that, even though no two persons are uniformly accurate, some persons are much better at accurately perceiving others. Taft (1955) and Vernon (1964) summarize the early research on person perception accuracy by pointing out that accuracy is not associated with age (in adults), there is little difference in accuracy between males and females (although females are slightly better), and accurate perceptions of others are positively associated with intelligence, artistic/dramatic interests, social detachment, and good emotional adjustment. Authoritarian personalities tend to be poor judges. In most instances, accuracy is related to similarity in race and cultural backgrounds (Malpas & Kravitz, 1969; Shapiro & Penrod, 1986). Interestingly, accuracy by psychologists may be only slightly related to their amount of clinical experience (Garb, 1989) and psychologists may be no better than certain groups of nonprofessionals, such as physical scientists and personnel workers (Taft, 1955; Ziskin & Faust, 1988). Relatively higher rates of accuracy were achieved when clinical judgments based on interviews were combined with formal assessments and when statistical interpretive rules were used. When subjective test interpretation was combined with clinical judgment, it was questionable whether any increase in accuracy was obtained.

Lanyon and Goodstein (1982) summarize the research on improving the accuracy of clinical judgment with the following points. When inaccuracies did occur, it was because clinicians were not paying attention to relevant types of information. When judges were made aware of relevant signs and cues, their judgments improved. For example, persons taught valid statistical prediction formulas for the MMPI increased the accuracy of their predictions (Oskamp, 1962). However, this was only true when using an actuarial approach. Immediate feedback regarding the relative accuracy or inaccuracy of conclusions was also found to increase later accuracy. Finally, the amount of knowledge regarding theoretical relationships and the predictor "target" was positively associated with accuracy. For example, persons having greater theoretical knowledge regarding specific categories, such as sexual offenders or personality disorders, would be expected to more accurately describe these persons.

It would be logical to assume that the more confidence clinicians feel regarding the accuracy of their judgments, the more likely it would be that their judgments would be accurate. Unfortunately, studies have indicated that confidence was often not related to accuracy (Kelly & Fiske, 1951; Oskamp, 1965). Kelly and Fiske (1951) even found that degree of confidence was inversely related to predicting the success of trainees in a V.A. training program. Several studies (Fischoff, Slovic, & Lichtenstein, 1977; Lichtenstein & Fischoff, 1977) concluded that persons were generally overconfident regarding judgments and, when outcome knowledge was made available, clinicians typically overestimated what they thought they knew prior to having received outcome knowledge. As knowledge and experience increase regarding an area, there was generally a decrease in confidence regarding judgments.

This observation was found to be true unless the clinicians were very knowledgeable, in which case they were likely to have a moderate level of confidence. A review by Garb (1989) concluded that highly experienced clinicians assessing personality were generally no more accurate than less experienced clinicians. However, the more experienced clinicians were able to more accurately rate their degree of confidence related to their judgments.

The research mentioned so far on accuracy in clinical judgment implies specific guidelines clinicians should follow. First, statistical rules for prediction, whenever these are available, should be used to reach conclusions. Clinicians should also seek feedback, whenever possible, regarding the accuracy and usefulness of their judgments. For example, psychological reports should ideally be followed up with rating forms (that can be completed by the referral sources) relating to the clarity, precision, accuracy, and usefulness of the information and recommendations contained in the reports (see Ownby & Wallbrown, 1983). However, when evaluating success, caution should be exercised by taking into account base rates (number of correct identifications occurring by chance) and the inflated success rate created by the possible inclusion of universally valid statements (judgments that would apply to everyone). Thus, beginning practitioners should be cautious regarding confidence in the accuracy of their judgments, especially since confidence for all but the most experienced clinicians seems to have little relationship with accuracy. Finally, clinicians should learn as much as possible regarding the theoretical and empirical material on the person or group they are assessing.

Clinical versus Actuarial Prediction

Over 30 years ago, Meehl (1954) published a review of research comparing the relative accuracy of clinical judgment versus statistical formulas when used on identical sets of data (life history, demographic data, test profiles). The clinical approach used a clinician's judgment, whereas the actuarial approach used empirically derived formulas, such as single/multiple cutoffs and regression equations, to come to decisions regarding a client. His review covered a large number of settings including military placement, college success, criminal recidivism, and benefit from psychotherapy. He concluded that statistical decisions consistently outperformed a clinician (Meehl, 1954, 1965). This resulted in some lively debate in the journals, with Meehl's conclusions generally being supported (Goldberg, 1965; Wiggins, 1973). Dawes and Corrigan (1974) even found that an actuarial formula based on specific clinicians' own decision making processes yielded more valid future predictions than the clinician's own predictions. This was probably due to the formula reducing the influence of uncontrolled errors in the clinician's procedures.

Despite the empirical support for an actuarial approach, several practical and theoretical issues need to be considered. A clinical approach to integrating data and arriving at conclusions allows a clinician to explore, probe, and deepen his or her understanding in many areas. These frequently involve areas that tests or statistical formulas cannot measure. Often an interview is the only means of obtaining observations of behavior and unique aspects of history. Idiosyncratic events with a low frequency of occurrence may significantly alter a clinician's conclusions although no formulas take these events into account. It is quite common for unique, rare events to have occurred at some time in a client's life and, during the process of assessment, they are frequently relevant and can often alter the conclusions of many, if not most, clinical assessments. Not only do unique aspects of a person change interpretations, but typically an assessment for a person needs to be focused for a specific context and specific situation that he or she is involved in. When the focus changes from institutional to individual decision making, the relevance of statistical rules becomes less practical (Vance & Guarnaccia, 1989). Not only are individuals too multifaceted, but their unique situations, contexts, and the decisions facing them are even more multifaceted.

A further difficulty with a purely actuarial approach is that development of both test reliability and validity, as well as actuarial formulas, requires that the world be conceived as stable and static. For such approaches to be useful, the implicit assumption is that neither people nor criteria change. In contrast, the practitioner must deal with a natural world that is imperfect, constantly changing, does not necessarily follow rules, is filled with constantly changing perceptions, and is subject to chance or at least impossible to predict events. Thus, even when statistical formulas are available, they may not apply. This distinction between the statistical orientation of the psychometrician and the natural environment of the practitioner underlies the discrepancy between their two worlds. Practitioners must somehow try to combine these two modes of analysis, but often find the task difficult. The fact that controlled studies generally favor a statistical approach over a clinical one may be true but, at the same time, the fact is also usually useless to the practitioner involved in the changing and unique world of practice (Bonarius, 1984). Often, there is no alternative other than to rely on clinical judgment to combine a wide variety of relevant information. This return to a "pre-Meehl" perspective is unfortunate and is accepted by most clinicians with hesitation.

Bonarius (1984) presents a conceptual alternative to the above dilemma. The first step is to alter mechanistic views of prediction. Instead, clinicians might avoid the term "prediction" altogether and use "anticipation." Anticipating future possibilities implies a cognitive constructional process rather than a mechanical process. It admits that the world can never be perfect in any mechanistic sense and that there is no such thing as an average person in an average situation engaged in an average interaction. Furthermore, the creation of future events is shared by coparticipants. Clients take an active part in formulating and evaluating their goals. The success of future goals is dependent on the degree of effort they are willing to put into them. Responsibility for the future is shared by coparticipants. Thus, the likelihood that future events will occur is related to both cognitive constructions of an idiosyncratic world, and interaction between participants.

The ideal approach might be for clinicians to be aware of and to use, whenever available, actuarial approaches such as multiple cutoffs and regression equations. The conclusions reached from actuarial approaches also need to be integrated with data and inferences obtainable only through clinical means. If unusual details regarding a client are discovered and result in altering an interpretation, then the basis for this alteration should be noted in the psychological report. Sensitivity should also be given to individual differences in person perception accuracy between one clinician and the next. These differences may depend on experience, training, knowledge, personality, and the amount and quality of feedback regarding the perceptions of different clinicians. Clinicians also need to be aware of possible increases and decreases in clinical judgment resulting from the incremental validity of their instruments.

The Psychological Report

An accurate and effective psychological report requires that clinicians clarify their thinking and crystallize their interpretations. The report serves to tie together all sources of information. Often, complex interprofessional and interpersonal issues are combined. All the advantages and limitations involved with clinical judgment either directly or indirectly affect the report. The focus should be a clear communication of the clinician's interpretations, conclusions, and recommendations. Chapter 12 provides in-depth information on the psychological report as it relates to relevant research, guidelines, format, and sample reports.

PHASES IN CLINICAL ASSESSMENT

An outline of the phases of clinical assessment can provide both a conceptual framework for approaching an evaluation and a summary of some of the points already discussed. Although the steps in assessment will be isolated for conceptual convenience, in actuality they often occur simultaneously and interact with one another. Throughout these phases, the clinician should fulfill the role of an integrator of data and an expert on human behavior, rather than merely an interpreter of test scores. This is consistent with the belief that a psychological assessment can be most useful when it addresses specific individual problems and provides guidelines for decision making regarding these problems.

Evaluating the Referral Question

Many of the practical limitations of psychological evaluations are due to an inadequate clarification of the problem. Since clinicians are aware of the assets and limitations of psychological tests and since clinicians are responsible for providing useful information, it is their duty to clarify the nature of the requests that are made of them. Furthermore, it cannot be expected that initial requests for an evaluation will be adequately stated. Clinicians may need to uncover hidden agendas, unspoken expectations, and complex interpersonal relationships, as well as to explain the specific limitations of psychological tests. One of the most important general requirements is that clinicians have an understanding of the vocabulary, conceptual model, dynamics, and expectations of the referral setting in which they will be working.

Clinicians are rarely asked to give a general or global assessment, but are instead asked to answer specific questions. To address these questions, it is sometimes helpful to contact the referral source at different stages in the assessment process. For example, it is usually important in an educational evaluation to observe the student in the classroom environment. The information derived from such an observation might be relayed back to the referral source for further clarification or modification of the referral question. Likewise, an attorney may wish to somewhat alter his or her referral question based on preliminary information derived from the clinician's initial interview with the client.

Acquiring Knowledge Relating to the Content of the Problem

Before beginning the actual testing procedure, examiners should carefully consider the nature of the problem, the adequacy of the tests they will be using, and the specific applicability of that test to an individual's unique situation. The consideration of these factors may require referring both to the test manual and to additional outside sources. Clinicians should clearly be aware of operational definitions for such problems as anxiety disorders, psychoses, personality disorders, or organic impairment so that they can be continually alerted to their possible expression during the assessment procedure. Competence in merely administering and scoring tests is insufficient to conduct effective assessment. For example, the development of an I.Q. score does not necessarily indicate that an examiner is aware of differing cultural expressions of intelligence or of the limitations of the assessment device. It is essential that clinicians have in-depth knowledge regarding the variables they are measuring or else the results of the evaluations are likely to be extremely limited.

Related to this is the relative adequacy of the test in measuring the variable being considered. This includes evaluating certain practical considerations, the standardization sample, and reliability and validity (see Table 1–1). It is important that the examiner also considers the nature of the problem in relation to the adequacy of the test and decides whether a specific test or tests can be appropriately used on an individual or group of individuals. This involves knowledge relating to such areas as the client's age, race, educational background, motivation for testing, anticipated level of resistance, social environment, and interpersonal relationships. Finally, clinicians need to assess the effectiveness or utility of the test in aiding the treatment process.

Data Collection

After the referral question has been clarified and knowledge relating to the problem has been obtained, clinicians can then proceed with the actual collection of information. This may come from a wide variety of sources, the most frequent of which are test scores, personal history, behavioral observations, and interview data. Clinicians may also wish to obtain school records, previous psychological observations, medical records, police reports, or discuss the client with parents or teachers. It is important to realize that the tests themselves are merely one tool or one source for obtaining data. The case history is of equal importance since it serves to provide a context for understanding the client's current problems and, through this understanding, renders the test scores meaningful. In many cases, a client's history is of even more significance in making predictions and in assessing the seriousness of his or her condition than his or her test scores. For example, a high score on depression on the MMPI is not as helpful in assessing suicide risk as are historical factors like the number of previous attempts, age, sex, details regarding any previous attempts, and length of time the client has been depressed. Of equal importance is the fact that the test scores themselves will usually not be sufficient to answer the referral question. For specific problem solving and decision making, clinicians must rely on multiple sources and, using these sources, check to assess the consistency of the observations they make.

Interpreting the Data

The end product of assessment should be a description of the client's present level of functioning, considerations relating to etiology, prognosis, and treatment recommendations. Etiological descriptions should avoid simplistic formulas and should instead focus on the influence exerted by several interacting factors. These factors can be divided into primary, predisposing, precipitating, and reinforcing causes (Carson, Butcher, & Coleman, 1988), and a complete description of etiology should take all of these into account. Further elaborations may also attempt to assess the person from a systems perspective in which patterns of interaction, mutual two-way influences, and the specifics of circular information feedback are evaluated. Clinicians should also pay careful attention to research on, and the implications of, incremental validity and continually be aware of the limitations and possible inaccuracies involved in clinical judgment. If actuarial formulas are available, they should be used whenever possible. These considerations indicate that the description of a client should not be a mere labeling or classification, but should rather provide a deeper and more accurate understanding of the person. This understanding should allow the examiner to perceive new facets of the person in terms of both his or her internal experience and his or her relationships with others.

To develop these descriptions, clinicians must make inferences from their test data. Although such data is objective and empirical, the process of developing hypotheses, obtaining support for these hypotheses, and integrating the conclusions is dependent on the experience and training of the clinician. This process generally follows a sequence of developing impressions, identifying relevant facts, making inferences, and supporting these inferences with relevant and consistent data. Maloney and Ward (1976) have conceptualized a seven-phase approach (Figure 1–1) toward evaluating data. They note that, in actual practice, these phases are not as clearly defined as indicated in Figure 1–1. Oftentimes they occur simultaneously. For example, when a clinician reads a referral question or initially observes a client, he or she is already developing hypotheses about that person and checking to assess the validity of these observations.

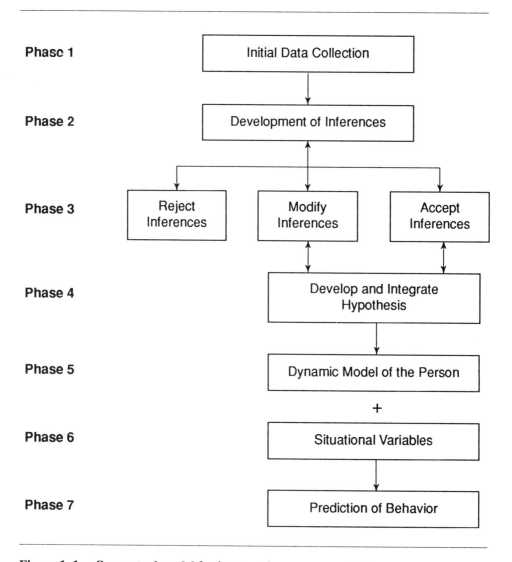

Figure 1–1.   Conceptual model for interpreting assessment data
Adapted from Maloney and Ward, 1976, p. 161. Reprinted, by permission, from *Psychological Assessment: A Conceptual Approach*, by M.P. Maloney and M.P. Ward, Oxford University Press, 1976.

Phase 1   The first phase involves collecting data about the client. It begins with the referral question and is followed by a review of the client's previous history and records. At this point, the clinician is already beginning to develop tentative hypotheses and to clarify questions that can be investigated in more detail. The next step is actual client contact, in which the clinician conducts an interview and administers a variety of psychological tests. The client's behavior during the interview, as well as the content or factual data, are noted. Out of this data, the clinician begins to make his or her inferences.

Phase 2   Phase 2 focuses on the development of a wide variety of inferences about the client. These inferences serve both a summary and explanatory function. For example, an examiner may infer that a client is depressed, which also may explain his or her slow performance, distractibility, flattened affect, and withdrawn behavior. The examiner may then wish to evaluate whether this depression is a deeply ingrained trait or more a reaction to a current situational difficulty. This may be determined by referring to test scores, interview data, or any additional sources of available information. The emphasis in the second phase is on developing multiple inferences that should initially be tentative. They serve the purpose of guiding future investigation to obtain additional information that is then used to confirm, modify, or negate later hypotheses.

Phase 3   Since the third phase is concerned with either accepting or rejecting the inferences developed in Phase 2, there is constant and active interaction between these phases. Often, in investigating the validity of an inference, a clinician will alter either the meaning or the emphasis of an inference, or will develop entirely new ones. It is rare that an inference will be entirely substantiated, but rather the validity of that inference can become progressively strengthened. This is achieved by evaluating the degree of consistency and the strength of data that support a particular inference. For example, the inference that a client is anxious may be supported by WAIS-R subscale performance, MMPI scores, and behavioral observations, or it may only be suggested by one of these sources. The amount of evidence to support an inference directly affects the amount of confidence a clinician can place in this inference.

Phase 4   As a result of inferences developed in the previous three phases, the clinician can move in Phase 4 from specific inferences to general statements about the client. This involves an elaboration of each inference in order to describe trends or patterns of the client. For example, the inference that a client is depressed may be due to self-verbalizations in which the client continually criticizes and judges his or her behavior. This may also be expanded to give information regarding the ease or frequency with which a person might enter into the depressive state. The central task in Phase 4 is to develop and begin to elaborate on statements relating to the client.

Phases 5, 6, 7   The fifth phase involves a further elaboration of a wide variety of the personality traits of the individual. It represents an integration and correlation of the client's characteristics. This may include describing and discussing such factors as need for achievement, dynamics involved in depression, level of anxiety, conflicting needs, intellectual potential, problem solving style, and relative level of social skills. Although Phases 4 and 5 are similar, Phase 5 provides a more comprehensive and integrated description of the client than Phase 4. Finally, Phase 6 places this comprehensive description of the person into a situational context and Phase 7 makes specific predictions regarding his or her behavior. Phase 7 is the most crucial element involved in decision making and requires that the clinician take into account the interaction between personal and situational variables.

Establishing the validity of these inferences presents a difficult challenge for clinicians since, unlike many medical diagnoses, psychological inferences cannot usually be physically documented. Furthermore, clinicians are rarely confronted with feedback regarding the validity of these inferences. Despite these difficulties, psychological descriptions should strive to meet the following four basic criteria: reliability, adequate descriptive breadth, descriptive validity, and predictive validity (Blashfield & Draguns, 1976). Reliability of descriptions refers to whether the description or classification can be replicated by other clinicians (interdiagnostician agreement) as well as by the same clinician on different occasions (intradiagnostician agreement). The next criterion is the breadth of coverage encompassed in the classification. Any classification should be broad enough to encompass a wide range of individuals and yet specific enough to provide useful information regarding the individual being evaluated. Descriptive validity involves the degree to which individuals who are classified are similar on variables external to the classification system. For example, are individuals who have similar MMPI profiles also similar on other relevant attributes—such as family history, demographic variables, legal difficulties, or alcohol abuse? Finally, predictive validity refers to the confidence with which test inferences can be used to evaluate future outcomes. These may include academic achievement, job performance, or the out-come of treatment. This is one of the most crucial functions of testing. Unless inferences can be made that effectively enhance decision making, the scope and relevance of testing are significantly reduced. Although these criteria are difficult to achieve and to evaluate, they represent the ideal standard for which assessments should strive.

RECOMMENDED READING

Anastasi, A. (1988). *Psychological Testing*. (6th ed.). New York: Macmillan.

Garb, H. N. (1985). The incremental validity of information used in personality assessment. *Clinical Psychology Review*, 4, 641-655.

Kaplan, R. M., & Sacuzzo, D. (1989). *Psychological Testing*: *Principles, Applications, and Issues*. Pacific Grove, CA.: Wadsworth.

McReynolds, P. (1989). Diagnosis and clinical assessment: Current status and major issues. *Annual Review of Psychology*, 40, 83-108.

Chapter 2

THE CONTEXT OF CLINICAL ASSESSMENT

Although general knowledge regarding tests and test construction is essential, practitioners also need to consider aspects of the referral setting, relevant guidelines and cautions, criteria for selecting testing instruments, and issues related to computer-assisted assessment. The overall purpose of such knowledge is to develop the ability to place testing procedures and test scores into an appropriate context. In particular, clinicians should keep in mind such issues as clarifying the referral question, determining who will read the final report, identifying possible abuses of assessment, selecting the most appropriate instrument for the variable or problem being studied, and making appropriate use of computer-assisted interpretations.

TYPES OF REFERRAL SETTINGS

Throughout the assessment process, clinicians should make efforts to clarify the referral question and understand the unique problems and demands encountered in different referral settings. In fact, examiners who do not take these issues into consideration, but who may otherwise be skilled in administering and interpreting tests, might provide a large amount of useless information to their referral source. Clinicians might even administer a needless series of tests. That is, if the clinicians had investigated the underlying motive behind the referral, they might have discovered that evaluation through testing was not warranted.

One of the more frequent sources of error in test interpretation occurs because clinicians do not develop a clear comprehension of the referral question in its broadest context (Levine, 1981). In turn, requests for psychological testing are often not made in a clear manner. They may be worded as vaguely as "I would like a psychological evaluation on Mr. Smith" or "could you evaluate Jimmy because he is having difficulties in school." The request is usually posed neither as a question to be answered nor a decision to be made, when in fact this is almost always the position that the referral source is in. For example, a school administrator may need testing to support a decision he or she has already made, a teacher may want to prove to parents that their child has a serious problem, or a psychiatric resident may not be comfortable with the manner in which he or she is managing a patient. An organization's surface motive for testing may even be as vague as testing someone as a matter of policy. Many of these situations need far more clarification before clinicians can provide useful problem solving information. Furthermore, many of these situations include issues other than those involved in the testing itself and are filled with hidden agendas that may not be adequately handled through psychological testing.

It must be stressed that the responsibility for exploring and clarifying the referral question lies with the clinician, who particularly should help the referring person organize the referral question. This clarification involves placing the client's difficulty within a workable context. Clinicians must understand the decisions that the referral source is facing, as well as the alternatives that are available and the relative usefulness of each of these alternatives. Clinicians also need to specify the relevance of the psychological evaluation in regard to determining different alternatives and the possible outcomes for each of these alternatives. They should make clear the advantages and usefulness of psychological testing, but should also explain the limitations inherent in test data.

In helping to clarify the referral question, as well as in developing a relevant psychological evaluation, clinicians should become familiar with the types of environments in which they will be working. The most frequent environments are the psychiatric setting, the general medical setting, the legal context, the educational context, and the psychological clinic.

The Psychiatric Setting

Levine (1981) has summarized the following points as being important for a psychologist working in a psychiatric setting. First, referrals typically come from a psychiatrist who may be asking the referral question in the role of administrator, psychotherapist, or physician. In each of these roles, unique issues confront the psychiatrist. The primary responsibility of clinicians is to develop a clear understanding of these roles so that their evaluations can directly address the problems with which the psychiatrist is likely to be faced.

One of the main roles a psychiatrist fills is as an administrator in a ward. Ward administrators frequently must make decisions about such problems as suicide risk, admission/ discharge, and the administration of a wide variety of medical procedures. In many situations, a psychiatrist will use other persons to help with decisions even though the psychiatrist is still primarily responsible for these decisions. This represents a change from the typical role of psychiatrists 25 years ago. Originally, psychiatrists were mainly concerned with diagnosis and treatment, but current issues about custody, freedom of the patient, and the safety of society have taken over as the primary focus. From the perspective of psychologists making assessments, this means it is insufficient to make a classical psychiatric diagnosis. For example, if a patient is labeled manic-depressive, this label does not, in itself, provide information regarding the level of dangerousness that the patient poses to him- or herself or to others. Once patients have been admitted to a psychiatric setting, many practical questions have to be answered, such as the type of ward in which to place them, the types of activities in which they should be involved, and the method of therapy that would be likely to benefit them the most.

The task confronting the psychologist is to initially determine and clarify the questions he or she receives from the administrator of a psychiatric ward, particularly in regard to any decisions that must be made concerning the patient. Sometimes psychologists in psychiatric settings are given the vague request for "a psychological" without further elaboration. Thus, a standard evaluation is developed based on the psychologist's preconception of what is involved in "a psychological." This may include a discussion of the patient's defense mechanisms, diagnosis, cognitive style, and psychosocial history. Often this evaluation is conducted without addressing the specific decisions that have to be made or perhaps only addressing two or three relevant issues and omitting others. To maximize the usefulness of an evaluation, examiners must both clarify and address these issues. This implies an awareness of, and sensitivity to, psychiatric administrators' legal and custodial responsibilities.

In contrast to ward administrators, the standard referral question from psychiatrists who are conducting psychotherapy is whether a particular patient they are considering working with is suitable for therapy. This type of assessment is usually clear-cut and typically does not present any difficulties. Such an evaluation can elaborate on likely problems that may occur during the course of therapy, defenses, capacity for insight, cognitive styles, affective level, and diagnosis. However, if a referral is made during therapy, a number of difficulties surrounding the referral might not be readily apparent from the referral question.

An area of potential conflict arises when psychiatrists are attempting to fulfill roles of both administrator (caretaker) and psychotherapist, and yet have not attempted to clearly define these roles either for themselves or for their patients. The resulting ambiguity may cause defensiveness and resistance on the part of the patient and a feeling on the part of the psychiatrist that the patient is not living up to the therapist's expectations. Thus, the resolution of this conflict cannot be found in the elaboration of a specific trait or need within the patient, but must occur from the context in which the therapist and patient are interacting. A standard psychological evaluation investigating the internal structure of the patient will not address this issue.

A second possible problem area for clients referred in the midst of therapy can often be the result of personal anxiety and discomfort on the therapist's part. Thus, such issues as countertransference and possibly unreasonable expectations on the part of the therapist may be equally or even more important than looking at a patient's characteristics. The possibility of role ambiguity, countertransference, or unreasonable expectations needs to be investigated and, if present, elaborated and communicated in a sensitive manner.

When psychiatrists are acting in the role of physician, they and the psychologist may have different conceptual models for describing a patient's disorder. Whereas psychiatrists function primarily from a disease or medical model, psychologists may speak in terms of difficulties in living with people and society. In effectively communicating the results of psychological evaluations, examiners must be able to deal with this conceptual difference. For example, a psychiatrist may ask whether a patient is schizophrenic, whereas a psychologist may not believe that the label "schizophrenia" is useful or even a scientifically valid concept. However, the larger issue is that the psychiatrist is still faced with some practical decisions. In fact, the psychiatrist may even share some of the same concerns regarding the term "schizophrenia," but this conceptual issue may not be particularly important in dealing with the patient. For example, legal requirements or hospital policies might require that the patient be given a traditional diagnosis. The psychiatrist may also have to decide whether to give antipsychotic medication, electroconvulsive therapy, or psychotherapy. If a patient is diagnosed as schizophrenic rather than brain damaged or personality disordered, then, given a hospital's current and economic policy considerations, the psychiatrist may decide upon antipsychotic medication. An effective examiner should be able to see beyond possible conceptual differences and instead address practical considerations. A psychiatrist may refer a defensive patient who cannot or will not verbalize his or her concerns and ask whether this person is schizophrenic. Beyond this are such factors as the quality of the patient's thought processes and whether the person poses a danger to him- or herself or to others. Thus, the effective examiner must translate his or her findings into a conceptual model that is both understandable by a psychiatrist and useful from a task-oriented point of view.

The General Medical Setting

It has been estimated that as many as two-thirds of patients seen by physicians have significant emotional components to their illnesses. Somewhere between 25% to 50% have specifically psychological disorders in addition to medical ones (Lipowski, 1977). Most of these psychological difficulties are neither diagnosed nor referred for treatment (Borus, Howes, Devins, & Rosenberg, 1988; Follette & Cummings, 1967). In addition, many traditionally "medical" disorders—such as coronary heart disease, asthma, allergies, rheumatoid arthritis, ulcers, and headaches—have been found to possess a significant psychosocial component (Friedman & Booth-Kewley, 1987; Olbrisch, 1977; Schwartz, 1982). Not only are psychological factors related to disease, but are, of equal importance, related to the development and maintenance of health. A complete approach to the patient, then, involves an awareness of the interaction between physical, psychological, and social variables (Schwartz, 1982). Thus the contributions that psychologists can make are potentially extremely important. To adequately work in general medical settings, psychologists must become familiar with medical descriptions, which often means learning a complex and extensive vocabulary. Another important consideration is that, even though physicians must often draw information from a variety of sources to aid in their decision making, they must take ultimate responsibility for whatever decisions are made.

The most frequent situations in which physicians might use the services of a psychologist involve possible emotional factors associated with medical complaints, assessment for neuropsychological deficit, psychological treatment for chronic pain, and the treatment of chemical dependency (Bamgbose, Jesse, Smith, & Groth-Marnat, 1980; Groth-Marnat, 1988). Even though the physician has conducted a medical exam without finding any physical basis for the patient's complaints, the physician still has to devise some form of treatment or at least an appropriate referral. This is crucial in that a significant portion of patients referred to physicians do not have any detectable physical difficulties and their central complaint is likely to be psychological (Borus et al., 1988; Jencks, 1985). Within this situation, the psychologist can elaborate and specify how a patient can be treated for possible psychological difficulties.

Another area that has greatly increased in importance is the psychological assessment of a patient's neuropsychological status. Whereas physicians attempt to detect physical lesions in the nervous system, the neuropsychologist has traditionally been more concerned with the psychological status of higher cortical functions. Another way of stating this: Physicians evaluate how the *brain* is functioning, whereas the neuropsychologist evaluates how the *person* is functioning as a result of possible brain abnormalities. The typical areas of assessment focus primarily on the presence of possible intellectual deterioration in such areas as memory, sequencing, abstract reasoning, and spatial organization. In the past, neuropsychologists have been asked to help determine whether a patient's complaints were "functional" or "organic." Currently, the focus is more on whether the person has neuropsychological deficits that may contribute to or account for observed behavioral difficulties than on either/or distinctions. Physicians often want to know whether a test profile suggests a specific diagnosis—particularly malingering, conversion disorder, hypochondriasis, organic brain syndrome, or depression with pseudoneurological features. Further issues that neuropsychologists often address include the nature and extent of identified lesions, localization of lesions, emotional status of neurologically impaired patients, extent of disability, and suggestions for treatment planning—such as recommendations for cognitive rehabilitation, vocational training, and readjustment to family and friends.

A physician might also request a psychologist to conduct a presurgical evaluation to assess the likelihood of a serious stress reaction to surgery. Finally, physicians—particularly pediatricians—are often concerned with detecting early signs of serious psychological disorder, which may have been brought to their attention by parents, other family members, or teachers. In such situations, the psychologist's evaluation should assess not only the patient's present psychological condition, but also the contributing factors in his or her environment, and should provide a prediction of the patient's status during the next few months or years. When the patient's current condition, current environment, and future prospects have been evaluated, the examiner can then recommend the next phase in the intervention process. A psychologist may also consult with physicians to assist them in more effectively disclosing the results of an examination to the patient or the patient's family.

The Legal Context

During the past 15 years, the use of psychologists in legal settings has become more prevalent, important, and accepted. Psychologists might be called in at any stage of legal decision making. During the investigation stage, they might be consulted to assess the reliability of a witness or to help evaluate the quality of information by a witness. The prosecuting attorney might also need to have a psychologist evaluate the quality of another mental health professional's report, evaluate the accused person's competency, or help determine the specifics of a crime. A defense attorney might use a psychologist to help in supporting an insanity plea, to help in jury selection, or to document that brain damage has occurred. A judge might use a psychologist's report as one of a number of factors to help determine a sentence, a penal officer might wish consultation to help determine the type of confinement or level of dangerousness, or a parole officer might need assistance to help plan a rehabilitation program. Even though a psychologist might write a legal report, he or she is likely to actually appear in court in only about one in every ten cases.

Since psychology has only recently been used extensively in the legal/justice system, the psychologist's role lacks clear definition. This is further complicated by certain legal terms the psychologist has to deal with that are not clearly defined within the legal profession itself (for example, insanity). In addition, many attorneys are familiar with the same professional literature that psychologists read and may use this information to either attack the qualifications of psychologists or the assessment tools they have used to reach their conclusions (Ziskin & Faust. 1988).

Each psychologist appearing in court must have his or her qualifications approved. Important areas that are considered include the presence of clinical expertise in treating specialty disorders and relevant publication credits. Despite these qualification standards, psychologists are generally viewed favorably by the courts and may be reaching parity with psychiatrists (Hall, Catlin, Boissevain, & Westgate, 1984).

As outlined by the American Board of Forensic Psychology, the practice of forensic psychology includes training/consultation with legal practitioners, evaluation of populations likely to come into contact with the legal system, and the translation of relevant technical psychological knowledge into usable information. Psychologists are used most frequently in child custody cases, competency of a person to dispose of property, juvenile commitment, and personal injury suits in which the psychologist documents the nature and extent of the litigant's suffering or disability (stress, anxiety, cognitive deficit). In contrast, psychiatrists are far more likely to be used in assessing a person's competency to stand trial, degree of criminal responsibility, and mental defect. Although psychologists can testify in these cases, physicians need to sign any commitment certificates and are therefore more likely to be used.

One essential requirement when working in the legal context is for psychologists to modify their language. Many legal terms have exact and specific meanings that, if misunderstood, could lead to extremely negative consequences. Words such as "incompetent," "insane," or "reasonable certainty" may vary within different judicial systems or from state to state. Psychologists must familiarize themselves with this terminology and the different nuances involved in its use. Psychologists may also be requested to explain in detail the meaning of their conclusions and how these conclusions were reached. Whereas the actual data that psychologists generate is rarely questioned, the inferences and generalizability of these inferences are frequently placed under scrutiny or even attacked. Often this questioning can seem rude or downright hostile but, in most cases, attorneys are merely doing their best to defend their client. Proper legal protocol also requires that the psychologist answer questions directly rather than respond to the implications or underlying direction suggested by the questions. Furthermore, attorneys (or members of the jury) may not be trained in or appreciate the scientific method, which is the mainstay of a psychologist's background. In contrast, attorneys are trained in legal analysis and reasoning, which subjectively focuses on the uniqueness of each case rather than on a comparison of the person to a statistically relevant normative group.

Two potentially problematic areas lie in evaluating insanity and evaluating competency. Even though physicians are more typically called on to testify in these areas, psychologists can also become involved. Although the insanity plea has often received considerable publicity, very few people make the appeal and, of those who do, few have it granted. It is usually difficult for an expert witness to evaluate such cases because of the problem of possible malingering in order to receive a lighter sentence and the possible ambiguity of the term "insanity." Usually a person is considered insane in accordance with the McNaughton Rule, which states that persons are not responsible if they did not know the nature and extent of their actions and if they cannot distinguish that what they did was wrong according to social norms. In some states, the ambiguity of the term is increased because defendants can be granted the insanity plea if it can be shown they were insane at the time of the incident. Other states include the clause of an "irresistible impulse" to the definition of insanity. Related to insanity is whether the defendant is competent to stand trial. Competence is usually defined as whether or not the person can cooperate in a meaningful way with the attorney, understand the purpose of the proceedings, and understand the implications of the possible penalties. To increase the reliability and validity of competency and insanity evaluations, specialized assessment techniques have been developed such as the Competency Screening Test (Lipset, Lelos, & McGarry, 1971; Nottingham & Mattson, 1981) and the Rogers Criminal Responsibility Scales (Rogers, 1984).

The prediction of dangerousness has also been a problematic area. Since actual violent or self-destructive behavior is a relatively unusual behavior (low base rate), any cutoff criteria are going to typically produce a high number of false positives. Thus, people incorrectly identified may potentially be detained and understandably be upset. However, the negative result of failure to identify and take action against people who are potentially violent makes erring on the side of caution more acceptable. Attempts to use special scales on the MMPI (Overcontrolled Hostility Scale; Megargee & Mendelsohn, 1962) or a 4-3 code type (see Chapter 7) have not been found to be sufficiently accurate for individual decision making. However, significant improvements have been made in predicting dangerousness by using actuarial strategies, which include relevant information on developmental influences, possible events that lower thresholds, arrest record, life situation, and situational triggers such as interpersonal stress and substance intoxication (Hall et al., 1984; Klassen & O'Connor, 1989). The legal/justice system is most likely to give weight to those individual assessment strategies that combine recidivism statistics, tests specifically designed to predict dangerousness, and double administrations of psychological tests to assess change over time. Clinical judgment combined with a single administration of tests is usually considered to be only mildly useful (Hall et al., 1984).

Psychologists are sometimes requested to help with child custody decisions. The central consideration is to determine which arrangement will be in the child's best interest.

Areas to be considered include the mental health of the parent, the quality of love and affection between the parent and child, the nature of the parent/child relationship, and the long term effect of the different decisions on the child. Often, psychological evaluations are conducted on each member of the family using traditional testing instruments. Specific tests have also been developed, such as the Bricklin Perceptual Scales (Bricklin, 1984).

A final, frequently requested service is to aid in the classification of inmates in correctional settings. One basic distinction is between merely managing the person and attempting a program of rehabilitation. Important management considerations are levels of suicide risk, appropriateness of dormitory versus a shared room, possible harassment from other inmates, or degree of dangerousness to others. Rehabilitation recommendations may need to consider the person's educational level, interests, skills, abilities, and personality characteristics related to employment.

The Educational Context

Psychologists are frequently called upon to assess children who are having difficulty in or may need special placement within the school system. Sattler (1988) has summarized school assessments into these relevant areas: evaluating the nature and extent of a child's learning difficulties, measuring intellectual strengths and weaknesses, assessing behavioral difficulties, creating an educational plan, estimating a child's responsiveness to intervention, and recommending changes in a child's program or placement. Any educational plan should be sensitive to the interactions among a child's abilities, the child's personality, the characteristics of the teacher, and the needs and expectations of the parents.

An assessment should first include a visit to the classroom where a child's behavior can be observed under natural conditions. A valuable aspect of this is to observe the interaction between the teacher and child. Typically, any behavioral difficulty is closely linked with the child-teacher interaction. Sometimes the teacher's style of responding to a student can be as much a part of the problem as the student. Consequently, classroom observations can produce discomfort on the part of teachers and should be handled sensitively.

Observing the child in a wider context is, in many ways, contrary to the tradition of individual testing. However, individual testing all too frequently provides a relatively limited and narrow range of information. If it is combined with a family or classroom assessment, additional crucial data may be collected, but there is also likely to be significant resistance. This resistance may result from legal or ethical restrictions regarding the scope of the services the school can provide or the demands that a psychologist can make on the student's parents. Often there is an initial focus on, and need to perceive, the student as a "problem child" or "identified patient." This may obscure larger, more complex, and yet more significant issues such as marital conflict, a disturbed teacher, misunderstandings between teacher and parents, or a conflict between the school principal and the parents. All or some of these individuals may have an investment in perceiving the student as the person with the problem rather than acknowledging that a disordered school system or significant marital turmoil may be respon-sible. An individually oriented assessment may be made with excellent interpretations, but unless wider contexts are considered, understood, and addressed, the assessment may very well be ineffective in solving both the individual difficulties and the larger organizational or interpersonal problems.

A typical assessment of children within a school context will include behavioral observations, a test of intellectual abilities—such as the WISC-R, Stanford Binet, or Kaufman Assessment Battery for Children (K-ABC), and tests of personality functioning. In the past, assessment of children's personality generally relied on projective techniques. However, many projectives have not been found to meet psychometrically accepted standards for adults. This difficulty is magnified with children. Projectives that have been found to meet more scientific standards with children are the Blacky Pictures Test (Blum, 1968), Rotter Incomplete Sentences (Rotter & Rafferty, 1950), and Incomplete Sentences Test (Lanyon, 1980). In contrast to older projective techniques, a variety of sound objective instruments have been relatively recently developed such as the Personality Inventory for Children (PIC; Wirt, Lachar, Klinedinst, & Seat, 1977). The inventory was designed along similar lines as the MMPI, but is completed by a child's parent. It produces four validity scales to detect faking and 12 clinical scales, such as Depression, Family Relations, Delinquency, Anxiety, and Hyperactivity. The scale was normed on 2,400 children, empirically developed, extensively researched, and has yielded good reliability. Additional well designed scales that show excellent promise within a school context are the Child Behavior Check List/Child Behavior Profile (Achenbach, 1978; Achenbach & Edelbrock, 1979), Adaptive Behavior Inventory for Children (Mercer & Lewis, 1978), Vineland Adaptive Behavior Scales (Sparrow, Balla, & Cicchetti, 1984), and the Revised Behavior Problem Checklist (Hogan, Quay, Vaughn, & Shapiro, 1989; Quay & Peterson, 1987).

Any report written for an educational setting should focus not only on a child's weaknesses, but also on his or her strengths. Understanding a child's strengths can potentially be used as a way to increase a child's self-esteem as well as to create change within a wide context. Recommendations should be realistic and practical. This can most effectively be developed when the clinician has a thorough understanding of relevant resources in the community, the school system, and the classroom environment. This understanding is particularly important since the quality and resources available between one school or school system and the next can vary tremendously. Recommendations typically specify which skills need to be learned, how these can be learned, a hierarchy of objectives, and possible techniques for reducing behaviors that make learning difficult. Recommendations for special education should only be made when a regular class would clearly not be equally beneficial. However, the recommendations are not the end product. They are beginning points that should be elaborated and modified depending on the initial results. Ideally, a psychological report should be followed up with continuous monitoring.

Messick (1984) suggests that the assessment of children should be carried out in two phases. The first phase should assess the nature and quality of the child's learning environment. If the child is not exposed to adequate quality instruction, then he or she cannot be expected to perform well. Thus it must first be demonstrated that a child has not been learning even with appropriate instruction. The second phase involves a comprehensive assessment battery, which includes measures of intellectual abilities, academic skills, adaptive behavior, and screening out any biomedical disorders that might disrupt learning. Intellectual abilities might involve memory, spatial organization, abstract reasoning, and sequencing. Regardless of students' academic and intellectual abilities, they will not perform well unless they have relevant adaptive abilities, such as social skills, adequate motivation, and ability to control impulses. Raven (1983) has stressed that assessing a child's values are of utmost importance since they determine whether the student is willing to use whatever resources he or she may have. Likewise, the person's level of personal efficacy helps to determine whether the person is able to perform behaviors leading toward attaining the goals he or she values. Physical difficulties that might interfere with learning include poor vision, poor hearing, hunger, malnutrition, or endocrine dysfunction.

The above considerations clearly place the assessment of children in educational settings into a far wider context than merely the interpretation of test scores. Relationships among the teacher, family, and student need to be assessed, along with the relative quality of the learning environment. Furthermore, the child's values, motivation, and sense of personal efficacy need to be taken into consideration, along with possible biomedical difficulties. Examiners need to become knowledgeable regarding the school and community resources as well as to learn new instruments that have demonstrated relatively high levels of reliability and validity.

The Psychological Clinic

In contrast to the medical, legal, and educational institutions where the psychologist serves only as a consultant to the decision maker, the psychologist working in a psychological clinic is often the decision maker. A number of typical referrals come into the psychological clinic. Perhaps the most common ones are individuals who are self-referred and are seeking relief from psychological turmoil. For most of these individuals, psychological testing is not relevant and, in fact, may be contraindicated because the delay between the time of testing and the feedback of the results is usually time that could best be applied toward treatment. There may be certain groups of self-referred clients about whom the psychologist may question whether the treatment available in a psychological clinic is appropriate. These clients can include persons with extensive medical problems, individuals with legal complications that need additional clarification, and persons who may require inpatient treatment. With these cases, it might be necessary to obtain additional information through psychological testing. However, the main purpose of the testing would be to aid in decision making rather than to serve as a direct source of help for the client.

Two other situations in which psychological assessment may be warranted involve children who are referred by their parents for school or behavioral problems and referral from other decision makers. Where referrals are made for poor school performance or behavioral problems involving legal complications, special precautions must be taken prior to testing. Primarily, the clinician must develop a complete understanding of the client's social network and the basis for the referral. This may include a history of previous attempts at treatment and a summary of the relationship among the parents, school, courts, and child. Usually a referral comes at the end of a long sequence of events, and it is important to obtain information regarding these events. Once the basis of the referral has been clarified, the clinician may decide to have a meeting with different individuals who have become involved in the case—such as the school principal, previous therapists, probation officer, attorney, or teacher. This meeting may uncover a myriad of issues that require decisions, such as referral for family therapy, placement in a special education program, a change in custody agreements between divorced parents, individual therapy of other members of the family, and a change in school. All of these may affect the relevance of, and approach to, testing, but these issues may not be apparent if the initial referral question is taken at face value. Sometimes psychologists are also confronted with referrals from other decision makers. For example, an attorney may want to know if an individual is competent to stand trial. Other referrals may involve a physician who wants to know whether a head-injured patient can readjust to his or her work environment or drive a car, or the physician may need to document changes in a patient's recovery.

So far, this discussion on the different settings in which psychological testing is used has focused both on the issue of when to test and how to clarify the manner in which tests can be most helpful in making decisions. Several additional summary points must be stressed. First, it is sometimes unrealistic to believe that a referral source will be able to adequately formulate the referral question. In fact, the referral question will usually be neither clear nor concise. This is further complicated by the fact that a psychologist is typically only used for consultation in the most difficult and complex cases. This means it is the clinician's responsibility to look beyond the referral question and understand the basis for the referral in its widest scope. Thus, an understanding must be developed of the complexity of the client's social setting—including interpersonal factors, family dynamics, and the sequence of events leading to the referral. In addition to clarifying the referral question, a second major point is that psychologists are responsible for developing knowledge about the setting for which they are writing their reports. This includes learning the proper language, the roles of the individuals working in the setting, the choices facing decision makers, and the philosophical and theoretical beliefs they adhere to. It is also important that clinicians understand the values underlying the setting and assess whether these values coincide with their own. For example, psychologists who do not believe in aversion therapy, capital punishment, or electroconvulsive therapy may come into conflict while working in certain settings. Psychologists thus should clearly understand how the information they give their referral source will be used. It is essential for them to appreciate the fact that they have a significant responsibility, since decisions made regarding their clients, which are often based on assessment results, can frequently be major changing points in a client's life. If the possibility exists for the information to be used in a manner that will conflict with the clinician's value system, then he or she should reconsider, clarify, or possibly change his or her relationship to the referral setting.

A final point is that clinicians should not allow themselves to be placed into the role of a "testing technician" or psychometrist. This role ultimately does a disservice to the client, the practitioner, and the profession. In other words, clinicians should not merely administer, score, and interpret tests, but should also understand the total referral context in its broadest sense. This means they also take on the role of an expert who can integrate data from a variety of sources. Tests, by themselves, are limited in that they are not flexible or sophisticated enough to address themselves to complex referral questions. Levine (1981) writes:

> [The formal research on test validity is] not immediately relevant to the practical use of psychological tests. The question of the value of tests becomes not "Does this test correlate with a criterion?" or "Does the test accord with a nomological net?", but rather "Does the use of the test improve the success of the decision making process?" by making it either more efficient, less costly, more accurate, more rational, or more relevant. (p. 292)

All of these concerns are consistent with the emphasis on an examiner fulfilling the role of an expert clinician performing psychological assessment rather than a psychometrist acting as a technician.

GUIDELINES AND CAUTIONS FOR USING TESTS

Over the past 30 years, there has been extensive criticism of, and resistance to, the use of psychological tests. Such criticism has included the use of tests in inappropriate contexts, cultural bias, invasion of privacy, and the continued use of tests that are inadequately validated. The result has been restrictions on the use of certain tests, greater clarification within the profession regarding ethical standards, and increased skepticism from the public. Criticism of testing has been partially responsible for a decrease in the use of psychological tests. However, the decrease in traditional tests has also been due to the availability of alternative methods of assessment that are more specific, objective, and observable—such as structured interviews, behavioral assessment, and tests of narrow specific domains. There has also been a relative increase in the use of objective tests in favor of projective instruments. However, some clinicians continue to adhere to unvalidated or outdated procedures and have not familiarized themselves with relevant research that might have led them to modify their testing instruments or procedures.

The main damage done to the field stems from two general sources. The first is an over-reliance on, and excessive faith in, psychological tests by such people as psychiatrists, judges, physicians, social workers, educators, and businesspeople. Such uncritical faith and overoptimism can potentially result in the misuse of test data, and may also eventually result in disillusionment when expectations of test-based decisions do not adequately solve problems. The second area of difficulty arises from the possible misuse of tests on the part of clinicians themselves. To conduct useful and accurate assessments, clinicians must be aware of the types of misuse they could potentially make of their tools. The American Psychological Association (APA) and other professional groups have published guidelines for examiners in their *Standards for Educational and Psychological Tests* (1985), principles 5 and 8 of *Ethical Principles of Psychologists* (1981), "General Guidelines for Providers of Psychological Services" (APA, 1987), and *Guidelines for Computer-based Test Interpretations* (APA, 1986).

Cautions in Administration and Scoring

The relationship between the examiner and the client can influence the outcome of test scores, and this influence typically occurs without the examiner being aware of it. Thus, it is the examiner's responsibility to recognize the possible influences he or she may exert on the client and to closely adhere to the standardized conditions specified in the manual. If these are not adhered to, the result is likely to be unreliable and inaccurate test scores.

One important variable is rapport, which has been found in many cases to significantly alter test performance. For example, enhanced rapport with older children (but not younger ones) involving verbal reinforcement and friendly conversation has been shown to increase WISC-R scores by an average of 13 I.Q. points as compared with an administration involving more neutral interactions (Feldman & Sullivan, 1971). This is a difference of nearly one full standard deviation. It has also been found that mildly disapproving comments such as "I thought you could do better than that" resulted in significantly lowered performance when compared with either neutral or approving ones (Witmer, Bornstein, & Dunham, 1971). In a review of 22 studies, Fuchs and Fuchs (1986) concluded that, on the average, I.Q. scores were four points higher when the examiner was familiar with the child being examined than when he or she was unfamiliar with the child. This trend was particularly pronounced for lower socioeconomic status children.

Whereas there is little evidence (Lefkowitz & Fraser, 1980; Sattler, 1973a, 1973b; 1988; Sattler & Gwynne, 1982) to support the belief that black students have lower performance when tested by white examiners, it has been suggested that black students are more responsive to tangible reinforcers (money, candy) than white students, who generally respond better to verbal reinforcement (Schultz & Sherman, 1976). However, in a later study, Terrell, Taylor, and Terrell (1978) demonstrated that the main factor was the cultural relevance of the response. They found a remarkable 17.6 point increase in I.Q. scores when black students were encouraged by black examiners with culturally relevant comments such as "nice job, blood" or "good work, little brother." Thus the rapport and feedback, especially if that feedback is culturally relevant, can significantly improve test performance. As a result, the feedback and level of rapport should, as much as possible, be held constant from one test administration to the next.

One variable extensively investigated by Rosenthal and his colleagues is that a researcher/examiner's expectations can influence another person's level of performance (Rosenthal, 1966). This has been demonstrated with humans as well as laboratory rats. For example, when an experimenter was told to expect better performances from rats who were randomly selected from the same litter as "maze bright" (compared with "maze dull"), the descriptions of the rats' performance given by the experimenter conformed to the experimenter's expectations (Rosenthal & Fode, 1963). Despite criticisms that have been leveled at his studies (Barber & Silver, 1968; Elashoff & Snow, 1971; Thorndike, 1968), Rosenthal maintains that an expectancy effect exists in some situations and suggests that the mechanisms are through minute nonverbal behaviors (Cooper & Rosenthal, 1980). He states that the typical effects on an individual's performance are usually small and subtle, and occur in some situations but not others. The obvious implication for clinicians is that they should continually question themselves regarding their expectations of clients and check to see if they may in some way be communicating these expectations to their clients.

An additional factor that may affect the nature of the relationship between the client and the examiner is the client's relative emotional state. It is particularly important to assess the degree of the client's motivation and his or her overall level of anxiety. There may be times in which it would be advisable to discontinue testing because situational emotional states may significantly influence the results of the tests. At the very least, examiners should consider the possible effects of emotional factors and incorporate these into their interpretations. For example, it might be necessary to increase the estimate of a client's optimal intellectual functioning if the client was extremely anxious during administration of an intelligence test.

A final consideration, which can potentially confound both the administration and—more commonly—the scoring of responses, is the degree to which the examiner likes the client and perceives him or her as warm and friendly. Several studies (Sattler, Hillix, & Neher, 1970; Sattler & Winget, 1970) have indicated that the more the examiner likes the client, the more likely he or she will be to score an ambiguous response in a direction favorable to the client. Higher scores can occur even on items in which the responses are not ambiguous (Donahue & Sattler, 1971; Egeland, 1969; Simon, 1969). Thus, "hard" scoring, as opposed to more lenient scoring, can occur at least in part due to the degree of subjective liking the examiner feels toward the client. Again, examiners should continually check themselves to assess whether their relationship with the client is interfering with the objectivity of the test administration and scoring.

Use with Minority Groups

One of the most controversial issues regarding psychological tests is their use with ethnic minorities. Critics believe that psychological tests are heavily biased in favor, and reflect the values of, white, middle-class society. They argue that such tests cannot adequately assess intelligence or personality when applied to minority groups. Whereas the greatest controversy has arisen from the use of intelligence tests, the presence of cultural bias is also relevant in the use of personality testing. For example, blacks usually score significantly higher than whites on MMPI scales F, 8, and 9 (Greene, 1980; Pritchard & Rosenblatt, 1980), and controversy has arisen over whether interpretations based on these elevations are accurate (Greene, 1987; Green & Kelly, 1988; Gynther, 1979b). Thus, the possibility exists that personality tests, such as the MMPI, may also have discriminatory bias.

The basic issue lies in determining whether tests are as valid for minority groups as for nonminorities. Clearly, differences do exist, however the meaning that can be attributed to these differences has been strongly debated. A further question lies in identifying the cause of these differences. Some theorists believe that the differences are primarily the result of environmental factors (Kamin, 1974; Rosenthal & Jacobson, 1968), whereas others stress hereditary determination (Jensen, 1969, 1972; Munsinger, 1975). Even though the debate is far from resolved, guidelines have been established by the Equal Employment Opportunity Commission (EEOC) for the use of psychological tests with minority groups in educational and industrial settings. The basic premise is that a screening device (psychological test) can have an adverse impact if it screens out a proportionally larger number of minorities than nonminorities. Furthermore, it is the responsibility of the employer to demonstrate that the procedure produces valid inferences for the specific purposes for which the employer would like to use it. If an industrial or educational organization does not follow the guidelines, as defined by the EEOC (1978), then the Office of Federal Contract Compliance has the direct power to cancel any government contract that the institution might have.

The degree of validity contained within the tests also is of significance to the legal issues, research data, and guidelines for the individual clinician. If investigated from the perspective of content validity, popular individual intelligence tests appear on the surface to be culturally biased. This conclusion is based largely on early intuitive observations that many black children and other minorities usually do not have the opportunity to learn the types of material contained in many of the test items (Kagan, Moss, & Siegel, 1963; Lesser, Fifer, & Clark, 1965). Thus, their lower scores may represent not a lack of intelligence, but merely a lack of familiarity with white, middle-class culture. Critics of the tests point out that it would clearly be unfair to assess a white person's intelligence based on whether he or she knows what the "funky chicken" is or what "blood" means, or for that matter, to ask him or her the meaning of British terms such as "shilling" or "lorrie." Low scores would simply measure an individual's relative unfamiliarity with a specific culture rather than his or her specific mental strengths. If one uses this reasoning, many I.Q. and aptitude tests may appear on the surface to be culturally biased. However, studies in which researchers, to the best of their ability, eliminated biased test items or items that statistically discriminate between minorities and nonminorities, have not been successful in altering overall test scores. A representative study was one in which 27 items were removed from the Scholastic Aptitude Test (SAT) that consistently differentiated minorities from nonminorities. This did little to change either the test taker's individual scores, or the differences between the two groups (Flaugher & Schrader, 1978). Thus, the popular belief, based on a superficial appraisal of many psychological tests that biased items are responsible for test differences, does not appear to be supported by research.

Although test differences between minority and nonminority groups have frequently been found, the meaning and causes of these differences is open to debate. It has been demonstrated that blacks consistently score lower than whites on the WISC-R (Jensen & Reynolds, 1982) WAIS-R (Kaufman, McLean, & Reynolds, 1988) and SAT (Temp, 1971). However, when blacks and whites of equal socioeconomic status were compared, their I.Q. scores became similar. Likewise, the 5 T-score point differences found on MMPI scales F, 8, and 9 were also decreased or even insignificant when blacks and whites were comparable in age, education, and other relevant demographic characteristics (Dahlstrom, Lachar, & Dahlstrom, 1986). This suggests that many differences in test scores may be due more to factors such as socioeconomic status than to ethnicity.

Another consideration is the adequacy of the predictive validity of various tests when used with minority groups. Since one of the main purposes of these tests is to predict later performance, it is essential to evaluate the extent to which the scores in fact adequately predict such areas as a minority's performance in college. A representative group of studies indicates that the SAT actually overpredicts how well minorities will perform in college (Jensen, 1984; Kallingal, 1971; Pfeifer & Sedlacek, 1971; Reynolds, 1986). Furthermore, both the WISC and the WISC-R are equally as effective in predicting the academic achievement of both blacks and whites in primary and secondary school (Reynolds & Hartlage, 1979). However, in actually working with minority groups, it is important to become familiar with different subgroup norms and to know the confidence with which predictions can be made based on the scores of these subgroups.

The above discussion of content and predictive validity represents the traditional defense of psychological tests. For many individuals, these defenses are still not sufficient. The two main choices, then, are either to outlaw all psychological tests for minority groups or to develop more appropriate psychological assessment approaches. A half-serious attempt toward a more appropriate measuring device is the Dove Counterbalance General Intelligence Test (Dove, 1968). It has since become referred to as the "Chitling Test" and includes items relevant for a black inner-city culture, such as "a 'handkerchief head' is: (a) a cool cat, (b) a porter, (c) an Uncle Tom, (d) a haddi, (e) a preacher." A similar attempt by Williams (1974) is his development of the Black Intelligence Test of Cultural Homogeneity (BITCH). Although neither test has been standardized and validated, both contain vocabulary words and experiences with which most black children would be familiar but with which white children would be unfamiliar.

A number of additional tests have been developed with the partial intent of using them in the assessment of ethnic minorities. These tend to emphasize nonverbal tasks and include the Leiter International Performance Scale, Culture Fair Intelligence Test, Raven's Progressive Matrices, and the Goodenough-Harris Drawing Test. Unfortunately, available research indicates that most of these "culture-fair" tests do not show greater validity for minorities as compared with nonminorities (Sattler, 1988). One relatively recent development that does show good potential for the assessment of minorities is the Kaufman Assessment Battery for Children (K-ABC; Kaufman & Kaufman, 1983). Mean I.Q. scores for whites, blacks, and Hispanics are relatively close, and there is some evidence that concurrent validity is comparable for different ethnic populations (Kaufman & Kaufman, 1983). The test is based on empirical developments in cognitive psychology and has a good record of reliability and validity. Although it looks promising, further validity studies will be necessary to clearly establish its accuracy in evaluating ethnic minorities.

The System of Multicultural Pluralistic Assessment (SOMPA; Mercer, 1979; Mercer & Lewis, 1978) provides an alternative and more complex method of evaluating minorities by using traditional assessment tools but correcting the bias involved with these tools. The assumption underlying this approach is that all cultural groups have the same average potential and any adequate assessment device should be able to accurately test this potential for a particular individual. One of its primary goals is to differentiate between members of minorities who have been incorrectly labeled mentally retarded due to test bias and those who are in fact mentally retarded. The SOMPA method involves medical, social system, and pluralistic components. The "medical component" assesses whether students have any physical disorders that may be interfering with their level of performance. This assessment includes tests of hearing, vision, and motor function. The rationale for the medically oriented assessment is that children from lower income groups are both more likely to have medical difficulties, due to their harsher environment, and less likely to obtain treatment for these difficulties, due to financial constraints. The "social system" component uses traditional assessment tools, such as the WISC-R, to measure whether the student is functioning at a level consistent with social norms. The problem with this component is that it provides a narrow definition of successful functioning because the criteria are based on the dominant culture's definition of success. Thus, the final "pluralistic" component attempts to correct for the narrow approach in the social system component by evaluating an individual's test scores against a culturally similar group, thereby—it is hoped—adjusting for such variables as socioeconomic status and cultural background. Thus, comparisons are made between performances within a specific subgroup, rather than with the performance, values, and criteria of the dominant culture. The resulting adjusted scores are referred to as an individual's Estimated Learning Potentials (ELPs).

SOMPA has had many critics, most of whom argue that the criterion for judging it should be the adequacy with which it can predict school performance (Brown, 1979; Johnson & Danley, 1981; Oakland, 1979). Studies indicate that, whereas WISC-R scores correlate at a level of .60 with grade point average, SOMPA scores have a correlation of only .40 (Oakland, 1979). ELPs have also been found to have lower correlations with other forms of achievement than traditional I.Q. measures (Wurtz, Sewell, & Manni, 1985), and it is difficult to relate ELP results to specific applications in the classroom (Brooks & Hosie, 1984). Mercer refutes these criticisms by pointing out that her intent was not so much to predict school performance, as to identify students who have been falsely classified as mentally retarded. Proponents of SOMPA have been so persuasive that it has been adopted by several states. Many people hoped that SOMPA would create more accurate labeling of mentally retarded students. However, students who are now labeled "normal" through the SOMPA approach, but were previously labeled "mentally retarded" or "learning disabled," might still require some additional form of special instruction. In fact, reclassifying students as normal through a calculation of ELPs may bar access of these students from special educational services. In addition, studies indicate that a high proportion of students classified as mentally retarded using the SOMPA are still likely to be minorities (Heflinger, Cook, & Thackrey, 1987) and that scores may be biased in favor of urban children, regardless of their ethnicity (Taylor, Sternberg, & Partenio, 1987). Due to the above difficulties, SOMPA has probably not achieved its goal of equalizing educational opportunities for ethnic minority children, and thus its use for individual educational decision making should be used with caution.

As is true for ability tests and tests of scholastic aptitude, personality tests also have the potential to be biased. The main research in this area has been performed on the MMPI and has consistently indicated that minority groups do score differently than nonminorities. In general, blacks scored higher than whites on scales F, 8, and 9 (Green & Kelly, 1988; Gynther & Green, 1980), but this pattern was not consistent across all populations (Greene, 1987). Even if consistent score differences were found, this does not mean these differences will be of sufficient magnitude to alter a clinician's interpretations, nor does it mean that predictions based on empirical criteria will be different. Studies using empirical criterion for prediction indicate that the MMPI does not produce more accuracies for whites than blacks (Elion & Megargee, 1975; Green & Kelly, 1988). In a review of MMPI performance for Asian Americans, blacks, Hispanics, and Native Americans, Greene (1987) concluded that "the failure to find a consistent pattern of scale differences between any two ethnic groups in any publication suggests that it is premature to begin to develop new norms for ethnic groups" (p. 509). What seems to affect MMPI profiles more than ethnicity are moderator variables—such as socioeconomic status, intelligence, and education. Furthermore, the existing differences may be due to true differences in behavior and personality caused by the greater stresses often encountered by minorities. Graham (1987) suggests that, when MMPI scores are deviant, the clinician should tentatively accept these scores but make special efforts to explore the person's life situation and level of adjustment, and integrate this information with the test scores.

From this discussion, it should be obvious that the problems are both complicated and far from being resolved. Several general solutions have been suggested. These include improving selection devices, developing different evaluation criteria, and changing social environments. Improving the use of selection devices would involve paying continual attention to, and obtaining greater knowledge of, the meaning of different scores for different subgroups. This may include tailoring specific test scores to the types of decisions individuals may make in their lives. For example, blacks typically make scores equal to whites on the verbal portion of the SAT, but their average scores on math are lower. This suggests that black students have a greater development in their verbal skills than in their quantitative ones. This conclusion is further reflected by, and consistent with, the fact that blacks are more likely to choose verbally oriented majors in college. Based on this, it may be more accurate to predict the future college performances of blacks from their SAT verbal scores than their SAT math scores.

Another approach toward solving the problem of test bias is to develop different and more adequate criterion measures. For example, it has been found that WISC-R scores correlate highly with teacher/classroom ratings for nonminorities, but not for minorities (Goldman & Hartig, 1976). This indicates that using teacher/classroom ratings as a criterion of academic achievement is not appropriate for minorities. In contrast, the WISC-R accurately predicts grade point average for both minorities and nonminorities, which suggests that grade point average is a better criterion measure. Perhaps of greater relevance is the actual prediction of an individual's career performance. Current test predictors for graduate schools (Law School Aptitude Test, Medical School Aptitude Test, etc.) give generally satisfactory predictions for later academic performance, but do not predict whether an individual will be, for example, a good attorney or physician. In fact, it has been shown that medical school grades themselves are not associated with later success as a physician (Loughmiller, Ellison, Taylor, & Price, 1970). This issue may become particularly pronounced in comparing the relative effectiveness of minorities and nonminorities when working in different cultural settings. For example, if a white and a Hispanic attorney are both placed in settings in which they will be working with Hispanics, it is probable that the Hispanic attorney would be more effective because he or she will have an increased rapport and greater familiarity with the language and values of his or her clientele.

Another solution involves changing the social environment. Part of the rationale for emphasizing this approach is the belief held by many researchers that the differences in test scores between minorities and nonminorities are not due to test bias but rather because tests accurately reflect the effects of an unequal environment and unequal opportunities (Flaugher, 1978; Green, 1978). Even though, in some situations, different minority norms and additional predictive studies on minority populations are necessary, the literature suggests that tests are not as biased as they have been accused of being. For example, removal of biased or discrim-inating SAT items still results in the same mean scores, the WISC-R provides accurate predictions of grade point average for both minorities and nonminorities, and the MMPI is usually equally as accurate for making behavioral predictions for blacks as for whites. Tests themselves are not the problem but merely the means of establishing that, often, unfortunate inequalities do exist between ethnic groups. The goal should be to change unequal environments that can ideally increase a population's skills as measured by current tests of aptitude, I.Q., and achievement. Whereas improving selection devices and developing different criterion measures are still important, future efforts should also stress more equal access to educational and career opportunities.

All of these solutions can give some direction to the profession in general, but it is the responsibility of individual clinicians to keep abreast of research relating to minority groups and to incorporate this knowledge into the interpretations they make of test scores. As Mercer (1979) has emphasized, test scores are neither valid nor invalid, but inferences by clinicians based on these scores are.

Examiner Qualifications

To correctly administer and interpret psychological tests, an examiner must be properly trained. This training generally includes an adequate amount of graduate course work, combined with a long period of supervised experience. Clinicians should have a knowledge of tests and test limitations, and should be willing to accept responsibility for competent test use. Intensive training is particularly important for individually administered I.Q. tests and for the majority of personality tests. Students who are taking or administering tests as part of a class requirement are not adequately trained to administer and interpret tests professionally. Thus, test results obtained by students have questionable validity, and they should clearly inform their subjects that the purpose of their testing is for training purposes only.

In addition to the above general guidelines for training, examiners should acquire some specific skills. These include the ability to evaluate the technical strengths and limitations of a test, the selection of appropriate tests, and a knowledge of issues relating to the test's reliability and validity. Examiners need to be aware of the material in the test manual as well as relevant research both on the variable the test is measuring and the status of the test since its publication. This is particularly important with regard to newly developed subgroup norms and possible changes in the meaning of scales as a result of further research. Once examiners evaluate the test itself, they must also be able to evaluate whether the purpose and context for which they would like to use it are appropriate. Sometimes an otherwise valid test can be used for purposes that it was not intended for, resulting in either invalid or useless inferences based on the test data. Examiners must also be continually aware of, and sensitive to, conditions affecting the examinee's performance. These conditions may include expectations on the part of the examiner, minor variations from the standardized instructions, degree of rapport, mood of the examinee, or timing of the test administration in relation to an examinee's life changes. To help develop accurate conclusions, examiners should have a general knowledge of human behavior. Particularly relevant areas include personality theory, abnormal psychology, and the psychology of adjustment. Furthermore, interpretations should only be made after evaluating other relevant information beyond the mere test scores. A final consideration is that, if interns or technicians are administering the tests, then an adequately trained psychologist should be available as a consultant or supervisor.

Specific data-based guidelines for test user qualifications have been recently developed by relevant professional groups (American Psychological Association, 1988) and these guidelines have been incorporated by most organizations selling psychological tests. Qualification forms request information regarding the purpose for using tests (counseling, research, personnel selection), area of professional expertise (marriage and family, social work, school), level of training (degrees, licenses), specific courses taken (descriptive statistics, career assessment), and quality control over test use (test security, appropriate tailoring of interpretations). Persons completing the forms certify that they possess appropriate training and competencies and agree to adhere to ethical guidelines and legal regulations regarding test use.

Communicating Test Results

The knowledge areas just discussed refer primarily to the test or test situation itself. However, no matter how accurate are the collection and interpretation of data, the data will be meaningless unless the results can be communicated effectively. This involves understanding the needs and vocabulary of the referral source, client, and other persons who may be affected by the test results—such as parents or teachers. Initially, there should be a clear exploration of the rationale for testing and the nature of the tests being administered. This may include the general type of conclusions that will be drawn, the limitations of the test, and common misconceptions surrounding the test or test variable. If a child is being tested in an educational setting, a meeting should be arranged with the school psychologist, parents, teacher, and other relevant persons. Such an approach is crucial for I.Q. tests, which are more likely to be misinterpreted, than for achievement tests. Feedback of test results should be given in terms that are clear and understandable to the receiver. Descriptions are generally most meaningful when performance levels are clearly indicated along with behavioral references (Ownby, 1987). For example, in giving I.Q. results to parents, it will only be minimally relevant to say that their child has an I.Q. of 130 with relative strengths in spatial organization, even though this may be appropriate language for a formal psychological evaluation. A more effective description might be that their child is currently functioning in the top 2% when compared with his or her peers and is particularly good at organizing nonverbal material—such as piecing together puzzles, putting together a bicycle, or building a playhouse.

In providing effective feedback, the clinician should also consider the personal characteristics of the receiver, such as his or her general educational level, relative knowledge regarding psychological testing, and possible emotional response to the information. The emotional reaction is especially important when a client is learning about his or her personal strengths or shortcomings. Facilities should be available for additional counseling, if needed. Since psychological assessment is often requested as an aid in making important life decisions, the potential impact of the information should not be underestimated. Clinicians are usually in positions of power and, that power involves responsibility, since the information that clients receive and the decisions they make based on this information will often be with them for many years.

Unwarranted Applications

One of the more frequent misuses of psychological tests occurs when an otherwise valid test is used for purposes for which it was not intended. Ordinarily such misuses are done in good faith and with good intentions. For example, an examiner might use a TAT or Rorschach as the primary means of inferring an individual's I.Q. Similarly, the MMPI, which was designed to assess the extent of psychopathology in an individual, might be inappropriately used to assess a normal person's level of functioning. Although some conclusions can be drawn from the MMPI relating to certain aspects of a normal person's functioning, or although I.Q. estimates based on projectives can be made, they should be considered extremely tentative. These tests were not designed for these purposes and, as a result, such inferences do not represent their strengths. A somewhat more serious misuse can occur when a test such as the MMPI is used to screen applicants for personnel selection. Results from MMPI type tests are likely to be irrelevant for assessing most job-related skills. Of equal importance is the fact that the type of information derived from the MMPI is typically of a highly personal nature and, if used in personnel selection, is likely to represent an invasion of privacy.

Invasion of Privacy

One of the main difficulties examinees can encounter in relation to psychological tests is that the examiner might discover aspects of the client which he or she would rather keep secret. Also of concern is that this information may be used in ways that are not in the best interest of the client. The Office of Science and Technology (1967), in a report entitled *Privacy and Behavioral Research*, has defined privacy as "the right of the individual to decide for him/herself how much he will share with others his thoughts, feelings, and facts of his personal life" (p. 2). This right is considered to be "essential to insure dignity and freedom of self determination" (p. 2). The invasion of privacy issue usually becomes most controversial with personality tests since items relating to motivational, emotional, and attitudinal traits are sometimes disguised. Thus, persons may unknowingly reveal characteristics about themselves that they would rather keep private. Similarly, many persons consider their I.Q. scores to be highly personal.

Public concern over this issue culminated in an investigation by the Senate Subcommittee on Constitutional Rights and the House Subcommittee on Invasion of Privacy. Neither of these investigations found evidence of deliberate or widespread misuse of psychological tests (Brayfield, 1965). Dahlstrom (1969) has argued that public concern over the invasion of privacy is based on two basic issues. The first is that tests have been oversold to the public, with a resulting exaggeration of their scope and accuracy. The public is usually not aware of the limitations of test data and may often feel that tests are more capable of discovering hidden information than they actually are. The second misconception is that it is not necessarily wrong to obtain information about persons that they either are unaware of themselves or would rather keep private. The more important issue is the use to which the information will be put. Furthermore, the person who controls where or how this information will be used is generally the client. The ethical code of the APA (1981) specifically states that information derived by a psychologist from any source can be released only with the permission of the client. Although there may be exceptions regarding the rights of minors, or when clients are a danger to themselves or others, the ability to control the information is usually clearly defined as being held by the client. Thus, the public is often uneducated regarding its rights and typically underestimates the power it has in determining how the test data will be used.

Despite ethical guidelines relating to testing, dilemmas sometimes do arise. For example, during personnel selection, applicants may feel pressured into revealing personal information on tests because they aspire to a certain position. Also, applicants may unknowingly reveal information due to subtle, nonobvious test questions, and, perhaps more important, they have no control over the inferences that examiners will make in relation to the test data. Lovell (1967), in referring to the function of tests in personnel selection, argues that they are unacceptable based on ethical, scientific, and community service reasons. He states that, ethically, these tests often have no place in a free society, scientifically they do not have adequate validity for special institutional settings, and in the long run, they do not serve the public's best interests. However, if a position requires careful screening and if serious negative consequences may result from poor selection, then it is necessary to evaluate an individual as closely as possible. Thus, the use of testing for personnel in the police, delicate military positions, or important public duty overseas may warrant careful testing. A complete discussion of the restriction for tests in personnel selection can be found in the "Guidelines on Employee Selection Procedures" established by the Equal Employment Opportunity Commission (1970).

In a clinical setting, obtaining personal information regarding clients usually does not present problems. The agreement that the information will be used to help clients develop new insights and change their behavior is generally clear and straightforward. However, should legal difficulties arise relating to such areas as child abuse, involuntary confinement, or situations in which clients may be a danger to themselves or others, then ethical dilemmas are often present. Usually, there are general guidelines regarding the manner and extent to which information should be disclosed. These are included in the APA's *Ethical Principles of Psychologists* (1981), and test users are encouraged to familiarize themselves with these guidelines.

Adequate handling of the issue of an individual's right to privacy involves both a clear explanation of the relevance of the testing and obtaining informed consent. Examiners should always have a clear conception of the specific reasons why the tests are given. Thus, if personnel are being selected based on their mechanical abilities, then tests measuring such areas as general maladjustment should not be administered. Examiners must continually evaluate whether a test, or series of tests, is valid for a particular purpose, and whether each set of scores has been properly interpreted in relation to a particular context. Furthermore, the general rationale for test selection should be provided in clear, straightforward language that can be understood by the client. Informed consent involves communicating not only the rationale for testing, but also the kinds of data obtained and the possible uses of the data. This does not mean the client should be shown the specific test subscales themselves beforehand, but rather that the nature and intent of the test should be described in a general way. For example, if a client is told that a scale measures "sociability," this foreknowledge might alter the test's validity in that the client may answer questions based on popular, but quite possibly erroneous, stereotypes. If the test format and intent are introduced in a simple, respectful, and forthright manner, the chance that the client will perceive the testing situation as an invasion of privacy will be significantly reduced. This explanation should include a clear statement of the relevance, intent, and nature of the testing, and should inform clients of their rights to confidentiality and to information regarding the test results.

Inviolacy

Whereas concerns about invasion of privacy relate to the discovery and misuse of information that clients would rather keep secret, inviolacy involves the actual negative feelings created when clients are confronted with the test or test situation. Inviolacy is particularly relevant when clients are requested to discuss information they would rather not think about. For example, the MMPI contains questions about many ordinarily taboo topics relating to sexual practices, toilet behavior, bodily functions, and personal beliefs about human nature. Such questions may produce anxiety by making the examinees more aware of deviant thoughts or repressed unpleasant memories. Many individuals obtain a certain degree of security and comfort by staying within familiar realms of thought. Even to be asked questions that may indicate the existence of unusual alternatives can serve as an anxiety-provoking challenge to personal rules and norms. This problem is somewhat related to the issue of invasion of privacy and it, too, requires one-to-one sensitivity as well as providing clear and accurate information about the assessment procedure.

Labeling and Restriction of Freedom

When individuals are given a medical diagnosis for physical ailments, the social stigmata are usually relatively mild. In contrast are the potentially damaging consequences of many psychiatric diagnoses. One main danger is the possibility of creating a self-fulfilling prophecy based on the expected role associated with a specific label. Many of these expectations are communicated nonverbally and are typically beyond a person's immediate awareness (Cooper & Rosenthal, 1980; Rosenthal, 1966). Other self-fulfilling prophecies may be less subtle: for example, the person who is labeled as a chronic schizophrenic is not given treatment because chronic schizophrenics rarely respond and therefore does not improve—perhaps mainly because he or she has not received treatment. Another negative consequence of labeling is the social stigma attached to different disorders. Thus, largely due to the public's misconceptions of such terms as schizophrenia, labeled individuals may be socially avoided.

Just as labels imposed by others can have negative consequences, self-acceptance of labels can likewise be detrimental. Thus, clients may use their label as a way to excuse or deny responsibility for their behavior. This is congruent with the medical model, which usually assumes that a "sick" person is the victim of an "invading disorder." Thus, in our society, "sick" persons are not considered to be responsible for their disorders. However, the acceptance of this model for behavioral problems may perpetuate behavioral disorders because persons see themselves as helpless, passive victims under the power of mental health "helpers" (Szasz, 1987). This sense of helplessness may serve to lower their ability to deal effectively with new stress. In contrast to this is the belief that clients require an increased sense of responsibility for their lives and actions in order to effectively change their behavior.

A final difficulty associated with labeling is that it may unnecessarily impose limitations on either an individual or a system by restricting progress and creativity. For example, an organization may conduct a study to determine the type of person who has been successful at a particular type of job and may then develop future selection criteria based on this study. This can result in the future selection of a relatively homogeneous type of employee, which in turn could prevent the organization from changing and progressing. There may be a narrowing of the "talent pool," in which people with new and different ideas are never given a chance. In other words, what has been labeled as adaptive in the past may not be adaptive in the future. One alternative to this predicament is to look at future trends and develop selection criteria based on these trends. Furthermore, diversity might be incorporated into an organization so that different but compatible types can be selected to work on similar projects. Thus, clinicians should be sensitive to the potential negative impact resulting from labeling by outside sources or by self-labeling, as well as to the possible limiting effects that labeling might have.

SELECTING PSYCHOLOGICAL TESTS

Generally, psychological tests used in clinical work are selected based on each clinician's training and experience, personal preferences, and familiarity with relevant literature. For example, a clinician who has received training in the MMPI might be concerned about its ability to assess personality disorders (Widiger & Frances, 1987) and may rather choose to use an instrument such as the Millon Clinical Multiaxial Inventory (Millon, 1985). Clinicians might also select an instrument because it has practical efficiency in terms of time and economy. Thus, they may wish to use simple behavioral predictions made by the client rather than use more expensive, time consuming, and, quite possibly, less accurate tests (Bandura, 1977; Bem & Funder, 1978).

Typically, test batteries are likely to include the tests discussed in the following chapters. These include the traditional tests of cognitive abilities, objective and projective personality tests, and various strategies of behavioral assessment. Often a test battery will also include tests directed specifically toward assessing a particular type of population or specific type of problem. For example, an assessment of neurological patients might use tests sensitive to cerebral deficit, depressed patients might be given the Beck Depression Inventory (Beck, 1967), and pain patients might be given the McGill Pain Questionnaire (Melzack, 1975), MMPI, or Illness Behavior Questionnaire (Pilowski, Spence, Cobb, & Katsikitis, 1984).

Various sources are available for finding information about tests. Such sources can provide important information for deciding whether to obtain the tests and incorporate them into a battery. Probably the most useful is the *Mental measurements yearbook*, which contains a collection of critical test reviews that include evaluations of the meaning of the available research on each test. The ninth *Mental measurements yearbook* was published in 1985 (Mitchell, 1985) and the tenth edition became available in 1989 (Canoley & Kramer, 1989). The reviews are available in book form as well as online computer (*Mental measurement database*). *Tests in print II* (Buros, 1974) is associated with the *Mental measurements yearbook* but, rather than focusing on evaluating tests, lists information on each test such as its title, population it was designed for, available subtests, updating, author(s), and publisher. Similar publications are Sweetland & Keyser's (1983) *Tests: A comprehensive reference for assessment in psychology, education, and business*, which provides descriptive information on over 3500 tests, and *Test Critiques* (Keyser & Sweetland, 1985), which reviews specific topics related to psychological testing. If clinicians are interested in obtaining information on rating scales used in psychiatric research, they might consult the *Handbook of psychiatric rating scales* (Research and Education Association, 1981). A careful review of the information included in the above references will frequently answer questions clinicians might have related to a test's psychometric properties, usefulness, appropriateness for different populations, details for purchasing, and strengths and limitations. Most of the questions listed in Table 1–1 can be answered by consulting the above resources.

A current trend in research on psychological assessment is to clearly establish the functional utility of assessment in treatment (Hayes, Nelson, & Jarrett, 1987). Indeed, a basic objective of psychological assessment is that it should provide useful information regarding the planning, implementation, and evaluation of treatment. With the increased specificity of both treatment and assessment, this goal is becoming easier to achieve. For example, subgroups of depressed persons with irrational thoughts (but adequate social skills) responded better to a cognitive change module than to a module emphasizing social skills (McKnight, Nelson, & Hayes, 1984). In contrast, patients who score low on social skills (but with relatively rational thoughts) responded better to a module emphasizing social skills than to a cognitive module. Thus, an assessment of a depressed person's relative level of irrational thoughts rather than his or her social skills has clear implications for the treatment process. Likewise, chronic pain patients are more likely to respond to treatment if their MMPI scales are average or below average on somatic concerns (Prokop, 1988). Clinicians should not select tests based simply on their diagnostic accuracy or psychometric properties; they should also be concerned with the functional utility of the tests in treatment.

Two special concerns in selecting tests are faking and the use of short forms. In many situations, clinicians might be concerned that persons will either consciously or unconsciously provide inaccurate responses. Thus, these clinicians may want to be sure to include and pay particular attention to such tests as the MMPI and CPI, which have validity scales incorporated into them (Greene, 1988). Although controversial, many projective techniques may be resistant to attempts at faking. Concerns regarding the time required for assessment may cause examiners to select short forms of instruments, such as the WAIS-R, WISC-R, or MMPI. Although many of these seem sufficiently valid for screening purposes, their use as substitutes for the longer forms is questionable (Watkins, 1986) and they may be appropriate for some populations but not for others (Fauschingbauer & Newmark, 1978; Newmark & Thibodeau, 1979).

During the evaluation of single cases, such as in clinical diagnoses and counseling, clinicians do not usually use formal combinations of test scores. Rather, they rely on their past judgment, clinical experience, and theoretical background to interpret and integrate test scores. However, for personnel decisions, academic predictions, and some clinical decisions (recidivism rate, suicide risk), clinicians may wish to use statistical formulas. The two basic approaches for combining test results are multiple regression equations and multiple cutoff scores. Multiple regression equations are developed by correlating each test or subtest with a criterion. The higher the correlation, the greater the weight in the equation. The correlation of the entire battery with the criterion measure gives an indication of the battery's highest predictive validity. For example, high school achievement can be predicted with the following regression equation, which combines I.Q. and CPI subtests:

$$\text{Achievement} = .786 + .195 \text{ Responsibility} + .44 \text{ Socialization} - 130 \text{ Good Impression} \\ + .19 \text{ Achievement via Conformance} + .179 \text{ Achievement Imagery} \\ + .279 \text{ I.Q.}$$

This equation raises the correlation with grade point average (GPA) to .68 as compared with .60 when using I.Q. alone (Megargee, 1972). This correlation indicates that academic achievement is dependent not only on intellectual factors, but also on psychosocial ones, such as responsibility, socialization, achievement imagery, and achievement via conformance—all of which are measured by the CPI. The second strategy, multiple cutoff scores, involves developing a minimum cutoff for each test or subtest. If the person is below a certain optimal score (i.e. not in the brain damaged or schizophrenic range), then this score is rejected. Although not all tests have equations or cutoffs developed for them, the decision to include a test in a battery may in part depend on the presence of such formal extensions of the tests.

COMPUTER-ASSISTED ASSESSMENT

During the past 20 years, computer-assisted assessment has grown exponentially. In 1984, it was estimated that over 500 clinicians had their own terminals for computerized assessment and over 300,000 computer-assisted reports were processed annually (Johnson, 1984). In excess of 300 software packages are available and listed in such publications as Krug's (1989) *Psychware Sourcebook, 1988-1989*, the American Psychological Association's *Computer Use in Psychology: A Directory of Software* (Stoloff & Couch, 1988), Moreland's (1987) "Computerized Psychological Assessment: What's Available," and the Association for Measurement and Evaluation in Guidance's (1984) *Guide to Microcomputer Software in Testing and Assessment*. It has been estimated that by the year 2000 the vast majority of psychological tests will be automated and many will include such features as speech analyzers, physiological monitoring devices, and verbal and pictorial stimulus presentations. Computing in mental health has included not only computer-assisted assessment but also computer interviews, computerized diagnosis, computer-aided instruction, direct treatment intervention, clinical consultation, and simulated psychiatric interviews (Hedlund, Vieweg, & Cho, 1985).

The use of computer-assisted assessment has a number of advantages. Computers can save valuable professional time, potentially improve test-retest reliability, reduce possible tester bias, and reduce the cost to the consumer by improving efficiency. Even greater benefits may someday be realized by incorporating more complicated decision rules in interpretation, collecting data on response latency and key pressure, incorporating computer-based models of personality, tailoring future questions to a client based on past responses, and estimating the degree of certainty of various interpretations (Butcher, 1987; Butcher, Keller, & Bacon, 1985; Yossef, Slutske, & Butcher, 1989).

However, the use of computer-assisted assessment has resulted in considerable controversy within mental health publications (Matarazzo, 1986; Groth-Marnat & Schumaker, 1989), the popular media (Hall, 1983), and professional publications outside the mental health area (Groth-Marnat, 1985). A primary issue is untested validity. It has been assumed that, if a paper-and-pencil version of the test is valid, then a computerized version will also have equal validity. However, a computer administration may change the nature of the task and alter a subject's responses to the task, thereby resulting in questionable validity. Even though computer acceptance has been well documented (French & Beaumont, 1987), patients who are given computer administrations may alter their level of truthfulness (Johnson & Williams, 1977; Lucas et al., 1977), and blacks have been found to score better on computer-administered ability tests (Johnson & Mihal, 1973). Other studies have suggested equivalence between computer administered and conventionally administered tests (Lee, Moreno, & Sympson, 1986; Lukin, Down, Plake, & Kraft, 1985). Honaker (1988) concluded his review of studies on the equivalence of computerized and conventional administration of the MMPI by stating it is premature to conclude that the two formats result in equivalent scores. Of greater concern is that little consideration has been given to the differences between test validity and either the validity of individually computer-generated interpretations or the validity of computer-generated narrative reports. This is further complicated by software manuals that typically have not provided enough information to judge the adequacy of their decision rules. Persons might also tend to give greater credibility to the narrative reports due to their objective appearance, yet there is little evidence that these narrative summaries are valid (Lanyon, 1984; Matarazzo, 1986; Walker & Myrick, 1985). The few validity studies of narrative reports have not evaluated an entire system and have been almost exclusively restricted to the MMPI.

A further concern is that many software packages are available to persons who clearly do not possess appropriate professional qualifications. In many cases, no agreed-upon and enforced standards are in place to determine who is a qualified user. Ideally, qualified persons should be those who meet the requirements for using psychological tests in general. The American Psychological Association (1986) has attempted to clarify these standards in their *Guidelines for Computer-based Test Interpretation* and "Guidelines for Test User Qualifications" (American Psychological Association, 1988), but Krug's (1984) *Psychware Sourcebook, 1987-1988* indicated that 19% of the programs could be sold to the general public. The American Psychological Association guidelines specify that users "have an understanding of psychological or educational measurement, validation problems, and test research" and that practitioners "will limit their use of computerized testing to techniques which they are familiar and competent to use" (American Psychological Association, 1986, p. 8). Users should also "be aware of the method used in generating the scores and interpretation and be able to evaluate its applicability to the purpose for which it will be used" (American Psychological Association, 1986, pp. 8-9).

A further problem is that clinicians may subtly be encouraged to take the role of a technician without properly integrating the test results into a client's overall situation. Similarly, a narrative report is unsigned and therefore the results do not have the same legal and professional accountability that a signature might have. Matarazzo (1986) compares this to a physician randomly selecting another physician from the phone book and accepting an unsigned report of a consultation from this physician. Thus, clinicians need to critically analyze and evaluate the results derived from a narrative report to such an extent that they feel legally and professionally comfortable in signing it. Finally, there are few mechanisms for correcting obsolete software. As a result, incorrect interpretations might continue to be generated indefinitely.

The above difficulties associated with computer-assisted instruction suggest a number of guidelines for users (Groth-Marnat & Schumaker, 1989). First, they should not blindly accept computer-based narrative statements, but rather should insure, to the best of their ability, that the statements are both linked to empirically based research and placed within the context of the unique history and unique situation of the client. Computers have, among other benefits, the strong advantage of offering a wide variety of possible interpretations to the clinician, but these interpretations still need to be critically evaluated. It is clear that far greater research needs to be performed on both the meaning of computer-administered test scores and on the narrative interpretations based on these scores. The developers of software should also be encouraged to provide enough information in the manual to allow proper evaluation of the programs and should develop mechanisms to insure that obsolete programs are updated. Finally, some form of licensing might be required for users of computer-assisted assessment.

RECOMMENDED READING

Blau, T. (1984). *The psychologist as expert witness*. New York: John Wiley & Sons.

Groth-Marnat, G., & Schumaker, J. (1989). Computer-based psychological testing: Issues and guidelines. *American Journal of Orthopsychiatry, 59*, 257-263.

Hayes, S. C., Nelson, R. O., & Jarrett, R. B. (1987). The treatment utility of assessment: A functional approach to evaluating assessment quality. *American Psychologist, 42*, 963-974.

Chapter 3

THE ASSESSMENT INTERVIEW

Probably the single most important means of data collection during psychological evaluation is the assessment interview. Without interview data, most psychological tests are meaningless. The interview also provides information that is often unobtainable through other means. Such information includes potentially valuable behavioral observations, idiosyncratic features of the client, and the person's reaction to his or her current life situation. In addition, interviews are the primary means by which rapport is developed and can serve as a check against the meaning and validity of test results.

Sometimes an interview is mistakenly thought to be simply a conversation. In fact, the interview and conversation differ in many ways. An interview is meant to achieve defined goals and, as such, will typically have a clear sequence and be organized around specific, relevant themes. The assessment interview, unlike a normal conversation, may even require that the interviewer and interviewee discuss unpleasant facts and feelings. Its general objectives are to gather information that cannot easily be obtained through other means, establish a relationship that is conducive to obtaining the information, develop greater understanding in both the interviewer and interviewee regarding problem behavior, and provide direction and support in helping the interviewee deal with problem behaviors. The interviewer must not only direct and control the interaction to achieve specific goals, but must also have knowledge related to the areas that the interview is intended to explore.

One basic dimension of interviews is the degree to which they are structured versus unstructured. Some interviews allow the participants to freely drift from one area to the next, whereas others are highly directive and goal oriented, often using structured ratings and checklists. The more unstructured formats offer flexibility, possibly high rapport, the ability to assess how clients organize their responses, and the potential to attend to unique details of a client's history. There have, however, been frequent criticisms of unstructured interviews, resulting in widespread distrust regarding their reliability and validity. As a result, highly structured and semistructured interviews have been developed that provide sound psychometric qualities, the potential for use in research, and the capacity to be administered by less trained personnel.

Regardless of the degree of structure, any interview needs to accomplish specific goals, such as assessing the client's level of adjustment, client strengths, the nature of the problem, history of the problem, diagnosis, and relevant personal and family history. Techniques for accomplishing these goals vary from one interviewer to the next. Most practitioners use at least some structured aids, such as intake forms, which provide identifying data and basic elements of history. Obtaining information through direct questions on intake forms frees the clinician to investigate other aspects of the client in a more flexible, open-ended manner. Clinicians might also use a checklist to help ensure that all relevant areas have been covered. Other clinicians continue the structured format throughout most of the interview by using one of the formally developed structured interviews, such as the Diagnostic Interview Schedule (DIS) or Structured Clinical Interview for the DSM-III (SCID).

HISTORY AND DEVELOPMENT

Early Developments   The earliest form of obtaining information from clients was through clinical interviewing. At first, these interviews were modeled after question-and-answer medical formats, but later the influence of psychoanalytic theories resulted in a more open-ended, free-flowing style. Parallel to the psychoanalytically oriented interview was the development of the more structured and goal-oriented mental status examination originally formulated by Adolf Meyer in 1902. The mental status examination assessed relevant areas of a client's current functioning, such as general appearance, behavior, thought processes, thought content, memory, attention, speech, insight, and judgment. Early interest was also expressed regarding the relationship between biographical data and the prediction of occupational success or prognosis for specific disorders.

Regardless of the style used, the interviews all had these common objectives: to obtain a psychological portrait of the person, to conceptualize what is causing the person's current difficulties, to make a diagnosis, and to formulate a treatment plan. The difficulty with unstructured interviews is that they were (and still are) considered to have questionable reliability, validity, and cost-effectiveness. The first standardized psychological tests were developed to overcome these limitations. Tests could be subjected to rigorous psychometric evaluation and were more economical in that they required less face to face contact with the person(s) being evaluated.

Developments during the 1940s and 1950s   During the 1940s and 1950s, researchers and clinicians began conceptualizing and investigating important dimensions of interviews, including:

1. content versus process
2. goal orientation (problem solving) versus expressive elements
3. degree of directiveness
4. amount of structure
5. the relative amount of activity expressed by the participants

These issues have been the focus of numerous research studies. A representative and frequently cited study on interviewer style was reported by Snyder (1945), who found that a nondirective approach was most likely to create favorable changes and self-exploration in a client. In contrast, a more directive style using persuasion, interpretation, and interviewer judgments typically resulted in client defensiveness and resistance to expressing their difficulties. Strupp (1958) investigated the experience-inexperience dimension and found, among other things, that experienced interviewers expressed more warmth, a greater level of activity, and a greater number of interpretations. Level of empathy did not alter, regardless of the interviewer's degree of experience. Further, representative studies include Porter's (1950) in-depth evaluation of the effects of different types of responses (evaluative, probing, reassuring) and Wagner's (1949) early review, which questioned the reliability and validity of employment interviews.

Developments during the 1960s   A considerable amount of research in the 1960s was stimulated by Rogers (1961), who emphasized understanding the proper interpersonal ingredients necessary for an optimal therapeutic relationship (warmth, positive regard, genuineness). Elaborating on Rogers' ideas, Truax and Carkhuff (1967) developed a five-point scale to measure interviewer understanding of the client. This scale was used for research on interviewing, therapist training, and as support for a client-centered theoretical orientation. Additional research efforts were also directed toward listing and elaborating on different categories of interactions—such as clarification, summarizing, and confrontation.

Other investigators conceptualized interviewing as an interactive system in which the participants simultaneously influenced each other (Matarazzo, 1965; Watzlawick, Beavin, & Jackson, 1966). This emphasis on an interactive, self-maintaining system became the core for most early and later formulations of family therapy. The 1960s also saw the development and formalization of behavioral assessment, primarily in the form of goal-directed interviews that focused on understanding current and past reinforcers as well as on establishing workable target behaviors. Proponents of behavioral assessment also developed formal rating instruments and self-reports used in such areas as depression, assertiveness, and fear.

Some attempts were made at integrating different schools of thought into a coherent picture, such as Beier's (1966) conceptualization of unconscious processes being expressed through nonverbal behaviors that could then be subject to covert social reinforcement. However, the 1960s (and part of the 1970s) was mostly characterized by a splintering into different schools of conflicting and competing ideologies. For example, client-centered approaches emphasized the importance of staying with the client's self-exploration, behavioral interviews emphasized antecedents and consequences of behavior, and family therapy focused on interactive group processes. Parallel progress was made within each of these different schools and within different disciplines, but little effort was devoted to cross-fertilization and/or integration.

Throughout the 1950s and 1960s, child assessment was primarily conducted through interviews with parents. Direct interviews with the child were considered to be for therapeutic purposes rather than for assessment. Differential diagnosis was unusual; almost all children referred to psychiatric clinics were either undiagnosed or diagnosed as "adjustment reactions" (Rosen, Bahn, & Kramer, 1964). Early research by Lapouse and Monk (1958; 1964), using structured interviews, indicated that mothers were more likely to report overt behaviors that are bothersome to adults (thumbsucking, temper tantrums), but children were more likely to reveal more covert difficulties (fears, nightmares). Somewhat later, Graham and Rutter (1968), using structured interviews of children (rather than a parent), found inter-rater agreement was high for global psychiatric impairment (.84), moderate for attentional deficit, motor behavior, and social relations (.61–.64), and low for more covert difficulties such as depression, fears, and anxiety (.30).

Developments during the 1970s   Assessment with adults and children during the 1970s saw a further elaboration and development of the trends of the 1960s, as well as increased emphasis on structured interviews. The interest in structured interviews was fueled largely by criticisms about the poor reliability of psychiatric diagnosis. A typical structured interview would be completed by the interviewer either during or directly after the interview, and the data would be transformed into such scales as organicity, disorganization, or depression-anxiety.

Initial success with adult structured interviews (e.g., Present State Examination, Renard Diagnostic Interview) encouraged thinking regarding the further development of child structured interviews both for global ratings as well as for specific content areas. Child assessment became concerned not only with information derived from parents, but also with the child's own experience. There was a trend toward direct questioning of the child, greater emphasis on differential diagnosis, and the development of parallel versions of structured interviews for both the parent(s) and child.

Behavioral strategies of interviewing for both children and adults emphasized not only the interviewee's unique situation, but also provided a general listing of relevant areas to consider. For example, Kanfer and Grimm (1975) outlined the areas an interviewer should assess as:

1. behavioral deficiencies
2. behavioral excesses
3. inappropriate environmental stimulus control
4. inappropriate self-generated stimulus
5. problem reinforcement contingencies

In a similar categorization, Lazarus (1973) developed his BASIC ID model, which describes a complete assessment as involving behaviors (B), affect (A), sensation (S), imagery (I), cognition (C), interpersonal relations (I), and need for pharmacological intervention/drugs (D).

Additional themes in the 1970s included interest in biographical data, online computer technology, and the training of interviewer skills. Specifically, efforts were made to integrate biographical data for predicting future behavior (suicide, dangerousness, prognosis for schizophrenia) and for inferring current traits. Johnson and Williams (1975) were instrumental in developing some of the earliest online computer technology to collect biographical data and to integrate it with test results. Although training programs were devised for interviewers, a central debate was whether interview skills could actually be significantly learned or improved (Weins, 1976).

Whereas most reviews of the literature in the 1970s emphasized the advantages of a comprehensive structured format, family therapists were dealing with group processes in which formal interview structure was typically deemphasized. Since most family therapists were observing fluid interactional processes, they needed to develop a different vocabulary than that used in traditional psychiatric diagnosis. In fact, DSM categories were usually considered irrelevant since they described static characteristics of individuals rather than ongoing group processes. Few, if any, structured formats were available to assess family relationships.

Developments during the 1980s   Many of the trends, concepts, and instruments developed in the 1960s and 1970s were further refined and adapted for the 1980s. One important effort was the adaptation of many instruments to the DSM-III (1980) and DSM-III-R (1987). In addition, the increased delineation of childhood disorders required greater knowledge related to differential diagnosis and greater demand for structured interviews as adjuncts to assess-ment. Many of the efforts were consistent with the use of specific diagnostic criteria along with a demand for efficiency, cost-effectiveness, and accountability. Despite concerns regarding computer-based interpretations (Groth-Marnat & Schumaker, 1989), some of the above functions were beginning to be performed by specific computer programs. Since interviews were becoming increasingly structured, with the inclusion of scales and specific diagnostic strategies, the distinction between tests and interviews was becoming less clear. In some contexts, aspects of interviewing were even replaced with computer-requested and computer-integrated information and combined with fairly simple programs to aid in diagnosis, such as DIANO III (Spitzer, Endicott, & Cohen, 1974) and CATEGO (Wing, Cooper, & Sartorius, 1974). During the mid- and late 1980s, most clinicians, particularly those working in large institutions, used a combination of structured interviews along with open-ended unstructured approaches. Some research focused on the importance of the initial interview regarding clinical decision making and later therapeutic outcome

(Turk & Salovey, 1985; Hoge, Andrews, Robinson, & Hollett, 1988). There was also a greater appreciation and integration of the work from different disciplines and from differing theoretical persuasions (i.e., Hersen, 1988).

Future Directions   The future is likely to see an increased use and sophistication of computers to integrate interview data with test results and to aid in developing treatment planning through the generation of useful suggestions. In addition, greater efforts are likely to be directed toward making the assessment interview relevant and accountable to later treatment effectiveness (assessment utility). Such efforts will probably represent an integration of different schools and disciplines rather than be based in particular ideologies. There is also likely to be greater sophistication and choice in adult and child structured interviews for both comprehensive assessment as well as specialized subareas.

ISSUES RELATED TO RELIABILITY AND VALIDITY

Although the interview is not a standardized test, it is a means of collecting data and, as such, can and should be subjected to some of the same types of psychometric considerations as a formal test. This is important since interviews might introduce numerous sources of bias, particularly if the interviews are relatively unstructured. Reliability of interviewers is usually discussed in relation to interrater (interviewer) agreement. Wagner's (1949) early review of the literature found tremendous variation, ranging from .23 to .97 (Mdn = .57) for ratings of personal traits and -.20 to .85 (Mdn = .53) for ratings of overall ability. Later reviews have generally found similar variations in interrater agreement (Arvey & Trumbo, 1982; Ulrich & Trumbo, 1965). The problem then becomes how to determine which ratings to trust and which to view with skepticism. Of particular relevance is why some interviewers focus on different areas and have different biases. One consistent finding is that, when interviewers were both given narrow areas to assess, and were trained in interviewer strategies, interrater reliability increased (Dougherty, Ebert, & Callender, 1986; Sedeck, Tziner, & Middlestadt, 1983). The consensus was that highly structured interviews were more reliable. However, greater structure undermines one of the greatest strengths of interviews—their flexibility. In many situations, a free form, open-ended approach may be the only way to obtain some types of information (Weins, 1983).

Research on interview validity has typically focused on sources of interviewer bias. For example, halo effects result from the tendency of an interviewer to develop a general impression of a person and then group other seemingly related characteristics. For example, clients who are considered to express warmth may be seen as more competent or mentally healthy than they actually are. This grouping may be incorrect, thereby producing distortions and exaggerations. Similarly, first impressions have been found to bias later judgments (Cooper, 1981). Confirmatory bias might occur when an interviewer makes an inference regarding a client and then directs the interview in a way that will elicit the type of information that confirms the original inference. For example, a psychoanalytically oriented interviewer might direct questions related to early childhood traumas possibly incorrectly confirming traditional psychoanalytic explanations of current adult behaviors. It has also been found that one specific outstanding characteristic (educational level, physical appearance, etc.) can lead an interviewer to judge other characteristics that he or she incorrectly believes are related to the outstanding one. For example, physical attractiveness has been found to create interviewer bias in job applicants (Gilmore, Beehr, & Love, 1986). Interviewers might also be prone to incorrectly focus on explanations of behavior that emphasize traits rather than situational determinants (Ross, 1977). This is particularly likely to happen when the interpretation of interview data relies heavily on psychological tests, since tests, by their nature, conceptualize and emphasize static characteristics of the person rather than ongoing interactional processes.

In addition to perceptual and interactional biases on the part of an interviewer, the interviewees might be likely to distort their responses. For example, they might present an overly favorable view of themselves, particularly if they are relatively naive regarding their motivations. Distortions might be particularly likely in such sensitive areas as sexual behavior. Some specific areas of distortions are represented by the finding that victims of automobile accidents typically exaggerated the amount of time they lost from work, 40% of respondents provided incorrect estimates of their contributions to charity, and 17% of respondents reported their ages incorrectly (Kahn & Cannell, 1961). More extreme cases of falsification occur with outright (conscious) lies, delusions, confabulations, and lies by pathological (compulsive) liars that they partially believe themselves (Kerns, 1986).

Reviews of interview validity, in which interviewer ratings were compared with outside criterion measures, have, like reliability measures, shown tremendous variability—ranging from -.05 to +.72 (Arvey & Campion, 1982; Ulrich & Trumbo, 1965). However, this data refers mainly to unstructured types of interviews. A brief review of reliability and validity on selected structured interviews is provided at the end of this chapter. The above information on relatively unstructured interviews does strongly suggest that the information derived from them enables the development of tentative hypotheses that need to be supported by other means. Interviewers should also continually question the extent to which their particular style, attitudes, and expectations might be compromising interview validity.

ASSETS AND LIMITATIONS

Both structured and unstructured interviews allow clinicians to place test results into a wider, more meaningful context. In addition, biographical information derived from interviews can be used to help predict future behaviors; what a person has done in the past is an excellent guide to what he or she is likely to continue doing in the future. Factors for predicting suicide risk, success in certain occupations, and prognosis for certain disorders can usually be most effectively accomplished by attending to biographical data rather than test scores. Since tests are almost always structured or "closed" situations, the unstructured or semistructured interview is typically the only time during the assessment process when the clinician can observe the client in an open, ambiguous situation. Observations can be made regarding how persons organize their responses, and inferences can be derived from subtle, nonverbal cues. These inferences can be followed up with further, more detailed questioning. This flexibility inherent in unstructured and semistructured interviews is frequently their strongest advantage over standardized tests. The focus during unstructured interviews is almost exclusively on the individual rather than on how that individual does or does not compare to a larger normative comparison group. Some types of information can only be obtained through this flexible, person-centered approach, which allows the interviewer to pay attention to idiosyncratic factors. In crisis situations—when relatively rapid decisions need to be made—it can be impractical to take the time required to administer and interpret tests, leaving interviews and rapid screening devices as the only means of assessment. Finally, interviews create an opportunity to establish rapport and encourage client self-exploration.

Rarely will clients reveal themselves nor will they perform optimally on tests unless they first feel there is trust, openness, and a feeling that they are understood.

The greatest difficulty with unstructured interviews is interviewer bias that results from such perceptual and interactional processes as the halo effect, confirmatory bias, and the primacy effect. This typically results in wide variation for both reliability and validity as well as in difficulty comparing one subject with the next. A further difficulty is the high cost of using trained interviewers for large-scale epidemiological studies.

Structured interviews have many distinct advantages over unstructured approaches. Since structured interviews have more psychometric precision, the results enable comparability between one case or population and the next. For many years, structured interviews have been exclusively used in research settings, but are becoming progressively more common in clinical practice. The efficiency and cost-effectiveness of using less trained interviewers for such instruments as the Diagnostic Interview Schedule enable these tests to be used in large-scale epidemiological studies. Their efficiency is further enhanced through the development and availability of computer administration and scoring programs.

Even though structured interviews generally have higher psychometric properties than unstructured formats, they tend to overlook the idiosyncracies and richness of the person. In many cases, these unique aspects of the person may go undetected and yet may make a significant difference in interpreting test scores or making treatment recommendations. Although still somewhat controversial (Helzer & Robins, 1988), another criticism made by many clinicians/researchers is that a highly structured approach is less likely to create enough rapport for the client to feel sufficiently comfortable to reveal highly personal information. This is more true for the highly structured interviews such as the Diagnostic Interview Schedule than for a semistructured instrument such as the Schedule for Affective Disorders and Schizophrenia, which includes an initial, relatively unstructured component.

Although many of the structured interviews have demonstrated adequate reliability, studies relating to validity have primarily focused on the general level of impairment or simple discriminations between psychiatric and nonpsychiatric populations. There has been considerable controversy over what exactly is an acceptable outside criterion measure regarding the "true" diagnosis. In-depth studies of construct validity or incremental validity have yet to be performed. Furthermore, far more work needs to be done on the treatment utility of structured interviews in such areas as prognosis, selection of treatment, and likely response to specific forms of pharmacological or psychotherapeutic interventions.

THE ASSESSMENT INTERVIEW AND CASE HISTORY

General Considerations

The previously mentioned historical and psychometric considerations clearly indicate that no single correct way exists to conduct an unstructured interview. Interviewer style will be strongly influenced by theoretical orientation and by practical considerations. Persons strongly influenced by client-centered theories will tend to be nondirective and avoid highly structured questions. This is consistent with the assumption that persons have the inner ability to change and organize their own behaviors. The goal of a client-centered interview, then, would be to create the type of interpersonal relationship most likely to enhance this self-change. In contrast, a behavioral interview is more likely to be based on the assumption that change occurs as a result of specific external consequences. As a result, behavioral interviews will be relatively structured since they will be directed toward obtaining specific information that would help to design strategies based on altering external conditions.

Often, interviewers might wish to construct a semistructured interview format by listing in sequence the types of questions they would like to ask the person. To construct such a list, interviewers might consult Table 3–1 to note possibly relevant areas. Each of these areas might then be converted into specific questions. For example, the first few areas might be converted into the following series of questions:

"What are some important concerns that you have?"
"Could you describe the most important of these concerns?"
"When did the difficulty first begin?"
"How often does it occur?"
"Have there been any changes in how often it has occurred?"
"What happens after the behavior(s) occurs?"

Since clients vary regarding their personal characteristics (age, educational level, degree of cooperation) and type of presenting problem (childhood difficulties, legal problems, psychosis), the questions will necessarily need to vary from person to person. Furthermore, any series of questions should not be followed in any rigid manner, but with a certain degree of flexibility to allow the exploration of unique but relevant areas that arise during the interview.

Good interviewing is difficult to define, partly because different theoretical perspectives exist regarding clinician-client interaction. Furthermore, the success of an interview is determined not so much by what is done or what is said, but by making sure the proper attitude has been expressed. Whereas clinicians from alternative theoretical persuasions might differ regarding such areas as the degree of directiveness or the type of information that should be obtained, they would all agree that certain aspects of the relationship are essential. These include the interviewer's expression of sincerity, acceptance, understanding, genuine interest, warmth, and a positive regard for the worth of the person. If these are not expressed, it is unlikely that the goals of the interview, no matter how they are defined, will be achieved.

Patient ratings of the quality of interviews have been found to be dependent on the extent to which interviewers can understand the patient's emotions and detect emotional messages that are only partially expressed, particularly since these emotions are likely to be indirect and conveyed through nonverbal behaviors (Dimatteo & Taranta, 1976). This is especially relevant in clinical interviews that focus on a client's personal difficulties. Typically, words are inadequate to accurately describe problem emotions, so interviewers must necessarily infer them from paraverbal or nonverbal expression. This is highlighted by the assumption that nonverbal aspects of communication are likely to be a more powerful method of conveying information. For example, eye contact is most likely to convey involvement, rigidity of posture might suggest client defensiveness, and hand movements often occur beyond the person's conscious intent—suggesting nervousness, intensity, or relaxation. Mehrabian (1972) has estimated that the message received is 55% dependent on facial expression, 38% by tone, and only 7% by the content of what is said.

Interviewers vary in the extent to which they take notes during the interview. Some argue that notetaking during an interview might increase a client's anxiety, raise questions regarding anonymity, increase the likelihood that he or she will feel like an object under investigation, and might create an unnatural atmosphere. In contrast, many interviewers counter these arguments by pointing out that a loss of rapport is rarely due solely to notetaking during the interview, assuming, of course, that the interviewer can still spend a

Table 3–1.   Checklist for an assessment interview and case history

HISTORY OF THE PROBLEM:
    Description of the problem   Intensity and duration
    Initial onset   Previous treatment
    Changes in frequency   Attempts to solve
    Antecedents/consequences   Formal treatment

FAMILY BACKGROUND:
    Socioeconomic level   Cultural background
    Parent's occupation(s)   Parent's current health
    Emotional/medical history   Family relationships
    Married/separated/divorced   Urban/rural upbringing
    Family constellation

PERSONAL HISTORY:

Infancy;
    Developmental milestones   Early medical history
    Family atmosphere   Toilet training
    Amount of contact with parents

Early and Middle Childhood;
    Adjustment to school   Peer relationships
    Academic achievement   Relationship with parents
    Hobbies/activities/interests   Important life changes

Adolescence;
    (all areas in early and middle childhood)
    Presence of acting out   Early dating
    (legal, drugs, sexual)   Reaction to puberty

Early and Middle Adulthood;
    Career/occupational   Marriage
    Interpersonal relationships   Medical/emotional history
    Satisfaction with life goals   Relationship with parents
    Hobbies/interests/activities   Economic stability

Late Adulthood;
    Medical history   Reaction to declining abilities
    Ego integrity   Economic stability

MISCELLANEOUS
    Self-concept (like/dislike)   Somatic concerns
    Happiest/saddest memory   (headaches, stomach aches, etc.)
    Earliest memory   Events that create happiness/sadness
    Fears   Recurring/noteworthy dreams

sufficient amount of time attending to the client. Ongoing notetaking is also likely to capture more details and result in less memory distortion than recording material after the interview has been completed. Thus, an intermediate amount of notetaking during the interview is recommended. If the interview is taped or videorecorded, the reasons for this procedure need to be fully explained, along with the assurance of confidentiality and a signed agreement. Although tape or video recording is often awkward at first, usually the interviewer and client quickly forget that it is occurring.

Interview Tactics

Directive Versus Nondirective   The degree to which clinicians chose to be structured and directive during an interview will depend on both theoretical and practical considerations. If time is limited, the interviewer will need to be direct and to the point. The nature of the interview will be quite different for a person who has been referred for an interview and will be returning to the referring person than for an interviewer who is assessing the person prior to conducting therapy with him or her. An ambiguous, unstructured approach will probably make an extremely anxious person even more anxious, while a direct approach may prove more effective. A resistant, uncooperative client will also be likely to require a more direct question-and-answer style. As stated previously, a less structured style often encourages deeper client self-exploration, enables clinicians to observe the client's organizational abilities, and may result in greater rapport, flexibility, and sensitivity to the client's uniqueness.

Frequently, behavioral interviews are characterized as being structured and directed toward obtaining a comprehensive description of actual behaviors and conscious thoughts, attitudes, and beliefs regarding different behaviors (see Chapter 4). This is often contrasted with the more unstructured psychodynamic approach, which investigates underlying motivations and hidden dynamics, and assesses information that may not be within the person's ordinary awareness. Typically, these approaches are perceived as competing and mutually exclusive. Haas, Hendin, & Singer (1987) point out that this either/or position is not only unnecessary but unproductive. Rather, each style of interviewing provides different types of information that could potentially compensate for the other's weaknesses. By using both approaches, interview breadth and validity might be increased. This is also similar to Leary's (1957) designation of client descriptions as being based on direct behavioral data (public communication), self-description, and private symbolization. Each of these levels may be useful for different purposes, and the findings from each level might be quite different from one another.

Style and Sequence of Responses   Numerous tactics or types of statements have been proposed and studied. These include the clarification statement, verbatim playback, probing, confrontation, understanding, active listening, reflection, feedback, summary statement, random probing, self-disclosure, perception checking, use of concrete examples, and therapeutic double binds. Additional relevant topics include the importance of eye contact, self-disclosure, active listening, and touch. These areas are beyond the scope of this chapter, but the interested reader is referred to excellent discussions by Harper, Wiens, and Matarazzo (1981), Pope (1979), Sattler (1988), and Wiens (1983). Several highly relevant and practical tactics have been isolated and are discussed below.

Maloney and Ward (1976) have suggested that interviewers begin with open-ended questions and, after observing the client's responses, then use more direct questions to fill in gaps in their understanding. Although this sequence might begin with open-ended questions, it should typically lead to interviewer responses that are intermediate in their level of directiveness such as facilitating comments, requesting clarification, and possibly confronting the client regarding inconsistencies.

Maloney and Ward (1976) clarify that an open-ended question requires clients to comprehend, organize, and express themselves with little outside structure. This is perhaps the only occasion in the assessment process that makes this requirement of clients, since most tests or structured interviews provide guidance in the form of specific, clear stimuli. When clients are asked open-ended questions, they will be most likely to express significant but unusual features about themselves. This may require that interpretations of test data be modified or altered. Verbal fluency, level of assertiveness, tone of voice, energy level, hesitations, and areas of anxiety can be noted. Hypotheses can be generated from these observations and further open-ended or more direct questions used to test these hypotheses.

Interviewer responses that show an intermediate level of directiveness are facilitation, clarification, and confrontation. Facilitation of comments is done to maintain or encourage the flow of conversation. This might be accomplished verbally ("Tell me more...," "Please continue...") or nonverbally (eye contact, nodding). These requests for clarification might be used when clients indicate, perhaps through subtle cues, that they have not fully expressed something regarding the topic of discussion. Requests for clarification can bring into the open material that was only implied. In particular, greater clarification might be achieved by requesting the client to be highly specific, such as asking him or her to provide concrete examples (a typical day or a day that best illustrates the problem behavior).

Sometimes interviewers might wish to confront or at least comment upon inconsistencies in a client's information or behavior. Carkhuff (1969) has categorized the potential types of inconsistencies as being between what a person is versus what he or she wants to be, what he or she is saying versus what he or she is doing, and discrepancies between the person's self-perception versus the interviewer's experience of the person. A confrontation might also involve a challenge regarding the improbable content of what he or she is reporting ("tall" stories).

The purpose of confrontations during assessment is to obtain more in-depth information regarding the client. In contrast, therapeutic confrontations are used to encourage client self-exploration and behavior change. If a practitioner is using the initial interview and assessment as a prelude to therapy, then this distinction is less important. However, a confrontational style can produce considerable anxiety, which should only be created if sufficient opportunity exists to work through the anxiety. Usually, a client will be most receptive to confrontations when they are posed hypothetically—as possibilities to consider—rather than as a direct challenge. Confrontations also require a sufficient degree of rapport in order to be sustained; unless this rapport is present, confrontations will probably result in client defensiveness and a deterioration of the relationship.

Finally, direct questions can be used to fill in gaps in what the client has stated. Thus, a continual flow can be formed between client-directed or client-organized responses and clinician-directed responses. This sequence—beginning with open-ended questions, then moving to intermediately structured responses (facilitation, clarification, confrontation), and finally ending in directive questions—should not be rigid but should continually vary throughout the interview.

Comprehensiveness   The basic focus of an assessment interview should be to define the problem behavior (nature of the problem, severity, related areas that are affected) and its causes (conditions that worsen or alleviate it, origins, antecedents, consequences (see Chapter 4). Interviewers might wish to use a checklist, such as the one in Table 3–1, to ensure they are covering most relevant areas. In using such a checklist, the interviewer might begin with a general question, such as "How were you referred here?" or "What are some areas that concern you?" Observations and notes can then be made about the way the client organizes his or her responses, what he or she says and the way he or she says it. The interviewer could use facilitating, clarifying, and confronting responses to obtain more information. Finally, the interviewer could review the checklist on family background to see if all relevant areas were covered sufficiently. If some areas or aspects of areas weren't covered, then the interviewer might ask direct questions, such as "What was your father's occupation?" or "When did your mother and father divorce?" The interviewer could then begin the same sequence for personal history related to infancy, middle childhood, etc. Table 3–1 is not comprehensive, but rather is intended as a general guide that is applicable in most interview situations. If practitioners have specific types of clients that they typically evaluate (child abuse, suicide, brain impaired), then this checklist may need to have specific additions to it and/or be used as an adjunct to commercially available structured interviews, such as the Neuropsychological Status Examination (Schinka, 1983) or Lawrence Psychological-Forensic Examination (Lawrence, 1984).

Avoidance of "Why" Questions   One tactic to avoid is the use of "why" questions, since they are likely to increase client defensiveness. A "why" question typically sounds accusatory or critical and thus forces the client to account for his or her behavior. In addition, clients are likely to become intellectual in this situation, thereby separating themselves from their emotions. An alternative approach is to preface the question with "how" rather than "why." This is more likely to result in a description rather than a justification and to keep clients more centered on their emotions.

Nonverbal Behaviors   Interviewers should also be aware of both their own as well as their client's nonverbal behaviors. In particular, interviewers might express their interest by maintaining eye contact, being facially responsive, and attending verbally and nonverbally, such as through occasionally leaning forward.

Concluding   Any interview will be bound by time constraints. An interviewer might help to insure that these constraints are observed by alerting the client when only 5 or 10 minutes remain until the arranged completion of the interview. This allows the client or interviewer to obtain final relevant information. It also allows the interviewer to summarize the main themes of the interview and, if appropriate, make any recommendations.

MENTAL STATUS EXAMINATION

The mental status exam was originally modeled after the physical medical exam; just as the physical medical exam is designed to review the major organ systems, the mental status exam similarly reviews the major systems of psychiatric functioning. Over the past 80 years it has become the mainstay of patient evaluation in most psychiatric settings. In many ways, the data derived from the mental status exam is handled by psychiatrists in much the same way as psychological test results are handled by psychologists. The mental status exam "raw" data is selectively integrated with general background information to present a coherent portrait of the person and arrive at a diagnosis. Whereas psychiatry has placed considerable emphasis on the mental status exam (and more recently on structured clinical interviews), psychology and other related mental health disciplines have chosen to focus more on psychological tests and case histories.

It is rare for a psychological report to include a traditional mental status examination. However, it is included and outlined below since it is such an essential means of interviewing within the broader mental health field. This form of interviewing is not typically used by psychologists partly because many areas reviewed by the mental status exam are already covered during the assessment interview and through the interpretation of psychological test results. Many psychological tests cover these areas in a more precise, in-depth, objective, and validated manner. A client's appearance, affect, and mood is usually noted by attending to behavioral observations. A review of the history and nature of the problem is likely to pick up such areas as delusions, misinterpretations, and perceptual disorders (hallucinations). Likewise, interview data and psychological test results typically assess a client's fund of knowledge, attention, insight, memory, abstract reasoning, and level of social judgment. However, the mental status examination reviews all of the above areas in a systematic manner. Furthermore, there are situations, such as intakes in an acute medical or psychiatric hospital, where insufficient time is available to evaluate the client with psychological tests.

Numerous sources in the psychiatric literature provide thorough guidelines to conducting a mental status exam (Crary & Johnson, 1981; Nicholi, 1978; Taylor, 1981), and structured mental status exams have been developed to assist the interviewer. For example, the Mental Status Examination Record (Spitzer & Endicott, 1971) is a four-page computer form that includes 121 checklist items and 156 rating scales. It is intended to be completed after the interview is finished and is designed to produce 20 derived scales in such areas as somatic concern, judgment, hallucinations, and anger-negativism. Another similar instrument is the Missouri Automated Mental Status Examination Checklist (Hedlund, Sletten, Evenson, Altman, & Cho, 1977), which requires the examiner to make ratings on the following nine areas of functioning: general appearance, motor behavior, speech and thought, mood and affect, other emotional reactions, thought content, sensorium, intellect, and insight and judgment. The checklist includes a total of 119 possible ratings, but the examiner makes ratings in only those areas he or she judges to be relevant. Should clinicians wish to develop skills in conducting mental status examinations, they are encouraged to consult these sources.

The following outline of the typical areas covered will serve as a brief introduction to this form of interviewing. The outline is organized around the categories recommended by Crary and Johnson (1981) and a checklist of relevant areas is included in Figure 3–1. Interviewers can answer the different areas on the checklist either during or after a mental status examination. The tabled information can then be used to answer relevant questions relating to the referral question, to help in diagnosis, or to add to other test data.

General Appearance and Behavior

This area assesses similar material as that requested in the "behavioral observations" section of a psychological report (see Chapter 12). A client's dress, posture, gestures, speech, personal care/hygiene, and any unusual physical features such as physical handicaps, tics, or grimaces are noted. Attention is given to the degree to which his or her behavior conforms to social expectations, but this is placed within the context of his or her culture and social position. Additional important areas are facial expressions, eye contact, activity level, degree of cooperation, physical attractiveness, and attentiveness. Is the client friendly, hostile, seductive, or indifferent? Do any bizarre behaviors or significant events occur during the interview? In particular, speech might be fast or slow, loud or soft, or include a number of additional unusual features. A systematic checklist of relevant areas of behavior and appearance is included in Figure 3–1.

Name ———————————————————— Observer's Name ————————————————————

			No Data	Present	Absent
APPEARANCE		1. unkempt, unclean, disheveled............			
		2. clothing and/or grooming atypical........			
		3. unusual physical characteristics.........			

COMMENTS RE APPEARANCE:

			No Data	Present	Absent
BEHAVIOR	Posture	4. slumped................................			
		5. rigid, tense..........................			
	Facial Expression Suggests	6. anxiety, fear, apprehension..............			
		7. depression, sadness...................			
		8. anger, hostility......................			
		9. absence of feeling, blandness...........			
		10. atypical, unusualness..................			
	General Body Movements	11. accelerated, increased speed............			
		12. decreased, slowed.....................			
		13. atypical, unusual....................			
		14. restlessness, fidgetiness................			
	Speech	15. rapid speech..........................			
		16. slowed speech........................			
		17. loud speech..........................			
		18. soft speech..........................			
		19. mute................................			
		20. atypical quality, slurring, stammer......			
BEHAVIOR	Therapist-Patient Relationship	21. domineering, controlling................			
		22. submissive, overly compliant, dependent..			
		23. provocative, hostile, challenging.......			
		24. suspicious, guarded, evasive...........			
		25. uncooperative, non-compliant............			

COMMENTS RE BEHAVIOR:

		No Data	Present	Absent
FEELING (AFFECT AND MOOD)	26. inappropriate to thought content.........			
	27. increased lability of affect.............			
	predominant mood is:			
	28. blunted, dull, bland....................			
	29. euphoria, elation.....................			
	30. anger, hostility......................			
	31. anxiety, fear, apprehension..............			
	32. depression, sadness.....................			

COMMENTS RE FEELING:

		No Data	Present	Absent
PERCEPTION	33. illusions............................			
	34. auditory hallucinations.................			
	35. visual hallucinations.................			
	36. other types of hallucinations...........			

COMMENTS RE PERCEPTION:

			No Data	Present	Absent
THINKING	Intellectual Functioning	37. impaired level of consciousness..........			
		38. impaired attention span, distractible....			
		39. impaired abstract thinking..............			
		40. impaired calculation ability............			
		41. impaired intelligence..................			
	Orientation	42. disoriented to person...................			
		43. disoriented to place..................			
		44. disoriented to time..................			
	Memory	45. impaired recent memory..................			
		46. impaired remote memory................			
	Insight	47. denies presence of psychological problems................................			
		48. blames others or circumstances for problems................................			
	Judgment	49. impaired ability to make routine decisions................................			
		50. impaired impulse control...............			
THINKING	Thought Content	51. obsessions...........................			
		52. compulsions..........................			
		53. phobias.............................			
		54. depersonalization......................			
		55. suicidal ideation.....................			
		56. homicidal ideation....................			
		57. delusions...........................			
	Stream of Thought	58. associational disturbance...............			

COMMENTS RE THINKING:

DIAGNOSIS:—————————————————————————————
  as manifested by the following M.S.E. items

————— ————— ————— ————— —————
————— ————— ————— ————— —————

Figure 3–1. Format for mental status and history

Reproduced by permission of MTP Press Ltd., Lancaster, England, from Crary, W.G. & Johnson, C.W. (1981). Mental status examination. In Johnson, C.W., Snibbe, J.R., & Evans, L.A. (Eds.), *Basic Psychopathology: A Programmed Text* (2nd ed.). Lancaster: MIP Press, pp. 55-56.

Feeling (Affect and Mood)

A client's mood refers to the dominant emotion expressed during the interview, whereas affect refers to the client's range of emotions. This is inferred from the content of the client's speech, facial expressions, and body movements. The type of affect can be judged according to such variables as its depth, intensity, duration, and appropriateness. The client might be cold or warm, distant or close, labile, and, as is characteristic of schizophrenia, his or her affect might be blunted or flattened. The client's mood might also be euphoric, hostile, anxious, or depressed.

Perception

Different clients perceive themselves and their world in a wide variety of ways. It is especially important to note whether there are any illusions or hallucinations. The presence of auditory hallucinations are most characteristic of schizophrenics, whereas vivid visual hallucinations are more characteristic of persons with organic brain syndromes.

Thinking

Intellectual functioning   Any assessment of higher intellectual functioning needs to be made within the context of a client's educational level, socioeconomic status, and familiarity and identification with a particular culture. If a low level of intellectual functioning is consistent with a general pattern of poor academic and occupational achievement, then a diagnosis of intellectual disability might be supported. However, if a person performs poorly on tests of intellectual functioning and yet has a good history of achievement, then organicity might be suspected.

Intellectual functioning typically involves reading and writing comprehension, general fund of knowledge, ability to do arithmetic, and the degree to which the client can interpret the meaning of proverbs. Throughout the assessment, clinicians typically note the degree to which the client's thoughts and expressions are articulate versus incoherent. Sometimes clinicians might combine assessments of intellectual functioning with some short, formal tests such as the Bender, with an aphasia screening test, or even with portions of the WAIS-R or WISC-R.

Orientation   The ability of clients to be oriented can vary regarding the degree to which they know who they are (person), where they are (place), and when current and past events have occurred or are occurring (time). Clinical observation indicates the most frequent type of disorientation is for time, whereas disorientation for place and person occur less frequently. However, when disorientation does occur for place, and especially for person, the condition is relatively severe. Disorientation is most consistent with organic conditions. If a person is oriented in all three spheres, this is frequently abbreviated as "oriented X3."

Related to the orientation of clients is their sensorium, which refers to how intact their physiological processes are to receiving and integrating information. Sensorium might refer to hearing, smell, vision, and touch and might range from being clouded to clear. Can the client attend to and concentrate upon the outside world or are these processes interrupted? The client might experience unusual smells, hear voices, or have the sense that his or her skin is tingling. Sensorium can also refer to the client's level of consciousness, which may vary from hyperarousal and excitement to drowsiness and confusion. Disorders of a client's sensorium often reflect organic conditions, but may also be consistent with psychosis.

Memory, Attention, and Concentration   Since memory retrieval and acquisition requires attention and concentration, these three functions are frequently considered together. Long term memory is often assessed by requesting information regarding the client's general fund of information (e.g. important dates, major cities in a country, three major heads of state since 1900). Some clinicians include the Information or Digit Span subtests from the WAIS-R/WISC-R or other formal tests of a similar nature. In addition, long term memory might be evaluated by measuring recall of their major life events and the accuracy of their recall can be compared to objective records of these events (e.g., year graduated from high school, date of marriage). It is often useful to record any significant distortions of selective recall in relation to life events as well as to note the client's attitudes toward his or her memory.

Short term memory might be assessed by either requesting that clients recall recent events (most recent meal, how they got to the appointment) or by having them repeat digits forward and backward. Again, the WAIS-R/WISC-R Digit Span subtest might be used or at least a similar version of it. Serial sevens (counting forward by adding seven each time) can be used to assess how distractable or focused they are. Persons who are anxious and preoccupied will have a difficult time with serial sevens as well as with repeating digits forward and especially digits backward.

Insight and Judgment   Clients vary in their ability to interpret the meaning and impact of their behavior on others. They also vary widely in their ability to provide for themselves, evaluate risks, and make future plans. Adequate insight and judgment involves developing and testing hypotheses regarding their own behavior and the behavior of others. Clients also need to be assessed to determine why they believe they were referred for evaluation and, in a wider context, their attitudes toward their difficulties. How do they relate their past history to current difficulties, and how do they explain these difficulties? Where do they place the blame for their difficulties? Based on their insights, how effectively can they solve problems and make decisions?

Thinking

A client's speech can often be considered to be a reflection of his or her thoughts. The client's speech may be coherent, spontaneous, and comprehensible or may contain unusual features. It may be slow or fast, be characterized by sudden silences, or be loud or unusually soft. Is the client frank or evasive, open or defensive, assertive or passive, irritable, abusive, or sarcastic? Consideration of a person's thoughts is often divided into thought content and thought processes. Such thought contents as delusions might suggest a psychotic condition, but delusions may also be consistent with certain organic disorders, such as dementia. The presence of compulsions or obsessions should be followed up with an assessment of the client's degree of insight into the appropriateness of these thoughts and behaviors. Such thought processes as the presence of rapid changes in topics might reflect flightive ideas. The client might also have difficulty producing a sufficient number of ideas, include an excessive number of irrelevant associations, or ramble aimlessly.

INTERPRETING INTERVIEW DATA

Interpreting and integrating interview data into the psychological report inevitably involves clinical judgment. Even with the use of structured interviews, the clinician still must determine which information to include or exclude. Thus, all the potential cautions associated with clinical judgment need to be taken into account. This is particularly important since life decisions and the success of later treatment may be based on conclusions and recommendations described in the report.

Several general principles can be used to interpret interview data. The interview is the primary instrument that clinicians use to develop tentative hypotheses regarding their clients. Thus, interview data can be evaluated by determining whether these hypotheses are supported by information outside the interview. Interview data that is supported by test scores can be given greater emphasis in the final report. However, material should only be emphasized if it is relevant to the referral question. Even material that is highly supported throughout different phases of the interview process should not be included unless it relates directly to the purpose of the referral.

Enelow and Wexler (1966) suggest reducing interview data into short phrases and categorizing them into either process or content areas. Process areas might include unusual behaviors, tone of voice, or level of tension. Content areas might include a client's thoughts, preoccupations, interests, or significant life events. A convenient summary can be reached by listing key phrases under each category. For example, the following list might summarize some of the data recorded during a legal evaluation:

PROCESS	CONTENT
1. excited	1. fearful of imprisonment
2. poorly focused	2. arrested for burglary
3. disheveled appearance	3. abused as a child
4. loud	4. dropped out of school
	5. two previous arrests

The data can then be more easily screened and placed into appropriate sections of the report. A worksheet like the one shown might be used in conjunction with Ownby's (1987) recommendation to list the topic for consideration (e.g., learning difficulties, depression) followed by relevant data (test scores, behavioral observations, relevant biographical details) leading to a listing of possible constructs, diagnoses, or conclusions and finally to treatment recommendations (see Chapter 12, Figure 12–1). The previous listing of interview data into either process or content areas can be used as one source of information that might be included in a worksheet such as Figure 12–1.

Interview data might also be organized and interpreted based on the presence of different themes. For example, one person's history might be characterized by frequent difficulties with authority figures. Specific details relating to these difficulties might emerge, such as the client feeling like a martyr and eventually inappropriately expressing extreme anger toward the authority figures(s). A careful review of the client's history might reveal how he or she becomes involved in these recurring relationships and how he or she typically attempts to resolve them. Other persons who are frequently depressed might distance themselves from others by their behavior and then be confused about why relationships seem to be difficult. Often these themes will emerge during a carefully conducted interview, yet aspects of the themes (or the entire themes themselves) will not be apparent to the interviewee.

There is no one strategy for sensitizing interviewers to the types and patterns of recurring themes that might be encountered during interviews. Inevitably, clinical judgment will be a significant factor. The accuracy and types of judgments will depend on the theoretical perspective of the interviewer, knowledge regarding the particular difficulty the interviewer is investigating, past experience, types of questions asked, and purpose of the interview.

STRUCTURED CLINICAL INTERVIEWS

Standardized psychological tests and structured interviews were developed to reduce the problems associated with open-ended interviews. They both serve to structure the stimuli presented to the person and reduce the role of clinical judgment. Since structured interviews generate objective ratings on the same areas, they have advantages in making comparisons between one case and the next. Typically these interviews vary in their degree of structure, the relative expertise required to administer them, and the extent to which they serve as screening procedures designed for global measurement or as tools used to obtain specific diagnoses.

Before structured interviews could be developed, clear, specific criteria needed to be created relating to symptom patterns and diagnoses. This ideally helped to reduce the amount of error caused by vague guidelines for exclusion or inclusion in different categories (criterion variance). These criteria then needed to be incorporated into the interview format and interview questions. Information variance refers to the variability in amount and type of information derived from interviews with patients. In most unstructured interviews, information variance is caused by the wide differences in content and phrasing due to such factors as the theoretical orientation of the interviewer. Structured interviews correct for this by requesting the same or similar questions from each client.

The first popular system of specific criterion-based diagnosis was developed by Feighner et al. (1972), and provided clear, behaviorally oriented descriptions of 16 psychiatric disorders based on the DSM-II. Clinicians using the Feighner criteria were found to have an immediate and marked increase in interrater diagnostic reliability. The descriptions of and relevant research on the Feighner criteria are published in Woodruff, Goodwin, and Guze's (1974) book, *Psychiatric Diagnosis.* Several interviews—such as the Renard Diagnostic Interview (Helzer, Robins, Croughan, & Welner, 1981)—incorporated the Feighner criteria. Spitzer, Endicott, & Robins (1978) further altered and elaborated the Feighner criteria to develop the Research Diagnostic Criteria. Simultaneous with the development of the Research Diagnostic Criteria, Endicott and Spitzer (1978) developed the Schedule for Affective Disorders and Schizophrenia (SADS), which was based on the new Research and Diagnostic Criteria. When the DSM-II (1968), DSM-III (1980), and DSM-III-R (1987) were published, revisions of older interviews and more recently developed interviews typically incorporated the DSM-III/DSM-III-R along with elements of the Feighner criteria and/or the Research Diagnostic Criteria.

As noted earlier, the reliability of structured interviews has been found to vary depending on the specificity or precision of the rating or diagnosis. Whereas the highest reliabilities have been found for global assessment (i.e., presence/absence of psychopathology), much lower reliabilities have generally been found for the assessment of specific types of behaviors or syndromes. Likewise, high reliabilities have been found for overt behaviors, but reliability has been less satisfactory for more covert aspects of the person—such as obsessions, fears, and worries. Reliability also tends to be lower when clinicians are requested to attempt exact estimates regarding behavioral frequencies and for inferences of multifaceted aspects of the person derived from complex clinical judgments.

Most early studies on validity were based on item content (content validity) or degree of accuracy in distinguishing between broad areas of psychopathology (psychiatric/nonpsychiatric). More recent trends have attempted to assess the accuracy of far more specific areas. However, most validity studies have suffered from an absence of clear, commonly agreed-upon criteria. Even though structured interviews were attempts to improve on previous, imperfect instruments (unstructured interviews, standardized tests), the structured interviews themselves could not be compared with anything better. For example, the "procedural validity" strategy is based on comparing lay interviewers' diagnoses with diagnoses derived from trained psychiatrists. Even though the psychiatrist's diagnosis may be better than the lay person's, diagnoses by trained psychiatrists still cannot be said to be an ultimate, objective, and completely accurate standard. Furthermore, there is confusion about whether actual validity is being measured (which would assume psychiatrists' diagnoses are the true, accurate ones) or merely a version of interrater reliability.

Future studies need to involve aspects of what has previously been discussed as construct validity. Specifically this means looking more carefully at structured interviews in relationship to etiology, course, prognosis, and treatment utility relating to such areas as the appropriate selection of types of treatments and the likelihood of favorable responses to these treatments. Validity studies also need to look at the interaction between and implications of multiple criterion measures, including behavioral assessment, checklists, rating scales, self-report inventories, biochemical indices, and neuropathological alterations.

During the past 15 years, there has been a proliferation of structured interviews for a wide range of areas. Clinicians working in specific areas will often select structured interviews directed toward diagnosing the disorders they are most likely to encounter. For example, some situations might benefit from using the Anxiety Disorders Interview Schedule (DiNardo, O'Brien, Barlow, & Waddel, 1983) to make clear distinctions between anxiety disorders and substance abuse, and between psychosis and major affective disorders. Other contexts might be best served by the Schedule for Schizotypal Personalities (Baron, Asnis, & Gruen, 1981) or the Structured Interview for DSM-III Personality Disorders (Stangl et al., 1985). A consideration is that, since most structured interviews are undergoing continuous revisions, the most up-to-date research should be consulted to ensure that practitioners obtain the most recently revised versions. The following is an overview of the most frequently used and most extensively researched structured interviews.

Schedule for Affective Disorders and Schizophrenia

The Schedule for Affective Disorders and Schizophrenia has been the most widely used structured interview for clinical research purposes. Even though it was originally designed for differential diagnosis between affective disorders and schizophrenia, it actually covers a much wider range of symptoms and allows the interviewer to consider many different diagnostic categories. A wide range of disorders are considered within the SADS, but its primary strength lies in obtaining fine detail regarding different subtypes of affective disorders and schizophrenia. The interview is semistructured and was designed from clear, objective categories derived from Spitzer, Endicott, and Robins' (1978) Research Diagnostic Criteria (RDC).

Adult Version   The adult version of the Schedule for Affective Disorders and Schizophrenia (SADS; Endicott & Spitzer, 1978) is designed to be administered in two different parts, the first focusing on the client's present illness and the second on past episodes. This division roughly corresponds with the three different versions of the SADS. The first is the regular version (SADS), the second is the lifetime version (SADS-L, which is actually the second half of the SADS), and the third is the SADS-C, which measures changes in the client. The SADS-L is directed toward diagnosing the possible presence of psychiatric disturbance throughout the person's life. The SADS and SADS-L are the most extensively used. Since the questions in the SADS are directed toward current symptoms and those symptoms experienced one week before the illness, it is most appropriate for administration when the client is having current difficulties. In contrast, the SADS-L is most appropriate when there is no current illness. To make accurate ratings, interviewers are allowed to use a wide range of sources (client's family, medical records) and ask a number of different questions. Final ratings are made on a Likert-type scale. Administration takes from 1.5 to 2 hours and should only be conducted by a psychiatrist, clinical psychologist, or psychiatric social worker.

Interrater reliabilities for the specific diagnostic categories were quite high, with the exception of the Formal Thought Disorder Scale (Endicott & Spitzer, 1978). The low reliability of this scale may have been due to the fact that few of the patients in the Endicott and Spitzer (1978) sample showed clear patterns of disordered thoughts, which resulted in high variability for the ratings. Test-retest reliabilities were likewise good, ranging from .88 for Manic Disorders to .52 for Chronic and Intermittent Depressive Disorder (Spiker & Ehler, 1984). The exception was a low reliability for schizoaffective, Depressed (.24), but this was probably due to the small number of patients included in this category, which resulted in limited variance. Using a different and possibly more appropriate statistical method, reliability increased to .84. Incremental validity might be increased by having clients referred for a medical exam to screen out medical difficulties that might be resulting in central nervous system dysfunction. The authors also recommend that interviewers try to increase validity by always including the best available information (family history, structured tests, other rating schedules) prior to making final ratings.

Child Version   The SADS for School Age Children (Kiddie-SADS-P, K-SADS-P; Puig-Antich & Chambers, 1978) is a semistructured interview developed for children between 6 and 17. The test is scored using the Research Diagnostic Criteria and focuses on current level of pathology according to how it was at its worst and how it has been during the past week. Although much of the K-SADS-P is based on research with major depressive disorders of prepubertal children, it also covers a wide range of disorders—such as phobias, conduct disorders, obsessive-compulsive disorders, and separation anxiety.

The interview should be administered by a professional clinician who has been trained in the use of the K-SADS and is familiar with DSM-III criteria. Administration time is approximately one hour, but it usually takes longer with younger children. Separate interviews are given to the parent and then the child, and any discrepancies between the two sources of information are clarified before final ratings are made. The first phase is a 15 to 20 minute unstructured interview in which rapport is developed as well as an overview of relevant aspects of history, including the frequency and duration of presenting symptoms, their onset, and whether the parents have sought previous treatment. This is followed by structured questions regarding symptoms, which are rated on a Likert scale, with 1 representing "not at all" and 7 indicating that they are "extreme." A skip structure is built into the format so that interviewers can omit irrelevant questions. Interviewers are allowed to use their judg-ment regarding the wording and the type and number of questions. Finally, ratings are made regarding behavioral observations (appearance, attention, affect). Interviewers are also requested to rate the completeness and reliability of the interview and to make a global assessment of pathology (degree of symptomatology and level of impairment).

Test-retest reliability on the K-SADS has been good for conduct disorders and symptoms related to depression, but poor for anxiety disorders. Overall reliabilities have been lower for the K-SADS than for the adult SADS, but this is to be expected, given the relative changeableness and less well developed language skills found with children (Chambers et al., 1985).

Diagnostic Interview Schedule

In contrast to the SADS, which is semistructured and requires administration by trained professionals, the Diagnostic Interview Schedule (DIS; Robins, Helzer, Croughan, & Ratcliff, 1981) is highly structured and was designed specifically by the National Institute of Mental Health (Division of Biometry and Epidemiology) to be administered by nonprofessional interviewers for epidemiological studies (see Helzer & Robins, 1988). Clinical judgment is reduced to a minimum through the use of verbatim wording, specific guidelines, and a clear flow from one question to the next. Thus, the DIS is far more economical to administer than the SADS. Studies have generally indicated that results are comparable between trained clinicians and nonprofessional interviewers (Helzer, Spitznagel, & McEvoy, 1987).

Adult Version   The original version of the DIS was derived from the format of the earlier Renard Diagnostic Interview. Diagnosis is currently based on both the DSM-III and Research Diagnostic Criteria. Initially, questions are directed toward obtaining information regarding the client's life, and information is also requested regarding more current symptoms based on the past two weeks, past month, past six months, and past year. Specific probe questions distinguish whether a symptom is clinically significant. Administration time is approximately 60 to 90 minutes. Also, a computer scoring program is available that can generate diagnoses based on the DSM-III, Research Diagnostic Criteria, or Feighner criteria.

Computer administration is available and this has been found to generate an average of 5.5 possible diagnoses as compared with an average of 2.56 for nonstructured interviews (Wyndowe, 1987). Patient acceptance for the computer administration has been found to be high, although the average administration time of 111.6 minutes is somewhat longer than the clinician-interviewed version. The schedule is undergoing continual updating and revision. The current version (Version III-A) includes 43 DSM-III diagnoses and future projects include a screening DIS, a more in-depth multisystem version, and the incorporation of further advances in computerized interviewing (Helzer & Robins, 1988).

Studies of the reliability and validity of the DIS have generally been favorable. In particular, the comparability of diagnosis by professionals and nonprofessionals using the DIS has been supported. This suggests that nonprofessionals can effectively use it to help gather data for large epidemiological studies. Robins et al. (1981) found diagnostic agreement between psychiatrists and nonprofessional interviewers to be .69. The sensitivity (percent interviewees correctly identified) of the DIS varied according to type of diagnosis, but had a mean of 75% with a mean specificity (percent noncases correctly identified) of 94%. However, data on sensitivity and specificity were based on using psychiatrists' diagnoses as the true index of diagnostic accuracy. The difficulties in considering psychiatrists' ratings as the truly accurate criterion for validity have already been noted, so it is probably best to consider the above data on sensitivity and specificity as forms of interrater reliability.

Helzer et al. (1985) found that, when compared with psychiatrists, nonprofessional interviewers tended to overdiagnose major depression. However, for most diagnoses Helzer, Spitznagel, and Envoy (1987) found that agreement between nonprofessional interviewers and physicians tended to be comparable. In contrast, Folstein et al. (1985) did not find a sufficiently high rate of agreement between diagnoses by a panel of psychiatrists and diagnoses by the DIS to warrant its use in epidemiological studies. Specifically, they found that the DIS generated more cases of depression and schizophrenia and fewer cases of alcoholism and antisocial personality (Folstein et al., 1985). However, determining the relative accuracy of the psychiatrists or the DIS is more difficult. The DIS has also been found to be comparable with other commonly used psychiatric rating devices such as the Psychiatric Diagnostic Interview, but both of these may contain inaccuracies and, as in the Folstein et al. (1985) study, it is difficult to tell in which areas these inaccuracies occurred (Weller et al., 1985). The DIS has had the greatest difficulty accurately diagnosing border-line conditions and patients in remission, but this is to be expected since these are the most problematic diagnoses for any assessment strategy (Robins, Helzer, Ratcliff, & Seyfried, 1981).

Child Version   The Diagnostic Interview Schedule for Children (DISC; Costello, Edel-brock, Duncan, & Kalas, 1984) is similar to the adult version in that it is highly structured and designed for nonprofessional interviewers. It differs in that it is designed to be given as both a child interview (DISC-C) having 264 items and parent interview (DISC-P) involving 302 items. Ratings are coded as 0 (not true), 1 (somewhat true), or 2 (very often true). DSM-III diagnoses are generated based on the combined ratings for the child and parent interviews. Some of the more problematic diagnoses (autism, pervasive developmental disorder, pica) are based on an interview with the parent only. The entire interview usually takes one hour, but an explicit skip structure can enable some interviews to be somewhat shorter.

Test-retest reliability for DSM-III diagnosis and symptom scores were .84 for parent interviews and .75 for child interviews (Edelbrock, Costello, Duncan, Kalas, & Conover, 1985). Children's reliability increased with age which would be expected considering their increase in intellectual abilities, greater memory, and improved language comprehension and expression. In contrast, reliabilities based on ratings from interviews with the parents decreased with the child's age, probably due to the parents having progressively less con-tact with their child. Comparisons between psychiatric and pediatric referrals indicated that psychiatric referrals had more symptom scores and more psychiatric diagnoses than pedi-atric referrals (Costello, Edelbrock, & Costello, 1985). Discriminations between psych-iatric and pediatric groups were good for children with severe diagnoses and severe symp-toms but not for children with a mild to moderate level of difficulties. Discriminations based on interviews with parents were generally more accurate than those based on child interviews.

Diagnostic Interview for Children and Adolescents

The Renard Diagnostic Interview (Helzer et al., 1981) inspired both the DIS and the Diag-nostic Interview for Children and Adolescents (DICA; Herjanc & Campbell, 1977; Her-janc, 1983). It has been through several revisions, which have incorporated the DSM-III and elements of the DIS. The DICA is designed for children between 6 and 17 years. Sepa-rate questionnaires are available for parents and children. The format is highly structured and primarily organized around different themes, such as behavior at home, behavior at school, and interpersonal relationships with peers. Additional content areas are substance abuse and the presence of such syndromes as anxiety disorders, mania, and affective disor-ders. Elaborate instructions are given for skipping irrelevant items, and total administration time is between 60 and 90 minutes. The administration begins with an interview of both the parent and child, which is designed to establish baseline behaviors and to obtain relevant chronological information. The parent is then questioned about the child in an effort to determine the possible appropriateness of 18 DSM-III diagnostic categories. The final step is to administer a "Parent Questionnaire," which requests additional medical and developmental history and addresses possible diagnoses that have not been covered by previous questioning.

Early studies on the psychometric properties of the DICA indicated that it could effectively discriminate between middle to older aged children who were referred to a psychiatric clinic and those referred to a pediatric clinic (Herjanic & Campbell, 1977). However, there was considerable overlap for children between six and eight, thus suggesting that a greater possibility of misdiagnosis exists for children in this age range. The interview was found to be most effective for assessing relationship problems, less effective for academic difficulties, and least effective for assessing school problems, somatic complaints, and neurotic symptoms (Herjanic & Campbell, 1977). Agreement between mother and child was 80% for the 207 items, but when this figure was adjusted for base rates, agreement was significantly lower (Herjanic, Brown, & Wheatt, 1975; Reich, Herjanic, Welner, & Gandhy, 1982). The highest level of agreement was for the oldest children and the lowest for younger groups. Whereas mothers reported more behavioral symptoms, children were more likely to report subjective complaints.

The Structured Clinical Interview for the DSM-III

The Structured Clinical Interview for the DSM-III (SCID; Spitzer, Williams, & Gibbon, 1987) is a recently developed broad-spectrum instrument that adheres closely to the DSM-III decision trees for psychiatric diagnosis. A certain degree of flexibility is built-in so that administration can be tailored to different populations and contexts. Thus, slightly different forms are used for psychiatric inpatients, outpatients, and nonpatients. The diagnosis of personality disorders is enhanced by a series of 120 items, which are completed by the patient. The SCID includes several open-ended questions as well as a skip structure, which enables the interviewer to branch into new areas dependent on the client's previous responses. The importance of clinical judgment is essential throughout the interview. In addition, the authors encourage the inclusion of relevant additional data to help increase diagnostic validity.

Reliability and validity studies on the SCID have been encouraging. For example, several difficult-to-distinguish diagnostic categories have been found to have relatively good levels of interrater agreement. These include generalized anxiety disorders (.79, 86% agreement), depressive disorders (.72, 82% agreement; Riskind, Beck, Berchick, Brown, & Steer, 1987), panic disorders (kappa = .86), and major depression (kappa = .81; Reich & Noyes, 1987). A representative validity study used comparisons of DSM-III-R diagnoses of personality disorders with the SCID and diagnoses by a panel of mental health professionals who relied on intrapanel consensus and inpatient ward observations over an extended period of time (Skodol, Rosnick, Kellman, Oldham, & Hyler, 1988). Agreement was generally satisfactory, but highest for disorders defined by specific behaviors (antisocial and schizotypal) than for those requiring a greater degree of inferences (narcissistic and self-defeating personality disorders).

RECOMMENDED READING

Cline, T. (1985). Clinical judgment in context: A review of situational factors in person perception during clinical interviews. *Journal of Child Psychology and Psychiatry and the Allied Disciplines*, 26, 369-380.

Gordon, R. L. (1987). *Interviewing: Strategy, techniques,and tactics* (4th ed.). Chicago: Dorsey Press.

Matarazzo, J. D. (1983). The reliability of psychiatric and psychological diagnosis. *Clinical Psychology Review*, 3, 103-145.

Weins, A. N. (1983). The assessment interview. In I. B. Weiner (Ed.). *Clinical methods in psychology* (2nd ed.). New York: John Wiley & Sons, Inc.

Chapter 4 —————————————————————————

BEHAVIORAL ASSESSMENT

Behavioral assessment is one of a variety of assessment traditions—such as projective testing, neuropsychological assessment, and objective techniques. Behavioral assessment distinguishes itself by being both a set of specific techniques as well as a way of thinking about behavior disorders and how these disorders can be changed. One of its core assumptions is that behavior can be most effectively understood by focusing on preceding events and resulting consequences. Out of this core assumption has come a surprisingly diverse number of assessment methods, including behavioral interviewing, different strategies of behavioral observation, measurement of relevant cognitions, psychophysiological assessment, and a variety of different self-report inventories.

Behavioral assessment can be most clearly defined by contrasting it with traditional assessment (see Table 4–1). One of the most important comparisons is the emphasis that behavioral assessment places on situational determinants of behavior. This emphasis means that behavioral assessment is concerned with a full understanding of the relevant antecedents and consequences of behavior. In contrast, traditional assessment is more likely to view behavior as the result of enduring, underlying traits. It is this underlying difference in conceptions of causation that explains most of the other contrasts between the two traditions. An extension of this conceptual difference is that behavioral assessment goes beyond the attempt to understand the contextual or situational features of behavior and, more importantly, concerns itself with ways in which these behaviors can be changed. There is a close connection between assessment itself and its implications for treatment. Thus, behavioral assessment is more direct, utilitarian, and functional.

The perceived limitations of traditional assessment were a major factor in stimulating the development of behavioral assessment. Specifically, traditional assessment was considered to focus too extensively on abstract, unobservable phenomena that were distant from the actual world of the client. In addition, behaviorists felt that traditional clinical psychology had stagnated because its interventions were not sufficiently powerful and too much emphasis was placed on verbal therapy. The concepts of traditional assessment seemed to exist in an abstract world divorced from the immediate realities and requirements of behavior change. The result of many traditional procedures seemed to be a large quantity of information that had little direct relevance to treatment intervention and outcome.

In contrast, behavioral assessment is concerned with clearly observable aspects in the way a person interacts with his or her environment. A typical behavioral assessment might include specific *measures of behavior* (overt and covert), *antecedents* (internal and external), *conditions surrounding behaviors*, and *consequences*. This knowledge can then be used to specify methods for changing relevant behaviors. Even though some behavioral assessers might take selected personality traits into account, these traits would only be considered relevant if they had direct implications for therapy. For example, locus of control has been found to predict success in self-regulation training (Carlson, 1982) and introversion/

Table 4–1. A summary of the aims, assumptions, and applications of the behavioral and traditional approaches to assessment

	BEHAVIORAL APPROACHES	TRADITIONAL APPROACHES
I. Aims	To assist in the identification of problem behaviors and their maintaining conditions To assist in the selection of an appropriate treatment To assist in the evaluation of treatment effectiveness To assist in the revision of treatment	To assist in the diagnostication or classification of problem conditions To assist in the identification of etiological factors To assist in prognostication
II. Assumptions		
1. Causes of performance	Performance is thought to be a function of situational variables or the interaction of situational and person variables	Performance is thought to be a function of intrapsychic or person variables
2. Meaning of performance	Test performance is viewed as a sample of a person's repertoire in a specific situation	Test performance is viewed as a sign of an enduring, underlying state or trait or person variable
III. Applications		
1. Instrument construction	Adequate representation of the contextual features of the setting of interest is emphasized (in that performance is seen as situationally determined) Adequate representation of the repertoire of interest is emphasized (in that the test performance is seen as a sample of the repertoire)	Little emphasis on the representation of contextual features (in that performance is seen as consistent across time and settings) Adequate representation of the underlying state or trait or person variable of interest is emphasized (in that test performance is seen as sign of the underlying variable)
2. Scope of assessment	Broad focus encompassing the problem behaviors and their maintaining conditions, treatment prerequisites, treatment administration, treatment outcome, etc.	Narrow focus encompassing the problem condition
3. Schedule of assessment	Repeated assessment: at key junctures in the course of treatment or throughout the course of treatment	Infrequent assessment: typically prior to and after treatment
4. Method of assessment	Preference for direct methods of measurement	Methods of measurement are by definition indirect (in that test performance is seen as a sign of an underlying state or trait)

Note: Table adapted from Barrios & Hartman (1986) and Barrios, Hartmann, Roper, & Bradford (1979). Entire table reprinted, with permission, from *Behavioral Assessment: A Practical Approach.* A.S. Bellack & M. Hersen (Eds.), 1988, p. 5, Pergamon Press PLC.

extroversion can help predict response to different types of therapy (Eysenck, 1976). This focus on the person and his or her unique situation is quite different from psychodynamic, biochemical, genetic, or normative trait models.

One important consideration is that the different behavior disorders are typically expressed in a variety of different modes. These might include overt behaviors, cognitions, changes in physiological states, and different patterns of verbal expressions. This implies that different assessment strategies should be used for each of these different modes (Lazarus, 1976). An inference based on one mode will not necessarily generalize to another. For example, depression for one person may be caused and maintained primarily by the person's cognitions and only minimally by poor social skills. Another person might have few cognitions relating to depression but be depressed largely because of inadequate social skills. The person with inadequate social skills would be most effectively treated through social skills training and only minimally helped through approaches that alter irrational thoughts (McKnight, Nelson, Hayes, & Jarrett, 1984). Furthermore, altering a person's behavior in one mode is likely to effect other modes, and these effects might have to be taken into account.

Whereas the above information presents a relatively rigid and stereotyped distinction between traditional and behavioral assessment, most practicing clinicians typically combine and adopt techniques from both traditions. This is especially true since behavioral assessment is now usually perceived as part of mainstream assessment rather than as a new, recent, and contrasting alternative. Traditional and behavioral approaches have now come to resemble each other in many areas. In particular, behavioral assessment has gone through both a turning inward as well as a turning outward. The turning inward is most clearly apparent in that aspects of cognition are seen as essential for a complete understanding of the person. Specific cognitive techniques include having the person think aloud as he or she is involved in a specific situation, sampling thoughts when a beeper goes off, and a wide variety of self-statement inventories. Second, behavioral assessment has turned outward in that it has become increasingly concerned with traditional psychometric considerations. This has included evaluating the reliability and validity of behavioral observations, self-report inventories, and diagnoses.

The assumptions and perspectives of behavioral assessment have resulted in an extremely diverse number of approaches and an even wider variety of specific techniques. These approaches and their corresponding techniques can be organized into the areas of behavioral interviewing, behavioral observation, cognitive behavioral assessment, psychophysiological assessment, and self-report inventories. Each of these areas was developed within a wider historical context extending over several decades.

HISTORY AND DEVELOPMENT

Treatment based on behavioral principles has a long history, dating back to the days of Little Albert and his fear of white, furry objects (Jones, 1924; Watson & Raynor, 1920). However, extensive, well-defined behavioral assessment strategies that were consistent with behavioral therapy were relatively slow to develop. The earliest formal use of behavioral assessment occurred in industrial and organizational settings (Hartshore & May, 1928; OSS Assessment Staff, 1948), but behavioral assessment did not become popular within the clinical context until the mid- to late 1960s. This was probably due to the powerful influence of psychodynamic approaches among clinicians who were taught to "look beneath the surface" in order to understand the "true" causes of behavior. Perhaps in part as a reaction to this indirect and inferential approach to understanding the person, the earliest forms of behavioral assessment focused almost exclusively on observable behaviors. Although organismic variables—such as cognitions, feelings, and psychophysiological responses—were acknowledged, they were not considered important regarding causal aspects of behavior. As a result they were not considered important for assessment and treatment. Instead, behavioral assessment was consistent with the then dominant operant conditioning paradigm in that it focused on identifying discrete behavioral responses, target behaviors, and reinforcers that could change specific behaviors. Measurement of these areas typically quantified the frequency, rate, and duration of relevant behaviors (Ullman & Krasner, 1965). The result was numerous, highly innovative assessments of overt behaviors. Typically, interventions involved single cases, which was consistent with their idiographic approach.

Early definitions of behavioral assessment were created partially by making contrasts with traditional psychodynamic approaches. Each had different aims (identification of problem behaviors versus classification), assumptions (behavior is caused by situations versus enduring traits), and applications (direct observation versus indirect inferences). In particular, Mischel (1968) attacked the very nature of traits by arguing that they were fictions based on distortions of language (a preponderance of static descriptions), the result of consistency of roles and situations (not inner traits), perceptual bias based on needs for predictability, and the rarity of disconfirmation when traits are (incorrectly) inferred. This attack fueled a lengthy controversy, which was relevant to behavioral assessment in that Mischel's perspective was used to argue for a focus on situational determinants of behavior. Proponents of behavioral assessment (along with psychiatry itself) were also dissatisfied with traditional DSM II diagnosis, which not only had poor reliability and validity, but did not seem to relate to the real world of the client nor did it have direct treatment utility.

During the 1970s, there was a much greater emphasis on a wider approach. The typical single case study format gave way to assessment within a much larger context—such as schools, businesses, families, and differing sociocultural frameworks. This assessment approach was based partially on the observation that these larger contexts could have considerable influence on the person, so that effective individual change often required change in these wider contexts. A refocusing on larger contexts was also motivated by challenges to the strict operant paradigm in that, while effective in controlled situations (hospital ward, Skinner box, prison), it had questionable social validity and doubtful long-term clinical impact (Goldfried, 1983; Milne, 1984). Assessment was also widened by arguments to focus on the wider aspects of the person, which meant not only behavior, but also feelings, sensations, internal imagery, cognitions, interpersonal relations, and psychophysiological functioning (Lazarus, 1976). This emphasis on a multimodal or multifaceted approach forced the mainstream of behavioral assessment to accept a number of indirect measures such as self-reports, ratings by significant others, and cognitions (Cone, 1977; 1978). Relevant publications were the first editions of *Behavioral Assessment: A Practical Handbook* (Hersen & Bellack, 1976), *Handbook of Behavioral Assessment* (Ciminero, Calhoun, & Adams, 1977), and the journals *Behavioral Assessment* and the *Journal of Behavioral Assessment*, both of which began in 1979.

The 1980s have seen a proliferation of publications within the field of behavioral assessment, a dramatic reevaluation of some of its most basic assumptions, as well as the incorporation of influences from other traditions and disciplines. In particular, psychiatry had similar difficulties with the DSM-II as behavioral assessment, and began to develop strategies quite similar to those of behavioral assessment. For example, the Problem

Oriented Record (Weed, 1969) was introduced into many general hospital and psychiatric settings. It was designed to improve diagnostic and treatment practices by providing behavior-specific databases, problem lists, treatment plans, and follow-up data. It thereby more effectively tied in the relationship between assessment and treatment, and more clearly delineated diagnostic issues. Perhaps of greater importance, the DSM-III and DSM-III-R were similar to the efforts of behavioral assessment in that each diagnostic category was developed using behavior-specific descriptions. Numerous publications have worked to integrate behavioral assessment with traditional psychiatric diagnosis (Hersen, 1988; Hersen & Bellack, 1988) in such areas as depression (Nelson & Maser, 1988), the diagnosis of childhood disorders (Kazdin, 1988), and the understanding of different models of causation (Haynes & O'Brien, 1988). The perspectives of psychiatry and behavioral assessment have been further linked by the *Journal of Behavior Therapy and Experimental Psychiatry*. The development and expansion of behavioral medicine has also drawn extensively on behavioral assessment strategies in the evaluation of headaches, coronary heart disease, Reynaud's disease, asthma, chronic pain, sleep disturbances, and eating disorders (see Williamson, Davis, & Prather, 1988). Not only did behavioral assessment begin to accept the contributions of other disciplines, but many of the most honored behavioral techniques were challenged (Goldfried, 1983). For example, clinical judgment within the context of structured interviews has been accepted, diagnostic classification is now considered potentially useful, reliance solely on behavioral observations is perceived in some contexts as inappropriate, and indirect measurement is seen as not only important, but essential. In essence, the 1980s have witnessed a significant reappraisal and expansion of what is involved in behavioral assessment. Since there has clearly been a significant blurring and cross-fertilization between behavioral assessment and other forms of assessment, the future may eventually result in behavioral assessment and traditional assessment being indistinguishable.

ISSUES RELATED TO RELIABILITY AND VALIDITY

Traditional psychometric considerations for behavioral assessment are difficult to summarize due to the wide diversity of techniques and to the differences in assumptions regarding the focus, nature, and causes of behavior. Whereas traditional assessment stresses the relative stability of various characteristics, behavioral assessment assumes variability based largely on environmental factors. A finding such as low test-retest reliability is more likely to be interpreted within the behavioral context as being due to true variance resulting from environmental conditions rather than error within the data collection procedure. Furthermore, behavioral assessment stresses the importance of individually tailored approaches emphasizing the client's idiosyncracies. Within this context, normative comparisons are frequently seen as both irrelevant and inappropriate. Despite these issues, many from within the area of behavioral assessment have successfully argued for the importance of evaluating behavioral assessment techniques using traditional psychometric approaches (Anderson, Cancelli, & Kratochill, 1984; Gresham, 1984). For example, interobserver agreement for behavioral observations is essential before the data gathered from this approach can be trusted. This is typically determined by calculating the percentage of interrater agreement (see Cooper, Heron, & Heward, 1987). Likewise, data derived from self-reports in such areas as assertiveness and fear needs to demonstrate that the findings can be generalized to other situations—such as role plays, simulations, and especially daily life.

The earliest forms of behavioral assessment relied primarily on behavioral observation and assumed that the direct observation of specific behaviors was sufficiently clear, reliable, and accurate. The emphasis was primarily on determining a functional analysis between behavior and its antecedents and consequences. In an activity such as pressing a bar for reinforcement, the behavior could be easily recorded by an electronic detector and therefore the reliability of the measure could be considered to be quite high. However, with behaviors that are more difficult to define, the reliability of measurement, especially measurement based on behavioral observation, cannot be assumed. For example, finger-nail-biting might be defined merely by the person touching his or her face, or it may involve touching the mouth, actually chewing the nail, or removing part of the nail or perhaps the entire nail. The issue of precise definition and accurate measurement of the behavior becomes even more problematic when dealing with internal cognitions, where the clinician is completely dependent on self-reports rather than on direct observation.

The level of reliability across different observational strategies has been found to vary. In general, material derived from behavioral observation during behavioral assessment can be influenced by observer expectations in similar ways, as has been found by experimental research (Cooper & Rosenthal, 1980; Orne, 1962; Rosenthal, 1966). In such situations as natural observation—where observer bias, outside factors such as interference from non-target persons, and a lack of clear definitions are likely to create variability in observer responses—reliability can be expected to be relatively low. Further sources of observer error include halo effects, primacy effects, failure to score a behavior that has occurred, rating toward the center of the scale, and leniency or generosity of scoring. When bias is reduced through the use of highly structured procedures, then reliability has increased. Thus, a procedure such as systematic sampling—in which clear strategies are used to determine when and how the behavior will be measured—has generally been found to be more reliable and accurate than naturalistic observation (Cunningham & Thorp, 1981). Although reliability has been found to increase in controlled situations where the observers know that they, themselves, are being evaluated for accuracy (Romanczyk, Kent, Diament, & O'Leary, 1973), this outside monitoring of observers rarely occurs in clinical situations. Thus, the reliability found in clinical situations cannot be assumed to be as high as for controlled studies in which evaluators are themselves being evaluated. General guidelines for increasing reliability in clinical situations include having two observers compare their results, providing clear and careful instructions when a client is requested to monitor his or her own behavior, clearly specifying target behaviors, clearly wording items on self-reports, taking care in the construction of instruments, and carefully training observers—such as parents or teachers.

During the 1960s and 1970s, the validity of various assessment procedures depended primarily on informal content validity. Questionnaires and observational strategies were based on rational considerations regarding what was to be studied and how these measurements were to be made. Few efforts were made to develop empirically derived categories. For example, the assessment of depression might have been based on knowledge regarding the typical thoughts depressed people seem to have as well as additional variables that seem important regarding social supports and typical antecedent events. The various areas of observation were mostly selected based on what rationally seemed to be the most important areas to consider. Since the early 1980s, increased work has gone into assessing the validity of various methods of behavioral assessment. In general, few validity studies have been performed on behavioral interviews and naturalistic observations, whereas much more has been done on behavioral questionnaires (Morrison, 1988). Most validity studies have been conducted by using relevant outside criteria. Many of the same issues have come up with criterion validity for behavioral assessment as for traditional assessment, including difficulty generalizing to different populations, settings, and methods of administration.

The early behavioral self-report questionnaires relied on content and face validity. Since these questionnaires were considered new techniques with a different underlying philosophy, it was believed that thcy did not have to be judged using the same criteria as the older and more traditional psychometric tests. They were considered to be direct reports of client behaviors thus, little psychometric validity was reported. Kaplan and Sacuzzo (1989) criticize this by stating that behavioral assessment may be "repeating history and reinventing the wheel" (p. 423). They further point out that the "early paper-and-pencil structured personality tests which were finally abandoned in the 1930s are indeed difficult to distinguish from many present-day self-report procedures" (p. 423). The problems of response bias, questionable reliability and validity, no norms, and assumed client truthfulness are problems that need to be addressed for any standardized instrument, including behavioral procedures. Many behavioral self-report questionnaires might be best referred to as "idiosyncratic clinical tools" rather than psychometrically sound tests. The familiar argument used for traditional tests is that different assessment procedures serve to provide checks and balances for one another. Although it is often argued that self-reports are supported by other sources of data (direct observation, psychophysiological measurement, internal dialogue), few actual studies on the incremental validity of these procedures have been conducted.

Many behavioral self-report inventories have been developed but have had widely varying degrees of success demonstrating acceptable psychometric qualities. For example, the Rathus Assertiveness Schedule (RAS; Rathus, 1973) has been subjected to traditional psychometric procedures and can serve to illustrate the types of difficulties encountered in this as well as other behavioral inventories. Whereas Heimberg, Harrison, Goldberg, Desmarais, & Blue (1979) did not find a very high correspondence between scores on the RAS and observational reports of role plays in an inmate population, the RAS did relate to nonassertiveness in a group of dental students (Rathus, 1972) and communicator apprehension (Kearney, Beatty, Plax, & McCroskey, 1984). However, a difficulty with relating assertiveness in role play situations, which most of the above studies used, is that assertiveness in role plays may not relate to assertiveness in naturalistic situations (Bellack, Hersen, & Turner, 1979). Perhaps when subjects are requested to role play they can alter their daily level of assertiveness to "act the part" correctly (Higgins, Alonso, & Pendleton, 1979). The RAS similarly has poor criterion validity based on instructor evaluations of observed assertive behavior and grades in a communication course (Tucker, Weaver, Duran, & Redden, 1983). Even though the RAS is a frequently used device in both research and clinical settings, the above suggests that the meaning of the scores might be difficult to evaluate. Other behavioral self-report questionnaires have experienced similar problems.

ASSETS AND LIMITATIONS

Probably the greatest advantage of behavioral assessment is that its practitioners have continually paid attention to its relevance toward treatment. Any measurement of problem behaviors is usually directly tied to how these behaviors can be changed. Furthermore, relevant behaviors are given an empirical functional analysis, which enables clinicians to make baseline measurements of behavior and to assess the antecedents and consequences of these behaviors. An initial functional analysis can then allow clinicians to evaluate whether change has actually occurred during or after treatment. Even though many of the techniques have not been through rigorous traditional validity studies, the emphasis on treatment validity has proven to be attractive to many practitioners. Thus, behavioral assessment is particularly useful for persons using a hypothesis testing approach and for those who wish to have clear accountability that change has actually taken place. In some situations, however, behavioral assessment can be tied too closely to treatment. This is particularly the case in legal assessments or other situations where assessment and therapy are separate.

A further asset is that behavioral assessment offers a wide range of possible techniques for use in an extremely varied number of contexts. Possible strategies include self-reports, naturalistic observation, physiological monitoring, structured observation, and self-monitoring. This variation in technique is consistent with the view that a complete understanding of the person requires multiple modes of assessment. These assessment modes might involve relevant aspects of person-situation interaction, physiological changes, cognitions, interpersonal relationships, overt behaviors, feelings, imagery, and aspects of the person's larger social system. Many behavioral assessment models organize their approach around stimulus, organism, response, and contingencies (Goldfried, 1982). Other approaches rely on Lazarus' BASIC ID, or on Kanfer and Saslow's (1969) functional analysis of behavioral excesses and deficits. These approaches place the person into a much wider context than traditional assessment procedures.

Behavioral assessment is particularly appropriate when a presenting problem is determined primarily by environmental factors. In most cases, a clear, functional relationship (environmental interaction) can be established for such disorders as phobias, marital difficulties, acting out, temper tantrums, and inappropriate classroom behavior. Behavioral assessment is somewhat less relevant when environmental factors account for a smaller portion of the variance. For example, organic factors may be more important than environmental ones in chronic schizophrenia, certain types of headaches, and head injuries. Although behavioral assessment and intervention can still be effective for such problems, greater difficulties are involved, since the environment is relatively less important.

One major drawback of many behavioral assessment strategies is that they have poor or at least untested psychometric properties. In the past, the attitude was taken that, since behavioral assessment was interested in "direct" measures, there was little need to be accountable in the same way as for the traditional, more indirect measures. More recently, intensified efforts have been made to establish the reliability and validity of self-report measures, but the results have often been disappointing. Similar to traditional techniques, behavioral interviewing and observation can also be distorted by observer bias, halo effects, primacy effects, low interobserver agreement, and confirmatory bias.

Although cognitive behavioral assessment has been given increased importance, in many ways it is contrary to the original spirit of behavioral assessment's emphasis on direct observation. Cognitive assessment is necessarily nonobservable and relies on client self-reports. Difficulties might include differences in meaning between the client and the clinician, response biases, assumed honesty of reporting, and assumptions regarding the equivalence of internal dialogue and the verbal descriptions of these dialogues.

A final limitation of behavioral assessment is that it often requires extensive resources in terms of time, personnel, and equipment. This is particularly true for psychophysiological and observational methods. Wade, Baker, and Hartman (1979) surveyed 257 behaviorally oriented professionals, and 43.8% felt that behavioral assessment was impractical in applied settings. As a result, behavioral assessment is frequently limited to interviews and questionnaires (Bornstein, Bridgwater, Hicky, & Sweeney, 1980). A further area relating to impracticality is that many behavioral instruments have not been designed to deal with problems frequently encountered in clinical practice, such as dissociative disorders, paranoia, and hypochondriasis (Haynes & Wilson, 1984).

STRATEGIES OF BEHAVIORAL ASSESSMENT

Behavioral assessment has given rise to a highly varied and large number of techniques. For example, Barrios and Hartmann (1988) found over 100 instruments that have been developed to assess children's fears and anxieties. Despite this diversity, behavioral assessment strategies can be organized into the general categories of behavioral interviewing, behavioral observation, cognitive behavioral assessment, psychophysiological assessment, and self-report inventories. Each of these approaches varies in the degree to which they emphasize direct versus indirect measures of the person, as well as in the extent to which they rely on inference. For example, cognitive assessment is more indirect than behavioral observation and relies much more on inferences regarding the degree to which cognitions affect and interact with overt behavior. However, all of these techniques stress the importance of developing a functional analysis of behavior through understanding person-environment interaction. They also place considerable importance on each aspect of assessment being directly relevant to treatment planning and evaluation.

Behavioral Interviewing

Behaviorally oriented interviews generally focus on describing and understanding the relationships between antecedents, behaviors, and consequences (ABC). In addition, a baseline or pre-treatment measure of behavior is developed through a systematic consideration of the frequency, intensity, and duration of relevant behaviors. Behaviors might also be provided with a description of specific behavioral excesses and deficits (Kanfer & Saslow, 1969). Any goal must be able to be measured and tested in an objective and reliable way, and its relevance should be agreed-upon by the client (Gresham, 1984). Although the above approach might seem long and involved, the process is simplified by considering only those areas relevant toward treatment.

Despite this emphasis on treatment utility, it is also important to place each aspect of the information derived from a behavioral interview into a wide context. A basic description of a target behavior is simplistic since it does not take into account an interactionist model. For example, a phobia is likely to create difficulties in the client's relationships, and these difficulties might combine to undermine the person's sense of competence. The person might then react by becoming highly dependent on his or her primary relationship, which reinforces a sense of helplessness. The helplessness might then reinforce a fear of not being able to cope, which can then interact with and quite possibly exacerbate the phobia. Thus, a complete interview would need to consider not only the existence of and nature of the phobia, but also evaluate the effect of the phobia on such areas as relationships, work effectiveness, and self-statements.

The initial phase of a behavioral interview needs to take into consideration many of the issues relevant for traditional interviews. A sufficient degree of rapport needs to be established, a statement needs to be developed of the general and specific purposes of the interview, and a review should be made of the client's relevant history. However, history tends to be deemphasized in favor of current behaviors. This is because the main cause of client behavior is considered to be situational rather than historical. Common types of clinician approaches might involve reflective comments, probing, understanding, and expressed empathy. Open-ended questions might be followed up with more direct questioning.

However, the extensive use of nondirective techniques is inappropriate in that the clinician must set a clear direction and have the client answer direct questions relevant to a behaviorally oriented approach.

Sometimes clients provide excellent descriptions of their problems and can clearly specify relevant antecedent and consequent conditions. Other clients frequently experience difficulty describing such areas as the events surrounding the decision to seek treatment, elaborating on their feelings, stating who referred them, or providing information regarding how other people might be perceiving their problem. Since a careful behavioral analysis requires a complete description of problem behaviors, the client and therapist must work to establish the extent of the difficulty, where it occurs, when it occurs, and the effects it has on relationships. Sometimes it is helpful to have the client keep a diary of relevant events and observations. Often clients will describe and define their difficulties by relying extensively on trait descriptions rather than on more behaviorally oriented ones. A behavioral interviewer, then, needs to work with the client to operationalize these trait descriptions into ones that are specific and easily observable. For example, if a client says he or she is a "depressed type of person," this might translate into specific types of behaviors (slow movement, spending too much time in bed, avoiding people, being nonassertive), cognitions (that he or she is no good, a failure), and feelings (hopelessness, apathy). In other words, the belief in an underlying permanent trait (illness) needs to be reframed as a group of specific behaviors that are potentially changeable. This reframing process, in itself, is likely to be beneficial to clients because they will be better able to see specific things they can do to change how they feel. Speaking in concrete behavioral terms rather than abstractions is also likely to increase mutual understanding between client and therapist.

A wide-based behavioral assessment should include not only detail regarding the specific presenting problem, but also the manner in which the problem has generalized into other areas. In particular, this assessment might involve information regarding the larger social system. Often, the client's school, work, or family situation can be incorporated into the assessment and treatment program to ensure immediate and long-term success. In contrast, if a narrow approach to change is taken, the client may attempt to express his or her newly acquired behavior in contexts that will not be supportive of it. As a result, previous problem behavior might once again develop to the exclusion of newer, more adaptive behavior. This might be true if the client developed new effective behaviors that were learned only within the narrow context of the practitioner's office.

An interview should end by providing the client with a summary of the information that has been obtained, an explanation regarding additional information that is required, and an estimate of the likely success of treatment (Morganstern, 1988). If further information is required, the clinician and client need to agree upon the type of information required and the possible ways it can be obtained. This might involve instructions for keeping an effective diary, requests for observations from other people, or techniques for self-monitoring of different behaviors. If the interview is intended as a prelude to therapy, additional information should be given regarding possible strategies for intervention, the length of treatment, possible financial and emotional costs, and assurances that the client will have input into all decisions.

Most interviews tend to be somewhat informal and haphazard. Such informality can often result in low reliability and validity regarding the information obtained. For example, Wilson and Evans (1983) found a low level of reliability among clinicians trying to specify appropriate target behaviors. Some authors urge that behavioral interviews be structured and standardized. For example, Kratochwill (1985) has suggested that interviews be planned around a four-stage problem solving process. The first stage is *problem identifi-*

cation in which the problem is specified and explored, and procedures are established to measure current performance and desired target behaviors. The vague and generalized descriptions that clients typically come in with are developed into specific behavioral descriptions. Next, a *problem analysis* is performed by assessing the client's resources, and by noting the relevant environmental conditions influencing behavior and the context in which the behavior excesses or deficits occur. An interview also needs to establish how a *plan might be implemented*, which would also include ongoing procedures for collecting data relevant to the progress of the treatment. Finally, strategies for *treatment evaluation* should be specified by considering the pre- and post-treatment measures to determine whether the intervention was successful.

Witt and Elliott (1983) provide the following somewhat similar outline of expected accomplishments for any behavioral interview:

1. Initially, provide the client with an overview of what needs to be accomplished and why a clear and detailed specification of the problem behavior is important.
2. Identify the target behavior(s) and articulate them in precise behavioral terms.
3. Identify the problem frequency, duration, and intensity ("How many times has it occurred today," "How long has it been going on," etc.).
4. Identify conditions in which the problem occurs in terms of its antecedents, behaviors, and consequences.
5. Identify the desired level of performance. An estimate of how realistic this is and possible deadlines should be considered.
6. Identify the client's strengths.
7. Identify the procedures for measuring relevant behaviors. What will be recorded, who will record it, how will it be recorded, when and where will it be recorded?
8. Identify how the effectiveness of the program will be evaluated.
9. When discussion regarding the above areas has been completed, summarize it for the client to ensure that it has been understood and is agreed upon.

The above outline should not be followed rigidly, but rather should be used as a general guideline. However, each behavioral assessment should have accomplished all nine areas prior to its completion.

Behavioral Observation

In some cases, the behavioral interview is itself sufficient to obtain an adequate assessment. However, some form of actual behavioral observation is usually required before, during, and/or after treatment. The particular method for observing behavior is usually decided upon during the initial interview. Whereas the interview is primarily directed toward obtaining verbal information from the client, behavioral observation is used to decide upon and actually carry out specific strategies and techniques of measuring the relevant areas of behavior discussed during the interview. In some cases—such as assessing the developmentally disabled, resistant clients, or very young children—behavioral observation may become one of the most important means of assessment. These observations might be made by the professional who is actually conducting the treatment or by someone else who is more involved in the client's life—such as a teacher, parent, spouse, or self-monitoring by the client. The most frequent approaches are narrative recording, interval recording, event recording, and ratings recording.

The first behavioral observation task is to select relevant target behaviors, which can vary from a single response set to a larger interactive unit. The target behavior needs to either involve the problem behavior itself or relate to it in a meaningful way. Decisions must be made regarding the number of behaviors to record and the relative complexity of the recording method. Both the recording method and the target behavior need to be manageable and should avoid being overly complex. The target behavior can best be clarified by beginning with a narrative description of the client's difficulty and then further specified by considering the antecedents and consequences related to the problem behavior.

All behaviors to be measured must have objective, clear, and complete definitions. A definition should allow measures of the behavior to be clearly observed. In particular, this means the definition should avoid abstract and highly inferential terms, such as "apathy" or "sadness," and instead translate such terms into specific behaviors. Any description of the target behavior should involve an easy-to-read dictionary-type definition, an elaboration of the behavior, and specifications regarding precisely when the behavior occurs as well as descriptions of borderline examples and clear nonexamples (Foster et al., 1988). In measuring behavioral frequencies, the practioner must clearly define when the behavior begins and ends. This might be easy for measuring the number of cigarettes a person smokes or number of times a child bangs his or her head, but is more difficult when measuring less clearly defined behaviors, such as the number of aggressive acts a person makes or frequency of nonassertive behaviors. Recordings also need to measure the duration of behaviors and their intensity. For example, how hard a child bangs its head and the overall length of time engaged in the activity has implications regarding the urgency and strength of the treatment approach.

The different devices used to make recordings might include various combinations of golf counters, stopwatches, pencil-and-paper forms, or electromechanical devices such as an event recorder with buttons that can be pressed when various categories of behaviors occur. Sometimes the recordings of behaviors might be entered into a computer and summarized or audio and video recordings might be made for later review.

The settings of behavioral observation can range from those that are natural to those that are highly structured. Natural or "in vivo" settings might include the home, classroom, business, or playground. Observations made from these types of settings are likely to be directly relevant to and reflective of the client's life. Natural settings are most effective when assessing high frequency behaviors and/or more global behaviors, such as attentional deficits, social withdrawal, or depressive behaviors. They are also useful when measuring the amount of change the client has made following intervention. However, natural settings present difficulties due to the extensive amount of time required to make observations. Furthermore, natural settings are problematic when trying to measure infrequently occurring behaviors (aggression, nonassertiveness) or behaviors that occur only in the absence of others (firesetting, suicide). To counter the difficulties inherent in naturalistic observation, practitioners may wish to create structured environments (role plays, work simulations) that elicit specific types of behaviors. Such environments are especially important for behaviors that occur infrequently. However, inferences derived from observations made in these structured or "analog" situations need to be made cautiously since they may not generalize into the client's actual life.

When clinicians are concerned that observations made by a person outside the client's environment might contaminate the results, they may wish to train persons who are already a part of the client's natural setting—such as parents, teachers, or spouses. This might help prevent subjects from changing their behaviors simply because they are aware that they are being observed (reactivity). These more natural observers can be much less obtrusive than an outside professional. The training of observers needs to include a clear rationale for measuring the behavior and emphasis needs to be placed on the importance of making accurate and objective recordings. Observers need to memorize the recording code, practice making the recordings, and receive feedback regarding the relative accuracy of their recordings. Precautions should be taken to avoid observer error, such as through observer bias, leniency, lapses in concentration, and discussing data with other observers. Sometimes reliability might be checked by comparing the degree of agreement between different observers rating the same behaviors. Caution should be made when using trained observers since widely varying levels of interobserver agreement have been noted (Margolin, Hattem, John, & Yost, 1985).

A system of coding behaviors usually needs to be developed so that recordings are abbreviated and simplified. If too many codes are used, then it will be difficult for recorders to recall them, especially if a series of behaviors occur in rapid succession. Both the type of recording method (narrative recording, event recording, etc.) and the coding system will depend largely on the goals of assessment. A coding system that is clear, simple, and is closely connected to the presenting problem is likely to be both useful and reliable. Important considerations in selecting a recording and coding system are the number of times the behavior needs to be observed, the length of observation periods, when to make the recording, the type of recording to be made, and the target behaviors to be recorded (Sattler, 1988). The following sections describe the most frequently used recording systems along with examples of different methods of coding.

Narrative Recording   Narrative recording requires that the observer simply make note of behaviors of interest. There is little quantification and the observations can vary regarding the degree of inferences that are made. For example, an observer may stick close to direct descriptions of behavior, such as noting that someone frequently laughs and smiles at his or her friends, or may infer from these behaviors that the client has good peer relations. The primary value of narrative recordings is that they may help define future, more specific areas, which can then be measured in a more quantitative manner. Thus, narrative recording is usually a precursor to alternative forms of measurement. It has the advantages of potentially discovering relevant behaviors; it can elaborate on these behaviors, it requires little, if any, equipment; and numerous hypotheses can be generated from the narrative descriptions. Limitations are that it doesn't enable the observer to quantify the observations, may have questionable validity, and the usefulness of the observations depends largely on the individual skill of the observer.

Interval Recording   A clinician may choose to record selected aspects of behavior within predetermined intervals of time. As a result, this technique is also referred to as time sampling, interval sampling, or interval time sampling. Usually the intervals vary from between 5 and 30 seconds and may be based either on set schedules for each observation period (i.e., every 5 minutes) or may be selected randomly. Interval recording is most appropriately used when measurements of overt behaviors with moderate frequencies (e.g., once every 5 to 20 seconds) are required and when these behaviors do not have any clear beginning or end. This might include such behaviors as walking, listening, playing, reading, or looking up/down.

When developing a strategy for interval recording, clinicians must decide on the length of time between each observation, the method of recording, and the length of the observation period. This will depend largely on the type of behavior. For example, different types of verbal interaction may vary in length and, as such, the observation periods must be adjusted to take this into account. Some strategies might require the observer to alternate back and forth between recording (i.e., for 10 seconds), then observing (i.e., for 20 seconds), and then going back to recording the observation that has just been made. Cues regarding the beginning and end of each behavior must be specified. The target behaviors for observation will be derived from information based from such sources as the initial interview, self-report inventories, narrative observations, and especially from descriptions of the presenting problem. The focus of observation may also vary between different people—such as the husband, wife, teacher, child, or client. Sometimes clinicians or researchers arrange to have an outside person observe the same client behaviors. The interrater reliability of the observations can then be established by calculating the percentage of agreement between the two raters (see Cooper et al., 1987). A representative interval recording chart, with instructions on how to develop such a chart, are provided in Figure 4–1.

Interval recording is time efficient, highly focused on specific behaviors, and allows almost any behavior to potentially be measured. Unfortunately, interval recording is not designed to assess the quality of the target behaviors and can be artificial or may overlook other additional important behaviors.

Event Recording   Whereas interval recording depends on measurements defined by units of time that are imposed on target behaviors, event recording depends on the occurrence of the behavior itself. The observer must wait for the target behavior to occur, and then record relevant details of the behavior. Examples of behaviors most appropriate for event recording are aggressive actions, greetings, or use of such verbal expressions as assertion or profanity.

The basic design of event recording systems is to make note of the behavior's frequency, duration, and intensity, and to record the behavior on such devices as a checklist, golf counter, or hand counter. Although the main emphasis is on quantifying the frequency of responding, its duration also can be measured with a stopwatch. The intensity of the behavior can be noted by simply specifying whether it was slight, moderate, or strong. A representative example of an event-recording chart is included in Figure 4–2.

Event recording is especially good for recording behaviors having low frequencies, measuring changes in behaviors over time, and for use in studying many different types of behaviors. However, event recording is relatively poor at measuring behaviors that do not have clear beginnings and endings, and presents difficulties in keeping the attention of observers for behaviors of long durations. Since event recording does not provide information regarding sequences of behaviors, it is difficult to make inferences regarding how and why behaviors occur.

Ratings Recording   Rather than recording direct observations of behaviors, clinicians may wish to obtain general impressions of relevant dimensions of behaviors and have these impressions rated on a checklist or scale. Such measures tend to be more global and may involve more abstract terms, such as the client's level of cooperativeness or ability to maintain self-care. Typically, ratings recordings are made after a period of observation. A typical format might request the evaluator to rate, on a scale from one to five or one to seven, the client's frequency of temper tantrums, quality of peer relations, or conscientiousness. Representative items from the Cognitive Behavior Rating Scales (Williams, Little, Davis, & Haban, 1987) are included in Table 4–2.

Ratings recordings potentially can be used for a wide variety of behaviors. Other advantages are that the data can be subjected to statistical analysis, the ratings can be made either for individuals or groups, and, due to the time efficiency of ratings recordings, they are likely to be cost-effective. Disadvantages include possibly low interrater agreement due to the subjectivity of the ratings, little information regarding antecedent and consequent events, and possibly inaccurate ratings, especially if much time has elapsed between the observations and when the ratings are made.

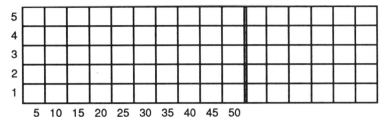

a. Graph paper with series of columns, each five blocks high. Double heavy line marks off 10 columns, for a 50-minute period.

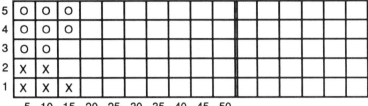

b. Chart after 13 minutes of monitoring pupil's behavior. First two columns are completed and the third is partially completed. If the pupil behaves appropriately during the next (14th) minute, the observer will mark an "X" in the third column just above the other "X." If the pupil misbehaves, the observer will mark an "O" in that column just under the other two "Os."

c. Chart after observer has completed the 50-minute period.

Figure 4–1. Example of interval recording

To set up a self-graphing data recording system, start with a piece of graph paper. Mark 2 heavy lines across the paper so that 5 blocks are between the lines. You have now a series of columns, all 5 blocks high. Each block will represent an interval (e.g. minute) of observation time. Mark off the number of 5-block columns needed for the scheduled observation period: a 50-minute period would need 10 columns of 5 blocks; a 30-minute period would need 6 columns; a 45-minute period would need 9 columns; and a 5-minute period would need only 1 column of 5 blocks. For now, let's assume you have scheduled a 50-minute period for your observations, as shown in Figure 4–1 a–c. You have marked off 10 columns on your paper, each 5 blocks high, for a total of 50 blocks: 1 block for each minute scheduled.

For each interval (minute) in which the behavior occurs, you will place an "X" in a box. For each interval in which the behavior does not occur, you will place an "O" in a box. Start with the left column and work toward the right. In each column, work from the bottom up with the "Xs", but from the top down with the "O" marks. When the "Xs" and "Os" meet in the middle, the column is filled. Move to the next column to the right and continue: "Xs" from the bottom, "Os" from the top down, until they meet. As you move across the row of 5 columns, the data recorded will automatically form a graph without any extra effort on your part. With this method, trends in data across the session can be easily identified and shared with school personnel or parents. By focusing on the "Xs" in Figure 4–1c, it is clear that the amount of 'on task' behavior by the pupil is steadily increasing during the observation session (i.e., there are fewer "Xs" in the first column, and more "Xs" in the later columns).

Note: From "Behavioral observation for the school psychologist: Responsive-Discrepancy model" by G.J. Alessi, 1980, *School Psychology Review*, p. 40.

Note: All explanatory material is verbatim from Alessi (1980).

Intervals in minutes

Behavior	Totals	Person Observed	5	10	15	20	25	30
Getting out of seat	29	Subject	▢	L'	▢	⦂	•	••
	8	Comparison	••	,	⦂,	•		•
Request-ing help	5	Subject		•		⦂⦂		,
	11	Comparison	••	⦂•	⦂•	,	,	◆

Figure 4–2.   Example of event recording within 5-minute intervals

Figure 4–2 illustrates an event recording for 2 different types of behaviors, the first of which (getting out of seat) the subject's teacher would like to see less of and the second (requesting help) the subject's teacher would like to see more of. In addition to recording the subject's behavior, another student was selected as a basis for comparison. The coding of the number of responses was developed by Tukey (1977) and uses dots and lines to indicate the number of responses which were made. One dot equals one response. Any number above 4 responses is indicated by a line connnecting two dots. For example, in the first 5 minute block for "getting out of seat" the subject got out of his seat 8 times. By noting the increases and decreases in the different recordings, observers can be alerted to possible environmental events that might have caused these changes. In the above example there was both a decrease in "getting out of seat" and an increase in "requesting help" beginning at the 20-minute interval.

Table 4–2.   Representative items from the Cognitive Behavior Rating Scales

Respondents are requested to read each item and rate the person they are evaluating on a scale between 1 and 5 where 1 is "not at all" like the person and 5 is "very much" like the person.

28. Cannot tolerate frustration.
64. Repeats the same story over and over again.
41. Needs a constant routine.
80. Has a short attention span.
89. Has many accidents.
97. Is upset about memory and thinking problems.
101. To simple questions, says "I don't know" rather than attempting an answer.

Cognitive Behavioral Assessment

Over the past 20 years, considerable research has been conducted on understanding the cognitive processes underlying behavior disorders. Relevant areas include the self-statements associated with different disorders, the underlying structure or cognitive organization related to these disorders, differences between cognitive distortions in pathological versus normal behavior, and cognitive alterations that occur during therapy. This research has considerably influenced and altered the nature of behavioral assessment. In particular, researchers have developed specific techniques for assessing cognitive processes, such as having the person think aloud, listing different thoughts, thought sampling at various intervals, and a wide variety of self-statement inventories.

This internal perspective is quite different from the early emphasis of behavioral assessment, which focused almost exclusively on observable overt behavior. This transition has come about due to persuasive evidence regarding the relationship between behavior and cognitions (Bandura, 1986; Kendall & Hollon, 1981; Klinger, Barta, & Mahoney, 1976; Meichenbaum, 1976). Cognitive processes not only change during the course of effective therapy, but may be causally related to both the development as well as the maintenance of different types of disorders. Some approaches assume that altering cognitions can be sufficiently powerful to change behaviors. However, there are also a number of significant limitations with cognitive behavioral assessment. All material is necessarily derived from the client's self-reports of his or her internal processes and, as such, may be subject to a number of distortions. Clients usually can recall and describe the results of their cognitive processes, but have much greater difficulty describing the processes they went through to arrive at these conclusions (Nisbett & Wilson, 1977). The actual processes may need to be inferred based on complicated analyses of the results derived from intricate assessment strategies. In addition, remembering events seems to be a reconstructive process in which each successive recall can be altered based on the person's needs, biases, and expectations (Loftus & Loftus, 1980). These inherent difficulties have led some traditional behaviorists to question the theoretical and practical appropriateness of cognitive assessment.

One relevant finding is that the popular belief in the "power of positive thinking" is simplistic in that it is not a very good predictor of adjustment. What seems more important is the absence of negative statements or, what Kendall and Hollon (1981) have referred to as "the power of nonnegative thinking." Furthermore, the effect of negative self-talk is greater than the ability of positive thinking to counter negative internal dialogue. As might be expected, gains in therapy have been associated with reductions in negative self-statements (Kendall & Hollon, 1981).

Specific Content Areas   Theories of the cognitive processes of *depression* suggest that it is maintained by characteristic and repetitive thoughts that are self-maintaining. For example, Beck (1967) listed the cognitions associated with depression as involving *arbitrary inference* (making inferences without substantiating evidence), *selective abstraction* (making a broad judgment based on a minor aspect of an event), *overgeneralization* (extrapolating in an unjustified fashion from a minor event), and *magnification/minimization* (overemphasizing negative events; minimizing positive ones). Although these processes do seem to be clearly related to depression, a simple cause-effect model between depression and specific cognitions does not seem to be warranted and further clarification is required (Brewin, 1985).

A wide number of self report-type inventories have been developed for the cognitive assessment of depression. The most time-honored and frequently used of these is the Beck Depression Inventory (BDI; Beck, Rush, Shaw, & Emery, 1979). A more complete coverage of the BDI is included in the section on self-report inventories. A further test based on Beck's theory of depression is the Dysfunctional Attitudes Scale (Weissman & Beck, 1978) which requests the extent to which people endorse the attitudes and beliefs held by persons subject to depression. The Cognitive Bias Questionnaire (Hammen & Krantz, 1976; Hammen, 1978), is a fairly well developed endorsement-type inventory that measures the likelihood of distorted thinking. It presents a series of vignettes, and requests the client to answer depressed/nondepressed and distorted/nondistorted options. Both child and adult versions are available. Persons who have been diagnosed as depressed are more likely to endorse "depressotypic distortions" (Michael & Funabiki, 1985), and scores have been found to change as depression lifts (Miller & Norman, 1986).

Several additional cognitive self-report inventories have also become frequently used in research and clinical practice. The Attributional Styles Questionnaire (Seligman, Abramson, Semmel, & von Baeyer, 1979) is based on the relationship between self attribution and learned helplessness. Since causal attributions—which are internal, stable, and global in their relationship to negative outcomes—are related to depression, the Attributional Styles Questionnaire systematically assesses the occurrence of these attributions. The Automatic Thoughts Questionnaire (Hollon & Kendall, 1980) is a 30-item endorsement-type inventory that shows good discrimination between depressed and nondepressed persons, but may be overly state-dependent. The Cognitive Response Test (Watkins & Rush, 1983) uses an open-ended sentence format (incomplete sentences) and requests the person to respond to vignettes relating to occupation, family, marriage, and friendships.

The main cognitions that seem to characterize *social phobias* are interpersonal threat along with beliefs that positive interpersonal feedback is incorrect (Sewitch & Kirsch, 1984). The importance of a cognitive assessment of social phobias is underscored by research suggesting that cognitive deficits and distortions are more important in causing and maintaining the difficulty than deficits in social skills (Galassi & Galassi, 1979). Social phobics are more likely to recall negative information, interpret ambiguous feedback negatively, underestimate their own performance, expect more negative evaluations from others, and have more negative self-statements prior to interactions (Smith & Sarason, 1975; Cacioppo, Glass, & Merluzzi, 1979). Assessment of the relative rate of occurrence of each of these areas can provide specific treatment suggestions regarding which processes need to be modified. The cognitive assessment of social phobias is frequently made with the Social Interaction Self-statement Test (Glass, Merluzzi, Biever, & Larson, 1982), which has demonstrated relatively good psychometric properties. Many of the self-statements described by research on social phobias and measured by such tests as the Social Interaction Self-statement Test are quite similar to the ones described by Beck (1967) as being characteristic of depression. These similarities raise the as yet unresolved issue of whether specific irrational beliefs are related to specific types of disorders, or whether there is a nonspecific (yet generally negative) effect of irrational beliefs.

Although less work has been done on *generalized anxiety*, two relevant assessment devices have been developed. The Irrational Beliefs Test (Jones, 1969) provides the client with 100 items that cover 10 different categories of irrational beliefs. The test has demonstrated adequate psychometric properties that suggest satisfactory validity in that scores have been found to change when a person is under distress (Jones, 1969; Nelson, 1977) and are correlated with other measures of anxiety and depression (Cook & Peterson, 1986). In support of the nonspecificty view of irrational beliefs, test scores have not been found to relate to specific problem areas. The somewhat similar 70-item Rational Behavior Inventory (Shorkey, Reyes, & Whiteman, 1977) has also been used in the assessment of irrational beliefs and their relationship to anxiety.

Self-efficacy has received considerable interest, particularly since it has been related to a variety of different predictions relevant to treatment (Bandura, 1986). A person having a high level of self-efficacy is likely to have positive expectations regarding his or her effectiveness to judge and deal effectively with situations. Self-efficacy is determined by the attainments someone has achieved in the past, vicarious (observational) experiences, verbal persuasion, and physiological states. An assessment of self-efficacy is especially important in understanding the antecedent and retrospective accounts of the effect and quality of the behavior. The relative level of self-efficacy has been found to predict a wide number of variables, including general therapy outcome (O'Leary, 1985), the prediction of success in the treatment of smoking (Baer & Lichtenstein, 1988; Baer, Holt, & Lichtenstein, 1986; DiClemente, 1986), and relapse rate from self-regulatory training (Carlson, 1982). Useful distinctions should be made between the level of strength of self-efficacy and its generalizability from one situation to the next. Since some question exists regarding the degree to which self-efficacy can be related from one situation to the next, specific measurements are often used for different areas (depression, assertion, smoking, etc.).

An area needing further development is the *clinical assessment of imagery*. It has frequently been observed that a person's presenting problem is significantly related to his or her fantasies/daydreams and different dreaming states. A depressed person may continually repeat images of being criticized, the anxious person might replay scenes of danger, and the paranoid might frequently review images of persecution. Knowing a person's relative ability to produce and control images may be important in predicting response to treatment that requires the formation of images—such as systematic desensitization, covert desensitization, covert aversive conditioning, and certain types of relaxation procedures. Extensive experimental work has been conducted on imagery in such areas as the different dimensions of imagery (Parks, 1982), differences between waking and nonwaking imagery (Cartwright, 1986), and the effects of conscious and unconscious images on behavior (Horowitz, 1985). However, little material has been published regarding the clinical assessment of imagery. Of studies that have been published, most have related to measures of imagery ability (Sheehan et al., 1983) rather than to the effect of clinically relevant images on the person. Persons wishing to assess both clinical imagery as well as other aspects of cognitions might use one or several of a variety of the following strategies that have been developed to assess cognitions.

Recording Cognitions   In addition to the many self-report inventories available, a number of strategies have been developed for recording cognitions in a less-structured manner. Parks and Hollon (1988) have listed and summarized the following methods used by previous researchers:

> *Thinking aloud*   Clients are requested to verbalize their ongoing thoughts, with these verbalizations usually extending for five to ten minutes. A similar technique is free association, where the client is asked to simply say whatever comes to mind rather than report on his or her ongoing inner thoughts. One potential problem is that the procedure may feel unnatural and therefore provide a sample different from normally occurring internal thoughts. Also, the client may have no opportunity to verbalize competing thoughts—reported thoughts will most likely be a limited portion of the total cognitions, and clients may not report everything honestly. One factor that is likely to make the verbally reported thoughts different from actual ongoing processes is that typically people change the topic of ongoing internal dialogues every five to six seconds, whereas verbal reports of these dialogues may only have topic changes on the average of every 30 seconds.

Private speech   Sometimes, children's cognitions can be assessed by paying close attention to barely audible speech they make while engaged in various activities. It is believed that these private verbalizations are closely aligned to inner thoughts.

Articulated thoughts   Clinicians may wish to create structured situations or simulations that are parallel to the types of problems the client reports. For example, a situation may be created that demands the client to be assertive or be exposed to criticism or phobic stimuli. The person can then be requested to articulate the thoughts he or she is experiencing during these situations. Typical thoughts can be noted and inferences made regarding how they relate to the problem behaviors.

Production methods   Instead of requesting clients to articulate their thoughts during a simulation, an actual naturalistic situation can occur (criticism, phobic stimuli, etc.), with clients then noting and recording the typical thoughts they have related to these situations. As such, these methods might also be referred to as "in vivo" self-reports.

Endorsement method   The client might be presented with either a standardized (i.e., Irrational Beliefs Test, Cognitive Bias Questionnaire) or an informally developed list of items and then is requested to make ratings regarding their frequency of occurrence, strength of belief, and how the item might be uniquely represented in the person's cognitions. These items might include ratings of the frequency of such thoughts as "What's the use" or "I can't do anything right." Potential difficulties with this technique are the effects of the demand characteristics of the situation and social desirability. An underlying and questionable assumption behind the technique is that the relevant cognitions are within the client's conscious awareness.

Thought listing   Instead of developing a continuous description of ongoing thoughts, clients might be requested to simply list summaries of their relevant thoughts. The thoughts to be listed might be elicited by a specific stimulus, problem area, or by merely attending to or anticipating a stimulus.

Thought sampling   A sample of a person's thoughts might be obtained by setting a prompt (i.e., a beep on a timer), then having the client describe the thoughts he or she was having just prior to being interrupted by the prompt.

Event recording   The client might be requested to wait until a relevant event occurs (i.e., handwashing for an obsessive-compulsive), at which point, the thoughts related to these events are written down. Instead of merely waiting for a problem or spontaneously occurring behavior, a client might also be requested to describe the thoughts related to the expression of new and desired behaviors, such as assertion. The relevant thoughts about these behaviors might then be used to increase the likelihood of their continued occurrence.

Psychophysiological Assessment

A complete understanding of the person involves an assessment of not only behavioral, affective, and cognitive modes, but also of the ways these interact with and are dependent on physiological functioning. Such psychophysiological assessments have recently become easier to make due to increased interest and knowledge regarding instrumentation (electronics, computers), operant conditioning of behaviors that at one time were considered involuntary, physiological and neurochemical aspects of behavior, and behavioral medicine (Sturgis & Gramling, 1988). The most frequently assessed physiological responses are heartrate, blood pressure, skin temperature, muscle tension, vasodilation, galvanic skin response (GSR), and brain activity as measured by electroencephalograms (EEGs). By quantifying data gathered through the above areas, psychological problems can be translated into more precise physiological indices.

One of the first relevant studies to relate psychological and physiological modes indicated that fear and anger had different physiological responses in blood pressure and skin conductance (Ax, 1953). This result suggested that these and other psychological variables might be measured in ways other than through self-report inventories. More recently, it has been found that persons scoring high on psychological indices of intelligence had relatively small pupillary dilations (Ahern & Beatty, 1979), lower heartrate variability, and less skin conductance when requested to perform tasks (Geiselman, Woodward, & Beatty, 1982). This suggests that persons with higher intelligence not only require less effort to complete a task, but that, potentially, intellectual assessment might increasingly be based on psychophysiological measurement. A further representative area of research has involved the relationship between different personality variables and psychophysiological measurement. Schizophrenics (when unmedicated) and persons with anxiety disorders have been found to have a relatively higher level of sympathetic responsiveness as compared with parasympathetic responsiveness. In contrast, antisocial personalities are characterized by parasympathetic dominance and low levels of sympathetic responsiveness (Porges & Fox, 1986; Wenger, 1966). Attempts to detect lying by using physiological indicators, while still extensively practiced, have not been found to have adequate psychometric properties (Kleinmuntz & Szucko, 1984; Saxe, Dougherty, & Cross, 1985). While most of the studies mentioned above represent very general correlations among such variables as emotions, intelligence, and behavioral disorders, they show considerable potential for future assessment should these measures become more refined. Physiological baseline measures for an area such as anxiety can and have been used to monitor the effectiveness of treatment for social phobias, generalized anxiety disorders, and obsessive-compulsive disorders.

In addition to the usual knowledge relating to psychological assessment, clinicians who obtain and interpret psychophysiological data must have knowledge in anatomy, electronics, and the physiology of cardiovascular, musculoskeletal, neurological, respiratory, electrodermal, ocular, and gastrointestinal response systems. This extensive background is particularly important since instrumentation presents a number of special problems. A variety of confounding factors may be present, such as the effect of slowing respiratory rate to alter cardiac output or the effect of eye roll on measured brain activity. Filters might be necessary to exclude noise in the system. The techniques are also intrusive, thereby making the situation artificial and, partially as a result, generalizations to outside aspects of the client's life or between different response modes may be inappropriate. A wide variety of difficulties may arise regarding meaningful psychological interpretations that are based on the physiological data. In the future, it is likely that the development of better instruments and improved methods of computer analysis may greatly increase the utility of psychophysiological assessment and overcome many of these difficulties.

SELF-REPORT INVENTORIES

An extremely wide number of self-report inventories have been developed for behavioral assessment. Typically, they involve between 20 to 100 items, with respondents requested to indicate their degree of endorsement to each item on a Likert-type scale. Most of these instruments have been developed for a specific topic-area such as assertiveness, depression, anxiety, fear, dysfunctional attitudes, control of visual imagery, ability to resolve conflict, or irrational thoughts. Many of these inventories have extremely poor or even nonexistent psychometric properties. Also, normative data is rarely provided. In contrast to many behavioral inventories, the following inventories on depression, assertiveness, and fear have been selected because they have been extensively used in clinical and research settings and because they have had relatively extensive evaluations of their psychometric properties.

The Beck Depression Inventory

The Beck Depression Inventory (BDI) was first introduced in 1961 by Beck, Ward, Mendelson, Mock, and Erbaugh (1961) and was later revised in 1971 and copyrighted in 1978 (Beck, Rush, Shaw, & Emery (1979). Although the later version involved a clarification and modification of the items, the two versions were found to be highly correlated (.94; Lightfoot & Oliver, 1985). The BDI has been widely used for the assessment of cognitions associated with depression—for both psychiatric patients (Piotrowsky, Sherry, & Keller, 1985) as well as depression in normals (Steer, Beck, & Garrison, 1986). The popularity of this instrument is amply demonstrated in that, in the 30 years since its introduction, over 1,000 research studies have been performed either on or using it.

The items included in the BDI were originally derived from observing and summarizing the typical attitudes and symptoms presented by depressed psychiatric patients (Beck et al., 1961). A total of 21 symptoms were included; respondents were requested to rate the intensity of these symptoms on a scale from 0 to 3. Typical questions relate to such areas as sense of failure, guilt feelings, irritability, sleep disturbance, and loss of appetite. The inventory is self-administered and takes from 5 to 10 minutes to complete.

Several forms have been developed, including a card form (May, Urquhart, & Tarran, 1969), several computerized forms, a normal 21-item form, and a 13-item short form (Beck & Beck, 1972). Correlations between the short and long forms have ranged between .89 to .97 (Beck, Rial, & Rickels, 1974). A fifth- to sixth-grade reading level is required to adequately comprehend the items. The total possible range of scores extends from a theoretical low of 0 to a high of 63. Within clinical populations, no or minimal depression is indicated by a score of less than 10 (M = 10.9, SD = 8.1), mild to moderate depression ranges from 10 to 18 (M = 18.7, SD = 10.2), moderate to severe depression from 19 to 29 (M = 25.4, SD = 9.6), and severe depression from 30 to 63 (M = 30.0, SD = 10.4; Beck, 1967). However, high scores within nonclinical populations can also indicate maladaptive functioning (Tanaka-Matsumi & Kameoka, 1986).

Reliability and Validity   Since its initial development nearly 30 years ago, the BDI has been subjected to extensive psychometric evaluation. A meta-analysis of the different efforts to establish internal consistency has shown them to range from .73 to .92 with a mean of .86 (Beck, Steer, & Garbin, 1988). Similar reliabilities have been found with the 13-item short form. Test-retest reliabilities have ranged from .48 and .86, depending on the interval between retesting and type of population (Beck et al., Steer, & Garbin, 1988). However, some controversy exists over whether the variable(s) the BDI is measuring is a state or trait. The practical implication of this is that, if the variable measures a state, then relatively wide fluctuations can be expected and thus the lower test-retest reliabilities would be more acceptable.

Evaluation of content, concurrent, and discriminant validity as well as factor analysis has generally been favorable. The content of the BDI items was derived by consensus from clinicians regarding symptoms of depressed patients (Beck et al., 1961), and six of the nine DSM-III categories for the diagnosis of depression are included. Concurrent validity is suggested by high to moderate correlations (.55 to .96, Mdn r = .72) with clinical ratings for psychiatric patients (Beck et al., 1988). In addition, moderate correlations have been found with similar scales that also rate depression, such as the Hamilton Psychiatric Rating Scale for Depression (.73), Zung Self Reported Depression Scale (.76), and the MMPI Depression Scale (.76; see Beck et al., 1988). The BDI has been able to discriminate psychiatric from nonpsychiatric populations (Byerly & Carlson, 1982) as well as discriminate the level of adjustment in seventh-graders (Albert & Beck, 1975). Although Delay, Pichot, Lemperiere, and Mirouze (1963) were unable to make fine distinctions between endogenous, involutional, and psychogenic depression, Steer, Beck, Brown, & Berchick (1987) reported that patients with major depressive disorders had relatively higher scores than those with dysthymic disorders. Furthermore, the BDI has been used to discriminate persons who were lonely (Gould, 1982), under stress (Hammen & Mayol, 1982), and persons self-reporting anxiety (Baker & Jessup, 1980). Factor analytic studies indicate that the BDI measures a general factor of depression as well as the more specific factors of negative attitudes toward self, performance impairment, and somatic disturbance (Tanaka & Huba, 1984).

Interpretation   An ipsative interpretation of BDI responses can be used to specify irrational beliefs and relevant symptoms that are likely to be related to a person's depression. Identification of these beliefs and symptoms can be useful in specifying those which need to be worked on in therapy. Any of the following can be assumed to be an area of difficulty if a score of 3 is indicated on the numbered item:

1. sadness	12. social withdrawal
2. pessimism	13. indecisiveness
3. sense of failure	14. change in body image
4. dissatisfaction	15. retardation in work
5. guilt	16. insomnia
6. expectation of punishment	17. fatigability
7. dislike of self	18. loss of appetite
8. self-accusation	19. loss of weight
9. suicidal ideation	20. somatic preoccupation
10. episodes of crying	21. low level of energy
11. irritability	

The following scores can be used to indicate the general level of depression:

5 to 9	No or minimal depression
10 to 18	Mild to moderate depression
19 to 29	Moderate to severe depression
30 to 63	Severe depression
Below 4	Possible denial of depression, faking good; this is below usual scores for normals.
Above 40	This is significantly above even severely depressed persons, suggesting possible exaggeration of depression; possibly characteristic of histrionic or borderline personality disorders. Significant levels of depression are still possible.

Fear Survey Schedule

The Fear Survey Schedule (FSS; Wolpe & Lang, 1964, 1969, 1977) is one of the most thoroughly researched behavioral instruments and has been used for a variety of purposes, including the measurement of the types of fears in children and adults, the evaluation of phobic disorders, and as an index of pre- and post-treatment change. In particular, the FSS has been used as an ipsative instrument to identify the typical situations that result in avoidance so effective treatment can be based on the identified fears. The first version of the FSS was a 50-item inventory by Akutagawa (1956), but several variations have since been developed of which the most frequently used (Caldwell-Colbert & Robinson, 1984) is the 78-item FSS-III by Wolpe and Lang (1964). Ratings on the different Fear Survey Schedules are made either on a 5- or 7-point Likert scale that indicates the extent of fear to such situations or stimuli as snakes, open places, surgery, dead animals, or speaking in public. The different fear categories were selected based on clinical observation, actual cases, and laboratory experiments (Geer, 1965; Wolpe & Lang, 1964).

At least seven variations of the FSS have been developed (Tasto, 1977). One noteworthy version is the Fear Questionnaire (Marks & Mathews, 1979), a shortened 20-item scale developed to produce scores on a person's main phobia, global phobia, total phobia, and overall level of anxiety/depression. An 80-item version was developed for children (Fear Survey for Children; Scherer & Nakamura, 1968) and later modified as the Revised Fear Survey for Children (Ollendick, 1978). A 100-item version is the Temple Fear Survey Inventory (Braun & Reynolds, 1969), which includes items from previously developed surveys. The 108-item FSS (Wolpe & Lang, 1969) is probably the most readily available and frequently used form. Unfortunately, it is not known which of the many versions is best. There is also no unified standardized administration for the different forms and no clear procedures for scoring and interpretation.

Reliability and Validity   Due to the many variations of the FSS, it is difficult to evaluate as a unitary instrument. Furthermore, authors have sometimes not specified which variation they have used in their studies. Internal consistency of the original Wolpe and Lang (1964) scale was reported as greater than .90 (Geer, 1965; Spinks, 1980). The following subscales based on FSS items answered by college students have likewise demonstrated satisfactory internal consistencies: Hostile-dependent (males, .91; females, .90), Body Assault (.97 for both males and females), Developmental Fear (males, .83; females, .66), Performance Evaluation (males, .80; females, .69), Death Evasion (males, .80; females, .73), and Nuisance Animals (.81 for both males and females; Gulas, McClanahan, & Poetter, 1975). A somewhat different categorization of subscales based on the responses of agoraphobics likewise indicated adequate internal consistency ranging from .62 to .76 (Arrindell, 1980). A review of FSS test-retest (3 to 10 weeks) reliability studies indicated a range of .72 to .90, with shorter intervals generally producing higher reliabilities (Arrindell, Emmelkamp, & van der Ende, 1984).

Content validity by Wolpe & Lang, 1964 based on a rational consideration of the items indicated the following six, broad, fear-related categories:

1. animal fears
2. tissue damage, illness, death, or associated stimuli
3. classical phobias
4. social stimuli
5. noises
6. miscellaneous (Wolpe & Lang, 1964)

Some of the meanings behind responses to the items might be clarified by improved wording. For example, if a respondent reports anxiety related to flying in an airplane, a wide variety of reasons are possible, including excessive noise, being in an enclosed place, height, fear related to travel/transport, or a combination of the above (Arrindell, Emmelkamp, & van der Ende, 1984). More formal factor analytic studies have often served to confuse the FSS's underlying factors due to the wide number of often overlapping categories. Frequently, different factors have been found according to patient versus nonpatient populations. A representative factor analysis done on a large sample of phobics using a 76-item FSS-III listed social fears (9.7% of the variance), agoraphobia (9.1%), fears relating to bodily injury, death, and illness (8.2%), fears relating to the display of sexual or aggressive themes (7.2%), and fears relating to harmless animals (7.0%; Arrindell, 1980; Arrindell, Emmelkamp, & van der Ende, 1984). Adequate, concurrent validity of the FSS is suggested by high scores being related to a person's sensitivity to becoming anxious (Reiss, Peterson, Gursky, & McNally, 1986) and FSS results being able to predict phobic avoidance behaviors (Lick, Sushinsky, & Malow, 1977).

Relatively extensive psychometric data is available for the 80-item Fear Survey Schedule for Children-Revised (FSSC-R; Ollendick, 1978, 1983). Internal consistency was .94, and test-retest reliability over a one-week interval was .82, but this dropped to a low of .55 after a three-month retesting period (Ollendick, 1978; 1983). Validity studies indicate a relationship between trait anxiety, high self-concept (in girls), and the ability to discriminate school-phobic children from normals (Ollendick, 1983). A tentative factor analysis suggests the following five factors: fear of failure (giving an oral report, being teased, failing a test), fear of the unknown (mystery movie, dark places, nightmares), fear of injury and small animals (lizards, sharp objects, getting in a fight), fear of danger and death (earthquakes, being hit by a car, death or dead people), and medical fears, (going to the dentist, riding in a car, getting car sick; Ollendick, 1983).

Research using the FSSC-R indicates that girls have consistently reported more fears and a greater intensity to their fears. However, the following seven greatest reported fears (rank ordered) were the same for both girls and boys: a burglar breaking into house, being sent to the principal, bombing attacks, being hit by a car or truck, falling from high places, being in earthquakes, and not being able to breathe (Ollendick, 1983). In contrast, anxious adult female patients reported that the five most frequent fears were, in rank order, the prospect of a surgical operation, speaking in public, losing control of self, feeling rejected by others, and failure (Thyer, Tomlin, Curtis, Cameron, & Nesse, 1985). The five most frequent fears of anxious adult male patients were speaking in public, losing control of self, failure, feeling rejected by others, and looking foolish (Thyer et al., 1985).

Interpretation   Most clinicians use an ipsative analysis of client responses to determine clusters of self-reported fears. Some clients might have a preponderance of medical fears—such as having surgery, getting sick, or going to the dentist. Others might report concerns related to social situations—such as speaking in public, interpersonal rejection, or social disapproval. By knowing the specific fears or clusters of fears, the clinician can help focus the interview toward developing more information regarding the antecedents and consequents of these concerns. Client scores can also later be used as baseline measures for evaluating the effectiveness of interventions.

Although they provide less specific information, FSS total fear scores can also be used diagnostically to compare client scores. Tomlin et al. (1985) reported that the overall mean for patients with diagnosed anxiety disorders was 108.6 (SD = 61.5). Scores for specific anxiety subgroups were provided for simple phobias (M = 89.9, SD = 53.5), social phobias

(M= 86.9, SD = 63.5), agoraphobias (M = 152, SD = 58.9), obsessive-compulsives (M = 117.6, SD = 43.1), and panic disorder (M = 113.5, SD = 61.4). Although some researchers have reported higher scores for females, the Tomlin et al., (1985) study did not find significant differences. Fischer and Tomlin (1977), using a normal college population, have reported extensive normative data for individual items, but no means and standard deviations are available for total scores for normal populations.

Rathus Assertiveness Schedule

The assessment of assertiveness is typically measured by either observing role play situations or through self-report inventories. A wide variety of self-report inventories have been developed, including the Wolpe-Lazarus Assertion Inventory (Wolpe & Lazarus, 1966), Gambrill Assertion Inventory (Gambrill & Richey, 1975), Bakker Assertiveness Inventory (Bakker, Bakker-Rabdau, & Breit, 1978), and the Conflict Resolution Inventory (McFall & Lillesand, 1971). However, the Rathus Assertiveness Schedule (RAS; Rathus, 1973) has been the most extensively used, and relevant normative data is available for normal college students (Quillan, Besing, & Dinning, 1977) as well as for psychiatric populations (Rathus & Nevid, 1977). The 30 items on the schedule were derived from diaries kept by the author's undergraduate students, from the Wolpe-Lazarus Assertion Inventory, and, to a lesser extent, from relevant items from Allports's A-S Reaction Study and Guilford and Zimmerman's Temperament Survey (1956). Respondents are requested to rate, on a six-point scale, how descriptive each statement is to themselves. A -3 indicates that the statement is "very uncharacteristic of me" and a +3 indicates that it is "very characteristic." Sixteen items have been reversed to reduce the likelihood of response bias. Scores can theoretically range between -90 to +90, with higher scores indicating high levels of assertiveness.

In addition to the original 30-item schedule, two other versions have been developed for special populations. The modified RAS (MRAS; Del Greco, Breitbach, & McCarthy, 1981) was developed for young adolescents. Moderate test-retest reliability (.74; three-week interval) has been reported with means of 8.58 (SD = 19.42) for adolescent males and -.29 (SD = 19.70) for adolescent females (Del Greco, Breitbach, Rumer, McCarthy, & Suissa, 1986). A simplified version of the RAS is available that requires a minimum sixth-grade reading skills level in contrast to the tenth-grade reading level required for the regular version (SRAS; McCormick, 1984). The simplified version was found to have high correlations with the regular RAS (.94) and produce similar means and standard deviations.

Reliability and Validity   Moderate levels of internal consistency have been reported, ranging from .59 to .86 with a mean of .78 (Beck & Heimberg, 1983). Test-retest reliabilities have been moderately high (.80; Norton & Warnick, 1976). A number of criterion validity studies have been reported that suggest adequate concurrent and predictive validities. A moderate correlation (.72) was reported with the Wolpe-Lazarus Assertion Inventory (Henderson & Furnham, 1983), although this would be expected given that the RAS and Wolpe-Lazarus Assertion Inventory share nine items in common. A positive correlation has been reported with communicator apprehension (Kearney et al. 1984) and an inverse relationship with depression (Sanchez & Lewinsohn, 1980). The relation with depression is particularly associated with RAS items that deal with inhibited social expression (Culkin & Perrotto, 1985). A decrease in RAS scores has been reported following successful treatment (Rathus, 1972, 1973) as well as high correspondence between RAS scores and the frequency of assertive responses in role plays (Futch & Lisman, 1977).

The different components of assertive behavior that Gambrill (1977) has described include positive assertion (complimenting others, expressing affection), negative assertion (expressing annoyance or irritation), behavior initiation (beginning a conversation with a stranger), and responding to another (participating in a conversation started by another). Assertive skills may not generalize from one area to the next—such as the person who can freely express compliments but has difficulty dealing with conflict. Most factor analytic studies of the RAS indicate that it emphasizes negative types of situations that require assertion and responding to another, and focuses to a much lesser extent on behavior initiation and positive situations requiring assertion. A representative factor analytic study by Henderson and Furnham (1983) indicated that the strongest factor (22.4% of the total variance) was "standing up for rights in a public place." This factor was most related to items 25, 3, 27, and 28, which deal with making complaints about poor service, making complaints about food in a restaurant, and asking noisy theater patrons for quiet. The second most important factor, accounting for only 6.6% of the variance, was "initiating and maintaining interaction with nonintimate others." Relevant items for this factor were 10, 2, 11, and 5, which relate to enjoying a conversation with a stranger and hesitating over dates through shyness. However, the number of different factors that have been isolated has ranged from 3 to 12, and this variation along with the different, often imprecise and overlapping categories, has often added to confusion rather than simplification of the underlying factors. A further difficulty is that the RAS often seems to confuse aggression and assertion, as represented by the lack of clarity in "Most people seem to be more aggressive and assertive than I am."

Interpretation As with previously discussed behavioral self-report inventories, the RAS can be used as an ipsative instrument as well as to make normative comparisons. If used ipsatively, the client's responses on the specific items can be interpreted based on their content. These responses can be used to provide information for treatment planning or evaluation. Such information might be particularly important if a client's difficulties with assertion are restricted to a specific area. The result might be responses indicating low assertiveness for certain items, yet the overall score might still be within normal limits. Thus, in certain cases, simply noting their total scale score may be misleading.

Normative data derived from a normal college population found that males had a mean of 9.68 (SD = 22.36) and females had a mean of 8.35 (SD = 18.65; Brenner & Bertsch, 1983). Although these means are quite similar, differences in specific items were noted that indicated males tend to be more assertive in public situations and more willing to question high-status persons, but are shier in dating situations. In contrast, females reported being more assertive in private interpersonal settings (Brenner & Bertsch, 1983). A similar normative study of normal college students by Quillen et al. (1977) revealed the following percentile rankings for total RAS scores.

Overall RAS raw score	Percentile ranking
35	95
25	90
21	85
15	75
11	70
10	65
6	60
2	55
0	50
-4	45

Overall RAS raw score	Percentile ranking
-5	40
-9	35
-13	30
-14	25
-19	20
-20	15
-25	10
-35	5

RECOMMENDED READING

Bellack, A. S., & Hersen, M. (Eds.). (1988). *Behavioral assessment: A practical handbook* (3rd ed.). New York: Pergamon Press.

Cooper, J. O., Heron, T. B., & Heward, W. L. (1987). *Applied behavior analysis.* Columbus, OH: Merrill.

Alessi, G. J. (1980). Behavioral observation for the school psychologist: Responsive-discrepancy model. *School Psychology Review, 9,* 31-45.

Chapter 5

THE WECHSLER INTELLIGENCE SCALES

The Wechsler Adult Intelligence Scale-Revised (WAIS-R) and the Wechsler Intelligence Scale for Children-Revised (WISC-R) are individually administered, composite intelligence tests in a battery format. They assess different areas of intellectual abilities and create a situation in which personality functioning can be observed. Both the WAIS-R and the WISC-R provide three different I.Q. scores: an overall or Full Scale I.Q., a Verbal I.Q., and a Performance I.Q. The WAIS-R Verbal I.Q. and Performance I.Q. are derived from averaged scores on 11 subtests: six are verbal and primarily measure a verbal comprehension factor; five are performance and measure visual-spatial abilities. The WISC-R has essentially the same subtests as the WAIS-R, except that the content of the items is designed for children and an optional performance subtest (Mazes) is included, which brings the total number of WISC-R subtests to 12. Although the Wechsler intelligence scales have several limitations, they have become the most frequently used tests in clinical practice and are considered to be a model to which other assessment instruments aspire.

THE NATURE OF INTELLIGENCE

Attempts to develop an accurate definition for "intelligence" have been fraught with difficulty and controversy (see Weinberg, 1989). This is largely because intelligence is an abstract concept and has no actual basis in concrete, objective, and physical reality. It is a general label for a group of processes that are inferred from more observable behaviors and responses. For example, it is possible to observe problem solving techniques and to measure the results of these techniques objectively, but the intelligence assumed to produce these techniques cannot be observed or measured directly. Thus, the concept of intelligence is somewhat like the term "force" in physics: it can be known by its effects, yet its presence must be inferred. Both "intelligence" and "force," however, provide terms that allow a person to approach, discuss, and generalize certain types of objective events. However, the ambiguity in the term "intelligence" has also enabled it to become influenced by and framed within the context of different philosophical assumptions, political agendas, social issues, and legal restrictions.

Numerous attempts have been made to define intelligence. One of the earliest was Binet and Simon (1916) who conceptualized it as:

> "...judgement, otherwise called good sense, practical sense, initiative, the faculty of adapting ones self to circumstances. To judge well, to comprehend well, to reason well, these are the essential activities of intelligence" (pp. 42-43).

One of the most frequently used definitions of intelligence was developed by Wechsler in 1958. He considered intelligence to be a global concept that involved an individual's ability to act purposefully, think rationally, and deal effectively with the environment. He further emphasized that "general intelligence cannot be equated with intellectual ability, however broadly defined, but must be regarded as a manifestation of the personality as a whole" (in Matarazzo, 1972, p.79). Thus, for Wechsler, intelligence can be social, practical, or abstract, but it cannot be measured or even considered independently from certain nonintellectual aspects of functioning—such as persistence, drive, interests, or need for achievement. A review of most definitions of intelligence reveals that they all imply, include, or elaborate on the following five areas:

1. Abstract thinking
2. Learning from experience
3. Solving problems through insight
4. Adjusting to new situations
5. Focusing and sustaining one's abilities in order to achieve a desired goal

The practical significance of a clear conceptualization of intelligence is to allow clinicians to fully appreciate the complexity of what they are attempting to evaluate. Such an appreciation should allow them to estimate more adequately which aspects of a client's intelligence have been measured and which have not. It should also help them evaluate the assets and limitations involved in using a specific test by contrasting the test items with the theoretical nature of intelligence. For example, an "intelligence" test that emphasizes verbal abilities will be limited because it will not give an assessment of such areas as nonverbal problem solving or adjusting to new situations. A thorough overview of the history and nature of intelligence is beyond the scope of this chapter, but interested readers can find excellent discussions in Maloney and Ward (1976), Sattler (1988), or Sternberg (1982, 1985). Most of the different discussions of intelligence focus on 4 major traditions that have emerged over the past 80 years. These include:

1. the psychometric approaches
2. neurological-biological approaches
3. developmental theories
4. information processing

Psychometric Approaches

The psychometric approach assumes that intelligence is a construct or trait in which there are individual differences. However, many of the early psychometrists such as Binet, Ebinghaus, and Wernicke were concerned not so much with understanding the nature of intelligence as with the practical issues of correct classification and prediction. It was generally only after intelligence tests were constructed that theoricians became curious about exactly which constructs were being measured by these tests. Thus, it is important to understand that, within the psychometric movement, two directions have characteristically been taken: one practical, which was oriented toward solving problems; and another, more conceptual and concerned with theory. The following summary focuses primarily on the development of theoretical concepts relating to the nature of intelligence. However, a pressing concern, which will be discussed later is, and has been, whether I.Q. is a scientifically valid construct and whether intelligence tests actually measure intelligence as it is theoretically understood.

In 1904, Binet petitioned the French government for a grant for funds to develop a tool that could distinguish those capable of learning at normal rates from those in need of a slower-paced, specially designed educational program. His basic task was one of correct classification, and it was not necessary for him to develop a theoretical understanding of that which he sought to measure. His early scales (1905, 1908) were based on the premise that each individual possesses both a "chronological age" (C.A.) or actual age in years, and a "mental age" (M.A.), indicative of the average intellectual abilities present within a specific age group. After computing a student's mental age, a comparison could be made with his or her chronological age to determine his or her relative standing in relation to persons with similar chronological ages.

Binet was already an accomplished lawyer, playwright, psychologist, and hypnotist, and, after creating his "intelligence" test, he became one of the world's first psychometrists. He began the development of his initial scales by selecting a large number of problems that, at face value, seemed to test a student's ability to benefit from instruction. Next, he tested these items with a random sample of students to determine which were "good" items and which were "poor." "Good" items were those for which, as the age of the student increased, the number of items answered correctly also increased. Thus, as the students within the sample became chronologically older, they were able to obtain progressively higher scores since they could answer more and more of the items correctly. "Poor" items, on the other hand, were comprised of questions that did not demonstrate a relationship between the number of correct answers and chronological age. For example, a poor item was a question that all the students, regardless of age, answered incorrectly or which, as the students grew older, fewer and fewer of them answered correctly. By compiling and organizing the good items, and discarding the poor ones, Binet was able to develop a test that ranked questions by age so that the student's mental age could be determined. For example, at age 7 or 8, relatively few children can define the word "connection." At 10 years of age, 10% can, and at 13 years, 60% are able to do so correctly. Therefore, a student's ability to define "connection" indicates a mental ability comparable to that of the average 13-year-old and would be one of several items reflecting a mental age of 13. The student's mental age could then be compared with his or her chronological age to determine the extent to which the person is ahead of, equal to, or behind his or her age-related peers.

Binet's original scale, which was first used in 1905, has gone through numerous revisions—the most significant ones being in 1916, 1937, 1960, and the most recent fourth edition was published in 1986. One of the more important revisions was the reconceptualization of the intelligence quotient, or I.Q., by Terman in 1916. The problem with Binet's early I.Q. (the difference between M.A. and C.A.) was its differing meaning for various age groups. A one-year lag for a child of 3 has a quite different meaning from that for a child of 14. This is because the greatest absolute change in intelligence occurs in the early years, so that a one-year lag for a 3-year-old is much more severe than a one-year lag for a 14-year-old. This problem was countered to a certain extent by Terman's (1916) computation of I.Q. as being equal to M.A./C.A. X 100. If one uses this formula, a child of 3 with a one-year lag would have an I.Q. of 66, whereas a 14-year-old with a one-year lag would have a relatively higher I.Q. of 93. Thus, Terman's revision more adequately reflected the severity of a lower M.A. than C.A. for different age groups. However, it was assumed that mental age reaches a peak around the age of 16. Difficulties would then occur when evaluating adult I.Q.s since adults' chronological ages would be greater than their mental ages. Furthermore, decreases in mental age due to aging or adult brain damage could also not be estimated accurately. For this reason, the 1960 and 1986 revisions of the Stanford-Binet used Wechsler's concept of the deviation I.Q. This is simply a standard score on an ability test that can be compared with the performances of others in an age group. The result is that more meaningful comparisons can be made between persons of different ages.

Whereas Binet did not specifically develop a theory of intelligence, Spearman (1927) became concerned with what it was that intelligence tests were supposed to be measuring. He stated that a general factor, or "g factor," is common to all types of intellectual activity, in addition to specific factors, or "s factors," which are unique to particular problems. Spearman stressed that the different tests of intelligence were highly correlated and further observed that persons who dealt effectively in one area generally were effective in others as well. This led him to believe that there is a g factor operating that serves to integrate and enhance most, if not all, of a person's abilities. Although Spearman's work has often been referred to as a two-factor theory, he clearly emphasized the importance of a single global factor (g) and attempted to assess the relative importance of g within any single test of intelligence.

Thurstone (1938) developed a theory that was a radical departure from Spearman's in that he did not believe in the existence of a unifying g factor. Rather, he believed that intelligence was made up of specific and separate abilities. This theory was developed through the factor analysis of different tasks in which Thurstone attempted to conceptualize and isolate the different skills required for the performance of these tasks. His factor analytic studies suggested that intellect was comprised of the following components, which he referred to as Primary Mental Abilities:

- Verbal Ability
- Verbal Fluency
- Numerical Ability
- Spatial Ability
- Perceptual Ability
- Inductive Reasoning
- Memory

Some vivid examples exist that do suggest a specific factor can exist without a corresponding general unifying (g) factor. Among so-called idiot savants, there is typically the extreme development of only one ability, whereas in other areas of their lives they may be functioning at an extremely low level. Cases have been documented in which an idiot savant could correctly and almost immediately compute the day of the week on which a certain date occurred several years ago or could reproduce a long piece of music after hearing it one time. Such a specific differentiation of abilities gives some support to Thurstone's contention that, at least potentially, s factors can exist without a globally unifying g factor. However, in most recent studies, Thurstone's seven factors have been found to be highly correlated. This suggests that Thurstone's factors are not completely independent and that a g factor also is common throughout the seven primary abilities.

A more recent conceptualization of specific intellectual factors by Gardner (1983) has expanded intelligence into a much wider scope than most other theorists. He has described the following seven relatively independent competencies:

- Linguistic
- Musical
- Logical-mathematical
- Spatial
- Bodily-kinesthetic
- Interpersonal
- Intrapersonal

He has included not only the traditional types of competencies assessed by I.Q. tests (verbal, mathematical, spatial abilities) but also gives credence to intelligence as encompassing athletic ability, knowledge of self and others, and musical talent. Thus, an outstanding gymnast or keyboard player who performs poorly in school (or on I.Q. tests) might still be considered to be extremely intelligent. Unfortunately, Gardner has not developed any formal assessment procedures, but rather recommends evaluation through behavioral observation and informal tasks appropriate for different ages. Someday, his concepts may stimulate more standardized procedures assessing his six different competencies.

For many years, the main issue in conceptualizing intelligence was whether it could be best represented by Spearman's single, unitary, generalized factor or Thurstone's multiple-factor theory (so called "lumpers" versus "splitters"). Vernon (1950) took an intermediate position, stating that intelligence is integrated and unitary but is also comprised of a number of both large and small specific abilities. His model (Figure 5–1) is basically hierarchical, with the g factor at the top to indicate that it unifies all the abilities occurring at lower levels. The next level is comprised of verbal-educational and spatial-mechanical abilities. Smaller subdivisions at lower levels refer to increasingly more specific and discrete abilities such as verbal fluency, numerical reasoning, and creativity. Blaha and Wallbrown (1984) have indicated that the WISC and WISC-R ability arrangement can be categorized using Vernon's model. They have found that a general factor seemed to unify most abilities, with more specific minor abilities being organized by Verbal Comprehension, Perceptual Organization, and Freedom From Distractability. A similar hierarchical model by Horn (1985) emphasized a developmental hierarchy (sensory reception, association processing, perceptual organization, relation education) based on distinct functions, such as short-term acquisition and retrieval, clerical ability, broad auditory thinking, and fluid ability.

Guilford used a highly sophisticated series of factor analytic techniques to develop a conceptualization of intelligence that centered around specific interactions among different factors (Structure of Intellect, or SOI). He examined a far larger and more varied number of test items than previous researchers and broke down intelligence into 120 different factors. He reasoned that each intellectual skill involved a particular operation, on a particular type of content, to yield a particular product or outcome. Thus, Guilford believed that intelligent behavior involves an interaction of operations, contents, and products. Through his factor

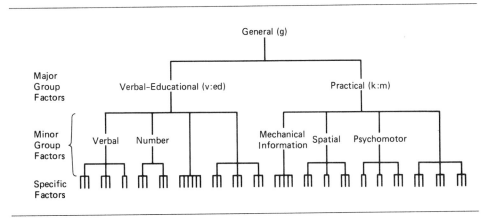

Figure 5–1.   Vernon's hierarchical model of intelligence
Adapted from Vernon, 1960, p. 22. Reprinted, by permission, from *The Structure of Human Abilities* by P.E. Vernon, Methuen & Co., Ltd., 1960.

analytic techniques, he determined five operations or cognitive processes (Recognition, Memory, Divergent Production, Convergent Production, and Evaluation), four contexts (Figures, Symbols, Semantics, and Behaviors), and six outcomes or products (Units, Classes, Relations, Systems, Transformations, and Implications; see Figure 5–2). Each specific intellectual skill involves one of the operations, performed on one of the types of contexts, to produce one of the outcomes. The total (5 x 4 x 6) possible interactions yields Guilford's 120 specific intellectual skills, which he uses to define the structure of intellect.

Although Guilford's conceptualization of intelligence appears highly theoretical, it demonstrates a wide variety of intellectual skills and can potentially give insight into practical difficulties. For example, it can help educators determine which skills are emphasized in our educational system and which are neglected. In general, most educational systems train students to deal with the physical world far more than the social world and to approach problems with logical thinking more than creative thinking. Using Guilford's terminology, students are usually far better trained to "converge" from a number of possible answers to one externally defined "correct" answer, rather than to "diverge" from one question to a number of possible answers.

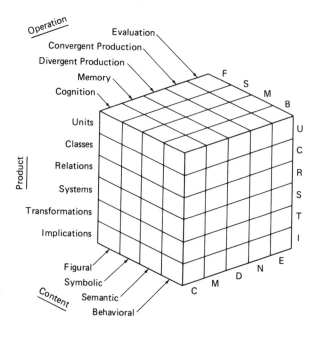

Figure 5–2.   Three-dimensional model of the structure of intellect
From Guilford, 1967, p. 63. Reprinted, by permission, from *The Nature of Human Intelligence*, by J.P. Guilford by McGraw-Hill Book Co., 1967.

Although Binet originally began the study of intelligence from a global and somewhat poorly defined concept, the understanding of cognitive functioning has become increasingly more specific and complex. This progression began with Binet's (1908) implied global factor and proceeded to the contrasting views of Spearman's (1927) two-factor theory, with an emphasis on g, as opposed to Thurstone's (1938) multiple-factor theory. A resolution was attempted with Vernon's (1950) and Horn's (1985) hierarchical models, which described specific abilities arranged according to increasing specificity or developmental complexity. One of the more current major theories is Guilford's (1967) classification of 120 separate abilities. From a practical standpoint, the views of intelligence presented here can help clinicians to understand and describe more precisely a client's intellectual abilities. However, a significant limitation of the psychometric approach is that, even though theories relating to the nature of intelligence have been expounded, the tests of intelligence that have been developed may not actually measure these constructs. This discrepancy between theory and practicality should be taken into consideration when interpreting I.Q. test scores. Thus, I.Q. tests are generally quite effective when used to predict later academic performance, but they may not actually measure "intelligence." In a review of tests and theories of intelligence, Maloney and Ward (1976) state:

> In terms of scientific validity, the tests do seem to be inadequate. They bear little or no relationship to the theories we have examined and thus lack an adequate theoretical foundation or superstructure. Nevertheless, the items of intelligence tests have proven their practical value, such as the prediction of school achievement. Thus, while not conforming to any theoretical notions per se, the tests do relate to the types of performances that almost everyone agrees reflect the operation of intelligence, that is, school achievement. It is in terms of these practical effects that tests are designated "successful." (p. 224-225)

This is not to say that theories of intelligence are useless; they serve the important function of enabling clinicians to perceive and discuss aspects of the client that were not accessible before they were conceptualized. Such theories potentially increase the depth and breadth of understanding. Likewise, I.Q. tests have relevance and usefulness in relation to specific types of predictions. The apparent discrepancy between theories of intelligence and tests of intelligence also suggests that this gap must be narrowed, and indicates future directions for research and test construction. So far, the traditional psychometrically based tests (Stanford-Binet and Wechsler scales) have dominated intelligence assessment. It remains to be seen whether neuropsychological, information processing, and cognitive theories will significantly impact future assessment strategies.

Neurological-Biological Approaches

All four of the general approaches to understanding intelligence assume that there is an underlying neurological substrate on which intelligence is ultimately dependent. It is therefore important to somehow conceptualize and search for the neuroanatomical and neurophysiological processes underlying the behaviors that are referred to as intelligent. This might include a greater understanding of anatomical structures, electrochemical processes, or physiological correlates of intelligence. The most simplistic approach might be to study the relationship between brain size and measurements of intelligence, which have indicated only a small positive correlation. This type of theorizing has been the general trend, but it has been conducted in a far more complex and theoretical manner.

Halstead (1961), for example, has proposed a theory of biological intelligence. He stated that a number of brain functions relating to intelligence are relatively independent of cultural considerations. They are biologically based and pertain to the brain functions of all individuals. The four factors he delineates are central integrative (C), abstraction (A), power (P), and directional (D). These are summarized as follows:

1. The *central integrative* (C) factor involves one's ability to organize experience. A person's background of familiar experiences and past learning works with and integrates new incoming experiences; its main purpose is adaptive.

2. The *abstraction* (A) factor is the ability to group things into different categories, and to perceive similarities and differences among objects, concepts, and events.

3. The *power* (P) factor refers to cerebral power—the undistorted strength of the brain. It involves the ability to suspend affect so that rationality and intellectual abilities can grow and develop.

4. The *directional* (D) factor provides direction or focus to a person's abilities; it specifies the manner in which intellect and behaviors will be expressed.

Two other contributors to biological approaches are Cattell (1963) and Hebb (1972). Cattell's conceptualization of fluid and crystalized intelligence, and Hebb's A and B intelligence, are sufficiently similar so that they will be discussed together. Both Cattell and Hebb emphasized the existence of certain areas of intelligence that are directly tied to brain function. Hebb refers to this as intelligence A and stresses that it is innate and biological, requires an intact nervous system, relates to problem solving abilities, and cannot be measured by psychological tests. Cattell's fluid intelligence is similar and enables a person to perceive relations, similarities, and parallels. It is dependent on the brain's efficiency and relative intactness, and is sensitive to the effects of brain damage. Furthermore, it is primarily nonverbal and culture free, and can be measured by such tests as progressive matrices, figural analyses, and number/letter series. Fluid intelligence increases until around the age of 14, at which time it levels off until age 20, when it shows a gradual decline.

In addition to the more fluid, biologically based aspects of intelligence, Cattell and Hebb also refer to more environmentally determined, content-oriented dimensions. Hebb labels this "intelligence B," and indicates that it is based on experience and can be reflected in the extent of a person's accumulated knowledge. It is this dimension of intelligence that most intelligence tests measure. Cattell's term "crystallized" intelligence suggests that it is relatively permanent and generally less susceptible to the effects of brain damage. It is developed from the interaction between a person's innate fluid intelligence and such environmental factors as culture and education. Cattell states that it grows and develops until the age of 40, at which time it generally shows a slow decline. Representative tests that measure crystallized intelligence are those which relate to acquired skills and knowledge such as vocabulary and general information. However, Cattell differs from Hebb in that he believes both fluid and crystallized intelligence can be measured, whereas Hebb believes that psychometric tests cannot adequately measure intelligence A.

Moderate success has been achieved in relating intelligence to different types of psychophysiological responses. For example, Ahern and Beatty (1979) found that more intelligent subjects showed smaller pupillary dilations while performing tasks. Similarly, more intelligent subjects required less effort and energy (as measured by skin conductance and heartrate variability) while performing a cognitive task (Geiselman, Woodward, & Beatty, 1982). In contrast, studies on the relationship between brain wave patterns and intelligence have found only minimal relationships. Visually evoked response latencies (speed at which

EEG readings respond to a visual stimulus) were related to the intelligence of most adults but not to the intelligence levels of older persons (Engel & Fay, 1972; Henderson & Engel, 1974; Perry, McCoy, Cunningham, Falgout & Street, 1976). However, the above studies are merely correlates of intelligence and, while implying an underlying neurological process, do not help explain either its nature or structure.

Biological approaches to intelligence generally have serious methodological and theoretical difficulties. So far, no specific neurological substrates have been found that clearly relate to intelligence. Also, it is extremely difficult to actually separate the effects of learning and culture from a hypothesized underlying biological structure. However, other theories clearly depend on this underlying neurological structure. It is hoped that, as the techniques of psychological measurement parallel increases in knowledge relating to neuroanatomy and neurophysiology, this approach will become more integrated and the actual links between intelligent brain-behavior relationships will become more adequately understood (see Eysenck & Barrett, 1985; Vernon, 1987).

Developmental Theory

One criticism directed at the psychometric approach is that test constructors have been more concerned with quantitative scores than the quality of, or reasoning behind, an examinee's responses (Embretson, 1986; Siegler & Richards, 1982; Sigel, 1963). In contrast, Piaget studied the incorrect responses of children to different questions or tasks as a means of understanding their internal processes. He was concerned not so much with whether the answers were right or wrong but rather with why they were right or wrong. Piaget soon noticed that certain patterns of responses characterized different age groups. Further studies suggested to him that qualitative differences existed in the thinking of persons of certain ages. This led him to the following general conclusions regarding cognitive abilities:

1. Mental growth follows definite patterns and is nonrandom.
2. There are qualitative differences in the thinking of younger as opposed to older children.
3. As a person develops, there is corresponding development in new cognitive structures and abilities.
4. Mental growth is complete somewhere during late adolescence.

Piaget (1950) viewed intelligence as a special form of biological adaptation between a person and his or her environment. It involves an interaction in which a person must somehow fit his or her personal needs into some workable relationship with environmental demands. As persons grow and develop, they are in a continual process of reorganizing their psychological structures to deal more effectively with the environment. Piaget believes that this process occurs through both "assimilation" and "accommodation." Assimilation is primarily an inward process in which a person incorporates input from his or her environment into some sort of internal organized structure. It is a relatively active process beyond merely coping with the environment. Assimilation also involves a certain degree of independence from the environment, which allows for the growth and development of internal cognitive structures. For example, make-believe play with objects requires that a child act as if the objects are something else. This necessitates a certain degree of independence from the object, an active interaction with it, and the use and growth of new cognitive structures in relation to it. Whereas assimilation is more inward and active, accommodation looks outward in an effort to adapt and change cognitive structures in accordance with external demands. Thus, the changing or "accommodating" mental constructions must have a direct correspondence with the real world. Piaget stressed that both assimilation and accommodation occur simultaneously, independently of age, but also within all age groups. However, within these general processes there are specific age-related differences. Horn (1985) has further drawn and elaborated on some of these principles to conceptualize that the earliest forms of "intelligence" depend on sensory reception followed by association processing, perceptual organization, and, during adolescence and adulthood, understanding relations and implications becomes most important (relation education).

Piaget described four major stages of cognitive development:

I.   Sensorimotor Period (Approx. Birth to 2 years)
     The child passes through six different stages. These begin with simple reflex actions and grow in complexity until simple mental schemata are developed to more effectively deal with the world. The stage ends with the first sign of internal or symbolic constructs.

II. Preoperational Period (Approx. 2 to 7 years)
     The child develops language and basic symbolic constructs. The child can begin to think internally; is aware of the past, present, and future; can engage in symbolic play, can search for hidden objects; and can engage in delayed imitation.

III. Concrete Operational Period (Approx. 7 to 11 years)
     At this stage, the child acquires conservation skills (in which independence from the stimulus properties of objects is developed, and the child is not fooled by mere perceptual transformations). He or she can add, subtract, classify, and serialize, and is less egocentric and more social. The child still has difficulty performing operations independently from his or her environment.

IV. Formal Operations Period (Approx. 11+ years)
     This stage marks the development of adult thinking in which the child can think abstractly, form and test hypotheses, use deductive reasoning, and evaluate solutions.

The above cognitive stages are action-oriented in that a developing person actively operates on the environment and develops internal constructs based on these interactions. Piaget also emphasized the qualitative changes that occur in a person's cognitive processes. He believed that it is more important to describe the nature and style of these changes than to quantitatively measure them. The different stages also occur within all cultures, and the sequence cannot be varied. The later stages are dependent on earlier ones. However, even though the sequence cannot be changed, there is some variability in the ages at which these stages occur between one individual and another, and from culture to culture. Thus, it may be important to determine what variables slow these stages down or accelerate them. In summary, Piaget's central theme is that intelligence is a developmental phenomenon of adaptation in which a person moves toward constructing reality in progressively more symbolic terms.

Information Processing Approaches

The greater cognitive emphasis in psychology during the late 1970s and 1980s has resulted in models of intelligence that focus on ongoing processes rather than contents. This has involved an understanding of operations, mental processes, transformations, manipulations, and the different stages of acquisition and retrieval. An information-processing model usually considers the manner in which information is received, stored, and retrieved and the ways these processes eventually result in a response. The combinations and transformations that occur at various stages in this procedure are defined and elaborated. Most information processing models include both structural (memory storage, short/long term memory, sensory reception) as well as functional (transformations, processes) components.

A representative information processing theory is the work of Campione and Brown (1978), which was later elaborated by Borkowski (1985). Their theory includes both an architectural and an executive system. The architectural system refers to and depends on an intact central and peripheral nervous system. Its three components are *capacity* (the amount of memory that can be stored and worked with), *durability* (the hardiness of the system, resistance to disruption, time taken to lose information), and *efficiency* (speed of processing; rate of encoding/decoding). Whereas the architectural system relates to relatively fixed abilities or structures, the executive system is more concerned with ongoing fluid processes. Within the executive system, the *knowledge base* encompasses not only stored information, but how that information is received. *Schemas* are used in much the same way as Piaget (framework for incoming information) and *control processes* are the strategies and rules used to focus, monitor, and rehearse for a task. Finally, *metacognition* is the ability to stand back and observe one's thoughts. It involves retracing various cognitive processes and understanding why these processes were effective/ineffective in problem solving. It is through the effective functioning of both control processes (focusing, concentration, monitoring) and metacognition (self-reflection, retracing, puzzlement) that new solutions are developed.

Another example of an information processing approach is Sternberg's (1985) triarchic theory, which is composed of:

1. metacomponents
2. performance
3. knowledge

Similar to other theories, he has emphasized that intelligence must be purposeful, goal oriented, relevant, and must also involve the development of effective information processing. An important aspect of his theory is its focus on both the internal experience of the person (particularly novelty) as well as the social context of the experience. In particular, intelligence is a sociocultural phenomenon; what is considered adaptive within one culture may not be considered adaptive in another culture. Furthermore, intellectual assessment is importantly a "folk concept" in that day-to-day human interaction (at a party, in the office) involves intuitively evaluating the level of intelligence of each other. A final contribution to human information processing approaches has been made by Das and his colleagues (Jarman & Das, 1977) in their conceptualization of *simultaneous processing* (integrated, semi-spatial) versus *successive processing* (orderly sequence, recall of numbers, reading).

Although significant developments have occurred in understanding the processes underlying intelligence, it remains to be seen if these advances will have a significant impact on the mainstream approaches used by practitioners. Assessment in general has adhered fairly closely to past traditions, with changes occurring only very slowly and with a frequent lack of impact from research findings. Possible future changes might include tests that are based more on broad, sound theories, increased emphasis on the assessment and remediation of specific cognitive deficits, and greater concern with the predictive power of intelligence tests within broader areas than are currently considered. In particular, tests might pay more attention to real-life criteria. The assessment of intelligence might also become more dependent on computer-assisted techniques and be concerned with a more sophisticated understanding of the interactions among test formats, characteristics of the subject, and the settings that the subject is concerned with.

THE TESTING OF INTELLIGENCE: PRO AND CON

The testing of intelligence has had a consistent history of misunderstanding, controversy, and occasional misuse (Houts, 1977; Weinberg, 1989). Criticisms have ranged from moral indictments against labeling individuals, to cultural bias, and even to accusations of flagrant abuse of test scores. Although certainly valid criticisms can be made against testing intelligence, there are also a number of advantages to continuing with such procedures.

One of the main assets of intelligence tests is their accuracy in predicting future behavior. Initially, Binet was able to achieve a certain degree of predictive success with his scales, and, since that time, test procedures have become progressively more refined and accurate. More recent studies indicate that the WAIS-R/WISC-R can predict an extremely wide number of variables (Appelbaum & Tuma, 1982; Grossman & Johnson, 1982; Kitson & Vance, 1982; Matarazzo & Herman, 1984; Reilly, Drudge, Rosen, Loew, & Fischer, 1985; Ryan & Rosenberg, 1983; Sutter & Bishop, 1986). In particular, I.Q. tests are excellent predictors of academic achievement (Appelbaum & Tuma, 1982; Grossman & Johnson, 1982; Ryan & Rosenberg, 1983). However, certain liabilities are also associated with these successes. First, intelligence tests can be used to classify children into stereotyped categories, which can limit their freedom to choose fields of study. Furthermore, I.Q. tests are extremely limited in predicting nontest or nonacademic activity, yet they are sometimes incorrectly used to make these inferences (Snyderman & Rothman, 1987). It should also be stressed that intelligence tests are measures of a person's present level of functioning and, as such, can only provide short-term predictions. Long-term predictions, although attempted frequently, are less accurate because there are many uncontrolled, influencing variables. Similarly, even short-term academic placements made solely on the basis of an I.Q. score have a high chance of failure since all the variables that may be crucial for success are not and cannot be measured by an intelligence test (Zigler & Farber, 1985). It can sometimes be tempting for test users to extend the meaning of test scores beyond what they were originally intended, especially in relation to the predictions they can realistically be expected to make.

Another important asset of intelligence tests, particularly the WAIS-R and WISC-R, is that they provide valuable information about a person's cognitive strengths and weaknesses. They are standardized procedures whereby a person's performance in various areas can be compared with their age-related peers. In addition, useful comparisons can be made regarding a person's pattern of strengths and weaknesses. The WAIS-R, WISC-R, and other individually administered tests provide the examiner with a structured interview within which a variety of tasks can be used to observe the unique and personal ways in which cognitive tasks are approached. Through a client's interactions with both the examiner and the test materials, an initial impression can be made of the individual's self-esteem, behavioral idiosyncrasies, anxiety, social skills, and motivation, while at the same time a specific picture of intellectual functioning is obtained.

Intelligence tests often provide clinicians, educators, and researchers with baseline measures for use in determining either the degree of change that has occurred in an individual over a period of time or how an individual compares with other persons in a particular area or ability. This may have important implications for evaluating the effectiveness of an educational program or for assessing the changing abilities of a specific student. In cases involving recovery from a head injury or readjustment following neurosurgery, it may be extremely helpful for clinicians to measure and follow the cognitive changes that occur within a patient. Furthermore, I.Q. assessments may be important in researching—and understanding more adequately—the effect of environmental variables, such as educational programs, family background, and nutrition on cognitive functioning. Thus, these assessments can provide useful information about cultural, biological, maturational, or treatment-related differences among individuals.

One criticism leveled at intelligence tests is that almost all have an inherent bias toward emphasizing convergent, analytical, and scientific modes of thought. Thus, a person who emphasizes divergent, artistic, and imaginative modes of thought may be at a distinct disadvantage. Guilford (1967, 1971) has specifically stated that the single I.Q. score does not do justice to the multidimensional nature of intelligence. Some critics have even stressed that the current approach to intelligence testing has become a social mechanism used by people with similar values to pass on educational advantages to children who resemble themselves. Not only might I.Q. tests tend to place creative individuals at a disadvantage, but they are limited in assessing nonacademically oriented intellectual abilities (Frederiksen, 1986; Snyderman & Rothman, 1987). Thus, social acumen, success in dealing with people, the ability to handle the concrete realities of one's daily world, social fluency, and specific tasks such as purchasing merchandise are not measured by any intelligence test. More succinctly, people are capable of many more cognitive abilities than can possibly be measured on an intelligence test.

One frequent misunderstanding—and an area for potential misuse of intelligence tests—occurs when scores are treated as measures of innate capacity. I.Q. is not a measure of an innate fixed ability, nor is it representative of all problem solving situations. It is rather a specific and limited sample, made at a certain point in time, of abilities that are subject to numerous alterations. It reflects, to a large extent, the richness of an individual's past experiences. Although interpretation guidelines are quite clear in pointing out the limited nature of a test score, there is a tendency to look at test results as absolute facts reflecting permanent characteristics within an individual. People often want a quick, easy, and reductionist method to quantify, understand, and assess cognitive abilities, and the I.Q. score has become the most widely misused test score to fill this need.

One important limitation of intelligence tests is that, for the most part, they are not concerned with the underlying processes involved in problem solving. They focus on the final product or outcome rather than on the steps involved in reaching the outcome. In other words, they look at the "what" rather than the "how" (Embretson, 1986; Sigel, 1963). Thus, if a person gives the correct response to the question "How are a desk and couch similar?" the examiner does not know if the response results from past learning, perceptual discrimination, syllogistic reasoning, or a combination of these (Sigel, 1963). The extreme example of this "end product" emphasis is the global I.Q. score. When the myriad assortment of intellectual abilities is looked at as a global ability, the complexity of cognitive functioning is simplified to the point of being almost useless. Labels can be applied quickly and easily, without any attempt made to examine specific strengths and weaknesses, thereby eliminating opportunities to make precise therapeutic interventions or to provide knowledgeable recommendations. This type of thinking detracts significantly from the search for a wider, more precise, and more process-oriented understanding of mental abilities (Siegler & Richards, 1982).

A further concern about intelligence tests involves their limited usefulness in assessing minority groups with divergent cultural backgrounds. It has been stated that intelligence-test content is strongly biased in favor of white, middle-class values. Critics stress that minorities tend to be at a disadvantage when taking the tests due to deficiencies in motivation, lack of practice, and difficulties in establishing rapport. Numerous arguments against using intelligence tests for the assessment and placement of minorities have culminated in recent legal restrictions on the use of I.Q. scores. However, traditional defenses of I.Q. scores suggest that they are less biased than has been accused. For example, the removal of biased items has done little to alter overall test scores, and I.Q.s still provide mostly accurate predictions for many minorities (see Chapter 2 for a further discussion). The issue has certainly not been resolved, but clinicians should continue to be aware of this dilemma, pay attention to subgroup norms, and interpret minority group I.Q. scores cautiously.

Finally, many people feel that their I.Q.s are deeply personal pieces of information. They would prefer that others, even a psychologist who is expected to observe confidentiality, not be allowed access to this information. This problem is further compounded when I.Q. scores might be given to several different persons, such as during legal proceedings or personnel selection.

In summary, intelligence tests provide a number of useful and well-respected functions. They can adequately predict short-term scholastic performance, provide an assessment of an individual's relative strengths and weaknesses, reveal important personality variables, and permit the researcher, educator, or clinician to trace possible changes within an individual or population. However, these assets are only helpful if the limitations of intelligence tests are adequately understood and appropriately taken into consideration. They are limited in predicting occupational success and such nonacademic skills as creativity, motivational level, social acumen, and success in dealing with people. Furthermore, I.Q. scores are not measures of an innate, fixed ability, and their use in classifying minority groups has been questioned. Finally, there has been an overemphasis on understanding the end product of cognitive functioning and a relative neglect in appreciating underlying cognitive processes.

HISTORY AND DEVELOPMENT

During the 1930s, Wechsler began studying a number of standardized tests and selected 11 different subtests to form his initial battery. His search for subtests was in part guided by his conception that intelligence is global in nature and represents a part of the greater whole of personality. Several of his subtests were derived from portions of the 1937 revision of the Stanford-Binet (Comprehension, Arithmetic, Digit Span, Similarities, and Vocabulary). The remaining subtests came from the Army Group Examinations (Picture Arrangement), Koh's Block Design (Block Design), Army Alpha (Information, Comprehension), Army Beta (Digit Symbol, Coding), Healy Picture Completion (Picture Completion) and the Pinther-Paterson Test (Object Assembly). These subtests were combined and published in 1939 as the Wechsler-Bellevue Intelligence Scale. The Weschler-Bellevue had a number of technical deficiencies primarily related to both the reliability of the subtests and the size and representativeness of the normative sample. Thus, it was revised to form the Wechsler Adult Intelligence Scale (WAIS) in 1955, and another revised edition (WAIS-R) was published in 1981. The 1981 revision was based on 1,880 individuals who were representative of the 1970 census and categorized into nine different age groups.

The original Wechsler-Bellevue Scale was developed for adults, but in 1949 Wechsler developed the Wechsler Intelligence Scale for Children (WISC) so that children down to the age of 5 years, 0 months could be assessed in a similar manner. Easier items, designed for children, were added to the original scales and standardized on 2,200 white American boys and girls selected to be representative of the 1940 census. However, some evidence shows that Wechsler's sample may have been overrepresentative of children in the middle and upper socioeconomic levels. Thus, ethnic minorities and children from lower socio-economic levels may have been penalized when compared with the normative group. The WISC was revised in 1974 and standardized on a new sample that is more accurately representative of children in the United States. It is currently published as the WISC-R. There are plans to publish a further revision of the WISC-R sometime in the early 1990s.

In 1967, the Wechsler Preschool and Primary Scale of Intelligence (WPPSI) was first published for the assessment of children between the ages of 4 and $6\frac{1}{2}$. Just as the WISC is a downward extension of the WAIS, so the WPPSI is generally a downward extension of the WISC in which easier but similar items are used. Although most of the scales are similar in form and content to the WISC, a number of them are unique to the WPPSI. A 1989 revision has been published that includes an expanded age range (3 to 7), extensive standardization, and modifications in the stimulus materials.

RELIABILITY AND VALIDITY

WISC-R Reliability and Validity

The WISC-R has generally excellent reliability. The average WISC-R internal consistency reported by Wechsler (1974) across all 11 age groups was .96 for the Full Scale I.Q., .94 for the Verbal Scale, and .90 for the Performance Scale. Internal consistency for the specific subtests was far more variable, ranging from a low for Object Assembly of .70 to a high of .86 for Vocabulary. The average reliabilities for Verbal subtests ranged between .77 to .86 (Mdn r = .80), while the Performance subtests were somewhat lower, ranging between .77 and .86 (Mdn r = .72). However, the reliabilities vary somewhat according to different age levels.

Test-retest reliabilities are likewise quite high for the three scales and somewhat lower for the specific subtests. Full Scale I.Q. reliability over a one-month retesting was .95 and the Verbal and Performance Scales were .93 and .90 respectively (Wechsler, 1974). The average increase in scores for retesting over a one-month interval was seven points for the Full Scale I.Q., four points for the Verbal I.Q., and ten points for the Performance I.Q. This can mainly be accounted for by practice effects that seem to be particularly pronounced for the Performance Scale. The practical implication for this is that clinicians should incorporate the meaning of these short-term increases into their interpretations. Specifically, moderate short-term increases in scores of 5 to 10 points should not usually be considered to indicate true improvement in ability. Longer term retesting over a two-year interval (which is more typical in clinical settings) has shown somewhat more stability with less than an average three-point difference (Haynes & Howard, 1986). Test-retest reliabilities for the specific subtests ranged from a low of .65 for Mazes and a high of .88 for Information with an overall Median of .78 (see summary in Appendix A).

The standard error of measurement (indicated in I.Q. points) for the Full Scale I.Q. was 3.19, Verbal I.Q. 3.60, and Performance I.Q. 4.66. The standard error of measurement (given in subscale scores) for the Verbal subtests ranged from 1.15 to 1.44, with the narrowest range of error for Vocabulary (1.15) and the widest for Digit Span (1.44). The Performance subtests ranged from 1.17 to 1.70, with the narrowest range for Block Design (1.17) and widest for Object Assembly and Mazes (1.70; see specific listings in Appendix A). Further information for incorporating specific standard error of measurement scores into WISC-R (and WAIS-R) interpretations is included in the section on "Interpretation Procedures."

The validity of the WISC-R has primarily been established by extensive correlations with relevant criterion measures, including other ability tests, school grades, and achievement tests. Selected median correlations reviewed and reported by Sattler (1988) include those for the Stanford-Binet: Fourth Edition (.78), K-ABC (.70), group I.Q. tests (.66), WRAT (.52–.59), Peabody Individual Achievement Test (.71), and school grades (.39). The underlying factor structure, while still somewhat controversial, has generally supported Wechsler's conceptualization of abilities into a Verbal Comprehension factor that roughly corresponds with the Verbal Scale, and a Perceptual Organizational factor that generally corresponds with the Performance Scale (Kaufman, 1975, 1979). A third factor, variously referred to as Freedom from Distractability (Kaufman, 1975, 1979), Memory, or Sequencing (Bannatyne, 1971, 1974), has also typically emerged. Thus, the WISC-R has been found both to predict relevant variables in the subject's life and to be based on a conceptually sound framework.

WAIS-R Reliability and Validity

Reliabilities for the three scales of the WAIS-R are comparable to those for the WISC-R. Wechsler (1981) reported that the split half reliability for the Full Scale I.Q. was .97; Verbal I.Q., .97; and Performance I.Q., .93. The specific subtests were far more variable (Mdn r = .83), with the highest split half reliability being for Vocabulary (.96) and the lowest for Object Assembly (.52). Similar to the WISC-R, the split half reliabilities were higher for the Verbal subtests than for the Performance subtests.

Test-retest reliabilities over a one- to seven-week interval were quite high. Full Scale I.Q. reliabilities averaged .97; Verbal I.Q., .97; and Performance I.Q., .93. The specific subtests were somewhat less satisfactory. with an average low of .67 reported for Object Assembly and a high of .94 for Vocabulary (see specific listings in Appendix B). The mean increase in scores during a two- to seven-week interval was 6.2 for the Full Scale I.Q., 3.3 for the Verbal I.Q., and 8.4 for the Performance I.Q. (Matarazzo & Herman, 1984). As is true for the WISC-R, the increase was primarily due to short-term practice effects; these expected increases should be taken into consideration when making interpretations of clients' abilities over a short retesting interval. However, caution should be exercised due to the wide range that was recorded; although the average scores were higher, some persons also showed significant losses. The above pattern of average gains was found for both a normal population as well as for various clinical groups (Ryan, Georgemiller, Geisser, & Randall, 1985).

Standard error of measurements (SEMs) for the WAIS-R scales indicate that the greatest confidence can be placed in the Full Scale and Verbal Scale I.Q.s (SEMs for I.Q. points = 2.53 and 2.74 respectively). Somewhat lesser confidence can be placed in the Performance I.Q. (4.14) and specific subtests (SEMs range between .61 and .25). The highest standard error of measurement was found for the Verbal subtests (.61 to 1.24) with the narrowest range of error for Vocabulary (.61) and the widest for Information (.93). The Performance subtests ranged from .98 for Block Design to 1.54 for Picture Completion (see specific listings in Appendix B).

When the WAIS-R was first published, the extensive and impressive validity studies on the WAIS were used as support for the validity of the newer revision. This seemed reasonable given that the two tests were conceptually quite similar and shared many of the same items. As would be expected, correlations between the two tests were quite high. Median WAIS/WAIS-R correlations reported by Sattler (1988) were .94 for the Full Scale I.Q., .94 for the Verbal I.Q., and .86 for the Performance I.Q.. These high correlations were used as one of the strongest sources of support for the validity of the WAIS-R. However,

Kaufman (1983) indicated that the WAIS-R norms were quite different than the norms used for the WAIS. As a result, the assumed validity of the WAIS-R may have been accepted prematurely. In particular, mean I.Q.s obtained by most populations have produced lower scores on the WAIS-R than on the WAIS (Ryan, Nowak, & Geisser, 1987). The median WAIS-R lowerings were 6.6 for the Full Scale I.Q., 6.4 for the Verbal I.Q., and 6.8 for the Performance I.Q. (Sattler, 1988). However, this lowering for obtained WAIS-R I.Q.s may occur only for the midranges of intelligence and not for I.Q.s derived from either extreme (Mitchell, Grandy, & Lubo, 1986; Spitz, 1986). For example, Spruill and Beck (1988) found that WAIS/WAIS-R I.Q.s were equal for a mildly retarded population, but WAIS-R scores were actually higher for moderately retarded persons. Thus, the WAIS and WAIS-R are not interchangeable and comparisons should be made with either the test's validity or individually derived scores, taking the differences into consideration.

Since the publication of the WAIS-R, a sufficient number of validity studies on the WAIS-R have been specifically published to establish the validity of the newer revision without having to rely on research from the older version. Full Scale WAIS-R I.Q.s have been found to correlate with a wide number of criterion measures, including the Stanford-Binet (.85), WRAT (Reading, .62; Spelling, .60; Arithmetic, .76), Slosson Intelligence Test (.78), and number of years of education (.54; Sattler, 1988). Furthermore, the construct validity has been found to be strong. For example, factor analytic studies have indicated that all the subtests have moderate to high correlations with general intelligence. The factor structure also supports the basic distinction originally made by Wechsler between the Verbal I.Q. (Verbal Comprehension factor) and the Performance I.Q. (Perceptual Organization factor; Leckliter, Matarazzo, & Silverstein, 1986; Naglieri & Kaufman, 1983). Theoretical predictions related to scores that decline with age have also been supported. Verbal abilities are relatively stable throughout the life span, which is consistent with the view that Verbal Scales primarily measure crystallized intelligence. Performance abilities, which are associated more with fluid intelligence, show a slow decline with age until after age 70, at which time the decline becomes much sharper.

ASSETS AND LIMITATIONS

Since their initial publication, the Wechsler scales have been evaluated in numerous research studies and have become widely used throughout the world. Thus, they are familiar to both researchers and practitioners and also have a long and extensive history of continued evaluation. Furthermore, the subtests are easy to administer, and the accompanying manual provides clear instructions, concise tables, and excellent norms.

Perhaps of even more practical importance to the clinician is the clear, precise data obtained regarding the person's cognitive functioning from the pattern of responses to the subtests. It is relatively easy for an examiner to determine a person's psychological strengths and weaknesses by comparing the results of each subtest. For example, relatively high scores on Block Design and Object Assembly suggest that the person is strong in perceptual organization, whereas an individual with relative peaks on Arithmetic and Digit Span is most likely strong in immediate memory and is not easily distracted. A clinician can become extremely sensitive to the different nuances and limitations of each of these subtests and the pattern of their results. In addition, a quick review of a person's Verbal, Performance, and Full Scale I.Q.s can point to areas of concern that may need further evaluation.

A final, but extremely important, asset of the Wechsler scales is their ability to aid in assessing personality variables. This can be done by directly observing the individual as he or she interacts with the examiner, studying the content of test item responses, or evaluating information inferred from the individual's pattern of subtest scores. For example, a person scoring low on Digit Span, Arithmetic, and Digit Symbol is likely to be experiencing anxiety, to have an attentional deficit, or a combination of both. On the other hand, another person who scores high in both Comprehension and Picture Arrangement is likely to have good social judgment. Despite attempts to establish descriptions of the manner in which different clinical groups perform on the WAIS-R/WISC-R, few clear findings have emerged (Piedmont, Sokolove, & Fleming, 1989a, 1989b). Thus, the Wechsler scales should not be seen as similar to "personality scales." Rather, the subject's behavior surrounding the test and qualitative responses to the items should be considered as means of generating hypotheses related to personality. Within this context, the Wechsler scales are unique in the degree to which they can provide personality variables and clinical information.

Despite these strengths, a number of weaknesses and limitations do exist. The Wechsler scales do not adequately measure extreme ranges of intelligence (below 40 and above 160) when compared with such tests as the Stanford-Binet. It is only with the average and moderately below-average ranges that the Wechsler scales and the Stanford-Binet provide means that are comparable. Thus, the Stanford-Binet and WISC-R are closely correlated for the average or moderately below-average child, but not for the child of either superior intelligence or extremely low intelligence.

Both the WISC-R and WAIS-R have some peculiar aspects of their norms, which makes the interpretation of I.Q. results for certain ages difficult or even questionable. On either end of the age spectrum for the WISC-R (6-0 to 6-3 years, and 16-8 to 16-11 years), no children were included in the standardization sample. Even though a small group (N = 50) who were 6-0 years were included and extrapolations made for the 3 months between 6-0 to 6-3, no children actually within this range were used. Thus, the accuracy of I.Q. scores for the 6-0 to 6-3 and 16-8 to 16-11 age ranges may be questionable.

A peculiar feature of the WAIS-R was its use of the scaled scores for the age group between 20 and 34 (N = 500) as the comparison for all other age groups. This age group produced scaled scores with a mean of 10 and an average standard deviation of 3. When the 16 to 17 and 18 to 19-year-olds included in the standardization sample are compared with the 20 to 34-year-olds, they scored surprisingly low, especially on the verbal subtests. For example, the mean Vocabulary score for 16 to 17-year-olds was only 7.8 whereas the 18 to 19-year-olds scored only slightly higher, with a mean of 8.1. It might be reasoned that their knowledge was not yet fully developed, but even this does not explain the substantial increase in scores within the 20 to 34-year-old group. Thus, there may be some bias in the sample perhaps due to its being unrepresentative of the overall population in some unknown way (Gregory, 1987). The practical implication for practitioners is that the validity of intelligence results (and especially subtest scores) may not be as high for persons under 20 as for other age groups.

Another area of caution relates to the use of WAIS-R profile analysis for older persons, particularly if they are 70 or older. A clear finding is that subtest scores decrease with age but do so quite differently for different subtests. For example, the mean subtest scores for Block Design and Digit Symbol for 70 to 74-year-olds is only 6.4 and 4.9 respectively. In contrast, the mean Vocabulary score is 9.2. A practitioner might be tempted to incorrectly interpret this normal subscale scatter and thus reach erroneous conclusions regarding an elderly person's strengths and weaknesses. A partial solution is the use of conversions based on age-corrected scaled scores (see Table 21 in Wechsler's 1981 Manual). However, this may make the protocol unwieldy and increase the risk of clerical errors. Any practitioner should always use these age-corrected scores when making subscale comparisons for older persons.

There are several additional limitations to the Wechsler scales. Some critics believe that norms may not be applicable for ethnic minorities or persons from lower socioeconomic backgrounds. Furthermore, there is a certain degree of subjectivity when scoring many of the items on Comprehension, Similarities, and Vocabulary. Thus, a "hard" scorer may develop a somewhat lower score than an "easy" scorer. This is particularly true for Similarities, Comprehension, and Vocabulary, where scoring criteria are less clear than for other subtests. The Wechsler scales, like other tests of intelligence, are also limited in the scope of what they can measure. They do not assess such important factors as need for achievement, motivation, creativity, or success in dealing with people. As a result, the scales tend to be relatively poor at predicting such factors as occupational success.

Perhaps the most significant criticism leveled at the Wechsler scales has been the lack of a sufficient variety of data related to their validity (Anastasi, 1988). Although they have been correlated with other measures, including the Stanford-Binet and academic achievement, for the most part there has been a notable lack of comparisons with behavior external to the scales themselves. This is despite the belief that many significant areas of a person's functions, such as adaptive behavior, are separate (but related) constructs (Keith, Fehrmann, Harrison, & Pottebaum, 1987). In particular, the meanings associated with subtest scores should be investigated in far more depth. For example, Picture Completion has traditionally been considered to be a measure of a person's ability to distinguish relevant from irrelevant details in his or her environment, yet this assumption has not been adequately tested. Likewise, no studies have been made to determine if high or low Digit Span scores relate to actual day-by-day behaviors, such as recalling telephone numbers, facility with computer programming sequences, or following directions that have been given to the person.

THE MEANING OF I.Q. SCORES

Since only a weak and vague relation exists between theories of intelligence and the tests themselves, it is important for all persons involved with testing to understand the meaning of I.Q. scores. Untrained persons are particularly likely to misinterpret I.Q. scores, which may result in poor decisions or negative attitudes related to the client. The meaning of I.Q. scores can be partially clarified by elaborating on some of the more common misinterpretations. I.Q. is often incorrectly believed to be fixed, unchangeable, and innate. To the contrary, I.Q. measurement is subject to a wide variety of environmental influences. Second, I.Q. scores are not exact, precise measurements; rather, they are estimates in which there is an expected range of fluctuation between one performance and the next. Furthermore, such tests as the Wechsler scales measure only a limited range of abilities, and a large number of variables usually considered to be "intelligent" are beyond the scope of most intelligence tests. No test or battery of tests can ever give a complete picture; rather, they assess various areas of functioning. In summary, an I.Q. is an estimate of a person's current level of functioning as measured by the various tasks required in a test.

An assumption of any global I.Q. score is that it derives from a wide array of interacting abilities. For example, a subtest such as Information assesses the specific area of a person's range of knowledge and is related to general intelligence. It is also influenced by achievement orientation, curiosity, culture, and the person's interests. More general prerequisites are that the client must comprehend what has been requested, follow directions, provide a response, and understand English. Factors such as persistance and drive are also likely to influence any type of task presented to the person. The tasks included in I.Q. tests are those, based on judgments by psychometrists, most valued by Western society. In other words, they relate to and are predictive of relevant skills outside of the testing situation. It is certainly possible to test a much wider range of areas (as in Guilford's Structure of Intelligence), but many of these would be of little relevance to the practical aspects of work and academic achievement.

Despite the many relevant areas measured by I.Q. tests, practitioners need to observe some humility when making predictions based on them. Gregory (1987) has pointed out that many persons with quite average I.Q.s achieve little or nothing. Having a high I.Q. is in no way a guarantee of success, but merely means that one important condition has been met. In contrast, persons with relatively low I.Q.s will have more severe limitations placed on them. As a result of their relatively narrower range of options, predictions regarding their behavior tend to be more accurate.

Regardless of the I.Q. range a person is in, clinicians should be clear regarding the likely band of error. Statistically this can refer to the standard error of measurement that is provided for the different WISC-R and WAIS-R I.Q.s (see Appendixes A and B). It is often useful to include the standard error of measurement into a report. For example, the WAIS-R Full Scale I.Q. has an average standard error of measurement of 2.53. Thus, a particular I.Q. will have a 95% chance of being within ± 5 I.Q. points of a person's obtained I.Q. Error can also be the result of unforeseen events beyond the context of I.Q. tests. Even though approximately 75% of the variance of children's academic success is dependent on nonintellectual factors (persistence, personal adjustment, curiosity), most of a typical assessment is spent evaluating I.Q. Some of these nonintellectual areas might be quite difficult to assess and others might even be impossible to account for. For example, a student might unexpectedly develop an excellent relationship with a teacher, which results in transforming his or her attitude toward school and stimulates his or her interest to passionately pursue a specific area. Thus, any meaning attached to an I.Q. score should acknowledge the possible effects of uncertainty both within the measurement itself as well as from the wider context of the person's life.

Another important aspect of I.Q. is the statistical meaning of the different scores. Binet originally conceptualized intelligence as the difference between a person's mental age and his or her chronological age. This was found to be inadequate and has been replaced by the use of the deviation I.Q. The assumption behind the deviation I.Q. is that intelligence falls around a normal distribution (see Figure 5–3). The interpretation of an I.Q. score, then, is straightforward in that it gives the relative position of a person compared with his or her age-related peers. The I.Q. can thus be expressed in deviation units away from the norm. Each of the three Wechsler I.Q.s (Full Scale, Verbal, Performance) has a mean of 100 and a standard deviation of 15. Scores also can be easily translated into percentile equivalents. For example, an I.Q. of 120 is $1\frac{1}{3}$ standard deviations above the mean and places an individual in the ninety-first percentile (see Appendix C). Thus, this person's performance is better than 91% of his or her age-related peers. The I.Q. cutoff for mental retardation is 70, which indicates that such individuals are functioning in the lower 2% when compared with their age-related peers. Appendix C can be used to convert Wechsler I.Q. scores (M = 100, SD = 15) into percentile rankings.

A final consideration is the different classifications of intelligence. Table 5–1 lists commonly used diagnostic labels and compares them with I.Q. ranges and percentages. These terms are taken from the 1981 WAIS-R manual and the designations for high average, low average, and mentally retarded correspond to the earlier 1955 WAIS manual terms of bright normal, dull normal, and mental defective, respectively. Thus, an I.Q. can be

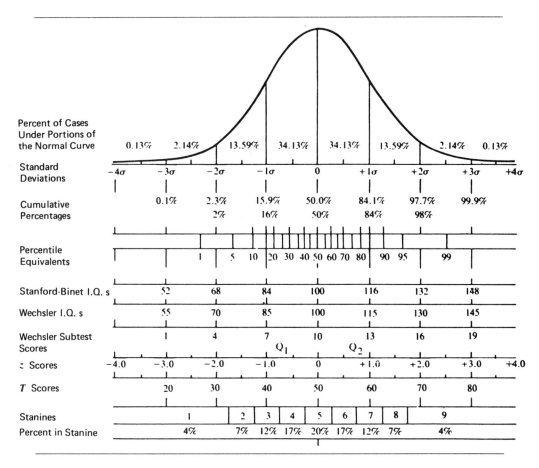

Figure 5–3. Relationship of Wechsler scores to various types of standard measures

Table 5–1. Intelligence classifications

| I.Q. | CLASSIFICATION | PERCENT INCLUDED | |
		THEORETICAL NORMAL CURVE	ACTUAL SAMPLE
130 and above	Very Superior	2.2	2.6
120–129	Superior	6.7	6.9
110–119	High average	16.1	16.6
90–109	Average	50.0	49.1
80–89	Low average	16.1	16.1
70–79	Borderline	6.7	6.4
69 and below	Mentally retarded	2.2	2.3

Note: From Wechsler (1981, p. 28). Reproduced, by permission, from the *Wechsler Adult Intelligence Scale—Revised Manual.* Copyright © 1981 by The Psychological Corporation. All rights reserved.

expressed conceptually as an estimate of a person's current level of ability, statistically as a deviation score which can be transformed into percentile equivalents, and diagnostically using common terms for classification.

INTERPRETATION PROCEDURES

Sattler (1988) has recommended the following successive-level approach to interpreting Wechsler scores. This approach provides the clinician with a sequential, six-step format for working with and discussing a person's performance. Later in this chapter, a listing and brief discussion of the more frequently encountered interpretive hypotheses will be provided. This later section can serve as a summary and quick reference for clinicians, especially in analyzing test profiles (levels II, III, and IV).

Level I—The Full Scale I.Q.

An examinee's Full Scale I.Q. should be considered first since it provides the basis and overall context for evaluating other cognitive abilities. It is generally the single most reliable and valid score. The Full Scale I.Q. score gives the person's relative standing in comparison with his or her age-related peers and provides a global estimate of his or her overall mental abilities. It is often useful to transform the Full Scale I.Q. into a percentile rank (see Appendix C) or intelligence classification (see Table 5–1). This is especially important when relating test results to untrained persons since both percentile rank and intelligence classifications are usually less subject to misinterpretation than I.Q. scores. Many examiners also prefer to include the standard error of measurement (SEM) as an estimate of the confidence that can be placed in the obtained score. For example, a WAIS-R Full Scale I.Q. of 110 has a 95% probability of falling between 105 and 115 I.Q. points (see Appendixes A and B).

Level IIa—Verbal and Performance I.Q.s

The second step is to consider the Verbal and Performance I.Q.s, especially the relative difference between them. The Verbal I.Q. is an index of a person's verbal comprehensive abilities, while the Performance I.Q. provides an estimate of his or her perceptual organizational abilities. However, clinicians should be aware that a pure test of verbal comprehension or perceptual organization does not exist. For example, a seemingly simple task, such as repeating numbers, involves not only verbal comprehension but also adequate rapport, ability to concentrate, number facility, and adequate short-term memory. If there is a wide discrepancy between verbal and performance I.Q.s, then an explanation for the reason for these differences should be developed. As with the Full Scale I.Q., it may also be helpful to convert the Verbal and Performance I.Q. scores into percentile rankings.

One area of difficulty (and controversy) lies in deciding what should be considered an interpretable difference between Verbal and Performance scores. In terms of statistical significance, a 9-point difference is significant at the .15 level, 12 points at the .05 level, and a 15-point difference is significant at the .01 level. Thus, a difference of 15 points or greater should be investigated further. It should still be noted that a full 25% of the WISC–R (and 20% of the WAIS–R) standardization samples obtained a Verbal/Performance difference of 15 points or greater (Grossman, 1983; Kaufman, 1976a, 1979). This means that, although a 15-point difference is statistically significant, it is still a fairly common occurrence. The difference, then, may represent merely useful information rather than "lurking pathology"

(Gregory, 1987). The possibility of pathology is far more likely with a 25-point or more difference.

Sattler (1988) has summarized the possible interpretations associated with significant Verbal/Performance differences as relating to cognitive style, patterns of interests, sensory deficits, pyschopathology (such as emotional disturbance or brain damage), deficiencies or strengths in information processing, or deficiencies or strengths in ability to work under pressure. Further specific interpretations related to the direction of the difference (Verbal versus Performance being relatively higher) are included under the sections on Verbal and Performance Scales and in the discussions of special populations. In addition, Appendix F provides implications and instructional recommendations for high and low scores (for Full Scale, Verbal, and Performance I.Q.s, and Freedom from Distractability). Any interpretations relating to Verbal/Performance discrepancies should be made taking a person's demographics into account. In particular, persons from higher socioeconomic backgrounds or with higher I.Q.s are likely to have verbal scores significantly higher than their performance scores (Bornstein, Suga, & Prifitera, 1989). In contrast, unskilled workers are more likely to have higher performance scores relative to verbal. If these trends are reversed (i.e., an attorney with higher performance scores), then the importance of that result becomes greater.

Level IIb—Factor Scores

An alternative to interpreting Verbal/Performance differences is to consider the meaning associated with factor scores. The factor structure of the Wechsler scales has been controversial, with different researchers coming up with somewhat different numbers and types of factors. However, most authors refer to Verbal Comprehension, Perceptual Organization, and Freedom from Distractability (see Gregory, 1987; Kaufman, 1975, 1979; Leckliter et al., 1986; Nagleiri & Kaufman, 1983; and Sattler, 1988).

The *Verbal Comprehension* factor on both the WAIS-R and WISC-R is comprised of Information, Similarities, Vocabulary, and Comprehension, and represents a somewhat purer measure of verbal abilities than the Verbal scale itself. The *Perceptual Organization* factor is likewise a somewhat purer measure of perceptual abilities and, on the WISC-R, is comprised of Picture Completion, Picture Arrangement, Block Design, and Object Assembly. On the WAIS-R, Picture Completion, Block Design, and Object Assembly comprises Freedom from Distractability but, unlike the WISC-R, Picture Arrangement is not included. Perceptual Organization has been found to be least related to educational level on the WAIS–R (Kaufman, McLean, & Reynolds, 1988).

The *Freedom from Distractability* factor, a more complex and controversial construct, has been extensively studied with children but only minimally with adults. It is comprised of Arithmetic, Digit Span, and Coding on the WISC-R. The WAIS-R subtests of Arithmetic and Digit Span are likewise related to Freedom from Distractability, but Digit Symbol has only been found to be related for certain age groups (18 to 19 and 45 to 54; Parker, 1983a). This means interpretations for adults should be made with somewhat more caution.

Freedom from Distractability has primarily been related to concentration, attention, and memory but is believed to be effected by poor number facility, anxiety, ability to make mental shifts, and skill at self-monitoring. Bannatyne (1971, 1974) has stressed the importance of sequencing since each of the relevant subtests requires that the respondent place numbers/symbols in proper order. A low Freedom from Distractability factor is also likely to lower performances in other areas, and this should be taken into account when estimating the person's overall potential.

The relative magnitude of differences between the factor scores can be calculated by finding the mean subtest scores for each group of subtests related to the different factors. There is some subjectivity involved in this process, but a general rule is to consider that one scale score standard deviation is generally three points. Thus, a difference of six points could be considered to occur infrequently. More precise procedures and several useful tables have been provided by Sattler (1988). Appendix F includes possible interpretive and instructional implications for high and low factor scores. Factor scores can be used for interpreting a person's relative strengths and weaknesses but should not be reported in the same formal way as the Full Scale, Verbal, and Performance I.Q.s.

Level III—Subtest Variability within Scales

The third step is to consider the degree to which the individual subtests deviate from the verbal or performance scale means and to make comparisons between the different subtests. The outcome should be a description of a person's relative cognitive strengths and weaknesses. A listing and discussion of the meaning of each subtest and the abilities it measures is provided in the next section of this chapter. Clinicians can refer to this section—as well as to information on how to assess special populations—in order to develop their own hypotheses about important dimensions of intersubtest scatter. Readers may also wish to refer to Sattler (1988), who has provided a detailed list of hypotheses for various combinations of high and low subtest scores.

The varying performance on subtests can occur for many reasons, and the clinician must determine which of these reasons is most accurate. This can be accomplished not only by referring to the skills involved in each subtest, but also by making careful behavioral observations and testing the limits of an examinee's abilities. For example, a clinician may speculate that a person scored low on Block Design due to poor spatial abilities. If this was the case, it would be expected that his or her arrangement of blocks would be poor, perhaps characterized by rotations. On the other hand, if the clinician had tested the limits and observed that the individual could complete the task if given enough time, then the poor performance would be more the result of slow spatial problem solving skills rather than an actual inability to perform.

The interpretation of subtest variability (profile analysis) is one of the more complex and controversial areas of Wechsler scale interpretation. One of the most important strategies is to account for the implications of the mostly modest reliabilities associated with the different subtests. This means each clinician needs to seriously consider whether the variability is due to a reliably measured strength or weakness, or merely due to the error inherent in the subtest. This issue has caused some authors to question whether profile analysis should even be undertaken (Hanson, Hunsley, & Parker, 1988; Ziskin & Faust, 1988).

At the center of this controversy is the importance of determining what should be considered a significant deviation (Matarazzo, Daniel, Prifitera, & Herman, 1988; Piedmont, Sokolove, & Fleming, 1989a, 1989b). Silverstein (1982) has provided tables for the WAIS-R (also reproduced in Gregory, 1987) that take into account each subtest's relative reliability (and therefore, band of error). For example, the WAIS-R Vocabulary, with a high reliability of .96, would only need to deviate by a scaled score of 2.2 to achieve a .01 level of significance. In contrast, Object Assembly, with a relatively low reliability of .68, would need to have a much larger deviation of 4.8 scaled scores to achieve the same .01 level of significance. A rough estimate of the band of error for each subtest can be obtained by consulting the data on reliability and the standard error of measure found in Appendix A (for the WISC-R) and Appendix B (for the WAIS-R). Kaufman (1979) recommends the following less rigorous and simpler approach:

1. Average all the scaled scores for the Verbal subtests.

2. If a subtest is three or more subscale points below the mean Verbal subtests, it should be labeled as a relative weakness.

3. If a subtest is three or more subscale points above the mean Verbal subtests, it should be labeled as a relative strength.

4. Steps 1, 2, and 3 should be repeated for the Performance subtests. If no deviations occur within either the Verbal or Performance scales, then no interpretations need to be made. In some cases, it may not be possible to make a profile analysis.

5. Examine all strengths and weaknesses to determine possible commonalities and differences. Integrate this information to form more clear, congruent hypotheses. This will often require a thorough study and knowledge relating to each of the meanings associated with the different subtests.

The above procedure should be undertaken with an awareness of its inherent limitations. Clinicians need to take into account the implications of the possible band of error of the subtests and be cautious regarding those with relatively low reliabilities. This cautiousness is particularly important for Object Assembly (r = .68) and Picture Arrangement (r = .74) on the WAIS-R, and for Object Assembly (r = .70), Coding (r = .72), and Mazes (r = .72) on the WISC-R. It should further be noted that, similar to Verbal/Performance discrepancies, a fairly high range (number of total subscale scores between highest and lowest subtest) is a fairly common occurrence. The *average* range on the WISC-R is seven points (SD = 2.1) for the Full Scale, four points for the Verbal Scale, and five points for the Performance Scale (Kaufman, 1976b). A full two-thirds of the standardization sample had subscales that ranged from five to nine points. Similarly, a subtest range of nine points on the WAIS-R Full Scale (and seven points on the Verbal and Performance Scales) was not unusual (Matarazzo et al., 1988). Persons with low obtained I.Q.s were less likely to have a high amount of subtest scatter than persons with a high I.Q. Thus, the diagnostic significance would be greater for low I.Q. persons who have a high amount of subscale scatter. However, a high range may merely indicate cognitive style rather than pathology or exceptionality. The criteria for an unusually high range is seven points for the Verbal subtests, nine points for the Performance subtests, and ten if the comparison is made for the total highest and lowest subtests used to calculate the Full Scale I.Q. It should also be noted that the above procedure (Steps 1 to 5) makes comparisons relative *only* to the clients themselves. Clinicians who wish to make profile analysis comparisons with the standardization sample will need to take this into account and, when appropriate, use age-corrected conversions (for the WAIS-R).

Level IV—Intersubtest Variability

Rather than investigate the deviation of subtests from within the Verbal and Performance scales, examiners might wish to compare intersubtest variability throughout all the subtests that were given. A procedure similar to that used for Level III interpretations can be followed, except that subtests are compared with a mean derived from the total subtests administered. Note that the range is likely to be somewhat higher (see Level III). In addition, all the cautions that apply to Level III interpretations also apply at Level IV.

Level V—Intrasubtest Variability

A further, important area of analysis involves looking at the patterns of performance found within the items of each subtest. These items are arranged in sequences that become progressively more difficult. Thus, a normal and expected pattern would be for the examinee to pass the initial items and slowly but evenly begin to fail more difficult ones. A more sporadic pattern, in which the examinee misses initial easier items but passes later more difficult ones, may suggest an attentional deficit or specific memory losses. If performance is highly sporadic, the reason for this should be explored further. For example, clients might be consciously faking if they miss every other item, miss extremely easy items, and/or appear much more alert than their obtained I.Q. Sporadic performance might also be characteristic of brain-damaged patients with diffuse cortical involvement (Mittenberg, Hammeke, & Rao, 1989). An analysis of the intrasubtest scatter can thus provide a type of information different from that obtained by merely looking at the quantitative-scaled scores.

Level VI—Qualitative Analysis

The final step is to look at the content of responses, especially on Information, Vocabulary, Comprehension, and Similarities. The presence of unique, highly personal, or unusual responses can often suggest some important dimensions of an individual's intellectual or personality functioning. For example, some responses may reflect aggressive tendencies, concrete thinking, or unusual associations. A highly aggressive person might provide unusual responses on the Vocabulary item of knife, or a paranoid might provide rigid, cautious, and legalistic responses. Similarly, impulsivity might be suggested by persons who draw lines beyond the walls of the Mazes or by persons who say they would "yell" if they noticed a fire in a theater.

THE WECHSLER SUBTESTS

To interpret the Wechsler scales adequately, it is essential to understand the various abilities that each subtest measures. This section presents the different abilities involved in each of the 12 subtests, followed by a discussion of their relevant features, including the possible meanings associated with high or low scores.

Data on factor loadings presented for most of the subtests are based on the work of Kaufman (1975, 1979) for the WISC-R and research reviewed by Sattler (1988) for the WAIS-R. Summaries of reliabilities, standard error of measurement, and average factor loadings across all age groups for the WISC-R (Full Scale, Verbal, Performance I.Q.s and all subtests) can be found in Appendix A. A similar table can be found for the WAIS-R in Appendix B. Clinicians may wish to consult these tables to determine relevant information on standard error of measure and factor loadings that can serve as guidelines for profile interpretation, which could then be considered for inclusion in their reports.

In keeping with the overall approach of this book, any interpretations suggested in the discussion of the subtests should be considered tentative. They are merely beginning possibilities, and must be explored further and placed in a proper context. A further consideration is that no subtest is a pure measurement of any one intellectual ability; rather, each represents a combination of skills. It is important to emphasize that a low or high score on a specific subtest can occur for a variety of reasons, which the examiner must consider during his or her interpretation of the overall profile. This section will be most helpful only after practitioners are familiar with the subtest stimuli and administration procedure outlined in the WAIS-R and WISC-R manuals.

Verbal Scales

The Wechsler verbal scales assess an individual's proficiency in the following areas:

1. the ability to work with abstract symbols
2. the amount and degree of benefit a person has received from his or her educational background
3. verbal memory abilities
4. verbal fluency

The WAIS-R and WISC-R verbal scales are generally more subject to cultural influences, whereas the performance scales are considered to be somewhat more culture free. If an individual does significantly better (15 points or more) on the verbal scales compared with the performance subtests, this difference may indicate a number of interpretative possibilities, including a relatively high level of education, a tendency toward overachieving, psychomotor slowing due to depression, difficulty working with practical tasks, deficits in performance abilities, poor visual-motor integration, a slow, deliberate work style that results in relatively lower scores on timed tests (but higher scores on verbal tests), or a quick, impulsive work style resulting in relatively more errors on performance subtests.

Information:

Old learning or schooling
Intellectual curiosity or urge to collect knowledge
General fund of accumulated information
Alertness to day-to-day world
Remote memory

The Information subtest samples the type of knowledge that average persons with average opportunities should be able to acquire (Matarazzo, 1972). This knowledge is usually based on habitual, overlearned material, particularly in the case of older children and adults. Both Information and Vocabulary are highly resistant to neurological deficit and psychological disturbance (Blatt & Allison, 1968), and are two of the most stable subtests on the WAIS-R. Due to this stability, Wechsler referred to them as "hold" tests as opposed to "no hold" tests, which he theorized were more sensitive to deterioration and such situational variables as anxiety and fatigue (i.e., Arithmetic, Digit Symbol, Block Design). Furthermore, these subtests are both good measures of general intelligence and are highly correlated with educational level (Kaufman, McLean, & Reynolds, 1988) and WISC-R and WAIS-R Full Scale I.Q.s. The WAIS-R Information and Vocabulary subtests have also been found to predict college grade point average as accurately as well-established college aptitude tests (Feingold, 1983). Although performance on the Information subtest involves remote memory and alertness to the environment, it is only influenced to a small extent by conscious effort and is believed to be only minimally affected by such factors as anxiety. In order to score well, the individual must have been exposed to a highly varied past environment, have an intact long-term memory, and possess a wide range of interests.

A high score on this subtest suggests that the examinee has good long-term memory, cultural interests, strong educational background, positive attitude toward school, good verbal ability, and possibly intellectualization as his or her most frequently used defense mechanism. Low scorers may show superficiality of interests, lack of intellectual curiosity, cultural deprivation, or lack of familiarity with Western (primarily American) culture.

Digit Span:

Short-term memory or immediate auditory memory
Concentration and attention

Ability to shift thought patterns (from Digits Forward to Digits Backward)
Sequencing
Rote learning

Digit Span is considered to be a test of short-term memory and attention. The subject must recall and repeat auditory information in the proper sequence. Bannatyne (1974) has further described this as "auditory vocal sequencing memory." Correct responses require a two-step process. First, the information must be accurately received, which requires attention and encoding. Persons who are easily distractible have difficulty in this phase. Second, the examinee must accurately recall, sequence, and vocalize the information. Persons who can perhaps receive the information correctly may have difficulty at this phase because they cannot hold the memory trace long enough. Sometimes, the previous digit is forgotten as they are attempting to vocalize a present one. Whereas Digits Forward is a simpler, more straightforward task requiring rote memory, Digits Backward is more complex. The examinee must usually hold the memory longer and also transform it prior to making a restatement. Thus, a good performance on Digits Backward is likely to reflect a person who is flexible, can concentrate, and is tolerant of stress. High Digits Backward scores may also involve the ability to form, maintain, and scan visual mental images formed from the auditory stimulus.

Passive, anxiety-free individuals seem to do best on this test. It requires an effortless and relatively unhampered contact with reality, which is characterized by open receptivity to incoming information. Performance is greatly hampered by increased anxiety or tension, and the Digit Span subtest is considered to be the most susceptible to the effects of anxiety. In addition to Digit Span, the other two subtests that are sensitive to the effects of anxiety are Arithmetic and Coding (Digit Symbol). These three subtests are sometimes referred to as the "anxiety triad." Digit Span, along with Coding (Digit Symbol), is one of the most sensitive tests to brain damage, mental retardation, and learning disabilities (Mishra, Ferguson, & King, 1985).

Persons who score high have good auditory short-term memory and excellent attention, and may be relatively unaffected by stress and anxiety. However, it should be stressed, that just because a person has good short-term auditory memory for digits does not necessarily mean that his or her memory for more complicated information, such as music or verbally relevant information, will also be good. These more complex features of memory may have to be assessed by other means. Low scorers show a lack of ability to concentrate, which may be the result of anxiety or unusual thought processes. A large discrepancy between Digits Forward and Digits Backward can suggest the presence of an organic deficit, particularly if the overall backward Digit Span score is below scores for such tests as Information and Vocabulary. (See section on estimating premorbid I.Q. in the assessment of brain-damaged populations.) Whereas Digits Forward is more likely to be lowered by left hemisphere lesions, lowered Digits Backward is more consistent with right frontal involvement (Lezak, 1983; Swierchinsky, 1978).

Vocabulary:

General verbal intelligence
Language usage and accumulated verbal learning ability
Rough measure of the subject's optimal intellectual efficiency
Educational background
Range of ideas, experiences, or interests that a subject has acquired

The Vocabulary subtest is a test of accumulated verbal learning, and represents an individual's ability to express a wide range of ideas with ease and flexibility. It may also involve one's richness of ideas, long-term memory, concept formation, and language development. Vocabulary is noteworthy in that it is the most reliable verbal subtest (test-retest WISC-R = .86; test-retest WAIS-R = .96) and, like Information, it is highly resistant to neurological deficit and psychological disturbance (Blatt & Allison, 1968). Although the Vocabulary subtest holds up with age, it tends to fall off with those people for whom words are not necessary in order to adapt. Vocabulary generally reflects the nature and level of sophistication of one's schooling and cultural learning. Vocabulary is primarily dependent on the wealth of early educational environment, but it is susceptible to improvement by later experience or schooling. It is the least variable of all the subtests, and subtest scores below the Vocabulary level often imply a drop of efficiency in that function. Vocabulary is the best single indicator of general intelligence, with 64% of its variance accounted for by g on the WISC-R and 76% on the WAIS-R. Because of its high degree of stability, vocabulary is often used as an indicator of a person's intellectual potential and to make an approximate assessment of premorbid level of functioning. (See more precise method in section on assessing brain damage.)

The Vocabulary responses are similar to Comprehension and Similarities in that a qualitative analysis often provides a great deal of information relating to the examinee's thought processes, background, life experiences, and response to frustration. It is often important to explore incorrect responses to determine whether they were guesses, clang associations (i.e., "ponder" meaning "to pound"), concrete thinking, bizarre associations, or overinclusive reasoning. Even when a response is correct, a consideration of the style used to approach the word and specific content can be helpful.

High scores suggest high general intelligence, and indicate that the examinee can adequately recall past ideas and form concepts relating to these ideas. Persons with high scores have a wide range of interests and a good fund of general information. Clinical populations who score high on Vocabulary may use compulsive or intellectualizing defense mechanisms. Low scores suggest a limited educational background, low general intelligence, poor language development, lack of familiarity with English, and/or poor motivation.

Arithmetic:

Numerical reasoning and speed of numerical manipulation
Concentration and attention
Reality contact and mental alertness; that is, active relationship to the outside world
School learning (earlier items)
Logical reasoning, abstraction, and analysis of numerical problems (later items)

The Arithmetic subtest requires a focused concentration as well as basic mathematical skills and an ability to apply these skills. The skills required to complete this test are usually acquired by the time a person reaches junior high school, so that low scores are more likely to be the result of poor concentration. Arithmetic is likely to be more challenging and stressful than such tests as Information and Vocabulary both because the task itself is more demanding and because it is timed. Thus, persons who are susceptible to the disruptive effects of anxiety are likely to be adversely affected. However, examiners may want to establish whether the person simply lacked the necessary skills or rather had difficulty concentrating. This can be assessed by giving the person previously missed items a second time, but allowing them to use a paper and pencil without a time limit. Under these circumstances, persons with adequate mathematical knowledge who are distractible should be able to complete the items correctly.

Individuals from higher socioeconomic backgrounds, obedient teacher-oriented students, and persons with intellectualizing tendencies usually do well on this subtest. A helpful formula is that Information plus Arithmetic equals school achievement. Since numbers come from the outside environment, and create rule and direction, some individuals react rebelliously. This is particularly true for antisocial personalities. Histrionic personalities, who do not readily accept outside direction and generally refuse to take responsibility for their behaviors, may likewise do poorly. This is not to suggest that lowered arithmetic scores are diagnostic of these clinical groups, but rather that this lowering may at times be consistent with the way these individuals interact with their environment.

High scorers show alertness, capacity for concentration, freedom from distractibility, and may use intellectualizing defenses. Low scorers show poor mathematical reasoning, lack of capacity to concentrate, and distractibility. A poor educational background in which adequate mathematical skills have not been developed can also account for lowered performance.

Comprehension:

Social judgment, common sense, or judgment in practical social situations

Grasp of one's social milieu; for example, information and knowledge of moral codes, social rules, and regulations

Ability to evaluate past experience; that is, proper selection, organization, and emphasis of facts and relationships

Reality awareness, understanding, and alertness to the day-to-day world

Abstract thinking (later items only)

Comprehension has often been considered to reflect the extent to which an examinee adheres to conventional standards, has benefited from past cultural opportunities, and has a well-developed conscience. This is somewhat supported in that Comprehension (and Picture Arrangement) have been found to be related to measures of social intelligence on the CPI (Sipps, Berry, & Lynch, 1987). In contrast, Nobo and Evans (1986) did not find Comprehension (or Picture Arrangement) to be related to introversion, social adroitness, conformity, or social self-esteem. Comprehension is also, at least in part, a test of information, which is supported by its high correlation (low- to mid-70s, depending on age) with the Information and Vocabulary subtests. Comprehension involves an adaptive response by the individual to a situation that requires him or her to select the most efficient way of dealing with a specific problem. The examinee not only must possess relevant information but must appropriately use this information for decision making. In this sense, the Comprehension subtest goes one step beyond the degree of complexity and synthesis required for the Information subtest. The examinee must not only have the necessary information, but must apply it in a coherent, problem-oriented manner. Thus, a Comprehension score significantly below the Information score suggests that an examinee is not effectively using his or her knowledge.

In assessing an examinee's responses, it can be important to distinguish between actually dealing with the material to develop an original response and merely repeating overlearned concepts. For example, parroting answers to "forest" or "bad company" does not indicate full comprehension and may simply be based on past experience rather than on accurate problem solving or good judgment. Thus, basic rule-of-thumb answers can significantly increase the total number of correct responses. However, in the later items, a correct response requires higher-level problem solving, and these items, therefore, can still be a good measure of general intelligence instead of merely rote memorization.

Personality variables, especially those relating to judgment, are important areas to consider in this subtest. Thus, clinicians should note the pattern of responses, cliches, literalness, and any circumscribed responses. Good judgment involves the ability to engage in discriminative activity. Failure on the easy items indicates impairment of judgment, even though later, more difficult ones are passed. It is important to note emotional implications on this subtest since emotional responsiveness influences the way in which a person evaluates environmental events. For example, individuals who are highly analytical and use these analytical abilities to avoid emotions may have difficulty understanding the social components of situations as presented in Comprehension.

High scorers show reality awareness, capacity for social compliance, good judgment, and emotionally relevant use of information. Low scorers, especially if they have four subscale points or more below Vocabulary, might have poor judgment, impulsiveness, and hostility against their environment (Weiner, 1966). Mentally disturbed persons often do poorly on Comprehension, which may be the result of disturbed perceptions, idiosyncratic thinking, impulsiveness, or antisocial tendencies.

Similarities:

Verbal concept formation or conceptual thinking
Logical abstract reasoning
Associative ability combined with language facility

The Similarities subtest requires verbal concept formation and abstract reasoning ability. These functions mediate for the individual an awareness of the belonging-togetherness of objects and events of the day-to-day world. An essential aspect of adjusting to one's environment is the use of these abilities to clarify, reduce, and classify the style and manner to which a response will be made. Inductive reasoning is required since the examinee must move from particular facts to a general rule or principle. Implicit in the test is the ability of individuals to use remote memory and to apply elegant expressions in their responses. The more precise and abstract the expression, the higher the score, which indicates that verbal fluency is an important determinant. However, correct responses to the last few items indicate a particularly high level of abstraction. Individuals with a good ability for insight and introspection tend to perform highly on this subtest; thus it may be used as an indicator of favorable prognosis for psychotherapy. Scores decrease significantly in schizophrenics, rigid or inflexible thinkers, and patients with senile conditions. Examiners can therefore use this subtest to gain further information regarding the nature of an examinee's idiosyncratic or pathological form of concept formation.

High scorers show good verbal concept formation, which, if unusually high, may reflect intellectualizing tendencies. Low scorers show poor abstraction abilities, literalness, and inflexible thinking.

Performance Scales

The performance scales reflect:

1. the individual's degree and quality of nonverbal contact with the environment
2. the ability to integrate perceptual stimuli with relevant motor responses
3. the capacity to work in concrete situations
4. the ability to work quickly

The performance subtests are generally less affected by educational background than are the verbal scales. If an individual does significantly better (15 points or more) on the performance scales than on the verbal subtests, this may indicate a number of interpretive possibilities, including superior perceptual organizational abilities, ability to work under time pressure, a tendency toward low academic achievement, possible acting out, an individual who could be described as a doer rather than a thinker, a person from a relatively low socioeconomic background, presence of a language deficit, poorly developed auditory conceptual/processing skills, or that immediate problem solving is better developed than problem solving based on accumulated knowledge.

Picture Completion:

Visual acuity; awareness of environmental detail; reality contact
Perception of the whole in relation to its parts; visual conceptual ability
Ability to differentiate essential details from nonessential details
Perceptual alertness and concentration combined with an ability to visually organize material

The Picture Completion subtest is a measure of visual concentration and is a nonverbal test of general information. It involves discovering consistency and inconsistency by paying close attention to the environment and accessing remote memory. It is dependent on, and also draws upon, an individual's experience with his or her culture. Thus, a person who is unfamiliar with common features of American society will often make errors due to a lack of experience rather than a lack of intelligence. A person will also make errors if he or she is unable to detach him- or herself emotionally from the material, thereby making accurate discriminations difficult. For example, passive, dependent personalities often make errors because they notice the absence of people controlling the actions in the pictures. Typical responses might be that "there's nobody holding the pitcher," "there are no people rowing the boat," or "there's no flag pole." Schizophrenic patients also make certain characteristic responses, such as responding to number 4 (playing card) with "the other 48 cards are missing" or to number 12 (crab) with "there's no scales" (Weiner, 1966).

High scorers are able to recognize essential visual information, are alert, and demonstrate good visual acuity. Low scores indicate poor concentration and inadequate visual organization. Impulsiveness can often produce lowered performance since the examinee may make a quick response without carefully analyzing the whole picture.

Picture Arrangement:

Accurately understanding interpersonal situations
Ability to comprehend a total situation and evaluate its implications
Visual organization and perception of essential visual cues
Ability to anticipate consequences of initial acts and plan ahead in social relations

The Picture Arrangement test is primarily a test of the ability to plan, interpret, and accurately anticipate social events within a given cultural context. Thus, an individual's cultural background can affect his or her performance on the test; normal subjects with poor or different cultural backgrounds often do poorly. Since many of the tests require subtle knowledge of American sociocultural values, the scores derived from persons of differing cultural backgrounds should be treated with caution. Wechsler (1958) has stated that the test requires an examinee to use general intelligence in nonverbal social situations. In fact, each of the items requires a person to respond to some practical interpersonal interaction. Solving the correct sequence also requires at least some sense of humor. However, interpretive caution should be exercised in that, even though Picture Arrangement has been found to be related to social intelligence on the CPI (Sipps et al., 1987), other authors have not found expected relationships using different measures of social functioning (Nobo & Evans, 1986; Ramos & Die, 1986). Both Picture Arrangement and Block Design are measures of nonverbal intelligence. However, Picture Arrangement is far more dependent on cultural variables than is Block Design. Picture Arrangement also requires the person to grasp or "size up" the complete situation before proceeding to a correct response. In contrast, persons can achieve good scores on Block Design by approaching the task in small segments and then contrasting their performance on each segment with the whole design.

Picture Arrangement is not usually sensitive to the effects of brain damage, although injuries that disrupt nonverbal social skills are likely to produce lowered scores (Lezak, 1983; Golden, 1979). An unusually low Picture Arrangement score in a protocol in which there is little difference between Verbal and Performance I.Q.s implies an organic impairment consistent with a static lesion to the right anterior temporal lobe (Reitan, 1974). More generalized right hemisphere lesions are likely to lower not only Picture Arrangement but also Block Design, and Object Assembly scores (Russell, 1979).

There are two approaches that can be followed to obtain additional qualitative information from Picture Arrangement. The first is to observe and record the manner in which the person attempts to solve the problem. Does he or she carefully consider the overall problem or rather impulsively begin altering the cards? Is he or she easily discouraged or does he or she demonstrate a high degree of persistence? Once the entire subtest has been completed, an examiner may also want to obtain projective stories relating to the pictures. This might be initiated by simply asking the examinee to "tell me what is happening in the pictures" or "make up a story about the cards." The cards that usually produce the richest information on the WAIS-R are 2, 8, and 10. The following questions are especially important: Are the stories logical, fanciful, or bizarre? Are they original or rather stereotyped and conventional? Do examinees reveal any emotional attitudes relating either to themselves or to their interpersonal relationships? Were errors the result of incorrectly perceiving specific details or rather of neglect in even considering certain details? Did the examinee consider all the different relationships in the pictures or were important aspects omitted?

Persons who score high in Picture Arrangement are usually sophisticated, have a high level of social intelligence, and demonstrate an ability to anticipate consequences of initial acts. Low scorers may have a paucity of ideas, lack of ability to plan ahead, poor sense of humor, difficulty in interpersonal relationships, and poor rapport.

Block Design:

Analysis and synthesis of spatial relations
Nonverbal concept formation
Visual-motor coordination and perceptual organization
Capacity for sustained effort; concentration
Visual-motor-spatial coordination; manipulative and perceptual speed

The Block Design subtest involves nonverbal problem solving skills due to its emphasis on analyzing a problem into its component parts and then reintegrating these parts into a cohesive whole. The examinee must apply logic and reasoning in a manner that will solve spatial relationship problems. As a test of nonverbal concept formation, Block Design demands skills in perceptual organization, spatial visualization, and abstract conceptualization. The Block Design subtest is sturdy and reliable, correlating highly with general intelligence, and is not likely to be lowered except by the effects of depression or organic impairment (Schorr, Bower, & Kiernan, 1982). To perform well, examinees must be able to demonstrate a degree of abstraction that is free from literal concreteness. They must also make a distinction between part and whole by demonstrating analysis and synthesis skills. This test involves an ability to shift the frame of reference while maintaining a high degree of flexibility. The examinee must be able to inhibit his or her impulsive tendencies and to persist in a designated task.

An important feature of Block Design is that it enables an examiner to actually observe the examinee's response. Some subjects are easily discouraged and give up, while others insist on completing the task even if they have to work beyond the time limit. In approaching the task, one might impulsively place the blocks together in a nonrandom sequence, whereas another subject might demonstrate a meticulously sequential style. Potentially valuable information can be obtained by observing and recording these differences in problem solving.

Block Design is also a nonverbal, relatively culture-free test of intelligence. It is reliable in that it correlates highly with general intelligence (approximately 53% of its variance may be attributed to g), but it has a relatively low correlation with education (.40 to .46). Thus, the Block Design subtest is only minimally biased by an examinee's cultural or educational background. Block Design scores can, therefore, be an important tool in assessing the intellectual potential of persons from divergent cultural and intellectual backgrounds.

High scorers show a capacity for visual-motor-spatial perception, a good ability to concentrate, and excellent nonverbal concept formation. Low scores suggest poor perceptual abilities, difficulties with visual integration, and problems in maintaining a sustained effort. These problems can sometimes be the result of cerebral impairment—especially right parietal lesions, but also right hemisphere lesions in general (Lezak, 1983; Golden, 1979).

Object Assembly:

Visual-motor organization

Synthesis; putting things together in a familiar configuration

Ability to differentiate familiar configurations

Manipulative and perceptual speed in perceiving the manner in which unknown objects relate to each other

Object Assembly is a good test of motor coordination and control, as are Digit Symbol (Coding) and Block Design. It measures the ability to differentiate familiar configurations, and also involves some anticipation and planning. However, scores are subject to a high degree of fluctuation, primarily due to the potential for accidentally fitting together parts. A further, but related, area that may create some confusion is that persons who are in the lower ranges of intelligence (60 to 75) sometimes do quite well, whereas persons with above-average I.Q.s can do quite poorly. Object Assembly is only a moderate measure of general intelligence (38 to 40% of its variance may be attributed to g) and is not highly correlated with Full Scale I.Q. scores (.56 to .65). Furthermore, its correlation with other subtests is generally low (.30 to .69) as is its reliability (.65 to .71). Thus, it is psychometrically one of the poorest subtests, and scores should be treated with caution. Sattler (1988) notes that it lacks a sufficient amount of subtest specificity for adequate interpretation of the test's underlying abilities. One advantage to Object Assembly is that, similar to Block Design and Picture Arrangement, an examiner can directly observe a person's problem solving style and reactions to success or failure.

The test presents an "open" situation, and those who can work freely within this context usually do well. However, those with rigid visual organizations will stick with one clue without allowing themselves to change their frame of reference. This process is often true of obsessive-compulsives. On the other hand, a flexible visual organization permits a rapid integration of new clues and an adaptation of these clues toward completing the task.

Persons scoring high on Object Assembly show good perceptual-motor coordination, have superior visual organization, and can maintain a flexible mental outlook. Low scorers show visual-motor disorganization, concreteness, and difficulties with visual concept formation. As noted, given the test's inadequate test specificity and low reliabilities, these interpretations should be very tentative.

Digit Symbol (Coding):

Visual-motor speed and coordination
Ability to learn an unfamiliar task; capacity for learning and responding to new visual material
Some degree of flexibility; ability to shift
Capacity for sustained effort, attention, concentration, and mental efficiency
Associative learning and ability to imitate newly learned visual material
Short-term memory

Visual-motor integration is implied by good performance on Digit Symbol. However, the most important function necessary for a high score is psychomotor speed. This test involves appropriately combining the newly learned memory of the digit with the symbol, as well as adequate spatial-motor orientation followed by executing the half-habituated activity of drawing the symbol. The subtest also requires the ability to learn an unfamiliar task, accuracy of eye-hand coordination, attentional skills, short-term memory, and the ability to work under pressure. This is a delicate and complex interaction, which can be disturbed due to difficulties with any of the above skills. Whereas Vocabulary is a highly stable subtest, Digit Symbol is extremely sensitive to the effects of either organic or functional impairment. In particular, depressed and brain-damaged patients have a difficult time with this subtest.

Whereas Coding has a high factor loading on Freedom from Distractibility on the WISC-R, its WAIS-R counterpart, Digit Symbol, has only a low Freedom from Distractibility loading on the WAIS-R. This means interpretations based on inferring Freedom from Distractibility on the WISC-R should include high or low scores on Digit Span, Arithmetic, and Coding, but, for the WAIS-R, should include only Digit Span and Arithmetic. Whereas Coding (WISC-R) is a poor measure of g (only 17% of its variance), its equivalent subtest on the WAIS-R (Digit Symbol) is a fair measure of g (40% of its variance).

Since visual-motor coordination—particularly visual acuity and motor activity—is implied, it is not surprising to find that those individuals with high reading and writing experience are among the high scorers. Functions that are implicit in the task are rapid visual, spatial, and motor coordination, as well as the executive action of drawing the symbol. Since this task requires sustained attention and quick decision making, anxious hesitancy and obsessive doubt significantly lower scores. Furthermore, persons who are extremely competitive but also become highly anxious in competitive situations may be adversely affected. Not only can Digit Symbol scores be lowered by anxiety, but the psychomotor slowing found in depressive states or the confused orientation of schizophrenics likewise produces a decrease in performance. Thus, a rough index of the severity of a person's depression can be assessed by comparing the relative lowering of Digit Symbol with other more stable subtests. Of particular significance is that Digit Symbol is one of the most sensitive subtests to the effects of any type of organic impairment (Lezak, 1983; Swiercinsky, 1978) and it tends to be one of the lower scores found in learning-disabled individuals (Bannatyne, 1974).

High scorers show excellent visual-motor ability, mental efficiency, capacity for rote learning of new material, and quick psychomotor reactions. Lower scorers show reduced capacity for visual associative learning, impaired visual-motor functioning, and poor mental alertness.

Mazes (WISC-R only):

    Planning ability or foresight
    Perceptual organization
    Visual-motor coordination and speed

The Mazes subtest is an optional portion of the WISC-R and is not extensively used. Its correlation with the Full Scale I.Q. is not especially high (r = .44), and it is also a poor measure of g (20% of its variance may be attributed to g). Mazes does provide an additional and often useful test, particularly with nonverbally oriented children or when a further assessment of planning, sequencing, and perceptual organization is required. Its main advantage is that it is a relatively pure measure of perceptual planning ability.

    Individuals with high scores have an efficient ability to plan ahead and maintain a flexible mental orientation, which further suggests an excellent ability to delay impulsive action (Glasser & Zimmerman, 1967; Ireland-Galman, Padilla, & Michael, 1980). Low scores reflect impulsivity and poor visual-motor coordination. Often, unusually low scores may suggest poor reality orientation or organic cerebral impairment, particularly to the frontal areas (Waugh & Bush, 1971).

ASSESSING BRAIN DAMAGE

The WAIS-R and WISC-R measure many abilities that are likely to be lowered by brain damage. These include memory, learning, perceptual organization, problem solving, and abstract reasoning. As a result, the WAIS-R and WISC-R have become one of the most important assessment instruments used in clinical neuropsychology. At one time, it was hoped that the WAIS-R/WISC-R, along with other more specialized psychological tests, could be used in the actual diagnosis of brain damage. Despite some noteworthy success in this area, it is currently more typical for psychological tests to be used in the assessment (and often localization) of the effects a known lesion is likely to have on a person's cognitive and adaptive functioning.

    During the earlier development of the WAIS and WISC, Wechsler (1958) hoped that brain damage could be discriminated based on relative lowerings in subtests that were most sensitive to neurological impairment. He referred to these brain-sensitive tests as "no hold" tests (Digit Span, Digit Symbol, Similarities, Block Design) and contrasted them with "hold" tests, which were believed to be far more resistant to impairment (Information, Object Assembly, Picture Completion, Vocabulary). Although the distinction between "hold" and "no-hold" tests has some truth, the use of such a distinction in diagnosing brain damage has been found to result in too many misclassifications. Vogt and Heaton (1977) have summarized the reasons for this lack of success by pointing out that:

1. there is no single pattern of brain damage, so it would be expected that highly variable test responses would occur

2. the "hold"/"no hold" distinction does not account for other significant factors, such as the age when the brain damage occurred, environmental variables, education, location of the lesion, and whether the lesion is recent versus chronic

3. many important abilities related to brain damage still are not measured by the WAIS-R or WISC-R.

More recent work indicates that there is no specific brain damage profile (Aram & Ekelman, 1986; Bornstein, 1983; Lezak, 1983; Todd, Coolidge, & Satz, 1977). Some persons with brain damage produce low I.Q.s, whereas for others, I.Q.s are still high. Sometimes there is a high level of subtest scatter and at other times the scores on the subtests are quite even. Some brain-damaged persons produce a high Verbal/Performance split and others do not. This is further complicated by the fact that a Verbal/Performance split is more likely to occur for males than for females (Bornstein & Matarazzo, 1982). Brain damage may cause a general lowering on all or most subtests and, at other times, there may only be a lowering of specific abilities. The most general indicator for the detection of brain damage is whether a person's scores (either general or specific) are lower than expected given his or her socioeconomic status, age, education, occupation, and other relevant areas of his or her history.

One of the older conventional wisdoms about brain damage is that left hemisphere involvement is more likely to lower the Verbal Scales, whereas right hemisphere involvement results in relatively lower scores on the Performance Scales. Reviews of this issue have shown that sometimes this laterality effect has occurred and at other times it has not (Aram & Ekelman, 1986; Bornstein, 1983; Larrabee, 1986). Probably the safest approach is that a Verbal/Performance split is not *diagnostic* of either brain damage in general or, more specifically, damage to one or the other hemisphere. However, a Verbal/Performance split (especially if 15 points or greater) can at times be *consistent with* this hypothesis. This is especially true if the Verbal/Performance difference is 25 points or greater. More specifically, a lowered Verbal Scale (15 points or greater) suggests the possibility of language impairment. Noteworthy subtests within the Verbal Scales are Arithmetic and Digit Span, which, if lowered, suggest difficulties with attending and concentrating. A Performance scale that is 15 or more points lower than the Verbal Scale suggests impaired perceptual organization abilities. Appropriate caution should be taken to avoid the risk of overinterpreting a person's results and to use further means of investigation including knowledge of health status, medical history, and additional specialized psychological tests.

Another frequent belief is that brain damage is more likely to lower performance than verbal tests. Some good reasons can be given to suggest this may be true. The performance subtests are timed and, since many persons with brain damage tire easily and have difficulties with concentration and attention, they would be expected to have a particularly difficult time with these tests. From a theoretical perspective, fluid intelligence is more tied to an intact brain structure and is also more clearly assessed by the ongoing problem solving tasks presented in the performance subtests. Thus, a destruction of brain tissue would be more likely to lower fluid intelligence, which would be reflected in lowered performance subtest scores. Although there is some basis for accepting the above assumptions, there are also many exceptions. More specifically, Russell (1979) found that left hemisphere damage caused a lowering in both WAIS performance *and* verbal subtests, whereas right hemisphere and diffuse damage resulted in the expected lowering in primarily performance subtests.

Many of the inferences related to brain damage depend on profile analysis. Useful material relevant to brain damage can be found in the discussion of Levels III and IV under "Interpretation Procedures" and in the relevant discussions on each subtest in the previous Wechsler Subtests section of this chapter. Interpretation is based primarily on the presence and extent of subtest deviation from other subtests. Much of this interpretation is an art, based on integrating knowledge about the person, brain function, Wechsler subtests, and past clinical experience. Often, no clear, empirically based guidelines exist. Inferences are accepted and rejected based on testing different hypotheses. Accuracy of any inferences are based partially on whether they make neuropsychological sense. However, one generally accepted principle is that intersubtest scatter is most likely to occur with focal lesions of recent origin. In contrast, general lowering of all abilities (low subtest scatter) is more likely with either chronic lesions or with diffuse degenerating diseases (i.e. Alzheimer's).

When the above cautions and principles are taken into account, clinicians can generate and test useful hypotheses developed from different patterns of subtest scores. The following summary provides a description of some of the most frequently supported hypotheses about specific subtests or patterns of subtests:

1. Digit Symbol (Coding) is the most brain-sensitive subtest and can be lowered by lesions in any location. A lowering implies difficulties with sequencing, rote learning, concentration (especially with lowerings in Digit Span and Arithmetic), visual-motor abilities, and speed of processing or speed of learning.

2. Block Design is highly brain sensitive, especially to either left or right parietal lesions (Golden, 1979; Lezak, 1983; McFie, 1960, 1969). A lowering implies visual spatial problems (especially combined with a lowering in Object Assembly) and possible difficulty in constructing objects (constructional apraxia; note quality of drawings).

3. Picture Arrangement lowering is consistent with right frontal and right temporal lesions (Reitan, 1974; Russell, 1979). It suggests difficulty with sequencing and nonverbal social judgment. In some cases, Picture Arrangement might also be lowered by left hemisphere lesions if there is a resulting impairment in following directions and/or conceptual skills.

4. Both Digit Span and Arithmetic are frequently lowered in brain-damaged populations, particularly with left hemisphere lesions (McFie, 1960, 1969). It suggests poor concentration and attention and, if Digits Backward is significantly lower than Digits Forward, a loss in mental flexibility and/or difficulty forming and maintaining a visual image of the digits.

5. Vocabulary, Information, and Picture Completion can generally be used as rough estimates of a person's premorbid level of functioning since they are usually unaffected by lesions, regardless of their location (McFie, 1969). An important exception is that brain-damaged children often score lowest on the Vocabulary subtest (Boll, 1974; Reitan, 1974). Picture Completion, although usually resistant to brain damage, might be sensitive to difficulties involving vision, especially visual agnosia (difficulty recognizing objects). Both Vocabulary and Picture Completion might also be lowered by expressive language difficulties.

6. Similarities is most likely to be lowered with left temporal lesions and suggests difficulty with verbal concept formation.

7. Qualitative responses on the subtests (even when the subtests are not lowered) can provide useful information related to brain damage. Some responses might suggest poor judgment and impulsivity, whereas others might indicate concrete thinking in which the person is bound by the stimulus value of the item (i.e. winter defined as "wet, cold" rather than the more abstract reference to a season or the "clang" response that "ponder" means "to pound"). Other persons might report they once knew the answer but have forgotten. Diffuse brain damage (but not focal) might also be consistent with a high degree of intratest scatter in which the client misses easy items but correctly answers later, more difficult ones (Mittenberg, et al., 1989). This suggests retrieval failure and/or the random loss of previously stored information.

This intrasubtest scatter is most likely to occur on Vobulary, Comprehension, Information, Similarities, and Picture Completion.

Neuropsychologists are frequently confronted with the need to make estimates of a client's premorbid level of functioning. This requires taking into account both factors outside the WAIS-R/WISC-R (previous work history, age, size of the lesion, etc.) as well as indicators from within the scales themselves. A very rough estimate can be obtained by considering the performance on tests most resistant to neurological impairment (Information, Picture Completion, and especially Vocabulary). These can be considered to reflect the person's past level of functioning. A related technique is to consider the person's two or three highest subtests (regardless of whether the subtests are brain sensitive or non-brain sensitive) and then use these as an estimate of the person's premorbid level of functioning. However, the above procedures are likely to result in a high number of misclassifications since they do not take into account such crucial factors as the person's age, educational level, or location of the lesion (Matarazzo & Prifitera, 1989). As noted previously, Vocabulary is frequently one of the lowest subtests for brain-damaged children and Picture Completion might be lowered by visual agnosia. Thus, always considering Vocabulary and Picture Completion as indicators of premorbid functioning can potentially result in incorrect inferences.

A more accurate and sophisticated technique for determining premorbid I.Q. is the Barona Index (Barona, Reynolds, & Chastain, 1984). It was developed through a stepwise multiple-regression procedure to create formulas that take into account a person's relevant demographic characteristics. The following formula can be used to estimate premorbid Full Scale I.Q.:

Estimated Full Scale I.Q. = 54.96 + 0.47 (age) + 1.76 (sex) + 4.71 (race) +
5.02 (education) + 1.89 (occupation) + 0.59 (region).

The specific codes to complete the formula are as follows:

age: 16 to 17 = 1, 18 to 19 = 2, 20 to 24 = 3, 25 to 34 = 4, 35 to 44 = 5, 45 to 54 = 6, 55 to 64 = 7, 65 to 69 = 8, 70 to 74 = 9

sex: male = 2, female = 1

race: black = 1, other ethnicity = 2, white = 3

education: 0 to 7 years of school = 1, 8 years = 2, 9 to 11 years = 3, 12 years = 4, 13 to 15 years = 5, 16 or more years = 6.

occupation: professional and technical = 6; managers, officials, proprietors, clerical and sales workers = 5; craftspersons and foremen (skilled workers) = 4; not in the labor force = 3; operatives, service workers, farmers, and farm managers (semi-skilled) = 2; farm laborers , farm foremen, and laborers (unskilled workers) = 1

region (U.S.A.): South = 1, North Central = 2, West = 3, Northeast = 4.

Barona et al. (1984) also provide formulas for estimating Verbal and Performance premorbid I.Q.s (also reproduced in Eppinger, Craig, Adams, & Parsons, 1987 and Gregory, 1987).

The following similar formula (Reynolds & Gutkin, 1979) was developed for use with the WISC-R:

Estimated Full Scale I.Q. = 126.9 – 3.65 (SES) – 9.72 (race) – 1.79 (sex) –
1.20 (residence) – 0.41 (region).

The specific codes to complete the formula are as follows:

SES: (based on father's occupational group): upper = 1, upper middle = 2, middle = 3, lower middle = 4, lower = 5

race: white = 1, black = 2, other = 3

sex: male = 1, female = 2

residence: urban = 1, rural = 2

region (U.S.A.): Northeast = 1, North Central = 2, South = 3, West = 4.

Reynold & Gutkin (1979) also provide formulas for estimating WISC-R Verbal and Performance I.Q.s.

Although the above formulas are likely to be more accurate than clinical judgment, they should be used with caution. Less accuracy is likely with either extremely high (above 120) or extremely low (below 69) I.Q.s (Barona et al., 1984) and the formulas are likely to over-estimate most premorbid I.Q. levels (Eppinger et al., 1987). Also, these formulas produce a relatively wide band of error (SEM = 12.14 for the WAIS-R and 13.50 for the WISC-R).

ASSESSING ADDITIONAL SPECIAL POPULATIONS

Learning Disabilities

Learning disability is a complex, loosely defined disorder with a wide variety of manifestations and many different theories regarding causation (see Houk, 1984; Mercer, 1983; Myers & Hammill, 1982; or Sattler, 1988). A central component of all definitions is that learning disabilities involve difficulties in developing skills in reading (most commonly), writing, listening, speaking, reasoning, or math. This is sometimes summarized as poor information processing. Further essential features are that learning-disabled persons have adequate intelligence, a significant discrepancy between achievement and intellectual ability, and the disorder is considered primarily intrinsic to the person, presumably due to central nervous system dysfunction. The underachievement cannot be primarily the result of an intellectual disability (mental retardation), brain damage, behavior problems, sensory handicaps, or environmental disadvantage.

The major purpose of learning-disability assessment is to identify a client's strengths and weaknesses in order to decide on an appropriate placement and to design an optimal program. Relevant areas to assess include developmental-cognitive processes, achievement skills, environmental demands, reactions of others to the client's difficulties, and the possible interaction of additional factors, such as fear of failure and overall level of interpersonal adjustments (Barkly, 1981). The WISC-R is typically considered essential as a means of identifying the client's overall level of functioning, specific cognitive strengths and weaknesses, and to eliminate the possibility of intellectual disability (mental retardation). Other tests are usually required—such as achievement tests, measures of adaptive behavior, visual-motor tests (Bender), and assessments of auditory and visual processing.

Considerable effort has been placed into searching for a specific WISC-R profile that is unique to learning-disabled populations. There is some evidence that many persons who are learning disabled have lowered performance on Arithmetic, Coding, Information, and Digit Span (the so-called ACID profile; Ackerman, Dykman, & Peters, 1976; Kaufman, 1979). A more refined and multifaceted approach is the use of Bannatyne's factors, which conceptualize learning-disabled performances as highest on subtests requiring spatial abilities

(Object Assembly, Block Design, Picture Completion) in which little or no sequencing is required (Bannatyne, 1974). Conceptual skills are intermediate (Comprehension, Similarities, Vocabulary), and subtests requiring sequencing abilities (Digit Span, Digit Symbol, Picture Arrangement) are lowest. Thus, their spatial abilities are believed to be greater than their conceptual abilities, which in turn are greater than their sequential abilities. Bannatyne used a fourth category, Acquired Knowledge (Information, Arithmetic, Vocabulary) as a rough index of the extent to which the person has accumulated school-related facts and skills.

Unfortunately, reviews and cross-validation of Bannatyne's factors have produced inconsistent results. Only some groups of learning-disabled students in some studies showed the hypothesized Spatial>Conceptual>Sequential pattern (Kavale & Forness, 1984). This is not surprising given the many different modes of expression found under the umbrella term of "learning disabilities." In addition, Bannatyne's pattern has not been found to be unique to learning disabilities, but frequently occurs in juvenile delinquents (Groff & Hubble, 1981) and emotionally handicapped children (Thompson, 1981). Despite the fact that only minimal support exists for Bannatyne's factors as a diagnosis for learning disabilities, they are far from useless. The four categories (Spatial, Conceptual, Sequential, Acquired Knowledge) can be invaluable for interpreting relative strengths and weaknesses both for learning-disabled persons as well as for other groups. While research has not been able to produce a "learning disabled profile," the research placed into this effort has resulted in a useful means of analyzing WISC-R profiles.

Intellectual Disability

Intellectual disability (mental retardation, developmental disabilities) is a nonspecific, heterogenous disorder that occurs during a person's early developmental stages (birth to 18 years). It is defined in large part as involving subaverage general intellectual performance, which in turn is defined as less than two standard deviations below average. Of at least equal importance are difficulties in adaptive behavior, and any assessment of intellectual disability must demonstrate that the person cannot deal effectively with day-to-day life problems. Although the disorder is heterogenous, there is consensus that it consists of two general categories. *Familial retardation* is caused by low genetic inheritance, poor environment, and possibly some organic factors. Persons with familial retardation constitute the upper realms of intelligence (50 to 69) among persons with intellectual disabilities and can be educated to varying degrees. *Organic retardation* is more severe (I.Q. less than 50) and is more closely associated with neurological impairment. Persons with this disorder typically require close supervision and extensive care.

A typical assessment battery for the diagnosis and assessment of mental retardation includes the WISC-R, achievement tests, and measures of adaptive functioning. Further information from interviews, behavioral observations, and medical records is also essential. An important purpose of a test such as the WISC-R is to establish the client's intelligence classification into one of the following categories described by the American Association of Mental Deficiencies (AAMD, 1973): Mild (69 to 55), Moderate (54 to 40), Severe (39 to 25), Profound (less than 25). Whereas the WISC-R can be successfully used in the assessment of the higher ranges of intellectual disabilities, it is not adequate for the lower ranges since the minimum WISC-R "floor" is 50. The WISC-R also cannot distinguish between brain-damaged persons and non-brain-damaged persons with intellectual disabilities. The most difficult subtests for mentally retarded persons are Information, Similarities, and Vocabulary (primarily the Verbal Comprehension factor), while the easiest subtests are

Picture Completion and Object Assembly (primarily the Perceptual Organization factor; Mueller, Dash, Matheson, & Short, 1984).

Gifted Children

Gifted children are frequently defined as having Verbal or Performance I.Q.s of 130 or higher. Children who have a single outstanding ability—such as in art, music, or math—are also frequently classified as gifted even though their I.Q.s may not necessarily be above 130. Although the WISC-R is frequently used to identify giftedness, the Stanford-Binet may be somewhat more effective since it has a higher ceiling than the WISC-R. However, neither may be particularly good if a single outstanding ability is used to determine whether a particular child is gifted. Additional assessment strategies for children should include samples of their work, achievement tests, rating forms, or designation by a highly qualified person.

An essential goal of assessing for giftedness is to optimize (rather than "normalize") the child's abilities so that a greater likelihood exists that the child will eventually make a significant contribution to society. This implies that the assessment will be able to recommend an appropriate placement and provide general guidelines for program planning. I.Q., in itself, is in many ways a limited definition of giftedness. Many persons with extremely high I.Q.s do not accomplish anything of significance. A high I.Q. (or outstanding talent in a specific area) is merely one of a variety of prerequisites. The interaction between internal motivation, discipline, and appropriate instruction are of equal importance.

Caution should also be used when using a test such as the WISC-R to assess gifted persons who demonstrate high creativity. Often, highly intelligent people are not particularly creative, which is supported by the low correlation between intelligence tests and creativity (Amabile, 1983). For such abilities as artistic or musical creativity, measures outside I.Q. testing may prove to be of greater importance. These might include a list of creative achievements, nomination by a qualified person, and specific tests of creativity.

Ethnic Minorities

Intelligence tests have frequently been criticized for being limited in assessing ethnic minorities. A detailed discussion of this issue is included in Chapter 2 (Use with Minority Groups). However, several additional guidelines should be noted. Often, it is essential to be familiar with the values and beliefs of the client's culture as well as relevant research. This is underscored by the observation that the degree of cultural difference between an interviewer and client has been found to be related to the amount of inaccurate perceptions (Malpass & Kravitz, 1969; Shapiro & Penrod, 1986). A clinician should determine which language is most familiar to the client and establish the extent and manner in which any language difference might bias the test results. Of related and equal importance is the degree to which clients have assimilated into the dominant culture. Directions and pronunciation should be particularly clear. The examiner also needs to pay particular attention to the importance of rapport and motivation.

Probably the most important strategy is to maintain a flexible attitude combined with the use of alternative assessment strategies. This strategy might include a variety of nonverbal techniques, such as the Draw-A-Person, Raven's Progressive Matrices Test, or emphasizing the Performance Scales on the WAIS-R/WISC-R. Material beyond merely tests should also have a greater significance (teacher reports, discussions with parents, history, behavioral observations).

Delinquency

Delinquent, acting-out persons usually score significantly higher on performance subtests than on verbal ones (Sacuzzo & Lewandowski, 1976; Wickham, 1978). In particular, scores on subtests that reflect academic achievement (Information, Vocabulary, and Arithmetic) are likely to be low, with difficulties in judgment often reflected by a lowered performance in Comprehension (Brandt, 1982). Although most verbal scales will tend to be lower, Similarities—which is a test of abstract thinking relatively independent of education—may still be relatively elevated. This pattern reflects the difficulty these individuals have in adapting and conforming to a structured academic environment, which results in a general lowering in tests that depend on an adequate assimilation of traditional academic information.

SHORT FORMS

Dozens of short forms for the WAIS-R and WISC-R have been developed to provide a more time-efficient means of estimating I.Q. Although time efficient, short forms tend to result in a loss of information regarding a person's cognitive abilities, produce a wider band of error than a full administration, result in a loss of clinical information, and are often of questionable accuracy when used to make intelligence classifications. However, short forms can serve appropriately as screening devices, which are best used when the purpose of evaluation is other than for intellectual assessment. The results can either be used as a rough indicator of intelligence, or as a basis for determining whether a more complete cognitive assessment is necessary. However, none of the short forms should be confused with a full intellectual assessment or even with a valid indicator of I.Q. (Watkins, 1986). For this reason, it is important to clearly specify on the report that a "brief WAIS-R/WISC-R" was given. If this is not specified, the I.Q. derived from the short form may be confused with a full administration and later decisions may be incorrectly based on the misleadingly described results.

The basic requirement for any short form is a minimum correlation of .90 with the full administration. Even at the .90 level, the band of error will be considerably wider than for an I.Q. derived from a full administration. Schwartz and Levitt (1960) calculated that, with a .90 correlation, two-thirds of the I.Q.s will fall within nine points of a person's actual I.Q. and a full one-third will be ten or more points away from the actual I.Q.

Most clinicians calculate short form I.Q.s by prorating the subtest scores. Unfortunately, prorating may produce error by failing to take into account the relative reliabilities of the different subtests that were used. Clinicians who wish to reduce this source of potential error for the WAIS-R might consult conversion tables developed by Silverstein (1982) and by Brooker and Cyr (1986). Similarly, Sattler (1988) has provided a formula for obtaining deviation I.Q.s from WISC-R short forms.

Best Two Subtest Short Forms

One of the most frequently used and conceptually sound two subtest short forms are for the administration of Vocabulary and Block Design. Length of administration varies from 15 to 17 minutes and correlations are generally in the .90 range (Brooker & Cyr, 1986; Hoffman & Nelson, 1988; Silverstein, 1982). In two-thirds of the cases, I.Q.s will fall within seven points of a person's actual I.Q., and one-third of the scores will have an error of eight points or greater. Conceptually, Vocabulary and Block Design are good tests to use since they are both good measures of g, are quite stable, and represent a sample subtest from both the performance and verbal scales. However, they may potentially underestimate the I.Q.s from blacks since these two subtests are typically their lowest scores (Kaufman, McLean, & Reynolds, 1988). If examiners wish to add a third subtest, the inclusion of Similarities, Information, Comprehension, Picture Arrangement, and Picture Completion have each been found to increase correlations into the low .90s (McNemar, 1974).

Best Four Subtest Short Forms

A frequently used tetrad is comprised of Vocabulary, Arithmetic, Block Design, and Picture Arrangement. Administration time is approximately 30 minutes and correlations with the full administration range from .93 to .95 for both the WAIS-R and WISC-R (McNemar, 1974; Silverstein, 1982). The above four subtests are usually excellent in detecting abnormal cognitive functioning (Ryan, Georgemiller, & McKinny, 1984). The inclusion of Arithmetic to Vocabulary and Block Design provides an assessment of auditory attention along with an important indicator of how effectively the person functions in the real world. Picture Arrangement provides information on a person's knowledge regarding sequencing and his or her relative perceptiveness regarding common social situations. However, an important caution is that any short-form combination of Vocabulary, Block Design, Arithmetic, or Picture Arrangement is likely to overestimate the I.Q.s of patients referred for neuropsychological evaluation (Roth, Hughes, Mankowski, & Crosson, 1984). Additional short forms using any four combinations of Vocabulary, Block Design, Arithmetic, Picture Arrangement, Information, Comprehension, Similarities, or Picture Completion are also likely to produce correlations in the low to mid .90s (McNemar, 1974).

The Satz-Mogel and Yudin Approaches

An alternative to administering various combinations of subtests is to use every subtest but limit the number of items used from within each of the subtests. The most frequently used variation is the Satz-Mogel (1962) approach, which was originally developed for the WAIS but has been more recently updated for the WAIS-R (Adams, Smigielski, & Jenkins, 1984). The procedure is to administer every third item for Information and Vocabulary and multiply the scores by three to obtain the scaled scores. Only odd items are administered for Similarities, Arithmetic, Comprehension, Block Design, Object Assembly, and Picture Completion and each score is multiplied by two to obtain the respective scaled scores. Full administrations are given for Digit Span and Digit Symbol. The entire procedure takes approximately 30 minutes and the derived I.Q.s have correlations similar to the best four subtest variations. A distinct advantage over four subtest variations is that the Satz-Mogel approach samples a wider range of areas. This is likely to increase the stability of scores over a wider variety of populations and also allows clinicians to develop inferences over a larger number of behaviors. For example, results of the Satz-Mogel and a full administration were comparable for an elderly demented population (Osato, Van Gorp, Kern, Satz, & Steinman, 1989). Intelligence classifications using the Satz-Mogel method have been found to be 93% accurate and 97% of I.Q.s are within 15 I.Q. points of I.Q.s derived from a full administration (Watkins, Edinger, & Shipley, 1986). A caution is that, even though a score is provided for each subtest, it is inappropriate to attempt a profile analysis since the individual subtests will not be sufficiently reliable.

A WISC-R equivalent of the Satz-Mogel approach was developed by Yudin (1966) and has the same advantages and follows a nearly identical procedure. The main difference is that Digit Span is not administered since it is an optional subtest, but Coding, like Digit Symbol on the WAIS-R, is given in its entirety.

Modified Format

A final approach is the elimination of early, easy items on each of the subtests. This is most appropriate for relatively bright subjects but should be used cautiously with persons of below-average intelligence. Cella (1984) has provided guidelines for the number of items to be omitted based on a subject's performance on the Information subtest. Such a procedure has been found to have an almost exact correlation (.99) with a full administration and yet can reduce the total administration time by 25%.

PROFILE FORMS

The forms in Appendixes D and E may be used to plot WAIS-R or WISC-R scores so that an individual's test results can be quickly and easily observed. The skills required for the 11 WAIS-R and the 12 WISC-R subtests are summarized on the far right side, and the scaled scores are plotted in the center. This provides persons reviewing the test results with a listing of the three I.Q.s as well as a summary of their relative strengths and weaknesses. However, this should be done cautiously due to the previously discussed difficulties with profile analysis. The profiles should clearly not be perceived as interpretations but as hypotheses that may or may not be confirmed by additional information.

INSTRUCTIONAL RECOMMENDATIONS

Once a WAIS-R or WISC-R has been scored and interpreted, an examiner must still develop practical recommendations. Appendix F gives the interpretive rationales, implications of high and low scores, and possible instructional recommendations for persons scoring low on either the Full Scale, Verbal, or Performance I.Q. sections. Appendix G has a similar format but enables a clinician to develop instructional recommendations (activities) for commonly occurring groups of subtests. Although these tables were originally developed for the analysis of children's (WISC-R) scores, a clinician can also utilize the recommendations for adult (WAIS-R) scores by developing tasks that are similar but somewhat more difficult.

RECOMMENDED READING

Gregory, R.J. (1987). *Adult intellectual assessment*. Boston: Allyn & Bacon.

Kaufman, A.S. (1979). *Intelligent testing with the WISC-R*. New York: John Wiley & Sons.

McLoughlin, J. A., & Lewis, R. B. (1981). *Assessing special students*. Columbus, OH: Charles E. Merrill.

Sattler, J.M. (1988). *Assessment of children* (3rd ed.). San Diego: Sattler Publishing Co.

Wechsler, D. (1974). *Manual for the Wechsler Intelligence Scale for Children-Revised*. New York: Psychological Corporation.

Wechsler, D. (1981). *Manual for the Wechsler Adult Intelligence Scale-Revised*. New York: Psychological Corporation.

Weinberg, R.A. (1989). Intelligence and I.Q.: Landmark issues and great debates. *American Psychologist, 44*, 98-104.

Chapter 6

THE BENDER VISUAL MOTOR GESTALT TEST

The Bender Visual Motor Gestalt Test, usually referred to as the Bender Gestalt Test or simply the Bender, is used primarily as a screening device to detect the possible presence of brain damage. It consists of nine designs that are sequentially presented to subjects, with the request that they reproduce them on a blank $8\frac{1}{2}$ x 11-inch sheet of paper. The subject's designs are then rated on their relative degree of accuracy and overall integration.

Although the Bender has most frequently been used as a screening device for brain damage, its research and clinical applications extend well beyond this area. Within child populations, it has been used to screen for school readiness, predict school achievement, diagnose reading and learning problems, evaluate emotional difficulties, study developmental disabilities, and has also been used as a nonverbal intelligence test (see review in Koppitz, 1975). For adults and adolescents, the Bender has proved useful in the diagnosis of brain damage (see Lacks, 1984; Marley, 1982) and as a projective test for the assessment of various personality functions (see Hutt, 1988; Oas, 1984; Rossini & Kaspar, 1987). Thus, the Bender, whose task appears simple at first glance, has given rise to a surprisingly diverse and flexible number of clinical and research uses. The diversity of the Bender and the amount of interest it has engendered have also resulted in a variety of administration procedures, scoring guidelines, and interpretation systems. Its popularity can be partially accounted for in that it is brief, economical, flexible, nonthreatening, nonverbal, and extensively researched.

HISTORY AND DEVELOPMENT

The Bender Gestalt Test was originally assembled by Lauretta Bender in 1938 and discussed in her monograph *A Visual Motor Gestalt Test and Its Clinical Use*. The nine designs were adapted from a set of 30 configurations developed by Wertheimer (1923), which he used to demonstrate the Gestalt laws of perception. Wertheimer emphasized the normal individual's ability to respond to the designs in an integrated and coherent manner. Bender developed this theme further and demonstrated how an individual's level of performance could be impaired by delayed perceptual-motor maturation as well as by either a functional or an organically induced pathological state. Bender's primary use for her test was to provide an index of perceptual-motor maturation, which could be inferred from the degree of integration reflected in the nine reproductions of the designs.

For many years after Bender's publication, the data derived from test administration was not reported in an objective and systematic matter. This made it initially difficult to evaluate the test's effectiveness. Many clinicians still use a subjective, intuitive approach, although several objective methods have made possible a more accurate and empirical assessment of the test's effectiveness. One of the earliest and most widely accepted scoring systems for adults was developed by Pascal and Suttell (1951). They viewed the approach the individual takes toward the test as a reflection of the person's approach toward his or her environment. They reasoned that the more adapted and adjusted individuals were, the more likely they would be to respond to the designs in a coherent, integrated manner. Conversely, individuals who lacked integrative capacities or who had poor emotional adjustment would do poorly. On the basis of matched samples of normals and abnormals, Pascal and Suttell were able to develop a scoring system with a mean of 50 and a standard deviation of 10. Test-retest reliabilities for normals over a 24-hour interval were approximately .70, inter-scorer reliabilities for trained examiners were reported to be .90 (Pascal & Suttell, 1951), and split half reliabilities were .70 (Wagner & Flamos, 1988). Some research has indicated that optimal cutoff scores were able to differentiate between normal, neurotics, and psychotics (scoring 50, 68.2, and 81.8, respectively), as well as to differentiate organics from both normals and psychotics (Tolor & Schulberg, 1963). The Pascal and Suttell approach is the most frequently cited system in research publications but has not received wide acceptance in clinical settings, primarily due to its relatively time-consuming and complex scoring procedures.

Starting in the mid 1940s Hutt began conceptualizing the Bender as a projective test that could be interpreted based on psychoanalytic principles. He also developed a set of stimulus cards that were slightly different from those published by Bender (1938). Hutt believed his set to be more representative of Wertheimer's original gestalt formulations. Hutt's set of cards were formally printed and made available to professionals in 1960 (Hutt & Briskin, 1960). His interest has primarily focused on using the Bender for projective personality assessment. He recommends administering the test in three different phases. Initially, the client is requested to copy the designs as they are presented (copy phase), then to elaborate on the designs by redrawing them in a way that is more pleasing (elaboration phase), and finally to describe what the designs remind the client of (association phase). The interpretation of the client's responses is based largely on clinical experience and accumulated clinical lore. Two objective scales have been developed to assess the global presence or absence of psychopathology (Psychopathology Scale) and the degree to which the person is open versus closed in his or her perception of the world (Perceptual Adience-Abience). The projective portion of the system has been criticized as unwieldy (20 minutes to score), having poor norms, applicable only to adults and adolescents with nine years or more of education, and possessing poor empirical support. Also, this portion of the system has difficulty discriminating chronic schizophrenics from persons with brain damage (Sattler, 1985).

Hutt (1960) also listed "12 essential discriminators of intracranial damage" (Fragmentation, Closure Difficulty, etc.) but did not provide substantial empirical verification. Lacks (1984) adapted Hutt's scoring categories and prepared a detailed scoring manual, which is included in Appendix H. Studies using her guidelines have reported diagnostic accuracies of from 64% to 84% with a mean of 77%, which is superior to the Pauker (1976) and Hain (1964) systems (Lacks & Newport, 1980). The Lacks adaptation also takes three minutes or less to score each protocol, but is limited to persons 17 years of age or older.

Although Pascal and Suttell—as well as Hutt—recognized the effects of maturation on the test of young children, they used young children's test results merely as a means of comparison with adult records and did not develop norms or scoring procedures for children. To correct this limitation, Koppitz (1963, 1975) developed a scoring system for children and carried out an extensive standardization of 1,104 children from kindergarten through fourth grade. Interscorer reliabilities were excellent (.88 and .96), although test-retest reliabilities over a four-month interval were somewhat low (.58 to .66). The correlations found between Koppitz's scoring method on the Bender and the WISC-R performance subtests ranged from –.51 (Block Design) to –.08 (Coding; Redfering & Collins, 1982), which suggests that the quality of Bender performance is moderately related to ability to perform well on Block Design but not on Coding. Moderate correlations (–.57) have also been found between the K-ABC Simultaneous Scale and Bender error scores (Haddad, 1986). Significant correlations have been reported between the degree of mental retardation and the number of errors (Andert, Hustak, & Dinning, 1978), as well as between first-graders' Bender scores and their level of performance in reading and arithmetic (Ackerman, Peters, & Dykman, 1971; Koppitz, 1958a). Koppitz (1963, 1975) reports significant differences between the scores of brain-damaged children and those of normals. However, she cautions that, for a diagnosis of brain damage, the examiner should consider not only the child's scores but also such additional observations as the time required to complete the test, the amount of space used, behavioral observations, and an inquiry into the relative degree of awareness the child has regarding his or her errors. The Koppitz system is designed for children since, after the age of 10, the scores no longer correlate either with intelligence test results or with age. After age 10, most individuals obtain nearly perfect scores. However, McIntosh et al. (1988) provided adolescent norms (ages 12 to 16) that suggest the Koppitz system can be used to distinguish normals and emotionally disturbed adolescents from those who are neurologically impaired and/or developmentally disabled. The Koppitz interpretive guidelines are summarized later in this chapter, and her manual for scoring children's protocols can be found in Appendix A of her book *The Bender Gestalt Test for Young Children* (1975). A simplified outline and scoring sheet are included in Appendix I to aid in scoring protocols using her system.

Hain (1964) developed an adult scoring method that was somewhat different from the Pascal and Suttell system. Whereas Pascal and Suttell approached the designs card by card and identified 106 different potentially scorable characteristics, Hain approached the test performance as a whole. By a careful and systematic study of the Bender protocols of brain-damaged patients, he developed a 15-category scoring system. Any example of a scorable characteristic would earn a ranked score for that category. For example, a rotation or reversal of a design would earn four points, whereas an omission (leaving out part of a design) would only score one point. The Hain (1964) system is somewhat brief (requiring less than three minutes to score) and easy to learn, yet Hain reports that it still correctly distinguishes approximately 80% of brain-damaged patients from psychiatric and other non-brain-damaged patients. However, subsequent studies of the Hain system have found relatively low rates of diagnostic accuracy (73%), a high number of false negatives (Pardue, 1975; Tolor & Brannigan, 1980) and a scoring system which produces less accurate results than either the Pauker or Hutt-Briskin systems (Lacks & Newport, 1980).

Numerous additional scoring systems (Jansky & de Hirsch, 1972; Keogh & Smith, 1961; Marley, 1982; Pauker, 1976; Plenk & Jones, 1967; Thweatt, Obrzut, & Taylor, 1972) have also been developed and have all met with varying degrees of success, popularity, and controversy (see Field, Bolton, & Dana, 1982; Lacks, 1984; McIntosh, Belter, Saylor, Finch, & Edwards, 1988; Tolor & Brannigan, 1980). The ones most frequently quoted in the literature are those by Pascal and Suttell (1951), Koppitz (1963, 1975), and Hutt (1969, 1977, 1985). However, all the scoring systems are similar in their attempt to rearrange, tabulate, and assign different weights to the same commonly occurring responses—such as lack of closure, perseveration, and rotations. Each system has various advantages and disadvantages, and none has yet become the dominant scoring method.

Despite a number of poor reviews and ambiguous research findings, the Bender has consistently been one of the four or five most frequently used tests. Lubin et al. (1985) found that, overall, it was the third most frequently used test, which is consistent with other studies on test usage dating back to 1969. This relatively high usage exists despite the fact that other, similar tests—such as the Minnesota Perceptual Diagnostic Test-Revised—are theoretically and psychometrically superior (Vance, Fuller, & Lester, 1986). A survey of the National Academy of Neuropsychologists found that the Bender was ranked fourth (used by nearly half the members), with the three highest-rated tests being the Wechsler intelligence tests, portions of the Halstead-Reitan, and the Wide Range Achievement Test. The extensive research and clinical interest in the Bender is also reflected in the fact that well over 1,000 studies were listed in the ninth edition of the *Mental Measurements Yearbook* (1985).

RELIABILITY AND VALIDITY

The Bender is similar to projective drawings and the Rorschach in that it cannot be considered a single unitary test. No agreed upon standard procedure exists for administration, at least eight different scoring systems are in use, the stimulus cards differ, and authors disagree about the purposes for which it can legitimately be used (Dana, Field, & Bolton, 1983). The dominant scoring systems are those developed by Koppitz (1963, 1975), Pascal and Suttell (1951), and Hutt (1985), and the most frequently used cards are those published by the American Orthopsychiatric Association. Almost all authors agree that the Bender can legitimately be used as a screening device for neurological impairment, whereas fewer authors agree on its use as a measure of intelligence, personality, psychopathology, maturational level, and as an index of treatment effectiveness. The above diversity complicates the evaluation of its psychometric qualities in that, ideally, the different scoring systems and the different uses must be evaluated separately rather than as a comprehensive unit.

Reliabilities across the different scoring systems have generally been acceptable. Test-retest reliability using the Pascal and Suttell (1951) system on a sample population of normals over a 24-hour interval revealed a reliability of .70. Test-retest reliabilities for the Koppitz (1975) system range from .53 to .90 (Mdn r = .77), depending on age and time between retesting. The test-retest reliabilities for the total-error score was .83, but reliabilities for specific errors (distortion, rotation, integration, perseveration) were too low to be dependable. Thus the major focus should be on the total-error score rather than the specific features of the reproductions. The Hutt (1985) test-retest reliabilities were .87 for the Psychopathology Scale, with a two-week retesting interval. Using the Lacks adaptation, test-retest reliabilities were .79 for protocols from neuropsychiatric patients, .66 for patients with Alzheimer's disease, and from .57 to .63 for older adults (Lacks, 1984). Retesting intervals ranged from 3 to 12 months (Lacks, 1984). Interscorer reliabilities have been consistently high, with the Koppitz method being in the range of .91 (Koppitz, 1975; Neale & McKay, 1985), and ranging from .98 to .95 for the 12 organic signs of the Hutt-Briskin system (Lacks & Newport, 1980).

Validity studies on the Bender have been controversial. Proponents of the Bender typically report positive validity studies, whereas critics—some of whom provide reviews of the literature—report negative findings. In many studies, the Bender has been able to demonstrate its ability to discriminate brain-damaged from non-brain-damaged populations (Hain, 1964; Lacks, 1984; Marley, 1982). Even though most authors agree that screening for brain damage is clearly the most legitimate use for the Bender, it has been considered ineffective when subtle neuropsychological deficits are present, such as among many epileptics (Delaney, 1982), or when a differentiation is attempted between functional psychotic patients and brain-damaged patients (Hellkamp & Hogan, 1985). The differentiation between brain-damaged and psychiatric patients has been found to be particularly difficult to identify when distinguishing severely disturbed chronic schizophrenics from brain-damaged patients. However, this distinction may be inappropriate given that schizophrenia is being progressively more conceptualized as an organically based disorder that may even be caused by an as-yet-unidentified lesion (Weinberger, 1987; Weinberger & Berman, 1988).

The validity of Koppitz's (1975) developmental system depends primarily on the purpose for which it is used. Validity is fairly good as an index of perceptual-motor development since error scores decrease with age, between the ages of 5 and 9 (Koppitz, 1963, 1975). Concurrent measures of visual-motor perception also suggest a moderate level of validity based on correlations with the Developmental Test of Visual Motor Integration (Mdn r = .65) and the Frostig Developmental Test of Visual Perception (Mdn r = .47; Breen, 1982; Wright & Demers, 1982). Correlations with intelligence and academic achievement have been low to moderate (Koppitz, 1975; Lesiak, 1984; Vance, Fuller, & Lester, 1986). Thus, it in no way can substitute for a formal intelligence test or a standardized test of academic achievement.

Whereas the use of the Bender in screening for brain dysfunction has been generally accepted, its use in personality assessment has been questionable. Clearly, single-sign indicators have rarely been found to be valid. For example, "edging" (consistently drawing the designs along the edge of the paper) has not generally been found to indicate personality variables (Holmes, Dungan, & Medlin, 1984; Holmes & Stephens, 1984). Likewise, projective interpretations that rely heavily on psychoanalytic theory and clinical lore have neither been generally accepted nor sufficiently validated (Sattler, 1985). However, global ratings that typically sum a series of indicators (size increases, collisions, scribbling, etc.) have been more valid indicators. For example, accurate discriminations have been made for impulsivity by comparing total scores for impulsive versus nonimpulsive indicators (Oas, 1984). Likewise, Koppitz (1975) has listed emotional indicators that have been found to be good predictors of the general presence of psychopathology when three or more are present (Koppitz, 1975; Rossini & Kaspar, 1987). Thus, the Bender has generally been found to be valid in the prediction of the absence or presence of psychopathology based on clusters of indicators rather than on single signs. With the possible exception of impulsivity and anxiety, the Bender is probably ineffective in identifying specific personality characteristics or specific psychiatric diagnoses.

ASSETS AND LIMITATIONS

The relatively fast and easy administration of the Bender has been a primary reason for its popularity. The Bender can usually be administered in three to five minutes and is an excellent way to initiate a testing session since it is typically perceived to be straightforward and nonthreatening. Furthermore, the test is flexible in that it can serve both as a projective test for studying personality and as a visuographic task for the assessment of organic impairment. In addition to these assets, most clinicians are familiar with the Bender, and it can also be used as a nonverbal developmental scale.

Although the research on the Bender has often been contradictory, it has been extensive. This enables researchers and clinicians to more clearly understand the Bender's psychometric qualities and clinical utility. The extensive research can potentially be a strong asset of the Bender. However, it is also possible for individuals to become lost in the sheer volume of studies and also possible for proponents of a particular position to selectively cite studies to support their position.

One basic assumption behind the Bender is that the manner in which subjects perceive and approach their world parallels the way they approach the task of reproducing the nine designs. Much of the validity research on the Bender has attempted to demonstrate that this parallel occurs. For example, disoriented patients might rotate the designs (Mermelstein, 1983), manic patients might produce irregular sequences (Donnely & Murphy, 1974) that reflect their impulsivity and attentional deficits, and the degree of anxiety the person is experiencing might influence the size of the drawings (Rao & Potash, 1985). Additional clinical information can be derived by observing anxious patients who might erase and retrace their drawings. Similarly, compulsives might begin their drawings by making extensive preliminary guidelines and often take three to five minutes to complete each design. Thus, the Bender can potentially be useful in revealing the general style and manner of approach the individual takes toward his or her world.

Although the Bender has a good track record of achievements, a number of cautions and limitations surround its use. The test has often been described as "assessing" brain damage, yet it is perhaps more accurate to say that it is a "screening" device for brain damage assessment. It does not provide in-depth information about the specific details and varieties of such damage. In fact, the Bender is limited to relatively severe forms of brain damage, especially in the right hemisphere—particularly the right parietal region (Filskov, 1978; Garron & Cheifetz, 1965; Hirschenfang, 1960). Thus, a patient may have significant lesions or subtle deficits that could easily go undetected if a traditional scoring of the Bender was the sole method used to assess the presence of cerebral impairment (Delaney, 1982). It is more correct to say, then, that the Bender is a screening device for generalized impairment and/or right parietal involvement. If more detailed information is required to assess left hemisphere deficits, subtle neurological dysfunction, or the nature of the deficits, then more specialized tests should be used—such as the Halstead Reitan or Luria Nebraska.

A certain degree of overlap often exists between emotional and organic indicators on the Bender, which adds to the risk of misdiagnosis. For example, one of the better indicators for organic impairment is the presence of rotations (Bender, 1938; Hain, 1964; Lacks & Newport, 1980; Symmes & Rapaport, 1972), yet moderate rotations, although less frequent, can also occur in the reproductions of psychotics or even neurotics (Billingslea, 1948; Fuller & Chagnon, 1962; Hutt & Gibby, 1970; Mermelstein, 1983). Likewise, line tremors are often present in the drawings of chronic alcoholics, particularly with Korsakoff's syndrome (Kaldegg, 1956; Pascal & Suttell, 1951), but these tremors may also reflect nonorganic causes related to the anxiety, tension, and pent-up aggression often found in adolescent delinquent populations (Oas, 1984; Pascal & Suttell, 1951; Zolik, 1958). The degree of overlap occurring in the scores of different populations has led some reviewers (Dana, Field, & Bolton, 1983; Sattler, 1985) to seriously question the clinical usefulness of the Bender. From a clinical perspective, this means an examiner must carefully consider and investigate all possibilities to determine why a subject produced certain types of responses on the test.

A further difficulty with the Bender is the absence of a commonly accepted and verified scoring and interpretation system. The result is that different research studies have often used different systems, which makes it somewhat difficult to compare their conclusions. Clinicians generally begin by learning a system of scoring and interpretation, but end up with their own unique, subjective approach based on clinical impressions (Robiner, 1978). Although this may result in a highly workable, flexible approach, disagreements between "experts" can occur due to their differences in approaching the designs. Another difficulty in depending on clinical impressions is continued, unwarranted reliance on unsubstantiated and possibly incorrect clinical "lore." Lacks (1984) has presented evidence to demonstrate that clinicians could increase their diagnostic accuracy for organic impairment on the average of 10 to 15% by using a brief, easily learned, objective scoring system.

When the Bender is used as a projective test, the same general criticisms that are true for any projective test are also true for Bender interpretations. These include a frequent—although often challenged—reliance on intuitive clinical guidelines, subjectivity of scoring, inadequate validation studies, test sensitivity to situational variables, and reliance on unsubstantiated psychoanalytic theory. Furthermore, projective approaches have often been subject to overinterpretation when clinicians use single signs as certainties rather than as hypotheses in need of further validation. Generally, composite ratings—such as the total number of emotional or impulsive indicators—have proven to be far more accurate. Also, global judgments—such as the presence or absence of psychopathology—have been found to be more accurate than attempts to make specific interpretations regarding personality. Thus, to maximize its utility, Bender results should be interpreted globally and be used in, and understood as, one test in an overall battery.

Despite its limitations, the Bender remains an extremely popular, easily administered, reliable, and frequently valid device for the clinician, particularly when an objective empirical method for scoring and interpretation is used. The most confidence seems to be in its use for screening for organicity (particularly severe and/or right hemisphere dysfunction) and in making global judgments regarding such areas as the presence of psychopathology or level of maturational development. The least confidence is in making specific personality interpretations (particularly when a single-sign approach is used), assessing for subtle or left hemisphere cerebral dysfunction, or differentiating between brain damage and severe forms of psychopathology.

ADMINISTRATION

When administering the Bender, the examiner presents the cards one at a time and the person is asked to copy each design with a number 2 pencil on a single, blank, $8\frac{1}{2}$ x 11-inch sheet of white paper that has been presented to the client in a vertical position. The following verbal directions are taken from Hutt (1977) and are recommended as a standard procedure:

> I am going to show you these cards, one at a time. Each card has a simple drawing on it. I would like you to copy the drawing on the paper, as well as you can. Work in any way that is best for you. This is not a test of artistic ability, but try to copy the drawings as accurately as possible. Work as fast or as slowly as you wish. (p. 64)

A somewhat simpler variation of the above instructions may be given to children. When the person has completed the design, the next card is presented. No comments or additional instructions are to be given while the person is completing the drawings. If the person asks a specific question, he or she should be given a noncommittal answer. For example, "Make it look as much like the picture on the card as you can." If the person begins to count the dots on figure 5, the examiner may say, "You don't have to count the dots, just make it look like the picture." If the person persists, this may show perfectionistic or compulsive tendencies, and the behavioral observation should be considered when evaluating the test results and formulating diagnostic impressions. Although examinees are allowed to pick up the cards, they are not allowed to turn them unless they are in the process of completing their drawing. If it looks as if they have turned the design and are beginning to copy it in the new position, the examiner should straighten the card and state that it should be copied from this angle. As many sheets of paper may be used as desired, although the client is presented with only one sheet initially. There is no time limit, but it is important to note the length of time required to complete the test, since this information may be diagnostically significant.

In addition to the standard procedure for using the Bender, an additional, somewhat different administration of the designs is often diagnostically useful. Common procedures for an altered administration include:

1. a memory task in which the person, after having first copied the designs during the standard administration, is asked to reproduce as many designs as possible from memory

2. asking the person to draw the designs in any way he or she chooses—altering, combining, or elaborating at will

3. presenting the cards and asking the person what they remind him or her of

The second and third techniques emphasize the projective possibilities of the Bender and can theoretically provide information about the emotional adjustment of the person, much as a projective drawing or a free association test would do. The first variation provides an assessment of an individual's level of short-term, visual-motor recall. Typically, adult brain-injured subjects will not be able to recall the designs as well as persons who are non-brain-injured. Tolor (1956) found that organic patients could only recall an average of 3.69 designs, whereas convulsive (epileptic) patients and patients with psychological difficulties successfully recalled an average of 5.5 and 5.53 of the designs accurately. The recall method has not been found to be successful for the screening of children (Koppitz, 1975). A further variation from the initial administration, which assesses a person's immediate visual memory, is to present the person with a design for five seconds, remove it, and then have him or her reproduce it from memory.

A variety of group administrations have also been described. These include the use of enlarged stimulus cards simultaneously shown to the group, providing each person with individual decks of Bender cards, and projecting the designs using an overhead projector. The use of group rather than individual administrations does not seem to significantly alter test performance (Keogh & Smith, 1961; Dibner & Korn, 1969; Jacobs, 1971).

An important addition to Bender administration procedures for adolescents and adults is the Background Interference Procedure (BIP; Canter, 1963, 1966, 1976; Heaton, Beade, & Johnson, 1978). This requires the subject to first complete a standard administration and then complete the Bender designs on a specially designed sheet of paper that contains a confusing array of curved, intersecting lines. It has been demonstrated that brain-damaged patients show significant decrements in their BIP performance compared with their performances using a standard administration (Canter, 1966, 1971, 1976; Norton, 1978; Pardue, 1975). This is in contrast to functionally disordered patients and normals who typically do not show significant differences between the two administration procedures.

INTERPRETATION GUIDELINES: CHILDREN

The Developmental Bender Test scoring system (Koppitz, 1963, 1975) is the dominant system used for children. The primary focus is on understanding children's visual-motor abilities as they relate to developmental maturation. Koppitz (1963, 1975) also lists typical errors associated with emotional indicators and brain damage, but places these within the context of what would be expected for a particular individual having a specified chronological age. Bender protocols are scored based on the presence of 30 mutually exclusive items. Composite scores can thus range from 0 to 30. The system is relatively easy to learn and interscorer reliability is typically .89 or better (Koppitz, 1975; Neale & McKay, 1985). The following section is primarily a summary of Koppitz's approach and provides general interpretative guidelines based on indicators for developmental maturation, organicity, visual-motor perception difficulties, and emotional indicators.

The specific scoring criteria developed by Koppitz (1963, 1975) for developmental level can be found in Appendix B of *The Bender Gestalt for Young Children* (Volume 2, 1975). A summary outline of the scoring criteria is included in Appendix I of the present handbook. A different set of scoring criteria for emotional indicators has also been developed by Koppitz and is included in *The Bender Gestalt Test for Young Children* (1963). To obtain specific scores, clinicians should consult these criteria and use the outline in Appendix I as a scoring guide. Both texts by Koppitz (1963, 1975) include important guidelines, cautions, and reviews of research, and clinicians are encouraged to consult these for further elaboration and discussion.

The Bender can be used to provide information regarding a person's perceptual maturity, degree of emotional adjustment, or extent of neurological impairment. Many of the different systems (including Koppitz's) include different scoring guidelines for each of these areas. A particular clinician may wish to assess only one of these areas, or may consider them all. However, if all of the above areas are considered, it is crucial to be cautious of the possible overlap among them since many of the signs also occur throughout the different scoring guidelines.

A suggested sequence in approaching the Bender is to initially develop a global impression of the relative quality of the reproductions as a whole. It is also important to note any relevant behavioral observations made while the child is completing the designs. These observations might include such areas as the child's level of confidence, awareness of errors, completion time, and any comments that are made. The clinician might then look at specific features of the drawings, including figure size, placement, line quality, order and organization of the designs, distortions, erasures, reworking, omissions, and any other unusual treatment. Finally, objective scoring can be made for developmental maturity, organicity, visual-motor perception, and emotional difficulties.

Developmental Maturation

As is true with all areas of development, visual-motor perception skills increase with the growth of the child. Although children mature at different rates, the following guidelines developed by Bender (1938) and outlined by Clawson (1962) can be used to understand the typical pattern of visual-motor development.

Age	Typical patterns of reproductions
2	Has not developed the skills necessary to reproduce the designs with any degree of accuracy but is able to keep their pencil on the paper and make scribbles, dots, and dashes.

3   Ability to draw loops, lines, arcs, and circles.

4   Can arrange circles or loops in a horizontal left-to-right direction.

5   Figures are characterized by having a square appearance, many different designs can be created, horizontal and vertical lines are crossed.

6   A relatively accurate reproduction of the Bender designs can be created since visual perception is more mature and they are able to integrate this with kinesthetic and tactual perception. Designs A, 1, 4, and 5 are likely to be particularly accurate.

7   Good ordering of designs, relatively accurate reproduction of oblique lines, subparts to designs A and 8 are joined. There are no major additions to the child's drawing ability beyond the age of 7 but there is an increasing number of successful reproductions, greater combinations of basic forms, and more refinement in technique.

8   Accuracy in joining subparts and making dots, and an improvement in the contours on curved figures; figure 2 is drawn with vertical rather than oblique columns, figure 3 has columns of arcs instead of angles; figure 6 is accurate except for an obliqueness in vertical support.

9   Further improvements are present in that rotations occur with less frequency, there is a subtle improvement in the detail of the designs, and the tendency to draw the designs vertically is no longer present.

10   Accurate hexagons are drawn for figure 7 and the subparts are correctly joined, oblique columns are drawn for figure 2.

11   All designs are reproduced accurately in that the sequence, organization, and size are correct.

Visual examples of the above maturational guidelines are provided in Appendix J. The table in Appendix J lists the relevant ages in the left-hand column and the specific designs on the top row. The percentage in each box represents the percentage of persons from a particular age group who produce an accurate reproduction of the designated design. As can be seen, the percentage of accurate reproductions gradually increases for design A until the age of 11, at which time 95% of all children produce an accurate design. A clinician can develop a rough indication of the person's maturational level by referring to the visual norms included in Appendix J.

A more specific rating of developmental level can be determined for children from 5 to 12 by scoring with the criteria developed by Koppitz (1975) and outlined in Appendix I. However, the decrease in errors with age is not even and steady but rather decreases rapidly around age 8. This results in a skewed distribution, with most of the errors occurring among the ages of 5 to 8 (Taylor, Kaufman, & Partenio, 1984). Thus, it should not be considered developmental past the age of 8 or 10. If there is a significant lag between the child's chronological age and the level at which he or she reproduces the Bender designs, the possible causes should be explored with a more complete evaluation of the protocol as well as a review of other relevant data.

Indicators for Organicity

When screening for organicity using the Bender, it is important to be aware that many of the indicators for brain damage are also indicators for emotional disturbance. This raises the serious possibility of misclassification. Thus, the results of the Bender alone are rarely sufficient to make a differential diagnosis between brain damage and emotional disturbance; additional information is needed to determine both the nature and cause of the individual's problems.

The error categories listed below have been reported in the literature to be significant indicators of brain damage both for children and for adults. Although the presence of these errors may indicate impairment, it must be remembered that, even if none of these factors is present, the person may still be suffering a neurological impairment. Conversely, a poor Bender performance may reflect a variety of factors, only one of which is neurological impairment. The most common types of errors associated with organicity for both children and adults are rotations of all or part of a design, perseveration within one design or from one design to another, distortion of figures, fragmentation or omission of parts of a design, substitution of lines for dots, and closure problems. The above are relatively consistent errors described in most of the different scoring systems. The presence of only one of these is rarely likely to indicate organic impairment. However, the likelihood of organic deficit increases with the increased presence of these indicators.

The assessment of organic impairment using the Bender requires a number of important considerations and cautions. Perhaps the most clear and specific indicator is a score greater than one standard deviation above the mean normative score for a given age group (see Appendix K). However, alternate considerations should still be made. The high score might be the result of emotional factors, poor motivation, fatigue, a poor understanding of the instructions, or developmental delay. A high score that is due to developmental delay may merely reflect individual differences in the rate of maturation. The possibility then exists that significant improvement might occur with increased age. Furthermore, a normal score on the Bender does not necessarily rule out organic impairment. Often, organic difficulties affect other abilities that may not have a relationship to Bender performance. Koppitz (1975) points out that there is little to be gained by scoring for both developmental level and brain damage since they are both equally as effective in detecting organic impairment. This overlap between the two scoring guidelines also underlies the difficulty in differentiating between developmental delay and a more pathological injury to the brain.

When using the neurological indicators described and listed in Table 6–1, clinicians should note the overall number of indicators. An abbreviated list of nine indicators is given below and can be used as a brief reference and summary. Whereas normal children from the ages of 5 to 8 might be expected to make some of these errors, persons above the age of 8 or 9 should be expected to have few or no errors (Taylor, Kaufman, & Partenio, 1984). If four or more of the following characteristics are present, then central nervous system impairment is a strong possibility.

1. Simplification of two or more figures to a level three or more years below the child's chronological age

2. Collision of a figure with another figure or a reproduction in which a figure runs off the edge of the paper

3. Fragmentation of one or more figures

4. Rotation of one or more figures 90 degrees or more

5. Incorrect number of units in three or more figures

6. Perseveration from figure to figure of one type or unit

7. Tremulous line quality

8. Lines instead of dots

9. Drawing a straight line when a curved one is indicated

Table 6–1. Bender indicators of brain injury for children 5 to 10 years of age*

Extra or missing angles:
    Figure A — Significantly† more often in BI at all age levels.
    Figure 7 — Common in BI and NBI though more frequently in BI at all age levels; *no* BI drew correct angles before age 8.
    Figure 8 — Common in BI and NBI through age 6, significant† for BI thereafter.

Angles for curves:
    Figure 6 — Common in BI and NBI but significantly† more often in BI at all age levels; *all* BI drew angles up to age 7.

Straight line for curves:
    Figure 6 — Rare but highly significant‡ for BI when present.

Disproportion of parts:
    Figure A — Common in BI and NBI through age 6, significant† for BI thereafter.
    Figure 7 — Common in BI and NBI through age 7, significant† for BI thereafter.

Substitution of five circles for dots:
    Figure 1 — Present in BI and NBI but significantly† more often in BI at all ages.
    Figure 3 — Present in BI and NBI through age 6, significant† for BI thereafter.
    Figure 5 — Present in BI and NBI through age 8, significant† for BI thereafter.

Rotation of design by 45°:
    Figures 1, 4, and 8 — Highly significant‡ for BI at all age levels.
    Figures A and 5 — Significant† for BI at all age levels.
    Figure 7 — Present in BI and NBI through age 6, significant† for BI thereafter.
    Figure 3 — Present in BI and NBI through age 7, significant† for BI thereafter.
    Figure 2 — Present in BI and NBI through age 8, significant† for BI thereafter.

Failure to integrate parts:
    Figures A and 4 — Significant† for BI at all age levels.
    Figure 6 — Rare but significant† for BI at all age levels.
    Figure 7 — Common for BI and NBI through age 6, significant† for BI thereafter.

Omission or addition of row of circles:
    Figure 2 — Common in BI and NBI through age 6, highly significant‡ for BI thereafter.

Shape of design lost:
    Figure 3 — Present in BI and NBI through age 5, significant† for BI thereafter.
    Figure 5 — Rare and does *not* differentiate between BI and NBI at any age.

Line for series of dots:
    Figures 3 and 5 — Rare but highly significant‡ for BI at all age levels.

Perseveration:
    Figures 1, 2, and 6 — Common in BI and NBI through age 7, highly significant‡ for BI thereafter.

†Significant = occuring more often, but not exclusively, in BI group.
‡Highly significant = occuring almost exclusively in BI group.
*BI = brain injured; NBI = non-brain injured.

Note: Reprinted, by permission, from E.M. Koppitz, *The Bender Gestalt Test for Young Children*, New York: Grune & Stratton, Inc., 1963.

Visual-Motor Perception Difficulties

Difficulties in visual-motor perception might be caused by emotional factors, developmental delay, brain damage, or a combination of all of these. Often, it will be the task of the clinician to understand both the underlying causes of the visual-motor difficulties as well as the manner in which these difficulties affect the child. The specific pattern of effects can be noticed by observing the types of behavior surrounding the test as well as the type and severity of errors on the reproductions of the designs. Some children might have primary difficulties with rotations, which might reflect mirror reversals involved with other tasks, such as reading. In contrast, other children might have difficulties in sequencing, which could be suggested by a poorly confused sequence in the reproduction of their Bender designs. This qualitative analysis of Bender protocols should always be conducted within the context of additional material in the client's history as well as other test data.

Sometimes children have learned to compensate for visual-motor difficulties caused by brain damage. As a result, their actual Bender reproductions might be relatively accurate. This compensation is particularly likely if an injury is not too extensive, there was above-average premorbid intelligence, the location of the lesion is not too critical, and the injury has not been recently acquired. If children have achieved an adequate level of compensation, then their actual Bender reproductions might be quite accurate. However, clinicians can sometimes detect compensatory strategies and thereby infer the possible presence of brain damage by becoming sensitized to a wide range of possible compensatory mechanisms. Koppitz (1975) has listed some of these as:

1. Excessive length of time for completion
2. "Anchoring" designs by placing their finger on them as they attempt to reproduce it
3. Reproducing a design from memory after first glancing at it
4. Checking and rechecking the number of dots yet still being uncertain regarding the correct number that should be included
5. Rotating either their sheet of paper or the Bender card itself as an aid in reproducing the design
6. Designs that are quickly and impulsively drawn and then corrected with extreme difficulty
7. Expressions of dissatisfaction with the poorly reproduced designs followed by repeated efforts to correct them

It is sometimes useful to attempt to determine whether a child's poor Bender reproductions are the result of inadequate reception (difficulty in visual perception) or inadequate expression (difficulty in reproducing that which might have been accurately perceived). This distinction can sometimes be determined by asking the child to evaluate the accuracy of the drawing he or she has made. Children who feel that their poorly reproduced drawings are accurate will most likely have receptive difficulties and possibly difficulties with expression. If they recognize that their drawings were done poorly, this suggests their problem might be primarily expressive. Even though they might be aware of the inaccuracy of their drawings, they would have extreme difficulty in correcting the inaccuracies.

Emotional Indicators

The most clearly supported use of the Bender is as a screening device for neurological impairment and as an index of developmental delay. However, it has also been used as a projective device to measure various personality functions (Clawson, 1959; Koppitz, 1963,

1975; Rossini & Kaspar, 1987). This usage has been most successful when cutoff scores have been established for various indicators of emotional difficulties. However, often children with visual-motor difficulties due to developmental delay also have a high number of emotional indicators. Despite this, a significant number of cases still have a large number of emotional indicators without necessarily having scores that indicate developmental delay. In these cases, the emotional indicators assess different levels of functioning. As Koppitz (1975) summarizes, "Not all youngsters with poor Developmental Bender test scores necessarily have emotional problems, nor do all children with Emotional Indicators on their Bender records inevitably show malfunctioning or immaturity in the visual-motor area" (p. 83).

Koppitz (1963, 1975) has listed a total of 12 emotional indicators and developed a scoring manual for 10 of these, which is included in her 1963 text. Each of these indicators has specific interpretive hypotheses associated with it. However, these specific hypotheses have not received sufficient empirical support, so any interpretation based on these indicators should be speculative. In contrast, far greater success has been achieved at predicting such difficulties as psychopathology, acting out, and anxiety by using summed totals of indicators (McCormick & Brannigan, 1984; Oas, 1984; Rossini & Kaspar, 1987). Koppitz (1975) recommended using three or more indicators as the cutoff for inferring emotional difficulties. She reports that over 50% of children with three indicators were emotionally disturbed and 80% with four or more indicators had serious emotional problems. Any person with three or more indicators should be given a more complete evaluation to determine the nature and extent of possible difficulties. However, it is likely that a high number of persons with less than three indicators may still have significant difficulties and yet might be misclassified as normal. Rossini and Kaspar (1987) suggest that one indicator is not uncommon for normal controls, children with adjustment problems often have two to three, and three or more indicators are typical among behavior-disordered children. Thus, they recommend a more conservative approach: two or more indicators suggest psychopathology. Although the total number of indicators has been used to successfully distinguish psychotic from neurotic levels of psychopathology in children (McConnel, 1967), it has not been successful in discriminating difficulties within nonclinical samples of school children (Gregory, 1977).

Koppitz (1963) originally listed 10 emotional indicators and later expanded these to 12 in her 1975 update of her system. Boxed figures, confused order, and large size have been supported in the most recent validity study (Rossini & Kaspar, 1987) and, along with their interpretive hypotheses, are listed below. However, the Rossini & Kaspar (1987) study merely supported the presence of these indicators as suggesting emotional difficulties and the interpretive hypotheses are derived from other authors.

1. **Confused order**: poor planning, difficulty organizing information, and possible mental confusion (Koppitz, 1963); associated with learning-disabled children if 8 to 10 years of age (Ackerman, Peters, & Dykman, 1971) and with acting out (Naches, 1967)

2. **Large size**: tendency toward acting out (Koppitz, 1963, 1975; Naches, 1967)

3. **Box around design**: impulsive tendencies with weak inner control in which external limits are needed to control behavior (Koppitz, 1975)

The following five indicators were found less frequently in Rossini and Kaspar's (1987) control group of normals. Although they did not relate significantly to psychopathology, their less frequent occurrence in the normal controls suggested some possible relationship with emotional difficulties.

4. **Expansion**: impulsive, acting out behavior (Brown, 1965; Naches, 1967) especially for older children who also have neurological impairment (Koppitz, 1963)

5. **Fine line**: shyness, timidity, withdrawal (Koppitz, 1963, 1975)

6. **Careless overwork** (or heavily reinforced lines): impulsive, aggressive behavior consistent with children who act out (Handler & McIntosh, 1971; Koppitz, 1963, 1975); overt hostility (Brown, 1965); however, careful reworking and erasures also might suggest high intelligence and good achievement (Bravo, 1972; Keogh, 1968)

7. **Second attempts** (without correcting the original): aggressiveness (Handler & McIntosh, 1971), impulsiveness, anxiety (Koppitz, 1963, 1975); indicates awareness that the first attempt is incorrect, yet individuals do not have sufficient inner control to correct the original

8. **Small size**: constriction, withdrawal, anxiety, and/or timidity (Koppitz, 1963, 1975)

The following four indicators did not relate to psychopathology in Rossini and Kaspar's (1987) sample, but have been found to be indicators by other researchers.

9. **Wavy line**: lack of stability in motor coordination, expression, or both (Koppitz, 1963); emotional instability may cause poor motor coordination, or poor coordination can cause or exacerbate emotional instability

10. **Dashes for circles**: impulsiveness (Brown, 1965), aggressiveness (Handler & McIntosh, 1971), or, in young children, a lack of interest or attention; suggests a preoccupation with personal difficulties to the extent that children may attempt to avoid tasks presented to them (Koppitz, 1963)

11. **Increased size**: poor ability to tolerate frustration, possible explosiveness (Koppitz, 1963), and acting out tendencies (Naches, 1967)

12. **Elaboration** (spontaneous additions to designs): intense fears, anxieties, preoccupation with inner thoughts (Koppitz, 1975)

Quite possibly, indicators 4 to 12 may relate to types of pathology other than the adjustment and behavior disorders used in Rossini and Kaspar's (1987) sample of 7 to 10 year olds. Also, older populations (e.g., adolescents) having emotional problems might be more likely to have a wider variety of emotional indicators. Future research will hopefully refine Koppitz's 12 indicators and eventually only include those indicators that have been demonstrated to be the most powerful predictors.

INTERPRETATION GUIDELINES: ADULTS

Many of the general interpretive considerations and scoring categories for adults are similar to those for children. Clinicians should approach adult and child protocols from a multidimensional perspective in which both quantitative scoring of pathological indicators and projective considerations relating to personality can be made. This section will provide general guidelines for organic as well as emotional indicators. Quantitative scoring or organic indicators can be obtained by using the "Detailed Scoring Instructions" included in Appendix H and developed by Lacks (1984) in her adaptation of the Hutt-Briskin scoring system. The results can be summarized and tabulated on the "Bender Gestalt Test scoring summary" included at the back of the "Detailed Scoring Instructions."

The projective interpretation of the Bender follows the same general approach as for other projective drawings (Draw-A-Person, Kinetic Family Drawing, etc.). The style and manner of drawing, including behavioral observations, should be noted during administration. Such observations can often be as important as the drawings themselves and provide a context in which to understand the examinee's approach to the task. For example, drawing times between different groups have been found to vary. Character disorders take an average of 3.5 minutes, 4.5 for schizophrenics, 5.8 for depressives, 6.25 for organics (Armstrong, 1965), and 7 to 9.75 minutes for adults with intellectual disabilities (Andert, Hustak, & Dinning, 1978). Next, the examiner can evaluate general features of the drawing—such as line quality, organization, size, and number of erasures. The meaning of these responses can then be interpreted within the context of results from the quantitative scoring, history, and other relevant test data. For example, a person with no indications of organicity who takes a greater than average length of time (five minutes or more), has a high number of erasures, and has a sketchy line quality is most likely expressing a general trait of hesitancy and self-doubt. Another person with documented brain damage who also takes a greater than average time but insists on counting each dot precisely may be attempting to compensate for his or her impairment by developing obsessive behaviors.

The quantitative method of scoring adult Benders using the Lacks adaptation of the Hutt-Briskin scoring system is a relatively brief and straightforward procedure. The 12 "essential discriminators of intracranial damage" outlined in the Lacks adaptation were originally derived from Hutt and Briskin (1960). They include rotation, overlapping difficulty, simplification, fragmentation, retrogression, perseveration, collision or collision tendency, impotence, closure difficulty, motor incoordination (line tremor), angulation difficulty, and cohesion. Descriptions and examples of each of these categories are included in Appendix H. Once a protocol has been scored using the manual's criteria, a clinician can then check to see if the examinee's score falls within the brain-damaged range. Lacks (1984) gives the normal range as 0 to 4 and the optimum cutoff for organic impairment as 5 or more errors (see Table 6–2).

The clinical utility of the Lacks adaptation for the Bender can be evaluated by its ability to differentiate organic populations from normals and psychiatric populations other than organics. The hit rate must exceed the typical base rate of 20 to 30% organics and 20 to 30% schizophrenics found in most psychiatric settings. Lacks (1984) presents evidence that it is unusual for nonorganic persons to have 5 or more essential discriminators (error categories). Table 6–2 indicates that 74% to 96% of nonorganics scored less than 5, whereas only 18% of diagnosed organics did. Using a cutoff score of 5 or more indicators results in a hit rate for accurately identifying organics that ranges from 82% to 86% (Lacks, 1984; Lacks & Newport, 1980). McIntosh et al. (1988) suggest that the Lacks adaptation can also be used for adolescent populations from age 12 to 16 by using a similar cutoff score. The hit rate found with the Lacks adaptation compares favorably with other Bender scoring systems. Under equal conditions, the Lacks adaptation had an 84% hit rate whereas the Pauker was 79%, Hain 71% , and, when only scoring for rotations, the hit rate was 63% (Lacks & Newport, 1980). The Lacks adaptation also has a lower rate of false negatives than either the Hain or Pauker systems. The Lack's adaptation also compares favorably with the Halstead Reitan composite impairment index, which has a hit rate of 84% for identifying organic impairment (Dean, 1982; Reitan, 1974). However, the Bender takes three to eight minutes to administer, whereas the Halstead Reitan can take up to three to four hours. For screening purposes, the Bender has a clear advantage simply due to its greater time efficiency. However, the Halstead Reitan, along with the WAIS-R, provides important, detailed information regarding the nature of cognitive deficits.

Table 6–2. Percentile distributions of Hutt-Briskin total scores for various comparison groups

Number of Errors	Nonpatient Adults (N = 495)	Nonpatient Older Adults (N = 334)	Nonorganic Psychiatric Inpatients (N = 264)	Organic Psychiatric Inpatients (N = 85)
0	20	5	3	0
1	51	17	10	0
2	75	35	31	4
3	87	52	55	9
4	96	74	74	18
5	98	85	85	51
6	99	92	93	71
7	100	96	96	80
8		99	99	87
9		99	100	95
10		100		99
11				100
12				

Note: The cutoff score for organic dysfunction is 5 or more errors.
Note: From Lacks, P. *Bender Gestalt Screening for Brain Dysfunction*, p. 52. Copyright ©1984 by John Wiley & Sons, Inc. Reprinted by permission of John Wiley & Sons, Inc.

Most neuropsychological tests, including the Bender, have difficulty identifying subtle neuropsychological deficit (Delaney, 1982) or differentiating between severe forms of psychopathology and organic impairment (Hutt, 1985; Verma, Wig, & Shaw, 1962). This difficulty can be reduced and the number of correct classifications of psychotics and organics increased through the use of Canter's Background Interference Procedure, since schizophrenics perform significantly better than organics when background interference is introduced (Heaton, Beade, & Johnson, 1978). However, this procedure may still have difficulty identifying subtle neuropsychological deficit (Delaney, 1982).

Like other tests requiring visual spatial organization, the Bender is most sensitive to right hemisphere and especially right parietal involvement (Garron & Cheifetz, 1965). There are often qualitative differences in the performance of persons with lesions in different areas of the brain. Whereas right hemisphere patients are more likely to make errors related to visuospatial abilities (e.g., rotations, asymmetry, fragmentation, unrecognizable drawings, unjoined lines), persons with left hemisphere lesions often make drawings that are shaky (line tremors) and smaller in size, with rounded corners and missing parts (oversimplification; Filskov, 1978). However, the Bender is still more likely to miss patients who have left hemisphere lesions.

Specific Indicators of Organicity

Lacks (1984) has listed Hutt's 12 essential discriminators of organic impairment. However, perseveration, rotations, closure difficulty, cohesion, and concretism require special elaboration since they have been found to be highly characteristic of brain damage and have been included in most scoring systems.

Perseveration can be defined as the continuation of a response well beyond the required number expected, based on the stimulus presented to the person. For example, a person is perseverating if he or she produces 14 or more dots on design 1, which only requires him or her to reproduce 12 dots. Perseveration is most common on designs 1, 2, and 3, but can occur on any design if the person draws the same design one or more times, does not ask if he or she can repeat the design, and/or fails to erase previous attempts. Although perseveration has been found to exist both in schizophrenic and organic populations (see Tolor & Brannigan, 1980), it is more strongly associated with organicity (Hain, 1964; Lerner, 1972; Lacks, 1984). Lacks (1984) reports that perseveration occurs in 56% of the protocols of brain-damaged patients, whereas only 31% to 32% of personality disordered persons had perseverations on their protocols.

Marley (1982) has expanded the definition of perseveration and divided it into three different types. While each type is considered an indicator of organic impairment, she also associated different areas of mental functioning with each one. Type A occurs when numbers, letters, or other shapes are substituted for those elements found in the original Bender design (similar to Koppitz's "elaboration" on her emotional indicators). This suggests a loosening of associations, impaired planning, diminished attention, poor concentration, and a difficulty with immediate and delayed memory. It is characteristic of dementia and is associated with frontal, frontotemporal, or bilateral involvement. Type B perseveration occurs when additional elements are drawn into designs 1, 2, 3, and 5 or when additional curves are included in design 6 (the same as the Lacks adaptation's definition of perseveration). Possible areas of mental functioning are an inability to shift-set, dissociation from the task, diminished attention, poor concentration, concrete thinking, and perseverating behavior outside the testing situation. This is characteristic of dominant hemisphere temporal involvement. The final form of scorable perseveration (Type C) occurs when the examinee redraws his or her design without any effort to erase or cross out the previous one (similar to Koppitz's "second attempt" on her emotional indicators). This can be the result of impaired concentration, intermittent confused ideation, difficulty with planning, and impaired visual-motor functions. Type C perseveration is characteristic of cortical impairment in the parieto-occipital areas of the dominant hemisphere. These findings represent possibilities for determining the nature of cognitive impairments and the location of lesions, which may either support other data or point out future directions for exploration.

Ample research effort has been given to the presence of rotations, which emphasizes the importance of this scoring category. A rotation is defined as the duplication of a design in which it is rotated 45 degrees or more from its axis. Reversals, in which the figure is turned anywhere from 90 to 270 degrees, are considered to be special cases of rotations and, according to most scoring systems, are still scored under the same category as rotations. Rotations occur most frequently on designs 3 (28% of the instances) and A (17%), and least frequently on designs 6 (2%), 2 (5%), and 1 (6%; Freed, 1966). Rotations occur both for organics and nonorganic psychiatric patients, such as hospitalized persons with intellectual disabilities (Silverstein & Mohan, 1962), and for schizophrenics (Hutt, 1985; Mermelstein, 1983). Thus, differentiated diagnosis between the two groups cannot be made based on the presence of rotations alone. Lacks (1984) has reported that 26% of persons with organic dysfunction made rotations, whereas only 13% and 9% of personality disordered persons did. It has been noted that organics produce more spontaneous rotations, but they also have more difficulty in creating a rotation when specifically requested to do so (Royer &

Holland, 1975). This suggests that assessment of the relative difficulty a person experiences in making deliberate rotations may have relevance for differential diagnosis. The primary mental functions associated with rotations are impaired attention, limited capacity for new learning (Marley, 1982), and disorientation (Mermelstein, 1983). As with other visuographic disabilities, the most likely area of the brain to be affected is the parietal lobe (Garron & Cheifetz, 1965). Although Bender rotations can occur with either right or left hemisphere lesions, the incidence is about twice as frequent for right hemisphere patients as for left (Billingslea, 1963; Diller et al., 1976).

Two frequently occurring errors listed by Lacks (1984) were closure difficulty and cohesion. Closure difficulty occurs when the patient has repeated difficulty connecting pieces of the designs, such as closing circles or joining the circle and square in design A. This was the most frequent error among Lacks' (1984) population of organics, with 79% of them demonstrating closure difficulties. The percentages were also fairly high for psychotics (53%) and personality disorders (55%). Cohesion is the tendency for significant increases in size to occur either in relationship to other designs or to other portions of a specific design. These occurred with 68% of the organics, compared with 50% and 47% of the psychotics and personality disorders, respectively.

Concretism is scored when a patient reinterprets a Bender design so that it resembles another object, such as drawing design 3 to look like a tree or design 6 to resemble a snake. Patients who create such concrete responses appear to need a specific stimulus object to make the more abstract Bender design meaningful. Although concretism has not been the subject of the same amount of research as perseveration and rotations, Hain (1964) found it occurred almost exclusively in the protocols of organic patients. In some cases, it might also suggest serious regression (Halpern, 1951) consistent with some schizophrenics (Kahn & Giffen, 1960).

Emotional Indicators

The more serious indicators outlined by the different scoring systems (perseveration, rotations, concretism) are most characteristic of brain-damaged populations. However, these can also occur in the protocols of emotionally disturbed persons. Distinguishing between the two categories of disorders based on Bender responses can often be difficult. This is further complicated by the fact that organically impaired persons will almost always have emotional responses to their deficits. It is often difficult, if not impossible, to differentiate precisely the extent to which their current problems are organic as opposed to functional. Related to this is the fact that schizophrenics may have a far greater number of abnormal neurological signs than was previously believed (Weinberger, 1984; Weinberger & Berman, 1988), which again makes a precise division into organic versus nonorganic categories difficult and sometimes inappropriate.

A consideration of the Bender cards themselves reveals that the same card may have different meanings for different persons. Thus, two persons may make the same response to a card for different reasons. For example, a rotation may result from a neurological processing deficit in one person, but for another it may result from a functionally based sense of disorientation. Within the context of these cautions, the following discussion approaches Bender responses from two perspectives. The first is a summary of possible interpretations associated with specific Bender responses, while the second is a discussion of the general types of responses associated with anxiety and depression, impulsivity, and schizophrenia. Since the empirical support for these hypotheses is usually either minimal or contradictory, any interpretations should be made cautiously. A more conservative approach having greater validity is to look at the total number of errors occurring in the following categories and make a global assessment of the presence and severity of psychopathology.

The following interpretive hypotheses are a listing and discussion of indicators frequently encountered in clinical practice and discussed in the literature. The first 8 categories are included in the 17 factors listed in Hutt's (1985) Psychopathology Scale and the remaining 7 are those frequently described in the literature but not included in Hutt's (1985) listing. Some of these errors are defined and illustrated in Appendix H (indicated as "see manual"), and those that are not are briefly defined in parentheses next to the error category.

1. **Perseveration** (see manual): rigid cognitive set (Hutt, 1985; Marley, 1982), as might be found in compulsive personalities (Hutt & Briskin, 1960); poor ego control and impaired reality testing (Hutt, 1977); difficulty with planning and poor concentration (Marley, 1982)

2. **Rotation** (see manual): a severe degree of dysfunction, possibly psychosis (Hutt & Gibby, 1970), oppositional tendencies (Hutt, 1985), poor attention with a limited capacity for new learning (Marley, 1982), disorientation (Mermelstein, 1983). Like perseveration, rotations are most frequent among organics. Sometimes, organics and nonorganics can be distinguished since, even with questioning, organics are often unaware of their errors and have difficulty altering the degree of rotation when requested to do so.

3. **Overlap** (see manual): insecurity and compulsive self-doubt (Hutt, 1977; Hutt & Gibby, 1970); potential for aggressive acting out (Brown, 1965; Hutt & Gibby, 1970)

4. **Elaboration or doodling** (spontaneous addition of lines, loops, curves, doodles): extreme preoccupation with inner needs (Halpern, 1951); intense anxiety and difficulty concentrating (Hutt, 1985; Hutt & Briskin, 1960).

5. **Simplification** (see manual): possibly negativism and/or low tolerance to frustration (Hutt & Briskin, 1960), impulsivity, possible malingering (Hutt, 1985)

6. **Closure difficulty** (see manual): anxiety, hesitancy, and self-doubt, with difficulty completing tasks (Hutt, 1977); relationships are usually seen as difficult and provoke anxiety (Hutt & Gibby, 1970); aggressive acting-out behavior (Brown, 1965).

7. **Confused sequence, chaotic arrangement** (confused, chaotic order): strong feelings of anxiety (Hutt, 1968); disorientation, poor comprehension, and impaired judgment (Marley, 1982). Arrangements that are scattered and expansive suggest aggressive and acting-out tendencies (Hutt, 1985; Hutt & Briskin, 1960) or expansiveness consistent with manic states (Murray & Roberts, 1956).

8. **Fragmentation** (parts grossly separated, distorted, or unfinished): poor abstracting and synthesizing ability (Hutt, 1985)

9. **Concretism** (drawing made to represent some concrete object): usually suggests brain damage but may also indicate regressive states (Halpern, 1951); difficulty with abstract thinking (Hain, 1964)

10. **Added angles** (new angles added): poor visual-motor coordination (Hain, 1964; Marley, 1982); insecurity and hesitancy (Halpern, 1951). Further difficulties with angles include an increase in width, suggesting problems with controlling affect,

and a decrease in width (more acute), suggesting a constricted, decreased affective response (Halpern, 1951; Hutt, 1969).

11. **Omission** (either of two subparts omitted from design): difficulty synthesizing and integrating, disturbance in coordinated motor acts (Marley, 1982), disrupted ego functions to the extent that the person cannot work with the more complex aspects of the design (Hutt, 1969)

12. **Expansion** (enlargement of designs): insufficient emotional control, impulsivity (Mundy, 1972; Brown, 1965); aggressive acting out, perhaps consistent with an antisocial personality (Halpern, 1951); grandiose expansiveness to compensate for underlying feelings of self-doubt and inadequacy (Hutt, 1985; Hutt & Briskin, 1960). A progressive and sequential expansion in the size of the figures suggests low tolerance for frustration, explosive acting out due to poor emotional controls, and/or social introversion (Hutt & Briskin, 1960).

13. **Reduction in size** (significantly decreased size): feelings of inadequacy, insecurity, tendency to withdraw, and emotional constriction (Hutt & Briskin, 1960; Mundy, 1972). A progressive and sequential reduction in size suggests acting-out behavior, a low tolerance for frustration, and/or a person who is introverted and depressed (Hutt, 1985; Hutt & Briskin, 1960). Size distortions (larger or smaller) may indicate anxiety (Rao & Potash, 1985).

14. **Rigid, methodological arrangement** (extremely well organized): rigidity and meticulousness (Hutt, 1985), possibly in an attempt to create a sense of security due to underlying feelings of vulnerability and inadequacy (Halpern, 1951)

15. **Constricted, compressed arrangement** (drawings compressed into less than one-half the sheet of paper): depression (White & McGraw, 1975), with feelings of insecurity and inferiority (Johnson, 1973; Murray & Roberts, 1956)

Although knowledge about the possible meaning of specific Bender responses can be helpful, a further approach is to understand categories of responses associated with different emotional states. The following three emotional states are not intended to be all-inclusive, but are commonly encountered in clinical practice and have also been well researched in relationship to Bender responses.

Anxiety and Depression

Anxiety and depression can be characterized as a person's withdrawal from and narrowing his or her contact with the world in an attempt to create security. Bender responses from either anxious or depressed persons likewise reflect a constriction (see emotional indicator 15 above) of the designs (Gavales & Millon, 1960; Johnson, 1973; White & McGraw, 1975). In addition to constricted placement, depressed or anxious persons also decrease the overall size (see emotional indicator 13 above) of their reproductions (Gavales & Millon, 1960) and make their lines in a sketchy, hesitant manner (Clawson, 1962; Hutt & Briskin, 1960). The possibility of suicidal behavior is raised if, in addition to constricted, hesitantly drawn designs, the examinee also encounters difficulty maintaining design 2 in a horizontal position (Leonard, 1973) and draws design 6 penetrating into the open semicircular areas of design 5 (Sternberg & Levine, 1965).

Rao and Potash (1985) found that persons who were typically relaxed (low trait anxiety) had few size distortions (larger or smaller) under nonstress conditions but, when placed in an anxiety-provoking situation, they did create size distortions. In contrast, persons who were ordinarily anxious (high trait anxiety) had size distortions during normal conditions but actually had few size distortions during an anxiety-provoking situation. Thus, anxiety and size distortions on the Bender may interact with both situational variables (level of stress) and personality characteristics (state or trait anxiety).

Impulsivity

Persons who frequently engage in acting-out behavior have a low tolerance for restraint or inhibition, difficulty in completing an exacting task, and a tendency to comply with requests in a superficial manner. If the Bender task is conceptualized as an exacting task requiring some degree of self-discipline, then acting-out persons would be expected to express their impulsiveness within this context. Oas (1984) found that impulsivity was likely to be characteristic of the person if five or more of the following indicators were present:

1. short time for completion
2. poor overall quality
3. discontinuing the task
4. omissions
5. collisions
6. transformations
7. size increases
8. angle changes
9. poor planning
10. perseveration
11. scribbling
12. aggression

A composite score of the above categories had a hit rate of 79% for discriminating impulsive from nonimpulsive adolescents, with 4.8 as a mean score for impulsives (S.D. = 2.0) and 2.3 as a mean for nonimpulsives (S.D. = 1.4). In contrast to impulsives, persons with good impulse control were most likely to take significantly longer to complete the task, more likely to have better, overall quality of their designs, and were more likely to count relevant details of the designs. The study was noteworthy in that it controlled for a wide number of variables, including I.Q., age, drawing ability, organicity, and motivation.

A somewhat similar listing of acting-out signs reported by McCormick and Brannigan (1984) but derived from previous authors (Brown 1965; Hutt, 1969; Koppitz, 1964, 1975) included:

1. figures spread widely on the page
2. progressive increase in figure size
3. overall increase in figure size
4. collisions
5. dashes for dots or circles
6. circles for dots
7. dots for circles
8. excessively heavy line
9. second attempt
10. acute angulation

McCormick and Brannigan (1984) found that a composite score on these signs was significantly related to adolescent acting-out behavior. Specific signs were that the presence of collisions was related to unethical behavior and that the creation of circles for dots was associated with inability to delay impulses.

Schizophrenia

Both acting out and anxiety or depression are usually less severe than a psychotic disorder such as schizophrenia. As the severity of a functional disorder increases, the Bender responses will be more likely to resemble the responses of organically impaired persons. For example, the presence of hallucinations for schizophrenics has also been found to cause greater disruption in the selective perception required to draw the Bender designs. Thus, schizophrenics reporting hallucinations will have significantly greater errors on their Bender responses than nonhallucinating schizophrenics (Rockland & Pollin, 1965). The following specific indicators have frequently been associated with schizophrenia: confused sequence (Hutt, 1985); concreteness (Halpern, 1951); fragmentation (Hutt, 1977; 1985); overlapping and crossing difficulty (Hutt & Gibby, 1970); perseveration (Gilbert, 1969; Hutt & Gibby, 1970); severe difficulties with closure (Hutt, 1985; Lacks, 1984); spontaneous elaborations, embellishments, or doodling (Gilbert, 1969; Hutt, 1985; Hutt & Gibby, 1970); expansion in size (Hutt, 1985; Kahn & Giffen, 1960; Lacks, 1984); extreme crowding; and collisions (Hutt, 1985; Lacks, 1984).

To differentiate organic impairment from schizophrenia, the best approach is to use information from both the patient's history and test scores. There are also several distinguishing signs related to the Bender. First, schizophrenics are more adept than organics at creating deliberate distortions. Second, schizophrenics are somewhat less likely to have the serious indicators of organicity and will probably have fewer of them. For example, in Lacks' (1984) sample of psychotics, they had rotations (13%), perseverations (32%), and closure difficulty (53%) in their protocols, but the frequency was significantly less than that found in organics (rotations, 26%, perseveration, 56%; closure difficulty, 79%). Only collisions did not show any significant statistical difference between the psychotic (53%) and organic (65%) groups. Finally, clinicians can use Canter's Background Interference Procedure (1966), which tends to decrease the performance of organics but not psychotics (Canter, 1976; Heaton, Baade, & Johnson, 1978).

RECOMMENDED READING

Hutt, M. L. (1985). *The Hutt adaptation of the Bender Gestalt Test* (4th ed.). New York: Grune & Stratton.

Koppitz, E. M. (1963 & 1975). *The Bender Gestalt Test for young children* (Vols. 1 & 2). New York: Grune & Stratton.

Lacks, P. (1984). *Bender Gestalt screening for brain dysfunction*. New York: John Wiley and Sons.

Marley, M. L. (1982). *Organic brain pathology and the Bender Gestalt Test: A differential diagnostic scoring system*. New York: Grune & Stratton.

Tolor, A., & Brannigan, G. C. (1980). *Research and clinical applications of the Bender Gestalt Test*. Springfield, IL.: Charles C. Thomas.

Chapter 7

THE MINNESOTA MULTIPHASIC PERSONALITY INVENTORY

The Minnesota Multiphasic Personality Inventory (MMPI) is a standardized questionnaire that elicits a wide range of self-descriptions scored to give a quantitative measurement of an individual's level of emotional adjustment and attitude toward test taking. Since its development by Hathaway and McKinley in 1940, the MMPI has become the most widely used clinical personality inventory, with over 8,000 published research references (Graham & Lilly, 1984; Lubin et al., 1985, Piotrowski & Keller, 1989). Thus, in addition to its clinical usefulness, the MMPI has stimulated a vast amount of literature and has frequently been used as a measurement device in research studies.

The original 1943 test format consisted of 504 affirmative statements that could be answered "true" or "false." The number of items was later increased to 566 through the inclusion of repeat items and scales 5 (Masculinity-Femininity) and 0 (Social Introversion). The 1989 restandardization retained the same basic format but altered, deleted, and/or added a number of items that resulted in a total of 567. The different categories of responses can be either hand or computer scored and summarized on a profile sheet. An individual's score as represented on the graph can then be compared with the scores derived from different normative samples.

Presently, the MMPI and MMPI-2 have a total of 13 standard scales of which 3 relate to validity and 10 to clinical or personality indices (see Table 7–1). These scales are known both by their scale numbers and by scale abbreviations. In addition, a large number of additional scales have been developed for research purposes and to aid in the interpretation of the traditional scales. Examples of such scales include ego strength (ES), dependency (Dy), dominance (Do), prejudice (Pr), and social status (St). New scales are frequently being reported in the literature.

The contents for the majority of MMPI questions are relatively obvious and deal largely with psychiatric, psychological, neurological, or physical symptoms. However, some of the questions are psychologically obscure in that the underlying psychological process they are assessing is not intuitively obvious. For example, item 68,* "I sometimes tease animals"** is empirically answered "false" more frequently by depressed subjects than normals. Thus, it was included under scale 2 (Depression) even though it does not, on the surface, appear to directly assess an individual's degree of depression. For the most part,

---

*Items from the MMPI are reproduced, by permission, from Hathaway, Starke R. and McKinley, J. Charnley, *The Minnesota Multiphasic Personality Inventory*, University of Minnesota Press, Minneapolis, MN.

**The item numbers are listed according to their numbering on the MMPI-2 unless otherwise indicated. Tables are available in the MMPI-2 *Manual for administration and scoring* for conversion to numbers on the MMPI Group Form or Form R.

Table 7–1. Basic Minnesota Multiphasic Personality Inventory Scales

Scale Name	Abbreviation	Code No.	MMPI No. of Item	MMPI-2 No. of Item
Validity Scales:				
Cannot say	?			
Lie	L		15	15
Infrequency	F		64	60
Correction	K		30	30
Clinical Scales:				
Hypochondriasis	Hs	1	33	32
Depression	D	2	60	57
Hysteria	Hy	3	60	60
Psychopathic deviate	Pd	4	50	50
Masculinity-Femininity	Mf	5	60	56
Paranoia	Pa	6	40	40
Psychasthenia	Pt	7	48	48
Schizophrenia	Sc	8	78	78
Hypomania	Ma	9	46	46
Social Introversion	Si	0	70	69

however, the statements are more direct and self-evident, such as item 56, "I wish I could be as happy as others seem to be" (true) or 146, "I cry easily" (true), both of which also reflect an examinee's level of depression. The overall item content is extremely varied and relates to such areas as general health, occupational interests, preoccupations, morale, phobias, and educational problems.

Once a test profile has been developed, the scores are frequently arranged or coded in a way that summarizes and highlights significant peaks and valleys. However, to accurately interpret the test, both the overall configuration of the different scales as well as relevant demographic characteristics of the client must be taken into consideration. In many instances, the same scaled score on one test profile can mean something quite different on another person's profile when the elevations or lowerings of other scales are also considered. For example, an elevated scale 3 (Hysteria) may indicate an individual who denies conflict, demands support from others, expresses optimism, and is somewhat interpersonally naive. However, if this elevation is also accompanied by a high 4 (Psychopathic deviate), there is likely to be a strong undercurrent of repressed anger. This anger is usually expressed indirectly, and any negative effects on others are likely to be strongly denied. Thus, it is important for the clinician to avoid the use of purely quantitative or mechanical formulas for interpreting the profile and instead examine the scores within the overall context of the other scale elevations and lowerings. Not only should a particular scale be examined within the context of the overall test configuration, but additional sources such as demographic characteristics (age, education, socioeconomic status, ethnicity), behavioral observations, other psychometric devices, and relevant history can often be essential in increasing the accuracy, richness, and sensitivity of personality descriptions.

A further important, general interpretive consideration is that the scales represent measures of personality traits rather than simply diagnostic categories. Although the scales were originally designed to differentiate normal from abnormal behavior, it is generally regarded as far more useful to consider that the scales indicate clusters of personality variables. For example, scale 2 (Depression) may suggest such characteristics as mental apathy, self-depreciation, and a tendency to worry over even relatively small matters. This approach characterizes the extensive research performed on the meanings of the two highest scales (two-point code types), which are summarized later in this chapter. Rather than merely labeling a person, this descriptive approach creates a richer, more in-depth, and wider assessment of the individual being tested.

HISTORY AND DEVELOPMENT

The original development of the MMPI was begun in 1939 at the University of Minnesota by Starke R. Hathaway and J. Charnley McKinley. They wanted an instrument that could serve as an aid in assessing adult patients during routine psychiatric case workups and that could accurately determine the severity of their disturbances. Furthermore, Hathaway and McKinley were interested in developing an objective estimate of the change produced by psychotherapy or other variables in a patient's life.

The basic approach taken during construction of the MMPI was empirical criterion keying. This refers to the development, selection, and scoring of items within the scales based on some external criterion of reference. Thus, if a clinical population was given a series of questions to answer, the individuals developing the test would select questions for inclusion or exclusion based on whether this clinical population answered differently from a comparison group. Even though a theoretical approach might be used initially to develop test questions, the final inclusion of questions would not be based on this theoretical criterion. Instead, test questions would be selected based on whether they were answered in a direction different from a contrasted group. For example, a test constructor may believe that an item such as "sometimes I find it almost impossible to get up in the morning" is a theoretically sound statement to use in assessing depression. However, if a sample population of depressed patients did not respond to that question differently from a normative group, then the item would not be included. Thus, if a person with hysterical traits answers "true" to the statement "I have stomach pains," it is not so important whether he or she actually does have stomach pains, but rather more important, from an empirical point of view, that the individual *says* he or she does. In other words, the final criterion for inclusion of items within an inventory is based on whether or not these items are responded to in a significantly different manner by a specified population sample.

Using this method, Hathaway and McKinley began with an original item pool of over 1,000 statements derived from a variety of different sources, including previously developed scales of personal and social attitudes, clinical reports, case histories, psychiatric interviewing manuals, and personal clinical experience. Of the original 1,000 statements, many were eliminated or modified. The result was 504 statements that were considered to be clear, readable, not duplicated, and balanced between positive and negative wording. The statements themselves were extremely varied and were purposely designed to tap as wide a number of areas in an individual's life as possible. The next step was to select different groups of normal and psychiatric patients to whom the 504 questions could be administered. The normals were primarily friends and relatives of patients at the University of Minnesota hospitals who were willing to complete the inventory. They consisted of 226 males and 315 females who were screened with several background questions about age, education, marital status, occupation, residence, and current medical status. Individuals who were under the care of a physician at the time of the screening were excluded from the study. This group was further augmented by the inclusion of other normal subjects, such as recent high school graduates, Work Progress Administration workers, and medical patients at the University of Minnesota hospitals. This composite sample of 724 individuals was closely representative—in terms of age, sex, and marital status—of a typical group of individuals from the Minnesota population, as reflected in the 1930 census. The clinical group was comprised of patients who represented the major psychiatric categories being treated at the University of Minnesota hospitals. These patients were divided into clear subgroups of approximately 50 in each category of diagnosis. If a patient's diagnosis was at all in question, or if a person had a multiple diagnosis, then he or she was excluded from the study. The resulting subgroups were hypochondriasis, depression, hysteria, psychopathic deviate, paranoia, psychasthenia, schizophrenia, and hypomania.

Once the normals and psychiatric patients had been administered the 504-item scale, Hathaway and McKinley could then compare their responses. Each item that correctly differentiated between these two groups was included in the resulting clinical scale. For example, item 40, "Much of the time my head seems to hurt all over," was answered "true" by 12% of the sample of hypochondriacs and by only 4% of the normals. It was thus included in the clinical scale for hypochondriasis. The comparisons, then, were between each clinical group and the group of normals rather than among the different clinical groups themselves. By use of this selection procedure, tentative clinical scales were developed.

Still another step was included in the scale constructions. The fact that an item was endorsed differently by the group of 724 Minnesota normals than by the patients from various clinical populations did not necessarily indicate that it could be used successfully for clinical screening purposes. Thus, an attempt was made to cross-validate the scales by selecting a new group of normals and comparing their responses with a different group of clinical patients. The items that still provided significant differences between these groups were selected for the final version of the scales. It was reasoned, then, that these items and the scales comprised of these items would be valid for differential diagnosis in actual clinical settings.

Whereas this procedure describes how the original clinical scales were developed, two additional scales that used slightly different approaches were also included. Scale 5 (Masculinity-Femininity) was originally intended to differentiate male homosexuals from males with a more exclusively heterosexual orientation. However, few items were found that could effectively perform this function. The scale was then expanded to distinguish items that were characteristically endorsed in a certain direction by the majority of males from those that were characteristically endorsed in a certain direction by females. This was accomplished in part by the inclusion of items from the Terman and Miles I Scale (1936). The second additional scale, Social Introversion (Si), was developed by Drake in 1946. It was initially developed by using empirical criterion keying in an attempt to differentiate female college students who participated extensively in social and extracurricular activities from those who rarely participated. It was later generalized to reflect the relative degree of introversion for both males and females.

It soon became apparent to the test constructors that persons could alter the impression they made on the test due to various test-taking attitudes. Hathaway and McKinley thus began to develop several scales that could detect the types and magnitude of the different test-taking attitudes most likely to invalidate the other clinical scales. Four scales were developed: the Cannot say (?), the Lie (L), the Infrequency (F), and the Correction (K). The Cannot say scale (?) is simply the total number of unanswered questions. If a high number of these are present, it would obviously serve to reduce the validity of the overall profile. High scores on the Lie scale indicate a naive and unsophisticated effort on the part of the examinee to create an overly favorable impression. The items selected for this scale were those that indicated a reluctance to admit to even minor personal shortcomings. The F scale is comprised of those items endorsed by less than 10% of normals. A high number of scorable items on the F scale, then, reflects that the examinee is endorsing a high number of unusually deviant responses.

K, which reflects an examinee's degree of psychological defensiveness is perhaps the most sophisticated of the validity scales. The items for this scale were selected by comparing the responses of known psychiatric patients who still produced normal MMPIs (clinically defensive) with "true" normals who also produced normal MMPIs. Those items that differentiated between these two groups were used for the K scale. Somewhat later, the relative number of items endorsed on the K scale was used as a "correction" factor. The reasoning behind this was that, if some of the scales were lowered due to a defensive test-taking attitude, then a measure of the degree of defensiveness could be added into the scale to compensate for this. The result would theoretically be a more accurate appraisal of the person's clinical behavior. The scales that are not given a K correction are those whose raw score still produced an accurate description of the person's actual behavior.

Since the publication of the original MMPI, special scales and numerous adjunctive approaches to interpretation have been developed. One primary strategy has been content interpretation. The most frequently used are the Harris and Lingoes subscales, Wiggins Content Scales, and several different listings of critical items whose contents can potentially provide important qualitative information regarding an examinee. In addition, many supplementary scales have been developed, such as the Anxiety Scale, the MacAndrew Scale to assess the potential for substance abuse, and the Ego Strength Scale to estimate the extent to which a person will benefit from insight-oriented therapy. Each of these approaches can be used as adjuncts in interpreting the traditional clinical scales and/or experimental scales for assessing or researching specific populations.

In addition to innovations in scales and interpretations, the MMPI has been used within a wide number of settings for an extremely diverse number of areas. The focus of most studies has been on the identification of medical and psychiatric disorders (Greene, 1988) and on expanding or further understanding the psychometric properties of the MMPI. Other frequent topics include alcoholism, aging, locus of control, computer-based interpretation, chronic pain, and the assessment of different occupational groups. In particular, the MMPI has been translated into a number of different languages and has been used in a wide range of different cross-cultural contexts (Butcher & Pancheri, 1976; Greene, 1987).

Criticisms of the MMPI have primarily centered on its growing obsolescence, difficulties with the original scale construction, inadequacy of its standardization sample, and difficulties with many of the items (Butcher & Pope, 1989). Problems with the items include sexist wording, possible racial bias, archaic phrases, and objectionable content. The original norms had poor representation of minorities and are inappropriate in making comparisons with current test takers. Further problems have related to inconsistent meanings associated with T-score transformations.

The above criticisms led to an extensive restandardization of the MMPI, which began in 1982. Despite the need to make major changes, the restandardization committee wanted to keep the basic format and intent of the MMPI as intact as possible so that the extensive research base collected over the past 50 years would still be applicable to the restandardized version. The specific changes were:

1. The deletion of obsolete or objectionable items
2. Continuation of the original validity and clinical scales
3. The development of a wide, representative normative sample
4. Norms that would most accurately reflect clinical problems and would result in a uniform percentile classification
5. The collection of new clinical data that could be used in evaluating the items and scales
6. The development of new scales (Butcher & Pope, 1989).

The restandardization used a special research form consisting of the original 550 items (of which 82 were modified) and an additional 154 provisional items used for the development of new scales. Even though 82 of the original items were reworded, their psychometric properties apparently were not altered (Ben-Porath & Butcher, 1989). The resulting 704-item form was administered to 1,138 males and 1,462 females from seven different states, several military bases, and a Native American reservation. The subjects were between the ages of 18 and 90 and were contacted by requests through direct mail, advertisements in the media, and special appeals. The resulting restandardization sample was highly similar to the 1980 U.S. census in almost all areas.

The new MMPI-2 (Butcher, Dahlstrom, Graham, Tellegen, & Kaemmer, 1989) differs from the older test in a number of ways. The T scores that subjects obtain are generally not as deviant as those from the earlier version. In addition, the T scores were designed to produce the same range and distribution throughout the traditional clinical scales (except for scales 5 and 0). The practical result is that T scores of 65 or greater are considered to be in the clinical range (versus T = 70 for the MMPI). Also, the percentile distributions are uniform throughout the different clinical scales (whereas they were unequal for the MMPI). The test booklet itself contains 567 items, but the order has been changed so that the traditional scales (three validity and ten clinical) can be derived from the first 370 items. The remaining 197 items (Nos. 371 to 567) provide different supplementary, content, and research measures. A number of new scales have been included with new, subtle, adjunctive measures of test validity, separate measures of masculinity and femininity, and 15 additional scales measuring specific personality factors (anxiety, health concerns, cynicism, etc.). It is hoped that the resulting instrument will retain the best features of the original MMPI while transforming the original into a more modern and accurate instrument providing a wider assessment of relevant dimensions.

RELIABILITY AND VALIDITY

Reliability studies on the MMPI indicate that it has moderate levels of temporal stability and internal consistency. For example, Hunsley, Hanson, and Parker (1988) performed a meta-analysis of studies performed on the MMPI between 1970 and 1981, and concluded that "all MMPI scales are quite reliable, with values that range from a low of .71 (scale Ma) to a high of .84 (Scale Pt)" (p. 45). Their analysis was derived from studies that included a wide range of populations, intervals that ranged from one day to two years, and a combined sample size exceeding 5,000. In contrast to Hunsley et al., (1988), some authors have reported that the fluctuations in some of the scales are sufficiently wide to question their reliabilities (Hathaway & Monachesi, 1963; Mauger, 1972). Proponents of the MMPI counter that some fluctuation in test scores are to be expected. This is especially true for psychiatric populations since the effects of treatment or stabilization in a temporary crisis situation are likely to be reflected in a patient's test performance (Graham, Smith, & Schwartz, 1986). Bergin (1971) has demonstrated that scale 2 (Depression) is particularly likely to be lowered after successful treatment. Thus, test-retest reliability may actually be an inappropriate method of evaluating this scale for certain types of populations. This defense of the test's reliability is somewhat undermined by the observation that test-retest reliability is actually slightly more stable for psychiatric populations than for normals. Whereas the median range for psychiatric patients is around .80, median reliabilities for normals are around .70. Split half reliabilities are likewise moderate, having an extremely wide range from .05 to .96, with median correlations in the .70s.

Reliability reported in the MMPI-2 manual indicates moderate reliabilities. However, test-retest reliabilities were calculated for a narrow population over short-term retesting intervals. Reliabilities for normal males over an average interval of 8.58 days (Mdn = 7 days) ranged from a low of .67 for scale 6 to a high of .92 for scale 0 (Butcher et al., 1989). A parallel sample of females over the same retesting interval produced similar reliabilities ranging from .58 (scale 6) to .91 (scale 0). Standard error of measurements for the different scales were found to range from 2 to 3 raw score points. Future studies will no doubt provide a further evaluation of the MMPI-2's reliability over longer intervals and for various population groups.

One difficulty with the MMPI lies in the construction of the scales themselves. More specifically, the intercorrelations between many of the scales are quite high, which is primarily due to the extensive degree of item overlap. Sometimes, the same item will be simultaneously used for the scoring of several different scales, and most of the scales have a relatively high proportion of items common to other scales. For example, scales 7 (Psychasthenia) and 8 (Schizophrenia) have fairly high overlap, which is reflected in correlations ranging from .64 to .87, depending on the population sampled (Butcher et al., 1989; Dahlstrom & Welsh, 1960). Scale 8, which has the highest number of items (78), has only 16 items that are unique to it (Dahlstrom, Welsh, & Dahlstrom, 1972). Several factor analytic studies have been conducted which have been motivated in part due to a need to further understand the high intercorrelations among scales. These studies have consistently found that two major variables could account for most of the variance (Block, 1965; Dahlstrom & Welsh, 1960; Dahlstrom et al., 1972, 1975; Welsh, 1956). All of this strongly suggests that a high degree of redundancy exists regarding what the scales measure.

The fact that the different scales correlate so highly can, in part, be understood by considering that the original selection of the items for inclusion in each scale was based on a comparison of normals with different clinical groups. The items, then, were selected based on their differentiation of normals from various psychiatric populations, rather than on their differentiation of one psychiatric population from another. Even though the psychiatric groups varied from the normals on several traits, this manner of scale construction did not serve to develop accurate measurements of these different traits. Rather, the scales are filled with many heterogeneous items and measure multidimensional, often poorly defined attributes. This approach has also led many items to be shared with other scales. In contrast, an approach in which specific psychiatric groups had been compared with one another would more likely have resulted in scales with less item overlap and with the ability to measure more unidimensional traits.

One difficulty relating to scale construction is the imbalance in the number of "true" and "false" items. In the L scale, all the items are scorable if answered in the "false" direction; on the K scale, 29 of 30 items are scored if answered "false"; and scales 7, 8, and 9 have a ratio of approximately 3 to 1 of "true" as compared with "false" items. The danger of this imbalance is that persons having response styles of either acquiescing ("yea saying") or disagreeing ("nay saying") will answer according to their response style rather than to the content of the items. A more theoretically sound approach to item construction would have been to include an even balance between the number of "true" and "false" answers. Some authors (Edwards, 1957, 1964; Messick & Jackson, 1961) have even suggested that test results do not reflect psychological traits as much as generalized test-taking attitudes. Thus, a controversy has arisen over "content variance," in which an examinee is responding to the content of the items in a manner that will reflect psychological traits rather than "response style variance," in which responses reflect more the examinee's tendency to respond in a certain biased direction. In a review of the literature, Koss (1979) concluded that, although response sets can and do exist, the examinee's tendency to respond accurately to the item content is far stronger. The restandardization has also developed the Variable Response Inconsistency (VRIN) and True Response Inconsistency (TRIN) scales to help detect invalid profiles caused by inconsistent or contradictory responding. These scales have been specifically designed to detect either response acquiescence or response nonacquiescence.

The difficulties associated with reliability and scale construction have led to challenges to the MMPI's validity. Rodgers (1972) has even referred to the MMPI as a "psychometric nightmare." However, even though the strict psychometric properties present difficulties, this has been somewhat compensated by extensive validity studies. More specifically, the meanings of two- and three-point profile code types have been extensively researched, as have the contributions that the MMPI can make toward assessing and predicting specific problem areas. Dahlstrom et al., (1975) in Volume 2 of their revised MMPI handbook, cite 6,000 studies investigating profile patterns. This number is continually increasing (see, for example, Archer, Gordon, Giannetti, & Singles, 1988; Bennet & Schubert, 1981; Conley, 1981; Sheppard, Smith, & Rosenbaum, 1988), and past studies provide extensive evidence of the MMPI's construct validity. For example, violence in women has been associated with elevations in scales 4 (Masculinity-Femininity) and 5 (Psychopathic deviate). These individuals can be described as defensive, lacking contact with their impulsiveness, nonconforming, and being at variance with the stereotyped definition of femininity (Huesmann, Lefkowitz, & Eron, 1978; McCreary, 1976). A further example is that alcoholics with elevations on scales 4 and 9 (49/94 code type) were more likely to drop out of a residential alcoholism treatment program than other code types (Sheppard et al., 1988). Individual clinicians can consult research on code types to obtain specific personality descriptions and learn of potential problems to which a client may be susceptible. The extensiveness and strength of these validity studies is one of the major assets of the MMPI and helps to explain its continued popularity.

In addition to studying the correlates of code type, another approach to establishing validity is to assess the accuracy of inferences based on the MMPI. Early studies by Kostlan (1954) and Little and Shneidman (1959) indicated that the MMPI is relatively more accurate than other standard assessment instruments, especially when the MMPI was combined with social case history data. This incremental validity of the MMPI has been supported in later reviews by Garb (1984) and Graham and Lilly (1984). For example, the accuracy of neurologists' diagnoses was found to increase when they added an MMPI to their patient data (Schwartz & Wiedel, 1981). Garb (1984) concluded that the MMPI was clearly more accurate than social history alone, was superior to projectives, and that the highest incremental validity was obtained when the MMPI was combined with social history.

ASSETS AND LIMITATIONS

The previous discussion on reliability and validity highlights several limitations associated with the original MMPI. These include moderate to low levels of reliability (especially over a long retesting interval) and problems related to the construction of the scales, such as item overlap, high intercorrelations among scales, multidimensional poorly defined scales, obsolete norms, and poorly worded items. Added to these difficulties are criticisms that the test is too long and that many of the items are considered to be offensive, especially those related to sex and religion.

A significant caution stemming from the construction of the original MMPI is that it is generally inadequate for the assessment of normal populations. The items were selected on the basis of their ability to differentiate—in a bimodal population—normals from psychiatric patients. Thus, extreme scores can be interpreted with a fairly high degree of confidence, but moderate elevations must be interpreted with appropriate caution. An elevation in the range of one standard deviation above the mean is more likely to represent an insignificant fluctuation of a normal population than would be the case if a normally distributed group had been used for the scale construction. This is in contrast to a test like the California Personality Inventory (CPI), which used a more evenly distributed sample (as opposed to a bimodal one) and, as a result, can make meaningful interpretations based on moderate elevations. Evaluation of normals is further complicated by the observation that normal persons often achieve high scores. Despite these difficulties, the use and understanding of nonclinical populations has been increasing (Graham & McCord, 1985). In particular, uses have included screening personnel for sensitive jobs such as air traffic controllers, police officers, and nuclear plant operators. This use should be more appropriate and accurate with the MMPI-2, which uses modern, broad-based norms for comparison and has developed uniform T scores that will allow a more even progression in scores between clinical and nonclinical populations.

Despite some clear improvements with the MMPI-2, significant issues have been raised regarding comparability between the two versions. In defense of their comparability are the many similarities in format, scale descriptions, and items. In particular, Ben-Porath and Butcher (1989) found that the effects of rewriting 82 of the MMPI items for inclusion in the MMPI-2 were minimal. Specifically, the rewritten items had no effect on any of the validity, clinical, or special scales when comparisons were made between administrations of the original and restandardized versions using college students. This provided some support for Butcher and Pope's contention that the MMPI-2 validity and clinical scales measure "exactly what they have always measured" (p. 11). They also stress that the correlations between the MMPI and MMPI-2 raw scores will be exactly the same. This suggests that the extensive research literature on the original MMPI is equally relevant for the MMPI-2. Despite this, Butcher et al. (1989) reported that use of the restandardization norms created differences in two-point codes in approximately one-third of the cases in a group of psychiatric patients. This seems to question the exact comparability of past research performed on the code types, since a sizable proportion of code types derived from the MMPI-2 will be different. This issue will no doubt be clarified by future empirical studies. Until research clarifies the meaning and difference in patterns between these changes, interpretations based on code types derived from the MMPI-2 should be made with caution.

One difficulty with both versions of the MMPI is that the scale labels can be misleading since they use traditional diagnostic categories. A person might read a scale such as "schizophrenia" and infer that a person with a peak on that scale therefore fits the diagnosis of schizophrenia. Although it was originally hoped that the MMPI could be used to make differential psychiatric diagnoses, it was soon found that it could not adequately perform this function. Thus, even though schizophrenics score high on scale 8, so do other psychotic and nonpsychotic groups. Also, moderate elevations can occur for normal persons. With the publication of the third edition (and revised third edition) of the *Diagnostic and Statistical Manual of Mental Disorders* (1980, 1987), the traditional labels upon which the scale names were based became somewhat outdated. This causes further confusion related to diagnosis since the scales reflect older categories. For example, scales 1, 2, and 3 are called the "neurotic triad," and scale 7 is labeled Psychasthenia; yet clinicians are often faced with the need to translate these outdated designations into DSM-III-R terminology. This difficulty has been somewhat alleviated through research focusing on the frequencies of DSM-III and DSM-III-R classifications, which are related to different code types (Morey, Blashfield, Webb, & Jewell, 1988; Vincent et al., 1983). DSM-III translations have been further aided through the use of different content and supplementary scales that allow for broader descriptions of symptom patterns (Butcher, Graham, Williams, & Ben-Porath, 1989; Caldwell, 1988).

To compensate for the difficulties related to scale labels, clinicians should become aware of the current meanings of the scales based on research rather than the meanings implied by the often misleading scale titles. This approach can be aided in part through the use of scale numbers rather than titles. For example, scale 8 suggests such attributes as apathy, feelings of alienation, philosophical interests, poor family relations, and unusual thought processes rather than "schizophrenia." It is the clinician's responsibility to determine which of these attributes are most characteristic of the person being evaluated. Clinicians should also be aware of the relationships among scales as represented by the extensive research performed on two- and three-point code types. Usually, the patterns or profiles of the scales are far more useful and valid than merely considering individual scale elevations. The extensiveness of research in this area represents what is probably the strongest asset of the MMPI. This volume of work has both prevented the MMPI from becoming obsolete and has been instrumental in transforming it from a test of psychiatric classification into a far more wide-band personality inventory.

A further significant asset is the MMPI's immense popularity and familiarity within the field. Extensive research has been performed in a variety of areas, and new developments have included abbreviated forms, new scales, the use of critical items, and computerized interpretation systems. The MMPI has been translated into many languages and is available in numerous countries. Normative and validity studies have been conducted on several different cultural groups (Butcher & Pancheri, 1976), which makes possible the comparison of data collected from varying cultures. In contexts where no norms have been developed, at least the test format lends itself to the development of more appropriate norms that can then be used in these contexts.

Although the MMPI has been used in the assessment of persons from different cultural contexts, such assessments should be made with caution. There are likely to be even larger cultural differences for a personality test such as the MMPI than for ability tests. Cultural differences are likely to be especially pronounced if a clinician used the original Minnesota norms rather than ones developed for the particular group being evaluated (Butcher & Pancheri, 1976). When interpreting the profiles of culturally divergent groups, clinicians should have a knowledge of the beliefs and values of that culture and should consult appropriate norms and relevant research when available. There are a wide variety of possible reasons why persons from different cultural groups score in a certain direction.

Although scores may be due to the accurate measurement of different personality traits, they may also be the result of cultural tendencies to acquiesce by giving socially desirable responses, differing beliefs about modesty, role conflicts, or varying interpretations of the meaning of items. Profiles may also reflect the results of racial discrimination in that scales associated with anger, impulsiveness, and frustration may be elevated.

Related to cultural issues is the importance of considering a variety of demographic variables. It has been demonstrated that age, sex, race, place of residence, intelligence, education, and socioeconomic status are all related to the MMPI scales. Often the same relative elevation of profiles can have quite different meanings when corrections are made for demographic variables. Some of the more important and well researched of these will be discussed here and should be taken into account when interpreting test profiles.

Age   Typically, elevations occur on scales 1 and 3 for older normal populations (Leon, Gillum, Gillum, & Gouze, 1980). On the other hand, scales F, 4, 6, 8, and 9 are commonly elevated for adolescent populations (Marks, Seeman, & Haller, 1974). As the sampled population becomes older, the deviations of the latter group of scales tend to decrease. A further finding has been that scale 9 is more commonly elevated in younger persons but decreases with age until it becomes the most frequent low point in older populations (Gynther & Shimkuras, 1966). As a general rule, the left side of the profile (scales 1, 2, and 3) increases with age, which parallels the trend in older persons toward greater concern with health (scales 1 and 3) and depression (scale 2). Conversely, the right side of the profile decreases with age, which parallels a decrease in energy level (scale 9), increased introversion (scale 0 as well as 2), and decreased assertiveness (scale 4). However, in specific cases there may also be a complex interaction with gender, health, socioeconomic status, and ethnicity. In addition to considering scale elevations related to aging, it may be helpful to evaluate individual item content. Swenson, Pearson, and Osborne (1973) provide a list of 30 items that are likely to be affected by aging, such as MMPI item 9, "I am about as able to work as I ever was" (false) and MMPI item 261, "If I were an artist I would like to draw flowers" (true). An analysis of these items indicates that older persons generally express a decrease in hostility (MMPI items 39, 80, 109, 282, and 438), have more "feminine" interests (MMPI items 132 and 261), and are more dutiful, placid, and cautious (Gynther, 1979a).

A significant feature found within adolescent populations is a general elevation in many of the MMPI scales. This has led to considerable controversy over whether adolescents have more actual pathology (based on external behavioral correlates) or whether they merely have higher scores without correspondingly higher pathology (Archer, 1984; 1987). The controversy has encouraged efforts to more clearly understand behavioral correlates of adolescent profiles (Archer, Gordon, Giannetti, & Singles, 1988; Spirito, Faust, Myers, & Bechtel, 1988). Most authors have encouraged the use of specific adolescent norms, such as those developed by Marks, Seeman, and Haller (1974). Although the Marks et al. (1974) norms may have been adequate for past assessment of adolescents (before and shortly after 1974), current adolescent populations may require the use of more recently developed norms (Archer, Pancoast, & Klinefelter, 1989; Pancoast & Archer, 1988; Williams & Butcher, 1989a, 1989b). Specific problems are that the traditional Marks, et al. (1974) norms produce a high percentage of false negatives for contemporary populations, adult descriptors may actually be more accurate than adolescent descriptors, scale 5 does not seem to have external correlates, and many of the more frequent adolescent code types have received only limited recent support (Williams & Butcher, 1989a, 1989b). Current researchers make the somewhat awkward recommendation that both adolescent and adult descriptors should be used for developing interpretations of adolescent profiles (Archer, 1984, 1987).

Adolescent normative comparisons will need to be clarified in relationship to the MMPI-2, and in fact this has been established as a priority by the restandardization committee.

Ethnicity   Past research has attempted to study the effects of ethnicity on MMPI perform-ance. Most of this work has centered on black-white differences and the use of the MMPI within different cross-cultural contexts. Past research on black-white MMPI performance has frequently indicated that blacks are more likely to score higher on scales F, 8, and 9 (Gynther & Green, 1980; Green & Kelly, 1988; Smith & Graham, 1981). This has resulted in considerable controversy over whether these differences indicate higher levels of actual pathology or merely reflect differences in perceptions and values without implying greater maladjustment. If the differences did not reflect greater actual pathology, then specialized subgroup norms would be required to correct for this source of error. However, a review by Greene (1987) demonstrated that, although black-white differences could be found for some populations, there was no consistent pattern to these differences across all popula-tions. What seemed of greater significance was the role of moderator variables, such as education or diagnosis. For example, when black and white psychiatric patients were compared according to level of education and type of pathology, their MMPI performances were the same (Davis, Beck, & Ryan, 1973). Unfortunately, the issue of actual behavioral correlates of black MMPI performances has received little research. The research which has been performed on behavioral correlates has generally not found differences between blacks and whites. For example, the main behavioral features of 68/86 code types between blacks and whites were the same (Clark & Miller, 1971) and predictions based on black and white juvenile delinquents' MMPI scores were equally as accurate for both groups (Green & Kelly, 1988). Based on the above findings, Greene (1987) and Pritchard & Rosenblatt (1980) concluded that it would be premature to develop and use separate norms for blacks. However, it is essential that clinicians be continually aware of the many possible factors that could cause differences in black-white MMPI scores and correct for these factors when appropriate.

Research with Asian Americans, Hispanics, and Native Americans has likewise not found consistent patterns of scale differences. Greene (1987) concluded his review of ethnicity and MMPI performance with three major points and recommendations:

1. It is premature to develop new norms for ethnic groups particularly since moderator variables (education, intelligence, socioeconomic status) seem to explain most of the variance in performance.

2. Future research needs to take into account the subject's degree of identification with his or her ethnic group.

3. More research needs to address actual empirical correlates of ethnicity and MMPI performance rather than merely reporting small mean differences.

Although black versus white scale differences within the United States are more frequently encountered in the literature, research has also been conducted, and norms developed, for using the MMPI within a cross-national context. This includes work on populations from China (Cheung, 1986; Cheung & Song, 1989), Israel (Merbaum & Hefetz, 1976), Pakistan (Mirza, 1977), South Africa (Lison & Van der Spuy, 1977), Chile (Rissetti et al., 1979), Mexico (Nunez, 1968, 1980), and Japan (Tsushima & Onorato, 1982). Whenever clinicians work with different cross-national groups, they should consult the specific norms that have been developed for use with these groups, as well as become familiar with any research that may have been carried out with the MMPI on these groups.

Useful sources are Butcher & Pancheri's (1976) handbook for cross-national MMPI research and reviews of cross-cultural research by Butcher & Clark (1979).

Intellectual Level   Individuals with higher intelligence and education frequently score higher on "feminine" interests (scale 5). Furthermore, scales L and F decrease as intellectual level increases (Gynther & Shimkuras, 1966). As a result, either low scores on scale 5 (Masculinity-Femininity) or higher elevations on the L or F scale take on increased significance with more educated populations. Thus, a university-educated male who has an average or moderate elevation (T = 50 to 65) on scale 5 (Masculinity-Femininity) may actually be more representative of men who place a strong emphasis on traditional expressions of masculinity. Likewise, highly educated persons having moderate elevations on L or F may be more characteristic of less educated persons who score somewhat higher. The significance of education and intelligence will be noted throughout the descriptions of single-scale interpretations. This will allow practitioners to take these factors into account when interpreting different scale elevations.

The advantages and cautions for using the MMPI and MMPI-2 clearly indicate that a considerable degree of psychological sophistication is necessary. Both the assets and limitations of the MMPI and MMPI-2 must be understood and taken into account. The limitations for the original MMPI are numerous and include moderately adequate reliability, problems related to scale construction, excessive length, offensive items, limited usefulness for normal populations, misleading labels for the scales, inadequacy of the original normative sample, and the necessity of considering demographic variables. Some of these limitations have been corrected by the MMPI-2, including an option to decrease the length (by giving only the first 370 items), increased appropriateness for normal populations, rewording of 82 of the items, and the use of a larger, more broad-based, modern normative sample. The limitations of the MMPI are also balanced by a number of significant assets, especially the extensive research relating to the meanings of the different scales and the relationships among scales. Further assets are the MMPI's familiarity in the field, the development of subgroup norms, and extensive research in specific problem areas. Of central importance is the fact that the MMPI has repeatedly proven itself to be of practical value to clinicians, especially because the variables that the scales attempt to measure are meaningful and even essential areas of clinical information. Butcher (1979) has poignantly summarized the status of the MMPI by calling it "an outmoded but as yet unsurpassed psychopathology inventory" (p. 34). The over 8,000 studies performed on or using it support its popularity. The 1989 restandardization should not only ensure that it continues to fill the position of an "unsurpassed psychopathology inventory" but that it will also eventually emerge as a more modern clinical tool.

ADMINISTRATION

The MMPI/MMPI-2 can be administered to persons who are 16 years of age or older with an eighth-grade reading level. Clients of any ages above 16 can be administered the test, and it has been successfully administered to clients down to the ages of 13 and 14. Completion times for all persons taking the test should be noted.

Various forms of the MMPI have been developed. The most frequently used are the Group (Booklet) Form and Form R. Both forms have 566 items that require special scoring templates for the validity, clinical, and supplementary scales. The Group (Booklet) Form requests clients to mark their answers on both sides of the answer sheet, and the number of darkened true or false items are then scored using the scoring templates and plotted on a profile sheet. Form R places the answer sheet over two pegs in the back of the booklet, which aligns the items with the correct spaces on the answer sheet. Clients are therefore prevented from accidentally entering their answers in the wrong spaces. Also with Form R, all items necessary for scoring the standard validity and clinical scales are included on the first 399 items.

For persons who have special difficulties, an individual (Box) form and a tape-recorded form have been developed. The Box form is most appropriate for persons who have difficulties concentrating and/or reading. Each item is presented on a card, which the person is requested to place into one of three different sections to indicate a "true," "false," or "cannot say" response. The tape-recorded form is used for persons who have reading difficulties due to such factors as illiteracy, blindness, or aphasia.

The MMPI-2 has only one booklet form. Completion of the first 370 items allows for the scoring of the validity and clinical scales. The final 197 items are used for scoring different supplementary and content scales. A tape-recorded (cassette) version is available, and in some contexts computer administration is possible.

Due to the sometimes prohibitive length of the MMPI, numerous short forms have been developed. However, none is sufficiently reliable or valid to be considered a substitute for the complete administration (Butcher, Kendall, & Hoffman, 1980; Dahlstrom, 1980). The only acceptable abbreviated form is to administer all the items necessary for scoring only the standard validity and clinical scales.

Some clinicians allow the client to take the MMPI under unsupervised conditions (such as at home). Butcher & Pope (1989) stress that this is not recommended, for the following reasons:

1. The conditions are too dissimilar from those used for the normative samples and any significant change in proceedings might alter the results.

2. Clients might consult others to determine which answers to make.

3. The clinician cannot be aware of possible conditions that might have compromised reliability and validity.

4. There is no assurance that the client actually completed the protocol him- or herself.

Thus, any administration should closely follow the administration used for the normative samples. This means providing clear, consistent directions, ensuring that these directions are understood, and providing adequate supervision.

INTERPRETATION PROCEDURE

Webb, McNamara, and Rodgers (1986) have recommended seven steps for interpreting an MMPI profile. These steps should be followed with a knowledge and awareness of the implications of demographic variables—such as age, culture, intellectual level, education, social class, and occupation. A summary of the relationship between MMPI profiles and some of the main demographic variables—including age, culture, and intellectual level—has already been provided. While looking at the overall configuration of the test (step 5), clinicians can elaborate on the meanings of the different scales and the relationships among scales by consulting the interpretive hypotheses associated with them. (These can be found in the sections on Validity Scales, Clinical Scales, and Two-point Codes.) The discussion of the various scales and codes represents an attempt to integrate and summarize the work of a number of different clinical and research sources, the most important of whom have been Butcher et al., (1989); Dahlstrom et al., (1972); Graham, (1987); Greene (1989); Marks et al. (1974); and Webb et al., (1986). Occasionally, additional relevant material has been cited that is not included in the above sources.

The seven steps in interpretation are:

1. The examiner should note the length of time required to complete the test. For a mildly disturbed person who is 16 years or older with an average I.Q. and eighth-grade education, the time for completion should be from 60 to 75 minutes. If two or more hours are required, the following interpretive possibilities must be considered:

   a. Major psychological disturbance, particularly a severe depression or functional psychosis
   b. Below-average I.Q. or poor reading ability resulting from an inadequate educational background
   c. Cerebral impairment

   If, on the other hand, an examinee finishes in less than an hour, one should suspect an invalid profile, an impulsive personality, or both.

2. Note any erasures or pencil points on the answer sheet. The presence of a few of these signs may indicate that the person took the test seriously and reduces the likelihood of random marking; a great number of erasures may reflect obsessive-compulsive tendencies.

3. Complete the scoring and plot the profile. Specific directions for tabulating the MMPI-2 raw scores and converting them into profiles are provided in Appendix L. If examiners would like to score the MMPI-2 content scales or the most frequently used supplementary scales, additional keys may be obtained through National Computer Systems. Compile additional information, including I.Q. scores, relevant history, demographic variables, and observations derived from steps 1 and 2.

4. Arrange the test scores in the following manner:

   a. Arrange the ten clinical scales in order of descending elevation and place the three validity scales last.
   b. Using the following Welsh code symbols, indicate the relative elevation of each scale:

Range	Elevation Symbol
Over 99 T	**
90-99 T	*
80-89 T	"
70-79 T	'
60-69 T	-
50-59 T	/
40-49 T	:
30-39 T	#
Under 30 T	No Symbol

In other words, all T scores above 99 have two asterisks (**) after them, all T scores between 90 and 99 have one asterisk after them, etc. The following example shows how to Welsh code a set of T scores:

Before Welsh coding:

No.	8	7	9	6	1	4	3	2	0	5			
Scale	Sc	Pt	Ma	Pa	Hs	Pd	Hy	D	Si	Mf	L	F	K
T score	92	85	83	80	75	65	66	60	50	43	56	63	46

After Welsh coding:

8*796"1'432–0/5:L/F–K:

An equally acceptable alternative is to simply note the highest and lowest clinical scales as well as relative scores on the validity scales. Code types can be determined by looking at the two or three highest elevations. If the scores need to be summarized, they can be arranged in descending order of elevation with the validity scales presented in their original order (L, F, K) at the end. A clinician might also wish to place them in the order in which they occur on the profile sheet (L, F, K; 1, 2, 3, etc.), with the corresponding T scores indicated directly after the scale numbers/abbreviations. However, any summary of scores should always include and be described in terms of T scores.

The above coding procedure not only allows for a shorthand method of recording the results, but is also used in many MMPI handbooks to designate code types used in interpreting profiles. For example, the test profile given above can be summarized as a 78/87, and personality description could be looked up under that abbreviation in different interpretive manuals or in the section on two-point codes in this chapter.

Mild elevations in a person's profile (T = 60–65) represent tendencies or trends in the individual's personality, although interpretations should be treated cautiously. Elevations above 70 on the MMPI and above 65 on the MMPI-2 are more strongly characteristic of the individual and are increasingly likely to represent core features of personality functioning. However, basing interpretations solely on specific T-score elevations may be misleading since it is crucial to take into consideration a client's demographic characteristics. For example, it is quite typical for college-educated persons to have K-scale elevations of 55 to 70. In contrast, lower-class clients usually have scores that range from 40 to 60. Any interpretation of K-scale scores needs to take this as well as other factors into account. As a result, specific T-score elevations along with their meanings have usually not been given. Instead, more general descriptions associated with high and low scores have been provided. Clinicians will need to interpret the accuracy of these potential meanings by taking into consideration not merely the elevations, but other relevant variables as well. In addition, each of the descriptions are modal. They should be considered as *possible* interpretations that will not necessarily apply to all persons having a particular score. They are merely hypotheses in need of further verification.

5. Examine the overall pattern or configuration of the test and note the relative peaks and valleys. Typical configurations, for example, might include the "conversion V" typical of conversion disorders or elevated scales 4 and 9, which reflect a high likelihood of acting-out behavior. The overall configuration can then be used to amplify or modify the interpretations derived from step 4. Note especially any scales greater than 70 or less than 40 as being particularly important for the overall interpretation. The meaning of two-point code configurations can be determined by

consulting the corresponding section in this chapter that discusses them. The examiner may also wish to consult one of the MMPI handbooks listed in the recommended readings for a more complete understanding and interpretation of the profile that has been obtained.

6. Score the critical items (see Appendix M) and note which ones indicate important trends. It is often helpful to review these items with the client and obtain elaborations. In particular, it would be essential to determine whether the person understood what the item was asking.

7. Examine the answer sheet and note which questions were omitted. A discussion with the client about why he or she chose not to respond might shed additional light on how he or she is functioning psychologically and what areas are creating conflict for him or her.

COMPUTERIZED INTERPRETATION

An important and frequently used adjunct to MMPI interpretation is the use of computerized interpretation systems. The number of such services has grown considerably since 1965 when the first system was developed by the Mayo Clinic. Major providers are National Computer Systems, Roche Psychiatric Service Institute (RPSI), Clinical Psychological Services, Inc. (using the Caldwell Report), Western Psychological Services, and Behaviordyne Psychodiagnostic Laboratory Service. A description and evaluation of many of these services is included in the eighth, ninth, and tenth editions of the *Mental Measurements Yearbook* (1978, 1985, 1989). Lists and descriptions of software packages available for personal computers can be found in Krug's (1989) *Psychware Sourcebook*, the Association for Measurement and Evaluation in Guidance's (1988) *Guide to Microcomputer and Software in Testing and Assessment*, or Stoloff and Couch's (1988) *Computer Use in Psychology: A Directory of Software*.

Caution in the use of different computer-based interpretive systems is important since the interpretive services and software packages are highly varied in terms of quality, and most of them have untested validity. Many do not specify the extent to which they were developed using empirical guidelines versus clinical intuition. Each computerized system has a somewhat different approach. Some provide screening, descriptive summaries, and cautions relating to treatment, whereas others are highly interpretive or may provide optional interpretive printouts for the clients themselves.

The rationale behind computerized systems is that they are efficient and can accumulate and integrate large amounts of information derived from the vast literature on the MMPI, which even experienced clinicians cannot be expected to recall. However, serious questions have been raised regarding misuse (Matarazzo, 1986; Groth-Marnat, 1985; Groth-Marnat & Schumaker, 1989). In particular, computerized services are limited to standard interpretations and are not capable of integrating the unique variables usually encountered in dealing with clinical cases. This is a significant factor, which untrained personnel may be more likely to either overlook or inadequately evaluate. In response to these issues, the American Psychological Association (APA) developed a set of guidelines to ensure the proper use of computerized interpretations (1986). It should be stressed that, although computerized systems can offer information from a wide variety of accumulated data, their interpretations are still not end products. Like all test data, they need to be placed in the context of the client's overall background and current situation, and integrated within the framework of additional test data.

VALIDITY SCALES

The ? "Scale"

The ? scale is not actually a formal scale but merely represents the number of items left unanswered on the profile sheet. The MMPI-2 does not even include a column for profiling a ? scale, but merely provides a section to include the total number of unanswered questions. The usefulness of noting the total number of unanswered questions is to provide one of several indices of a protocol's validity. If 30 or more items are left unanswered, the protocol is most likely invalid and no further interpretations should be attempted. This is simply because an insufficient number of items have been responded to, which means less information is available for scoring the scales. Thus, less confidence can be placed in the results. To minimize the number of "cannot say" responses, the client should be encouraged to answer all questions.

A high number of unanswered questions can occur for a variety of reasons. It might indicate difficulties with reading, psychomotor retardation, indecision, confusion, or extreme defensiveness. These difficulties might be consistent with severe depression, obsessional states, extreme intellectualization, or unusual interpretations of the items. Defensiveness might stem from legalistic overcautiousness or a paranoid condition.

The L Scale

The L or "lie" scale consists of 15 items that indicate the extent to which a client is attempting to describe him- or herself in an unrealistically positive manner. Thus, high scorers describe themselves in an overly perfectionistic and idealized manner. The items consist of descriptions of relatively minor flaws to which most people are willing to admit. Thus, a person scoring high on the L Scale might answer "false" to item 102, "I get angry sometimes." However, interpretations should take into account a client's demographic characteristics. Persons who are psychologically sophisticated, intelligent, college-educated, and from higher socioeconomic status groups will typically score quite low (raw scores of 0 or 1). On the original MMPI, the L score is scored by counting the total number of "false" responses to items 15, 45, 75, 135, 165, 195, 225, 255, 285, 30, 60, 90, 120, and 150. The MMPI-2 provides a separate scoring key.

High scores on L   Evaluating whether an L scale is elevated requires that the person's demographic characteristics first be considered. A raw score of 4 or 5 would be a moderate score for lower-class persons or persons from the middle class who are laborers. In contrast, a raw score of 4 or 5 would be considered high for college-educated persons unless it can be explained based on their occupation (i.e. clergy). If the client's score is considered high, then it may indicate the person is describing him- or herself in an overly favorable light. This may be due to conscious deception or, alternatively, might be due to an unrealistic view of him- or herself. Such clients may be inflexible, unoriginal, unaware of the impressions they make on others, and perceive their world in a rigid, self-centered manner. As a result of their rigidity, they may have a low tolerance to stress. Since they will deny any flaws in themselves, their insight will be poor. This is likely to make them poor candidates for psychotherapy. Extremely high scores would suggest that they are ruminative, extremely rigid, and will experience difficulties in relationships. This may be consistent with many paranoids who place considerable emphasis on denying their personal flaws and instead project them onto others. Extremely high scores might also be the result of conscious deception by antisocial personalities.

Low scores on L   Low scores suggest that clients were frank and open regarding their responses to the items. They are able to admit minor faults in themselves and may also be articulate, relaxed, socially ascendant, and self-reliant. Low scorers might also be somewhat sarcastic and cynical.

The F Scale

The F (Infrequency) Scale measures the extent to which a person answers in an atypical and deviant manner. The scale items were selected according to whether they were responded to in a scorable direction by less than 10% of the population. Thus, from a statistical definition, they reflect nonconventional thinking. For example, a response is scored if the client answers "true" to item 49, "It would be better if almost all laws were thrown away" or "false" to 64, "I like to visit places where I have never been before." However, the items do not cohere around any particular trait or syndrome. This indicates that a client who scores high is answering in a scorable direction to a wide variety of unusual characteristics. As might be expected, high scores on F are typically accompanied by high scores on many of the clinical scales. High scores can often be used as a general indicator of pathology. In particular, high scores can reflect unusual feelings due to some specific life circumstance to which the person is reacting. This might include grieving, job loss, or divorce. A person scoring high may also be "faking bad," which could serve to invalidate the protocol. Unfortunately, no specific cutoff score is available to determine whether a profile is invalid or is accurately reflecting pathology. Even T scores from 70 to 90 do not necessarily reflect an invalid profile. Further information can be obtained by consulting the F-K index (see section on F-K).

High Scores on F   Scores of 100 or greater indicate an invalid profile. This might have been caused by clerical errors in scoring, false claims by the client regarding symptoms, or distortions caused by a respondent's confused and delusional thinking. However, even severely disturbed patients who accurately respond to the items will very rarely have scores as high as 100. If their scores are in the range of 100, it indicates hallucinations, delusions of reference, poor judgment, and/or extreme withdrawal.

T scores of 80 to 99 suggest malingering, an exaggeration of difficulties, resistance to testing, or significant levels of pathology. If the scores accurately reflect pathology, clients will be disoriented, restless, moody, and dissatisfied. Scores of 70 to 80 suggest the client has unconventional and unusual thoughts and may be rebellious, antisocial, and/or having difficulties in establishing a clear identity. Scores from 70 to 90 might represent a "cry for help" in which persons are being quite open regarding their difficulties in an attempt to indicate they need assistance. If a client scores from 65 to 75 but does not seem to be pathological, he or she might be curious, complex, psychologically sophisticated, opinionated, unstable, and/or moody.

Low Scores on F   Low scores on F indicate that clients perceive the world like most other people. However, if their history suggests pathology, they might be denying difficulties ("faking good"). This distinction might be made by noting the relative elevation on K and interpreting the significance of the F-K index.

The K Scale

The K scale was designed to detect clients who are describing themselves in overly positive terms. It therefore has a similarity with the L scale. However, the K scale is different in that it is more subtle and effective. Whereas only naive, moralistic, and unsophisticated individuals would score high on L, more intelligent and psychologically sophisticated persons might have high K scores and yet be unlikely to have any significant elevation on L. In fact, college-educated persons can be expected to score higher on K (MMPI T scores from 55 to 70 and MMPI-2 T scores approximately 50 to 65). Thus, high scores would not occur until they reach above 65 or 70. In contrast, lower- to middle-class persons without college educations typically have scores that range from 40 to 60. Relatively high scores then, would begin above T = 55 or 60.

Moderate scorers often have good ego strength, effective emotional defenses, good contact with reality, and excellent coping skills. Typically, they are concerned with and often skilled in making socially acceptable responses. As might be expected, K scores are inversely related to scores on scales 8, 7, and 0. Elevations on K can also represent ego defensiveness and guardedness. This might occur with persons who are concerned with revealing themselves due to personality style or because something might be gained by conveying a highly favorable impression (i.e. employment). Unfortunately, there is no clear cutoff for differentiating between positive ego strength (adjustment), ego defensiveness, or "faking good." One general guideline is that the more ego defensive the person is, the more likely it is that some of the clinical scales might also be elevated. Helpful information can also be obtained through the F-K index, relevant history, and the context of the testing (legal proceedings, employment evaluation, etc.).

Since a defensive test-taking approach is likely to suppress the clinical scales, a K correction is added to some of them to compensate for this defensiveness. This correction is obtained by taking a designated fraction of K and adding it to the relevant scale (see directions in Appendix L).

High Scores on K   Scores that are much higher than would be expected given the person's education suggest that clients are attempting to describe themselves in an overly favorable light, deny their difficulties, or that they answered false to all items ("naysaying"). If the profile is considered to be valid, high scores indicate the person is presenting an image of being in control and functioning effectively, but they will overlook any faults they might have. They will have poor insight and resist psychological evaluation. Since they will resist being in a patient role, their ability to benefit from psychotherapy will be limited. They will be intolerant of nonconformity in others and perceive them as weak. Their typical defense will be denial and, due to their poor insight, will be unaware of the impression they make on others. They might also be shy, inhibited, and have a low level of social interaction.

Moderate Scores on K   Low scores suggest moderate levels of defensiveness, as well as a number of potential positive qualities. These clients may be independent, self-reliant, express an appropriate level of self-disclosure, and have good ego strength. Their verbal ability and social skills might also be good. Even though they might admit to some "socially acceptable" difficulties, they might minimize other important conflicts. They would be unlikely to seek help. Moderate scores in adolescents contraindicates acting out.

Low Scores on K   Low scores suggest a "fake bad" profile in which the person exaggerates his or her pathology. It might also suggest a protocol in which all the responses have been marked true. In an otherwise valid profile, the client might be disoriented and confused, extremely self-critical, cynical, skeptical, dissatisfied, and have inadequate defenses. He or she would be likely to have a poor self-concept with a low level of insight. Low scores among adolescents are not uncommon and may reflect a greater level of openness and sensitivity to their problems. It might be consistent with their undergoing a critical self-assessment related to establishing a clear sense of identity. Low scores are also quite common among clients from lower socioeconomic levels and, as such, would not be as likely to suggest difficulties with adjustment.

The F-K Index (Dissimulation Index)

The difference between scores on F and K can provide an index of the likelihood that a person is producing an invalid profile. This index can be determined by subtracting the raw score on K from the raw score on F. At the present time, F-K should be used cautiously for the MMPI-2 since not only have some of the items on F and K been worded differently from the MMPI, but 4 of the original 64 MMPI items have been removed from the F scale. This may result in subtle distortions of the meaning of the F-K index.

F-K = +11 or More   An F-K index in this range raises the possibility of an invalid profile due to "faking bad." This may be the result of malingering or may represent a "cry for help." However, faking should be approached with caution since it is possible for a person to have a high F-K index (greater than +11) and still have produced a valid profile. This may be true for persons who are experiencing a wide number of symptom-like behaviors due to a temporary reaction to situational stress. A moderately valid profile might also occur in persons who overdramatize their difficulties. They would then be expected to be self-indulgent, self-pitying, unstable, narcissistic, or histrionic. They might be using and even exploiting their current difficulties to manipulate others and/or gain attention (a "psycho-chondriac"). High F-K scores might also be found in severely disturbed psychiatric patients who have distorted self-perceptions, a wide range of symptoms, and who therefore provide very deviant responses to the items.

F-K = –11 or Less   Low F-K indexes indicate minimization of difficulties and defensiveness in which the client is attempting to present an overly favorable image. Interpretations of the rest of the clinical scales should thus be made with extreme caution.

F-K = –20 or Less   An index this low indicates extreme defensiveness. This may be due either to conscious deception or to the inability of persons to admit to any personal inadequacies. Their approach to evaluation will be extremely negative to the extent that they may refuse to cooperate. Since they will have a distorted image with low levels of insight, they would be poor candidates for psychotherapy.

Additional MMPI-2 Validity Scales

Fb (Back F) Scale   The 40-item Fb was developed in conjunction with the restandardization of the MMPI. It was designed to identify a "fake bad" mode of responding for the last 197 items. This might be important since the traditional F scale was derived only from items taken from what are now the first 370 questions on the MMPI-2. Without the Fb scale, no check on the validity of the later questions would be available. It might be possible for a person to answer the earlier items accurately and later change to an invalid mode of responding. This is important for the supplementary and content scales since many of them are derived from the last 197 questions. The Fb scale was developed in the same manner as the earlier F scale in that items with low endorsement frequency (less than 10% of nonpatient adults) were included. Thus, a high score suggests the person was answering the items in an unusual mode. As with the F scale, this could indicate either generalized pathology or that the person was attempting to exaggerate his or her level of symptomatology.

VRIN (Variable Response Inconsistency Scale)   The VRIN scale is also a new scale and was designed to complement the existing validity scales. It is comprised of pairs of selected questions that would be expected to be answered in a consistent manner if the person is approaching the testing in a valid manner. Each pair of items is either similar or opposite in content. It would be expected that similar items would be answered in the same direction. If a person answers in the opposite direction, then it indicates an inconsistent response and is therefore scored as one raw score on the VRIN scale. Pairs of items with opposite contents would be expected to be answered in opposite directions. If, instead, these pairs are answered in the same direction, this would represent inconsistent responding, which would also be scored as one raw score point on the VRIN scale. A high number of inconsistent responses (13 or more raw score points) suggests indiscriminate responding. Thus, the profile would be considered to be invalid and should not be interpreted.

TRIN (True Response Inconsistency Scale)   The TRIN scale is like the VRIN scale in that it is comprised of pairs of items. However, only pairs with opposite contents are included. This means there would be two ways for a person to obtain a response which would be scored on the VRIN scale. A "true" response to both items would indicate inconsistency and would therefore be scored as plus one raw score point. A "false" response to both pairs would also indicate inconsistency but would be scored as minus one point (negative scores are avoided by adding a constant). Very high scores (raw score of 13 or more), indicate that the person is indiscriminately answering "true" to the items (acquiescence or "yeasaying"). Very low scores (raw scores of 5 or less) indicate the person is indiscriminately providing "false" responses (nonacquiescence or "naysaying"). Either form of indiscriminate responses suggests an invalid profile. The restandardization committee has stated (Butcher et al., 1989) that both VRIN and TRIN are experimental scales and should be used cautiously until further research clarifies their meaning and potential utility.

CLINICAL SCALES

Scale 1: Hypochondriasis (Hs)

Scale 1 was originally designed to distinguish hypochondriacs from other types of psychiatric patients. Although it can suggest a diagnosis of hypochondriasis, it is most useful as a scale to indicate a variety of personality characteristics that are often consistent with but not necessarily diagnostic of hypochondriasis. High scorers not only show a high concern with illness and disease, but are also likely to be egocentric, immature, pessimistic, sour, whiny, and passive aggressive. Their complaints are usually related to a wide variety of physical difficulties. An important purpose of these complaints is to manipulate and control others. Low scores suggest an absence of these complaints.

Scale 1 may also be elevated along with scales 2, 3, and 7. This would reflect corresponding levels of depression, denial, conversions, or anxiety states. However, persons who score high on 1 typically experience little anxiety. A "conversion V" occurs when there are elevations on scales 1 and 3 along with a significant lowering (10 or more points) on 2. This profile suggests that the person converts psychological conflicts into bodily complaints (see 13/31 code type).

High Scores on Scale 1   Persons with high scores on scale 1 are described as stubborn, pessimistic, narcissistic, and egocentric. They will use their symptom-related complaints to manipulate others and, as a result, will make others around them miserable. Their symptom-related complaints are vague and diffuse and will often shift to various locations on their bodies. They often overuse the medical system and their histories might reveal numerous visits to a wide variety of practitioners. However, they refuse to believe assurances that their difficulties have no organic basis. Upon each visit to a physician, they will recite a long series of symptom complaints (sometimes referred to as an "organ recital"). Their symptoms are usually not reactions to situational stress but more of long-standing duration. They have often rejected and criticized the "help" that has been offered to them. They would be likely to resent any suggestion that their difficulties are even partly psychologically based. Since their level of insight is quite poor, they typically do not make good candidates for psychotherapy.

Persons with moderate scores may have a true organic basis for their difficulties. However, even moderately high scorers will be likely to exaggerate what physical difficulties they do have. If scale 7 is also elevated, this may indicate a better prognosis for psychotherapy since clients' level of anxiety is high enough to motivate them to change. Extremely high scores might suggest that the person has a wide variety of symptom-related complaints and will probably be extremely constricted. This might be consistent with a person with psychotic-like features (schizoid, schizoaffective, schizophrenic, psychotic depression) who is having bodily delusions (check elevations on scales 6, 7, 8, and 9).

Low Scores on Scale 1   Low scores primarily suggest an absence of physical complaints. This may even suggest an inappropriate lack of concern to the extent that the person would not seek medical consultation when indicated. They might also be generally alert, capable, responsible, and conscientious perhaps even to the point of being moralistic.

Scale 2: Depression (D)

Scale 2 is comprised of 60 items on the MMPI and 57 items on the MMPI-2. The Harris and Lingoes recategorization of the scale content suggests that these items are organized around the areas of brooding, physical slowness, subjective feelings of depression, mental apathy, and physical malfunctioning. Thus, high scores may indicate difficulties in one or more of these areas. Patients seeking inpatient psychiatric treatment are most likely to have scale 2 as the highest point on their profiles. As would be expected, elevations on 2 typically decrease after successful psychotherapy. The relative elevation on scale 2 is the single best predictor of a person's level of satisfaction, sense of security, and degree of comfort. Persons who score high on 2 are usually described as self-critical, withdrawn, aloof, silent, and retiring.

Any interpretation of scores on 2 need to take into account the person's age and the implications of possible elevations on other scales. Adolescents typically score 5 to 10 points lower than nonpatient adults. In contrast, elderly persons usually score 5 to 10 points higher. A frequent pattern often referred to as the "neurotic triad" occurs when 1, 2, and 3 are all elevated. This suggests that the person has a wide variety of complaints, including not only depression, but also somatic complaints, irritability, difficulties with interpersonal relationships, work-related problems, and general dissatisfaction (see code types 12/21, 13/31, 23/32). An accompanying elevation on scale 7 suggests that the self-criticalness and intropunitiveness of the depression also includes tension and nervousness. In some ways, moderate elevations on scales 2 and 7 are a favorable sign for psychotherapy. Such elevations indicate that persons are motivated to change due to the discomfort they experience and they are also likely to be introspective and self-aware. Scales 2 and 7 are often referred to as the "distress scales" since they provide an index of the degree of personal pain, anxiety, and discomfort the person is experiencing (see code types 27/72). If an elevation on scale 2 is also accompanied by an elevation on scale 8, it suggests that the depression is characterized by unusual thoughts, disaffiliation, isolation, and a sense of alienation (see code type 28/82).

An elevation on 2 raises the possibility of suicide. This is particularly true if the elevations are high to extremely high and if there are corresponding elevations on 4, 7, 8, and/or 9. Even though these elevations might raise the possibility of suicide, no clear "suicidal profile" has been found to be an accurate predictor. Any suggestion of suicidal behavior on the profile should be investigated further through a careful assessment of additional relevant variables (demographics, presence, clarity, lethality of plan, etc.). More specific information might also be obtained by noting relevant critical items (see Appendix M) and then discussing these with the client.

High Scores on Scale 2   Moderate elevations on 2 might suggest a reactive depression, particularly if 2 is the only high point. The person would likely be confronting his or her difficulties with a sense of pessimism, helplessness, and hopelessness. These may even be characteristic personality features that become exaggerated when the person is confronted by current problems. He or she may have a sense of inadequacy, poor morale, and difficulty concentrating, which may be severe enough to create difficulties in working effectively. The person might be described as retiring, shy, aloof, timid, inhibited but also irritable, high strung, and impatient. Since such persons are highly sensitive to criticism, they might attempt to avoid confrontations at all costs. Increasingly higher scores on 2 indicate an exaggeration of the above trends. They may worry excessively over even minor problems, and their ability to deal effectively with interpersonal problems could be impaired. Their sense of discouragement might result in psychomotor retardation, lethargy, and withdrawal. They are also likely to have a preoccupation with death and suicide. Decisions may need to be made to determine whether they would require inpatient or outpatient treatment. In particular this would require determining whether or not they were a danger to themselves.

Low Scores on Scale 2   Low scores generally indicate not only an absence of depression, but that the person is likely to be cheerful, optimistic, alert, active, spontaneous, and extraverted. They may also be undercontrolled, self-seeking, and even prone to self-display. Sometimes a low 2 score might indicate a person who is denying significant levels of underlying depression.

Scale 3: Hysteria (Hy)

Scale 3 was originally designed to identify patients who had developed a psychogenically based sensory or motor disorder. The 60 items primarily involve specific physical complaints and a defensive denial of emotional or interpersonal difficulties. The types of physical complaints are generally quite specific and include such areas as fitful sleep, nausea, vomiting, headaches, and heart or chest pains. The important feature of persons who score high on this scale is that they simultaneously report specific physical complaints but also use a style of denial in which they may even express an exaggerated degree of optimism. One of the important and primary ways in which they deal with anxiety and conflict is to channel or convert these difficulties onto the body. Thus, their physical complaints serve as an indirect expression of these conflicts. Their traits might be consistent with a histrionic personality in that they will demand affection and social support but do so in an indirect and manipulative manner. They are also likely to be socially uninhibited and highly visible. They can easily initiate relationships, yet their relationships are likely to be superficial. They will approach others in a self-centered and naive manner. They might act out sexually or aggressively, but have a convenient lack of insight into either their underlying motives or the impact they have on others.

Demographics are important to consider when interpreting scale 3. Specifically, persons who are more intelligent, better educated, and from higher socioeconomic groups are likely to score higher. In addition, scores are much more likely to be higher among females than males.

An elevated scale 3 is frequently found, with corresponding elevations on scales 1 and 2 (see code types 12/21, 13/31, and 23/32). If K is also elevated, the person is likely to be inhibited, affiliative, overconventional, and to have an exaggerated need to be liked and approved of by others. This is particularly true if scales F and 8 are also low. A high score on 3 reduces the likelihood the person will be psychotic, even though scales 6 and 8 might be relatively high.

High Scores on Scale 3   High scorers are likely to have specific functionally related somatic complaints. They will use a combination of denial and dissociation. Their insight regarding their behavior will be low since they both deny difficulties and have strong needs to see themselves in a favorable light. Persons with moderate scores, especially if educated and from higher socioeconomic groups, may have good levels of adjustment. However, with increasing scores there is an exaggeration of the above characteristics. In particular, they may be perceived as highly conforming, immature, naive, childishly self-centered, and impulsive. They will have strong needs for approval, support, and affection but will attempt to obtain these through indirect and manipulative means. Often, they will communicate with others in order to create an impact rather than to convey specific information. They will perceive events globally rather than attend to specific and often relevant details of a situation. Their physical difficulties typically worsen in response to increases in stress levels. When their level of stress decreases, their physical difficulties will be likely to disappear very quickly. This is particularly true for persons with T scores over 80.

Initial response to therapy is likely to be enthusiastic and optimistic, at least in part because the clients have strong needs to be liked. However, they will be slow to gain insight into the underlying motives for their behavior since they use extensive denial and repression. They would be likely to attempt to manipulate the therapist into a supportive and nonconfrontive role. As their defenses become challenged, they might become more manipulative, perhaps resorting to complaints of mistreatment and not being understood. At times, they may even become verbally aggressive. Their core conflicts are usually centered around issues of dependence versus independence.

Low Scores on Scale 3   Low scores might be consistent with persons who are narrow minded, cynical, socially isolated, conventional, constricted, and controlled. They might also have a difficult time trusting others and be difficult to get to know.

Scale 4: Psychopathic Deviate (Pd)

The purpose of scale 4 is to assess the person's general level of social adjustment. The questions deal with such areas as degree of alienation from family, social imperviousness, difficulties with school and authority figures, and alienation from self and society. The original purpose of the scale was to distinguish those persons who had continuing legal difficulties yet were of normal intelligence and did not report having experienced cultural deprivation. They were people who seemed to lack concern regarding the social consequence of their behavior and yet did not seem to suffer from neurotic or psychotic difficulties. An important rationale for developing the scale is that high scorers might not be engaged in acting out at the time of testing. In fact, they may often make an initial good impression, which could sometimes be described as "charming." Recent friends and acquaintances may not believe that they could even be capable of antisocial behavior. However, under stress or when confronted with a situation that demands consistent, responsible behavior, they would be expected to act out in antisocial ways. Even though they might get caught, these persons would still have a difficult time learning from their mistakes.

Since persons scoring high on 4 are usually verbally fluent, energetic, and intelligent, they might initially be perceived as good candidates for psychotherapy. However, their underlying hostility, impulsiveness, and difficulty with a long-term commitment would eventually surface. They are also likely to blame others for the problems they have encountered. As a result, they will eventually resist therapy and terminate as soon as possible. Their original motivation for therapy may not have been to actually change, but rather to avoid some form of punishment, such as jail. Thus, their long-term prognosis in therapy is poor.

Adolescents tend to score higher on 4 than nonpatient adults. This most likely reflects their often turbulent attempts to form a sense of identity and independence that is separate from their parents. Thus, the elevation might be part of a temporary phase of development rather than a permanent enduring trait. However, extremely high scores will still reflect significant levels of pathology. Different counterculture groups might often have high scores, which indicates their disregard for the values and beliefs of mainstream culture. Similarly, blacks often score higher, which might reflect their feelings that many of the rules and laws of the dominant culture are unfair and serve to disadvantage them. Graduate students in the humanities and social sciences often have somewhat elevated scores. More positive characteristics to be found with moderate elevations include frankness, deliberateness, assertion, sociability, and individualism.

Relating scale 4 with other corresponding scales can help to make more precise and accurate interpretations. If scales 4 and 9 are elevated, it indicates that the persons not only have an underlying sense of anger and impulsiveness, but also have the energy to act on these feelings (see 49/94 code type). Their histories will almost always reveal extensive impulsive behavior. This acting out has frequently been done in such a way as to damage their families' reputation. They may also have been involved in criminal activity. However, moderate elevations on scales 4 and 9 might suggest that the above behaviors were less extreme and the person may have even been able to have developed a good level of adjustment (see 49/94 code type). A psychotic expression of antisocial behavior might be consistent with elevations on both 4 and 8 (see 48/84 code type). A high 4 accompanied by a high 3 suggests that antisocial behavior might be expressed in covert or disguised methods or that the person might even manipulate another person into acting out for him or her (see 34/43 code type). Elevations on scales 4 and 2 suggest that the person has been caught performing antisocial behavior and is feeling temporary guilt and remorse for his or her behaviors (see 24/42 code type).

High Scores on Scale 4   High scorers typically have problems with persons in authority, frequent marital and work difficulties, and poor tolerance for boredom. They can be described as having an angry disidentification with their family, society, or both. Even though they might have been frequently caught for episodes of acting out, they are slow to learn from the consequences of their behavior. When confronted with the consequences of their actions, these individuals may feel genuine remorse, but this is usually short-lived. Their difficulty in profiting from experience also extends to difficulties in benefiting from psychotherapy. Usually, their relationships are shallow and characterized by recurrent turmoil and they have difficulty forming any long-term loyalties. Others often perceive these individuals as angry, alienated, impulsive, and rebellious. They usually have a history of involvement with the legal system as well as extensive alcohol or drug abuse. Since they resent rules and regulations, they will also have a history of work-related difficulties. Although they may often make an initial good impression, eventually they will have an outbreak of irresponsible, untrustworthy, and antisocial behavior.

Extremely high scorers might be aggressive or even assaultive. In addition, they will be unstable, irresponsible, self-centered, and most will have encountered legal difficulties due to their antisocial behaviors. In contrast, persons scoring in the moderate ranges might be described as adventurous, pleasure-seeking, sociable, self-confident, assertive, unreliable, resentful, and imaginative.

Low Scores on Scale 4   Scores below 45 reflect persons who are overcontrolled, self-critical, rigid, conventional, and overidentified with social status. They might also be balanced, cheerful, persistent, and modest, but are somewhat passive and have difficulties asserting themselves.

Scale 5: Masculinity-Femininity (Mf)

This scale was originally designed to identify males who were having difficulty with homosexual feelings and gender-identity confusion. However, it has been largely unsuccessful in that a high score does not seem to clearly and necessarily relate to a persons's sexual preference. Instead, it relates to the degree to which a person endorses items related to traditional masculine or feminine roles or interests. A high score is also highly correlated with intelligence and education. Thus, educated males will typically score relatively high and educated females usually score relatively low. Any interpretations need to take these crucial moderator variables into account. The item content seems to be organized around the following five dimensions: personal and emotional stability, sexual identification, altruism, feminine occupational identification, and denial of masculine occupations. The items are scored in the opposite direction for females. Thus, high scores for males indicate a nonidentification with traditional masculine roles, whereas a high score for females indicates an identification with these masculine roles.

Scale 5 is not an actual clinical scale in the same sense as are most of the other scales. It does not actually provide clinical information. However, it can be extremely useful in providing color or tone to the other scales. This means interpretations should first be made of the other scales and then the meaning of the relative score on 5 should be taken into consideration. For example, an elevation on scale 4 would indicate that the person is impulsive, might act out under stress, and feels alienated from his or her self or society. If the person is a male and also scores low on scale 4, then he would be likely to express his dissatisfaction through action, have low insight into his behavior, and place emphasis on physical strength. In contrast, a high scale on 4 accompanied by an elevated 5 suggests that the person will be more introspective, sensitive, articulate, and may channel his or her antisocial feelings toward creating social change. However, in deciding what should be considered to be a high or low 5, the person's level of education and socioeconomic status should always be taken into account.

A high score on 4 for males should never be used to diagnose homosexuality. High scores are more likely to suggest that the person has aesthetic interests, sensitivity to others, a wide range of interests, tolerance, passivity, and is capable of expressing warmth. Persons with moderate scores would be inner directed, curious, clever, and have good judgment and common sense. In some cases, extremely high scores might suggest homosexuality, but this is only raised as a possibility; the scores themselves are not diagnostic. The scale is also quite susceptible to faking since the meanings of the items are fairly transparent. Thus, a person wishing to conceal his or her gender-identity confusion could easily alter the items. In contrast, males with low scores could be expected to endorse traditional masculine interests and be described as easygoing, adventurous, but sometimes coarse.

Females who lack much education and score low on scale 5 are usually described as fulfilling traditionally feminine roles and occupations. They will be passive, submissive, modest, sensitive and yielding. In contrast, highly educated females who score in the same ranges are likely to be intelligent, forceful, considerate, insightful, conscientious, and capable. Females who score high are more likely to be involved in more traditionally male roles and occupational areas such as mechanics and science. They are frequently described as aggressive, competitive, confident, adventurous, and dominating.

Since the original development of scale 5, considerable change has occurred in society regarding the roles and behaviors of males and females. This, as well as other factors in scale construction, has caused some challenges to the current validity of 5 (Wong, 1984). Despite these challenges, the most recent study done on college students indicated that the behavioral correlates now were quite similar to what they were a generation ago (Todd & Gynther, 1988). A more complete resolution of this issue would require assessment of behavioral correlates within a wider number of contexts for persons of different ages and educational backgrounds.

Sometimes, males have elevations on both 4 and 5. Such a profile is likely to reflect a person who is not only unconventional, but will also be flamboyant about expressing this unconventionality. Thus, he may enjoy openly defying and challenging conventional modes of appearance and behavior (see 45/54 code type). In contrast, males who score low on 5 and high on 4 will be likely to make an obvious, perhaps even compulsive, display of their masculinity. Females with a high 5 and 4 will rebel against traditional expressions of femininity. As the elevation on 4 becomes progressively higher, this rebellion is likely to become correspondingly more deviant. Females having a profile with a high 4 and low 5 will similarly feel angry and hostile but will find it very difficult to express these feelings. This is likely to produce a considerable degree of inner tension and turmoil. Sometimes, males have high scores on 5 with corresponding high scores on 2 and 7, and occasionally on 4. These males will present themselves as self-effacing, weak, submissive, inferior, and guilty. In high school or college they may have taken on either the role of the self-critical school clown or a withdrawn "egghead." Females fulfilling these qualities would be likely to have the same pattern of scores, except they would have a valley rather than an elevation on 5.

High Scores on Scale 5 (Males)   High-scoring males are likely to be undemanding, shy, emotional, curious, creative, and to have a wide range of intellectual interests. Extremely high scores might suggest males who are not only involved in traditional feminine interests but also have gender-identity confusion. They might be effeminate, passive, experience homoerotic feelings, and have difficulty asserting themselves. Due to their passivity, they may experience marital problems since they have difficulty assertively fulfilling their partner's needs. In rare cases, some high scoring males might develop a reaction formation against their passivity and display an exaggerated expression of masculinity. Thus, they would be outwardly similar to low scoring males on scale 5 although their inner experience of these behaviors would be quite different. In contrast, moderate scorers will be expressive, demonstrative, empathic, individualistic, have interpersonal sensitivity, have aesthetic interests, be self-controlled, and exercise good common sense. They should be able to communicate their ideas effectively and are psychologically sophisticated, idealistic, and inner directed. College and seminary students usually score within the moderate ranges.

Low Scores on Scale 5 (Males)   Low-scoring males will be domineering and impersonal, and are perceived by their peers as being well-mannered. Their interests might be somewhat narrow and they will lack originality. They will show little interest in understanding the underlying motivation behind their own behavior or the behavior of others. In contrast, they will prefer action over contemplation and place considerable emphasis on athletic prowess and physical strength. Thus, they will act in a traditionally masculine manner. They might also be described as self-indulgent, independent, and narcissistic. Sometimes their masculine strivings might even be overdone and expressed in a rigid, almost compulsive manner. Extremely low scorers might even be expressing exaggerated masculine behavior to conceal serious doubts regarding their own masculinity.

High Scores on 5 (Females)   Since the scoring for females is reversed, a high score will mean the opposite for females as it would for males. Thus, high-scoring females would be endorsing traditional male interests and activities, and may be involved in traditionally masculine occupations. They will frequently be described as confident, spontaneous, bold, unsympathetic, competitive, logical, and unemotional. When compared with higher-scoring females, their physical health is likely to be better and they will more frequently be involved in active hobbies and interests. As the scale elevation increases, they correspondingly might be more aggressive, tough-minded, and domineering. They may often be rebelling against the traditional female role and feel uncomfortable in heterosexual relations.

Low Scores on 5 (Females)   College-educated females with low scores on 5 will be tender, emotional, have a balanced view of gender role behavior, express aesthetic interests, and be capable, competent, and conscientious. They may still endorse many traditionally feminine roles and behaviors. They are more likely to have a greater number of health-related complaints than high-scoring females, and their hobbies and interests will be more passive. In contrast to low-scoring educated females, low-scoring females with limited education are typically described quite differently. They may be caricatures of traditionally feminine behavior. They are likely to be modest, passive, constricted, and yielding. They may attempt to make others feel guilty by taking on an excessive number of burdens. As a result, they might be complaining and self-pitying, and might spend time finding faults in others. It is not unusual to have a low 5 accompanied by elevations in the "neurotic triad" (scales 1, 2, and 3). A low 5 accompanied by elevations on scales 4 and 6 has been referred to as the "Scarlet O'Hara" profile because the person is likely to express an exaggerated degree of femininity combined with covert manipulations, underlying antisocial feelings, and hypersensitivity.

Scale 6: Paranoia (Pa)

Scale 6 was designed to identify persons with paranoid conditions or paranoid states. It measures a person's degree of interpersonal sensitivity, self-righteousness, and suspiciousness. Many of the 40 items center on such areas as ideas of reference, delusional beliefs, pervasive suspiciousness, feelings of persecution, grandiose self-beliefs, and interpersonal rigidity. Whereas some of the items deal with overt psychotic content, other less extreme questions ask information related to perceived ulterior motives. The Harris and Lingoes subscales divide the items in scale 6 into ideas of external influence, poignancy, and moral virtue.

Mild elevations on scale 6 suggest that the person is emotional, soft-hearted, and experiences interpersonal sensitivity. As the elevation increases, a person's characteristics become progressively more extreme and consistent with psychotic processes. He or she may have delusions, ideas of self-reference, a grandiose self-concept, and disordered thought processes. In contrast, low-scoring persons are seen as being quite balanced. However, there are some differences between the descriptions given for low-scoring males as opposed to low-scoring females. Low-scoring males are described as cheerful, decisive, self-centered, lacking in a strong sense of conscience, and having a narrow range of interests. Females are somewhat differently described as mature and reasonable.

Persons scoring extremely low might actually be paranoid but are attempting to hide their paranoid processes. Thus, they would actually have characteristics quite similar to high-scoring persons.

In some ways, scale 6 is quite accurate in that high-scoring persons will usually have significant levels of paranoia. However, the contents of most of the 40 items are fairly obvious. Thus, a person wanting to conceal his or her paranoia, due to fear over the imagined consequences of detection, could do so quite easily. This means it might be possible for low or moderate scores to still be consistent with paranoia. This is especially true for bright and psychologically sophisticated persons. They might mask their paranoia not only on the test, but also in real life. Thus, they might be a member of some extreme political group or religious cult that provides some degree of social support for their underlying paranoid processes. However, if the scale is clearly elevated, it is an excellent indication of paranoia.

A pronounced elevation on scales 6 and 8 is highly suggestive of paranoid schizophrenia, regardless of the elevations on the other scales (see 68/86 code type). Another frequent combination is a corresponding elevation on 3. Such persons would then repress their hostile and aggressive feelings and appear naive, positive, and accepting. They might easily enter into superficial relationships, but once these relationships deepen, their underlying suspiciousness, hostility, ruthlessness, and egocentricity would become more clearly expressed (see 36/63 code type).

High Scores on Scale 6   Extremely high scores on 6 indicate persons who are highly suspicious, vengeful, brooding, resentful, and angry. They will feel mistreated and typically misinterpret the motives of others, feeling that they have not received a fair deal in life. They are likely to have a thought disorder with accompanying ideas of reference, delusional thinking, fixed obsessions, compulsions, and phobias. Their thinking will be extremely rigid and they will be quite argumentative. More specifics regarding their thought processes might be obtained by noting relevant critical items and asking them why they answered some of the items in the way that they did. Psychotherapy with them would be extremely difficult due to their rigidity, poor level of insight, and suspiciousness. They might attempt to manipulate the therapist by implicitly suggesting they will terminate.

Moderate elevations are much less likely to reflect overtly psychotic trends. However, the person is still likely to be suspicious, argumentative, potentially hostile, and quite sensitive in interpersonal relationships. They might easily misinterpret the benign statements of others as personal criticisms. They would then enlarge on and brood over these partially or wholly invented criticisms. It would be difficult to discuss emotional problems with them. They would be likely to defend themselves from anxiety through intellectualization and would use projection to deny underlying feelings of hostility. They might then express their own hostility through indirect means and yet appear outwardly self-punishing. They will feel as if they have gotten an unfair deal from life and feel particular resentment toward family members.

Persons with mild elevations on 6 are usually described in relatively favorable terms. These include hardworking, industrious, moralistic, sentimental, softhearted, peaceable, generous, and trusting unless betrayed. They are also likely to be intelligent, poised, rational, fair-minded, and have a broad range of interests. However, they might also tend to be submissive, prone to worry, high strung, dependent, and lacking in self-confidence. The above descriptions are particularly likely among nonpatient groups. Psychiatric patients with the same elevations are described somewhat differently as being oversensitive, slightly paranoid, suspicious, and feeling as if their environment is not sufficiently supportive.

Low Scores on Scale 6   Most persons with low scores on 6 are described as being quite balanced. Males tend to be cheerful, decisive, lacking in a sense of conscience, self-centered, and have a narrow range of interests. Females are somewhat more favorably described as being not only balanced, but also mature and reasonable. Both males and females are likely to be able to accept the challenges of life and are trusting, loyal, decisive, and self-controlled. Whereas the above descriptions tend to be true for nonpatient groups, persons having the same scores among patient groups are described as oversensitive, uninsightful, introverted, undependable, touchy, rough, and have poorly developed consciences and a narrow range of interests. Persons with extremely low scores might be paranoids who are attempting to hide their thought processes. Thus, they would be similar to high-scoring persons.

Scale 7: Psychasthenia (Pt)

The 48 items on scale 7 were originally designed to measure the syndrome of psychasthenia. Although psychasthenia is no longer used as a diagnosis, it was current during the time the MMPI was originally developed. It consisted of compulsions, obsessions, unreasonable fears, and excessive doubts. Thus, it is quite similar to an obsessive-compulsive disorder. However, there are important differences. Scale 7 measures more overt fears and anxieties that the person might be experiencing. In contrast, persons having an obsessive-compulsive disorder could potentially score quite low on 7 because their behaviors and obsessions are effective in reducing their levels of anxiety. Even though an elevation on 7 may suggest the possibility of an obsessive-compulsive disorder, other anxiety-related disorders or situational states could also produce an elevation.

Scale 7 is the clinical scale that most clearly measures anxiety and ruminative self-doubt. Thus, along with elevations on scale 2, it is a good general indicator of the degree of distress the person is undergoing. High scorers are likely to be tense, indecisive, obsessionally worried, and have difficulty concentrating. Within a medical context, they are prone to overreact to even minor medical complaints. They are usually rigid, agitated, fearful, and anxious. The most frequent complaints will be related to cardiac problems as well as difficulties related to their gastrointestinal or genitourinary systems. Within nonmedical and more normal populations, high scorers are likely to be high strung, articulate, individualistic, perfectionistic, and have extremely high standards of morality.

If both scales 7 and 2 are moderately elevated, it suggests a good prognosis for therapy since these individuals are sufficiently uncomfortable to be motivated to change. They are likely to stay in treatment longer than most other groups although their progress will be slow there is likely to be progressive improvement (see 27/72 code type). If their scores are extremely high, they might require anti-anxiety medication to enable them to relax sufficiently to be able to coherently discuss their difficulties. It might also be important to note the elevation of 7 in relationship to 8. If 7 is significantly higher than 8, it indicates the person is still anxious about and struggling with an underlying psychotic process. However, if 7 is quite low in comparison with 8, the person is likely to have given up attempting to fight the disorder and his or her psychotic processes are either of a chronic nature or likely to become more chronic (see 78/87 code type).

High Scores on Scale 7   Elevations on scale 7 suggest persons who are apprehensive, worrying, perfectionistic, apprehensive, tense and may have a wide variety of superstitious fears. Mild elevations suggest that, in addition to a certain level of anxiety, these persons will be orderly, conscientious, reliable, persistent, and organized—although they will also lack originality. Even minor problems might become a source of considerable concern. They will overreact and exaggerate the importance of events. Although they might attempt to use rationalization and intellectualization to reduce their anxiety, these defenses are rarely successful. With increasing elevations, they are likely to experience greater levels of self-doubt and be progressively more rigid, meticulous, apprehensive, uncertain, and inde-cisive. This could result in a variety of rituals and difficulty in concentrating. They will be highly introspective, self-critical, self-conscious, and feel a generalized sense of guilt. Extremely high scores might indicate a disruption in a person's ability to perform daily activities.

Low Scores on Scale 7   Low scorers are likely to be relaxed, warm, cheerful, friendly, alert, and self-confident. They will approach their world in a balanced manner and are often described as efficient, independent, placid, and secure. It is rare for persons referred for treatment to have low scores on this scale.

Scale 8: Schizophrenia (Sc)

Scale 8 was originally designed to identify persons who were experiencing schizophrenic or schizophrenic-like conditions. It has been partially successful in this goal in that a diagnosis of schizophrenia is raised as a possibility in the case of persons who score quite high. However, even persons scoring quite high would not necessarily fulfill the criteria for schizophrenia, in part because the items in the scale cover a highly diverse number of areas. Thus, elevations can occur for a variety of reasons, which means that the descriptions of high scorers would also be quite varied. The items assess such areas as social alienation, apathy, poor family relations, unusual thought processes, and peculiarities in perception. Other questions are intended to measure reduced efficiency, difficulties in concentration, general fears and worries, inability to cope, and difficulties with impulse control. The Harris and Lingoes subscales divide the contents of the items into social and emotional alienation, lack of ego mastery, and bizarre sensory experiences.

In general, an elevated score on 8 suggests the person feels alienated, distant from social situations, and misunderstood. He or she might have a highly varied fantasy life and, when under stress, will withdraw further into fantasy. Others will most likely perceive the person as eccentric, seclusive, secretive, and inaccessible. He or she will often have a difficult time maintaining a clear and coherent line of thought. Communication skills will be poor; often, other people will feel they are missing some important component of what this individual is trying to say. The person will typically not make clear and direct statements and often will have difficulty focusing on one idea for very long.

Age and race are important when deciding what should be considered a high versus a low score on 8. Many populations of blacks score somewhat higher on 8, which might reflect their greater level of social alienation and estrangement. However, this may be more related to education and socioeconomic status than ethnicity (Greene, 1987). Adolescents also score higher on scale 8, which might be consistent with their greater openness to unusual experiences, turmoil in establishing a solid sense of identity, and greater feelings of alienation. Thus, special adolescent norms might be considered as a means of correcting for these higher scores. However, such norms should be taken from relatively recent sources rather than from those developed 10 or 20 years ago (Pancost & Archer, 1988). Sometimes, persons who have had a variety of drug experiences may score somewhat higher on 8. This may reflect the direct effects of the drugs themselves rather than suggest greater levels of pathology.

Simultaneous elevations on 4 and 8 indicate persons who feel extremely distrustful and alienated from their world. They perceive their environment as dangerous and are likely to react to others in a hostile and aggressive fashion (see 48/84 code type). Another important but unusual profile is an elevation on 8 along with an elevation on 9. Such persons will be likely to constantly deflect the direction of conversation, frequently diverting it to unusual tangents. They are likely to not only have a distorted view of their world, but also to have the energy to act on these distorted perceptions (see 89/98 code type). Another important pattern is the prognostic significance associated with the relative height of 7 and 8 (see 78/87 code type) and the schizoid profile of elevated F, 2, 4, 8, and 0 (see scale 2).

High Scores on Scale 8   A high score suggests persons who have unusual beliefs, are unconventional, and may experience difficulties concentrating and focusing their attention. Within moderately elevated protocols, they might merely be aloof, different, and approach tasks from an innovative perspective. They may be interested in philosophical or religious matters, and have abstract interests in which they are not particularly interested in concrete matters. Others might describe them as shy, aloof, and reserved. Progressively higher scores would be likely to reflect individuals with greater difficulties in organizing and directing their thoughts. They might have aggressive, resentful, and/or hostile feelings yet are unable to express these feelings. At their best, they might be peaceable, generous, sentimental, sharp-witted, interesting, creative, and imaginative. Very high elevations suggest persons with bizarre mentation, delusions, highly eccentric behaviors, poor contact with reality, and possibly hallucinations. They will feel incompetent, inadequate, and be plagued by a wide variety of sexual preoccupations, self-doubts, and unusual religious beliefs. However, extremely high scores rarely occur, even among diagnosed schizophrenics. These extremes are likely to reflect unusual experiences reported by unusually anxious patients, adolescent adjustment reactions, prepsychotics, borderline personalities, or relatively well-adjusted persons who are malingering.

Since high-scoring persons have difficulty trusting others and developing relationships, therapy might be difficult—especially during its initial stages. However, such individuals tend to stay in therapy longer than many other types of clients and may eventually develop a relatively close and trusting client/therapist relationship. Due to the often chronic nature of their difficulties, their prognosis is frequently poor. If their thought processes are extremely disorganized, referral for medication might be indicated.

Low Scores on Scale 8   Persons scoring low are likely to be cheerful, good-natured, friendly, trustful, and adaptable. However, they are also likely to be overly accepting of authority, restrained, submissive, unimaginative, and avoid deep and involved relationships with others.

Scale 9: Hypomania (Ma)

The 46 items on scale 9 were originally developed to identify persons experiencing hypomanic symptoms. These symptoms might include cyclical periods of euphoria, increased irritability, and excessive unproductive activity that might be used as a distraction to stave off an impending depression. Thus, the items are centered around such topics as energy level, irritability, egotism, and expansiveness. The Harris and Lingoes subscales classify the content of the items under amorality, psychomotor acceleration, imperturbality, and ego inflation. However, hypomania occurs in cycles. Thus persons in the acute phase were unable to be tested due to the seriousness of their condition. Further, some persons might score quite low on scale 9, which might reflect the depressive side of their cycle. These low scorers, then, might still develop a hypomanic state and may have actually been hypomanic in the past.

The scale is effective not only in identifying persons with moderate manic conditions (extreme manic patients would be untestable) but also in identifying characteristics of non-patient groups. Thus, males with moderate to mild elevations and with no history of psychiatric disturbance might be described as warm, enthusiastic, outgoing, and uninhibited. They would most likely be able to expend a considerable amount of energy over a sustained period of time. They might also be easily offended, hyperactive, tense, and prone to periods of worry, anxiety, and depression. Others might describe them as expressive, individualistic, generous, and affectionate. Nonpatient females are likely to be frank, courageous, talkative, enthusiastic, idealistic, and versatile.

Age and race are important when evaluating what should be considered a high or low score. Some studies have indicated that blacks score higher than whites. Also, younger populations (adolescents and college-age students) score somewhat higher than nonpatient adults. In contrast, elderly persons often score quite low on scale 9.

Useful information can often be obtained by interpreting the significance of corresponding scores on 9, 2, 7, and K. Usually 9 and 2 are negatively correlated. However, they can sometimes both be elevated. This may reflect an agitated state in which the person is attempting to defend or distract him- or herself from underlying hostile and aggressive impulses. Sometimes such persons are highly introspective and narcissistically self-absorbed. Scales 9 and 2 can also be elevated for certain types of organically impaired patients. Profiles in which 2 and 7 are low (suggesting a minimum of psychological distress) combined with an elevation on 9, might be consistent with males who have an almost compulsive need to seek power and place themselves in narcissistically competitive situations. If the above profile is also accompanied by an elevation on K, then these males are likely to be managerial, autocratic, power hungry and expend a considerable degree of effort in organizing others. Their self-esteem would often be dependent on eliciting submission and weakness from others. What they usually receive from others is a grudging deference rather than admiration. Females having this profile are likely to be prone to exhibitionistic self-display and be extremely concerned with their physical attractiveness.

High Scores on Scale 9   Extremely high scores are suggestive of a moderate manic episode. These individuals will be maladaptively hyperactive and poorly focused, and will have flight-ive ideas, an inflated sense of self-importance, and low impulse control. Their appraisal of what they can actually accomplish is unrealistic. Thus they have an unwarranted sense of optimism. They are likely to become irritable at relatively minor interruptions and delays. Although they expend a considerable amount of energy, their activity usually will be unproductive since it is unfocused. Others might perceive them as restless and agitated. They will be able to quickly develop relationships with others, but these relationships will be superficial.

Persons with more moderate elevations are often more able to focus and direct their energy in productive directions. Nonpatients will be direct, energetic, enthusiastic, sociable, independent, optimistic, and have a wide range of interests. Sometimes scores alone are not sufficient to distinguish a person who is energetic, optimistic, and focused from a person who is scattered, ineffective, and hyperactive. Useful information might be obtained by noting relevant critical items, interpreting the Harris and Lingoes subscales, or integrating relevant historical information.

Low Scores on Scale 9   Persons scoring low on 9 are likely to have low levels of energy and activity. They are often described as dependable, responsible, conventional, practical, and reliable, but may also lack self-confidence. They might also be seclusive, withdrawn, quiet, modest, overcontrolled, and humble. Low scores are more frequently found among the elderly than among younger populations. Extremely low scores suggest serious depression, even if scale 2 is within normal limits.

Scale 0: Social Introversion (Si)

This scale was developed from the responses of college students on questions relating to an introversion-extraversion continuum. It was validated based on the degree to which the students participated in social activities. High scores suggest persons who are shy, have limited social skills, feel uncomfortable in social interactions, and withdraw from many interpersonal situations. In particular, they may feel uncomfortable around members of the opposite sex. They would prefer to be alone or with a few close friends than with a large group. One cluster of items deals with self-depreciation and neurotic maladjustment, whereas the other group deals with the degree to which the person participates in interpersonal interactions. The items have been divided to form subscales comprised of Shyness/Self-Consciousness, Social Avoidance, and Alienation-Self and Others (Ben-Porath, Hostetler, & Butcher, 1989). These subscales can be used in much the same way as the Harris and Lingoes scales in that they can provide more information to help determine why a person had a particular score on scale 0.

Scale 0 is similar to 5 in that it is used to "color" or provide a different emphasis to the other clinical scales. Thus, interpretations should first be made without considering 5 and 0 and, later, the implications of these scales should be included. As a result, code types involving 0 have not been included in the section on Two-Point Codes. Elevations on 0 help provide information on the other scales by indicating how comfortable persons are with interactions, their degree of involvement with others, the effectiveness of their social skills, and the likelihood that they will have a well-developed social support system. A low score on 0 will often reduce the degree of pathology that might otherwise be suggested by elevations on the other scales. A low 0 also suggests that, even if persons have a certain level of pathology, they are able to find socially acceptable outlets for these difficulties. In contrast, a high 0 suggests an exaggeration of difficulties indicated by the other scales. This is particularly true if 0, 2, and 8 are all elevated. This suggests that the person feels socially alienated, withdrawn, is self-critical, and has unusual thoughts. However, he or she is not likely to have an adequate social support group to help in overcoming these difficulties. Although an elevated 0 can suggest an increase in personal difficulties, it often reflects a decreased likelihood of acting out. This is further supported by corresponding elevations on 2 and 5 (for males or a lowering for females). As a result 0, 2, and 5 are often referred to as inhibitory scales.

High Scores on Scale 0   Persons scoring high on scale 0 will feel uncomfortable in group interactions and may have poorly developed social skills. They may be self-effacing, lacking in self-confidence, submissive, shy, and timid. Others might experience them as cold, distant, rigid, and difficult to get to know. Extremely high scorers are described as withdrawn, ruminative, indecisive, insecure, and retiring. They are both uncomfortable regarding their lack of interaction with others and sensitive to the judgments others make of them. Often they will not have a well-developed social support group to help them overcome difficulties. Persons with moderate scores on 0 are dependable, conservative, cautious, unoriginal, serious, and overcontrolled. Normal males who score high on 0 are described as modest, inhibited, lacking in self-confidence, and generally deficient in poise and social presence. Normal females who score moderately high are somewhat similarly described as modest, shy, self-effacing, sensitive, and prone to worry.

Low Scores on Scale 0   Low scorers are described as warm, outgoing, assertive, self-confident, verbally fluent, and gregarious. They are likely to be concerned with power, recognition, and status. They may even be opportunistic, exhibitionistic, manipulative, and self-indulgent. Normal males who score low are often perceived as being sociable, expressive, socially competitive, and verbally fluent. Normal females are similarly described as sociable, talkative, assertive, enthusiastic, and adventurous. Extremely low scores suggest a person who has highly developed social techniques but, behind their external image, may have feelings of insecurity with a strong need for social approval. They may also be hypersensitive and may have difficulties dealing with feelings of dependency. They are likely to have a large number of superficial friends, but probably do not feel close to anyone.

TWO-POINT CODES

Code-type interpretation often produces more accurate and clinically useful interpretations than merely interpreting individual scales. The basis of code-type interpretation depends on empirical correlations among various classes of nontest behavior. The two-point codes included in the following section have been selected based on their frequency of occurrence, the thoroughness of the research performed on them, and their relative clinical importance. Thus, not all two-point codes will be discussed.

Code-type interpretation is most appropriate for disturbed populations in which T-score elevations are at least 70 on the MMPI and 65 on the MMPI-2. The descriptions are clearly oriented around the pathological dimensions of an individual. The two-point code descriptions, then, do not have the same divisions into low, moderate, and high elevations as the individual scores but are directed primarily toward discussions of high elevations. When considering two-point codes that are in the moderate range (MMPI T = 65–70; MMPI-2 T = 60–65), interpretations should be made with caution and the more extreme descriptions should be considerably modified or even excluded.

Usually, the elevation of one scale in relationship to the other does not make much difference as long as the elevations are still somewhat similar in magnitude. A general approach is that, if one scale is 10 points or more higher than the other, then the higher one gives more color to, or provides more emphasis for, the interpretation. Specific elaborations are made for scales in which a significant difference between their relative elevations is especially important. If the scales have an equal magnitude, they should be given equal emphasis.

In some cases, three or more scales might be equally elevated, thereby making it difficult to clearly establish which scales represent the two-point code. In these cases, clinicians should look at the descriptions provided for other possible combinations. For example, if scales 2, 7, and 8 are elevated for a particular profile, then the clinician should look up the 27/72 code as well as codes 78/87 and 28/82. The descriptions for all three codes can then be integrated into a final description of the client. When three or possibly four scales are elevated along with the two-point code, all can be integrated into a description of the person.

In developing meaningful interpretations, it is important to continually consider the underlying significance of elevated scales. This requires taking into account such factors as the manner in which the scales interact, the particular category of psychopathology they suggest, and the recurring patterns or themes indicated. Whenever possible, DSM-III/DSM-III-R classifications have been used, but the term "neurosis" is used occasionally due to its ability to summarize a wide variety of disorders and/or its ability to refer to a cluster of related scales (e.g. "neurotic triad"). Some characteristics described in the code types will be highly accurate for a specific person while others will not be particularly relevant or accurate. Clinicians, then, will need to continually reflect on their data to develop descriptions and diagnoses that are both accurate and relevant.

12/21

Difficulties experienced by patients with the 12/21 code type revolve around physical symptoms and complaints that can be either organic or functional. Common complaints relate to pain, irritability, anxiety, physical tension, fatigue, and overconcern with physical functions. In addition to these symptoms is the presence of a significant level of depression. These individuals characteristically handle psychological conflict through repression and attending to real, exaggerated, or imagined physical difficulties. Regardless of whether these physical difficulties are organically based, these individuals will exaggerate their symptoms and use them to manipulate others. In other words, they elaborate their complaints beyond what can be physically confirmed, often doing so by misinterpreting normal bodily functions. Typically, they have learned to live with their complaints and use them to achieve their own needs. They lack insight, are not psychologically sophisticated, and resent any implications that their difficulties may be even partially psychological. This code pattern is more frequently encountered in males and older persons.

The three categories of patients that this code is likely to suggest are the generalized hypochondriac, the chronic pain patient, and persons having recent and severe accidents. General hypochondriacs are likely to have significant depressive features and to be self-critical, indirect, and manipulative. If their difficulties are solely functional, they are more likely to be shy and withdrawn, whereas persons with a significant organic component are likely to be loud complainers. Furthermore, complaints are usually focused around the trunk of the body and involve the viscera. This is in contrast to the 13/31 code in which complaints are more likely to involve the central nervous system and peripheral limbs. When the 12/21 code is produced by chronic pain patients with an organic basis, they are likely to have given in to their pain and learned to live with it. Their experience and/or expression of this pain is likely to be exaggerated, and they use it to manipulate others. They may have a past history of drug or alcohol abuse, which represents attempts at "self-medication." The most common profile associated with heavy drinkers consists of elevations in scales 1, 2, 3, and 4. Such persons will experience considerable physical discomfort, digestive difficulties, tension, depression, and hostility, and will usually have poor work and relationship histories. The third category of patient associated with the 12/21 code involves persons who are responding to recent, severe accidents. Their elevations on scales 1 and 2 reflect an acute reactive depression that occurs in response to the limiting effects of their condition.

The most frequent diagnosis with this code is hypochondriasis, and the somatic overconcern can be further supported if a corresponding elevation exists on scale 3. With a 127 profile, the likelihood of an anxiety disorder is increased. Such people will be fearful, anxious, nonassertive, dependent, and weak. Through the use of their helplessness, they will manipulate others into taking care of them. If scales 1 and 2 are elevated along with 8 and/or F, the person might be diagnosed as having a schizophrenic disorder with somatic delusions. With only moderate elevations in scale 8, the individual may still be hypochondriacal but with the presence of some mild somatic delusions, interpersonal alienation, and mild mental confusion. Less frequent patterns are 124, 126, and 1264, which may reflect a personality disorder, especially a passive aggressive personality experiencing depression.

13/31

The 13/31 code type is associated with the classic "conversion V," which occurs when scale 2 is significantly lower (10 points or more) than scales 1 or 3. As 2 becomes lower in relation to 1 and 3, the likelihood of a conversion disorder increases. This type of difficulty is strengthened in males who have correspondingly high scales 4 and 5, and in females with a correspondingly high 4 but lowered 5. However, the 13/31 code type is more frequent in females and the elderly than in males and younger persons. Typically, very little anxiety is experienced by persons with these profiles since they are converting psychological conflict into physical complaints. However, this can be checked by looking at the corresponding elevations of scales 2 and 7. If these are also high, it indicates that persons are experiencing anxiety and depression, perhaps because their conversions are currently unable to effectively eliminate their conflicts.

Persons with "conversion Vs" will typically engage in extensive complaining about physical difficulties. Complaints may involve problems related to eating, such as obesity, nausea, anorexia nervosa, or bulimia, and there may be the presence of vague "neurological" difficulties, such as dizziness, numbness, weakness, and fatigue. However, there is often a sense of indifference and a marked lack of concern regarding these symptoms. These individuals have a strong need to appear rational and socially acceptable, yet nonetheless control others through histrionic and symptom-related means. They defensively attempt to appear hypernormal, which is particularly pronounced if the K scale is also elevated. Usually, they are extremely threatened by any hint that they are unconventional and tend to organize themselves around ideals of service to others. Regardless of the actual, original cause of the complaints, a strong need exists to exaggerate them. Even if their complaints were originally caused by an organic impairment, there will be a strong functional basis to their problems. Interpersonal relationships will be superficial, with extensive repression of hostility, and often their interactions will have an exhibitionistic flavor. Others describe them as selfish, immature, and egocentric. They typically lack insight into their difficulties, use denial, and will often blame others for their difficulties. Since they lack insight and need to appear hypernormal, they typically make poor candidates for psychotherapy.

If scale 3 is higher than scale 1, this allows for the expression of a certain degree of optimism, and their complaints will most likely be to the trunk of the body. Thus, patients might complain of such difficulties as gastrointestinal disorders, or diseases of the lungs or heart. Furthermore, a relatively higher 3 suggests the strong use of denial and repression. These people are passive, sociable, and dependent; they manipulate others through complaints about their "medical" problems. Conversely, if scale 3 is lower than scale 1, the person tends to be significantly more negative, and any conversion is likely to be to the body extremities—such as the hands or legs. If scores are very high on scale 8, a corresponding peak on scale 1 is associated with somatic delusions.

When the "conversion V" is within the normal range (1 and 3 at or slightly below 70 on the MMPI or 65 on the MMPI-2), persons will be optimistic but somewhat immature and tangential. Under stress, their symptom-related complaints will usually increase. They can be described as responsible, helpful, normal, and sympathetic.

The most frequent diagnoses with 13/31 codes are major affective disorders (major depression, dysthymic disorder) hypochondriasis, conversion disorder, passive aggressive personality, and histrionic personality. Anxiety may be present if either scale 7 or 8 is elevated, but these corresponding elevations are rare. The 13/31 profile is also found in pain patients with an organic injury whose symptoms typically worsen under stress.

14/41

The 14/41 code is encountered somewhat rarely, but is important since persons with these elevations will be severely hypochondriacal. Their interpersonal interactions will be extremely manipulative but rarely antisocial. They will be able to maintain control over their impulses but will do so in a way that is bitter, pessimistic, self-pitying, and resentful of any rules and limits that are imposed on them. Furthermore, they will be egocentric, will demand attention, and will express continuous concern with their physical complaints. There will be some similarities to other high-scoring 4s in that these individuals may have a history of alcohol abuse, drug addiction, and poor work and personal relationships. Usually, they will be resistant to therapy, although they may have a satisfactory response to short-term, symptom-oriented treatment. However, long-term therapy will be difficult and characterized by sporadic participation.

The two most frequently encountered diagnoses will be hypochondriasis and a personality disorder, especially antisocial personality. Differentiation between these two can be aided by noting the relative strength of either scale 1 or 4, as well as other related scales. Profiles involving "neurotic" features (anxiety, somatoform, dissociative, and dysthymic disorders) are characterized by a relatively higher scale 1 with 2 and/or 3 also elevated. Personality disorders are more strongly suggested when scale 4 is the primary high point.

18/81

Peaks on scales 1 and 8 are found with persons who present a variety of vague and unusual complaints. They may also experience confusion, disorientation, and difficulty in concentrating. They focus on physical symptoms as a way to organize their thoughts, although the beliefs related to these symptoms may represent delusions. Their ability to deal effectively with stress and anxiety is extremely limited. They will experience interpersonal relationships with a considerable degree of distance and alienation. Often, they will feel hostile and aggressive but will keep these feelings inside. However, when such feelings are expressed, the expressions will be made in an extremely inappropriate, abrasive, and belligerent manner. Others will perceive these individuals as eccentric or even bizarre. They will distrust others and may disrupt their relationships due to difficulty in controlling their hostility. There may even be paranoid ideation, which will probably, but not necessarily, be reflected in an elevated scale 6. They might be confused, distractible, and disoriented. For the most part, their level of insight will be poor, which will make them difficult to work with in psychotherapy.

Common scales that are elevated along with 1 and 8 are 2, 3, and/or 7. These serve to color or give additional meaning to 18/81. Thus, an elevated scale 2 will emphasize self-critical, pessimistic dimensions; 7, the presence of fears and anxiety; and 3, the likelihood of conversions and/or somatic delusions.

The 18/81 code is frequently diagnosed as schizophrenia, especially if the F scale is also high. With a normal F, hypochondriasis is an important possibility, but if scale 7 is elevated, an anxiety disorder is also strongly suggested.

19/91

The 19/91 code is rarely encountered but is important in that it may suggest organic difficulties relating to endocrine dysfunction or to the central nervous system. There will be extensive complaining and overconcern with physical difficulties, but these patients may paradoxically attempt to deny and conceal their complaints at the same time. In other words, they may invest significant energy in avoiding confrontations relating to their complaints, yet will make a display of these techniques of avoidance. They will typically be extraverted, talkative, and outgoing, but also tense and restless. They might be in a state of turmoil and experience anxiety and distress. The expectations they have of themselves will be extremely high, yet their goals will be poorly defined and often unobtainable. If their complaints have no organic basis, then their behavior may be an attempt to stave off an impending depression. Often, this depression will be related to strong but unacceptable dependency needs. Psychotherapy will be difficult since these individuals are reluctant to accept a psychological explanation for their complaints.

Both hypochondriasis and manic states are frequent diagnoses and may occur simultaneously. These may be in response to, and exacerbated by, an underlying organic condition, an impending depression, or both. Corresponding elevations on scales 4 and 6 make the possibility of a passive aggressive personality an important diagnostic consideration.

23/32

Persons with elevations on scales 2 and 3 are lacking in energy, weak, apathetic, listless, depressed, and anxious. They feel inadequate and have difficulty accomplishing their daily activities. Much of their energy is invested in excessively controlling their feelings and behavior. Although situational stress may serve to increase their depression, usually this depression is longstanding, and they have learned to live with their unhappiness and general lack of satisfaction. They are often perceived as passive, docile, and dependent, and therefore often obtain nurturance from others. Their level of insight is poor, they will rarely volunteer for psychotherapy, and they usually do not show significant improvement during psychotherapy. This is primarily because their main dynamic is denial and situations such as therapy represent a threat to their style of avoidance. By keeping their relationships superficial, they achieve a certain level of security. Interpersonally, they appear immature, childish, and socially inadequate.

Some important male-female differences exist in the expression of this code type. Males are more ambitious, industrious, serious, and competitive, but also are immature and dependent. They strive for increased responsibilities, yet also fear them. They want to appear normal and receive recognition for their accomplishments, yet they often feel ignored and their level of work adjustment is often inadequate. In contrast, females are more apathetic and weak, and experience significant levels of depression. They have usually resigned themselves to long-term unhappiness and a lack of satisfaction. Although there is often significant marital strife, they rarely seek divorce. They also rarely seek treatment and seem resigned to live with their unhappiness.

Affective disorders represent the most frequent category of diagnosis given to this code. Corresponding elevations on scales 4, 6, and 0 may provide additional information relating to the personality of these persons. With a high scale 4, there is more likely to be an angry, brooding component to their depression, with underlying antisocial thoughts, yet their external behavior is usually overcontrolled. An elevated scale 6 suggests that their depression relates to extreme interpersonal sensitivity and distrust, whereas a high 0 indicates they are socially withdrawn and introspective. An additional diagnosis that should be considered is a major depression with psychotic features, especially if scales F and/or 8 are also elevated. Many patients with this code type are diagnosed as having a somatoform disorder. A 23/32 code type is frequently seen with chronic pain patients, especially if 1 is also elevated.

24/42

The most significant aspect of the 24/42 code is that these persons have an underlying antisocial trend to their personality, with difficulty maintaining control over their impulses. However, once they act on their underlying antisocial impulses, they experience guilt and anxiety regarding the consequences of their actions. This anxiety usually occurs too late to serve as an effective deterrent, and these individuals are unable to plan ahead effectively. The depression they experience is probably situational, and the distress they do feel may reflect a fear of external consequences rather than an actual internalized moral code. Once the situation has subsided, there is usually further acting out. For this reason, the 24/42 code is sometimes considered to reflect an antisocial personality who has been caught. Although such people may promise to change and their guilt is generally authentic, their acting out is usually resistant to change. Effective therapy must include clear limits, a change in environment, warm supports, and continual contact. However, the prognosis for long-term success in therapy is poor and the individuals will be likely to terminate when confronted with situational stress.

The history of persons with high scales 2 and 4 is often characterized by heavy drinking and/or drug abuse, which serves as a form of self-medication for their depression. Their interpersonal relationships are poor, which is reflected in numerous family difficulties and sporadic employment. Their prospects for long-term employment are rarely favorable. These problems have often resulted in numerous legal complications. Such persons respond to their failures with pessimism, self-criticism, and self-doubt. The initial impression they give may be friendly or even charming, and in a hospital setting they may attempt to manipulate the staff. At their best they can appear sociable, competent, and enthusiastic.

The hostility that is present with the 24/42 code may be expressed either directly or indirectly. A more direct expression is suggested if scale 6 is high, since these individuals may feel justified in externalizing their anger due to real or imagined wrongs that have been committed against them. In contrast, a low 6 may reflect a suppression or unconscious denial of hostility. If high energy levels are suggested by a high scale 9, the person may be extremely dangerous and volatile, and they may have committed violent behaviors.

The 24/42 code is associated with personality disorders, especially passive aggressive or antisocial personalities. This is further strengthened if scale 6 is also high. However, this code very frequently reflects an adjustment disorder with a depressed mood. An important distinction to make is whether the depression is reactive or chronic. If chronic, then difficulties related to anxiety, conversions, and depression (neurotic features) will be more likely to be predominant, especially if scales 1 and 3 are also high. A reactive depression is more likely to represent an antisocial personality who has been apprehended for his or her impulsive acting out. Substance abuse may be either their primary difficulty or may occur in addition to the other disorders suggested above. If scale 4 is extremely elevated (above 90), a psychotic or prepsychotic process may be present, especially if F and 8 are also high.

26/62

The most significant feature of the 26/62 code is extreme sensitivity to real or imagined criticism. These individuals will sometimes interpret the statements of others in a way that creates rejection, yet their conclusions will be based on insufficient data. Even minor criticism is brooded over and elaborated upon. Usually, they have long histories of difficulties with interpersonal relationships. Others describe them as resentful, aggressive, and hostile. To protect themselves from the impending rejection of others, they will often reject others first, which results in other people avoiding them. When they are avoided, these individuals then have evidence that they are being rejected which gives them a justification for feeling and expressing anger. They can then blame others for their difficulties. This cycle is thus self-fulfilling and self-perpetuating, yet such people have difficulty understanding the part they play in creating the interpersonal responses that are directed toward them.

If scales 7, 8, and possibly 9 are also high, a greater likelihood of a psychotic or prepsychotic condition exists, especially paranoid schizophrenia. A more controlled, well-defined paranoid system with a generally adequate level of adjustment may be suggested when scales 2, 6, and F are only moderately elevated. Further possible diagnoses with the 26/62 code are a dysthymic disorder and, if scale 4 is also elevated, a passive aggressive personality.

27/72

The 27/72 code is extremely common in psychiatric populations and reflects persons who are depressed, agitated, restless, and nervous. Their behavior may be accompanied by slowed speech and movements, as well as by insomnia and feelings of social and sexual inadequacy. Scales 2 and 7 reflect the relative degree of subjective turmoil the person is experiencing and therefore are often referred to as the "distress scales." Even though 27/72 persons usually express a great deal of pessimism regarding treatment and the future in general, their psychological distress is ordinarily reactive, and, in time, they can be expected to improve. With most patients, the disorder takes between one month and one year to develop, and, if they report for treatment, it will be their first need for such intervention. Most are married and their courtships were fairly brief, many marrying within one month of their initial dating. They can be characterized as perfectionistic, meticulous, and as having a high need for recognition. Their thinking is often obsessive, and they experience a wide variety of phobias and fears. Interpersonally, they have difficulty asserting themselves and will be self-blaming, self-punishing, and passive dependent. They will rarely be argumentative or provocative. Their consciences are strong and inflexible, and they will often be extremely religious in a rigidly fundamental manner. They worry excessively, often overreacting to minor stress, and anticipate possible situations with negative outcomes. Physical complaints may include weakness, fatigue, chest pain, constipation, and dizziness.

Moderate elevations on scales 2 and 7 can indicate a good prognosis for therapy, since this suggests that the person is introspective and is experiencing a sufficient amount of distress to be motivated to change. However, if these scales are extremely high, the person may be too agitated to focus and concentrate. In such cases, medication may be necessary to relax them sufficiently enough to function in a psychotherapeutic context. The presence of suicidal thoughts is a definite possibility, especially if scales 6 and 8 are also elevated, and the suicidal potential of these patients must be carefully evaluated.

The most frequent diagnoses are affective disorders, particular major affective disorder, although they might also have an adjustment disorder with depressed mood. Anxiety disorders are also a possibility, particularly obsessive-compulsive disorder. Possible personality disorders might be avoidant, compulsive, or passive aggressive. However, with only moderate elevations, they may be normals who are fatigued and exhausted, with a high degree of rigidity and excessive worry. This code occurs more frequently with males 27 years or older from higher educational backgrounds.

28/82

Persons with the 28/82 code complain of depression, anxiety, insomnia, fatigue, and weakness, as well as mental confusion, memory impairments, and difficulties in concentrating. They may also feel withdrawn, alienated, agitated, tense, and jumpy. Their motivation to achieve is characteristically low, as is their overall level of efficiency. Often, they will have fears relating to an inability to control their impulses, including suicide. They are suspicious and extremely sensitive to the criticisms of others. Typically they will underestimate the seriousness of their condition and are often resistant to psychotherapy. Delusions and hallucinations may also be present, especially if scale 8 is greater than 85. This list of complaints presents a highly diverse description of attributes, only some of which may be present in any specific case. The presence or absence of these complaints must be determined by examining data other than mere scale elevations. This may include the investigation of critical items, clinical interview data, personal history, and the use of additional scales, such as those developed by Harris and Lingoes. Of particular importance is the determination of the degree to which suicide is a possibility.

Most persons with this code type are diagnosed as having a major affective disorder (bipolar-depressed or major depression). Schizoaffective disorder is also a possibility. Personality disorders might include avoidant, compulsive, or passive aggressive.

29/92

Although anxiety and depression are present with the 29/92 code, a high level of energy also predominates. This energy may be associated with a loss of control, or it may also serve to defend against experiencing underlying depressive feelings. By speeding up their level of activity, these individuals can distract themselves from unpleasant depressive experiences. At times, this will be successful, but they may also use alcohol either to relax or to decrease their depression. With moderate elevations, this code will at least reflect tension and restlessness. Often, these persons will ruminate on feelings of worthlessness. They are typically perceived as self-absorbed and self-centered. Somatic complaints (especially upper-gastrointestinal) and difficulties with sporadic alcohol abuse are common.

If both scales are in the higher elevations, this suggests a mixed bipolar depression. However, both scales can change according to the particular phase the patient is in. This code can also reflect certain types of brain-injured patients or a cyclothymic disorder.

34/43

Persons having peaks on scales 3 and 4 are immature and self-centered, with a high level of anger that they have difficulty expressing. Thus, their anger will often be expressed in an indirect, passive-aggressive style. Outwardly, such individuals are continually trying to conform and please other people, but they still experience a considerable degree of anger and need to find ways of controlling or discharging it. This anger stems from a sense of alienation and rejection from family members. They might at times vicariously act out their aggression by developing a relationship with an individual who directly and spontaneously expresses his or her hostility. Such a relationship might be characterized by the 34/43 individual's covertly encouraging and fueling the other person's angry expressions, yet on a more superficial social level, disapproving of the other person. Typically, these individuals will have poor insight regarding their own behavior. If scale 6 is also high, their lack of insight will be even more pronounced since their hostility will be projected onto others. Usually, past interpersonal relationships have been difficult. There may be a history of acting out, marital discord, and alcohol abuse. Conflicts relating to dependence versus independence are significant since both of these needs are intense. Females are more likely than males to have vague physical complaints—such as headaches, blackouts, and upper-gastrointestinal complaints. Despite such complaints, these females are generally free from extensive levels of anxiety. Furthermore, their relationships will be superficial, and will be characterized by naive expectations and a perfectionistic view of the world, which they maintain by glossing over and denying conflicts.

The 34/43 code most clearly fits the pattern of a passive-aggressive personality. However, histrionic or borderline personalities are also common. Persons with 34/43 code types are also frequently diagnosed as having an adjustment disorder with depressed mood or mixed emotional features. If both scales are extremely elevated (T greater than 85), then there may be fugue states in which aggressive and/or sexual impulses will be acted out.

36/63

A 36/63 code type indicates that the person is extremely sensitive to criticism, and represses his or her hostile and aggressive feelings. These individuals are fearful, tense, and anxious, and may complain of physical difficulties—such as headaches or stomach problems. Overtly, they might deny suspiciousness and competitiveness, and might even see the world in naively accepting, positive, and perfectionistic terms. They can quickly and easily develop comfortable, superficial relationships. However, as a relationship's depth and closeness increases, their underlying hostility, egocentricity, and even ruthlessness becomes more apparent. If scale 6 is higher than scale 3 (by more than 5 points), these individuals will attempt to develop some sense of security in their lives by seeking power and prestige. Their ability to acquire personal insight is limited since they are psychologically unsophisticated and resent suggestions that their difficulties may be even partially psychological. They will usually blame their personal problems on others, which creates one of their major difficulties in relationships. In therapy, they will typically terminate abruptly and unexpectedly, and they can be ruthless, defensive, and uncooperative. If scale 3 is higher than scale 6 (by more than 5 points), their tendency to blame will be reduced, and such people will be more likely to deny any conflicts or problems. This will be consistent with a tendency to idealize both themselves and their world. They will be more likely to develop somatic complaints rather than paranoid ideation, and the chance of a psychotic process is significantly reduced.

38/83

The somewhat rare 38/83 code involves symptoms of anxiety, depression, and such complaints as headaches, gastrointestinal disturbances, and numbness. If scale 8 is significantly higher than scale 3, these individuals may also have thought disturbances—including mental confusion, disorientation, difficulties with memory, and at times, delusional thinking. They often experience considerable turmoil and feel tense, fearful, and worried. Outwardly, they might appear apathetic and withdrawn. Although they have unusual experiences related to their thought processes and feel socially alienated, they also have strong needs to appear normal and strong needs for affection. However, they feel that, if others knew how unusual their experiences were, they would be rejected. Thus, they are extremely afraid of dependent relationships. To protect themselves, they use extensive denial, which makes their capacity for insight poor. They typically will describe their difficulties in a vague, guarded, and nonspecific manner.

An important variation from the 38/83 code occurs when an elevated scale 3 is accompanied by an elevation on K, with low F and 8. Persons with this profile are likely to be affiliative, inhibited, and overconventional, and to have an exaggerated need to be liked and approved of by others. Frequently, they maintain an unrealistic yet unassailable optimism. They emphasize harmony, perhaps even at the cost of sacrificing their own needs, attitudes, and beliefs. Furthermore, individuals who have high 3s with low F scores are extremely uncomfortable with anger and will avoid it at all costs. Typically, they will also avoid independent decision making and many other situations in which they must exert their power. Since they have an exaggerated sense of optimism and deny their personal conflicts, these individuals rarely appear in mental health clinics. It is almost as if any feelings of anger, tension, or defeat are intolerable. Such feelings seem to represent both a personal failure and, perhaps more importantly, a failure in their attempts at controlling their world by developing an overconventional, exaggeratedly optimistic, and inhibited stance.

When scale 3 is relatively higher than scale 8, and 8 and/or F is less than 70, somatoform or dissociative disorders are important considerations. If 8 and F are highly elevated, the person might be schizophrenic.

45/54

High scores on scales 4 and 5 reflect persons who are immature, self-centered, and inner-directed, and are not only nonconformist but likely to openly express this nonconformity in a challenging, confrontive manner. They may also have significant problems with sexual identity and experience sexual dysfunction. A further area of conflict revolves around ambivalence relating to strong but unrecognized dependency needs. Overt homosexuals who make obvious displays of their orientation may have this code, especially if scales 4 and 5 are the only peaks in an otherwise normal profile. However, the 45/54 code should in no way be considered diagnostic of homosexuality but simply, at times, consistent with such an orientation. To obtain further information associated with this or any profile in which scale 5 is a high point, it is extremely helpful to interpret the third-highest scale and give it the degree of importance usually associated with the second-highest point. Thus, a profile in which 4, 5, and 6 are all high might be interpreted as though it were a 46/64 code type.

Some important differences exist between males and females who have this code. Males will be openly nonconformist, but if they are from higher educational levels, they will be more likely to direct their dissatisfaction into social causes and express organized dissent toward the mainstream culture. If 9 is correspondingly high, they will be dissatisfied with their culture, sensitive, and aware, but will also have the energy to attempt to create change. They are often psychologically sophisticated, and can communicate clearly and openly. In contrast, elevated scales 4 and 9 accompanied by a low scale 5 suggest a high probability of sexual acting out and the probable development of a "Don Juan" type personality. These men are self-centered and have difficulty delaying their gratification, and behind their overt display of affection is an underlying current of hostility.

Females with the 45/54 code will be openly rebelling against the traditional feminine role. Often, this rebellion is motivated by an intense fear related to developing dependent relationships. A further alternative interpretation is that these women are merely involved in a subculture or occupation that emphasizes traditionally male-oriented activities.

46/64

Persons with the 46/64 code type are hostile, brooding, distrustful, irritable, immature, self-centered, and usually unable to form close relationships. They have significant levels of social maladjustment often related to continually blaming others for their personal faults. This style of blaming prevents them from developing insight into their own feelings and behavior, since they are constantly focusing on the behavior of others rather than their own. They lack self-criticism, and are highly defensive and argumentative, especially if L and K are also high. Although they lack self-criticism, they are highly sensitive to real or imagined criticism from others, often inferring hostility or rejection when this was not actually intended. To avoid rejection and maintain a certain level of security, they become extremely adept at manipulating others. Often, they will have a history of drug addiction or alcohol abuse.

Frequent corresponding high points are on scales 2, 3, and/or 8. Males with high 8s are often psychotic, especially paranoid schizophrenic or prepsychotic, but with 2 and/or 3 also elevated, the chances of a borderline condition are significantly increased. These men are likely to be angry and to have significant conflicts relating to their own denied, but strong, needs for dependency. They are likely to rebel against authority figures and may use suicidal threats to manipulate others. Females with a 46/64 code type may be psychotic or prepsychotic, but they are more often passive-aggressive personalities. If scale 3 is also elevated, they will have intense needs for affection and will be egocentric and demanding. However, they will be resentful of the demands placed on them by others.

47/74

Persons with high scores on scales 4 and 7 experience guilt over their behavior, and are brooding and resentful. Although they are frequently insensitive to the feelings of others, they are intensely concerned with their own responses and feelings. They justify this insensitivity because they feel rejected or restricted by others. Their behavioral and inter-personal difficulties follow a predictable cycle in which they will alternately express anger and then feel guilty over their behavior. While they feel angry, they may have little control over their behavior, which results in impulsive acting out. This is then followed by a phase of excessive overcontrol accompanied by guilt, brooding, and self-pity. Frustrated by these feelings, they may then attempt to selfishly meet their needs through such means as alcohol abuse, promiscuity, or aggressive acting out. Thus, the cycle continues and is usually fairly resistant to change. These persons respond to limit-setting with anxiety and resentfulness, often either testing the limits or completely ignoring them. This frequently leads to legal problems and to difficulties in their work and home relationships. Although they do feel genuine and even excessive guilt and remorse, their self-control is still inadequate and their acting out continues. This is a chronic pattern, and therapeutic attempts to decrease the anxiety of these individuals may actually result in an increase in their acting out because the control created by their guilt and remorse might be diminished. Diagnostically, the 47/74 type is most likely to be either an antisocial personality or an anxiety disorder.

48/84

Persons with the 48/84 code are strange, eccentric, emotionally distant, and have severe problems with adjustment. Their behavior is unpredictable and erratic, and may involve strange sexual responses. Usually there will be antisocial behavior resulting in legal complications. These individuals also lack empathy, and are nonconforming and impulsive. Sometimes, they will be members of strange religious cults or unusual political organizations. In their early family histories, they learned that relationships were dangerous due to constant confrontation with intense family conflicts. They were rejected and, as a result, felt alienated and hostile, sometimes attempting to compensate with counterrejection and other forms of retaliation. Their academic and later work performance has usually been erratic and characterized by underachievement. In interpersonal relationships, their judgment is generally poor and their style of communication is likely to be inadequate. Often, others feel as if they are missing important elements or significant connotations of what the 48/84 individual is saying, but they cannot figure out exactly what or why.

If F is elevated with a low scale 2, these individuals are typically aggressive, cold, and punitive, and have a knack for inspiring guilt and anxiety in others. Often, they take on roles in which such behavior is socially sanctioned—for example, a rigid law enforcement officer, overzealous member of the clergy, or a strict school disciplinarian. Their behavior may range all the way from merely stern, punitive, and disapproving to actual clinical sadism. Underneath these overt behaviors, they usually have a deep sense of alienation, vulnerability, and loneliness, which may give rise to feelings of anxiety and discomfort.

Criminal behavior occurs frequently in males with a 48/84 code type, especially when scale 9 is also elevated. The crimes are likely to be bizarre, and often extremely violent, involving homicide and/or sexual assault. These behaviors are usually impulsive, poorly planned, without apparent reason, and generally self-defeating, eventually resulting in self-punishment. Females are less likely to act criminally, but their relationships will usually be primarily sexual and they will rarely become emotionally close. Often, they will form relationships with men who are significantly inferior to themselves and who could be described as losers.

The most likely diagnosis is a schizoid or paranoid personality. However, a psychotic reaction—often paranoid schizophrenia—is also common, especially with elevations on scale 6.

49/94

Persons with 49/94 codes not only feel alienated and have antisocial tendencies but also have the energy to act on these tendencies. They can be described as self-indulgent, sensation seeking, impulsive, oriented toward pleasure, irritable, extraverted, violent, manipulative, and energetic. They have poorly developed consciences, with a marked lack of concern for rules and conventions. Since they are free from anxiety, talkative, and charming, they can often make a good initial impression. However, their relationships are usually shallow because any sort of deeper contact with them brings out the more problematic sides of their personality. An investigation of their past history typically reveals extensive legal, family, and work-related difficulties. The 49/94 code, when found in persons over age 30, suggests that this pattern is highly resistant to change. In adolescent males, it is associated with delinquency.

There are numerous difficulties encountered in therapy with these persons. They are unable to focus for any length of time and are constantly embarking on often irrelevant tangents. Furthermore, they have difficulty delaying their gratification and usually do not learn from experience. They will often be irritable, and if confronted by a therapist, their fairly extensive hostility will be expressed. Thus, therapy is likely to be slow, frustrating, and often unproductive.

With a correspondingly low 0, this code is likely to reflect a person with highly developed social techniques who will use these skills to manipulate others. Thus, he or she may be involved in elaborate, antisocial "con" games. If scale 3 is correspondingly high, it decreases the chance of acting out. In these cases, the expression of hostility is likely to be similar to that of the 34/43 code in that it will be indirect and often passive-aggressive. When scale 6 is elevated along with scales 4 and 9, extreme caution should be taken since these individuals will be very dangerous and have poor judgment. Their acting out will often be violent and bizarre, and will appear justified to themselves due to strong feelings of resentment toward others.

The most likely diagnosis is an antisocial personality, although caution should be made, especially when categorizing adolescents since these scales are more commonly elevated for both normal and abnormal adolescents. If scale 8 is also high, it may reflect either a manic state or schizophrenia.

68/86

The key features of people with the 68/86 code type are suspiciousness and distrustfulness, and they often perceive the intentions of others as suspect and questionable. They will be extremely distant from others, with few or no friends. They can be described as inhibited, shy, resentful, anxious, and unable to accept or appropriately respond to the demands that are made of them. This is because they are highly involved in their fantasy world, uncooperative, and apathetic, and because they have poor judgment and experience diffi- culty concentrating. Their sense of reality is poor, and they often experience guilt, inferior- ity, mental confusion, and sometimes their affect will be flat. The content of their thoughts can be expected to be unusual if not bizarre, frequently containing delusions of grandeur and/or self-reference. Surprisingly, their past work history is often adequate, but an inten- sification of their symptoms brought on by stress will usually disrupt their ability to work. Persons with this code are more often single and younger than 26 years of age. If they are married, their spouses are frequently also emotionally disturbed.

The most frequent diagnosis is paranoid schizophrenia, especially if scale 4 is also elevated. These persons will experience depression, inappropriate affect, phobias, and paranoid delusions. If scale 7 is 10 points or more lower than scales 6 and 8, this pattern is referred to as the "paranoid valley" and emphasizes the presence of paranoid ideation. A highly elevated F with scales 6 and 8 above 80 does not necessarily indicate an invalid profile. A paranoid state is also a frequent diagnosis with the 68/86 code; less frequently, organic brain disorders or severe anxiety disorders may be diagnosed.

78/87

The 78/87 code often occurs among psychiatric patients and reflects a level of agitation sufficiently intense to disrupt their daily activities. Usually, this profile represents a reaction to a specific crisis. They may have been previously functioning at a fairly adequate level until some event or series of events triggered a collapse in their defenses. Their style of relating to others is passive, and they have difficulty developing and sustaining mature heterosexual relationships. They are lacking in self-confidence, often experience insomnia, and may have hallucinations and delusions. Common feelings include guilt, inferiority, confusion, worry, and fear, and they may have difficulties related to sexual performance.

There may be a significant suicidal risk, which can be further evaluated by looking at the relative elevation of scale 2, checking relevant critical items, taking a careful history, and asking relevant questions related to their thought processes.

The extent of elevations on scales 7 and 8, and the relative heights between them, have important implications both diagnostically and prognostically. If scale 7 is higher than scale 8, the person's psychological condition is more susceptible to improvement and tends to be more benign. This has a tendency to be true regardless of the elevation of 8, as long as 7 maintains its relatively higher position. The higher scale 7 suggests that the person is still actively fighting his or her problem and has some of his or her defenses still working. Thus, ingrained bizarre thought patterns and withdrawn behavior have not yet become established. A relatively higher scale 8, on the other hand, reflects more fixed patterns and is therefore more difficult to treat. This is particularly true if scale 8 is over 75. If scales 7 and 8 are both greater than 75 (with scale 8 relatively higher), this suggests an established schizophrenic pattern, especially if the "neurotic triad" is low. Even if schizophrenia can be ruled out, the condition tends to be extremely resistant to change, as for example, with a severe, alienated personality disorder. If scale 2 is also elevated, this raises the possibility of either a dysthymic or obsessive-compulsive disorder.

89/98

The 89/98 code suggests persons who are highly energetic, perhaps to the point of hyperactivity. They will be emotionally labile, tense, and disorganized, with the possibility of delusions of grandeur sometimes with a religious flavor, especially if scale 6 is also elevated. Their goals and expectations will be unrealistic; they often make extensive plans that are far beyond their ability to accomplish. Thus, their aspirations will be significantly higher than their actual achievements. Usually, they will have significant complaints related to insomnia. Their interpersonal relationships are childish and immature, and they will usually be fearful, distrustful, irritable, and distractible. This likewise makes psychotherapeutic approaches with them extremely difficult. Furthermore, their level of insight is poor, they resist psychological interpretations of their behavior, and they cannot focus on any one area for any length of time.

The most frequent diagnosis is schizophrenia, or possibly a schizoaffective disorder with manic states. If extensive delusions and hallucinations are present, antipsychotic medication may be indicated. Sometimes, the relative elevation of F can be used as an index of the relative severity of the disorder.

ALTERNATIVE SCALES

Since the initial publication of the MMPI, over 400 new scales have been developed. Some of these have been developed for normals and are unrelated to pathology, such as dominance (Do) and social status (St). Other scales relate more directly to pathological dimensions, and often use the data from Hathaway and McKinley's original standardization sample or the more recent restandardization group. The alternate scales have traditionally been categorized as either supplementary scales or content scales.

Supplementary Scales

Numerous scales have been developed as supplements to the standard clinical and validity scales. There is tremendous variation between the reliability and validity of each of these scales. Scoring is only possible if the entire 566 items are taken for the MMPI (or 567 items for the MMPI-2). Although exact cutoffs for determining high scores have not been specified, they are generally T = 70 for the MMPI and T = 65 for the MMPI-2. The most extensively used and validated of these scales are A (Anxiety), R (Repression), Es (Ego Strength), and the MAC/MAC-R (MacAndrew Alcoholism Scale/Revised).

A (Anxiety)   The 39-item Anxiety scale was developed by Welsh (1956) through a factor analysis of the standard validity and clinical scales. The content of the items center around negative thoughts and depression, low energy, pessimism, and malignant mentation. Split half and test-retest reliabilities were .88 and .87 to .90 respectively (Moreland, 1985; Welsh, 1956). The scale has been found to relate to predicted correlations with other scales and relevant dimensions of patient behavior (Block & Bailey, 1955; Welsh, 1956). High scores suggest that the person is upset, inhibited, uncertain, hesitant, conforming, under stress, and has extreme difficulty making decisions. In contrast, low scores suggest that the person is extraverted, energetic, competitive, and generally has an absence of emotional difficulties.

R (Repression)   The Repression scale was developed by Welsh (1956) at the same time and using the same procedure as the Anxiety scale. Split half reliability was reported to be .48, which is significantly lower than the A (Anxiety) scale, but test-retest reliability was similar (.84 to .85; Moreland, 1985; Welsh, 1956). High scorers tend to be submissive, slow, clear thinking, conventional, and go to great lengths to avoid unpleasant interpersonal situations. In contrast, low scorers are likely to be dominant, enthusiastic, excitable, impulsive, self-indulgent, and outspoken.

Es (Ego Strength)   Barron's (1953) Ego Strength scale consists of 68 items and was designed to assess the degree to which patients would benefit from psychotherapy. The revised scale for the MMPI-2 has only 52 items. Validity studies have produced somewhat mixed results. Graham (1978) summarizes these studies by suggesting that Es is successful in predicting the response of neurotic patients to insight-oriented therapy, but is not useful for other types of patients or other kinds of treatments. In a correlational study with other tests, Harmon (1980) found that Es relates to the degree to which a person has an underlying belief in self-adequacy, along with tolerant, balanced attitudes. High scores suggest these persons can benefit from psychotherapy since they are likely to be adaptable and possess personal resources, good reality contact, a sense of personal adequacy, and good physical health. Persons with low scores are likely to be poorly adjusted, lack personal resources, feel insecure, be rigid, and therefore will have difficulty benefiting from psychotherapy.

MAC/MAC-R (MacAndrew Alcoholism Scale/Revised)   The MacAndrew (1965) scale (MAC or the 1989 revision; MAC-R) consists of 49 items that significantly differentiate between outpatient alcoholics and nonalcoholic psychiatric outpatients. The scale has been found to effectively differentiate alcoholic from other psychiatric patients (Clopton, 1978b; Clopton, Weiner, & Davis, 1980; Svanum, Levitt, & McAdoo, 1982) and to identify persons who are at risk of later developing alcohol-related problems (Williams, McCourt, & Schneider, 1971). However, the scale has difficulty differentiating alcohol abusers from other substance abusers (Burke & Marcus, 1977), and appropriate caution should be taken in assessing males as opposed to females, since female alcoholics have consistently higher scores than males with similar difficulties (Butcher & Owen, 1978). Caution should also be taken in assessing blacks since nonalcoholic black psychiatric patients are likely to score in the higher ranges (Walters, Greene, Jeffrey, Kruzich, & Hastings, 1984). High scores on the MAC/MAC-R scale primarily suggest actual or potential substance abuse but may also suggest extraversion, assertiveness, risk taking, and the possibility of having experienced blackouts and possible difficulties in concentration. Low scores are not only a contraindication of substance abuse but may also suggest introversion, conformity, and low self-confidence.

Additional, frequently used supplementary scales included in the MMPI-2 Manual are OH (Overcontrolled Hostility), Do (Dominance), Re (Social Responsibility), Mt (College Maladjustment), GM/GF (Gender-Role Scales), and PK/PS (Post Traumatic Stress Disorder Scales). Most of the above as well as numerous additional scales are discussed in the 1989 Manual, Caldwell's (1988) *MMPI Supplemental Scale Manual*, and Graham's (1987) *The MMPI: A Practical Guide*.

Content Scales

Other scales have been derived from item content rather than empirically. These scales are most appropriately used as adjuncts in the interpretation of the basic validity and clinical scales. Although scoring keys are sometimes not commercially available, scoring directions can be obtained from such sources as Dahlstrom et al. (1972; 1975), Graham (1987), and the 1989 Manual. The content scales include the Harris and Lingoes subscales, MMPI-2 content scales, and critical items.

Harris and Lingoes Subscales   One of the more popular developments has been the reorganization by Harris and Lingoes (1955, 1968) of the standard scales into more homogeneous content categories. These subscales were constructed by intuitively grouping together items that seemed to reflect a single trait or attitude. The Harris and Lingoes subscales represent a specific breakdown of the already existing scales 2, 3, 4, 6, 8, and 9. The scales and a brief summary of the meanings associated with high scores are provided below. These summaries are derived from material by Harris and Lingoes (1968), and extensions of these materials are summarized by Graham (1987) and Butcher et al. (1989).

Scale 2 (Depression)

D1   **Subjective Depression:** unhappy, low energy, sense of inferiority, low self-confidence, socially uneasy

D2   **Psychomotor Retardation:** low energy, immobilized, socially withdrawn

D3   **Physical Malfunctioning:** reports wide variety of physical symptoms, preoccupied with health

D4   **Mental Dullness:** low energy, pessimistic, little enjoyment of life; difficulties with concentration, attention, and memory

D5   **Brooding:** may feel as if he or she is losing control of his or her thoughts; broods, cries, ruminates, and is hypersensitive

Scale 3 (Hysteria)

Hy1   **Denial of Social Anxiety:** extraverted, comfortable with social interaction, minimally influenced by social standards

Hy2   **Need for Affection:** strong needs for affection with fears that these needs will not be met, denies negative feelings toward others

Hy3   **Lassitude-Malaise:** subjective, discomfort, poor health, fatigued, poor concentration, insomnia, unhappy

Hy4   **Somatic Complaints:** wide variety of physical complaints, denial of hostility toward others

Hy5   **Inhibition of Aggression:** denial of hostility and anger, interpersonally hypersensitive

Scale 4 (Psychopathic Deviate)

Pd1   **Familial Discord:** family that was critical, unsupportive, and interfered with independence

Pd2   **Authority Conflict:** rebellion against societal rules, beliefs of right/wrong that disregard societal norms, legal/academic difficulties

Pd3   **Social Imperturbability:** opinionated, socially confident, outspoken

Pd4   **Social Alienation:** isolated from others, feels poorly understood

Pd5   **Self Alienation:** unhappy with self, guilt and regret regarding past behavior

Scale 6 (Paranoia)

Pa1   **Persecutory Ideas:** perceives world as dangerous, feels poorly understood, distrustful

Pa2   **Poignancy:** feels lonely, tense, hypersensitive, possibly high sensation-seeking

Pa3   **Naivete:** overly optimistic, extremely high moral standards, denial of hostility

Scale 8 (Schizophrenia)

Sc1   **Social Alienation:** feels unloved, mistreated, and possibly persecuted

Sc2   **Emotional Alienation:** depression, fear, possible suicidal wishes

Sc3   **Lack of Ego Mastery, Cognitive:** strange thoughts, sense of unreality, poor concentration and memory, loss of mental control

Sc4   **Lack of Ego Mastery, Conative:** depressed, worried, fantasy withdrawal, life is too difficult, possible suicidal wishes

Sc5   **Lack of Ego Mastery, Defective Inhibition:** sense of losing control of impulses and feelings, labile, hyperactive, cannot control or recall certain behaviors

Sc6   **Bizarre Sensory Experiences:** hallucinations, peculiar sensory and motor experiences, strange thoughts, delusions

Scale 9 (Hypomania)

Ma1   **Amorality:** selfish, poor conscience, manipulative, justifies amoral behavior by believing others are selfish and opportunistic

Ma2   **Psychomotor Acceleration:** restless, hyperactive, accelerated thoughts and behaviors, seeks excitement to reduce boredom

Ma3   **Imperturbability:** unaffected by concerns and opinions of others, denies feeling socially anxious

Ma4   **Ego Inflation:** unrealistic perception of abilities, resentful of demands placed on him- or herself

A similar set of subscales has been developed for the Social Introversion (Si) scale. The Si subscales were derived from a rational and empirical analysis of 1,312 college students' responses to the MMPI experimental form AX used by the restandardization committee (Ben-Porath et al., 1989).

Scale 0 (Social Introversion)

Si1   **Shyness:** easily embarrassed, socially uncomfortable, shy

Si2   **Social Avoidance:** dislike and avoidance of group activities, parties, social activities

Si3   **Self/Other Alienation:** poor self-esteem, self-critical, low self-confidence, sense of ineffectiveness

Scoring directions for the Harris and Lingoes and Social Introversion subscales can be found in the MMPI-2 Manual for Administration and Scoring (Butcher et al., 1989). The manual also provides tables indicating the item composition and linear T-score conversions for both sets of subscales. Although scoring templates for use with the MMPI-2 are not currently commercially available, they can be developed by using a transparency and marking the appropriate answers based on the item composition tables. A similar strategy can be used for the Harris and Lingoes subscales on the MMPI by consulting tables found in Dahlstrom et al. (1975) or Graham (1987).

Although the Harris and Lingoes subscales show high intercorrelations with the parent scales (Harris & Lingoes, 1968), the internal consistency of the subscales is somewhat low (.04 to .85; Gocka, 1965). Several initial validity studies are available (Boerger, 1975; Calvin, 1975; Gordon & Swart, 1973) that demonstrate the potential clinical usefulness of these subscales. The Social Introversion subscales have been found to account for 90% of the variance of the Si scale and convergent and discriminant validity was demonstrated based on an analysis of spouses' ratings of one another (Ben-Porath et al., 1989). The practical importance of both sets of subscales is that they provide a useful supplement for interpreting the original scales. For example, a clinician can assess whether a person scoring high on scale 4 (Psychopathic deviate) achieved that elevation primarily due to family discord (Pd 1) authority problems (Pd 2) or social imperturbability (Pd 3). This is likely to be most helpful in interpreting why a client received a high score that was unexpected given their history. It might also be quite useful in interpreting the significance associated with moderate elevations. Based on this knowledge, more accurate evaluations can be made in such areas as acting out potential or response to psychotherapy.

MMPI-2 Content Scales   In contrast to the attempt of Harris and Lingoes to develop subscales for already existing MMPI scales, Wiggins (1966, 1971) developed scales based on an overall analysis of the contents of the MMPI items. He began with item clusters that were based on such areas as authority conflicts and social maladjustment. These clusters were revised and refined using factor analysis and evaluations of internal consistency. During the 1989 restandardization of the MMPI, many of the items relating to the Wiggins scales were altered or deleted. As a result, Butcher et al. (1989) developed a new set of 15 different content scales. Provisional content scales were initially developed by rationally sorting the items into different content categories. These categories were then refined statistically by making item-scale correlations with psychiatric inpatients and correlations between the scales. These more recent content scales are summarized below, along with interpretations associated with high scores. The interpretations are derived from material provided in Butcher, Graham, Williams, & Ben-Porath, (1989).

ANX   **(Anxiety):** generalized anxiety, somatic difficulties, worries, insomnia, ambivalence, tension, life feels like a strain; symptoms are clearly perceived and admitted to by the client

FRS   **(Fears):** multiple specific fears (nuisance animals, blood, dirt, leaving home, natural disasters, etc.)

OBS   **(Obsessiveness):** ruminates, difficulty with decision making, resistant to change, needless repetitive counting, worried

HEA   **(Health Concerns):** numerous physical complaints regarding gastrointestinal, neurological, sensory, skin, cardiovascular and/or respiratory difficulties

BIZ   **(Bizarre Mentation):** psychotic thought processes, hallucinations (auditory, visual, olfactory), paranoid beliefs, strange thoughts, delusions

ANG   **(Anger):** difficulties in controlling anger, irritable, impatient, annoyed, episodes of loss of control, possibly physically abusive

CYN   **(Cynicism):** other people are distrusted, fear of being used, negativity toward friends and associates

ASP   **(Antisocial Practices):** past legal and/or academic problem behaviors, support of illegal behavior, enjoyment of criminal behavior of others

TPA   **(Type A):** driven, hard-working, irritable with time constraints, overbearing, annoyed with interruptions

LSE   **(Low Self-Esteem):** low self-confidence, feels insignificant, negative beliefs regarding self (clumsy, inept, unattractive), acutely aware of faults

SOD   **(Social Discomfort):** shy, withdrawn, uneasy with others, dislikes social events

FAM   **(Family Problems):** family discord, unhappy childhood, difficult marriages

WRK   **(Work Interference):** personal difficulties interfere with work; tension, worry, obsessiveness, career indecision and/or dissatisfaction, poor concentration, dislike of coworkers

TRT   **(Negative Treatment Indicators):** dislike or distrust of helping professionals, discomfort in discussing difficulties, resistance to change, disbelief in the possibility of change

The above content scales are intended to be used as adjuncts for interpreting the traditional clinical scales. The items included in these scales, their direction of scoring, and uniform T scores can be found in the 1989 Manual. Scoring templates are also commercially available through National Computer Systems. However, clients must answer all 567 items to enable scoring of the content scales.

Critical Items   An alternative method of constructing new scales is the interpretation of single items. Several attempts have been made to isolate those items considered critical to the presence of psychopathology. Answering in a significant direction on these items could represent serious pathology, regardless of how the person responded on the remainder of the inventory. These items have been referred to as "pathognomonic items," "stop items," or, more frequently, "critical items." It has been assumed that the direction in which a person responds represents a sample of the person's behavior and acts as a short scale that indicates his or her general level of functioning. Two frequently used lists of critical items are Grayson's (1951) list of 38 items and Caldwell's (1969) more comprehensive list of 69 items. Both of these were intuitively derived and are useful in differentiating which category of crisis a particular patient is in (acute anxiety, depressed-suicidal, mental confusion, etc.). In contrast, the Grayson items could indicate that the person is in crisis, but they are primarily used to specify the presence of psychotic complaints (mental confusion, persecutory ideas). Attempts to establish an efficient cutoff score for differentiating normals from psychiatric patients have met with only minimal success due to the extensive response overlap between the two groups (Koss et al., 1976).

Two more recent and comprehensive lists of critical items have been developed by Koss, Butcher, & Hoffman (1976) and Lachar & Wrobel (1976). They were developed through a combination of intuitive and empirical procedures. Although both sets are somewhat longer and have considerable item overlap with scales F and 8, they are generally more valid. The Koss-Butcher lists for both the MMPI and MMPI-2 are provided in Appendix M. They will be most useful if clinicians look at the individual item content in relationship to the specific types of information that the item reveals. This information might be used to guide further interviewing. In addition, the items themselves, along with the responses ("true" or "false") might be included in the psychological report to provide qualitative information regarding the client. However, some caution needs to be taken in their interpretation since they are both subject to an acquiescing response set (since most items are keyed in the "true" direction) and faking bad.

RECOMMENDED READING

Butcher, J. N. (Ed.). (1979). *New developments in the use of the MMPI*. Minneapolis: University of Minnesota Press.

Butcher, J. N., Graham, J. R., Williams, C. L., & Ben-Porath, Y. S. (1989). *Development and use of the MMPI-2 content scales*. Minneapolis: University of Minnesota Press.

Dahlstrom, W. G., Welsh, G. S., & Dahlstrom, L. E. (1972). *An MMPI handbook; Vol. 1. Clinical interpretation*. Minneapolis: University of Minnesota Press.

Graham, J. R. (1987). *The MMPI: A practical guide*. (2nd ed.). New York: Oxford University Press.

Greene, R. L. (Ed.). (1988). *The MMPI: Use with special populations*. San Diego: Grune & Stratton.

Webb, J. T., McNamara, K. M., & Rodgers, D. A. (1986). *Configural interpretation of the MMPI and CPI*. Columbus: Ohio Psychology Publishing.

Chapter 8

THE CALIFORNIA PSYCHOLOGICAL INVENTORY

The California Psychological Inventory (CPI) is a self-administered, paper-and-pencil test comprised of 462 true-false statements. The test is designed for group administration, although it can also be given individually. Even though the test has been used to evaluate individuals between the ages of 12 and 70, it was mainly constructed for use with young adults having a minimum of a fourth-grade reading ability. The CPI items request information concerning an individual's typical behavior patterns, usual feelings and opinions, and attitudes relating to social, ethical, and family matters. The results are plotted on 20 scales and 3 vectors (factors) focusing on aspects of interpersonal relationships that are presented in everyday, commonsense descriptions.

The philosophical orientation of the CPI is based on an appreciation of enduring, commonly discussed personality variables that are relevant throughout different cultures. Thus, it uses such familiar commonsense terms as dominance, tolerance, and self-control, which Gough has referred to as "folk concepts." The value of using such common, easy-to-understand constructs is that they already have "functional validity." In other words, they have immediate cross-cultural relevance, are readily understood by a wide range of people, and have a high degree of power in predicting behavior. This is not to imply that untrained persons should be allowed to interpret the CPI, but rather that the test's roots and original constructs are based on conceptions of human behavior held by most people within most cultures. It is up to the skilled clinician to go beyond these common constructs and into a more subtle, broad, and integrated description of the person. Thus, the test does not have as its primary goal psychometric elegance, nor is it derived from any specific personality theory. The main focus and concern of the CPI involves practical usefulness and the development of descriptions that strive to be relevant, understandable, and accurate in terms of behavioral predictions.

The CPI was originally developed by Harrison Gough and published in its original form in 1957. Although reviews of the test have been mixed, most reviewers generally describe it in favorable terms. For example, Anastasi (1982, p. 508) has stated that the "CPI is one of the best inventories currently available. Its technical development is of a high order and it has been subjected to extensive research and continuous improvement." The criticisms that have been directed at the CPI have stimulated extensive efforts toward refinement and improvement, including numerous studies on predictive validity, the development of alternate scales, and expanded normative data. Many of these improvements were incorporated into the 1987 revision. For these reasons, the CPI has become a respected and frequently used device in personality assessment, particularly in the areas of career development and personnel selection (McAllister, 1988).

HISTORY AND DEVELOPMENT

The CPI was developed as an inventory to assess enduring interpersonal personality characteristics within a normal population. Gough published his original scales in 1948, but the first copyrighted edition of the initial 15 scales appeared in 1951. However, it was not until 1957 that a completed set of 18 scales were published by Consulting Psychologists Press. It was further revised in 1987 and two new scales were included (empathy and independence), bringing the total number of scales to 20. These 20 scales measure such areas as social ascendency, social image, intellectual stance, and conceptual interests. Three of these are validity scales, which assess test-taking attitudes—including "fake bad" (Wb), "fake good" (Gi), and the extent to which highly popular responses are given (Cm).

The 1957 version of the CPI was derived from an original item pool of 3,500 questions. Of the 468 items that were eventually selected, 178 were identical to MMPI items, 35 were very similar, and the remaining 215 were developed specifically for the CPI. The items were selected on the basis of both empirical criterion keying and a rational approach in which questions were generated that, from a conceptual point of view, seemed to assess the characteristics the scales were trying to measure. These questions were then given to a sample group and accepted or rejected based on the extent of interitem correlation. However, the majority of the scales were not developed through the rational approach but rather through empirical criterion keying. Thus, series of questions, which had initially been developed rationally, were administered to different groups having specific, previously assessed characteristics that the scales were eventually intended to measure independently of these groups. Each group was selected through the use of a number of different criteria. For example, ratings, by friends and family, of an individual's degree of responsibility were used to select a person for inclusion in the sample group for the development of the scale on responsibility. The achievement via independence scale was based on college students' grade point averages; the socialization scale used delinquents and nondelinquents; and sociability involved the number of extracurricular activities that a student participated in. Items that were found to discriminate between the criterion group (responsibility, sociability, etc.) and a "normal" population were selected for initial inclusion in the scale.

It is important to emphasize that, similar to the MMPI items, the empirical relationships are more important than the "truth" of the content. For example, if a person in the group rated for responsibility answers "true" to the statement "I have never done anything hazardous just for the thrill of it," it does not matter whether or not he or she has actually performed hazardous behaviors for the thrill of it. The main consideration from a psychometric point of view is that he or she answers "true" to that question, which then indicates the item can be used to differentiate responsible from nonresponsible persons.

The final step was to cross-validate the items with other populations to determine the extent to which the variable the scale was attempting to measure could be accurately assessed. Of the 18 original scales, 13 used empirical criterion keying, 4 used the rational approach, and the final one (communality) cannot be easily categorized, although it primarily used a combination of the two techniques. The two new scales in the 1987 revision (Empathy and Independence) used a criterion keying approach to elicit and score items that already existed in the CPI.

Like the MMPI, the CPI scores are given a standard score (T score) with a mean of 50 and a standard deviation of 10. The 1957 scales were standardized on an original normative sample of 6,000 males and 7,000 females having a fairly wide range in age, socioeconomic status, and geographic area. The standardization for the 1987 revision was based on 1,000 males and 1,000 females who were selected from the CPI archives to be representative of the U.S. population in age, education, status, and other relevant variables. The 20 scales are arranged so that the first ones relate primarily to interactional, socially observable factors (sociability, social presence), the middle ones to more internal qualities (responsibility, self-control), and the final ones to "broadly stylistic variables related to different functional modes" (intellectual efficiency, flexibility; Gough, 1987). Interpretation is simplified in that higher scale values are associated with traditionally more favorable qualities and lower scores with more unfavorable qualities. The exception to this is the final scale, F/M, which measures traditionally feminine and masculine characteristics. The scales form four groupings or classes that are based more on conceptual convenience than on any psychometrically pure procedures. (Gough, 1987). The first class—containing six scales (Do, Cs, Sy, Sp, Sa, In, Em)—is centered on poise, social ascendancy, and self-assurance. The second class relates more to a person's social image—including socialization, maturity, and responsibility—and contains a total of seven scales (Re, So, Sc, To, Gi, Cm, Wb). Class 3 has only three scales (Ac, Ai, Ie) and assesses the variables of a person's intellectual stance. The final class, consisting of three scales (Py, Fx, Fe), measures conceptual abilities, such as intellectual and interest modes. Gough added three vectors or structural scales to the 1987 version. Rather than organizing these three scales conceptually, he developed them based on factor analysis to measure extraversion-introversion (externality-internality), norm-favoring versus norm-questioning, and degree of self-realization.

The CPI has been put to numerous uses since its initial development in 1957. Megargee (1972) reported that, when the test was first printed, researchers and practitioners used it for many of the more obvious purposes of a psychological test, such as the prediction of scholastic achievement, graduation from high school or college, and performance in specific areas, such as math and English. Later, its uses became much more diversified to the extent that work has now been done on managerial effectiveness, air traffic controllers, stock market speculators, the degree of creativity in such fields as architecture and mathematics, contraceptive practices, and performance in psychiatric residency programs. Furthermore, cross-cultural studies on validity have been performed in France, Israel, Italy, Japan, Poland, Switzerland, and Taiwan. Within the field of counseling, it has been used to predict response to therapy, to aid in the selection of a college major, predict college GPA, and to predict the degree of success in such graduate education programs as medicine, dentistry, nursing, and education. Piotrowski and Keller (1984) give evidence of the test's popularity by pointing out that directors of clinical psychology programs endorsed it as the second most important objective personality test. From 1969 to 1973, it was also the second most frequently used assessment device with adolescents (LeUnes, Evans, Karnei, & Lowry, 1980). Computerized scoring and interpretation services are currently available, and several alternate scales have been developed. Although the manual accompanying the CPI was first published in 1957, it was updated in 1969 and 1975, and along with a revision of the test itself, a new accompanying manual and administrators guide was published in 1987 (Gough, 1957, 1975, 1987). All of this attests to the CPI's extensive diversity, popularity, and success.

COMPARISON WITH THE MMPI

Since there is a similarity in both format and item content, comparisons between the CPI and MMPI are inevitable. Thorndike (1959) has referred to the CPI as "the sane man's MMPI," and there are a number of clear similarities. The CPI uses more than one-third (194 of 462) of the MMPI's questions; a conversion is made from raw to standard scale scores with a mean of 50 and standard deviation of 10; and the final values are charted on a graph with peaks and valleys.

Despite these similarities, it is essential for any clinician using the CPI to also appreciate the significant conceptual and psychometric differences between the two tests. The general intent of the MMPI is to assess a person's intrapsychic processes and emotional distress as these relate to specific psychodiagnostic categories. Each of these categories has a group of internal dynamics surrounding it—such as depression, which also includes apathy, lowered capacity for pleasure, and feelings of hopelessness and helplessness. The primary task of the MMPI is to identify either the presence or absence of these internal dynamics and to place the examinee in either a normal or one or more psychopathological categories. In contrast, the CPI focuses more on a normal population and is highly interpersonal in nature. In fact, there is a marked absence of symptom-oriented questions. Thus, the CPI is concerned with the presence or absence of specific interpersonal skills. In addition, the CPI avoids complex diagnostic nomenclature and instead emphasizes practical descriptions that are commonly used in most cultures.

From a psychometric perspective, the MMPI was developed from a bimodal distribution in which the main focus of the test was to be able to classify a specific client in either a pathological group or a normal one. The contrast groups were not high or low on a specific trait, but rather were high in pathology when compared with normals. For example, a group that was high in hysterical traits was contrasted not with a group of persons having superior health, but with individuals having only an average number of hysterical traits. In clinical assessment, members of the pathological group are considered to be anyone scoring greater than 2 standard deviations above the norm. As a result of this emphasis on differentiating pathological groups from "average" or normal groups, the interpretation of profiles within "normal" ranges (i.e., T = 35-64) is uncertain and should be approached with extreme caution. In contrast, the CPI uses a normal distribution within a standardized population. Furthermore, Gough used groups whose behavior was extreme on both high and low dimensions of the characteristic being measured. Thus, normal range scores of less than 2 standard deviations from the mean can be interpreted with a fairly high level of confidence. For example, a CPI score on Ac (achievement via conformance) of T = 60 indicates a fairly high level of this particular attribute and a T = 40 score indicates a fairly low level. However, an MMPI T score of 60 on scale 8 (schizophrenia) does not indicate a relatively high degree of schizophrenia, nor does a T score of 40 indicate a low level. Thus, relatively normal profiles on the CPI not only are to be expected, but can also be interpreted successfully.

RELIABILITY AND VALIDITY

In general, the reliability and validity studies on the CPI compare favorably with those done on other personality inventories. Test-retest reliabilities for individual scales have ranged between a low reported median of .53 for Empathy to a high median of .80 for Self-control. The overall median reliability was reported to be .70 (Gough, 1987). Measures of internal consistency indicate that there is considerable variability among the test items, but, overall, the scale constructions are adequate. Internal consistency is lowest for the scales of self-acceptance (.52), capacity for status (.58), and empathy (.58), and highest for vector 3 (degree of self-realization; .85), vector 1 (introversion-extraversion; .81), and self-control (.80; Gough, 1987).

Factor analytic studies have been reported for both a 2 factor and 4 factor solution. Megargee (1972) reported that the two factors of internal controls and interpersonal effectiveness accounted for a major portion of the variance on the original 1957 scales. Gough (1987) suggested four different factors for the 1987 revision. These included Extraversion (related to self-assurance, initiative, resourcefulness), Control (related to degree of rule-favoring, rule-following, conscientiousness, self-discipline), Flexibility (individuality, personal complexity, ingenuity, preference for change), and Consensuality (reliability, optimism, cooperation, agreeableness). These factors roughly corresponded with the three vectors or factor scorings that have been included in the 1987 revision. Vector 1 is a measure of introversion-extraversion and vector 2 measures the extent to which a person is norm-favoring versus norm-doubting. Vector 3 provides an index of a person's psychological integration and self-realization.

In line with Gough's practical orientation, the main work on validation has been predictive. Thus, Gough is less concerned with areas of psychometric elegance—such as whether the scales avoid overlap—than with the practical usefulness of the scales in providing accurate predictions. Specifically, persons scoring high on certain scales are more likely to be described in certain characteristic ways by those who know them. The scales themselves or the equations developed from various combinations of scales have also been able to predict a wide variety of different aspects of behavior. Many of the studies that have found useful levels of predictive validity are summarized later in this chapter under Configurational Interpretation.

ASSETS AND LIMITATIONS

The CPI focuses on diagnosing and understanding interpersonal behavior within normal populations. Instead of focusing on pathology, it assesses areas such as self-control, dominance, and achievement. However, even though its emphasis is on assessing normal variations, extreme scores can also provide important information about the specifics of a person's expression of maladjustment, particularly with regard to interpersonal relationships. Whereas the MMPI is limited to use with primarily pathologically oriented populations, the CPI is appropriate for normal persons. Thus, it addresses issues that interest a great many people.

The main thrust of the research and construction of the CPI has been toward developing accurate, long- and short-term behavioral predictions. The focus is not so much on evaluating and predicting a specific, internal, unidimensional trait, but more on interpersonal behaviors and orientations. Gough (1968, p. 56) clarifies this by stressing that "... a high score on a scale for social status does not mean that the individual has a 'trait' of high status; presumably, therefore, he may be already of high status, or possessed of those talents and dispositions that will lead him toward such attainment." Gough also stresses that certain interpersonal behaviors occur within specific contexts. For example, a person who scores high on "dominance" would be expected to assume control of a group requiring leadership. Thus, the longitudinal studies on the inventory have developed predictive strategies relating to such areas as graduating from high school (Gough, 1966), grades in college (Gough & Lanning, 1986), choice of major field in college (Goldschmid, 1967), assertive behavior (Harris & Brown, 1979), persistence among hospice volunteers (Lafer, 1989), and police performance (Hargrave & Hiatt, 1987). A number of special scales have been developed for assessing specific areas. These are available through the CPI computer-scored report and include Managerial Potential, Work Orientation, Leadership Potential

Index, Social Maturity Index, and Creative Potential Index (see McAllister, 1988). The test has generally proven to be a useful tool in the area of prediction and, as a result, has been particularly helpful in counseling high school and college students as well as in personnel selection.

Since the CPI's basic concepts were derived from day-to-day social interaction, it is relatively easily understood by a wide range of persons. Descriptions such as dominant, achievement oriented, and self-controlled are generally straightforward and are therefore not easily misinterpreted by untrained professionals. In contrast, providing feedback to clients who have taken the MMPI requires the clinician to rephrase psychiatric terminology into more approachable, easily understood "lay" terminology. Since the CPI relates to ongoing aspects of behavior, CPI interpretations are also likely to have more immediacy, relevancy, and impact on persons receiving feedback from their test results. These "folk concepts" also are generally found in all cultures and societies. Thus, Gough hoped that the inventory would have cross-cultural relevance and validity. Although some research has been conducted to test this hypothesis, more work still needs to be performed and subgroup norms should be applied when appropriate (Cross & Burger, 1982). Specific areas of future research should be the relationship between CPI scores and race, socioeconomic status, and other demographic variables. Gynther (1978b), in reviewing the literature on the CPI, stated that some of the research performed raises questions about Gough's assumption that the inventory has cross-cultural equivalence. He further questioned whether minorities produce valid results on the inventory. Although this issue is currently unresolved, studies that question the cross-cultural equivalence of the CPI are sufficient in number to advise that scores from persons of differing cultural backgrounds be treated cautiously.

A number of predictive studies have been conducted from a research perspective, and several useful regression equations have been developed as aids in predicting behavior. However, extremely few studies have been performed to test the validity of predictions made by clinicians in actual practice (Gynther, 1978b). It may be that clinical judgments are generally accurate, but at this point further empirical studies are needed to verify this. It is something of a contradiction that a test with an emphasis on practical usefulness has not been sufficiently evaluated within the clinical context. A further difficulty in developing accurate predictions is that few studies have been conducted to assess predictions of actual job performance. Most predictive studies have attempted to estimate such areas as future college attendance or grade point average in graduate programs. However, college attendance and grade point average do not necessarily correlate with later successful performance. For example, high medical school grades have not been found to correlate with later success as a physician (Loughmiller et al., 1970). This problem is certainly not unique to the CPI but is a general issue with many similar tests and relates to a difficulty in adequately establishing appropriate criterion measures. These issues suggest that test users should develop predictions based on test scores within limited and well-researched contexts. For example, if the CPI is being used to evaluate prospective medical students, it should be made clear that predictions are useful only with regard to the students' academic performance and not to their overall clinical skills or later success as physicians.

One major criticism directed toward the CPI is the lack of factor analysis in the development of the different scales (Eysenck, 1985). Factor analytic studies that have been conducted suggest that most of the variance can be accounted for by only two factors: interpersonal effectiveness and internal controls (Megargee, 1972). This conclusion is further supported in that many of the scales are highly correlated, are conceptually similar, and have extensive item overlap. Gough (1968) has responded to this by pointing out the scales were designed to assess constructs that are in most people's minds on a daily basis. Any scale overlap, then, might accurately reflect the conceptual overlap in common folk concepts used on a daily basis, such as the self-control and high degree of socialization involved in responsible behavior. Even if many of the scales are quite similar, there is accumulating evidence that the scales measure what they were designed to measure. The lack of factor analysis is further corrected in that the 1987 version has included three different factor analytically derived scales that measure extraversion-introversion (externality-internality), norm-favoring versus norm-questioning, and degree of self-realization (Gough, 1987).

A further limitation of the CPI is the insufficient number of studies undertaken on the meaning of pairs or triads of scales (Baucom, 1985). This may be partly due to the formidable number of possible CPI code types (compared with the MMPI's more manageable 45 possible combinations). In addition, many persons score within a relatively narrow range, which makes configural interpretation more difficult since there is less likely to be clearly defined clusters of high and low scales (Shaw & Gynther, 1986). In contrast, extensive fruitful research has been conducted on two- and three-point codes for the MMPI. Some of the work conducted on CPI code types is summarized later in the section on Configural Interpretation. Gough's more recent work on the 3 vectors (externality-internality, norm-favoring/norm questioning, and realization) has also provided information regarding composite subscale or factor scores (see section on Structural Scale Interpretations). In addition, McAllister (1988) has listed 132 different combinations of scale scores of which 40 have empirical support and the remaining 92 are based on a combination of rational considerations and clinical experience. However, more research needs to be done on the many possible two- and three-point codes that could potentially be derived from the CPI.

In developing accurate clinical interpretations from the CPI, it is essential to consider the implications of such factors as the overall life situation of the examinee. For example, the profile of a 15-year-old on the CPI scale for psychological mindedness (Py) has a meaning different from that of a person of 55. Another important consideration is the purpose for which the person believes he or she is being examined. A person who is taking the test in a conscious effort to receive a discharge from the military will be likely to bias his or her responses in a direction different from a person seeking employment. It is also essential to look at overall patterns of scores rather than "single sign" indicators. This is because corresponding elevations on other scales can elaborate or modify the meaning they have for one another. Thus, clinicians should always keep in mind the implications of an examinee's overall life situation, age, education, perceived reason for assessment, and pattern of scores.

A final caution relates to the degree of comparability between the 1987 revision and the previous version. In the 1987 revision, the total number of items was reduced (from 468 to 462), some of the scale items changed or deleted, and two new scales included. Gough attempted to improve the old scales and yet preserve their essential meanings. This is somewhat supported in that all correlations between the old and new scales were .91 or higher. Many of the prediction equations have been (and are being) updated. However, the new scales may be different in some yet-to-be defined ways. Thus, it may be questionable whether the extensive research on the previous scales is also relevant for the new ones. It may also be questionable whether clinical interpretation of the new scales should be made in the same manner as the older ones. As more research on the 1987 revision continues, many of these questions can be progressively addressed and interpretations altered (or reinforced).

The CPI, then, is an extremely useful test in the assessment of the interpersonal characteristics of relatively normal persons. It measures variables that interest a great number of people, providing helpful behavioral predictions, and uses routine, day-to-day interactional concepts. For these reasons, the CPI is extensively used in personnel selection and vocational guidance (McAllister, 1988). Significant limitations and cautions relate to limited validity studies in clinical settings, few empirical studies on the meaning of two- and/or three-point elevations, and the unknown (but continually emerging) comparability between the 1987 revision and the previous version.

INTERPRETATION PROCEDURES

Timing

The examiner should note the length of time it takes a person to complete the test. A person with an I.Q. within the normal range would be expected to complete the test in approximately one hour. If he or she takes $1\frac{1}{2}$ hours or more, it suggests one of the following:

1. a major psychological disturbance such as severe depression or functional psychosis
2. a low I.Q. combined with a poor reading ability
3. cerebral impairment

Tests that are completed in 20 minutes or less suggest:

1. an invalid profile
2. an impulsive personality
3. both 1 and 2.

An alternative form of administration is to use an oral or tape-recorded format, which would be particularly relevant for persons with unusually low reading skills. If time efficiency is important, two short forms are available. One is based on a factor analytic strategy (Factor Analyzed Short Form; Burger, 1975) and the other is based on incorporating items repeated on the MMPI (Repeated Item Short Form; Schut, Hutzell, Swint, & Gaston, 1980).

Scoring

In scoring the profile, examiners should check to make sure that scoring norms for the correct sex have been used. Examiners may also wish to extend the traditional scale information by using regression equations for such areas as high-school achievement, parole success, or medical-school performance (see Table 8–2). Alternate scales are also available and may be important in certain contexts.

Determining the Profile Validity

The CPI, similar to the MMPI, has built-in scales and relevant regression equations to detect invalid profiles. This is important since Gough (1987) has estimated that, in large-scale testing situations, approximately 1.7% of all profiles will be invalid (.6% "Fake good," .4% "Fake bad," .7% random answering).

An initial consideration in evaluating the profile validity is to note the number of items that have been left blank. If 30 or more spaces are blank, the test results may not be valid. The examiner should also make sure the subject has not marked a large number of questions

(30 or more) with both "true" and "false" on the same item. Yet another area that should be checked is the possibility of random answering. The subject may appear to have answered randomly simply because he or she was out of step between the number's questions in the answer sheet and test booklet, or may answer randomly in an attempt to hide his or her poor reading ability. A good indicator of random answering is a low score (T = 29 or less for males and 24 or less for females) on the communality (Cm) scale.

"Faking bad" can usually be detected based on the presence of extremely low scores on Well Being (Wb; T = 27 or less for males and 31 or less for females) and Communality (Cm; T = 29 or less for males and 24 or less for females). A low score (T = 39 or less for males and 40 or less for females) on Good Impression (Gi) is also frequently associated with "faking bad," especially in the profiles of males. It should be stressed that a subject who "fakes bad" is not necessarily maladjusted. Rather, it indicates that the specifics of his or her disorder cannot be evaluated due to the distorting effects of the person's need to create an impression of the seriousness of his or her problem. Thus, it is important to assess why the person is "faking bad." It might, for example, represent a "cry for help" in which suicide is a serious possibility, or the person might be malingering due to numerous secondary gains.

To determine whether a subject is "faking good," the most important scale to evaluate is good impression (Gi). "Fake good" profiles will usually have high scores (T = 69 or more for males and 71 or more for females) on this scale, and it will most likely be a relative peak in comparison with the other scales. Usually, when a person is asked to "fake good," all the scales with positive social connotations will be elevated but Gi will still be relatively higher than the others. Sometimes it may be difficult to differentiate between someone who has a superior level of adjustment and a person who is "faking good." The most significant consideration in making this distinction is the person's history. An individual with a history of poor adjustment combined with an unusually high Gi will probably be "faking good," whereas a person with a history of good adjustment and a moderately high Gi will probably be expressing his or her superior level of adjustment.

The above critical-scale values for the three validity scales can generally serve as clinical tools to detect invalid profiles. However, Gough (1987) notes that a significant number of errors are likely to occur. Instead, he recommends a sequence of equations devised by Lanning (1987). The first step is to determine the probability of "faking good" by seeing if the following equation results in a score of 56.65 or greater:

$$44.67 + .15Do + .18Em + .35Gi - .11Wb - .13To - .12Fx$$

Scores equal to or greater than 56.65 indicate a "faked good" profile. However, if scores are less than 56.65, the following equation should be calculated:

$$75.77 - .68Cm - .18Wb + .12Ac$$

Scores on this equation are considered "otherwise invalid" if they are equal to or greater than 58.55 or normal if they are less than 58.55. To determine if the profile is either "random" or "fake bad," the following equation should be calculated:

$$41.95 + .13In + .22Gi - .06Cm + .14Py + .13Fx$$

Scores equal to or greater than 50.00 indicate a randomly answered profile whereas a "fake bad" profile is indicated by scores less than 50.00. Use of the above decision tree is likely to significantly increase the accuracy of detecting invalid profiles when compared with clinical judgment based on single scale evaluations. However, circumstances surrounding test administration still need to be taken into account before a final conclusion can be reached.

Profile Interpretation

Once clinicians have determined that the test is valid, they should consider each of the following steps.

1. **Note the general patterns of elevations/lowerings.** Scores of T = 50 or more usually suggest a positive area of adjustment. If scales are well below T = 50, this indicates specific problem areas. However, the clinician must also interpret these scores within the overall context of assessment, taking into account such variables as the person's age, occupational level, cultural background, and educational level. For example, a high-school student with an intellectual efficiency (Ie) scale score of 60 represents a fairly high level of this characteristic, whereas the same score for a medical student represents a relatively low level when compared with his or her fellow students.

2. **Note patterns of elevations/lowerings on different clusters and classes.** After looking at possible areas of adjustment and maladjustment, the clinician can then further evaluate the profile by examining the average elevations on the different clusters or classes (Table 8–1) as organized by Gough (1987). For convenience, the clusters are separated on the profile sheets by gray, vertical lines. If most or all of the scales in a particular cluster are clearly above T = 50, then the qualities represented by the cluster are areas of strength. In contrast, scores well below T = 50 represent areas of difficulty.

    The clusters listed in Table 8–1 are organized according to conceptual similarity rather than statistically derived categories. In contrast, Gough (1987) also recommends examining the scales based on five factors that have been statistically derived from more empirical relations. Factor 1 (Do, Cs, Sy, Sp, Sa, In, Em) indicates a person's level of social poise and interpersonal effectiveness. Factor 2 (Wb, Re, So, Sc, To, Gi, Ac) provides a general index of mental health, adjustment, and social conformity. The third factor (Ai, Fx, To, Ie, Py) includes scales that are characterized by assessing the extent to which a person can think and behave independently. The fourth factor is comprised of scales Cm, Re, So, and Wb and measures the extent a person adheres to social norms and expectations. High scorers (all above T = 50) are likely to be conventional and place a high emphasis on doing

Table 8–1. Cluster analysis

Cluster	Scales	Interpretation
1	Do, Cs, Sy, Sp Sa, In, Em	Interpersonal effectiveness, style, and adequacy
2	Re So, Sc, To Gi, Cm, Wb	Intrapersonal controls, values styles, and beliefs
3	Ac, Ai, Ie	Intellectual stance, achievement, and academic ability
4	Py, Fx, F/M	Conceptual interests

and perceiving things, correctly whereas low scorers (all below T = 50) will be more unconventional, individualistic, and likely to perceive the world in more unusual ways. The final, fifth factor is comprised of Femininity/Masculinity and assesses a person's degree of aesthetic interests, dependency, and sensitivity. Clinicians can gain useful information by using either Gough's clusters (classes) or the more empirically derived five factors.

In the 1987 revision of the CPI, Gough formalized aspects of the CPI factor structure through the development and inclusion of three vectors. Each vector can be used to obtain general descriptions of personality. The first vector describes the person's degree of introversion/extraversion, the second the degree to which the person adheres to societal norms, and the third represents the extent to which the person has integrated and realized his or her personality. Scores on the first two vectors can be used to categorize personality into various combinations of introversion/extraversion and norm conformity (alphas, betas, gammas, deltas; see section on Interpretation of Structural Scales).

3. **Evaluate the meaning of the scores on each individual scale.** Whereas the different clusters, factors, or vectors provide general impressions for certain areas of functioning, the clinician can obtain more specific information by evaluating each scale individually. This involves looking at the relatively highest and lowest scales and developing a description of the dynamics involved with these scales. The meanings associated with specific high or low scores can be determined by considering the relevant scale descriptions in the section on Individual Scales. The general personality descriptions and discussions of the scales have been adapted and modified from the publications of Gough (1968, 1975, 1987), McAllister (1988), and Megargee (1972). Additional relevant material has also been included and is cited accordingly. The short list of most frequently used adjectives (provided at the end of the sections on high and low scores) is based on ratings reported by Gough (1987). The adjectives were included based on their occurring in two or more instances from within the different lists of ratings on the Adjective Check List made by peers, spouses, or CPI assessment staff.

4. **Note scale configurations and calculate regression equations.** Initial hypotheses can be further evaluated by consulting the section in this chapter dealing with typical scale configurations for different areas, including intellectual level, achievement, leadership, adjustment, and specific syndromes. This evaluation may also involve calculating and interpreting the regression equations, which are included in the section on configural interpretations and summarized at the end of the chapter in Table 8–2.

5. **Integration of data into a profile description.** The final step in interpretation is to integrate all the data into a profile description. An essential here is the clinician's ability to assess the interactions between two or more scales. This suggests that, once a specific trend has been established, the clinician should elaborate on it by evaluating how the other scales change their meaning for the individual (cf. Heilbrun, Daniel, Goodstein, Stephenson, & Crites, 1962; McAllister, 1988; Webb, McNamara, & Rodgers, 1981). For example, dominance may be expressed in numerous ways, including rebellion, high achievement, leadership, or delinquency. Once these elaborations have been made within the test data, the clinician can then seek outside confirmation through personal history, behavioral observations, and additional test data.

STRUCTURAL SCALE INTERPRETATION

The major addition to the 1987 revision was the development and inclusion of three structural scales. Each was based on a factor analysis of the different items on the CPI. The first theme or factor that seemed to emerge referred to elements of extraversion, self-confidence, assertive self-assurance, and social poise. Items measuring these dimensions were formerly used to develop a scoring for the first vector (or structural scale), which Gough (1987) referred to as *externality-internality*. The second factor was related more to the degree to which a person accepted societal norms and included such areas as social conformity, personal integrity, self-control, and disciplined effectiveness. Scoring for these qualities was formally developed into a second vector, which Gough (1987) referred to as *norm-favoring versus norm questioning*. The final, third vector was labeled *realization* and assesses the degree to which a respondent has developed a sense of self-realization and psychological integration.

On the CPI profile sheet, the first two vectors (externality-internality and norm-favoring versus norm-questioning) are combined to place a person into one of four specific types (alpha, beta, gamma, delta) based on the interaction between vectors 1 and 2. The primary emphasis on structural scale interpretation is to understand the meaning associated with these four types. The third vector is used to provide additional meaning to these four types by considering the degree to which the person has managed to integrate them into a fully developed (self-realized) person. Vector 3 is rated on a scale between 1 and 7, where 1 represents no or little integration/realization and 7 represents an unusually high level. Gough (1987) describes these more specifically as 1 = poor, 2 = distinctly below average, 3 = below average, 4 = average, 5 = above average, 6 = distinctly above average, and 7 = superior.

Any interpretation of type should take into account both the extent to which the person has realized his or her type (vector 3) as well as the relative strength with which he or she represents the type. For example, an alpha combines qualities of extraversion and norm-favoring. These qualities would be far stronger if they scored quite high on both extraversion and norm-favoring (vectors 1 and 2) than if they merely scored in the borderline areas. Specific interpretations and the implications of their degree of realization are described below and were derived from descriptions provided by Gough (1987).

Alphas

Persons scoring in this quadrant tend to be highly extraverted and to adhere to societal norms. They will be good leaders in that they are task-focused and productive but also interested in associating with others. Their social style may be somewhat managerial. Externally, they may be assertive, talkative, and have high levels of achievement and social presence. If highly realized (note vector 3), alphas may be charismatic leaders and help to create social change. If undeveloped, they might become manipulative, self-centered, and concerned only with achieving their own ends regardless of consequences to others.

Betas

Betas combine qualities of both introversion and norm-favoring. Thus, they prefer external structure and are generally most comfortable in the role of a follower. They will have a high degree of self-control, are highly dependable, conservative, value traditions, and may place the needs of others before their own. If highly realized, they can be nurturant, represent ideal models of goodness, and convey conventional sources of wisdom. Poorly developed betas might be nonresponsive, overly conformist, inflexible, constricted, and rigid.

Gammas

Gammas are extraverted and, at the same time, question traditional beliefs and values. Thus, they make their questions, beliefs, and challenges quite apparent. These are the skeptics, doubters, and persons who might try and change society. They perceive the world in highly individualistic ways but are still actively involved with others. Often, they might try to test limitations imposed on them and do so in a rebellious, self-dramatizing manner. At their best, gammas would be innovative, visionary, perceptive, and imaginative. They are likely to be inventors, create new ideas, and push their field to new limits. If inadequately developed, they would be intolerant, belligerent, self-indulgent, rebellious, and disruptive.

Deltas

Persons scoring in this quadrant have qualities of introversion and also question traditional values and beliefs. As a result, deltas will be highly reflective, somewhat detached, preoccupied, and possibly overly absorbed in their own fantasies and daydreams. They might prefer that others make decisions for them and, if extreme, may live primarily in their own private world. If fully developed, they might be highly imaginative, artistic, visionary, and innovative. However, they run the risk that their innovations may go unnoticed since they rarely make a production of their activities. If poorly developed, deltas may be poorly organized, withdrawn, aloof, self-defeating, and at risk of decompensating.

THE INDIVIDUAL SCALES

1. Dominance (Do)

The Do scale measures areas of leadership ability and has become one of the most validated scales on the CPI. It includes verbal fluency, persuasiveness, and the extent to which a person is likely to take charge of a situation. Thus, high scorers are persistent in approaching a task and will usually take the initiative in interpersonal relationships. However, this description is more characteristic of the style in which high-scoring males express their dominance. High-scoring females express their dominance either by initiating attempts to choose a leader, or by being somewhat coercive, aggressive, or impatient. The contents of the items deal with social poise, confidence, verbal fluency, persuasiveness, and a sense of duty.

It should be stressed that the conditions in which leadership occurs are at least as important as the actual trait. This means that, when a situation arises requiring leadership, high scorers will usually become leaders rather than followers. More specifically, they are more likely to be the ones to set limits, and will become more assertive, goal oriented, and clear and direct regarding their requests. They will adopt this role relatively comfortably and naturally. In contrast, low scorers experience discomfort when requested to take charge. They may be either more submissive, in which case they prefer others to control and direct them, or merely socially isolated and introverted, in which case they do not want to control others but also do not want others to control them. They may even actively resist efforts that are made to control them.

High Do (T = 65 or More)   High scorers on Do are strong in expressing their opinions and in reaching their goals. This may range from being highly assertive, in which they are clear and direct in expressing their needs, to being aggressive, in which they are more forceful. They would rather take charge of a situation and can effectively do so since they have excellent abilities to plan and are self-confident when directing others. Persons high in dominance can use and develop the resources available to them and often express a sense of optimism. They are generally able to define their goals and work persistently to attain them. They would not be particularly compromising nor would they be the type of person to whom others would feel comfortable admitting their weaknesses. The most frequent adjectives used to describe them are dominant, confident, aggressive, assertive, outgoing, ambitious, and (having) initiative.

Moderate Do (T = 50–65)   Moderate Do scale scorers have the capacity for leadership but do not, under ordinary circumstances, seek opportunities to use this ability.

Moderately Low Do (T = 40–50)   With moderately low Do, people usually feel uncomfortable when leadership is required and much prefer being in the follower role. They are participants rather than organizers. Although some persons who are low in dominance are effective in relatively high leadership positions, they are uncomfortable with this aspect of their job, and usually have a democratic and participative style of decision making. However, most persons scoring low on Do experience a difficult time planning and, as a result, may sometimes appear reckless and impulsive. They are likely to believe and adhere to the beliefs of others and can therefore be easily influenced. Often, they have a difficult time making direct requests, and are usually seen as nonassertive. Low scorers, particularly females, are seen as submissive, shy, timid, and inhibited.

Low Do (T = 40 or Less)   Extremely low scores on Do suggest a general pattern of maladjustment (Gregory & Morris, 1978). They are likely to be socially withdrawn, insecure, and shy. They see themselves as having little or no leadership ability and dislike being directly responsible for either their own actions or the actions of others. They may be passive, require prodding, and attempt to avoid situations that are likely to produce tension and pressure. The most frequently used adjectives to describe these persons are shy, timid, submissive, withdrawn, quiet, retiring, unassuming, silent, and inhibited.

2. Capacity for Status (Cs)

An individual's capacity for status has been defined by Gough (1968, p.61) as equal to the "relative level of income, education, prestige, and power attained in [his or her] social-cultural milieu." This definition focuses on status as it has been achieved, but the Cs scale looks at status more as a trait associated with such features as ambition and self-assurance. The specific trait of capacity for status suggests that, eventually, a person will achieve and maintain a position of status. Thus, in creating the scale, Gough looked at the specific trait variables that would eventually lead to a higher status position. These traits include perseverance, self-direction, ambition, and self-confidence. Persons seeking status are usually willing to go through a fairly high degree of discomfort and personal change in order to achieve their goals. In the scale construction, there is some overlap of test items with social presence (Sp), intellectual efficiency (Ie), and self-acceptance (Sa), indicating that capacity for status also includes dimensions of social poise, efficiency, and self-confidence. The item content also reflects an absence of fears or anxieties, a high degree of social conscience, an interest in belonging to various groups, and an interest in literary and aesthetic activities.

High Cs (T = 60 or More)   Individuals with high scores on Cs scales are characterized as independent, imaginative, and will take advantage of opportunities that are presented to them. They will be highly self-directed, achievement oriented, and able to respond to their environment in a manner designed to further their own goals. Their aspirations will be high and they will have excellent verbal fluency. Extremely high scores suggest they will be overbearing, arrogant, and will be aristocratic and feel superior. The most frequent adjectives used to describe these high scorers are ambitious, confident, intelligent, versatile, enterprising, interests wide, assertive, and (having) initiative.

Moderate Cs (T = 45–60)   As might be expected, moderate scorers are somewhat goal oriented and relatively highly motivated to achieve. They are willing to change and adapt their lives to a certain extent in their attempts to achieve status. They are also moderately ambitious and self-assured.

Moderately Low Cs (T = 35–45)   These individuals are minimally goal oriented, but their general lack of self-direction is not sufficiently low to impair their level of functioning. They are unwilling to make many personal sacrifices in order to achieve power, prestige, or a higher income.

Low Cs (T = 35 or Less)   Persons who score extremely low on Cs usually have a low level of energy and are relatively rigid and inflexible. Their interests are extremely narrow, and they are likely to have little curiosity about their environment. They are usually resentful of their current position, which results in tension, restlessness, and depression. In the face of difficulties, they will usually give up easily and withdraw. Their thinking is commonplace, unimaginative, literal, and slow. The most frequent adjectives used to describe them are shy, timid, silent, interests narrow, quiet, and simple.

3. Sociability (Sy)

The sociability scale was originally designed to measure the extent to which a person participates in social activities. It was later generalized to differentiate between a person who is outgoing, extraverted, and sociable versus one who is more introverted, withdrawn, and prone to avoid social visibility. There is a great deal of item overlap with intellectual efficiency (Ie), social presence (Sp), self-acceptance (Sa), and, to a much lesser extent, achievement via independence (Ai), dominance (Do), capacity for status (Cs), and achievement via conformance (Ac). The questions deal with enjoyment of social interactions, a sense of poise, self-assurance in dealing with others, and interest in cultural and intellectual activities.

High Sy (T = 60 or More)   High scorers on Sy have some of the same traits as persons scoring high on capacity for status (Cs), such as a greater sense of maturity and a wide range of interests. They are also described as outgoing, sociable, and confident. In general, they feel comfortable in social settings and can easily mix with others. They feel comfortable around large groups of people and would dislike working alone. They have well-developed social skills and generally make a good impression. The most frequently used adjectives to describe them are outgoing, sociable, confident, ambitious, aggressive, energetic, talkative, assertive, and enterprising.

Moderate Sy (T = 50–60)   Persons in this range have an average level of extraversion and are relatively comfortable in most social situations. Although they prefer to be around others, they do not, by any means, exclusively orient their lives in this direction.

Moderately Low Sy (T = 35–50)   Such persons are able to interact with groups of people without experiencing an excessive amount of discomfort, but they prefer to be alone. They feel somewhat anxious around strangers and strongly prefer to be with persons with whom they are already acquainted. Usually, they dislike being the center of attention.

Low Sy (T = 35 or Less)   Persons who score this low have a definite sense of awkwardness in social situations and frequently have bitter complaints about their lives. They have a marked lack of confidence in their social skills and, as a result, avoid most social encounters, especially in unfamiliar settings or with those they do not know. They might act in self-defeating ways, frequently perceive themselves as underachievers, and are prone to anxiety. The most frequently used adjectives to describe them are withdrawn, shy, retiring, quiet, timid, meek, quitting, reserved, and awkward.

4. Social Presence (Sp)

The social presence scale was intended to serve as a measure of a person's degree of poise, self-confidence, verve, and spontaneity in social interactions. It especially assesses the extent to which the person is self-assured and assertive. Sp is very similar to sociability in that an individual scoring high on Sp is outgoing, extraverted, and enjoys being around other people. However, a person who is sociable does not necessarily also have social presence even though this is often the case. Social presence implies not only that the person is sociable, but also that he or she has more of a need to have impact on others and is thus likely to be more verbally aggressive, irritable, and sarcastic. A person exerting social presence might manipulate and control others, especially by working on another person's defenses and self-deceptions. There is some overlap of items with sociability (Sy), self-acceptance (Sa), and, to a lesser extent, capacity for status (Cs) and intellectual efficiency (Ie). The primary content of the questions relates to a person's poise and the degree to which he or she enjoys social interactions.

High Sp (T = 65 or More)   High scorers are often described as being unconventional, spontaneous, witty, and perceptive. They are usually concerned with their own pleasure in interpersonal relationships and will often manipulate interactions in order to feel a sense of personal power. Thus, they not only like to be with other people, but also want to be in control. Their expression of ideas and vocabulary is excellent, as are their social skills. They are often perceived as imaginative, socially relaxed, and generally make a good impression. Extremely high scorers might be manipulative, highly energetic, and feel offended if people do not pay attention to them. The most frequently used adjectives to describe them are outgoing, confident, versatile, talkative, and adventurous.

Low Sp (T = 40 or Less)   Whereas high scorers are unconventional and uninhibited, low scorers are extremely cautious and concerned with proper etiquette. They feel that others should conform to set, predefined standards and are disapproving of nonconforming behavior. Their view of what is correct and incorrect falls within relatively narrow limits. In their relationships with others, they emphasize cooperation rather than manipulation and are likely to be kind, appreciative, patient, and serious. However, this kindness and appreciation are expressed only when the behavior of others falls within their definition of conventional. They would most likely feel anxious when expected to alter their routine. They are moralistic regarding the behavior of others, but also can be made to feel guilty regarding their own behavior. Extremely low scorers might lack energy, avoid being the center of attention, and feel uncomfortable when required to use their influence on others.

The most frequently used adjectives to describe them are shy, withdrawn, retiring, silent, quiet, timid, and inhibited.

5. Self-acceptance (Sa)

The self-acceptance scale was intended to "assess factors such as a sense of personal worth, self-acceptance, and capacity for independent thinking and action" (Gough, 1969, p. 10). Furthermore, it was hoped that Sa could "identify individuals who would manifest a comfortable and imperturbable sense of personal worth, and who would be seen as secure and sure of themselves whether active or inactive in social behavior" (p.10). Even though persons scoring high on self-acceptance would be less likely to become upset, the Sa scale should not be used as an index of adjustment and is not related to the absence or presence of pathology. For example, a person might be high in self-acceptance, yet still be rebellious, impulsive, and generally indulge in antisocial behavior. In fact, persons scoring extremely high on Sa are quite likely to be egocentric and indifferent, sometimes even to the point of narcissism. The scale questions have some overlap with sociability (Sy), social presence (Sp), and, to a lesser extent, capacity for status (Cs). There is some negative overlap in which answers are scored in the opposite direction from capacity for status (Cs). Thus, a number of statements deal with social poise and self-confidence. Additional areas of item content relate to an accepting attitude toward social prohibitions, attention to duty, consideration of others, and an acceptance of human frailties.

High Sa (T = 65 or More)   Individuals scoring high on Sa are comfortable with themselves, self-reliant and independent, and are usually polished, sophisticated, enterprising, and self-seeking in social relations. They also have a clear sense of self-definition, and are characterized as being self-confident and outgoing. However, Sa should not necessarily be tied with sociability since self-acceptance can be high regardless of the quantity of interaction with others. The scale is slightly correlated with hypomania, which has often been formulated as a defense against depression. Thus, extremely high scores may suggest an inflated sense of self-acceptance with underlying, but unacknowledged, feelings of self-criticism, pessimism, and hopelessness. The most frequently used adjectives to describe high scorers are outgoing, self-confident, talkative, ambitious, and assertive.

Moderate Sa (T = 50–65)   These persons have an average or somewhat above-average level of confidence, with a generally good sense of harmony and internal balance. They are somewhat adventurous and outgoing.

Moderate Low Sa (T = 35–50)   Moderately low scorers are somewhat low in self-confidence and have some significant doubts about themselves. For the most part, they can adequately cope with their lives, but they are prone to periods of insecurity and depression. One way in which they often attempt to adapt is through conformity and conventionality, which frequently has the desired effect of making their world safer and more predictable.

Low Sa (T = 35 or Less)   Such individuals have a pronounced lack of self-confidence. They are usually described as ordinary and have "flat" or unidimensional personalities. They achieve a moderate degree of safety in their world by withdrawing, quitting, and maintaining a relatively narrow range of interests. They are likely to have a strong sense of insecurity, are afraid to take risks, and have low levels of self-confidence. Although usually submissive and conventional, they may at times impulsively act out in a reckless manner, almost as a form of rebellion against their largely self-imposed conventionality. The most frequently used adjectives to describe them are shy, withdrawn, retiring, silent, quiet, timid, and inhibited.

6. Independence (In)

The independence scale is a new CPI scale (1987 revision) comprised of 30 items and originally developed by Kurtines (1974). It measures the extent to which a person strives toward vocational and interpersonal autonomy. Conceptually, it overlaps with Ai in that they both assess the value a person places on working away from the restrictions, expectations, and influence of others. It also has similarities with Sa since persons high in both In and Sa are likely to be self-assured and self-reliant. Similarities can also be found with Sp (both witty, animated) and Do (both like to be in control).

High In (T = 65 or More)   Persons scoring high on In are self-assured, confident, and possess social presence. Their vocabulary is likely to be wide, and they are intelligent, self-reliant, witty, animated and, as a result, are likely to make a good impression. However, they are not necessarily affiliative and friendly. They are perceived as resourceful, confident, self-sufficient, and capable. If they believe in a concept, position, or fact, they will defend it without bending to external pressure. Interpersonally, they are likely to be dominant; vocationally, they have high needs for achievement, and they are willing to work to achieve higher status. They will also tend to be morally responsible and have high levels of self-control. They are most frequently described as confident, independent, aggressive, (having) initiative, and assertive.

Moderately High In (T = 55–65)   Moderately high scorers have many of the above characteristics in that they will be confident, goal-oriented, and will be able to rely on their own evaluations and directions. They are assertive and usually can deal effectively with others.

Low In (T = 30–45)   Low scorers need to rely on others for decisions and directions. They are likely to avoid conflict, competition, and experience discomfort when having to assert themselves. Assets include an excellent ability to cooperate and blend with the requirements and needs of others.

Extremely Low In (T = 30 or Less)   If persons score in the extremely low range, it suggests they are dependent and lack self-confidence. They will probably accept domination from others, partially because they feel uncomfortable having to face uncertainty. Often they will experience worry and anxiety and be reluctant to express their own ideas. Assets include tolerance, adaptability, generosity, and helpfulness. Frequent adjectives used to describe them are timid, shy, cautious, meek, submissive, unassuming, nervous.

7. Empathy (Em)

The 38-item Empathy scale was a new edition to the 1987 version and was originally developed by Grief and Hogan (1973). The central construct it attempts to measure is the degree to which a person perceives and can feel the inner experience of others. It also measures related abilities, including social skills, confidence, social presence, leadership, and extraversion. The major underlying themes to the scale are that "empathic persons are characterized by a patient and forbearing nature, by affiliative but socially ascendant tendencies, and by liberal and humanistic political and religious attitudes" (Grief & Hogan, 1973, p. 284).

High Em (T = 65 or Above)   High scorers are intuitive, perceptive, verbally fluent, have a wide range of interests, and are usually perceived by others as interesting. In addition, they are highly creative, spontaneous, and able to use their imagination in a number of areas. They have social presence, and are animated, witty, and make a good impression. Thus, they will be interpersonally effective, independent, and flexible. They are most frequently described as sociable, outgoing, versatile, spontaneous, interests wide, confident, and humorous.

Moderately High Em (T = 55–65)   Moderately high scorers have some insight into the feelings and motives of others and are friendly, adaptable, and comfortable to be around.

Moderately Low Em (T = 30–45)   Persons with moderately low scores are typically slow to understand the feelings and motives of others. They are perceived as having narrow interests and as shy, withdrawn, narrow-minded, and conventional.

Very Low (T = 30 or Lower)   Extremely low scorers often feel bewilderment regarding the reasons others behave as they do. These individuals can often be insensitive and inconsiderate. Often they are shy, rigid, unfriendly, and others find it difficult to please them. They are uncomfortable with uncertainty and, as a result, might cling to a rigid set of morals and narrow range of behaviors, often becoming authoritarian and ethnocentric. Their fathers were probably distant, cold, and taciturn. The most frequent adjectives used to describe them are shy, silent, interests narrow, and conservative.

8. Responsibility (Re)

The intent of the Re scale was to assess the degree to which persons are "conscientious, responsible, dependable, [and] articulate regarding rules and order, and who believe life should be governed by reason" (Gough, 1968, p. 65). Although responsibility is somewhat related to sociability and self-control, it also stresses that values and controls are well-defined and significant factors in a person's life. The person who is highly responsible will sacrifice his or her own needs for the benefit of the group. Such people accept the consequences of their behavior, are dependable and trustworthy, and have a sense of obligation to the larger social structure. They are not necessarily leaders, but they do have a high sense of integrity and are committed to follow through on agreements they have made with others. In general, persons who express antisocial behavior score low on Re, whereas average or above-average scores are obtained by occupational groups in which responsible behavior and "attention to duty" are required. The Re scale is scored positively for items that reflect a high degree of commitment to social, civic, or moral values.

High Re (T = 60 or More)   High scorers respond well to tasks in which they are required to be conscientious, dependable, and reasonable. They will give up their own personal satisfactions for the sake of the group and will honor any commitments they have made. Their approach to problem solving is extremely rational and clear. Usually, they have strong religious beliefs, a clear sense of ethics, and are concerned with philosophical issues. Their work is productive since their aspiration levels are high and their work style is dependable and responsible. Their behavior is courteous, polite, alert, energetic, honest, and direct. The most frequent adjectives used to describe them are conscientious, responsible, dependable, thorough, industrious, and efficient.

Moderate Re (T = 40–60)   Such persons respond well to tasks in which they are required to be conscientious, dependable, and reasonable. Generally, they are not comfortable taking responsibility for the behavior of others, but they are seen by others as reasonably conscientious and straightforward.

Low Re (T = 40 or Less)   Individuals with scores this low show a lack of discipline, and are usually rebellious and impulsive. They have difficulty budgeting their finances and are seen by others as restless and careless. Their perceptions are tied to their own personal biases and they are mainly concerned with their own needs. They often behave in exploitive and immature ways. Their histories usually reveal they had their first sexual encounters at an early age, they were underachievers in high school, had considerable disagreements with their parents, engaged in borderline delinquent behavior, and that often their fathers were alcoholics. Their external behavior is typically crude, unpredictable, rebellious, nonconforming, and self-indulgent. Internally they feel dissatisfied, moody, cynical, and distrustful. The most frequent adjectives used to describe them are rebellious, reckless, and pleasure seeking.

9. Socialization (So)

The socialization scale was originally called the "delinquency scale," and, as the name suggests, its intent was to assess the likelihood of antisocial behavior. The scoring was later reversed, its name changed, and it gradually became a measure of an individual's social maturity, integrity, and rectitude. It is probably Gough's favorite scale and is based on his theory that antisocial behavior is the result of a role that certain individuals assume. There has been an extensive accumulation of literature on this scale, due at least in part to Gough's personal interest in it. The research indicates that the So scale has excellent concurrent, predictive, and cross-cultural validity, and is probably the most validated and most powerful scale on the CPI.

The socialization scale was designed to measure the degree to which social norms are accepted and adhered to. An individual, then, can score on a continuum from extremely well socialized to highly antisocial. The scale also estimates the probability that a person will engage in behavior considered incorrect within their culture. For example, the So scale has been able with relative accuracy to differentiate cheaters from noncheaters in a college population (Kipnis, 1968) and low So scores were related to a diagnosis of personality disorder (Standage, 1986). Schizophrenics making violent suicide attempts were found to have particularly low scores on So (Seeman, Yesarage, & Widrow, 1985). The So scale has also differentiated high-school dropouts from graduates (Gough, 1966; Hase & Goldberg, 1967). In a further study, Wernick (1955) demonstrated that 50% of the low scorers who were hired as temporary Christmas help stole from the store and none proved to be satisfactory workers. Several researchers have found a negative correlation between So scores and a past lack of family cohesiveness and poor quality of parental care (Glueck & Glueck, 1950; Rosenquist & Megargee, 1969; Standage, 1986). Thus, many items included in the scale are designed to determine whether the examinees experienced warmth and satisfaction within their family relationships. Some of the items also reflect the presence or absence of pessimism regarding one's life and environment. The content of several other questions centers on whether examinees can properly evaluate the effects of their behavior as well as the extent to which they can be empathetic and sensitive to the feelings of others.

High So (T = 65 or More)   Persons scoring high on So are organized, adaptable, and efficient. They are highly dependable, but maintain this level of dependability by being cautious, self-controlled, and inhibited. In general, they are willing to trust others and express a fairly high level of optimism. They are often described as kind, honest, and practical, and they typically come from a stable, cohesive family environment where warmth and concern were freely expressed. Often they were overprotected, and their current behavior is usually relatively conventional. Their external behavior is typically gentle, considerate, honest, tactful, well-organized, capable, and productive. Their values are conservative and, as a result, they behave in an ethically consistent manner. Internally, they feel optimistic, stable, and well controlled. They are most frequently described as reliable, organized, dependable, stable, and cooperative.

Moderate So (T = 50–65)   Individuals who score in this range are able to trust others and are generally accepting of the mores and rules established by society. They also tend to be inhibited and conventional, sometimes to the point of being overadapted, but not as much as those with higher So scores.

Moderately Low So (T = 30–45)   Individuals who score in the lower ranges of So are somewhat impulsive and unreliable, and often have a difficult time trusting others. They are not usually followers; rather, they frequently question the rules given to them and, in general, do not have a high degree of respect for society's prescribed forms of behavior. They will often express a moderate level of rebelliousness.

Low So (T = 30 or Less)   Such persons have a far greater likelihood of antisocial behavior and are usually unreliable, unconventional, rude, defensive, and impulsive. They reject past family ties, primarily because their past family life was filled with chaos and was unsatisfying. They were unhappy at home, experienced considerable friction with their parents, and were underachievers and sexually precocious. They experience a deep sense of alienation and have an extremely difficult time trusting people. Others see them as headstrong, unpredictable, deceitful, rebellious, and pleasure seeking. Internally, they feel cynical, moody, and often that their lives are meaningless. The most frequent adjectives used to describe them are reckless, impulsive, rebellious, unconventional, bitter, restless, and suspicious.

10. Self-control (Sc)

The original intent of the Sc scale was to measure the degree to which a person can self-direct his or her own behavior. More specifically, high scores suggest that a person can delay his or her behavior and redirect it in a clear, goal-oriented manner. Thus, a certain degree of similarity exists between self-control and both responsibility and socialization. Gough (in Megargee, 1972) clarifies these concepts by stating that responsibility reflects the "degree to which controls are understood," socialization measures the "extent to which they influence a person's behavior," and self-control assesses the "degree to which the individual approves of and espouses such regulatory dispositions" (pp. 65-66). Persons scoring high on Sc are self-directed, inhibited, and withhold their expressions of emotions and behavior. Some types of persons who score extremely high on Sc are often overcontrolled to the extent that, for short periods of time, they lose control and become explosive (Megargee, 1977d; Megargee, Cook, & Mendelsohn, 1967). Individuals with low scores are impulsive and pleasure seeking, have difficulty delaying their impulses, and are not good at evaluating the consequences of their behavior. Thus, both extremely high and extremely low scorers are similar in that they have significant issues dealing with the management of impulses; however, they use opposite strategies to cope with these impulses.

The primary overlap of items for Sc is with Gi, and several items are also scored in a direction opposite from Sp and Sa. Some of the most important items emphasize that thought and rationality are the primary determinants of behavior. Furthermore, high scorers usually endorse items that indicate they take precautions to avoid irrational behavior and are generally socially inhibited.

High Sc (T = 60 or More)   Persons who score high on Sc are considerate, self-denying, and dependable. They have a high need for precision and make every attempt to be reasonable. Other people perceive them as considerate, wholesome, and dependable, but also as stubborn, rigid, and overconforming. They avoid situations in which they might be tempted into acting impulsively, and are generally inhibited, lacking in spontaneity, and move slowly. Externally, their behavior is well organized, patient, capable, and fastidious.

They are conservative and moralistic, and behave in an ethical, conscientious, and consistent manner. Internally, they usually feel optimistic but serious. The most frequent adjectives used to describe them are moderate, calm, quiet, conservative, conventional, and conscientious.

Moderate Sc (T = 45–60)   Such persons are fairly conventional and somewhat inhibited. They carefully consider the consequences of their behavior before acting. Others usually see them as reasonable and dependable, although somewhat lacking in spontaneity.

Moderately Low Sc (T = 30–45)   Persons scoring in this range sometimes act in a spontaneous, impulsive manner but can usually delay their behavior. Thus, their level of impulsiveness is insufficient to impair their interpersonal and work relationships.

Low Sc (T = 30 or Less)   Low scorers have a marked difficulty delaying their behavior, are hasty in making decisions, and are usually individualistic and self-seeking. Their impulsiveness may sometimes cause tension in group activities, and they often regret having acted in inappropriate ways. At times, they can seem extremely unrealistic and headstrong. They are prone to develop relationships quickly, which often readily become chaotic and confused. The background of these individuals usually reveals they were sexually precocious, experienced considerable conflicts with their parents, and academically they were both underachievers and unhappy. Their external behavior is restless, excited, outgoing, rebellious, unpredictable, and they frequently perceive situations in sexual terms. The most frequent adjectives used to describe them are impulsive, mischievous, restless, humorous, pleasure seeking, and adventurous.

11. Good Impression (Gi)

Although Gi is mainly a validity scale designed to detect persons who are "faking good," it also reflects the degree to which a person with a valid profile is concerned with creating a favorable impression on others. There is a fairly high degree of item overlap with self-control (Sc), which suggests that an important component of creating a favorable impression is a good ability to delay impulses. Also, a number of items make fairly obvious statements concerning the person's level of functioning, amount of antisocial behavior, the extent to which he or she is goal oriented, and whether or not he or she has complaints regarding personal failings. High scorers are prone to exaggerate their positive points and minimize their negative qualities. Furthermore, they state that they have a high level of confidence and self-assurance, and minimize anxieties or insecurities. They emphasize that they can adapt well to stress and that they have a stable personality. Finally, there are several items related to the extent to which individuals behave in a socially approved manner and experience harmonious relationships with others.

The Gi scale has generally been successful in detecting invalid profiles. For example, Dicken (1960), by using a cutoff score of T = 60, was able to detect in 79% of the cases the profiles of persons attempting to make a favorable impression. With somewhat different criteria, only 3% of a total sample of profiles of mixed "normal" and "fake good" were incorrectly classified. In the same study, Dicken also demonstrated that even though persons were, in some of the cases, attempting to "fake good" on other scales, Gi still showed the greatest increase. The practical importance of this is that, even though a person might be attempting, for example, to exaggerate his or her level of responsibility, Gi would still be expected to increase. Thus, the use of Gi as a validity scale is not restricted to persons attempting to create a favorable impression in a global manner; it can be used to detect persons attempting to "fake good" along other specific dimensions as well. More precise and accurate classifications can be derived by using the equations devised by Lanning (1987) and included in the section on Determining the Profile Validity.

High Gi (T = 60 or More)   An examinee's personal history provides the best guide for determining whether a score in this range reflects a "fake good" profile or is more likely to indicate a person with an excellent level of adjustment. For example, an alcoholic with a high Gi is probably either consciously attempting to create a favorable impression or demonstrating the use of denial, which is often associated with that disorder. A further possibility for an extremely high Gi is that the person may be unaware of the impression he or she creates on others and has an inflated self-image based on rigidly selective perceptions. The self-image of such persons would then be likely to be maintained by ignoring the feedback they receive from others and manipulating others to agree with the perceptions they have of themselves. They may be people-pleasers who will do anything to fit in and, as a result, will probably be liked but not respected by others. Gough (1987) recommends that the ideal cutoff score for detecting a "fake good" profile is T = 69 for males and T = 71 for females.

If the profile is only moderately high and has been determined to be valid, then the person is likely to be conventional, adaptable, self-denying, and capable of a high degree of empathy. These people are often oversensitive to the criticisms of others, and usually respond by attempting to change and adapt in order to gain approval. They feel it is important to please others and to be seen in a favorable light. Others usually see them as kind, warm, considerate, and patient. They will probably attempt to overcontrol their needs and be moralistic, but will try and adapt by becoming considerate and tactful. The most frequent adjectives used to describe them are calm, conventional, conservative, and moderate.

Moderate Gi (T = 45–60)   Persons with a moderate score on Gi are usually unselfish and concerned with making a favorable impression. They are able to take feedback from others and use it in a constructive way. Others perceive them as peaceable, trusting, understanding, and highly concerned with living up to their social responsibilities.

Moderately Low Gi (T = 30–45)   Moderately low scorers are only minimally concerned with the impression they have on others to the extent that they are sometimes seen as insensitive. They feel that they alone are the judges of their behavior and thus rarely listen to the evaluations of others. They are often described as independent, witty, and occasionally temperamental and sarcastic.

Low Gi (T = 30 or Less)   Persons scoring in this range are typically arrogant and actively reject the judgments of others. They are even prone to exaggerate their negative behavior in a rebellious way, and then expect this behavior to be tolerated and even accepted. Others describe them as temperamental, cynical, sarcastic, and overly frank to the point of being disagreeable. This usually has the effect of disrupting their interpersonal relationships. Their external behavior will typically be rebellious, undiplomatic, critical, nonconforming, unpredictable, and self-indulgent. They might come from conflict-ridden families in which their mother was nervous and dissatisfied. They are often perceived as insensitive and lack qualities of nurturance. Internally, they may often feel cynical, distrustful, and dissatisfied. Frequent adjectives used to describe them are temperamental, restless, and rebellious. Scores of T = 35 or less suggest a "fake bad" profile.

12. Communality (Cm)

The Cm scale is a validity scale originally designed to detect random answering. The questions are keyed in such a way that normal populations answer 95% of the questions in the keyed direction. Although the scale was not designed to measure personality variables, some personality indicators can tentatively be derived from this scale. This is based mainly on the observation that the content of the items reflects the following areas: good socialization, conformity, optimism, denial of neurotic characteristics, and conventionality of behavior and attitudes. Gough points out that this is comparable to the "popular" response on the Rorschach in that it reflects the degree to which examinees see their surroundings in ways that are similar to others.

High Cm (T = 60 or More)   High scores suggest that the examinee adheres to highly conventional attitudes and is overly socialized, tending to see his or her world in a stereotyped manner. These individuals do not see themselves as particularly unique or special and are conscientious and serious. They are most frequently described as clear thinking, planful, practical, and tactful.

Low Cm (T = 30 or Less)   A low score sometimes suggests that persons have chaotic, conflict-ridden family backgrounds. Their attitudes toward the world would typically be unusual and idiosyncratic. They might also be generally upset, poorly motivated, self-defeating, and frail, and lack a sense of meaning in life. The most frequent adjectives used to describe them are reckless, distractible, unconventional, moody, and confused.

However, scores in this range primarily increase the likelihood that the test is of questionable validity, and scores below 20 almost always confirm that the profile is invalid. The ideal score for detecting a "fake bad" profile is T = 29 for males and T = 24 for females (see section on Determining the Profile Validity).

13. Sense of Well Being (Wb)

The scale for well being was originally developed to help recognize profiles in which the person was "faking bad." Thus, it was initially referred to as the dissimulation (Ds) scale, and "fake bad" profiles can usually be detected because they are significantly lower than even valid profiles for psychiatric patients. In contrast, persons who score high do not have a need to emphasize psychological or physical complaints. In fact, high scorers play down their worries and rather emphasize that they are enterprising, energetic, and experience a sense of security. They are also likely to have effective interpersonal relations, a high level of mental health, and a sense of psychological and physical well being. Low scorers usually have diminished health and experience difficulty meeting the daily demands of their environment. In general, the Wb scale has come to represent a rough estimate of a person's level of adjustment. However, it is more of a "state" scale than the others and is, therefore, somewhat changeable, depending on an individual's mood fluctuations.

The Wb scale has a low degree of item overlap with other scales since most of the questions were designed for exclusive use with this scale. The item content usually reflects a denial of various physical and psychological complaints. The second major content area reflects the extent to which a person is self-sufficient and independent.

High Wb (T = 55 or More)   Generally, high scorers on Wb have relaxed and satisfying interpersonal relationships, are able to trust others, and come from family backgrounds that were stable and supportive. They are dependable, responsible, and value intellectual interests. Usually, they are happily married and are stable, optimistic, and self-confident. The most frequent adjectives used to describe them are clear thinking and capable.

Moderately Low Wb (T = 35–50)   Although persons scoring in this range generally feel that life is not going well, they continue to meet this perceived adversity with a sense of apathy and listlessness. They are often passive, awkward, and defensive.

Low Wb (T = 35 or Less)   With a further decrease in Wb, there is a corresponding exaggeration of the trends just discussed. These individuals are usually highly alienated and dissatisfied, and experience a significant level of maladjustment. Characteristically, they are extremely distrustful in interpersonal relationships, with a tendency to dwell on real or imagined wrongs. Such people are seen by others as pessimistic, tense, restless, and moody. They feel their life lacks a sense of meaning and might cope by becoming absorbed in fantasy and daydreams. Individuals who use the test situation as a forum for complaining and attempt to exaggerate their difficulties will often score in this range. The most frequent adjectives used to describe these persons are confused, bitter, and nagging.

The interpretation of extremely low Wb scores requires two considerations. First, the scale lowering may in part reflect a downward but temporary mood shift of a person who is only somewhat maladjusted or even normal most of the time. More important, an extremely low score suggests an invalid profile in which the examinee is faking bad (see section on Determining the Profile Validity).

14. Tolerance (To)

The tolerance scale was designed to measure the degree to which persons are socially intolerant versus the extent to which they are accepting, permissive, and nonjudgmental in their social beliefs and attitudes. The content of most of the items focuses on openness and flexibility versus rigidity and dogmatism. Other content areas relate to an interest in intellectual and aesthetic activities, one's level of trust, and a lack of hostility or resentment toward others. A person scoring high on tolerance is also indicating that he or she is not alienated, does not feel isolated, rarely feels anxious, and is relatively poised and self-assured. There is a large variety of questions on this scale, but there is also a general lack of adequate validity studies. In fact, tolerance is one of the poorer scales on the CPI, and its validity has even been questioned. Thus, interpretations based on this scale should be made cautiously and tentatively.

High To (T = 60 or More)   High scorers are likely to be intelligent, have a wide range of interests, and be socially tolerant. They are also able to trust others, and may have a high degree of confidence and social poise. Furthermore, they are nonjudgmental, can easily accept divergent beliefs and values, and are forgiving, generous, and pleasant. They will typically have a wide vocabulary and varied interests. They are concerned with philosophical issues and can effectively understand and explain the core of many problems. They are likeable and make a good impression since they are tolerant, permissive, and benevolent. Extremely high scorers might be overly trusting to the extent that they are naive and underestimate potential difficulties. They might also be so worried about potential confrontations that they become overly adaptable and will fill any role in order to keep a situation peaceful. The most frequent adjectives used to describe them are fair minded, insightful, clear thinking, and interests wide.

Moderate To (T = 45–60)   Moderate scorers are likewise somewhat nonjudgmental and open to the beliefs of others. They usually have a wide range of interests, and are informal and independent.

Low To (T = 40 or Less)   Persons scoring in this range are likely to be judgmental and nonaccepting of the beliefs and values of others. This judgmental attitude tends to generalize into other areas of their lives so that, overall, they seem cold, smug, and stern. They are authoritarian and center their lives around a fixed and dogmatic set of beliefs. Furthermore, they are mannerly, fearful, arrogant, and sarcastic. If criticized, they will usually become extremely defensive, bitter, and rejecting. They are more likely to judge than to understand others. It is important for these individuals to exert power in relationships, and they may do so by becoming critical, outspoken, and holding unrealistic expectations. Internally, they often feel moody, distrustful, cynical, and dissatisfied. The most frequent adjectives used to describe them are prejudiced, interests narrow, and suspicious.

15. Achievement via Conformance (Ac)

The Ac scale involves not only an orientation toward achievement, but also a need for structure and organization as a means of channeling that achievement. This scale specifically relates to settings in which conformity is an asset and reflects the degree to which persons prefer to have their criteria of performance clearly specified by some outside source. The content of the items relates to how effectively they can perform within an academic setting and how high their relative levels of energy and efficiency are. High scorers also see themselves as being productive workers. Additional content areas relate to the extent to which the examinee is even-tempered, accepts the rules of socially approved standards of behavior, and dislikes frivolous, unconventional behavior.

The Ac scale has been one of the more thoroughly researched scales on the CPI, primarily due to its practical relevance for academic personnel. In a review of the literature, Megargee (1972) reports that it has good criterion validity and has been found to correlate significantly (.36 to .44) with grade point average (G.P.A.) and general achievement in high-school settings. The correlations are highest for high-school performance and somewhat lower for college settings.

High Ac (T = 60 or More)   Persons scoring above 60 are typically persistent and industrious, especially when conforming to some external standard. They strongly prefer specificity and structure, and may even have a difficult time when structure is lacking, especially if a high Ac is accompanied by a low Ai. Such persons are usually responsible, capable, and ambitious, but they express these behaviors in a conservative, reserved, and obliging manner. Furthermore, they place a high degree of value on intellectual effort. They are most comfortable when working in highly organized settings, where they excel when given specific, well-defined criteria for performance. The most frequent adjectives used to describe them are responsible, organized, ambitious, persevering, efficient, and conscientious.

Moderately High Ac (T = 50–60)   Moderate scorers may question the need for structure and organization. Although they may prefer not to have structure, they can adequately function in a structured situation when required to do so. They are usually stable, optimistic, dependable, and responsible.

Low Ac (T = 35 or Less)   Persons in this range are rejecting of authority and regulations. This rebellion may result in achievements far below their potential since their energy is directed more toward rejecting external organization and rules rather than working within the limits imposed on them. Such persons are often characterized as intellectual rebels, especially if their achievement via independence (Ai) scale is relatively high. When external demands for performance are placed on them, they may become disorganized and nonproductive. They will have difficulty committing themselves to organizations or people. The most frequent adjectives used to describe them are lazy, impulsive, reckless, rebellious, distractible, and mischievous.

16. Achievement via Independence (Ai)

Whereas Ac can be used to predict achievement in high school, Ai was designed to predict achievement in a college environment. Persons who are high in Ai succeed in settings that require creativity, self-actualization, and independence of thought. Gough (1968) has clarified this distinction by describing achievement via conformance (Ac) as "form enhancing" whereas Ai is "form creating." Ai correlates significantly with college students' G.P.A. (Gough & Lanning, 1986), yet there is only a low correlation with intelligence. Thus, students who have elevated Ai scales and who also achieve a high G.P.A. do so mainly on the basis of a high need for achievement and only secondarily on the basis of intelligence. They are able to tolerate a high level of ambiguity and usually reject authoritarian or overly stringent regulations. In some cases, high Ai scores can predict achievement in situations in which originality and independence are rewarded. Persons with high scores are unwilling to accept conventional advice unquestioningly but rather prefer to think for themselves. Also, some questions relate to the degree to which individuals appreciate activities involving the intellect. Other content areas attempt to assess their degree of adjustment and the extent to which they are concerned with the deeper aspects of interpersonal relationships.

High Ai (T = 60 or More)   Such persons prefer to work without rules and structures, and usually feel restricted within a highly organized environment. They value creativity and originality, and are self-motivated and rejecting of conventional standards of productivity. Their ability to produce and function is significantly impaired if a great deal of structure is required. They produce best and are most efficient when left to regulate their own behavior. Externally, they are verbally fluent, self-reliant, and make a good impression. They have a wide range of interests, high aspirations, and are concerned with philosophical interests. The most frequent adjectives used to describe them are intelligent, clear-thinking, logical, foresighted, insightful, and interests wide.

Moderate Ai (T = 40–50)   Persons scoring in this range are able to achieve based on their own self-direction but feel somewhat insecure when doing things completely on their own. Thus, they can work either with or without structure, but prefer a moderate degree of external organization. At times, they can be creative, but when they come to conclusions on their own, they still need external verification in order to feel comfortable.

Low Ai (T = 35 or Less)   Low scorers have difficulty trusting their own abilities, and this characteristic becomes more exaggerated as the scale score becomes lower. They require external definition in order to establish their self-concept and need others to specify their proper course of action. Due to this uncertainty and dependence on outside structure, these individuals are moderately anxious, depressed, and self-doubting. They are not intellectually inclined and tend to feel out of place in the world of abstract thinking. The most frequent adjectives used to describe them are confused and interests narrow.

17. Intellectual Efficiency (Ie)

The Ie scale was originally called a "nonintellectual intelligence test" and was designed to measure personality traits that coincided with a high level of intellectual ability. High scorers on Ie tend to be competent, clear thinking, and to make efficient use of the potential they possess. Thus, it is less an intelligence test than it is a measure of the degree to which persons make efficient use of the intelligence they do possess. There is a moderate amount of item overlap with sociability (Sy), achievement via independence (Ai), and social presence (Sp). One important content area of the items relates to the degree to which a person enjoys and is interested in wide-ranging intellectual activities. Also, a number of questions relate to self-confidence and assurance. Other questions relate to good physiological functioning, positive relationships with others, and an absence of irritability and suspiciousness.

A number of representative and noteworthy validity studies have been performed on Ie. It is positively correlated with measures of intelligence (Gough, 1969), and members of MENSA scored significantly higher on Ie than the national norms (Southern & Plant, 1968). The scale has also been able to successfully discriminate high-school dropouts from students who later graduated (Gough, 1966). The autobiographies of high scorers reveal that they see themselves as well organized, efficient, and committed to pursuing intellectual and cultural activities (Hill, 1967).

High Ie (T = 60 or More)   Persons scoring high on Ie have a wide range of interests, with an excellent ability to use their resources. They are capable and confident, with good planning abilities, and are independent, informal, and clear thinking. Their vocabulary is wide and they are verbally fluent, perceptive, and effectively understand subtle nuances of behavior. They value intellectual activities and have high levels of aspiration. The most frequent adjectives used to describe them are intelligent, clear thinking, alert, interests wide, and (having) initiative.

Moderate Ie (T = 40–60)   Moderate scorers may still be highly competent, but they are also likely to have some self-doubts regarding their intellectual capabilities.

Low Ie (T = 40 or Less)   Persons in this range may be insecure about their intellectual abilities, and are likely to experience enough self-doubt to create a mild degree of depression and anxiety. They typically appear awkward, shallow, and suggestible. They might give up easily and feel uncomfortable with uncertainties. As an alternative interpretation, low scorers may merely be uninterested in intellectual activities, which is also likely to be reflected in their choice of occupation. The latter interpretation would not imply the presence of self-doubt and insecurity suggested in the former, but rather merely a lack of interest. The most frequent adjectives used to describe individuals scoring low on the Ie are confused, nervous, and interests narrow.

18. Psychological Mindedness (Py)

The original intent of the Py scale was to identify persons who possess insight into the behavior of others in that they can accurately perceive the inner needs and motivations of others. This scale focuses on the ability to figure other people out, and does not necessarily indicate people who are empathic and nurturing. To assess the degree of empathy of individuals, it would be necessary to consult additional scales, such as empathy (Em), sociability (Sy) and well being (Wb). However, as further research was done on Py, it became clear that it was more an indicator of persons interested in pursuing psychology from an academic perspective. In fact, Megargee (1972) concludes his literature review by stating that the Py scale has limited usefulness as an indicator of a person's ability to accurately perceive the inner needs and motivations of others. The content of the items relates to one's ability to concentrate, one's effectiveness in dealing with ambiguity, and one's degree of enjoyment in his or her occupation. Other content areas deal with an ability to stick with long-term goals and an acceptance of unconventional opinions.

High Py (T = 65 or More)   High scorers are interested in academic pursuits, especially in the area of research. They can be highly original and creative in their approaches to abstract problems. They place a high level of importance on obtaining recognition for their efforts, and they demonstrate perseverance, the ability to concentrate for long periods of time, and a high degree of satisfaction from their chosen profession. Other people often see them as independent, individualistic, preoccupied, and reserved. They are excellent in dealing with abstract situations but generally avoid concrete problem solving situations. Extremely high scorers may be seen as distant, aloof, and detached. The most frequent adjectives used to describe them are logical, thorough, clear thinking, foresighted, and interests wide.

Low Py (T = 35 or Less)   Persons who score low on Py are generally not inclined toward research or scholarly activities. However, they are likely to be sociable, talkative, unassuming, and conventional. They usually accept the behavior and motivation of others at face value and are more comfortable with concrete situations. The most frequent adjectives used to describe them are simple and interests narrow.

19. Flexibility (Fx)

The Fx scale was designed to assess the degree to which an individual is flexible, adaptable, and changeable in his or her thinking, behavior, and temperament. It was originally based on questions relating to rigidity, but as the scale construction evolved, the scoring was reversed and the name changed from the "rigidity" scale to the "flexibility" scale. Other content areas relate to an ability to tolerate ambiguity, uncertainty, and impulsiveness, and to a nonjudgmental, tolerant attitude toward moral and ethical formulas of right and wrong.

The validity studies in part agree with the intent of the scale in that they do support the hypothesis that low-scoring individuals are somewhat rigid. However, there is little evidence to indicate that extremely high scores reflect a high degree of flexibility (Megargee, 1972). Gough (1975) suggests that scores in the higher ranges are curvilinear in that a moderately high score suggests that the person is relatively flexible, but with increasing elevation, a person becomes progressively more unstable and unpredictable. Megargee (1972) states that, given the weak evidence for the validity of this scale, especially for high Fx, it is one of the least valid scales on the CPI. Thus, any interpretations derived from it should be made with caution.

High Fx (T = 65 or More)   Persons having extremely high scores may feel rootless and are often emotionally unstable. Everything in their lives is open to question, including their sense of values and moral beliefs. Thus, it is difficult for them to internalize clear-cut standards. They can easily approach situations from a number of varying perspectives. This allows them to consider many alternatives but may create a disadvantage in that they have difficulty developing a clearly defined direction. Extremely high scorers might be volatile, distractible, restless, and poorly organized. The most frequently used adjectives to describe high scorers are logical, thorough, clear thinking, foresighted, and interests wide.

Moderate Fx (T = 50–65)   Moderate scorers are open to considering and experiencing alternative perspectives. They are nonjudgmental, intellectually flexible, original, and able to develop innovative ideas. They might also be independent, self-confident, optimistic, and value intellectual activities.

Moderately Low Fx (T = 35–50)   Persons scoring in this range prefer structure and like to have things clearly defined and specified. Although they can handle a certain degree of uncertainty, it usually creates discomfort. They are usually cautious and practical, and can be described as relatively rigid.

Low Fx (T = 35 or Less)   Low scorers generally dislike new ideas and experiences, and are continually seeking security. They have a strong need to control their thoughts and generally have a difficult time changing their decisions. They are usually rigid, stubborn, and defensive. Often, they have strong religious beliefs and are moralistic and conservative. Others perceive them as conscientious, serious, literal minded, and overcontrolled. The most frequently used adjectives to describe them are organized, efficient, rigid, conservative, interests narrow, conventional, and prejudiced.

20. Femininity/Masculinity (F/M)

The F/M scale was developed to assess the degree to which examinees were psychologically feminine or masculine, regardless of their actual sex. Its original intent was to detect significant conflicts over sexual identity, but this aspect of the scale has become progressively less emphasized. The scale is currently used to assess the extent to which individuals endorse beliefs, values, and occupations that are traditionally held either by males or by females. The intent of some items is fairly obvious whereas the intent of other items is more subtle. Many items relate to traditional masculine or feminine roles. Additional content areas refer to a person's degree of restraint and impulsiveness, as well as the extent to which one is emotional during interpersonal relationships. The items also reflect the degree to which a person is interested in politics, current affairs, and achievement. This scale has been well researched, and studies indicate it has a fairly high level of validity.

High F/M (T = 70 or More)   For males, scores within this range suggest the possibility of difficulties related to sexual identity. These males might also be highly introspective and have philosophical and aesthetic interests. Their interests might be wide ranging and their thought patterns unconventional. The most frequent adjectives used to describe them are nervous, worrying, weak, self-pitying, reflective, and sensitive.

Females with extremely high scores might be highly affiliative, dependent, submissive, and require continual reassurance. They might also be tolerant, permissive, giving, and oversensitive. Both male and female high scorers might use bodily symptoms to express anxiety and tension. The most frequent adjectives used to describe high-scoring females are warm, sympathetic, sentimental, and dependent.

Moderately High F/M (T = 60–70 or More)   Both males and females scoring within this range have significant needs for affiliation and dependency. They usually have a difficult time dealing with a high degree of autonomy and feel uncomfortable when independent action is required of them. They are both highly sensitive and quite concerned with not hurting others.

Moderate F/M (T = 40–50)   Persons scoring within this range can deal effectively with autonomy and have an average need for dependency and affiliation. They are generally practical and self-sufficient but not to an exaggerated extent.

Moderately Low F/M (T = 40 or Less)   Such persons are typically task oriented, practical, and emotionally self-sufficient with few dependency needs. They are often perceived as masculine, robust, tough, and even coarse.

Low-scoring males will generally fit the masculine stereotype in that they are described as masculine, emotionally independent, tough minded, self-sufficient, and self-centered. They often have a clear, stable, internally consistent personality and adhere to conservative values. The most frequent adjectives to describe low-scoring males are confident, independent, aggressive, and ambitious.

Females who score low will likewise be self-reliant, confident, independent, and deliberate. In addition, they might also be critical, distrustful, cynical, and outspoken. They tend to be motivated by power and have high aspirations for themselves. The most frequent adjectives to describe moderately low-scoring females are strong, tough, and independent.

Low F/M (T = 30 or Less)   An F/M score this low suggests an exaggeration of the above trends and, in females, the likelihood of difficulties related to sexual identity.

CONFIGURAL INTERPRETATION

The following material on configural interpretation summarizes most of the empirical research on different code types. Regression equations have been included and are summarized at the end of the section in Table 8–2. The material is organized according to different topics (leadership, achievement, etc.). In contrast, McAllister (1988) has provided a listing of 132 code types arranged according to different patterns of low and high scale scores. Readers wanting to interpret scale scores can refer to McAllister (1988) or, alternatively, use the topic listings below. They might also wish to make rational interpretations of patterns of scale scores by using the following sequence:

1. Note the high (generally above 60) and low (generally below 40) scale scores and read the individual descriptions that correspond with these scores.
2. The key phrases can then be written down which correspond with these single scales and the descriptions can be strengthened, weakened, or altered according to their relative elevations or lowerings and their relationships with other scales.
3. The descriptions can then be combined to create a more integrated description of the person.

Intellectual Level

Megargee (1972) has reported that To, Ac, Ai, Ie, Py, and Fx are all related to an individual's intellectual level. Elevations (T = 55 or more) on all or most of these scales strongly indicate that the person has a high interest in intellectual activities and good overall intelligence. Consistently low scores on all or most of the above scales reflects limited intellectual ability and is a strong indication that the person has a narrow range of interests. This narrowing of interests may, in part, be a response to an emotionally upsetting event either in the recent past or at a significant time during the person's earlier development.

The particular patterns of high and low scales can provide information on the specific expression of intelligence. For example, it might be noted whether individuals would be more likely to excel in structured (high Ac) or nonstructured (high Ai) environments (see next subsection). Similarly, an interpreter can note how tolerant, flexible, or efficient individuals might be.

Support for the CPI in measuring aspects of "social intelligence" lies in comparisons made with the Picture Arrangement and Comprehension subtests on the WAIS-R. Specifically, Comprehension has been found to be correlated with Cs, Fx, and Cm, and Picture Arrangement was similarly correlated with Cs, Fx, and also Fm (Sipps, Berry, & Lynch, 1987).

Achievement

Predicting and Assessing High-School Achievement   The CPI is generally effective at detecting bright high-school achievers. They typically have elevated scores on Ie and Ai, whereas underachievers are generally low on these scales. Bright achievers also have relatively high scores on Re, So, To, Ac, and Py. Persons who are high achievers but have average I.Q.s have relatively high scores (T = 55 or more) on Re and So and, to a lesser extent, on Wb, Ac, and Ie.

A number of equations have been developed for use in predicting achievement of high-school students (see Megargee, 1972). These equations are comprised of the weighted combinations of scales and, when computed, provide the best possible prediction of specific abilities. For predicting the achievement of both males and females with combined low, medium, and high I.Q.s, the following equation is recommended:

1. Achievement = 20.116 + .317 Re + .192 So − .309 Gi + .227 Ac + .280 Ai + .244 Ie

This equation correlates from .53 to .56 with overall High School G.P.A. (Gough, 1964). If a student's I.Q. scores are available, the following equation is recommended:

2. Achievement = .786 + .195 Re + .244 So − .130 Gi + .19 Ac + .179 Ai + .279 I.Q.

Since Ie is a relatively inefficient measure of I.Q., it has been excluded in this equation and instead the exact I.Q. is from intelligence testing. This equation raises the correlation with overall G.P.A. to .68, which is significantly better than the typical .60 correlation found when using only I.Q. scores.

To evaluate whether students will drop out of high school or graduate and continue on to college, social factors as measured by the CPI are at least as important as students' intellectual ability. The primary scales used to predict high-school graduation are Re, Ac, and, to a lesser extent, Wb, To, and Ie, all of which are usually significantly higher for students who graduate from high school than for students who are high-school dropouts (Gough, 1964). High-school students who later go on to college score significantly higher on Re, Ac, and Ie (Gough, 1968). The following formula correlates at a level of .52 with later college attendance for high-school students (Gough, 1968):

3. College Attendance = 17.822 + .333 Do + .539 Cs − .189 Gi + .740 Ac

Predicting and Assessing College Achievement   Several studies have been conducted on the relative importance of single-scale and combinations of scale scores in assessing college achievement. Significant correlations have been found among Re, So, Ai, and overall G.P.A. (Hase & Goldberg, 1967). Further studies (Flaherty & Reutzel, 1965; Griffin & Flaherty, 1964) likewise stress the importance of Re, So, and Ai but also include Ie and Cs, and, in female samples, Do was significantly correlated with G.P.A. as well (Flaherty & Reutzel, 1965). These scales are somewhat similar to those used to predict achievement in high-school students, except that Ai becomes more significant for college populations and Ac decreases in relative importance. Also, the likelihood of later upward social mobility is correlated with Cs and college G.P.A.

Although positive correlations were found among the above single scales, the magnitude of these correlations was not extremely high, with the highest correlation reaching only .36 for males on Ai. Most other significant correlations ranged from .20 and .26. However, weighted combinations of scores produced higher correlations ranging from .35 to .54, depending on the type of population being assessed. Gough (1964) has found a .41 correlation between the following formula and grades for both males and females in introduction to psychology classes:

4. Achievement (Introduction to Psychology) = 35.958 − .294 Sy − .180 Sp
     + .185 Re − .189 Sc − .152 Gi − .210 Cm + .275 Ac + .523 Ai + .241 Ie
     + .657 Py

Weighted combinations of scales in combination with SAT scores for males and females who were National Merit scholars were found to have a .32 and .23 correlation with college G.P.A., respectively:

5. Male G.P.A. = .16 SAT (Math) + .11 So − .19 Sp + .17 Fe

6. Female G.P.A. = .25 SAT (Verbal) − .14 Sp + .06 Re + .20 Ac + .08 Fe

Although the correlations derived from these formulas are somewhat low, they are an improvement on the use of SAT scores alone for this group.

Using a more general sample of college students' CPI scores to predict academic performance, Gough & Lanning (1986) found that Ai, Ie, and Py correlated at the levels of .28, .25, and .23 respectively. Multiple regression analysis produced the following equation, which had a correlation with later course grades of .38 for males and .36 for females:

7. G.P.A. = 30.60 − .26 Wb + .35 Re − .19 Gi + .39 Ai + .22 Ie + .36 Py

Although the correlation was modest, it was able to predict academic performance somewhat better than using SAT-V (.31 for males, .38 for females) and SAT-M (.30 for males, .24 for females).

These rather modest correlations indicate that it is more difficult to predict performance for college students than for those attending high school. This can be traced to the far greater number and complexity of variables involved in a college setting. Both the selection of curricula and the student's motivation for attending college can result from a variety of situations. Furthermore, significant changes have been made in the curricula and admissions policies of colleges since the early equations (4, 5, and 6) were developed. Finally, a student's lifestyle can be extremely varied. For example, some students may be attempting to struggle through college with a part- or even full-time job, whereas others may be taking relatively few classes and be supported exclusively by their parents. All of these variables are beyond the scope of what can be measured by a test such as the CPI. The practical implication for clinicians predicting college G.P.A. is to consider not only test scores but also as many of the other variables as possible.

Achievement in Vocational Training Programs

Student Teaching   Several studies have been performed to assess the effectiveness of teachers in student-teaching programs. Veldman and Kelly (1965) found that student teachers who were rated highly by their supervisors scored significantly higher on Ac, Cs, Do, Gi, and Py than those who were rated as less effective. Hill (1960) also emphasized the importance of Ac but did not find Do and Py to be important. A further study with a female population again stressed the importance of Ac but also included Re and Ie as significant factors (Gough, Durflinger, & Hill, 1968). Although these studies consistently emphasized the importance of Ac, none of the other individual scales were found to have either consistent or large correlations with teaching effectiveness. However, Gough, Durflinger, and Hill (1968) found a moderate correlation of .44 between CPI scores and teacher effectiveness by using the following equation based on weighted scales:

8. Teaching Effectiveness = 14.743 + .334 So − .670 Gi + .997 Ac + .909 Py − .446 Fx

Using this equation, they were able to predict with 65% accuracy the performance of student teachers.

Medical School   Several scales have been found to correlate positively with overall medical-school G.P.A., including Sy (.35), To (.34), and Ie (.40; Gough & Hall, 1964). An equation based on weighted combinations of scores was found to correlate at a magnitude of .43 with both faculty ratings of students and G.P.A. (Gough & Hall, 1964):

   9. Medical Promise = .794 Sy + .602 To + 1.114 Cm − .696 Cs

Dental School   Most studies using single-scale correlations with achievement in dental school have not produced significant correlations, although Kirk, Cumming, & Hackett (1963) did report a correlation of .28 between Ac and dental-school G.P.A. However, Gough and Kirk (1970) found a .38 correlation with G.P.A. by using the following equation based on weighted combinations of scales:

   10. Dental Performance = 29.938 − .110 Sp + .148 Re − .262 Gi + .727 Ac + .230 Py

Although this correlation is somewhat modest, it is higher than the Dental Aptitude Test's correlation of .29.

Seminary   Query (1966) performed a study on seminary students who were advised to discontinue and those who successfully completed the program. Although he did not develop any equations based on weighted scores, he did find that those who were unsuccessful tended to score higher on Sy and Sa.

Police and Military Training   Both Ie (Hogan, 1973) and Do (Hargrave, Hiatt, & Gaffney, 1986) have been found to be related to police effectiveness. Hogan (1973) found that Ie correlated .40 with ratings of effectiveness made by instructors during training and it correlated .43 after one year in training when ratings were made by field commanders (Mills & Bohannon, 1981). Other noteworthy correlations with other scales were for Ac (.31), Ai (.33), and Sy (.45; Hogan, 1973). Hargrave et al. (1986) described the most effective deputies as sociable, outgoing, and gregarious, whereas effective traffic controllers were characterized by a high capacity for rewarding social interactions. The most effective persons in both these groups (deputies and traffic controllers) were relatively dominant (high Do), energetic (high Ie), competitive (high Ac), independent (high Ai), flexible (high Fx), and socially ascendant (high Class 1 scales; Hargrave et al., 1986). Mills and Bohannon (1981) somewhat similarly described effective officers who had been in the field a year or more as independent (high Ai), energetic (high Ie), and flexible (high Fx).

   Pugh (1985) has pointed out that what determines successful police performance changes over time. During their training and first year of employment, the most effective officers were found to be those who were most able to obtain the trust of their coworkers and become an accepted member of their department. After two years, their ability to strive for improvement (high Cs) became the best predictor. In contrast, the best predictors after 4.5 years of employment were qualities that indicated a person was stable, socially skilled, and responsible (high Wb, Re, So).

   A study by Collins (1967) rated drill sergeants in a training program on the following four criteria of success: academic grades, an assessment of leadership ability, final class standing, and a field test of combat skills. The only scale to correlate significantly was Ie. It is interesting to note that the scales stressing conformity (Ac) and dominance (Do) had no correlation. This is in contrast to the frequent stereotype of drill sergeants as authoritarian, rigid, conformist, and autocratic. It has also been found that women who were successful in Air Force basic training scored higher in all scales except Sc, Cm, Py, and Fe than those who were unsuccessful (Elliott, 1960). A different study found that successful students graduating from an Army language training program scored significantly higher on Ai and Ie but not Ac than those who were unsuccessful (Datel, Hall, & Rufe, 1965).

Achievement through Conformance versus Independence   A comparison between Ac and Ai can provide useful information regarding an individual's typical style or preference toward working. This can have important implications for helping a person make a career choice or understanding existing job difficulties. If Ai is high (T = 50 or more) and significantly higher than Ac (50 or more), such persons usually place a high level of trust in their own judgments and conclusions, and are likely to reject conventional formulas. Their acceptance of decisions or ideas depends more on inward verification rather than a respect for, or adherence to, external standards. When left on their own, they are highly motivated to achieve, but they may feel restricted if placed in a structured environment. If Ai is exceptionally high (T = 65 or more), they may spend much of their time rejecting authority. This trend would be further exaggerated with high scores on Do and low scores on Sy. The result might be an almost obsessional quality in their thinking, characterized by strong themes of rebelliousness. In general, a significantly higher Ai than Ac is an excellent profile for authors, researchers, and persons in positions of independent leadership.

If Ac is high (T = 50 or more) and is significantly greater than Ai (10 or more), the opposite trend would be apparent. These persons would strongly prefer specificity and external structure. They would be more effective and feel more comfortable when "second in command," such as in a middle-management business position. An overall and generally effective combination occurs with high but evenly balanced scores on Ai and Ac. This suggests these individuals have the necessary flexibility both to work within a structured environment and to do effective work independently. The following is a listing of the descriptions given to persons scoring with different high and low combinations of Ac and Ai (Gough, 1968):

	Ac high			
	idealistic	mannerly	intelligent	logical
	cautious	shy	rational	interests wide
	praising	conscientious	realistic	inventive
	nervous	inhibited	independent	active
	helpful	dull	reasonable	stable
Ai low				Ai high
	irresponsible	show-off	spunky	tolerant
	careless	touchy	reckless	reliable
	distrustful	undependable	unexcitable	courageous
	disorderly	unstable	foresighted	distractible
	indifferent	restless	frank	pleasure seeking
		Ac low		

Leadership

The Do scale has consistently proven to be accurate in differentiating leaders from nonleaders. In discussing leadership, it is helpful to describe the difference between an executive leader who has been appointed and a social leader who has been elected. For both types of leaders, the Do scale is high. However, for the executive leader, there is considerably more variability among the other scales; the style of expressing leadership is more dependent on the conditions the person is in, and the achievement scales are relatively more important than the other measurements (summarized in Megargee, 1972). This seems reasonable since the success of an executive leader is based more on his or her administrative and supervisory abilities than on his or her popularity. Social leadership is more likely to have a general elevation in factor 2 scales as well as an elevated Do.

For example, if Do, Cs, and Sp are the high points, the leader is likely to be socially charismatic, persuasive, at the center of attention, and energetic (Heilbrun, Daniel, Goodstein, Stephenson, & Crites, 1962). If Do is high along with Sa and Ac, the person will have a high need for control, fear rejection, demand attention, dislike surprises, and emphasize clear structure (McAllister, 1988). If Do and Ai are the high points, these individuals will be independent achievers who may also be highly creative self-initiators (McAllister, 1988). Further interactions with Do can likewise be developed by taking into consideration the specific meanings of additional corresponding high and low scale scores.

Using a combination of weighted scales derived from social leaders in a high-school environment, Gough (1969) was able to obtain a modest correlation of .34 between social leadership and weighted CPI scales.

11. Leadership (Social) = 14.130 + .372 Do + .696 Sa + .345 Wb − .133 Gi + .274 Ai

Gough (1968) studied the relationship between Do and Re and found that the meaning of Do will be altered by the relative elevation of Re. If Do and Re are both high, a leader will be generally progressive, conscientious, and ambitious. In contrast, adjectives describing high Do persons with low Re indicate that they will be dominant in a more aggressive, rigid, and destructive way. The following is a list of adjectives used to describe various combinations of Do and Re:

Do high

touchy	dominant	dominant	ambitious
robust	strong	responsible	foresighted
cynical	tough	progressive	conscientious
hardheaded	aggressive	wise	formal
temperamental	opinionated	stern	alert

Re low ———————————————————————————— Re high

irresponsible	suggestible	quiet	calm
careless	foolish	peaceable	mild
unstable	pleasure seeking	modest	gentle
apathetic	changeable	reserved	thoughtful
confused	lazy	cooperative	honest

Do low

Executive Success   Success and effectiveness as an executive are frequently found in a profile in which T = 60 on Do, Cs, and Sp; T = 40-50 on Sa, Re, So, Sc; T = 55 or more on Sy; T = 40 or more on Wb; and T = 50 or less on Gi (in Webb et al., 1981). The most important variables are the indicated T scores on Do, Cs, Sp, Sa, Re, So, and Sc. This profile is common among business executives and managers. They are usually able to have others adapt to their plans, yet at the same time are flexible enough to adapt to the demands that are placed on them. Although they are generally excellent leaders, they may create a certain degree of family discord by attempting to be too demanding and autocratic in the home. If this combination of scores is present for a person under 25 years of age, it can suggest a naive sense of overconfidence in which the person cannot effectively assess his or her personal limitations. However, this profile is generally a good predictor of later success in leadership positions.

Leadership and Empathy   If an individual has elevations on both Do (T = 65 or more) and Gi (T = 60 or more), he or she is likely to not only possess excellent leadership abilities, but also to demonstrate a concern with, and empathy for, others (Heilbrun et al., 1962). If Gi is low in relationship to Do, then the leadership style will usually be more critical, domineering, egotistical, and autocratic, with a decreased concern for creating and maintaining harmonious interpersonal relationships in the group. A low score on both Gi and Do will reflect a somewhat passive and withdrawn person who is socially inept and resentful, and whose passivity may be expressed in a shy seeking of approval from others.

Decision Making   The interaction between Sa and Wb reflects the degree to which the examinee turns to him- or herself for decision making or depends on others. If Wb is low and Sa is moderate to high, these persons will usually rely on their own self-evaluations, and will feel that others are inferior and cannot be trusted. This may be because they are self-assured and independent as reflected by a Wb that is only moderate to slightly low, or they may only listen to their own judgments due to a deep sense of alienation and distrust of others—as reflected in a markedly low Wb and high Sa.

If Wb is moderate to high and Sa is low, such individuals will tend to believe that the judgment of others is superior to their own judgment. This may be because they are still fairly accepting of themselves (only slightly low Sa) but think even more highly of others. Thus, they may have a high level of loyalty to people who are in superior positions, such as an employer or parent. Such persons may also have a poorly developed ability to accurately perceive the faults and limitations of others, and may have developed this loyalty in response to overprotective parents. A further possibility could be that they do not respect their own judgments and perceptions because they are lacking in their own resources.

With both Sa and Wb low, there are likely to be significant doubts regarding oneself. There may be an excessive level of dependency, fearfulness regarding one's own competence, and a corresponding resentment of one's continual dependency on others.

Clinical Assessment

The CPI has generally not proven to be as effective in the assessment of psychopathology as it has in the educational and vocational areas. This can be traced to several reasons, but is primarily because it was not designed for clinical assessment and thus relatively little research has been conducted in this area. The organization and nature of the scales were not designed to differentiate among the various syndromes of pathology, nor do they provide information relating to a person's intrapsychic areas of functioning. Furthermore, devices such as the MMPI are clearly superior for the evaluation of pathology.

Despite these limitations, the CPI can make some general as well as specific contributions. Even though it does not distinguish between the different patterns of pathology, general maladjustment is usually indicated by lowered profiles. The CPI has also been effectively used to detect and assess criminal and delinquent individuals, which involves a more interpersonal or, more accurately, an individual versus societal type of conflict. Furthermore, the CPI is a good adjunct to more clinically oriented tests because it can assess the relative strengths in an otherwise pathological individual and answer questions relating to the type of educational and vocational programs this person might benefit from.

General Maladjustment   An individual's level of maladjustment is indicated by generally lowered profiles, which are often accompanied by an elevation on Fe (Gough, 1969; Webb, 1963). A lowering of factor 1 scales (especially Do, Re, So, and Sc) is often a good indicator of poor adjustment, and men with low Ac and Ie are especially likely to be maladjusted (Stewart, 1962).

Vulnerability to Stress   Persons with a "V" formation in which So is low (T = 35 or less), with Re and Sc significantly higher (T = 40 or more), are likely to be defensive and susceptible to the effects of situational stress (in Webb et al., 1981). They usually come from chaotic, stress-filled families in which there were episodes of irrational parental abuse. Thus, they have learned that the world is a dangerous place and have developed a precarious balance in which they feel constantly on guard. They keep their emotions carefully controlled, continually attempt to avoid conflict, and feel they need to be constantly prepared to diffuse potentially stress-filled interactions. Their conformity to their environment is based not on an expectation of achieving positive rewards, but more on fear and an avoidance of negative consequences. These people may have occasional explosive outbursts in which they have an almost dissociative loss of control. This explosiveness is especially likely if their spouse is manipulative, insensitive, and exploitive. As the discrepancy between So and Sc increases, these dynamics become more pronounced.

Depression   The social ascendency (Class 1) scales are generally lowered by depression, and a T score of 40 or less on Sy, So, Wb, and Ie is highly typical of depressed populations (Holliman & Montross, 1984). The scales that provided the best indicators of depression in males were Sy, So, and Ie, whereas for females the best discriminators were Wb, So, and Ie (Holliman & Montross, 1984). In most cases, the Wb scale is particularly important to notice, since a lowering on scales such as Do, Cs, Sy, Sp, and Sa might suggest merely a shy, unassertive, socially uninvolved person who is not necessarily depressed (McAllister, 1988). When the depression begins to lift and the person starts to have more optimism and a greater orientation to his or her environment, these scales generally increase. The mental and behavioral apathy often associated with depression can also be reflected by a lowering (T = 40 or less) in Ac, Ai, and Ie.

Psychosomatic Disorders   Although the CPI was not designed to diagnose psychosomatic disorders, it can assess certain personality characteristics that are consistent with individuals who are susceptible to this type of disturbance. Both male and female psychosomatics usually have lowered scores (T = 40 or less) on Wb and Sc and an elevation on Cm (Stewart, 1962). In addition, males often have a lowering on Ie. When the scores from male and female psychosomatics are compared with persons having behavior disorders, psychosomatics have a relatively higher So and Cm, with females also having a higher Re (Stewart, 1962). All of these scores suggest that psychosomatic patients have a significantly higher level of superego control and socialization. This agrees with most formulations of psychosomatic disorders that emphasize the suppression and repression of hostility and antisocial behavior as important predisposing factors. A pattern of psychosomatic disorders is especially likely if Wb has a T score of 35 or less, accompanied by an Fe of 60 or more. This pattern is associated with headaches, gastrointestinal upsets, or functional skin conditions. Such persons are likely to have moderately high needs for dependency, which are not being fulfilled, but they also tend to feel distrustful and alienated in their relationships with others.

Defense Mechanisms   Byrne (1964) has theorized that the two basic approaches to defense are either through repression or through sensitization. Whereas repressors attempt to avoid anxiety-arousing stimuli, sensitizers approach and attempt to control situations. Byrne, Golightly, and Sheffield (1965) found that high scorers on Sy, Wb, Sc, To, Gi, Ac, and Ie were more likely to use repression.

Certain types of assaultive offenders can usually be characterized as overcontrolled, but occasionally they drop all inhibitions and impulsively strike out (Megargee, 1964, 1965, 1966d). These persons score high on the "overcontrolled hostility" scale (OH) of the MMPI, and also have higher scores on Sc and Gi with a lowering on Sa (Megargee, Cook & Mendelsohn, 1967). This gives further support to the view that Sc and Gi are associated with the use of repressive defenses.

Juvenile Delinquency and Criminal Behavior   The assessment of antisocial behavior with the CPI has been well researched with generally useful findings. Both delinquents and criminals tend to have lower overall subscale scores, particularly on Re and So (Laufer et al., 1982). Scores are also somewhat lower on Wb, To, and Ac, and factors 3 and 4 are likewise decreased (Gough, 1969). This pattern suggests that the social poise of delinquents is usually about the same as that of other persons their age, but in most other respects their behavior is definitely unconventional and they usually do not channel these differences into creative or intellectual areas. Mizushima and DeVos (1967) have found significant differences on the CPI between solitary delinquents who have lower scores on Ie and Fe and more socially oriented delinquents who have significantly higher scores on Sy, Sp, and Sa. They also found violent offenders to be higher on Sp and Sa but low on Fe. However, delinquents who committed extremely violent offenses were especially high on Sc, which supports Gough's theory that excessive overcontrol in certain individuals periodically breaks down, leading to assaultive behavior (Megargee, 1966d). In summarizing this data on delinquency, it is most important to consider lowerings in Re and So. Further information regarding the style of delinquency can be derived by the lowered Ie and Fe for solitary delinquents; higher Sy, Sp, and Sa for social delinquents; higher Sp, Sa, and low Fe for violent social delinquents; and outstandingly high Sc for extremely violent offenders who have periodic excessive losses of control.

The likelihood of successful parole for delinquents can, in part, be predicted in that more successful parolees have higher scores on Sp and Sa, and less successful parolees have lower scores on So and Sc (Gough, Wenk, & Rozynko, 1965). Gough and his colleagues have developed the following regression equation to predict successful from unsuccessful parolees:

12.   Parole Success = $45.078 - .353$ Sp $- .182$ Sa $+ .532$ So $+ .224$ Sc

Using this equation, Gough et al. (1965) were able to predict with 60% accuracy which of a population of California Youth Authority parolees would be successful and which parolees would later become recidivists.

Chemical Dependency   The possibility of potential or actual substance abuse, perhaps to the extent of actual addiction, is suggested by high Sp and Sa accompanied by low scores on Re, So, Sc, and Wb (Kurtines, Hogan, & Weiss, 1975).

Social Maturity

The concept of social maturity includes So, but is more extensive and also includes areas other than that assessed by the So scale alone. Specifically, the person who is considered to be socially mature is not merely directed by blind conformance, but also has a high level of ethical standards that can even vary from the values held by the majority of people. He or she may, at times, feel a need to resist social pressure. Also, this person can accurately perceive the faults in a social system and attempt to deal with them in a mature way. Thus, the socially mature person is clearly different from someone who is merely oversocialized or hypernormal. Gough (1966) developed the following multiple regression equation to assess social maturity using combined weighted scores:

13. Social Maturity = 25.701 + .408 Re + .478 So − .296 Gi

Table 8–2.   Summary of CPI equations used for making predictions

1. Achievement (High School) = 20.116 + .317 Re + 192 So − .309 Gi + .227 Ac + .280 Ai + .244 Ie
2. Achievement (High School - Using I.Q.) = .786 + .195 Re + .244 So − .130 Gi + .19 Ac + .179 Ai + .279 I.Q.
3. College Attendance = 17.822 + .333 Do + .539 Cs − .189 Gi + .740 Ac
4. Achievement (Introduction to Psychology) = 35.958 − .294 Sy − .180 Sp + .185 Re − .189 Sc - .152 Gi − .210 Cm + .275 Ac + .523 Ai + .241 Ie + .657 Py
5. Male G.P.A. = .16 SAT (Math) + .11 So − .19 Sp + .17 Fe
6. Female G.P.A. = .25 SAT (Verbal) − .14 Sp + .06 Re + .20 Ac + .08 Fe
7. G.P.A. = 30.60 − .26 Wb + .35 Re − .19 Gi + .39 Ai + .22 Ie + .36 Py
8. Teaching Effectiveness = 14.743 + .334 So − .670 Gi + .997 Ac + .909 Py − .446 Fx
9. Medical Promise = .794 Sy + .602 To + 1.114 Cm − .696 Cs
10. Dental Performance = 29.938 − .110 Sp + .148 Re − .262 Gi + .727 Ac + .230 Py
11. Leadership (Social) = 14.130 + .372 Do + .696 Sa + .345 Wb − .133 Gi + .274 Ai
12. Parole Success = 45.078 − .353 Sp − .182 Sa + .532 So + .224 Sc
13. Social Maturity = 25.701 + .408 Re + .478 So − .296 Gi

RECOMMENDED READING

Gough, H. G. (1968). An interpreter's syllabus for the California Psychological Inventory. In P. McReynolds (Ed.), *Advances in psychological assessment*, (Vol. 1.) Palo Alto, CA: Science and Behavior Books.

Gough, H. (1987). *California Psychological Inventory administrator's guide*. Palo Alto, CA: Consulting Psychologists Press.

McAllister, L. (1988). *A practical guide to CPI interpretation* (2nd ed.). Palo Alto, CA: Consulting Psychologists Press.

Megargee, E.I. (1972). *The California Psychological Inventory handbook*. San Francisco: Jossey-Bass.

Chapter 9 ──────────────────

THE RORSCHACH

The Rorschach is a projective test consisting of a set of ten bilaterally symmetrical inkblots, in which subjects are requested to tell the examiner what the inkblots remind them of. The overall goal of the technique is to assess a client's structure of personality, with particular emphasis on understanding the unconscious manner in which he or she responds to and organizes his or her environment. Despite attacks from both within and outside the field of psychology, the Rorschach remains one of the most extensively used (Durand, Blanchard, & Mindell, 1988; Lubin et al., 1985) and well-respected assessment devices.

The central assumption of the Rorschach is that stimuli from the environment are organized by a person's specific needs, motives, conflicts, and certain perceptual "sets." This need for organization becomes more exaggerated, extensive, and conspicuous when subjects are confronted with ambiguous stimuli, such as inkblots. Thus, they must draw on their personal internal images, ideas, and relationships in order to create a response. This process requires that persons organize these perceptions as well as associate them with past experiences and impressions. The central thesis upon which Rorschach interpretation is based is that the process by which persons organize their responses to the Rorschach is representative of how they confront other ambiguous situations requiring organization and judgment. Once the responses have been made and recorded, they are scored according to three general categories: the "location," or the area of the inkblot on which they focused; "determinants," or specific properties of the blot they used in making their responses (color, shape, etc.); and the "content," or general class of objects to which the response belongs (human, architecture, anatomy, etc.). The interpretation of the overall protocol is based on the relative number of responses that fall into each of the above categories. Some systems also score for the extent to which subjects organize their response (organizational activity) and types of verbalizations related to the inkblots.

Although these scoring categories may appear straightforward, the specifics of scoring and interpreting the Rorschach are extremely complex. Furthermore, attempts to develop a precise, universally accepted coding system have not been entirely successful, which creates some confusion and ambiguity in approaching the Rorschach technique itself. Although the primary scoring systems have some agreed-upon similarities, there are also significant differences in the elements of these systems. These differences, in turn, reflect the complexity and ambiguity in the nature of the responses made to the cards. Thus, effective use of the Rorschach depends on a thorough knowledge of a scoring system, clinical experience, and adequate knowledge of personality and psychopathology.

The general purpose of this chapter is to provide an overview of administration, scoring, and interpretation using Exner's "Comprehensive System." Exner's system was selected because it is the most ambitious and psychometrically sound Rorschach system to date. Furthermore, the most frequently used scorings and interpretations from the other systems have been included and integrated into Exner's approach.

There has been some minor editing of Exner's system where certain features were either insufficiently researched and/or idiosyncratic to his system. For the most part, however, the approach of this chapter closely parallels Exner's "Comprehensive System." The Appendixes for this book include several tables that clinicians can use to compare the scores derived from their client's protocols with means and standard deviations developed for normal (nonpatient) adults and children. Clinicians who wish to use precise scoring tables and criteria, as well as a more extensive elaboration on interpretation, are encouraged to consult Exner and his colleagues' original works (Exner, 1978, 1986; Exner & Weiner, 1982).

This chapter cannot stand as a substitute for Exner's work. Its major intent is to familiarize persons with the Rorschach in general and, more specifically, with Exner's system of working with it. In addition, persons who are already familiar with Exner's system might wish to consult sections of this chapter to obtain summaries of different scoring categories and interpretive hypotheses. This might be most appropriate for persons who use the Rorschach only on an occasional basis. Finally, persons who use other scoring systems may wish to consult the different interpretive hypotheses as an aid to interpretation. This is theoretically possible since Exner incorporated the major approaches from other systems into his Comprehensive System. However, many minor variations are likely, so interpretations should be made with caution.

HISTORY AND DEVELOPMENT

Many inkblot-type tests and games had existed long before Rorschach published his original 10 cards in 1921. For example, Da Vinci and Botticelli were interested in determining how a person's interpretations of ambiguous designs reflected his or her personality. This theme was later considered by Binet and Henri in 1895, Whipple in 1910, and a popular parlor game named Blotto was developed in the late 1800s that required players to make creative responses to inkblots. However, Rorschach developed the first extensive, empirically based system to score and interpret responses to a standardized set of cards. Unfortunately, Rorschach died at 37, shortly after the 1921 publication of his major work, *Psychodiagnostik.* His work was continued to a limited extent by three of his colleagues; Emil Oberholzer, George Roeurer, and Walter Morgenthaler.

The main approach used by Rorschach and other early developers of inkblot techniques was to note the characteristic responses of different types of populations. Thus, the initial norms were developed to help differentiate between various clinical and normal populations. These early norms were developed for mental retardates, normals, artists, scholars, and other specific subgroups with known characteristics. Rorschach primarily wanted to establish empirically based discriminations between different groups; he was only minimally concerned with the symbolical interpretation of contents. Many of his original concepts and scoring categories have been continued within current systems of analysis. For example, he noted that depressed, sullen patients seemed to give the fewest responses. Persons giving a large number of very quick responses were likely to be similarly "scattered" in their perception and ideation to nontest situations. He also considered the importance of long latencies (so-called "shock" responses), and hypothesized that they were related to a sense of helplessness and emotional repression.

Had Rorschach lived longer, the history and development of his test might have been quite different. Without the continued guidance and research from a "founding father" such as Rorschach, the strands of the Rorschach technique were taken up by persons who had quite different backgrounds from one another. By 1957, five Rorschach systems were in wide use, the most popular of which were developed by Beck and Klopfer. These two approaches came to represent polarized schools of thought and were often in conflict.

Beck (1937) adhered closely to Rorschach's format for coding and scoring. He continually stressed the importance of establishing strong empirical relationships between Rorschach codes and outside criterion measures. Beck emphasized that the response to the Rorschach involved primarily a perceptual-cognitive process in which the respondents structure and organize their perceptions into meaningful responses. This perceptual-cognitive process was likely to reflect their responses to their world in general. For example, persons who broke down their perceptions of an inkblot into small details were likely to behave similarly for perceptions outside the testing situation.

In contrast, Klopfer (1937) was closely aligned to phenomenology and the theories of personality developed by Freud and Jung. As a result, he emphasized the symbolical and experential nature of a respondent's Rorschach contents. Thus, Klopfer believed that Rorschach responses were fantasy products triggered by the stimulus of the inkblots (Exner & Weiner, 1982; Weiner, 1977). For example, Rorschach responses that described threatening objects would suggest persons who perceive their world as similarly threatening. Although not as popular, additional systems were developed by Piotrowski, Hertz, and Rapaport. These additional systems represented a middle-ground between the two extremes taken by Beck and Klopfer.

With five distinct systems available, the Rorschach became not a unitary test but five different tests. Exner (1969) provided a comparative analysis of these different systems and later concluded that "the notion of *the* Rorschach was more myth than reality" (Exner, 1986, p.19). He pointed out that none of the five systems used the same verbal instructions and only two of the systems required identical seating arrangements. More importantly, each systematizer developed his or her own format for scoring, which resulted in many differences regarding interpretation; including the components required to calculate quantitative formulas, differences in the meanings associated with many of the variables, and differences in interpretive postulates.

The wide range of often competing approaches resulted in numerous detrimental practices. A survey of practitioners by Exner (1972) indicated that 22% of all respondents had abandoned scoring altogether and instead based their interpretations on a subjective analysis of contents. Of those who did score, 75% used their own personalized integration of scores from a variety of systems. In addition, the vast majority did not follow any prescribed set of instructions for administration. Since researchers had used a variety of approaches, it was also difficult to compare the results of different studies. Researchers in the early 1970s further reported difficulties recruiting subjects, problems with experimenter bias that needed to be corrected by using multiple examiners, statistical complexities of data analysis, inadequate control groups, and insufficient normative data (Exner, 1986).

The general conclusion based on the above findings was that the research on, and clinical use of, the Rorschach was seriously flawed in part due to the lack of clarity inherent in having five different systems. Surveys and analysis of research conducted in the early 1970s by Exner and his colleagues concluded that, although all five systems included some empirically sturdy elements, they also included elements that had no empirical basis or elements for which negative findings were predominant.

To correct the difficulties with both the research and clinical use of the Rorschach, Exner and his colleagues began the collection of a broad normative database and the development of an integrated system of scoring and interpretation. Their initial step was to establish clear guidelines for seating, verbal instructions, recording, and inquiry by the examiner regarding the examinee's responses. The best features for scoring and interpretation were adapted from each of the five different systems. They were included based on both empirical validation and commonality across systems. A scoring category was included in the new system only after it had achieved a minimum .85 level for interscorer reliability. The final product was first published in 1974 as *The Rorschach: A Comprehensive System* and in 1986 was released in its second edition. Two other volumes relating to current research and interpretation (Exner, 1978) and the assessment of children and adolescents (Exner & Weiner, 1982) have also been published.

Exner's integration of the different Rorschach approaches into a comprehensive system seems to have been largely successful. Most research studies during the 1980s have used his system, and it has become by far the most frequently taught system in graduate training (Ritzler & Alter, 1986). His close adherence to empirical validation combined with a large normative database have served to increase its acceptance and status. Access to training and interpretive aids has been facilitated through numerous workshops, a scoring workbook, ongoing research publications, new editions of earlier volumes, and computer-assisted scoring and interpretation (Exner, 1984, 1986).

RELIABILITY AND VALIDITY

Debates regarding the psychometric adequacy of the Rorschach have created one of the greatest controversies in the history of psychology. From the beginning, the Rorschach was met with skepticism in the United States. However, it developed a strong following in spite of this. At one point the Rorschach was the second most frequently used test and, in the 1940s and 1950s, the name Rorschach was almost synonymous with clinical psychology. Despite this initial (and continuing) popularity, reviews have generally been quite critical. As early as 1954 Shaffer declared that the Rorschach could no longer be considered a promising instrument and, 11 years later, Dana (1965) somewhat optimistically concluded that, "Indeed, we have come to the end of an era, preoccupation with the Rorschach as a test" (p.495). Jensen (1965) was even more critical when he recommended that "the Rorschach be altogether abandoned in clinical practice, and that students in clinical psychology not be required to waste their time learning the technique" (p.509). Despite these attacks, by 1956 there were almost 2,700 publications pertaining directly to the Rorschach. This number was estimated to be 2,000 by 1969 (Exner, 1969) and had increased to 6,000 by 1982 (Kobler, 1983).

Part of the difficulty in establishing the psychometric properties of the Rorschach has been in making meaningful comparisons across different studies. As Exner (1969; 1974; 1986) has repeatedly pointed out, there is not a Rorschach but rather at least five different Rorschachs have been created around the five major systems. Reliability and validity studies performed on one system did not necessarily mean that the findings from these studies could be generalized to any of the other systems. However, reviewers have often acted as if there was only one Rorschach. Furthermore, many studies were poorly conducted. They were characterized by inadequate controls for age, sex, race, I.Q., and socioeconomic status. In addition, many studies had extremely wide variations in the training required for scorers, insufficient protection from experimenter bias, poor validation criteria, and inadequate statistical models. These difficulties were amply demonstrated in that Exner (1986) and his associates found it necessary to discard 1,400 research studies of a total of 2,100 studies published prior to 1970.

Despite the above difficulties, estimates of reliability can be obtained by referring to a meta-analysis by Parker (1983) and data supplied by Exner (1983). Parker (1983b) analyzed 39 papers using 530 different statistical procedures published in the *Journal of Personality Assessment* between 1971 and 1980. He concluded that, overall, the Rorschach can be expected to have reliabilities in the low to mid .80s. During the development of Exner's Comprehensive System, Exner gave particular attention to reliability in developing his different scoring categories. No category was included unless it achieved a minimum .85 level between different scorers (Exner, 1974; 1986). Test-retest reliabilities were somewhat more variable. Retesting of 25 variables over a one-year interval for a nonpatient group produced reliabilities ranging between .26 to .91 (Exner, 1986). A total of 20 of the variables had correlations above .72, with 13 of them between .81 and .89 and 2 above .90. Exner has clarified that the five variables below .72 would all be expected to have had relatively low reliabilities since they related to changeable states (rather than trait) characteristics of the person. He also pointed out that the most important elements in interpretation are the ratios and percentages, all of which were among the higher reliabilities. Retesting for the same group over a three-year interval produced a similar but slightly lower pattern of reliability. In contrast, another group of nonpatient adults retested over a much shorter, three-week interval had somewhat higher overall reliabilities than for either the one-year or three-year retesting (Exner, 1986).

Long-term retesting for children has not shown near the same degree of stability as for adults (Exner & Weiner, 1982). Exner (1986) clarifies that this low stability for test results would be expected given that children undergo considerable developmental changes. However, short-term retesting over seven-day (for 8-year-olds) and three-week (9-year-olds) intervals did indicate acceptable levels of stability (Exner, 1986). Only 2 of 25 variables were below .70 with at least 7 above .90 and the remainder from .70 to .90. As with adults, the ratios and percentages demonstrated relatively high stabilities. Although acceptable short-term stability for young children's Rorschach variables were demonstrated, long-term stability was not found to occur until children reached the ages of 14 or older (Exner, Thomas, & Mason, 1985).

The primary focus of early validity studies was to empirically discriminate between different populations. This was based on past observations of a particular group's responses to the Rorschach, the development of norms based on these responses, and comparisons of an individual's Rorschach responses with these norms. For example, a schizophrenic might have a relatively high number of poor-quality responses or a depressed person might have very few human movement responses. In addition to this empirical discriminative validity, efforts have also been made to develop a conceptual basis for specific responses or response patterns (Weiner, 1986). Thus, it has been conceptualized that schizophrenics have poor quality responses because they do not perceive the world the way most people do; their perceptions are distorted and inaccurate, and their reality-testing is poor. A further approach, which was not extensively developed in the Comprehensive System (nor by Rorschach himself), was the validation of the latent meaning of symbolical content.

The above very general approaches have given rise to a surprisingly large number of specific scorings and interpretations, all of which have had various degrees of validation. Many of the early validity studies are difficult to evaluate due to the varying scoring systems and poor methodologies. In addition, most early studies depended on inadequate norms (especially for studies conducted on children, adolescents, and persons over 70). Test results might also have been significantly influenced by examiner-examinee variables, such as seating, instructions, rapport, sex, and personality of the examiner (see Exner, 1986). Harris (1960), for example, listed over 30 factors that could potentially influence

Rorschach performances. All of the above factors were (and are) likely to confound any attempts to develop consistent patterns of validity. It should then come as no surprise that, for every study supporting an interpretive hypothesis, there would often be another refuting the same hypothesis.

Establishing the validity of the Rorschach as a whole is difficult given the many scoring categories and quantitative formulas. Each category and formula has varying levels of validity. Some interpretations have greater validity than others even within a specific category. For example, the number of human movement responses (M) has been used as both an index of creativity and fantasy. A review of the research by Exner (1986) indicates that M relates fairly clearly to fantasy in that it has been correlated with daydreaming, sleep/dream deprivation, dream recall, and total time spent dreaming. However, associations between M and creativity have been weaker and more controversial. Validity might also depend on the context and population for which the test is used. For example, Exner (1986) reports that a depression index (DEPI) based on five Rorschach variables was able to adequately discriminate depressed patients from controls. However, among adolescent populations, the depression index was unimpressive in distinguishing depressives from schizophrenics (Archer & Gordon, 1988). Additional specific validity data on specific scoring categories and formulas is included in the Interpretation section of this text.

Perhaps the best way to provide a global index of validity is by combining the results from a large number of studies. In the meta-analytic study cited previously, Parker (1983b) reported that, when the studies he analyzed were well conducted, validity ranged from .40 to .50. This suggests that, overall, the Rorschach has achieved moderately acceptable levels of validity. However, interactions with type of scoring system, experience of the scorer, and type of population used is likely to have complicated the picture further. Clearly, more meta-analytic studies need to be conducted on both global aspects of the Rorschach as well as on more specific aspects. However, even though the psychometric properties of the Rorschach are not outstanding, it seems to have achieved acceptable levels of reliability and validity.

One major factor that may serve to lower Rorschach validity is the meaning associated with, and effects of, response productivity. Various interpretations have been associated with extremes of productivity—such as low productivity suggesting defensiveness, depression, and malingering, and extremely high productivity suggesting high achievement or an obsessive-compulsive personality. However, response productivity has also been found to be closely tied to age, intellectual level, verbal aptitude, and amount of education. Norms have been provided for different ages (Exner & Weiner, 1982), which can be helpful in correcting for the effects of age. However, intellectual level, verbal aptitude, and amount of education can potentially confound the meanings associated with response productivity. A high number of responses does not necessarily represent traditional personality interpretations (obsessiveness, creativity, good impulse control), but might merely indicate a high level of verbal aptitude. Most early validity studies rarely took these factors into account. More importantly, the number of responses will not only effect interpretations related specifically to response productivity, but productivity will also effect many other areas of interpretation. For example, a low number of responses are likely to increase the relative number of responses based on the whole inkblot (W). In contrast, a high number of responses would be likely to increase the relative number of small detail (Dd) responses. Since interpretations are frequently based on the relative proportions of different scoring categories (calculated in quantitative formulas), the overall number of responses is likely to influence and possibly compromise the validity of the formulas. Thus, protocols with either an extremely high or extremely low number of responses are often of questionable validity. Exner (1988) even recommends that brief protocols be discarded or a greater number of responses obtained. It is largely this problem with the meaning of various numbers of responses that led Holtzman to develop his alternate test (Holtzman Inkblot Test) in which subjects provide only one response for each inkblot (Holtzman, 1988; Holtzman & Schwartz, 1983; Holtzman, Thorpe, Swartz, & Herron, 1961).

A further area of difficulty in establishing validity is that Exner cites extensive validity studies throughout his three volumes, but the majority of these studies were not done using his Comprehensive System. Comparability between the different studies and systems is frequently assumed or at least implied. Presumably, the studies he cites are those with relatively sound methodologies. However, these studies were frequently done at a time when norms were inadequate, interscorer reliability was questionable, and little concern was given to the possible confounding effects of age, intellectual level, education, and verbal aptitude. The development of the Comprehensive System itself was largely motivated by the deficiencies (and strengths) inherent in each of the earlier systems. As progressively more studies accumulate using the Comprehensive System, there will be less need to rely on previous research. Eventually, the newer studies will help clarify Rorschach validity without the possible contaminating effects of previous work.

The main effort on Rorschach validity has been made in determining its ability to discriminate between different types of populations. Although the Rorschach has often demonstrated its success in making accurate discriminations, this is an important but limited form of validity. As Lanyon (1984) stresses, the Comprehensive System "still did not tackle (the) most urgent topic of external validity, one which continues to deny the Rorschach the status of scientific respectability" (p.680). Little success has been achieved in making accurate predictions to such relevant areas as response to therapy, academic achievement, or spontaneous improvement in a clinical condition. Ideally, a test such as the Rorschach should not merely infer characteristics regarding the ways in which persons organize their perceptions of their world, but also should translate these inferences into understanding types of behaviors relevant to both clinicians and the subjects themselves.

ASSETS AND LIMITATIONS

The history of the Rorschach has clearly been filled with controversy. Often, battle lines have been polarized into either "clinical loyalists" or "academic iconoclasts" (Parker, 1983b). It is surprising that, despite thousands of research studies, these positions have changed only minimally over the past 50 years. It is hoped the Comprehensive System will eventually represent a middle ground that will satisfy hardnosed empiricists and also will address areas relevant to clinicians.

Part of the reason the Rorschach has continued to have such high popularity is the number of attractive features associated with it. Perhaps part of its allure is the mystery it frequently seems to invoke. How could something as seemingly simple as 10 inkblots reveal inner aspects of a person's personality? Such metaphors as "X-rays of the mind" have certainly served to enhance its mystery and power. Often, a Rorschach protocol is perceived as something like a deep well in that the skilled clinician can dip into it again and again, continually coming up with rich and valuable information. It tends to frame the practitioner as a seer and artist rather than a technician. Indeed, studies do tend to support the belief that highly trained Rorschach experts can accurately describe a person's characteristics based on Rorschach responses (Karon, 1978). However, this accuracy has often been dependent more on intuition and clinical lore rather than on clearly validated interpretive rules.

One frequently quoted asset is that the Rorschach is excellent at bypassing a person's conscious resistance and instead assesses a person's underlying, unconscious structure of personality. This might be particularly important if a person appears to have an adequate surface level of adjustment yet the clinician suspects there may be some underlying pathology. In contrast, a structured test, such as the MMPI, may have difficulty assessing these more hidden levels of pathology. It is precisely the difficulty in organizing the ambiguous Rorschach stimuli that is likely to bring out these latent levels of pathology. There is some support for this view in that persons with borderline psychopathology have relatively normal performances on structured tests. In contrast, they tend to show extreme levels of thought disorder on the far less-structured Rorschach (Edell, 1987). Similarly, a relatively hidden trait such as alexthmia has been found as a feature in psychosomatic patients based on their Rorschach responses (Acklin & Bernat, 1987; Keltikangas-Jarvinen, 1986).

A related asset is that the Rorschach has often been described as highly resistant to faking. It is argued that, since the true meaning of the Rorschach responses are unknown to the subject, they cannot easily invent faked responses. Some proponents have even stated that it is virtually impossible to fake a Rorschach. Like many other statements about the Rorschach, this has become quite controversial. Exner (1986) has presented material from a theoretical and empirical perspective that suggests persons developing a Rorschach response go through a series of six stages, one of which is censorship. Subjects seem to come up with far more responses than they present to the examiner and select the ones they feel are most appropriate to reveal. Subjects who feel emotionally close to the examiner will tend to provide more responses and conceal less (Leura & Exner, 1978). This raises the possibility that they might also have enough control over responses to effectively fake a protocol. Thus, responses might depend to a certain extent on social desirability, perceptual accuracy, the context of the assessment, and personal needs. Despite the possibility of censorship and effective faking, Exner and Wylie (1975) have reported that only 1 student in 12 could simulate a schizophrenic profile, even though they were familiar with protocols from actual schizophrenics. Specifically, malingerers were likely to have longer free associations (presumably because they were censoring and elaborating on their responses), relatively accurate perceptions, and highly dramatic and idiosyncratic responses (i.e., "That's too awful to look at.") In contrast, Albert, Fox, and Kahn (1980) found that Rorschach experts did poorly when requested to blindly classify protocols from normals who were requested to fake paranoid schizophrenia, normals taking a standard administration, and diagnosed paranoid schizophrenics. Computer analyses of the same protocols were likewise unsuccessful in effectively detecting faking (Kahn, Fox, & Rhode, 1988). Although this clearly challenges the unfakability of the Rorschach, the Albert et al. (1980) and Kahn et al. (1988) studies did not simulate the manner in which the Rorschach is likely to be used in clinical practice. Typically, practitioners have knowledge regarding the history of the person and context of the assessment, which potentially sensitizes them to the possibility that a protocol might be faked.

One quite clear asset of the Rorschach is its ease of administration. The cards can be easily handled and administration (including inquiry) often takes less than ten minutes. This is somewhat offset in that the scoring and interpretation take considerably longer.

Despite some of the advantages associated with the Rorschach, a number of limitations do exist. Although both reliability and validity have reached adequate levels, they are far from being in the superior range when compared with other psychological tests. Furthermore, the established validity is often quite variable across different scoring categories and formulas. Typically, a wide number of scores and formulas are derived from the Rorschach responses, some of which have relatively good validity and some of which are moderate, controversial, or even nonexistent. It is usually difficult for the average user to appreciate and take into account the disparate levels of validity when actually making his or her interpretations.

The Rorschach is also one of the most complex psychological tests in use. Due to this complexity, error can potentially be introduced from many different directions—including censorship by the subject, scoring errors (particularly for infrequently used scorings), poor handling of the subtleties of interpretation, incorrectly incorporating the implications of age or education, or possible examiner bias (illusory correlation, primacy effects, etc.). One temptation is to reduce the complexity of the data by using a single-sign approach rather than viewing each sign within the context of the overall configuration. Since Rorschach "elevations" are often subject to a large number of possible interpretive hypotheses, a single-sign approach is particularly subject to error. Thus, interpretations must be continually checked and rechecked against both the overall Rorschach configuration and additional sources of data, specifically other test data and the patient's history.

The complexity of the Rorschach also requires that potential users undergo extensive training. Each new scoring category and index that is introduced often serves to add to this problem. In the past, graduate schools would sometimes provide an entire semester on the Rorschach. This is currently difficult for many programs to justify. First, other tests clearly have superior psychometric properties. Second, the 1970s and 1980s have seen a significant increase in the roles and skills required of graduate students. This includes both skills within the area of assessment (neuropsychology, behavioral assessment) as well as within other areas of clinical practice (family therapy, rehabilitation, new modes of intervention, treatment of chronic pain, etc.). Despite these increased requirements, the vast majority of training programs continue to expect trainees to have or to develop skills in the Rorschach (Piotrowski & Keller, 1984). Specifically, heads of training programs expected students to have had an average of 22.3 hours of training in the Rorschach and have given 6.4 administrations (Durand et al., 1988).

A further difficulty associated with the Rorschach is the previous lack of a single, standardized administration and scoring system. This is particularly important since numerous studies have clearly indicated that slight alterations in wording, rapport, and encouragement can significantly alter the numbers and types of responses. The numerous differences in administration and scoring will, it is hoped, be seen in the future as a historical aberration corrected by wide acceptance of the Comprehensive System.

The Rorschach has often been considered of limited use with children, particularly children under the age of 14 years (Klein, 1986). Although reliabilities have been found to be adequate for short-term assessments, they have been found to be clearly inadequate over a long-term basis. Thus, for such purposes as child custody decisions, where longer-term predictions are required, the Rorschach would be quite limited. Any use of the Rorschach for children should make clear that descriptions are for a short-term basis only.

Thus, the Rorschach is difficult to evaluate due to its complexity and frequent controversy, and to the contradiction between its popularity and its reviews. The voluminous research associated with the Rorschach is often both an asset and a limitation. It is often difficult to sort through the maze of often contradictory findings. It is especially difficult to direct this wealth of research toward a clear understanding of the interpretive meanings associated with certain patterns of scores. The specific assets of the Rorschach are its potential wealth of information, simplicity of handling, ability to bypass conscious resistance, and possible resistance to faking. Significant weaknesses are its moderate and widely varying reliabilities and validities, previous lack of standardization, limited use with children, extensive time required for training, and the possible introduction of error from a wide number of areas due to its complexity.

ADMINISTRATION

Examiners should standardize their administration procedures as much as possible. This is particularly important since research has consistently indicated it is relatively easy to influence a subject's responses. For example, saying the word "good" after each response can increase the overall number of responses on the Rorschach by as much as 50% (Hersen & Greaves, 1971). Similarly, examiners who were told that more experienced examiners elicited a greater proportion of human than animal responses actually produced this pattern from examinees even though the examiners believed they were providing a standard administration (Exner, Leura, & George, 1976). These findings are consistent with the view that subjects will be particularly responsive to subtle influences when attempting to create clarity in an ambiguous situation, such as projective testing. However, if the fluctuations in administration style are minor, it is unlikely that they will significantly influence a subject's responses (Phares, Stewart, & Foster, 1960; Williams, 1954). In general, examiners should minimize the variations in their administration procedures as much as possible. The following sequence of steps is recommended.

Step 1: Introducing the Respondent to the Technique

One of the most important goals an examiner must initially achieve is to allow the examinee to feel relatively comfortable with the testing procedure. Achievement of this goal is complicated by the fact that tests in most cultures are associated with anxiety. Although, in some cases, an increase in anxiety may provide some information that cannot be obtained when the subject is relaxed, anxiety is usually regarded as a hindrance. Typically, anxiety interferes with a person's perceptions and with the free flow of fantasy, both of which are essential for adequate Rorschach responses. Thus, subjects should be as relaxed as possible. Their relaxation can be enhanced by giving a clear introduction to the testing procedure, obtaining personal history, answering questions, and generally avoiding any behavior that might increase the subjects' anxiety. In describing the test, examiners should emphasize relatively neutral words—such as "inkblot," "interests," or "imagination"—rather than more potentially anxiety provoking words like "intelligence" or "ambiguous."

For the most part, any specific information regarding what subjects should do or say ought to be avoided. The test situation is designed to be ambiguous, and examiners should avoid any statements that might influence the responses. If subjects push for more detailed information about what they should do or what their responses may mean, they should be told that additional questions can be answered after the test is completed.

Step 2: Giving the Testing Instructions

Although some Rorschach systematizers recommend that the subject tell the examiner "everything you see" (Beck, 1961), the Comprehensive System attempts to keep the task as ambiguous as possible. Thus, Exner (1986) recommends that the examiner hand the subject the first card and ask, "What might this be?"

Commentary on, or discussion of, the cards by the examiner should be avoided as much as possible. At times, it might be acceptable to briefly describe how the designs were made or, ⌐ ⌐ ⌐ ⌐ ⌐ ⌐ ⌐ ⌐ ⌐ what one is supposed to see, the examiner might state that "people see all s⌐ ⌐ ⌐ ⌐ ⌐ ⌐ n the blots." Comments from the examiner that indicate the quantity or type of res, ⌐ ⌐ and whether or not the subject can turn the cards should be strictly avoided. If the subject asks specific questions, such as the type of responses he or she is supposed to give or whether he or she can turn the cards, the examiner might reply that it is up to him or her to decide.

The main objective is to leave the subject as much freedom as possible to respond to the stimuli in his or her own manner. To enhance this, Exner (1986) strongly recommends that the subject and the examiner not be seated face-to-face, but rather side-by-side to decrease the possible influence of the examiner's nonverbal behavior. The overall instructions and testing situation should be designed both to keep the task as ambiguous as possible and to keep examiner influence at a minimum.

Step 3: The Response (Association) Phase

Throughout the testing procedure, the basic conditions of step 2 should be adhered to as closely as possible. However, specific situations often arise as subjects are free-associating to the Rorschach designs. If a subject requests specifics on how to respond or asks the examiner for encouragement or approval, examiners should consistently reply that one can respond however one likes. The idea that there are no right or wrong answers might sometimes be mentioned.

The examiner should time the interval, beginning when subjects first see the card until they make their initial response, as well as the total time they spend with each card. These measurements can be helpful in revealing their general approach to the card and possible difficulties in coming up with responses. It should be noted that Cards II, III, and V are generally considered relatively easy to respond to and usually have shorter reaction times than Cards VI, IX, and X, which typically produce the longest reaction times (Meer, 1955). Since overt timing of subjects' responses is likely to produce anxiety, any recording should be done as inconspicuously as possible. It is recommended that, rather than using a stopwatch, the examiner should glance at a watch or clock and record the minute and second positions for the initial presentation, the first response, and the point at which the subject hands the card back to the examiner.

Exner (1986, 1988) has built in some safeguards to protect against unusually short or extremely long protocols. If a subject gives only one response to Card I, the examiner might provide a prompt by saying "If you take your time and look some more, I think that you will find something else, too" (Exner, 1986, p.68). If, in spite of these promptings, a subject still provides a brief protocol (less than 14 responses), they should be immediately retested and provided with a more clear request to provide more responses (Exner, 1988). However, if a subject provides more than one response to Card I and asks how many responses he or she should give, the examiner should simply state "its up to you." If a subject provides more than five responses to any of the inkblots, the examiner should remove the inkblot. No intervention is required if the subject provides five or less responses.

Exner (1986) stresses that all responses must be recorded verbatim. To simplify this process, most clinicians develop a series of abbreviations. One set of abbreviations used throughout all the Rorschach systems consists of the symbols ($\wedge$, <, $\vee$, >) in which the peak indicates the angle of the card. It is also important to note any odd or unusual responses to the cards, such as an apparent increase in anxiety, wandering of attention, or acting out on any of the percepts.

Step 4: Inquiry

The inquiry should begin after all ten cards have been administered. Its purpose is to collect additional information required for an accurate scoring of the responses. It is not intended to obtain new responses but rather to clarify the responses that have already been given. The inquiry should not end until this goal has been accomplished. Exner (1986) recommends that the instructions for the inquiry should closely approximate the following:

> O.K., we've done them all. Now we are going to go back through them. It won't take long. I want you to help me see what you saw. I'm going to read what you said, and then I want you to show me where on the blot you saw it and what there is that makes it look like that, so that I can see it too. I'd like to see it just like you did, so help me now. Do you understand? (p.72)

The inquiry should closely follow the general theme of the overall administration in not influencing the subject's responses. Thus, any questions should be as nondirective as possible. One should begin by merely repeating what the subject has said and waiting. Usually he or she will begin to clarify his or her response. If this information is insufficient to clarify how to score the response, the examiner might become slightly more directive by asking, "What about it made it look like a [percept]?" The examiner should not ask, "Is it mainly the shape?" or "How important was the color?" These questions are far too directive and are worded in a way that can exert influence on the subject's descriptions of his or her responses. The examiner should consistently avoid leading the subject or indicating how he or she should respond. Particular skill is required when clarifying a determinant that has been unclearly articulated but merely implied.

The outcome of a well-conducted inquiry is the collection of a sufficient amount of information to decide on scoring for location and determinants. If, on the location, information based on the subject's verbal response is insufficient, the examiner should have the subject point to the percept. An additional feature of the inquiry is to test the subject's awareness of his or her responses. For example, does a strange percept represent coherent creativity, or does it reflect a lack of contact with the environment in which the subject may have no awareness of the strangeness of his or her responses? The overall approach of the inquiry is to word questions in such a way as to be flexible without being too directive.

SCORING

The next step following administration is to code the different categories and calculate the different quantitative formulas in the structural summary. There is general agreement throughout the different Rorschach systems that these categories include location, determinants, content, and popularity. After these have been scored, a series of quantitative summaries is created based on reorganizations of, and comparisons among, the scores on the different categories.

This section summarizes most of Exner's categories of scoring. However, some areas have been deleted. The criteria for selecting specific subcategories were that:

1. They were the ones most frequently used in other systems.
2. They were most thoroughly researched.

Conversely, exclusions were made on the basis of areas that were generally less well researched and were found primarily in the Exner system only. Thus, omitted as determinants were form dimensionality (FD), active versus passive, pairs and reflections, organizational activity, and special scores. Several formulas were deleted, including Z sum - Zest, Zd, Adjusted D Score, active:passive, active:passive for movement, egocentricity index, suicide constellation, depression index, and schizophrenia. These deletions are further reflected in the sections on Interpretation and in the Appendixes. However, the majority of the scoring categories and formulas used by Exner are included.

It should be stressed that the following is merely an attempt to list and outline the scoring categories and quantitative summaries. To achieve accurate scoring, it would be necessary to consult Exner's scoring guides (see recommended readings), which include specific scoring criteria, tables, charts, and diagrams. The inclusion of specific scoring criteria is beyond the scope of this chapter. The focus is rather on providing a key to interpretation that is concise, accountable, and familiar. The following definitions and tables serve to outline and briefly define the primary Rorschach factors.

Location

The location of the responses refers to the area of the inkblot that is used (Table 9–1). This can vary from the use of the entire blot (whole response) to the use of an unusual detail (Dd). Unusual details were defined as location responses made by less than 5% of subjects. Exner also specifies coding for Developmental Quality, which is determined by evaluating each location score in relation to its degree of integration and organization (Table 9–2). Thus, each location response is given both a designation of the specific area of the blot and a symbol to indicate the degree of organization of that response.

Determinants

Determinants refer to the style or characteristic of the blot to which the examinee responds, such as its shape, color, or texture (Table 9–3). The determinants also receive a scoring for their level of form quality (Table 9–4). The form quality scoring refers to how accurately the percept relates to the form of the inkblot. For example, an angel on Card I is considered to be an "ordinary" form quality response, which is empirically reflected in the fact that nonpsychiatric populations perceive it far more frequently than psychiatric patients (see Appendix N). Initially, examiners should give a percept its appropriate classification regarding its determinants. This should then be followed by scoring the determinant for its

Table 9–1.   Symbols used for coding the location of Rorschach responses

Symbol	Definition	Criterion
W	Whole response	Where the entire blot is used in the response. All portions must be used.
D	Common detail response	A frequently identified area of the blot
Dd	Unusual detail response	An infrequently identified area of the blot
S	Space response	A white space area is used in the response (scored only with another location symbol, as in WS, DS, DdS)

Note: From Exner, J.E., Jr. *The Rorschach: A Comprehensive System. Volume 1: Basic Foundations* (2nd ed.), p. 91. Copyright © 1986 by John E. Exner, Jr. Reprinted by permission of John Wiley & Sons, Inc.

Table 9–2.   Symbols and criteria used for coding developmental quality

Symbol	Definition	Criterion
+	Synthesized response	Unitary or discrete portions of the blot are articulated and combined into a single answer. Two or more objects are described as separate but related. At least *one* of the objects involved must have a specific form demand, or be described in a manner that creates a specific form demand.
v/+	Synthesized response	Unitary or discrete portions of the blot are articulated and combined into a single answer. Two or more objects are described as separate but related. None of the objects involved have a specific form demand, or are articulated in a way to create a specific form demand.
o	Ordinary response	A discrete area of the blot is selected and articulated so as to emphasize the outline and structural features of the object. The object reported has a natural form demand or the description of the object is such to create a specific form demand.
v	Vague response	A diffuse or general impression is offered to the blot or blot area in a manner that avoids the necessity of articulating specific outlines or structural features. The object reported has no specific form demand, and the articulation does not introduce a specific form demand for the object reported.

Note: From Exner, J.E., Jr. *The Rorschach: A Comprehensive System. Volume 1: Basic Foundations* (2nd ed.), p. 96. Copyright © 1986 by John E. Exner, Jr. Reprinted by permission of John Wiley & Sons, Inc.

relative form quality. Descriptions of the different form qualities are included in Table 9–4, but, for specific empirically derived form quality codings, examiners need to consult Exner's (1986) tables.

In approximately 20% of all responses, more than one determinant is used to make a response. These *blends* are designated by indicating the two (or more) determinants and placing a full stop (.) between them.

Content

The scoring of content is based on the type and quantity of specific subjects that examinees perceive in their responses. Each Rorschach system uses different lists of content categories, although they all agree on such basic contents as human, human detail, and animal. Table 9–5 provides a listing of Exner's content categories along with the symbols and descriptions for each category.

Popular Responses

Rorschach popular or P scoring refers to the presence of frequently perceived responses. Although different systems have somewhat varying lists of populars, Exner (1986) has used the occurrence of at least once in every three protocols from nonpsychiatric populations as the cutoff for inclusion as a popular. Exner's list and description of popular responses are given in Table 9–6.

Table 9–3.   Symbols and criteria for determinant coding

Category	Symbol	Criteria
Form	*F*	*Form answers.* To be used separately for responses based exclusively on form features of the blot, or in combination with other determinate symbols (*except M & m*) when the form features have contributed to the formulation of the answer.
Movement	*M*	*Human movement response.* To be used for responses involving the kinesthetic activity of a human, or of an animal of fictional character in human-like activity.
	FM	*Animal movement response.* To be used for responses involving a kinesthetic activity of an animal. The movement perceived must be congruent to the species identified in the content. Animals reported in movement *not* common to their species should be coded as *M*.
	m	*Inanimate movement response.* To be used for responses involving the movement of inanimate, inorganic, or insensate objects.
Chromatic Color	*C*	*Pure color response.* To be used for answers based exclusively on the chromatic color features of the blot. *No* form is involved.
	CF	*Color-form response.* To be used for answers that are formulated *primarily* because of the chromatic color features of the blot. Form features *are* used, but are of secondary importance.
	FC	*Form-color response.* To be used for answers that are created mainly because of form features. Chromatic color is also used, but is of secondary importance.
	Cn	*Color naming response.* To be used when the colors of the blot or blot areas are identified *by name*, and with the intention of giving a response.
Achromatic Color	*C'*	*Pure achromatic color response.* To be used when the response is based exclusively on the gray, black, or white features of the blot, when they are clearly used as color. *No* form is involved.

continued

Table 9–3. *(continued)*

Category	Symbol	Criteria
	C'F	*Achromatic color-form response.* To be used for responses that are formulated *mainly* because of the black, white, or gray features, clearly used as color. Form features *are* used, but are of secondary importance.
	FC'	*Form-achromatic color response.* To be used for answers that are based *mainly* on the form features. The achromatic features, used clearly as color, are also included, but are of secondary importance.
Shading-Texture	*T*	*Pure texture response.* To be used for answers in which the shading components of the blot are translated to represent a tactual phenomenon, with no consideration to the form features.
	TF	*Texture-form response.* To be used for responses in which the shading features of the blot are interpreted as tactual, and form is used secondarily, for purposes of elaboration and/or clarification.
	FT	*Form-texture response.* To be used for responses that are based *mainly* on the form features. Shading features of the blot are translated as tactual, but are of secondary importance.
Shading-Dimension	*V*	*Pure vista response.* To be used for answers in which the shading features are interpreted as depth or dimensionality. *No* form is involved.
	VF	*Vista-form response.* To be used for responses in which the shading features are interpreted as depth or dimensionality. Form features are included, but are of secondary importance.
	FV	*Form-vista response.* To be used for answers that are based *mainly* on the form features of the blot. Shading features are also interpreted to note depth and/or dimensionality, but are of secondary importance to the formulation of the answer.
Shading-Diffuse	*Y*	*Pure shading response.* To be used for responses that are based exclusively on the light-dark features of the blot that are completely formless and do not involve reference to either texture or dimension.
	YF	*Shading-form response.* To be used for responses that are based primarily on the light-dark features of the blot. Form features are included, but are of secondary importance.
	FY	*Form-shading response.* To be used for responses that are based *mainly* on the form features of the blot. The light-dark features of the blot are included as elaboration and /or clarification and are secondary to the use of form.

Note: From Exner, J.E., Jr. *The Rorschach: A Comprehensive System. Volume 1: Basic Foundations* (2nd ed.), pp. 101-102. Copyright © 1986 by John E. Exner, Jr. Reprinted by permission of John Wiley & Sons, Inc.

Table 9-4.   Symbols and criteria for coding form quality

Symbol	Definition	Criterion
+	Superior-overelaborated	The unusually precise articulation of the use of form in a manner that tends to enrich the quality of the response without sacrificing the appropriateness of the form use. The + answer need not be original, but rather unique by the manner in which details are defined and by which the form is used and specified.
o	Ordinary	The obvious, easily articulated use of form features to define an object reported frequently by others. The answer is commonplace and easy to see. There is no unusual enrichment of the answer by overelaboration of the form features.
u	Unusual	A low-frequency response in which the basic contours involved are not significantly violated. These are uncommon answers that are seen quickly and easily by the observer.
–	Minus	The distorted, arbitrary, unrealistic use of form in creating a response. The answer is imposed on the blot structure with total, or near total disregard for the structure of the area being used in creating the response. Often arbitrary contours will be created where none exist.

Note: From Exner, J.E., Jr. *The Rorschach: A Comprehensive System. Volume 1: Basic Foundations* (2nd ed.), p. 148. Copyright © 1986 by John E. Exner, Jr. Reprinted by permission of John Wiley & Sons, Inc.

Table 9-5.   Symbols and criteria to be used in scoring for content

Category	Symbol	Criterion
Whole Human	H	Involving or implying the percept of a whole human form.
Whole Human (fictional or mythological)	(H)	Involving or implying the percept of a whole human form of a fictional or mythological basis, that is, gnomes, fairies, giants, witches, King Midas, Alice in Wonderland, monsters (human like), ghosts, dwarfs, devils, and angels.
Human Detail	Hd	Involving the percept of an incomplete human form, that is, a person but the head is missing, an arm, fingers, two big feet, and the lower part of a woman.
Human Detail (fictional or mythological)	(Hd)	Involving the percept of an incomplete human form of a fictional or mythological basis, that is, the hand of God, the head of the devil, the foot of a monster, the head of a witch, and the eyes of an angel.
Whole Animal	A	Involving or implying the percept of a whole animal form.

continued

Table 9–5.   *(continued)*

Category	Symbol	Criterion
Whole Animal (fictional or mythological)	*(A)*	Involving or implying the percept of a whole animal form of a fictional or mythological basis, that is, unicorn, flying red horse, black beauty, Jonathan Livingston Seagull, and a magic frog.
Animal Detail	*Ad*	Involving or implying the percept of an incomplete animal form, that is the hoof of a horse, the claw of a lobster, the head of a fish, the head of a rabbit.
Animal Detail (fictional or mythological)	*(Ad)*	Involving the percept of an incomplete animal form of a fictional or mythological basis, that is, the wing of the bird of prey, Peter Rabbit's head, the head of Pooh Bear, the head of Bambi, and the wings of Pegasus.
Abstraction	*Ab*	Involving the percept which is clearly an abstract concept, that is, fear, depression, elation, anger, abstract art, or any form of symbolism.
Alphabet	*Al*	Involving percepts of arabic numerals, such as 2, 4, and 7, or the letters of the alphabet, such as A, M, and X.
Anatomy	*An*	Involving the percept of anatomy (internal organs) of either human or animal content, that is, a heart, lungs, stomach, a bleached skull of a cow, a brain of a dog, and the insides of a person's stomach.
Art	*Art*	Involving percepts of paintings, plus other art objects, that is, a family crest, the seal of the president, and a sculpture of a bird.
Anthropology	*Ay*	Involving percepts which have a specific cultural relationship, that is, a totem pole, a helmet like those used by Romans, a Viking ship, or Lindberg's airplane.
Blood	*Bl*	Involving the percept of blood, either human or animal.
Botany	*Bt*	Involving the percept of any plant life, that is, flowers, trees, bushes, and seaweed.
Clothing	*Cg*	Involving the percept of any clothing ordinarily associated with the human, that is hat, boots, jacket, trousers, and tie.
Clouds	*Cl*	Involving the percept of clouds. Variations of this category, such as fog, mist, and so on, should be scored as *Na*.
Explosion	*Ex*	Involving percepts of an actual explosion, occurring most commonly to Card IX, as an atomic explosion or blast. The determinate for inanimate movement (*m*) should always accompany this content. Percepts of an explosion "aftermath" such as. "A blast has just occurred and things are lying all over the place." should be coded for other content, or written out in complete form.

continued

Table 9–5. *(continued)*

Category	Symbol	Criterion
Fire	*Fi*	Involving percepts of actual fire, smoke, burning candles, flame given off by a torch, and such. These percepts will ordinarily invoke the determinate scoring of *m* to denote the inanimate movement of the "fire" association.
Food	*Fd*	Involving the percept of any edible, such as ice cream, fried shrimp, chicken legs, a piece of steak, etc. The intent or meaning of the association must be clearly associated with "everyday" consumer produce, as in the instance of lettuce, cabbage, carrots, fried foods, etc., or must be presented in such a manner as to suggest that the object perceived is identified as a food substance, that is, "looks like a chicken like we used to have for Sunday dinner."
Geography	*Ge*	Involving percepts of any maps, specified or unspecified, that is, a map of Sicily, or a map of an island, peninsula, and continent. The percepts of *Ge do not* include the actual percept of definite or indefinite land masses which are "real" rather than representations. These types of percepts are scored as *Ls* (Landscape) or written out in rare cases.
Household	*Hh*	Involving percepts of interior household items, that is, chairs, beds, bedposts, plates, silverware, and rugs.
Landscape	*Ls*	Involving percepts of landscapes or seascapes, neither of which would be scored as *Bt* or *Ge*. A tree or a bush might legitimately be scored as *Bt*, whereas "trees" or "a bunch of shrubs" are more ordinarily scored *Ls*. This category includes some underwater scenes where specific animals are not identified, or in some instances as a secondary score as in Card X where a few specific animals may be cited but the bulk of the percept is left vague.
Nature	*Na*	Involving percepts of a wider natural scope than are included in *Bt*, *Ge*, or *Ls*, usually including sky, snow, water, racing sea, a storm, night, ice, rainbow, sun, etc.
Science	*Sc*	Involving percepts that are ordinarily associated with science or science fiction such as bacteria, germs, science fiction monsters, ray guns, rockets, rocket ships, space ships, etc. In some instances, the symbol *Sc* will be used as the primary content but in other responses, especially those involving science fiction objects, the symbol *(A)* or *(H)* may be assigned as primary and *Sc* secondary.
Sex	*Sx*	Involving percepts of sex organs or activities related to sex function, that is intercourse, erect penis, menstruation, vagina, testes, and breasts.

continued

Table 9–5. *(continued)*

Category	Symbol	Criterion
X-ray	*Xr*	Involving percepts of x-ray, most of which pertain to bone structure, that is, the x-ray of a pelvis, the x-ray of some bones, but may also involve x-rays of organs or organ like structures, that is, an x-ray of the stomach and an x-ray of the intestines. *Shading is always* involved in these percepts.
Vocational (supplementary)	*(Vo)*	Involving percepts which *may* be interpreted as related to the occupation of the subject. This scoring is *never* used as the primary or main content score but may be included as secondary or additional so as to alert the interpreter of a vocational or occupational percept.

Note: From Exner, J.E., Jr. *The Rorschach: A Comprehensive System. Volume 1: Basic Foundations* (2nd ed.), p. 148. Copyright © 1986 by John E. Exner, Jr. Reprinted by permission of John Wiley & Sons, Inc.

Table 9–6. Popular responses selected for the comprehensive system based on the frequency of occurrence of at least once in every three protocols given by nonpatient adult subjects and nonschizophrenic adult patients

Card	Location	Criterion	%†	%‡
I	W	Bat. The response always involves the whole blot.	48	38
I	W	Butterfly. The response always involves the whole blot.	40	36
II	D1	Animal forms, usually the heads of dogs, bears, elephants, or lambs; however, the frequency of the whole animal to this area is sufficient to warrant the scoring of *P*.	34	35
III	D1 or D9	Two human figures, or representations thereof, such as dolls and caricatures. The scoring of *P* is also applicable to the percept of a single human figure to area D9.	89	70
IV	W or D7	A human or human-like figure such as giant, monster, science fiction creature, etc.	53	41
V	W	Butterfly, the apex of the card upright or inverted. The whole blot *must* be used.	46	43
V	W	Bat, the apex of the card upright or inverted, and involving the whole blot.	36	38
VI	W or D1	Animal skin, hide, rug, or pelt.	87	35

† Percent of nonpatient reporting
‡ Percent of nonschizophrenic reporting

continued

Table 9–6. *(continued)*

Card	Location	Criterion	%†	%‡
VII	*D*1 or *D*9	Human head or face, specifically identified as female, child, Indian, or with gender not identified. If *D*1 is used, the upper segment (*D*5) is usually identified as hair, feather, etc. If the response includes the entire *D*2 area, *P* is coded if the head or face are restricted to the *D*9 area. If *Dd*23 is included as part of the human form, the response is *not* coded as *P*.	59	47
VIII	*D*1	Whole animal figure. This is the most frequently perceived common answer, the content varying considerably, such as bear, dog, rodent, fox, wolf, and coyote. All are *P*. The *P* is also coded when the animal figure is reported as part of the *W* percept as in a family crest, seal, and emblem.	94	91
IX	*D*3	Human or human-like figures such as witches, giants, science fiction creatures, monsters, etc.	54	24
X	*D*1	Spider with all appendages restricted to the *D*1 area.	42	34
X	*D*1	Crab with all appendages restricted to the *D*1 area. Other variations of animals are not P.	37	38

† Percent of nonpatient reporting
‡ Percent of nonschizophrenic reporting

Note: From Exner, J.E., Jr. *The Rorschach: A Comprehensive System. Volume 1: Basic Foundations* (2nd ed.), p. 158. Copyright © 1986 by John E. Exner, Jr. Reprinted by permission of John Wiley & Sons, Inc.

STRUCTURAL SUMMARY

After the examinee's responses have been coded according to locations, determinants, contents, and populars, they are then rearranged into quantitative formulas. These formulas reflect the proportions of, and comparisons between, various Rorschach factors. The primary interpretations are based on the different quantitative formulas as well as on sums for the different factors (locations, determinants, contents, populars).

1. EB (Experience Balance or Erlebnistypus):

$$\frac{\text{Sum of Human Movement}}{\text{Sum of Weighted Color}} \quad \text{or} \quad \frac{\text{Sum M}}{\text{Sum Weighted C}}$$

The different weighting for C responses is based on FC = 0.5, CF = 1.0, and C or Cn = 1.5. All human movement responses are included in the formula regardless of whether they are the major determinant of the response. Color naming responses are not included.

2. EA (Experience Actual):

Sum of Human Movement + Sum of Weighted Color

or

Sum M + Sum Weighted C

3. eb (Experience Base):

$$\frac{\text{Sum of All Nonhuman Movement}}{\text{Sum Shading or Achromatic Features}} \quad \text{or} \quad \frac{\text{Sum FM} + m}{\text{Sum C'} + T + Y + V}$$

4. es (Experienced Stimulation):

Sum of All Nonhuman Movement + Sum of All Shading or Achromatic Features

or

Sum (FM + m) + Sum (C' + T + Y + V)

5. FC / (CF + C) (Form-Color Ratio). The ratio FC/(CF+C) indicates the total number of form dominated chromatic color responses as compared with the absolute number of color dominant chromatic responses. To calculate this formula, each of the chromatic color determinants is weighted equally as a 1, which is in contrast to the different weightings of sum C used in the EB and EA. Cn determinants are included in this formula since they are color dominant responses.

6. Pure C. This consists of the total number of C + Cn responses.

7. Afr (Affective Ratio):

$$\frac{\text{Sum of Responses to Last 3 Cards}}{\text{Sum of Responses to First 7 Cards}} \quad \text{or} \quad \frac{\text{Sum R(VIII + IX + X)}}{\text{Sum R(I - VII)}}$$

8. L (Lambda):

$$\frac{\text{Pure Form Responses}}{\text{Sum of Responses - Form Responses}} \quad \text{or} \quad \frac{\text{Sum Pure FR's}}{\text{Sum R - F}}$$

In calculating Lambda, only responses involving form are used (F, M, CF, etc.) and not determinants without form (C, C', T, etc.).

9. Blends:R (Complexity Index). This compares the total number of blend responses with the total number of responses.

10. X+% (Conventional Form):

$$\frac{\text{Sum of All Good F Dominant Responses (+ and o)}}{\text{Total Number of Responses}}$$

or

$$\frac{\text{Sum F + and o}}{\text{Total R}}$$

X+% is an extension of F+% (see below) in that it is a measure of the degree to which good form is used in any response involving form (FY, M, CF, etc.). To calculate X+%, the sum of all + and o responses involving form is divided by the total number of R. The total number of R is used as the denominator because, where form is absent from a response (pure C, Y, etc.), it shows a disregard for form, which can be seen as a poor use of the stimulus similar to an F- response.

11. X-% (Distorted Form):

$$\frac{\text{Sum FQ-}}{R}$$

12. F+% (Conventional Pure Form):

$$\frac{\text{Sum F+ and Fo}}{\text{Sum F}}$$

13. **W:M (Aspirational Index).** The ratio of W to M represents a comparison between the total number of whole responses and the total number of human movement responses.

14. **W:D (Economy Index).** The ratio W:D compares the total number of whole responses with the total number of common details.

15. **Isolate:R (Isolation Index).** This is obtained by adding the total number of contents from Bt, Cl, Ge, Na, and Ls and comparing them with the total number of responses.

16. **Ab + Art:R (Intellectualization Index).** This is a comparison of the number of Ab and Art contents with the total number of responses.

17. **An + Xy (Body Concern).** This is merely a sum of the contents of Anatomy (An) and X-ray (Xy).

18. **H + (H):Hd + (Hd) (Human Interest).** This compares the total number of whole human or humanlike contents with the total number of human detail responses.

19. **Pure H (Conceptions of People).** This is merely a sum of the total number of whole human contents.

20. **(H) + (Hd):(A) + (Ad).** This summarizes the frequencies of parenthesized human and human details and compares them with the total number of parenthesized animal and animal detail responses.

21. **H + A:Hd + Ad.** This summarizes and compares the total number of whole human and animal contents with the total number of human and animal detail contents. Parenthesized human and animal contents are also included.

INTERPRETATION

The following description of interpretive information is meant to serve as a reference guide to alert Rorschach interpreters to a potentially wide range of possible interpretive hypotheses. Even though the format is as concise as possible, interpreters should be aware of the tremendous richness inherent in most Rorschach data. Effective interpreters should also have this richness reflected in the wide variety of possible interpretive hypotheses they generate. A mere labeling or simplistic "sign" approach should be avoided. Rather, clinicians must begin and end by continually being aware of the total overall configuration of the data. For example, the same number of C responses in two protocols can easily have entirely different meanings, depending on the implications from, and interactions with, other aspects of the Rorschach data.

The typical sequence for Rorschach interpretation should follow the general conceptual model for testing developed by Maloney and Ward (1976) and discussed in Chapter 1.

This requires that clinicians initially take a propositional stance toward the protocol (phase 2). The purpose of this stage is to develop as many tentative hypotheses as possible based on the quantitative data, verbalizations, and client history. The number and accuracy of these hypotheses will depend on the individual richness of the data as well as on the individual skill and creativity of the clinician. The final stage is the integration of the hypotheses into a meaningful and accurate description of the person (phase 4). This involves rejecting, modifying, or confirming previously developed hypotheses (phase 3). Once this is accomplished, clinicians can then integrate the Rorschach interpretations into the overall report itself (phases 5,6, and 7).

In the description of different interpretive hypotheses, continual reference is made to "high" and "low" scores. These relative weightings are based on extensive normative data that has been accumulated on the Rorschach. For comparisons of scores on individual protocols with normative ratings, clinicians can refer to Appendixes O and P, which provide means, standard deviations, and other relevant descriptive statistics for the different Rorschach factors and quantitative formulas. Although Exner (1986) describes the interpretation of Rorschach factors and quantitative formulas around different topics (characteristics of affect, interpersonal perception, etc.), the following list presents interpretive material in the order in which it was presented during the initial description of the Rorschach factors. This also parallels the order of presentation in Exner (1986) for the description of the Rorschach factors for scoring. It is hoped this organization will be clear, consistent, and will allow users to easily consult the relevant interpretive material and generate useful hypotheses.

Number of Responses

In using Exner's set of instructions, the mean for the total number of responses for nonpatient adults is 22.57 with a standard deviation of 5.54. However, different methods of administration can influence this number to a certain extent. For example, Ames, Metraux, Rodell, and Walker (1973) report an overall adult average of 26; Beck (1961) gives 32 for his adult mean; and both use instructions somewhat different from Exner's. Deviations from the normal range present the following possible interpretive hypotheses.

Low R (Adults, less than 17; Children, less than 15)   A low number of R suggests defensiveness, constriction, organicity, depression, or attempted malingering (Exner, 1986). A clinician cannot confirm any of these hypotheses based solely on the occurrence of a low number of R, but they are raised as possibilities. To confirm these hypotheses, factors from both within and outside the test must be used. Protocols having less than 13 responses are not likely to be valid and structural interpretation of the test should be avoided (Exner, 1988). Examiners should either discard the protocol, interpret the verbal material subjectively, or immediately retest the person with the request that he or she include more responses.

High R (Greater than 33)   A significantly higher-than-average number of responses suggests several possibilities, including an introversive character (Murstein, 1960; Wagner, 1971), above-average intelligence with a relatively high level of academic achievement (Beck, 1945; Goldfried, Stricker, & Weiner, 1971), and a high degree of creativity (Adams, Cooper, & Carrera, 1963; Dana & Cocking, 1968; Raychaudhuri, 1971). It can also suggest a high level of personal insight (Kagan, 1960) and good ego functioning, including the ability to plan ahead, adequate impulse control, and the ability to tolerate stress (Goldfried et al., 1971; Klopfer & Davidson, 1962). Among persons with psychopathology, high R is found among manics and obsessive-compulsives (Alcock, 1963; Beck, 1945, 1951; Pope & Scott, 1967).

A high number of R is likely to alter the meaning of, or render useless, specific formulas. There is likely to be a higher proportion of D and Dd responses since the number of W responses is usually exhausted sooner. Pure F responses will also tend to increase in frequency, the number of Populars will be increased, and there are usually relatively more R for Cards VIII and X, thus elevating the Affective Ratio (Afr). Thus, interpretations based on the quantitative formulas derived from a high number of R should be treated with appropriate caution.

Location

In general, the area of the inkblot to which examinees choose to respond is a reflection of the overall style in which they approach their world. This is especially true for the manner in which they confront uncertainties and ambiguities in their lives. For example, one person might perceive only the most obvious concrete aspects of a situation, whereas another might avoid important aspects of a stimulus by focusing on small details and neglecting dangerous, more significant issues. An analysis of Rorschach locations does not provide information regarding why people approach their world in a certain manner, but rather is limited to a description of their particular style.

Rorschach locations can be divided into usual and unusual features, depending on the area of the inkblot that was used. Frequently used locations, if they are within the normal number and of good quality, usually reflect good ties with reality, intelligence, ambition, good reasoning, and an ability to generalize. Unusual locations involving rarely used areas of the blot are associated with neurotic symptomatology, such as fears, anxiety, and obsessive or compulsive tendencies. An extreme use of unusual features may reflect more serious psychopathology.

Whole Response (W)   The whole response is related to the degree to which a person can interact in an efficient, active manner with his or her environment. This is particularly true if the quality and organization of the response is good. Whereas whole responses occur with the greatest frequency in children from 3 to 4 years of age (Ames et al., 1971; Exner & Weiner, 1982), there is a gradual decline in later childhood and adolescence until 30 to 40% of normal adult responses are wholes. The average adult ratio of whole:detail is approximately 1:2 (refer also to interpretation of W:M and W:D formulas).

High W   Rorschach (1921) originally believed that a high number of W responses reflected a person's ability to organize and integrate his or her environment. However, subsequent research has modified this in that W responses do reflect intellectual activity, but this activity can only be understood by looking at the quality of W responses (relative number of W+; Exner, 1986; Friedman, 1952) and the relative complexity of responses (Exner & Weiner, 1982). In considering the complexity of responses, it should be noted that W occurs with greatest frequency for Cards V, I, IV, and VI, and lowest for Cards X, IX, III, and VIII (Beck, 1945). Thus, W responses for the latter cards require significantly greater organizational activity. If good quality responses and a high degree of organizing activity are both present, then a high number of W responses would reflect good synthesizing and abstracting abilities (Smith, 1981), ambition (Schachtel, 1966), good ties with reality (Abrams, 1955; Levitt & Truuma, 1972), and excellent problem solving abilities (Beck, 1961; Rossi & Neuman, 1961).

Low R   Low W responses can reflect depression (Beck, 1960; Rapaport, Gill, & Shafer, 1968) or anxiety (Eichler, 1951). If the frequency, quality, and complexity are low, then more serious levels of maladjustment (Exner, 1974) are indicated, such as intellectual deterioration possibly related to brain damage (Goldfried et al., 1971) or mental retardation (Allison & Blatt, 1964).

Common Detail (D)   Rorschach (1921) originally conceptualized the D response as reflecting the degree to which a person reacts to and perceives the obvious aspects of a situation (Rorschach, 1921). This is supported by more recent normative data in which adult nonpsychiatric groups and outpatients gave 62% and 67% of their responses as D, whereas inpatient nonschizophrenics and inpatient schizophrenics gave 46% and 47% D responses, respectively (Exner, 1974). D tends to be most frequent for Card X (Exner, 1974). Any interpretations relating to D should take into account the fact that a greater number of R will be likely to increase the relative proportion of D when compared with other locations. (Also refer to the W:D ratio).

High D   D is often high in persons who overemphasize the concrete and obvious aspects of situations (Beck, 1961; Exner, 1986; Klopfer, 1954). It requires less energy and less integration than making a W response. A high emphasis on D may further suggest the person sacrifices the full use of his or her intellectual potential by merely focusing on the safe and obvious rather than probing into the more novel and unusual. This is sometimes reflected in the remitted schizophrenic who focuses on a relatively safe, conservative, and socially desirable response, which is suggested by pre- and post-treatment D% changes from 40% to 73%, respectively (Murillo & Exner, 1973).

Where D+ is high, there is the likelihood of an excellent level of developmental functioning and a concern with precision (Goldfried et al., 1971). On the other hand, if D is high but the quality of responses are low, a severe level of maladjustment is indicated (Exner, 1974).

Low D   Persons under stress show a decrease in D and a corresponding increase in Dd (Exner, 1974). Furthermore, low D can reflect inadequate perceptual habits (Klopfer, Ainsworth, Klopfer, & Holt, 1954), which may suggest brain damage (Reitan, 1955). The proportion of D is lowest in young children and gradually increases with age (Ames, Metraux, & Walker, 1974).

Unusual Detail (Dd)   The Dd response is considered to represent a retreat from a person's environment by focusing on details rather than either perceiving the whole situation or noticing the more obvious elements of the environment. A clinician would expect the number of Dd responses to comprise approximately 6% of the total R for a normal adult. However, Dd is frequently higher in the protocols of normal children and adolescents. For schizophrenics or severely impaired compulsives, the proportion of Dd can increase to 25% or more (Exner, 1974). When Dd is in good proportion to W and D, this reflects a healthy adjustment in which a person combines initiative with an appropriate ability to withdraw.

High Dd   Persons with high Dd scores reflect a need to pull back from the ambiguities that may be contained in a whole response. When this occurs in schizophrenics, it suggests an attempt to narrow their perceptions of their environment in order to make these perceptions more congruent with their inner world (Exner, 1986). If Dd perceptions are combined with movement, this gives further support to the hypothesis that the person's thought processes are impairing his or her perceptions (Exner, 1986).

Compulsives use Dd to focus on the details of a situation in an attempt to reduce their anxiety and exert more control over their perceptions. Their thought processes are not flexible enough to take in a sufficient number of whole responses. This rigidity becomes more exaggerated as the overall number of Dd responses increases and the size of each perception decreases.

Space (S)   A high number of S responses (three or more) is associated with negativism, difficulty in handling anger, and oppositional tendencies (Beck, 1961; Exner, 1986; Rapaport et al., 1968). However, within normal populations, a moderate number of S responses probably does not relate to hostility (Martin, Pfaadt, & Makinister, 1983) but may suggest some contrariness that is adaptive (striving for independence, constructive self-assertion). This is especially true if form quality is good (Klopfer et al., 1954; Piotrowski, 1957). If S responses are high (three or more), and occur with poor form quality and/or poor primitive movements, a clinician should consider the presence of anger, hostility, and potential acting out (Exner, 1986).

Determinants

Since the majority of research has been done on the determinants, they are frequently seen as the core of the Rorschach data. An analysis of a person's determinant score shows the psychological activity that he or she engaged in while the response was being created. It examines his or her unique style of perception and thinking, and how these interact with one another. In general, research has isolated specific details of the determinants that could possibly lure the clinician into a rigid and potentially inaccurate "single sign" approach. Again, a Rorschach interpreter should focus on the interaction among a large number of variables in order to modify, confirm, or reject tentative hypotheses derived from any single determinant score.

Form (F)   The amount of pure F in a protocol has generally been used to indicate the extent to which the person can remove affect from a situation. The presence of form in a response represents a certain degree of respect for the standards of the environment and reflects intact reasoning abilities. It is seen both as related to attention and concentration and as an index of affective control or delay. This is reflected in the fact that inpatient schizophrenics have a relatively higher percentage of Fw and F- responses than other groups (see Appendix N). However, schizophrenics have increases in pure F following treatment (Exner, 1986), and a higher level of pure F for schizophrenics is associated with a better prognosis (Exner & Murillo, 1977). The presence of a pure F response does not necessarily mean that no conflict is present, but rather that the person is able to suspend temporarily the affect associated with a conflict. Conversely, people in emotional turmoil are likely to produce a significantly lower number of pure form responses, reflecting their inability to remove their affect from their experience. (See also interpretation of Lambda).

High Pure F   Persons with a high pure F score either are highly defensive and constricted (Leavitt & Garron, 1982) or merely demonstrate a good ability to deliberately suspend or control their affect (Beck, 1945; Klopfer et al., 1954). When a person is in a more defensive position, the number of pure F responses increases. For example, pure F increases in populations of recovering schizophrenics (Goldman, 1960a), which may be the result of their attempting to cautiously give a socially acceptable answer in which they have to limit their affect. Also, pure F is higher among paranoid schizophrenics than other types of schizophrenics (Rapaport et al., 1968), reflecting their greater degree of organization and caution. Pure F also increases for persons who have been given some prior knowledge of the purpose of the test (Henry & Rotter, 1956) or who are requested to respond as quickly as possible (Hafner, 1958).

After ECT, pure F is usually higher (Kelly, Margulies, & Barrera, 1941), which corresponds with patients' subjective reports of decreased affect. Also, alcoholics give more pure F responses than do psychopaths (Buhler & LeFever, 1947), and Leavitt and

Garron (1982) have found an increase in F% in the protocols of patients having both psychological disturbances and lower back pain.

Low Pure F   If pure F is low, the likelihood exists that a person's level of turmoil is sufficiently high so that he or she cannot screen out his or her affective response to a situation. For example, acute schizophrenics who have difficulty reducing their level of affect also have a low number of pure F responses (Exner & Murillo, 1973). Likewise, certain characterological disorders (Buhler & LeFever, 1947) and organic disorders, in which there is difficulty controlling impulses, both have a low number of pure F responses (Exner, 1974).

Human Movement (M)   Probably more research has been done on the M response than on any other Rorschach variable. Most of this research is consistent in viewing M as reflecting inner fantasies connected to the outside world. More specifically, M represents the bridging of inner resources with reality or what might be described as "internalization of action" (Exner, 1974). M is also an inhibitor of outward behavior, even though that inhibition may only be temporary. It has been associated with creativity (Dudek, 1968; Hersh, 1962; Richter & Winter, 1966), and introverted thinking (Kunce & Tamkin, 1981), and there is a close relationship between M and daydreaming (Dana, 1968; Page, 1957). Schulman (1953) has shown M's relation to abstract thinking in that a high number of M responses reflects both an active inner process and a delay in expressing behavior. Thus, M can be generally understood as involving deliberate inner experience. In its positive sense, M can indicate good ego functioning, ability to plan, impulse control, and ability to withstand frustration. In a more negative vein, it can suggest an overdeveloped fantasy life.

While interpreting M, it is important to look carefully at the different components of the response. For example, does the movement involve conflict or rather cooperation? A high number of aggressive movements has been shown to reflect a person who is generally more aggressive him- or herself and also typically perceives relationships as characterized by aggressiveness (Exner, 1983). The degree of passivity in the movement is also likely to suggest that the person has more dependent and passive behaviors external to the test situation (Exner & Kazaoka, 1978). Specific interests might be projected into the movement responses, such as the increased number of dance movements perceived by physical education and dance students (Kincel & Murray, 1984). The clinician should also consider other data both from within the test and external to it. Further elaboration regarding M, especially as it relates to the person's degree of control of impulses, can be derived by referring to the EB and EA ratios.

High M   High M responses, especially if they are M+, are associated with high I.Q. (Abrams, 1955; Goldfried et al., 1971) and increased creativity (Dudek, 1968; Hersh, 1962; Richter & Winter, 1966). Dana (1968) has proposed that high M can represent any or all of several different psychological processes, including fantasy, an accurate sense of time, intellect, creativity, delay, and certain aspects of interpersonal relationships. Further studies include abstract thinking as an important correlate to M (Schulman, 1953) and to an introverted thinking orientation (Kunce & Tamkin, 1981).

A relatively high number of M responses suggests that the individual is overly invested in his or her fantasy life, which might be similar to a "Walter Mitty syndrome." With a high number of M- responses, the person is likely to be deficient in social skills and to have poorly developed interpersonal relationships (Molish, 1967; Weiner, 1966) or even psychotic symptoms (Phillips & Smith, 1953). Schmidt and Fonda (1954), for example, have found a high number of M responses in manic patients.

Low M   In many respects, a low M response indicates the opposite of what is suggested by a high M. Persons, especially depressives, who have a difficult time using their inner resources, usually have low M scores (Ames, 1959; Beck, 1945). Demented elderly patients have also been found to produce a low number of movement responses of all types (Insua & Stella, 1986). Low M is also associated with inflexible persons who have difficulty accepting and adjusting to change (Alcock, 1963; Goldfried et al., 1971; Rapaport et al., 1968). This inflexibility can at least in part be explained by a low level of empathy and a lack of imagination (Klopfer et al., 1954; Piotrowski, 1960, 1969). Since successful psychotherapy involves both flexibility and a relatively active inner life, low M is indicative of a poor prognosis (Goldfried et al., 1971; Klopfer et al., 1954). Conversely, a high number of good-quality M responses are a positive prognostic indicator.

Animal Movement (FM)   Whereas human movement responses serve to mediate between the inner and outer environment, animal movement reflects more unrestrained emotional impulses in which there is less ego control. The impulses are more urgent, more conscious, and provoked by situations beyond the person's control. This is reflected in the higher number of FM's in children (Ames et al., 1971) and the aged (Klopfer et al., 1956), and it correlates positively with MMPI scales that measure irresponsibility, aggressiveness, and distractibility (Thompson, 1948). If persons are in situations in which they have little control, FM is likely to be increased. For example, FM has been found to increase during physical restraint (Exner, 1979), in chronic amphetamine users (Exner, Zalis, & Schumacher, 1976), and among prostitutes who were addicted to drugs (Exner, Wylie, Leura, & Parrill, 1977). Whereas human movement responses involve delay, animal movements do not. FM responses correspond with persons who complain of "racing thoughts" and have too much on their minds (Exner, 1986).

High FM   A high number of FM responses suggests persons who are governed by their needs and urges. They generally have a difficult time delaying gratification and therefore rarely plan toward long-term goals (Exner, 1974). Typically, they will be highly defensive and will be using intellectualization, rationalization, regression, and substitution as their primary means of reducing anxiety (Haan, 1964). If the FM responses are aggressive, it is more likely that they will be assaultive (Sommer & Sommer, 1958). The general, overall theme of high FM responses is that thoughts or feelings are occurring beyond the person's control. The number of FM responses for children (8 to 16) is from 3.0 to 3.5, whereas adults have an average of approximately 3.5 (Exner, 1986).

Low FM   Low FM reflects persons who are overly inhibited in expressing their emotions and may deny their basic needs (Klopfer & Davidson, 1962). For example, Ames, Metraux, Rodell, and Walker (1974) have associated low FM with a decreased energy level in children.

Inanimate Movement (m)   Similar to FM, the number of inanimate movement responses also provides an index of the extent to which persons are experiencing drives or life events that are beyond their ability to control. The drives reflected by m are ones that threaten people's adjustment in that they are helpless to effectively deal with them (Klopfer et al., 1954). This helplessness is usually related to interpersonal activities (Hertz, 1976; Klopfer et al., 1954; Piotrowski, 1957, 1960). For example, Exner (1974) has found one or more m responses in the records of both inpatient and outpatient schizophrenics, and Piotrowski and Schreiber (1952) found no m scores in the records of successfully treated patients. The number of m responses is also more frequent with juvenile delinquents, to the extent that, by 16 years of age, they perceive an average of one per protocol (Majumber & Roy, 1962). The view that m represents threat from the external world is supported by the observation that sailors at sea produced significantly more m during a severe storm (Shalit, 1965). Similarly, paratroop trainees had an increase in m just before their first jump (Armbuster, Miller, & Exner, 1974) as did elective-surgery patients just prior to surgery (Exner, Armbuster, Walker, & Cooper, 1975). [See also interpretation of experience base (eb)].

High m   The presence of m should serve as a warning sign to indicate a marked presence of conflict and tension. Subjects probably see themselves as surrounded by threatening persons and are unable to reconcile themselves with their environment. A related finding by Thomas and Duszynski (1985) is that the word "whirl" (or similar words) was found more frequently in the protocols of persons who later committed suicide. Although the use of these "whirl all" words may not have necessarily been formally scored as FM or m, there are clear similarities between these classes of responses. To gain a more complete understanding of the individual meaning of m, clinicians should investigate the possible resources and the characteristic means of resolving conflict by looking at M, sum C, frequency of D and S, and the accuracy of their perceptions as reflected in F+% and X+%.

Color—Chromatic (C, CF, FC, Cn)   The manner in which color is handled reflects the style in which a subject deals with his or her emotions. If color dominates (C, CF, Cn), then their affect is likely to be poorly controlled and disorganized. In such cases, affect is disruptive and the person could be expected to be emotional, labile, and overreactive. If the responses are more dominated by form (FC), affect will be more delayed, controlled, and organized. For example, Gill (1966) demonstrated that subjects who could effectively delay their responses in a problem solving task had a higher number of FC responses in their protocols, whereas those who had difficulty delaying their responses had more CF and C responses. It has also been shown that a positive correlation exists between individuals having color-dominated responses and independent measurements of impulsiveness (Gardner, 1951). However, if the number of color-dominated responses is used to determine impulsiveness, the implications of the form quality, number of Y responses, and relative number of color-dominated responses (FC:CF + C) should also be taken into account. Furthermore, the chromatic cards produce a greater frequency of aggressive, passive, and undesirable contents than do the achromatic cards (Crumpton, 1956).

Adult nonpatients have between 1.5 to 2.5 times more form-dominated color to color-dominated responses [FC/(CF + C)]. This contrasts with the average patient group, which generally has an equal number of FC to CF + C responses (Exner, 1986). Pure C responses are also predominant in the protocols of very young children, as is color naming (Ames et al., 1974; Exner, 1986). (See also interpretation of the FC:CF + C formula.)

High C and Cn   Individuals with a high proportion of color dominated responses typically have little regard for the adaptiveness of their expressions, and discharge their emotions in an impulsive manner (Gardner, 1951). This suggests that a person's higher cognitive abilities have been suspended or possibly overwhelmed by affective impulses. Stormant and Finney (1953) were able to differentiate between assaultive and non-assaultive patients based on the assaultive patients having a higher number of poor-quality color responses. Likewise, Townsend (1967) found a higher level of aggressiveness in adolescents who produced a greater than average number of CF responses combined with an absence of human movement. In general, a high number of color-dominant responses suggests that the person is more labile, suggestible (Linton, 1954;

Mann, 1956; Steisel, 1952), sensitive, irritable (Allen, 1954; Shapiro, 1960), and has difficulty delaying his or her responses during problem solving tasks (Gill, 1966).

Color naming suggests that the person is giving a concrete response to the stimuli, and the response is primitive and poorly conceptualized. Although research is inconclusive, color naming typically seems to occur in severe disorders for adults, such as organic impairment. This is somewhat supported in that some brain-damaged subjects show an increased interest in color and seem to be more "stimulus bound" in their perception of it (Goldstein & Sheerer, 1941; Schilder, 1953). Color naming is not unusual in the protocols of young children.

Low C and CF   A total absence of C and CF occurs more frequently with depressed persons (Fisher, 1951; Kobler & Steil, 1953) and those with a low level of spontaneity who consistently dampen and overcontrol their emotional expression (Costello, 1958). If other suicidal indicators are present, a low color-dominant protocol may give additional support to the presence of suicidal tendencies (Goldfried et al., 1971). Low C and CF responses from schizophrenics can be a good sign for successful treatment (Stotsky, 1952).

High FC   A moderately high number of FC responses can indicate a good level of integration between controlling emotions and appropriately expressing them (Beck, 1945; Klopfer et al., 1954; Pope & Scott, 1967). Typically, this level of FC responses indicates that individuals have the ability to develop good rapport with others (Allison et al., 1968; Schafer, 1954) and can learn under stress (Phillips & Smith, 1953). The prognosis for therapy is good (Goldfried et al., 1971) because they can experience emotions yet also conceptualize and give form to the expression of these emotions. Beck (1945) has stated that a moderately high number of FC responses indicates that schizophrenia is unlikely. In children, it may reflect the effects of overtraining with a corresponding decrease in natural spontaneity (Klopfer et al., 1954; Shapiro, 1960). Within adult populations, it may also reflect overcompliance and a dependent personality (Schafer, 1954).

Low FC   Low FC suggests poor emotional control (Klopfer et al., 1954), which is likely to negatively affect interpersonal relationships (Piotrowski, 1957; Schafer, 1948). This can also indicate anxiety states (Rapaport et al., 1968) and gives support to a hypothesis of schizophrenia (Beck, 1945; Thiesen, 1952) if other indicators of schizophrenia—such as poor quality responses—are present.

Color—Achromatic (C', C'F, FC')   Achromatic color responses constitute one of the least researched areas of the Rorschach. However, it has been suggested that C' responses reflect constrained, internal, and painful affects. In other words, there is a dampened emotional expressiveness in which the person is cautious and defensive. Exner has referred to C' as the psychological equivalent of "biting one's tongue" in that "emotion is internalized and consequently creates some irritation" (Exner, 1986, p.341). Thus, it relates not only to painful emotions but also to affective constraint and defensiveness. Most Rorschach systematizers have consistently used C' as an index of depression (Klopfer, 1938; Piotrowski, 1957; Rapaport et al., 1968; Exner, 1983). In considering the meaning of achromatic color responses, a clinician should look at the relative influence of form. If form is dominant (FC'), there is likely to be definition and organization to the affect, with a stronger ability to delay the behavior. On the other hand, dominant C' responses suggest the immediate presence of painful emotions.

The average number of achromatic color responses for normals is 0.6. In contrast to this are outpatients who have an average of 1.3 per record and schizophrenics with an average of 1.2 (Exner, 1986).

High C' C' occurs most frequently among those patients who constrain their emotions, such as psychosomatics, obsessive-compulsives, and depressives (Exner, 1974). The pain and constraint associated with these emotions may adversely affect the person's overall level of adjustment. An absence of shading responses combined with a large proportion of C' responses has been suggested as predictive of suicidal gestures (Exner, 1974).

Shading-Texture (T, TF, FT) Texture responses represent painful emotional experiences combined with needs for supportive interpersonal relationships (Beck, 1945, 1968; Klopfer et al., 1954). For example, recently divorced or separated subjects averaged 3.57 texture responses per protocol (SD = 1.21) as compared with 1.31 for matched controls (SD = 0.96; Exner & Bryant, 1974). Persons with a high number of texture responses reach out, although they do so in a guarded and cautious manner (Hertz, 1976). If form plays a relatively insignificant role and texture is predominant, subjects tend to feel overwhelmed with painful experiences, which would probably be sufficiently intense to disrupt their ability to adapt. Conversely, if form dominates (FT), not only is the pain likely to be more controlled, but also the need for supportive contact from others would be of primary concern (Beck, 1968; Klopfer et al., 1954). Coan (1956) has suggested that a combination of movement and texture responses relates to inner sensitivity and empathy. If chromatic color and texture occur together, the subjects' behaviors would not only be less mature in seeking affection, but would also be more direct and unconstrained (Exner, 1974).

Responses in which texture dominates show an increase through childhood, reaching a maximum by 15 years of age, and gradually subsiding over the next few years until a form-dominated texture response is most characteristic in late adolescence and adulthood (Ames et al., 1971). Kallstedt (1952) hypothesized that this is due to the greater personal and sexual vulnerability of mid-adolescence. Nonpsychiatric populations average 1.4 texture responses per record, whereas psychiatric populations average 2 or more per record (Exner, 1961). They usually appear ten times more frequently on Cards IV and VI than on the other cards (Exner, 1961).

High T or TF High scorers for T or TF are characterized as having intense needs for affection and dependency. This might result in oversensitivity in personal relationships to the extent that they may have a difficult time in reconciling the intensity of these needs with what they can realistically expect from their relationships. They are open to their environment, but also approach it with a cautious sensitivity.

Low T The absence of any T responses may suggest an emotional "impoverishment" in which the person has ceased to look for meaningful emotional relationships (Exner, 1974). For example, inpatient depressives have the lowest average number of texture responses but the highest number of diffuse shading responses (Y; Exner, 1974). Likewise, psychosomatic patients give fewer T responses than other types of patients (Brown, 1953), which would correspond with their constrained expression of affect. In general, T, Y, and C' all represent an "irritating emotional experience" such as anxiety, tension, apprehension, and internal discomfort (Exner, 1978).

Shading-Dimension (Vista; V, VF, FV) Rorschach systematizers have generally considered Vista responses, especially pure V, to represent a painful process of self-examination in which the person creates a sense of distance from him- or herself in order to introspect (Klopfer & Davidson, 1962). This introspection usually involves depression and a sense of inferiority. However, if the V responses are dominated by form, introspection is still suggested, but the process is unlikely to be emotionally painful. This is in contrast to the negative type of self-examination associated with pure V. Even a single pure V response in a Rorschach protocol can be an important indicator.

Within normal populations, V responses occur an average of 0.48 per record. On the other hand, depressed inpatients averaged 1.25, while schizophrenics and character disorders averaged 0.63 and 0.25, respectively (Exner, 1986). It is extremely rare for V to appear in the protocols of children, but it occurs at about the same rate among adolescents and adults (Exner, 1986).

High V   Pure V responses created by depressed patients indicates a deep level of self-critical introspection (Klopfer & Kelly, 1942). Stutterers also produce more pure V responses (Light & Amick, 1956), as do alcoholics (Buhler & LeFever, 1947), which reflects the painful self-criticism that usually occurs in these patient groups. V responses have also been suggested as an index of suicidal risk and are an important part of Exner's Suicidal Constellation (Exner, 1986). Although shading (and combined color and shading) responses in themselves are probably ineffective in discriminating successful from nonsuccessful attempters, these responses may suggest a more stable suicidal trait (Hansell, Lerner, Milden, & Ludolph, 1988). However, Exner's Suicidal Constellation comprised of 12 possible signs (high number of morbid responses, es greater than EA, etc.) with a cutoff of eight or more, has been able to effectively discriminate persons who are serious suicidal risks (Exner, 1986).

Low V   The absence of V is usually a positive sign, and the presence of a single form-dominated V merely represents the ability to introspect (Exner, 1974). Although a certain degree of pain may be involved with the introspection, the more important fact is that the resulting information can be integrated and eventually used productively.

Shading-Diffuse (Y, YF, FY)   Klopfer et al. (1954) and Beck (1945) have described Y as representing a sense of helplessness and withdrawal, which is frequently accompanied by anxiety and is often a response to ambiguity. Beck (1945) further elaborated that subjects with a high number of vista responses are experiencing psychological pain and have also resigned themselves to their situation. The same general rule for looking at the influences of form (F) in relation to Vista (V), texture (T), and color (C, C') also applies for shading-diffuse. When F is dominant, subjects are more able to delay their behavior, and their experience is more controlled, organized, and integrated. This ability to delay behavior also gives them time to mobilize their resources. When Y is dominant, there is a much greater sense of being overwhelmed. Although these individuals are characteristically withdrawn, any expression of pain and helplessness is direct. Since there is little ability to delay their impulses, they do not have enough time to mobilize their resources.

Within the general population, 86% of people give at least one Y (Y, YF, or FY) response. Schizophrenics give more Y responses than nonpatients and outpatients, and nonschizophrenic patients give twice the number of Y responses than normals do (Exner, 1974). To accurately understand the meaning of Y responses, the clinician should look for other indicators of coping. In particular, these might include the number and manner in which pure form is used, the quality of organization, and the number of human movement responses. If there is a high number of Y and these "coping indicators" are absent, the person is likely to be overwhelmed and will probably be unable to adapt or respond effectively (Exner, 1974).

High Y   A high number of Y is associated with anxiety (Beck, 1961; Klopfer & Davidson, 1962) and a constrained expression of emotions, even though the experience of these emotions may be direct (Salmon, Arnold, & Collyer, 1972). It is more frequent in the protocols of depressed patients and outpatients (Exner, 1978). High Y is also associated with a sense of resignation to life events and an attempt to create distance between oneself and the environment (Elstein, 1965). Y is higher in alcoholics (Buhler & LeFever, 1947) and increases during stress, such as prior to examinations (Ridgeway & Exner, 1980), surgery (Exner, Thomas, Cohen, Ridgeway, & Cooper, 1981), and situational crises (Exner, 1986). Since m and Y assess similar constructs, they should be considered together.

Low Y   Since ambiguity is purposefully built into the test situation, it is expected that some Y, usually FY, will occur in any protocol. Exner's (1986) normative group of adult nonpatients had an average of 0.98 Y responses (SD = 1.60), compared with 1.56 for schizophrenics (SD = 2.00), and 1.31 for depressives (SD = 1.32). The total absence of Y suggests an extremely indifferent attitude toward ambiguity (Exner, 1974).

Content

The different content categories are generally regarded to contain information relating to a person's needs, interests, preoccupations, and social interactions. Several researchers have found positive correlations between a large variety of contents and intelligence (Paulker, 1963). Research has also shown that, whereas a high variety in content is associated with intellectual flexibility, a low variety suggests intellectual constriction and rigidity. Persons' occupational interests are often represented in a higher number of contents relating to their specific career choice. For example, biologists and medical personnel usually give a higher number of anatomy responses than the general population (Exner, 1974). This may merely indicate that these persons have an interest in their career, or it could also suggest that persons are overconcerned with their career to the extent that they neglect other areas of their life, perhaps even impairing their overall level of adjustment. For example, biologists who see only nature contents may be using a preoccupation with their careers to withdraw from interpersonal relationships (Exner, 1974).

While interpreting Rorschach content, it is important to look at the variety of contents, the number of each content, and their overall configuration, as well as the implications other Rorschach factors may have for the meaning of the content scorings. It is usually essential to consider the age of the subject and to use age-appropriate norms. For example, children usually have significantly fewer human and human detail responses than adults, and the variety of their contents is also lower (Ames et al., 1974; Exner & Weiner, 1982). Another important consideration is to study contents relating to aggressiveness (fire, explosions, etc.), facial features, and orality. Although the focus of the Comprehensive System is on a quantitative approach to the Rorschach, symbolical considerations can also be extremely important in conducting a more qualitative analysis. The following section provides general information on the meaning associated with human and animal contents. Further interpretive material can be found in the interpretation of quantitative formulas relating to contents (see formulas 15, 16, 17, 18, 19, 20, 21).

Human Contents (H, Hd, (H), (Hd))   Human responses constitute one of the most thoroughly researched contents. Beck (1961), in general agreement with other researchers, has found that H and Hd gradually increase with age until the median for 10-year-old children is from 16 to 18%. This remains unchanged through adolescence until the overall adult proportion of 17% is reached. Exner (1974) found that, whereas adult nonpatient H + Hd responses were 19%, adult outpatients and schizophrenics only had 13%. He also demonstrated that the ratio of human to human detail (H:Hd) for nonpatients was 3:1. In contrast to this were schizophrenics whose average ratio was approximately 1:1 and outpatients whose ratio was 2:1. Molish (1967), suggests that when there is an increase in Hd compared with H, the subject is prone to use constricted defenses. Others have theorized that it suggests intellectualization, compulsiveness, and a preoccupation with the self that restricts the degree of contact with others (Klopfer & Davidson, 1962). Beck (1945) associated high Hd with anxiety, depression, and a low intellectual level. [See also quantitative formulas for H + (H):Hd + (Hd), (H) + (Hd):(A) + (Ad), and H + A:Hd + Ad.]

High H   A high number of human contents occurs with individuals who have a wide-ranging interest in people (Beck, 1968), are more likely to have high self-esteem (Fisher, 1962), and possess greater intelligence (Beck, 1968; Rawls & Slack, 1968). A higher H content has been consistently found to be associated with a greater likelihood of successful psychotherapeutic treatment (Goldfried et al., 1971; Goldman, 1960; Halpern, 1940). As might be expected, human responses are more frequent in the records of psychologists and anthropologists (Roe, 1952).

Low H   An unusually low number of H contents suggests a low level of empathy and a withdrawal from interpersonal relationships (Allison et al., 1968; Kahn & Giffen, 1960). The overall H% has been found to be lower for schizophrenics than for normals (Duran, Pechoux, Escafit, & Davidow, 1949; Sherman, 1952). The prognosis for successful psychotherapy with low H scorers is poor (Piotrowski & Bricklin, 1961), and if this is accompanied by a low number of M responses, their termination from therapy is likely to be abrupt, probably due to a high level of anxiety combined with a low intellectual level (Affleck & Mednick, 1959; Rapaport et al., 1968). The complete absence of human content is unusual and, with the exception of very young children, is likely to indicate psychopathology characterized by difficulties with identity (Exner, 1978).

Animal and Animal Detail (A and Ad)   Most of the literature indicates that animal content is associated with the obvious aspects of adaptiveness and the most concrete features of reality testing (Draguns, Haley, & Phillips, 1967). Since animal contents are the easiest to perceive, their presence suggests that examinees are using routine and predictable ways of responding. Conversely, a low number of animal responses suggests highly individualistic persons who see their world in their own personal and unique ways.

Animal responses occur more frequently than any other content category and comprise 38 to 48% of the normal adult record (Beck, Rabin, Thieson, Molish, & Thetford, 1950; Cass & McReynolds, 1951; Wedemeyer, 1954) with a slightly higher amount for children (Beck, 1961). Schizophrenics and outpatients average 31% and 41%, respectively, whereas depressives score much higher with an average of 41% per protocol (Exner, 1974). Other studies have found that the percentage of A responses is low for manics (Kuhn, 1963; Schmidt & Fonda, 1954) and high for alcoholics (Buhler & LeFever, 1947).

High A   A high A suggests a predictable, stereotyped manner of approaching the world (Klopfer & Davidson, 1962; Levitt & Truumaa, 1972) often associated with depression and the use of constrictive and conforming defenses (Beck, 1945, 1960). There has been some evidence to suggest that high A responses are a sign of brain damage (Goldfried et al., 1971), but variables from without as well as within the test should be carefully considered before making this diagnosis.

Low A   Persons who are spontaneous, nonconforming, unpredictable, and of higher intelligence often have a low number of A responses (Allen, 1954; Kahn & Giffen, 1960).

Popular Responses

The number of popular responses reflects the subjects' degree of similarity to most people, the extent to which they conform to social standards, and the relative ease with which they can be influenced in interpersonal relationships. Persons who reject conventional modes of thinking give a significantly lower number of populars than those who are conforming and relatively conventional. With Exner's (1986) scoring system (see Table 9–6), the average number of P responses for nonpsychiatric subjects is 6.66 (SD = 1.66). Outpatients and nonschizophrenic patients, likewise, give approximately seven per record, whereas inpatient schizophrenics give four or less, characterological disorders give approximately five, and depressives have slightly more than five (Exner, 1986).

High P   High P suggests that the subject is experiencing anxiety related to a fear of making mistakes and, therefore, clings to common perceptions as a way to achieve approval. These individuals can be described as conventional, overconforming, guarded, and frequently, depressed (Exner, 1974; Levitt & Truumaa, 1972; Weiner, 1961).

Low P   The lowest number of P responses is given by inpatient schizophrenics, which is consistent with their poor contact with reality. They can be described as poorly adjusted, detached, aloof from their environment, and unable to see the world as others see it. Molish (1967) has suggested that if neurotic subjects, especially obsessive-compulsives, have low P, then the possibility of latent schizophrenia should be investigated. Patients diagnosed as having character disorders also have low P, which reflects their rejection of conventionality and their lack of conformity.

Since populars are extremely common for Cards I, III, V, and VIII, the absence of them from these cards is significant in that it more strongly suggests the trends just discussed. However, the assumption that low P responses alone confirm maladjustment should be approached with caution. For subjects who have good form quality (F+% and X+%) and whose organizational activity is also good, it is more likely that they are creative individuals who are avoiding common, ordinary perceptions and want to extend their imagination. If organization and form quality are poor, there is a high likelihood that the psychopathological dimensions are more predominant.

Structural Summary

The quantitative formulas used to develop the structural summary give the relationships between the determinants, locations, contents, and populars. Thus, the formulas provide a more extensive elaboration beyond these variables, and it is from them that some of the most important, reliable, and valid elements of interpretation are derived. The numbering of the quantitative formulas corresponds with the numbers given to them in the previous listing of the quantitative formulas in the description of the structural summary.

1. Experience Balance or Erlebnistypus [EB; (M:C)]   The Experience Balance formula or Erlebnistypus was originally devised by Rorschach and is the ratio between the sum of all M responses compared with the sum of all weighted color responses (FC = 0.5, CF = 1.0, pure C and Cn = 1.5). Rorschach systematizers and researchers have come to view the Experience Balance ratio as the extent to which a person is internally oriented as opposed to being more externally directed and behaviorally responsive to outside stimuli. Although the EB ratio is usually relatively stable (Exner, Armbuster, & Viglione, 1978), it can temporarily change during times of stress or become more permanently altered during the course of successful psychotherapy (Exner, 1974). Although the EB ratio is usually stable for adults, there is considerable variability in children until mid-adolescence (Exner, Thomas, & Mason, 1985; Exner & Weiner, 1982). In an extensive literature review, Singer (1960) described the two sides of the ratio as representing dimensions of "constitutional temperament." These dimensions are introversives (higher M scores) who have a preference for internal experience as opposed to extratensives (higher weighted C scores) who are more prone to activity and external expression. The introversive can more effectively delay his or her behavior, whereas the extratensive is more emotional and is likely to discharge his or her affect into some form of external behavior. Both types respond differently to stress and to problem solving tasks (Exner, 1978). It should be emphasized that, in their moderate forms, neither is any more or any less effective than the other, nor is either more prone to psychopathology (Molish, 1967). [See also interpretive meanings associated with M and C and to the quantitative formulas dealing with either of these factors (EA and W:M).]

Higher M (Introversives)   Rorschach stated that persons with a relatively higher number of M responses were more oriented toward using their inner fantasy life. Thus, they are directed inward and use their inner experience to satisfy most of their basic needs. This is not so much an absolute necessity as it is a preference. In fact, these individuals may, on a more superficial level, even appear to be extraverted. Researchers have found them to be cautious, deliberate, submissive (Kurz, 1963; Rosenthal, 1962), and less physically active than persons scoring relatively higher on the C side of the ratio (Mukerji, 1969). They approach problem-solving tasks by internalizing the situation, mentally reviewing possible alternatives, and engage in relatively few behaviors prior to reaching a solution (Exner, 1978).

Higher C (Extratensives)   Persons who have relatively lower M responses and higher C responses (extratensives) tend to use external interactions as the most important means of satisfying their needs. They characteristically direct their energy toward the outside world. Extratensives are usually spontaneous and assertive, but also have difficulty delaying their responses (Alcock, 1963; Exner, Thomas, & Martin, 1980; Palmer, 1970). In children, higher C scores may represent a lack of self-assurance (Palmer, 1970). Extratensives are likely to approach problem solving situations by experimenting with different behaviors (external trial and error) prior to achieving solutions (Exner, 1978).

M and C Equal (Ambitents)   If M and C are equal, the persons are more likely to be flexible during interpersonal relationships, but they are also less sure of themselves during problem solving and tend to vacillate (Exner, 1978). They usually need to verify every sequence in the solution of a problem at hand and do not profit as much from mistakes as either the introversive or the extratensive (Exner, 1978). Whereas the latter types are more sure of which response style to take in approaching an ambiguous situation, ambitents have a liability when flexibility is required (Exner, 1978). Thus, ambitents tend to be less consistent and efficient than either introversives or extratensives. Unusually high scores on both M and C suggest a manic condition (Beck, 1960; Singer, 1960).

2. Experience Actual [EA; (M + C)]   Whereas the Experience Balance ratio emphasizes the assessment of a person's type, the Experience Actual indicates the "volume of organized activity" (Beck, 1960). The M side of the formula shows the extent to which persons are able to organize their inner lives, and the C side indicates the extent to which emotions are available. The emphasis here is that both the M and C represent deliberate, organized activity, which is contrasted with the disorganization associated with nonhuman movement (FM, m) and responses related to the gray-black features of the blot (T, V, Y).

For the most part, the adult ratio between M and C is remarkably stable (Exner, 1986), yet the sum of M and C can sometimes fluctuate on a daily basis, which theoretically parallels the effects of changes in mood (Erginel, 1972). It has been further noted that, after successful treatment, M and C typically both increase (Beck, 1960; Exner, 1974; Piotrowski & Shreiber, 1952), indicating a greater increase in the degree of organization of the person's inner life and that more emotions have also become available. In fact, Exner (1974) found that EA increases significantly more for patients who improved in therapy than for those who showed little or no improvement. Furthermore, persons who underwent an insight-oriented treatment showed much more of an increase in EA than those in a treatment that emphasized a combination of support and environmental manipulation (Exner, 1974). This is consistent with the goal of insight therapy, which focuses on helping patients to understand and organize their internal resources. The mean changes for children show a gradual increase (rarely more than 0.5) with each year from the ages of 5 to 13 (Exner, 1986). Although brief retesting for children has shown good stability, long-term retesting (nine months or more), has resulted in wide fluctuations (Exner & Weiner, 1982; Exner, Thomas, & Mason, 1985).

3. Experience Base [eb; (FM + m)/(Y + T + V + C')]   The Experience Base ratio was originally suggested by Klopfer et al. (1954) and later developed in its present form by Exner (1974, 1986). The nonhuman movement side of the ratio reflects tendencies to respond in ways that are not completely acceptable to the ego. These tendencies appear out of control, impinge on the individual, and are disorganized (Klopfer & Davidson, 1962). Although the tendencies and feelings may have originally been produced by outside sources, the resulting internal activity is not within the person's control. The opposite side of the ratio, which is a sum of the responses relating to the gray-black features of the blot, is a reflection of the pain and disharmony the person is feeling as a result of unresolved stress. The eb ratio indicates which of these two areas of functioning is more predominant. If the eb is small on both sides, it suggests that the person is not experiencing very much pain and that his or her needs are well organized. Usually, the values on either side of the ratio will be from one to three from nonpatients. If either side becomes greater than five, its interpretive meaning becomes more clear. [See also additional interpretive meanings associated with material from the left side of the ratio (FM and m) and the right side (Y + T + V + C').]

4. Experienced Stimulation [es; (FM + m) + (C' + T + Y +V)]   Experienced Stimulation is the sum of the nonhuman movement responses and all responses relating to the gray-black features of the inkblot. These are all responses reflecting that the person's functioning is disorganized and that there are forces acting on the person that he or she feels are beyond his or her control. Thus, the es (previously referred to as experience potential in Exner's first volume of the Comprehensive System) sum is an index of a person's degree of disorganization and helplessness. Persons scoring high on es have a low frustration tolerance, and it is difficult for them to be persistent, even in meaningful tasks (Exner, 1978).

Important information can be obtained by comparing the amount of organization the person has as represented by EA with how much chaos and helplessness he or she experiences as represented by es. Normal populations usually have a higher EA than es, whereas psychiatric populations have a higher es than EA (Exner, 1974). Exner (1978) has suggested that the ratio between EA and es can provide an index of the degree to which a person can tolerate frustration. This difficulty dealing with frustration would be primarily due to high-scoring es persons having a limited ability to process and mediate cognitive information (Wiener-Levy & Exner, 1981). As would be expected, a correlate of successful psychotherapy is that there is a decrease in es and a corresponding increase in EA, which suggests that at least some of the patient's activity has become more organized (Exner, 1974; Gerstle, Geary, Himelstein, & Reller-Geary, 1988). This was supported by Exner (1974) who found that subjects rated as unimproved after therapy also showed little change in that their es still remained high in relationship to EA. In another study, Exner (1974) demonstrated that most persons in successful insight therapy had an increase in EA compared with es. This suggests that patients in successful insight therapy were able to either neutralize or reorganize the forces that were "acting on" them. In contrast, therapy emphasizing support or environmental manipulation produced no or little change in the es:EA ratio.

5. FC/(CF + C)   The ratio of form-dominated color responses to color-dominant responses provides a measure of the degree of control a person has over his or her impulses. If form is predominant (1.5 to 2.5 times greater), it suggests the person has good control over his or her impulses and satisfying interpersonal relationships (Exner, 1969, 1974; Klopfer & Davidson, 1962). Exner (1978), for example, has found that schizophrenics who have FC responses greater than CF + C have a better response to psychotherapy, with less likelihood of a relapse. The high form suggests they can integrate an accurate, reality-oriented interpretation into their perceptions. However, if no or very few color dominant responses (no CF + C) are present, the person will be overly constricted and have little contact with his or her emotions (Exner, 1978). This is consistent with the finding that most psychosomatic patients, who are typically constricted, had ratios of 4:1 or greater (Exner, 1986). If the CF + C side of the ratio is relatively high (1:1), it suggests a weak control over one's impulses in which there may be aggressive acting out, perhaps consistent with a narcissistic personality (Exner, 1969; Klopfer & Davidson, 1962). The perception of both internal and external events will typically be distorted and inaccurate, as will the responses to these events (Exner, 1974). The number of pure C responses increases with pathological groups, as indicated by only 26% of nonpatients giving pure C responses in contrast to 53% of depressives, 55% of nonpatients, 71% of schizophrenics, and 79% of character-disordered patients (Exner, 1978).

6. Pure C   The sum of C and Cn responses provides an index of the degree to which a person is likely to be overwhelmed by affective impulses. Among nonpatient adults, it is rare to have any C or Cn responses occurring in a protocol (M = 0.12, SD = 0.43), but this increases slightly for patient groups (see discussion in the section on interpretation of color).

7. Affective Ratio [Afr; (R for Cards VIII,IX,X)/(R for Cards I-VII)]   Since the last three cards are chromatic and the first seven are primarily achromatic, the Affective Ratio indicates the extent to which color makes an impact on the person. Normal adults usually show an Afr between .63 and .75, with a mean of .69.

> *High Afr*   (Greater than .75) A high Afr indicates an overresponsiveness to affect (Exner, 1974), reflecting that the person is more receptive to emotional inputs and more likely to respond immediately rather than to delay behavior (Exner, 1978). Afr is correlated with EB in that introversives will usually have a low Afr (mean of .62) and extratensives a high Afr (mean of .79; Exner, 1978). It is also important to evaluate the FC/(CF + C) proportion to assess the degree of control the person has over his or her emotions. In other words, the Afr measures the responsiveness and degree of affect, whereas the FC/(CF + C) indicates the ability to control what affect is present.

> *Low Afr*   (Less than .55) Persons with low Afr scores tend to withdraw from their emotions and, if they have an unusually low Afr, may attempt to exert an extreme amount of control over their affective responses (Exner, 1974).

8. Lambda [L; (Pure F:Non-Pure F)]   The lambda index was developed by Beck (1950) as an improvement on the F% that had been used by other Rorschach systematizers. The earlier F% used the total number of R as the denominator, whereas the Lambda uses the total number of non-pure F. The Lambda ratio is used as an overall index of the degree of responsiveness versus lack of responsiveness to stimuli (Exner, 1978, 1986). Thus, persons can range from highly constricted and withdrawn to completely emotionally flooded by their responses to stimuli. The Lambda for normals is between .52 and 1.12, with a mean of .82. In contrast to this are outpatients, .05 to .85; inpatient nonschizophrenics, .20 to .58; and inpatient schizophrenics, .23 to .63 (Exner, 1978). Although these statistics characterize psychiatric groups as having a generally lower Lambda ratio, this can be somewhat misleading. The more important factor is that psychiatric groups have a much wider range than normals, even though they tend overall to have lower scores. Thus, a maladjusted person may have a Lambda either greater than 1.2 or less than .50. The significance lies in Lambda's ability to provide specifics regarding the form this maladjustment takes. It is also important to look at other information within the test, such as form quality and Experience Balance, to obtain a more complete conceptualization of the meaning of L.

High L (L > 1.1)   Since pure F is a withdrawal from experiencing a situation fully and an avoidance of perceiving all the possibilities that may be present, the high L person is likely to be conservative, insecure, and fearful of involvement (Exner, 1974). Such individuals have also been described as defensive, constricted (Klopfer et al., 1954; Piotrowski, 1957), unimaginative (Alcock, 1963; Levi, 1976), and anxious (Riessman & Miller, 1958; Singer, 1960). Levitt and Truumaa (1972) have demonstrated the association of high L with depression, guilt, and an increased potential for suicide. Lambdas of 1.20 or greater are found in persons who have an excessive degree of affective detachment, often screening out relevant information (Exner, 1978, 1986). Thus, they avoid the complexities of a stimulus and often develop "tunnel vision" relating to certain ideas or perceptions. However, with adolescents, an interpretation that focuses on maladjustment should be made with caution since Ames (1959) and Ames et al. (1971) have found that adolescents usually have a higher proportion of pure F responses.

Low L (L < .50)   A low Lambda generally indicates that the person becomes overinvolved with stimuli to the extent that affect disrupts cognitive functioning (Exner, 1986). Nonpatients were the only group with a total absence of pure form responses. (Exner, 1974). Low L scorers have also been described as having inadequate control over their emotions, which results in difficulty maintaining satisfactory interpersonal relationships due to frequent, impulsive acting out (Allison et al., 1968; Exner, 1978; Klopfer & Davidson, 1972). Such people often have an impaired ability to attend to their environment (Alcock, 1963) and are often victims of their needs and conflicts (Exner, 1986). However, low Lambda might also be associated with persons who are achievement oriented and who deal effectively with their environment (Exner, 1986). These characteristics are often suggested by other indicators in their protocols reflecting control and flexibility (average X+%, average number of Populars, good organizational activity, above average W). This is consistent with the finding that increases in Lambda (along with decreases in es) have been associated with treatment improvement among children (Gerstle et al., 1988).

9. Blends:R (Complexity Index)   Approximately 20% of all Rorschach responses involve blends. To create a blend response, the person must appreciate the complexity of the inkblot. It requires both analysis and synthesis. Exner (1986) has pointed out that the pure F response is the exact opposite in that pure F requires attention to only the most simple, straightforward aspect of the stimulus. Usually one or more blends are found in a person's protocol. A complete absence of blends suggests narrowness and constriction. This is consistent with the finding that blends are less frequent in the protocols of depressives and persons with below average intelligence (Exner, 1974, 1986). In contrast, an extremely high number of blends (eight or more), suggests an unusual amount of complexity to the extent that the person may be overly burdened (Exner, 1986).

A thorough interpretation of blends also requires an understanding of their qualitative aspects. For example, a blend that includes color-dominated determinants implies that the person might be easily overwhelmed by affect, whereas the opposite would be true if they were form-dominated. The color-shading blend (combining color with C', Y, T, F, V) implies concern with painful, irritating, confusing emotional experiences and is associated with the protocols of depressives. Exner and Wylie (1977) found a moderate correlation with attempted suicide and this blend is included in Exner's (1986) Suicide Constellation. However, it does not seem to be an accurate predictor of suicide when used as a single sign (Hansell, Lerner, Milden, & Ludolph, 1988).

10. X+% (Conventional Form)   X+% includes the form quality of all the responses in a protocol and, as such, tends to be less subject to distortions than F+% (see F+% below). The X+% is essentially an indicator of the degree to which a person perceives things in a conventional, realistic manner. Most normal children and adults will have an X+% of 80% (Exner, 1986). An extremely high percentage (greater than 90%) means that persons will perceive their world in an overly conventional manner to the extent that they might sacrifice their individuality. They are likely to be hypernormal, inflexible, rigid, and overly conventional (Exner, 1974). This is further supported by, and is consistent with, an elevated number of Populars. In contrast, lowerings in X+% (less than 70%) suggest persons who perceive their world in an unusual manner. This might be simply because they are highly committed to their individuality or, particularly if X+% is unusually low, might suggest serious psychopathology. For example, schizophrenics have a mean X+% of only 53% (Exner, 1986). Thus, it is a critical indicator of schizophrenia, and an X+% of less than 70% is one of the five indicators on Exner's (1986) Schizophrenia Index.

11. X-% (Distorted Form)   In contrast to X+% (and F+%), X-% is a direct index of the degree to which a person has distorted perceptions of reality. The higher the X-%, the more likely it is that a person's level of impairment will be significant. For example, moderately high percentages (X-% = 15%) are found for depressives, and percentages of 31% are characteristic of schizophrenics (Exner, 1986). Any percentage above 15% suggests that the person will have difficulty since he or she will have poor ties with reality and difficulty developing accurate abstractions.

12. F+% (Conventional Pure Form)   F+% assesses the same dimension as X+% but is limited to a narrower number of responses since it only involves pure F responses rather than other responses such as C', Y, T, and V. Thus, interpretation is similar to the interpretation of X+% but should be done more cautiously. It reflects a person's respect for the conventional aspects of reality and perceptual clarity. Weiner (1966) reports data indicating that schizophrenics generally have F+% in the 60s whereas normals had percentages in the low to high 80s. In general a low F+% might suggest limited intellectual endowment (Beck, 1961), retardation (Klopfer & Kelly, 1942), organic impairment (Reitan, 1955), or schizophrenia (Beck, 1968; Kahn & Giffen, 1960).

13. W:M (Aspirational Index)   The W:M ratio is a rough formula that, at the present time, is somewhat lacking in research. It can be generally understood by reconsidering that the W response as an indicator of the degree to which subjects aspire to effectively organize and conceptualize their environments. It is an effort to encompass and include a number of different details in one coherent response. However, determining whether subjects have the resources to actually accomplish an effective organization depends also on M. Although M represents the degree of investment subjects have in their fantasy lives, it also suggests how effectively they can bridge their inner resources with external reality and perform abstract thinking. Thus, the W:M ratio provides a rough comparison between a person's aspiration level as represented by W and his or her actual capability as represented by M (Exner, 1974, 1986). Adults usually score from 1.5:1 to 2.5:1. If a person has a W:M ratio of 3:1 or more, his or her need to achieve would be expected to be greater than his or her actual ability. However, scores with extremely high W components are common in children, which is consistent with the observation that children often underestimate the actual effort required to accomplish a goal (Exner, 1986). On the other hand, a ratio of less than 2:1 suggests that the individual is performing below his or her actual ability level (Klopfer et al., 1954) but that he or she may have good creative potential (Klopfer & Davidson, 1962). If the ratio is 1:1 or lower, the person might be extremely cautious and conservative in defining achievable goals (Exner, 1986).

14. W:D (Economy Index)   The W:D ratio compares the degree to which an individual attempts to create a more challenging response requiring a high degree of organization (W) rather than choosing a less demanding and easily perceived area (D). Normals and outpatients usually have a ratio of 1:2 (Exner, 1974). If the person includes a relatively large number of D responses, it suggests that he or she takes the least challenging and possibly least productive way out of a conflict situation. It could be assumed that his or her characteristic way of dealing with ambiguity is to withdraw from it and focus on the obvious. If W is predominant, the person is perhaps overdriven in his or her attempts to organize his or her perceptions. If, with a high W, both the W and D responses are of poor quality, it suggests that a person is withdrawn and unrealistically striving for perfection (Exner, 1974). However, when W and D responses are both of good quality, it is more likely to represent the successful intellectual efforts of a creative person (Exner, 1974).

15. Isolate:R (Isolation Index)   Exner (1986) points out that the five contents (Botany, Clouds, Geography, Nature, and Landscape) used to develop the Isolation index are all "nonhuman, nonsocial, inanimate, and usually static objects" (p. 406). If a high proportion of these contents (one-fourth or more) occur in a person's protocol, it suggests the person may be withdrawn, alienated, or at least have some difficulties related to social isolation (Exner, 1986). This seems to be true for children, adolescents, and adults. However, the index should not be used as a diagnosis in itself but rather as a general indicator that suggests further exploration.

16. Ab + Art:R (Intellectualization Index)   The occurrence of three or more combined scorings for Abstraction (Ab) and Art (Art) suggests an excessive use of intellectualization (Exner, 1986). Both obsessives and paranoid schizophrenics generally had more than three combined Ab and Art frequencies in their protocols (Exner, 1986; Exner & Hillman, 1984), and both these groups are likely to use an intellectual approach to distance themselves from their emotions. This is in contrast to other patients and nonpatients who typically reported an average of approximately one per protocol (Exner, 1986).

17. Anatomy (An) and X-Ray (Xy) (Body Concern)   Since An and Xy both measure concern with the body, they are considered together. An responses have been well researched, and, along with human and animal contents, anatomy is one of the most frequently occurring responses (average of 0.6 for nonpatient adults). Anatomy content has an obvious connection with concern for the body, and the literature supports this connection in that it occurs more frequently for persons preparing to undergo elective surgery (Exner, Armbuster, Walker, & Cooper 1975) and among psychosomatic patients (Shatin, 1952). Anatomy responses also occur with greater frequency with the onset of psychological difficulties related to pregnancy (Zolliker, 1943). As might be expected, An responses occur more often in the protocols of biologists and persons with medical training (Dorken, 1954; Roe, 1952; Schactel, 1966). A review of the literature by Draguns et al. (1967) concluded that anatomy content can serve as an index of the degree of involvement persons have in their inner fantasy life or may reflect physical changes—such as illness, puberty, or pregnancy. It has also been suggested that anatomy content is associated with withdrawal from the environment and obsessive defenses (Exner, 1974).

It is important to take into consideration the relative proportion of anatomy to Xy responses. Although anatomy responses are generally low for both psychiatric and nonpsychiatric groups, a combined anatomy and Xy score allows for a more clear differentiation between the two groups. Whereas the combined An and Xy responses for a nonpsychiatric group give an average of only 0.6 responses, outpatients give 1.5, schizophrenics 1.4, and nonschizophrenic patients give 1.8 responses which, for the last group, accounts for 9% of the total number of responses (Exner, 1974). Xy responses have been found to be particularly high for schizophrenics with bodily delusions (average of 2.2) and depressed patients with concerns related to bodily functioning (1.7; Exner, Murillo, & Sternklar, 1979). Anatomy responses occur most frequently for Cards VIII and IX, and Xy responses are most frequent for Card I. Exner (1974) suggests Xy responses reflect a concern with the self that is painful, but that subjects are attempting to deal with this pain by distancing themselves from it or at least disguising their responses to it. On the other hand, anatomy responses reflect a process in which the person focuses more directly on the stress and there is more of a direct emotional release.

A high number of An and Xy responses are associated with hypochondriasis (Carnes & Bates, 1971; Wagner, 1973) and psychosomatic conditions (Shatin, 1952). In congruence with these disorders, there are likely to be intellectualizing defenses (Allison et al., 1968), anxiety (Wagner, 1961), obsessive traits, and withdrawal (Exner, 1974). High An may also reflect a concern with physical functioning due to aging (Ames et al., 1973) or career choice (Dorken, 1954), and it can reflect a greater-than-average level of narcissism in patients going through a physical rehabilitation program (Levi, 1951). Schizophrenic patients sometimes give an unusually high number (eight or more) of anatomy responses (Brar, 1970; Goldfried et al., 1971).

18. H + (H):Hd + (Hd) (Human Interest)   This ratio should be at least 3:1 and preferably greater. If the number of whole human responses compared with human details becomes less than 3:1, the person might be pedantic and possibly have distorted views of others (Exner, 1986).

19. Pure H (Conceptions of People)   If the number of Pure H responses is less than half the total number of human contents, it suggests the person's perceptions of people are based largely on nonreal (distorted) rather than real experiences (Exner, 1986). As the number of Pure H increases, the likelihood also increases that the person's knowledge and experience of social interaction are based on real experience. Within nonpatient adults, the proportion of Pure H is from one-half to two-thirds of all human contents (the mean is approximately three). The proportion is slightly less for children (8 to 13 years), with their proportions ranging from one-half to one-third of all human contents (Exner, 1986). Patient groups generally have lower means and proportions.

20. (H) + (Hd):(A) + (Ad)   This ratio combines and compares aspects of parenthesized content and, as such, Exner (1986) has described it as an index of possible detachment from reality. Whereas it is frequent for the left side of the ratio to be higher than the right (1:0 or 2:1), a higher right side or high combined total score (greater than three) can indicate significant misinterpretation and detachment from social interaction (Exner, 1986).

21. H + A:Hd + Ad   The general significance of human and animal responses has been discussed under the Contents section. However, the H + A:Hd + Ad ratio calls attention to the relative proportion of total whole human and animal versus the total human detail and animal detail responses. This is important to note since a high number of either human or animal detail responses is unusual. Nonpatient adults will typically have a ratio of 4:1, whereas patients with clear paranoid features will have 50% or more of their responses on the right side. Although a high proportion of contents on the right side does not necessarily indicate paranoia, it does suggest that the person perceives his or her interactions with others in an unusual manner (Exner, 1986).

RECOMMENDED READING

Exner, J. E. (1978). *The Rorschach: A comprehensive system: Vol. 2. Current research and advanced interpretation.* New York: John Wiley & Sons.

Exner, J. E. (1986). *The Rorschach: A comprehensive system: Vol. 1. Basic foundations* (2nd ed.). New York: John Wiley & Sons.

Exner, J. E., & Weiner, I. (1982). *The Rorschach: A comprehensive system: Vol. 3. Assessment of children and adolescents.* New York: John Wiley & Sons.

Wiener-Levy, D. & Exner, J. E. (1981). The Rorschach Comprehensive System: An overview. In P. McReynolds (Ed.), *Advances in psychological assessment Vol. 5.* San Francisco: Jossey-Bass.

Chapter 10

THE THEMATIC APPERCEPTION TEST

The Thematic Apperception Test (TAT) is a projective technique consisting of a series of pictures, in which the examinee is requested to create a story about what he or she believes is occurring in the events depicted by the pictures. The test was originally published in 1938 by Murray and his colleagues at the Harvard Psychological Clinic. Murray (1943) describes the TAT as:

> (a) method of revealing to the trained interpreter some of the dominant drives, emotions, sentiments, complexes, and conflicts of personality. Special value resides in its power to expose underlying inhibited tendencies which the subject is not willing to admit, or cannot admit because he is unconscious of them. (p. 1)

It is different from either projective drawings or inkblot-type tests such as the Rorschach or Holtzman in that the TAT cards present more structured stimuli and require more organized and complex verbal responses. In addition, the TAT relies on more qualitative methods of interpretation and assesses the "here and now" features of an individual's life situation rather than the basic underlying structure of personality. Since its origin, the TAT has become one of the more extensively used psychological tools in clinical practice and has also served as a model for the development of similar techniques.

The TAT materials consist of 20 cards with ambiguous pictures on them. The examinee is instructed to make up a story that includes a description of what is occurring in the picture, the thoughts and feelings of the characters, the events that led up to the situation, and the outcome of the story. The examiner can interpret the responses either quantitatively (using rating scales to measure intensity, duration, and frequency of needs) or qualitatively (evaluating the story themes using clinical judgment). The final results can be an important adjunct and supplement to other psychological tests since the TAT produces highly rich, varied, and complex types of information as well as personal data that theoretically bypasses a subject's conscious resistances.

HISTORY AND DEVELOPMENT

The TAT was first conceptualized in a 1935 article by Christina Morgan and Henry Murray but was later more fully elaborated in 1938 and 1943. Administrators were instructed to present all 20 cards in a given sequence in two separate sessions that, in total, could last up to two hours. The basic assumption was that a person's unconscious fantasies could be revealed by interpreting stories he or she told regarding ambiguous pictures. It potentially gave access to things that a client was either unwilling to tell or unconscious of. Initially, it was believed that the material derived from the test could serve as an "X-ray" of personality and reveal basic themes regarding the person, which might otherwise take months of psychoanalysis to understand. The TAT immediately received an enthusiastic reception and quickly became both a clinical instrument and research tool. By 1950, several books and over 100 articles were published either on or using it. The early research studies using the TAT investigated such areas as social attitudes, delinquency, abnormal personality, and variations in the use of language. By the late 1940s, many clinicians were using a limited number of cards and abbreviated scoring systems to reduce the time required for administration and scoring. These different TAT systems were elaborated in Shneidman's (1951) *Thematic Test Analysis.*

By 1971, over 1,800 articles had been written using the TAT yet, despite the extensive research, it is today still not considered to have achieved near the degree of standardization as the MMPI or WAIS-R. There is no clear, agreed-upon scoring and interpretive system, and controversy continues regarding the adequacy of its reliability and validity. Usually, clinicians vary the methods of administration, especially regarding the number, sequence, and types of cards that are given (Haynes & Peltier, 1985). As a result, the TAT is considered to be a highly impressionistic tool with interpretation frequently coming from a combination of intuition and clinical experience. Despite this, the TAT continues to be extremely popular and ranks as the seventh most frequently used test (Lubin et al. 1985). Fully 51% of psychologists in juvenile forensic settings reported using it (Haynes & Peltier, 1985). Also, the TAT was the projective test most frequently mentioned by clinical program directors as one that trainee psychologists should be familiar with (Piotrowski & Keller, 1984). Furthermore, it has been used in many countries, including all European countries, Australia, India, South Africa, China, South American and Asian countries, and the Soviet Union. The TAT (or TAT-type tests) has also been found to be the most frequently used assessment device for cross-cultural research (Retief, 1987).

A number of researchers were dissatisfied with the TAT because they wanted to study different populations (children, the elderly, minorities), specific problem areas (frustration, stress, social judgment), or felt that the TAT produced negative, low-energy stories. These concerns stimulated numerous variations. The most common is the Children's Apperception Test (CAT; Bellak, 1986, 1954) designed for children from age 3 to 10. Only ten cards are given, and animals are depicted instead of humans. Subsequently, another version of the CAT was developed that depicted humans instead of animals (CAT-Human or CAT-H). The rationale for using ten cards was that children have shorter attention spans and therefore should be given fewer cards. It was also believed that children could more easily identify with pictures of animals rather than humans. Both the Gerontological Apperception Test (Wolk & Wolk, 1971) and the more frequently used Senior Apperception Test (SAT; Bellak, 1975, 1986; Bellak & Bellak, 1973) are designed for elderly populations and show pictures of elderly people involved in scenes more likely to concern them, such as loneliness and family conflicts. The Tell Me A Story Test (TEMAS; Costantino, Malgady, & Rogler, 1988; Malgady, Costantino, & Rogler, 1984) is designed for use with minorities and includes 23 cards depicting Hispanic and black characters in situations of interpersonal conflict. There is also a parallel version of the TEMAS for nonminorities. Scoring of all versions of the TEMAS is made for nine different personality functions (aggression, anxiety, etc.) and has been found to effectively discriminate between outpatients and normal school children (Costantino, Malgady, Rogler, & Tsui, 1988).

Several TAT-type tests have been designed to study specific problem areas. The Rosenzweig Picture Frustration Study (Rosenzweig, 1976, 1977, 1978) was designed to more fully understand how persons perceive and deal with frustration. The Stress Tolerance Test is an older test that may begin to be used more frequently in understanding how a subject responds to stressful scenes of combat (Harrower, 1986). More recently, Caruso (1988) has developed a series of TAT-type cards to study the presence of and dynamics involved in child abuse. Three sets of cards are available, including the basic set of 25 cards depicting scenes pulling for possible child abuse, a 10-card set for neglect, and 5 cards to assess attitudes toward different courtroom themes. The Blacky Pictures Test (Blum, 1950, 1962, 1968) is another thematic-type test that is closely aligned to psychoanalytic theory. It presents to children pictures of a dog named Blacky who is involved in situations consistent with psychoanalytic theory, such as themes surrounding oral, anal, and phallic stages of development.

Ritzler, Sharkey, and Chudy (1980) have criticized the TAT for producing negative, low-energy stories and containing outdated pictures that are difficult for persons to identify with. To counter this, they developed the Southern Mississippi TAT (SM-TAT) using pictures derived from the *Family of Man* (Steichen, 1955) photo collection. They report that use of the SM-TAT pictures produces stories with more activity, greater emotional tone, and relatively few variations in thematic content (Sharkey & Ritzler, 1985). More importantly, the results derived from the SM-TAT were more effective than the TAT at discriminating different pathological groups. Depressives produced gloomy stories and psychotics demonstrated more perceptual distortions when compared with normals. Even though the SM-TAT is more modern, is based on a more rigorous methodology, and demonstrates greater diagnostic validity, the long tradition and extensive research associated with the TAT may make it difficult for the TAT to be supplanted.

In addition to the TAT's derivatives, a number of different approaches to scoring and interpreting the TAT itself have been developed. The original approach by Murray involves assessing which character in the story is the "hero," or focal figure, and then using a five-point scale to quantify the relative intensity of each expressed need. Murray's approach also includes measuring the forces of the hero/heroine's environment (press), types of outcomes, basic themes (thema), and interests and sentiments of the hero/heroine. Many variations of Murray's system have been developed by such authors as Arnold (1962), Bellak (1975, 1986), Chusmir, (1985), Dana (1955), Eron (1950), McClelland (1971), Thomas and Dudek (1985), and Wyatt (1949). The extensive diversity of different systems led Murstein, in his 1963 review of the TAT, to remark, "There would seem to be as many thematic scoring systems as there were hairs in the beard of Rasputin" (p. 23). Despite this, there is no one clearly preferred method. This chapter will focus primarily on Murray's original approach since it is both the original and most frequently used of the systems (Vane, 1981).

MURRAY'S THEORY OF PERSONALITY

The TAT is so integrally involved with Murray's concepts of personality that a survey of his basic theory is important. In constructing his theory, Murray emphasized the biological basis as well as the social and environmental determinants of behavior. He was also consistently aware of how individuals interact with their environment. This interaction includes how people are affected by external forces and how their unique set of needs, attitudes, and values influences their reaction to the world around them.

Perhaps more than any other theorist, Murray has analyzed and clarified the concept of needs. This has been the focus of his conceptual efforts, and the development of the TAT grew from his attempt to evaluate and assess the relative strength of the individual's specific psychological needs. Murray (1938) defined a need as:

> ...a construct which stands for a force...which organizes perception, apperception, intellectualization, connotation and action in such a way as to transform in a certain direction an existing, unsatisfying situation. Thus, it manifests itself by leading the organism to search for, or to avoid encountering, or when encountered, to attend and respond to certain kinds of press (environmental forces).... Each need is characteristically accompanied by a particular feeling or emotion and tends to use certain modes ... to further its ends. (pp. 123-124)

A need can either be provoked by internal processes or, more frequently, can be the result of specific environmental events, as shown in Table 10–1.

Table 10–1.   Murray's list of needs

A. Needs Motivated by Desire for Power, Property, Prestige, Knowledge, or Creative Achievement

1. n Achievement
2. n Acquisition
3. n Aggression
4. n Construction
5. n Counteraction
6. n Dominance
7. n Exposition
8. n Recognition
9. n Understanding

B. Needs Motivated by Affection, Admiration, Sympathy, Love, and Dependence

1. n Affiliation
2. n Deference
3. n Nurturance
4. n Sex
5. n Succorance

C. Needs Motivated by a Desire for Freedom, Change, Excitement, and Play

1. n Autonomy
2. n Change, Travel, Adventure
3. n Excitance, Dissipation
4. n Playmirth

D. Miscellaneous Needs

1. n Abasement
2. n Blame Avoidance
3. n Cognizance
4. n Harm Avoidance
5. n Passivity
6. n Rejection
7. n Retention
8. n Sentience

Note: Adapted from Murray (1938, pp. 152-226).

Although Murray makes a variety of distinctions among different types of needs, the most important is between primary or viscerogenic needs and secondary or psychogenic ones. Primary needs are linked to physiological events and are innate to each individual. They typically refer to physical satisfactions and can be illustrated by the need for air, water, food, or sex. Secondary needs are originally derived from primary needs and are acquired during the process of psychological development. They generally lack a strong connection to biological processes and are psychological in nature. Examples are needs for affiliation, achievement, recognition, dominance, autonomy, and acquisition.

Although it simplifies understanding to consider needs separately, in reality they do not function in isolation from one another. Rather, they interact with one another to create areas of mutual influence and effect. For example, needs may be in *conflict* with one another, as when a need for power is antagonistic to a need for affiliation, or a need for achievement is in opposition with a need for pleasure. There may also be a *fusion* of needs, in which separate needs such as power and achievement produce the same behaviors. Finally, there may be a *subsidization* of needs, in which one need is subsidized by, or works for, another. For example, an individual may express a high degree of aggressiveness, which is actually working to support an underlying need for acquisition.

When Murray uses the term "need," he refers to the significant determinants of behavior that reside in an individual. In contrast, "press" refers to the environmental determinants that elicit specific behaviors from an individual or constellate specific needs within him or her (see Table 10–2). "The press of an object is what it can do to the subject or for the subject—the power that it has to affect the well-being of the subject in one way or another" (Murray, 1938, p. 121). Murray conceptualizes press as either alpha or beta. Beta press refers to the individual's perceptions and interpretations of a specific aspect of the environment, and alpha press refers to the objective or real aspects of that environment. Most behaviors are a direct result of beta press, but it is important to be aware of the wide discrepancies between an individual's subjective interpretation of the world and the world as it actually is. A striking example of such a discrepancy is the delusional systems of paranoid patients who consistently distort external reality as a result of their inner psychological processes.

To conceptualize units of behavior that result from the interaction between needs and press, Murray developed the term *thema*. A thema is a small unit of behavior that can combine with other thema to form a *serial thema*. An individual's *unity thema* is the pattern of related needs and press that gives meaning to the largest portion of his or her behavior. For example, a core and overriding feature of an individual might be rebelliousness or martyrdom. This may be sufficiently well organized and powerful enough to override even primary needs, as amply demonstrated in the case of a martyr who is willing to die for his or her beliefs. A unity thema is derived from early infantile experiences and, once developed, repeats itself in many forms during an individual's later life. It operates largely as an unconscious force, and Murray (1938) described it as " ... a compound of interrelated—collaborating or conflicting—dominant needs that are linked to press to which the individual was exposed to on one or more particular occasions, gratifying or traumatic, in early childhood" (pp. 604-605). The TAT was designed to assess both small units of thema and the larger, core aspects of an individual's unity thema.

Figure 10–1 is a summary of the basic elements of Murray's theory. These elements are relatively simple and straightforward, but the specific details are complicated and comprehensive. The details include not only an extensive enumeration of a wide variety of needs and press, but also takes into account the complexities of their interactions.

In summary, Murray's theory is not a comprehensive understanding of personality but rather a listing and description of the various types and interactions among different needs. He also focuses on motivational aspects of the person, with tension reduction being the central theme to explain the individual's external behavior. Although these contributions are significant, the main achievement of Murray has been the development of the TAT, which is a direct result of his theories and has been used to provide support for them.

Table 10–2.   Murray's list of press

A. Press of Deprivation

   1. p Acquisition
   2. p Retention

B. Press Descriptive of an Empty, Alien, or Rejecting Environment

   1. p Lack
   2. p Loss
   3. p Rejection
   4. p Uncongenial Environment

C. Press of Coercion and Restraint

   1. p Dominance
   2. p Imposed Task, Duty, Training

D. Press Descriptive of a Hostile, Aggressive Environment

   1. p Aggression

E. Press of Danger, Injury, Death

   1. p Affliction
   2. p Death of Hero
   3. p Physical Danger
   4. p Physical Injury

F. Press of Friendliness, Sympathy, Respect, Dependence, Love

   1. p Affiliation
   2. p Deference
   3. p Nurturance
   4. p Sex
   5. p Succorance

G. Miscellaneous Press

   1. p Birth of Offspring
   2. p Claustrum
   3. p Cognizance
   4. p Example
   5. p Exposition
   6. p Luck

Note: Adapted from Murray (1938, pp. 152-226).

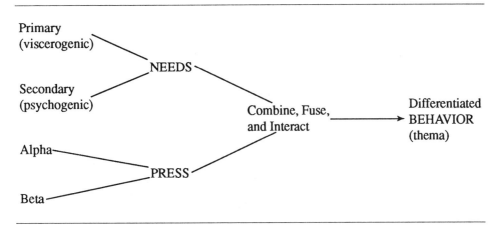

Figure 10–1.   Outline of Murray's theory of personality

RELIABILITY AND VALIDITY

The responses a subject makes to the TAT involve complex, meaningful verbal material. Due to the complexity of this material, exact quantitative analysis is difficult, and interpretations are typically based more on a qualitative analysis of story content. This makes most methods of determining reliability problematic. However, the development of quantitative scoring strategies and rating scales has led to some success in achieving adequate interscorer reliability. This is especially true for the work of McClelland (1961) and Atkinson and Feather (1966), all of whom developed complex scoring schemes for achievement, affiliation, and power. The interscorer reliability across different scoring systems has generally been found to be good, ranging from .37 to .90—with most reports in the higher ranges (Murstein, 1972). However, even though scorers can agree on the quantitative values assigned to different variables, these values still do not constitute conclusions but are, rather, raw data. In other words, it remains questionable whether clinicians will make the same inferences regarding personality based on the quantitative scores. Whereas good interscorer reliability has been achieved for such areas as the weighting of different needs, agreement between the conclusions based on these scores has typically not been adequately demonstrated. This is further complicated by the fact that, in actual practice, clinicians rely primarily on intuitive clinical judgment, use different sets of instructions, and vary the number, type, and sequence of cards from one client to the next (Haynes & Peltier, 1985). Thus, reliability in clinical contexts is likely to be considerably lower than under experimental conditions.

Another difficulty in determining reliability lies in the wide variability among different stories. If test evaluators wish to determine the internal consistency of the TAT, they are confronted with the fact that the various cards are not comparable (Entwisle, 1972). They were designed to measure separate areas of a person's functioning. Thus, a strategy such as split half reliability is inappropriate. Not only are different stories in the same administration likely to be different, but so are the stories between two different administrations. Thus, measures of temporal stability have been (and would be expected to be) low (Entwisle, 1972). Likewise, when subjects were requested to tell different stories on different administrations, the test-retest reliabilities derived from quantitative scorings of various needs were low (Lindzey & Herman, 1955). In contrast, Lundy (1985) found that, when subjects were requested to tell a similar story between one administration and the next, test-retest reliabilities achieved a respectable .56 (need for affiliation) and .48 (need for achievement). This suggests that the test-retest reliability of the TAT might be underestimated. However, the higher reliabilities found by Lundy (1985) might also reflect merely the quality of memory rather than the stability of personality variables as measured on the TAT (Kraiger, Hakel, & Cornelius, 1984).

Reviews of the TAT's validity have shown wide variability. Proponents of the test use terms like "impressive" and "strong" relationships, whereas critics have said that validity is "almost nonexistent." This can be partially accounted for by differing interpretations of the data. One reviewer might be impressed by a correlation of .45, which another might see as highly deficient. It would seem that not only is the TAT itself a projective test, but the research done on it likewise allows readers to project their biases, needs, and expectations onto it. One factor that might help explain the differences in results among studies is that the TAT has been found to be quite sensitive to the effects of instructions. Lundy (1988), for example, found that, under nonthreatening, neutral, and unstructured conditions, there were moderate correlations between outside criterion measures and needs for achievement, affiliation, and power. When instructions were used that presented the TAT as a structured formal test, especially if any words were used that might be interpreted as threatening (will "reveal imperfections" or "minor defects"), the correlations were nonsignificant. This suggests the interesting possibility that the wide variation in the findings of different studies may have been partially influenced by slight variations in instructions. This might also suggest that the differing correlations were due to faking. The threatening instructions could have increased subjects' motivations to fake good, thereby resulting in low correlations with external behavior. In contrast, the neutral instructions would have decreased the likelihood of faking with the result that correlations between TAT scores and external behavior were positive.

Studies attempting to determine criterion validity have shown a balance between positive and negative findings. One major problem lies in establishing agreed-upon external criteria. If overt behavior is used as the criterion, there is often little correspondence with test scores. For example, high aggression on TAT scores usually does not reflect the degree to which a person actually expresses aggressive behavior. However, it may still be valuable to understand a person's internal processes even though these are not outwardly expressed. When measures of needs on the TAT were compared with needs measured on such tests as the Edwards Personal Preference Schedule and the Adjective Check List, there was also little correspondence (Megargee & Parker, 1968). The above findings would seem to call into question the usefulness of TAT protocols. However, a number of positive findings have also been reported between the TAT and outside criteria. An early and frequently cited study by Harrison (1940) found that diagnosis by a trained clinician using the TAT was accurate 75% of the time when assessing broad diagnostic categories. Similarly, a correlation of .78 was found when comparing TAT inferences with data from hospital records. The most extensively studied constructs have been achievement, affiliation, and power (Lundy, 1988), and these, too, have had varying degrees of success when compared with outside criteria. Examples of recent positive results include a high need for achievement being associated with greater social attractiveness (Teevan, Diffenderfer, & Greenfield, 1986), need for affiliation being positively correlated with a preference for an internally directed orientation to tasks (Schroth, 1987), and need for achievement being positively related to grade point average (although this might have been confounded by verbal fluency; Lindgren, Moritsch, Thurlin, & Mich, 1986). Although a number of studies have not found a relationship between TAT scores and objective tests, Coche and Sillitti (1983) reported that the presence of depressive themes on the TAT was correlated with measures of depression on the MMPI and Beck Depression Inventory. Finally, the fantasies of highly effective executives differed significantly from relatively ineffective executives in that the more effective executives had more original themes, expressed a broader range of interests, were more intellectual, and could see beyond the individual details of their work (Maitra, 1983).

Similar to studies on criterion validity, the work on construct validity has shown varying results. A representative confirmatory study supported the hypothesis that subjects who were experimentally frustrated produced subsequent stories in which the focal characters in the stories expressed increased aggression (Lindzey & Kalnins, 1958). Likewise, persons who had used marijuana prior to testing showed an increase in primary process content in their stories (West, Martindale, Hines, & Roth, 1983).

An important issue in the interpretation of criterion validity studies on the TAT and other projective devices lies in understanding the implications of different levels of interpretation. Klopfer (1983) has summarized the earlier work of Leary (1956) by indicating that behavior can be based on outside observations (direct behavioral data, public communication), self-descriptions, or private symbolization. These three levels are often quite different from one another. For example, the observations by others are frequently quite discrepant from how a particular person perceives him- or herself. Likewise, a person's inner fantasy life (private symbolization) is often quite different from his or her public behavior. Projective tests such as the TAT primarily assess a person's inner life of private symbolization. Thus, it might be expected that this inner life would not relate to outside behavioral criterion measures. Furthermore, it may not even be desirable that TAT data relates to external behavior since this ability to access a person's inner life is precisely what makes projectives both unique and valuable. From a practical perspective, clinicians need to evaluate the above issue as well as establish the importance they place on having access to a person's inner world of private symbolization.

One argument against subjecting the TAT to strict psychometric scrutiny is that rigid objective studies do not represent the way in which the TAT is actually used in clinical practice. When experienced clinicians were requested to provide individual descriptions of persons based on TAT stories, the descriptions did tend to match independent descriptions based on case histories (Arnold, 1949; Harrison, 1940). However, even though the descriptions by individual clinicians were fairly accurate, there was usually little agreement among different clinicians evaluating the same person. It might be argued that, because of the complexity and richness of the material, each clinician was tapping into different aspects of the same person. The poor interrater reliability might not represent inaccuracy, but rather different approaches to the material, with each of these approaches having potentially relevant meanings for the client being evaluated.

ASSETS AND LIMITATIONS

Despite questions related to reliability and validity, the status of the TAT over the past 20 years has remained essentially unchanged (Lubin et al., 1985). It is still rated as the seventh most frequently used test and has produced the third largest number of research studies (behind the MMPI and Rorschach). One reviewer has summarized the incongruity between its popularity and its questionable validity by stating that "there are still enthusiastic clinicians and doubting statisticians" (Adcock, 1965). Considering this controversy, it is especially important that clinicians fully understand the general assets and limitations involved with the TAT.

Like most projective techniques, the TAT is potentially a valuable tool. Theoretically, it offers access to the covert and deeper structures of an individual's personality. There is also less susceptibility to faking than on many objective tests since the purpose of the projective techniques is usually disguised, and the subject often slackens his or her conscious defenses while releasing unconscious material. However, since the TAT deals with verbally familiar material, the potential is somewhat greater for the subject to bias and distort his or her responses when compared with other projective techniques such as the Rorschach. A further asset is that the TAT focuses on the global nature of personality rather than on the objective measurement of specific traits or attitudes. This focus includes not only emotional, motivational, and interpersonal characteristics, but also general intellectual level, verbal fluency, originality, and style of solving problems. A final advantage of the TAT involves ease of rapport. Most projective tests are regarded as intrinsically interesting and nonthreatening since there are no "wrong" answers. However, certain types of individuals might still feel quite anxious and insecure with the lack of structure of projective techniques.

In contrast to these assets, the following general criticisms have been leveled at projective techniques and therefore must be considered when using the TAT. There has typically been difficulty establishing adequate internal consistency and test-retest reliability. Inadequate normative data is generally lacking, with the result that clinicians often rely on clinical experience to interpret the responses. Standardization in administration and scoring is generally inadequate. Thus the effectiveness of the technique is often more dependent on the clinician's individual skill rather than on the quality of the test itself. Most studies on projectives, as well as the results coming from individual assessments, are confounded by age, sex, intelligence, and reading ability (Klein, 1986). Projectives have also been shown to be quite sensitive to situational variables, such as mood (McFarland, 1984), stress, sleep deprivation, and differences in instruction (Lundy, 1988). These variables can significantly alter test performance, thereby reducing the likelihood that stable aspects of personality are being measured. Finally, the validity studies on most projectives have been equivocal and, in particular, several researchers have found no increases in incremental validity when the TAT and most other projectives are used in a battery of tests (see Garb, 1985; Klein, 1986; Lanyon & Goodstein, 1982).

These general considerations must be understood when using projective techniques. However, a number of characteristics specific to the TAT should also be kept in mind. One important asset of the TAT is that the responses it produces from clients' (verbal stories) are familiar rather than hidden and mysterious. Even a relatively untrained person can appreciate the differing themes, moods, and perspectives portrayed in the stories. The experienced clinician also profits from this inherent familiarity or approachability of the test data.

A further asset of the TAT is its origin within an academic-humanistic environment. It is not closely aligned within any particular school of thought and therefore can be approached from, and interpreted by, a number of different theoretical orientations. Furthermore, the TAT was developed from the study of normal individuals rather than by case studies or normative comparisons with disordered populations. This orientation has evolved directly out of Murray's belief that the proper starting point for understanding personality is the intensive and detailed study of normal persons.

The TAT potentially provides a comprehensive evaluation of personality, which has sometimes been referred to as a "wide-band" approach (Rabin, 1968). For example, among the comprehensive dimensions that the TAT can assess are a person's cognitive style, imaginative processes, family dynamics, inner adjustment, emotional reactivity, general intelligence, and sexual adjustment (Bellak, 1986; Henry, 1956). The TAT also has some potential for evaluating such areas as creativity, level of affect, problem solving skill, and verbal fluency. Thus, although the primary use for the TAT is to provide insight into a person's fundamental needs and patterns of interaction, it can also provide important information about a far wider range of areas. In particular, the TAT may bypass conscious resistance to provide themes about the person that he or she may not reveal upon direct questioning. For example, alcoholics who reported high levels of internal locus of control on direct self-report questionnaires typically became highly externally oriented when locus of control was measured using a TAT-type instrument (Costello & Wicott, 1984). This might suggest that the TAT-type test bypasses their conscious denial and assesses a possibly more accurate, or at least different, level of private symbolization.

Although the TAT is potentially quite versatile, it is not self-sufficient, and a number of authors have emphasized that the TAT yields optimal results only when included in a battery of tests (Anastasi, 1988) and/or as a type of structured clinical interview (Obrzut & Cummings, 1983). In contrast to this, some reviewers have pointed out that the TAT and other projective tests do not help increase incremental validity in structured conditions and may even serve to reduce it (Garb, 1985; Klein, 1986).

One unresolved dispute with the TAT involves the relationship between inner fantasies and overt behavior. Most projective test originators, including Murray, have assumed that fantasy productions can be used to predict covert motivational dispositions. However, it is questionable whether high fantasy production in a certain area actually does reflect parallel overt behavior (Klinger, 1966; McClelland, 1966; Skolnick, 1966). In fact, fantasies may even serve to compensate for a lack of certain behaviors. It might be quite consistent for a highly repressed, overcontrolled person to have a high number of inner aggressive fantasies. In a 20-year longitudinal study of adolescents who obtained high TAT scores on need for achievement, these adolescents were often not among those who subsequently showed upward social mobility (McClelland, 1966). However, individuals who had shown upward social mobility typically obtained higher TAT need-for-achievement scores as adults. The interpretive significance of this: it might be better to consider fantasy productions as samples of thoughts that may or may not accurately predict overt behavior.

Practical difficulties associated with the TAT are the extensive amount of training required to properly learn the technique and its relatively poor cost-effectiveness in terms of the time required for administration and scoring (Haynes & Peltier, 1985). This is largely because the TAT does not lend itself to a manageable scoring system. Obtaining biographical information, asking direct questions during an interview, or using rating forms or questionnaires might yield the same or similar information in a simpler, quicker manner. Many clinicians feel that a projective test such as the Rorschach is both more efficient and less susceptible to faking than the TAT.

A further liability, which is particularly relevant for the TAT, is the subjectivity involved in both scoring and interpretation procedures. Although the various scoring methods have attempted to reduce the degree of subjectivity, intuitive judgment necessarily plays a significant role. This results in part from an inadequate development of norms, and the norms that have been created are only a rough approximation to common story themes (see section on Typical Themes Elicited). In clinical practice, individual clinicians frequently develop their own intuitive norms based on past experience. Thus, a clinician may have a general intuitive conception of what constitutes a "schizophrenic" or "narcissistic" story and will use this subjective image during diagnostic or interpretive procedures. This reliance on clinical experience is indirectly encouraged both by the lack of precise normative data and, more importantly, by the belief that norms tend to decrease the richness and comprehensiveness of the material being studied. A possible source of bias is that, since clinicians work predominantly with pathology, their firsthand experience of the characteristic reactions of normal people on tests such as the TAT is limited. Due to this lack of experience, clinicians may overemphasize the pathological features of stories and may have difficulty assessing fairly well-adjusted persons.

ADMINISTRATION

General Considerations

The TAT was intended to be administered in an interpersonal setting in which subjects verbally respond to pictures presented to them. However, when the examiner is absent, responses may be taped or written out by the individual him- or herself. The disadvantage of these latter procedures is that the subject's responses are often more contrived and cliché, since more time is available to censor fantasy material.

The TAT materials consist of 20 cards with ambiguous pictures on them. The cards are numbered so that a total of 20 cards can be presented to four different groups: males, females, boys, and girls, respectively. Thus, the back of each card is coded with a number and/or letters to designate which sex and/or age group the card is intended for. A number without a letter indicates the card is to be administered to all subjects, regardless of age or sex. A number with M or F designates that the card is intended for males or females, and B or G designates boys or girls, respectively. There may also be a number and either BM or GF indicating the card is to be given to boys/males or girls/females.

Some controversy exists in determining whether all 20 cards should be administered or a shorter version of selected cards. In actual practice, it is far more frequent to administer between 8 and 12 cards (Bellak, 1986; Dana, 1985; Haynes & Peltier, 1985). If less than 20 cards are administered, the selection of cards may be idiosyncratic to the patient's presenting problem or based on previous information derived from relevant history or other test data. For example, if depression and suicide are significant issues for the client, the examiner might administer cards 3BM, 13B, and 14 in an attempt to gather specific information on the dynamics of the client's condition. Specific cards may also be selected because they typically produce rich responses. Bellak (1986) reports that the best cards for adult males are 1, 2, 3BM, 4, 6BM, 7BM, 11, 12M, and 13MF. He further recommends that the best cards for adult females are 1, 2, 3BM, 4, 6GF, 7GF, 9GF, 11, and 13MF. If fewer cards are given, it may be preferable to give the cards in the sequence numbered in back, although Murstein (1963) presents evidence to suggest that the stimulus values of the cards themselves overshadow any effects produced as a result of altered sequencing. Dana (1985) urges that, if the TAT is the only means of assessment, or if the results of an assessment might be used in court proceedings, then all 20 cards should be administered. If the entire 20-card set is used, the cards should be administered in two separate sessions since clients can rarely continue for more than an hour without becoming fatigued and losing interest.

The subject should be seated beside the examiner, with his or her chair turned away so that the expressions on the examiner's face cannot be seen. Ideally, this creates a situation in which the subject is comfortable and relaxed so that his or her imagination can freely respond to the cards. However, some individuals do not feel comfortable when turned away from the examiner, in which case they should be allowed to sit in a position that is more relaxing for them. It is of primary importance to establish adequate rapport and to ensure that the subject is comfortable and relaxed.

Instructions

Murray's original instructions from the TAT Manual (1943) are as follows:

> This is a test of imagination, one form of intelligence. I am going to show you some pictures, one at a time; and your task will be to make up as dramatic a story as you can for each. Tell what has led up to the event shown in the picture, describe what is happening at the moment, what the characters are feeling and thinking; and then give the outcome. Speak your thoughts as they come to your mind. Do you understand? Since you have fifty minutes for ten pictures, you can devote about five minutes to each story. Here is the first picture. (p.3)

This set of instructions is suitable for adolescents and adults of average intelligence and sophistication. However, the instructions should be modified for children, adults with minimal education or intelligence, and psychotics. For these types of individuals, Murray (1943) suggests that the examiner state the following:

> This is a story-telling test. I have some pictures here that I am going to show you, and for each picture I want you to make up a story. Tell what is happening before and what is happening now. Say what the people are feeling and thinking and how it will come out. You can make up any story you please. Do you understand? Well, then, here is the first picture. You have five minutes to make up a story. See how well you can do. (pp. 3-4)

Such instructions may, of course, be modified, elaborated, or repeated to meet the individual needs of each subject. Lundy (1988) recommends that the instructions should be given in as neutral and nonthreatening a manner as possible so that the person does not become defensive, which would be likely to reduce the validity of the results. The clinician should even avoid referring to the TAT as a "test." However, the instructions should clearly encourage the client to use his or her imagination and not merely provide a description of the pictures. Variations on the instructions should also emphasize the four requirements of the story structure:

1. Current situation
2. Thoughts and feelings of the characters
3. Preceding events
4. Outcome

The instructions, either in whole or in part, may be repeated at any time, particularly if the subject has given a story that is too short or too long, or if he or she has left out one or more of the four requirements. Hurley and Sovner (1985) suggest that the TAT can potentially be excellent for the evaluation of mentally retarded persons, but that particular care needs to be taken to ensure that the instructions are concrete and explicit. The examiner may also want to check to ensure that the instructions have been clearly understood and may need to encourage the person at various times during the story telling.

Procedure

Time   Measurement of the time should begin when the picture is first presented and end when the subject begins his or her story. It is particularly important to notice any long pauses or hesitations, since these may reflect a struggle with conflictual or anxiety-laden material.

Recording   The subject's complete responses should be recorded, as well as any note-worthy behavioral observations. These may include exclamations, stuttering, pauses, blushing, degree of involvement, and changes in voice inflection. Thus, the general purpose of recording is not only to develop a reproduction of the verbatim story content, but to assess how the person interacts with the picture. As mentioned previously, ongoing verbal involvement with the cards is the preferable form of administration. Subjects would have time to critically evaluate and censor their responses if they were allowed to write the story on paper. There is no objection to the use of a tape recorder, although under such conditions it is also helpful to have the examiner record noteworthy behavioral observations and obtain the client's written consent.

Questioning and Inquiry   If a subject omits certain aspects of the story, such as the outcome or preceding events, the examiner should ask for additional information. Appropriate questions might be, "What led up to it?" or "How does it end?" However, these requests for clarification or amplification should not be stated in a way that could bias the stories or reveal the examiner's personal reaction. A more detailed inquiry may be undertaken either after the entire administration of the cards or directly after each story, although Murray recommends that the inquiry should occur only after the administration of all the cards. Sample inquiry questions may include, "What made you think of this story?" or "Do people you have mentioned in the story remind you of friends or acquaintances?" As with questioning, the inquiry should not be too forceful since this may produce defensiveness and withdrawal. The overall purpose of both the questioning and the inquiry is to produce an unhampered and free flow of the subject's fantasy material.

Order of Presentation   Usually, the cards should be administered according to the sequential numbering system. However, at times, the examiner may be interested in a specific problem and will therefore alter the sequence to more effectively obtain information concerning that problem area. For example, if the clinician is particularly interested in problems relating to family constellation in a male subject, the examiner might include some of the female series involving sisters, girlfriends, or wives. It is often helpful to include a sprinkling of "neutral" cards along with cards selected to indicate the presence of a specific conflict. This serves to ease the tension that may otherwise result from a constant confrontation with potentially conflictual stimuli.

Use of the TAT (or CAT) with Children   Instructions for children should, of course, be modified in accordance with their age and vocabulary. It is usually helpful to describe the test as an opportunity to tell stories or as an interesting game. In general, selection of cards from the TAT should be based on the likelihood and ease with which children may identify with the characters. The TAT cards that are appropriate for use with children and that have the highest number of interpretable responses and the lowest number of refusals, enumeration, or description are, in order of usefulness, 7GF, 18GF, 3GF, and 8GF (Bellak, 1986). In contrast, the least helpful are cards 19, 18BM, 11, and 12BG (Bellak, 1986).

It should be kept in mind that the stories of children are relatively easily influenced by recent events—such as those experienced through television, comic books, and movies. Children also tend to project their problems and conflicts into a story in a more direct and straightforward manner than adults. Often, there is little hidden meaning or masking of the relationships involved.

TYPICAL THEMES ELICITED

At the present time, no formal, normative standards have been developed for the TAT. However, a knowledge of the typical stories elicited by each of the cards and possible significant variations from the more frequent plots can serve to alert the examiner to unique—and therefore more easily interpretable—types of stories. Deviations from cliché or stereotypical responses may be significant because they might represent important areas of conflict, creative thinking, or important features of the subject's overall personality. If the clinician is equipped with expectations regarding typical versus unusual responses, it will enable him or her to:

1. More easily observe specific attitudes toward the central problem
2. Easily notice gaps where the inquiry can begin
3. Assess the type of information to which the subject shows resistance—as indicated by the use of noncommittal clichés
4. Notice any deviation from the expected information that may contain significant and interpretable responses

Both Murray's TAT cards and Bellak's original version of the CAT will be described and discussed here. The following descriptions of each TAT card are divided into three sections:

1. Description of the card's scene
2. Plots frequently encountered
3. A general discussion of the significance and overall usefulness of the card

The description of each TAT card is this author's characterization of the scene's content, while the CAT descriptions are from Bellak (1986, pp. 245-247). Unless otherwise cited, the discussion of each picture is a summary of the work of Bellak (1986), Murray (1943), and Stein (1981).

Thematic Apperception Test (TAT)

PICTURE 1

I. Description of card   A boy looking at violin on a table.

II. Frequent Plots   Typical stories emerging from this card revolve around a self-motivated boy who is daydreaming about becoming an outstanding violinist, or a rebellious boy being forced by his parents or some other significant authority figure to play the violin.

III. General Discussion   This is often considered to be the most useful picture in the entire TAT (Bellak, 1986). It usually elicits stories describing how the subject deals with the general issue of impulse versus control or, in a wider sense, the conflict between personal demands and external controlling agents. It also aids in providing information about the client's relationship with his or her parents, by making it relatively easy to see whether he or she views his or her parents as domineering, controlling, indifferent, helpful, understanding, or protecting (Bellak, 1986). This card frequently gives specific information regarding the need for achievement, and it is important to consider how any expressed achievement is accomplished.

Any variations from the frequent plots described should be taken into consideration because they are likely to provide important reflections of the subject's characteristic modes of functioning. For example, the attitude toward, and relationship with, any introduced figures, whether they are parents or peers, should be given special attention. Also of importance are the way in which the issue of impulse versus control is handled, any themes of aggression that may emerge, and particularly the specific outcome of the story.

PICTURE 2

I. Description of card   Country scene with a woman holding a book in the foreground and in the background there is a man is working a field with a woman watching.

II. Frequent Plots   Frequently encountered stories for this card involve a young girl who is leaving the farm to increase her education or to seek opportunities that her present home environment cannot provide. Usually the family is seen as working hard to gain a living from the soil. Often, the family values center on maintaining the status quo.

III. General Discussion   This picture usually provides an excellent description of family relations. As with Card 1, there are varying themes relating to autonomy from the family versus compliance with the status quo. It is one of the only cards in the series that presents the subject with a group scene and thus gives information relating to how the individual deals with the challenge of people living together. The card itself deals with a younger woman and an older male and female. Thus, it elicits stories dealing with parent-child and heterosexual relationships. Usually, an added dimension is included in which the new and the old are contrasted, and attitudes toward personal mobility and ambition are demonstrated. This card can also elicit stories relating to competition by the younger daughter for the attention of one or both of the parents. In these stories, her rivals are either siblings, particularly an older female, or the other parent. The extent to which separations or alliances occur among the three figures represented can also be quite revealing. For example, the two women may be united against the male, who is "merely a hired hand," or the older male and female may be united against the younger female. Within either of these possible formations, it is important to note the attributes of each person, and the patterns and styles of interaction with one another. Since this card is relatively complex and has a large number of details, compulsive patients often spend an inordinate amount of time commenting and elaborating on the detail.

PICTURE 3BM

I. Description of card   A boy is huddled next to a couch and on the floor next to him is a revolver.

II. Frequent Plots   The stories usually revolve around an individual who has been emotionally involved with another person or who is feeling guilty over some past behavior he has committed. Drug abusers often perceive the person in the figure as an addict and interpret the "revolver" as a hypodermic needle.

III. General Discussion   This has been identified as one of the most useful pictures (Bellak, 1986) since it evokes themes of guilt, depression, aggression, and impulse control. The manner in which the object on the left is seen and described often provides a good deal of information about problems concerning aggression. For example, if the object is described as a gun, is it used or intended to be used for intra-aggression (e.g., the subject is going to use it to do damage to him- or herself) or for extra-aggression (the subject has used it, or is going to use it, to harm another person)? If it is used for externally directed aggression, then what are the consequences, if any, for the focal figure as portrayed in the outcome? This picture is particularly important for depressed patients, regardless of whether they are male or female, since it can provide important dynamics regarding the manner in which the depression developed and how it is currently being maintained. For example, denial of aggressive conflict may be represented by completely overlooking the gun or rendering it harmless by depicting it as a toy pistol or a set of keys. On the other hand, excessive hesitation and detailed consideration of what the object might be could represent a compulsive defense surrounding conflictual aggressive feelings. Since this picture contains a lone figure, attitudes toward the isolated self are often aroused. The picture might be particularly useful for drug abusers since it frequently elicits themes and attitudes about overdosing, drug use, mechanisms for coping, self-destructive tendencies, and extent of social supports (Patalano, 1986).

PICTURE 3GF

I. Description of card   A woman is standing next to an open door with one hand grabbing the side of the door and the other holding her downcast face.

II. Frequent Plots   As with 3BM, the stories usually revolve around themes of interpersonal loss and contemplated harm directed internally due to guilt over past behavior.

III. General Discussion   The same general trends that hold for 3BM are also true for 3GF in that they both tend to bring out depressive feelings. Frequently, however, it is more useful to use 3BM, which brings out somewhat richer stories and allows both males and females to identify easily with the central figure.

PICTURE 4

I. Description of card   A woman is grabbing the shoulders of a man who is turning away from her.

II. Frequent Plots   The primary task is to form some sort of conceptualization for why the woman is restraining the man. Often, the woman is seen as the advice-giving moral agent who is struggling with the more impulsive and irrational man. In approximately half the stories, the vague picture of a woman in the background is brought into the story plot.

III. General Discussion   This picture typically elicits a good deal of information relating to the feelings and attitudes surrounding male-female relationships. Frequently, themes of infidelity and betrayal emerge, and details regarding the male attitude toward the role of women may be discussed. For example, the woman may be seen as a protector who attempts to prevent the man from becoming involved in self-destructive behavior or as a siren who tries to detain and control him for evil purposes. Likewise, a woman's attitude toward past male aggressiveness and impulsiveness may be revealed.

Yet a further area of interest is the vague picture of a seminude woman in the background. This often provokes themes of triangular jealousy in which one or more characters have been betrayed. When this picture is described, it is important to note whether the woman is depicted as a sexually threatening object or is seen as a more benign figure.

PICTURE 5

I. Description of card   A woman is looking into a room from the threshold of a door.

II. Frequent Plots   The most frequent plot is of a mother who either has caught her child misbehaving or is surprised by an intruder entering her house.

III. General Discussion   This picture often reveals information surrounding attitudes about the subject's mother in her role of observing and possibly judging behavior. It is important to note how the woman is perceived and how the situation is resolved. Is she understanding and sympathetic, does she attempt to invoke guilt, or is she seen as severely restricting the child's autonomy? Sometimes voyeuristic themes are discussed that may include feelings related to the act of observing others misbehave. The examiner should note whether these feelings include guilt, anger, indifference, or fear, and the manner in which these feelings are resolved. Often this card elicits paranoid fears of attack or intrusion from an outsider that may be represented by stories in which the woman is surprised by a burglar.

PICTURE 6BM

I. Description of card   An elderly woman is standing parallel to a window. Behind her is a younger man with his face down and holding onto his hat.

II. Frequent Plots   This picture typically elicits stories of a son who is either presenting sad news to his mother, or attempting to prepare her for his departure to some distant location.

III. General Discussion   Card 6BM is an extremely important one to include when testing males. It usually produces a rich source of information regarding attitudes and feelings toward mother or maternal figures in general. Since the stories usually revolve around a young man striving for independence, the specific manner in which the subject depicts this struggle is important. Does the struggle include an exaggerated amount of guilt, is there unexpressed or even overt anger toward the older woman, or does the young man succumb to the woman's wishes? Of equal importance is the mother's reaction to her son's behavior. To what extent does she control him, and how? It is also of interest to note whether the subject accepts the traditional mother-son version, or whether he or she chooses to avoid discussing this relationship directly. If such an avoidance is evident, how are mother-son type themes depicted in other cards that may have elicited discussions of this area (i.e., cards 1 or 5)?

PICTURE 6GF

I. Description of card   A young woman is seated and turning to see an older man with a pipe who is peering over her shoulder.

II. Frequent Plots   The man is usually seen as proposing some sort of an activity to the woman and the plot often includes her reaction to this suggestion.

III. General Discussion   This card was originally intended to be the female counterpart to 6BM, and it was hoped that it, too, would elicit attitudes and feelings toward paternal figures. However, since the two figures are often seen as being somewhat equal in age, the card frequently does not accomplish this purpose. When clear father-daughter plots are not discussed, then the picture reflects the subject's style and approach to unstructured heterosexual relationships. For example, the subject may describe the woman as startled or embarrassed or, on the other hand, may have her respond in a spontaneous and comfortable manner. It is important to note the manner in which the man is perceived by the woman. Is he seen as a seducer, does he offer her helpful advice, is he intrusive, or is he perceived as a welcome addition? A person who mistrusts interpersonal relationships will typically create a story in which the man is intrusive and the woman's reaction is one of defensiveness and surprise. Subjects who are more trusting and comfortable usually develop themes in which the woman responds in a more accepting and flexible manner.

PICTURE 7BM

I. Description of card   An older man is looking at a younger man who appears to be peering into space.

II. Frequent Plots   Stories usually describe either a father-son relationship or a boss-employee situation. Regardless of which of these variations is created, the older man is most frequently in the position of advising or instructing the younger one.

III. General Discussion   This card is extremely useful in obtaining information about authority figures and, more specifically, the subject's own father. The picture deals with hierarchical personal relationships and usually takes the form of an older, more experienced man interacting with a younger, less experienced one. Thus, the card can clearly show how the subject deals with external demands and his attitudes toward authority.

PICTURE 7GF

I. Description of card   A young girl is seated on a couch and is holding a doll in her hands. Behind her is an older woman who appears to be reading to her out of a book.

II. Frequent Plots   This picture is usually perceived as a mother and her daughter, with the mother advising, consoling, scolding, or instructing the child. Less frequently, there are themes in which the mother is reading to the child for pleasure or entertainment.

III. General Discussion   The intention of 7GF is to bring out the style and manner of mother-child interaction. With older women, it often elicits feelings and attitudes toward children. Since both figures are looking away, this is sometimes perceived as rejection by either figure of the other. Thus, the card often elicits negative feelings and interactions, and it is important to note how these feelings are resolved, expressed, or avoided. Sometimes, the older woman is described as reading a fairy story to the younger girl, at which time the most instructive data often comes from the fairy story itself.

PICTURE 8BM

I. Description of card   A young boy in the foreground of the picture is staring directly out of the picture. In the background is the hazy image of two men performing surgery on a patient who is lying down.

II. Frequent Plots   Stories revolve around either ambition, in that the young man may have aspirations toward becoming a doctor, or aggression. Frequently, the aggressive stories relate to fears of becoming harmed or mutilated while in a passive state. Another somewhat less frequent theme centers on a scene in which someone was shot and is now being operated on.

III. General Discussion   The picture can be seen as a thinly veiled depiction of a young man's oedipal conflicts, with the concomitant feelings of castration anxiety and hostility. Thus, it is important to note what feelings the boy or other characters in the story have toward the older man performing the surgery. If the story depicts a need for achievement expressed by the younger man, it is also likely that he will identify with the older one and perhaps use him as an example. If this is the case, the details of how the identification takes place and specific feelings regarding this identification may be helpful.

PICTURE 8GF

I. Description of card   A woman is sitting on a chair staring into space with her chin resting in her hand.

II. Frequent Plots   Since this picture is vague and nonspecific, extremely diverse plots are developed and there are no frequently encountered themes.

III. General Discussion   This picture is difficult to generalize about and typically produces somewhat shallow stories of a contemplative nature.

PICTURE 9BM

I. Description of card   Four men in a field are lying against one another.

II. Frequent Plots   Stories typically explain in some manner why the men are there and frequently describe them either as homeless wanderers or as working men who are taking a much-needed rest.

III. General Discussion   This picture is particularly helpful in providing information about relationships with members of the same sex. Are the men comfortable with one another? Is there any competitiveness? Is the central person in the story merely observing the four men, or is he one of the four men in the picture itself? Sometimes homosexual tendencies or fears regarding such tendencies become evident in the story plot. Often, social prejudice surrounding attitudes toward "lazy," lower class, or unemployed persons becomes apparent, particularly when the men in the picture are seen as homeless.

PICTURE 9GF

I. Description of card   A woman in the foreground is standing behind a tree. Below her is another woman running along a beach.

II. Frequent Plots   Usually the two women are seen as being in some sort of conflict, often over a man. Frequently, either in addition to this theme or in a separate story, the woman hiding behind the tree has done something wrong. It is very unusual to have a story in which cooperation between the women is the central plot.

III. General Discussion   This card basically deals with female peer relations and is important in elaborating on such issues as conflict resolution, jealousy, sibling rivalry, and competitiveness. Since the figure standing behind the tree is carefully observing the woman on the beach, stories may provide details surrounding paranoid ideation. At the very least, the dynamics of suspiciousness and distrust are usually discussed. Frequently, a man is introduced into the story who is often placed in the role of either a long-lost lover, whom one or both of the girls are running to meet, or a sexual attacker, from whom the girl on the beach is attempting to escape.

PICTURE 10

I. Description of card   A person is holding their head against another person's shoulder.

II. Frequent Plots   Stories usually center around some interaction between the male and the female, and may involve either a greeting between the two or a departure.

III. General Discussion   This card often gives useful information about the way in which the subject perceives male-female relationships, particularly those involving some degree of closeness and intimacy. It might be helpful to notice the relative degree of comfort or discomfort that is evoked by emotional closeness. If the story is one of departure or even termination of the relationship, this may be reflective of either overt or denied hostility on the part of the subject. Sometimes, males will interpret the embrace as involving two males, which may suggest the possibility of a repressed or overt homosexual orientation.

PICTURE 11

I. Description of card   A road in a chasm has several figures proceeding along a path towards a bridge. Above them and against the side of a cliff appears to be a dragon.

II. Frequent Plot   Typically, stories of attack and escape are elicited in which the subject takes into account the dragon, the path, and the obscure figures in the distance.

III. General Discussion   Since the form of this picture is quite vague and ambiguous, it is a good test of the subject's imaginative abilities and his or her skill in integrating irregular and poorly defined stimuli. The picture also represents unknown and threatening forces, and reflects the manner in which the subject deals with fear of attack. Thus, the examiner should take note of whether the characters in the story escape or become victims of their attackers. If they do escape, then how effective and coherent was the plan they devised to avoid danger, or on the other hand, were they saved by chance or by "the forces of fate"? A subject's story can often suggest the degree to which he or she experiences a sense of control over his or her environment and over the course of his or her life.

The dragon may be seen as representing aggressive forces in the environment or the need for protection. In this respect, the dragon may be seen as either coming out of the cliff and attacking people, or as a protecting creature whom the characters are using for refuge and safety. Such themes can suggest aspects of the subject's internal framework and mood. For example, subjects who report stories of "everything being dead" indicate a depressive and extremely impoverished inner state.

PICTURE 12M

I. Description of card   A man with his hand raised is standing above a boy who is lying on a bed with his eyes closed.

II. Frequent Plots   Stories center on illness and/or the older man using hypnosis or some form of religious rite on the younger, reclining figure.

III. General Discussion   The picture often elicits themes regarding the relationship between an older, usually more authoritative man and a younger one. This can have significance in predicting or assessing the current or future relationship between the therapist and the client. The manner in which the older man is perceived is particularly important. Is he sympathetic and giving aid, or is he described in more sinister terms? Thus the picture can represent specifics of the transference relationship and, as such, can be an aid in interpreting and providing feedback to the client regarding this relationship. It can also be used to predict a client's attitude toward, and response to, hypnotic procedures (White, 1941). Stories of this picture may also indicate whether passivity is compatible with the subject's personality or whether it is regarded with discomfort. In particular, subjects frequently reveal attitudes toward some external, controlling force.

PICTURE 12F

I. Description of card   A portrait of a woman in the foreground with an older woman holding her hand in her chin in the background.

II. Frequent Plots   Stories center on the relationship or specific communications between the two figures.

III. General Discussion   This picture elicits descriptions and conceptions of mother figures. The background figure is frequently seen as a mother-in-law, often with a variety of evil qualities. Often these negative qualities are feelings that the subject has toward his or her own mother but can indirectly, and therefore more safely, project onto the figure of a mother-in-law.

PICTURE 12BG

I. Description of card   A country setting depicting a tree with a rowboat pulled up next to it. No human figures are present.

II. Frequent Plots   Stories frequently center on themes of loneliness, peace, or the enjoyment of nature.

III. General Discussion   Suicidal or depressed subjects may elaborate on feelings of abandonment and isolation—for example, the case of someone being lost or having fallen from the boat. More stable, adjusted subjects are likely to discuss the peace of being alone in the woods and perhaps fishing or having gone fishing farther down the stream.

PICTURE 13MF

I. Description of card   A young man is standing in the foreground with his head in his arms. In the background is a woman lying in a bed.

II. Frequent Plots   The most frequent plot centers on guilt induced by illicit sexual activity. Themes involving the death of the woman on the bed and the resulting grief of the man, who is often depicted as her husband, are somewhat less frequent.

III. General Discussion   This picture is excellent for revealing sexual conflicts in either men or women. In a general way, it provides information on the subject's attitudes and feelings toward his or her partner, particularly attitudes just prior to and immediately following sexual intercourse. Stories in which there are overt expressions of aggression or revulsion are significant variations and should be noted as relatively unusual features. In particular, the relationship between a subject's aggressive and sexual feelings is frequently portrayed.

Since this picture has a relatively large number of details, obsessive-compulsive personalities frequently spend an excessive amount of time describing and explaining these details. This may be particularly evident because the picture often has a shock effect and may therefore create anxiety that evokes the obsessive-compulsive's style of handling anxiety by externally focusing on detail.

PICTURE 13B

I. Description of card   A boy is sitting in the doorway of a log cabin.

II. Frequent Plots   Themes of loneliness and stories of childhood are often elicited. However, since the stimulus is somewhat vague, the content and the nature of these stories tend to be extremely varied.

III. General Discussion   This picture may be helpful with both adults and children in revealing attitudes toward introspection or loneliness. In adults, it frequently elicits reveries of childhood memories.

PICTURE 13G

I. Description of card   A girl is climbing a flight of stairs.

II. Frequent Plots   The plots are similar to 13B in that they usually involve themes of loneliness and/or sometimes distant childhood memories.

III. General Discussion   This picture lacks the specificity and impact found in other TAT cards. It usually produces stories that are highly varied but lacking in richness and detail. Like 13B, 13G can sometimes be useful in depicting a subject's attitude toward loneliness and introspection.

PICTURE 14

I. Description of card   A person is silhouetted against a window.

II. Frequent Plots   This card produces themes of contemplation, wish fulfillment, depression, or feelings related to burglary.

III. General Discussion   If a subject's presenting problem is depression, especially if there is evidence of suicidal ideation, this card, along with 3BM, is essential. In these cases, subjects often describe the figure in the picture and, more importantly, discuss the events, feelings, and attitudes that led up to the current self-destructive behavior. It becomes important during the inquiry phase of examination to investigate the particular methods and styles of problem solving that the story character has attempted or is attempting. Also significant are the character's internal dialogues and personal reactions as he or she relates to different life stresses.

This picture may also reveal the subject's aesthetic interests and personal philosophical beliefs or wish fulfillments. If a story involving burglary is depicted, it can be useful to consider the character's level of impulse control, guilt, or the consequences of his or her behavior. For example, is the character apprehended and punished for his or her behavior, or is the character allowed to go free and enjoy the profits of his or her misdeeds?

PICTURE 15

I. Description of card   A man is standing among tombstones with his hands clasped together.

II. Frequent Plots   Themes usually revolve around beliefs or events surrounding death and a hereafter.

III. General Discussion   Stories from picture 15 reflect the subject's particular beliefs about, and attitudes toward, death and the dying process. For example, death may be viewed as a passive, quiet process, or in contrast, it can be experienced as a violent, aggressive situation. If the subject is having an extremely difficult time coping with the death of a friend or relative, the themes on picture 15 can provide useful information in determining why this difficulty is being experienced. For example, the story may reveal a method of adjustment based on excessive denial with a seeming inability to engage in grieving and a resulting lack of resolution. The story might also indicate unexpressed and problematic anger directed toward the dead person due to a sense of abandonment.

PICTURE 16

I. Description of card   Blank.

II. Frequent Plots   Stories from this card are highly varied, although the card frequently elicits stories related to a person's life situation (current marital, family, and personal) and, to a lesser extent, idyllic, defensive, catastrophic, and achievement-oriented concerns.

III. General Discussion   Instructions for this card are to imagine a picture and then tell a story about it. From subjects with vivid and active imaginations, this card often produces extremely rich, useful stories and the amount of detail and complexity from a person's stories have been found to correlate with different measures of creativity (Wakefield, 1986). The card does little to shape or influence the subject's fantasy material and can thus be seen as a relatively pure product from his or her unconscious. However, for anxious, resistant, or noncreative subjects, this card is often of little or no value since the stories are usually brief and lack depth or richness. In considering the story, it is helpful to note whether the depiction involves a scene that is vital and optimistic, or desolate and flat. Kahn (1984) suggests that this card's value can be increased by repeating instructions stressing that the person provide a complete story (preceding events, current situation, outcome) and giving the card as the last one in a series. He further stresses that its value derives partially from its total lack of structure but also because it is useful across different ages, ethnic backgrounds, and assessment goals.

PICTURE 17BM

I. Description of card   A naked man is climbing up (or down) a rope.

II. Frequent Plots   Stories usually involve someone escaping from a dangerous situation or an athletic event of a competitive nature.

III. General Discussion   Since the card depicts a naked man, attitudes regarding the subject's personal body images are often revealed. This may bring out themes of achievement, physical prowess, adulation, and narcissism. Possible homosexual feelings or anxiety related to homosexuality also become evident in the stories of some subjects. The particular direction in which the climber is going might reflect either an optimistic, positive outlook indicated by his climbing up, or a pessimistic, negative one as reflected by a downward movement.

PICTURE 17GF

I. Description of card   A female is standing on a bridge over water. Above the bridge is a tall building and behind the building the sun is shining from behind clouds.

II. Frequent Plots   A great variety of stories is elicited, although themes surrounding departure and social or emotional distance do occur with some frequency.

III. General Discussion   Attitudes toward a recent separation or the impending arrival of a loved one are sometimes described. This card can be particularly useful in cases of suicidal depression in which the figure on the bridge is perceived as contemplating jumping off as a last attempt to resolve her difficulties. As with cards 3BM and 14, an inquiry into the specific difficulties the story character has encountered and the manner in which she has attempted to resolve these difficulties can often reflect the subject's manner and style of coping with his or her own difficulties. Personal reactions to, and internal dialogue involving, life stresses can also be extremely informative. However, some of this material may be available only through a more detailed inquiry made after the initial story has been given.

PICTURE 18BM

I. Description of card   A man dressed in a long coat is being grabbed from behind.

II. Frequent Plots   Typical themes involve either drunkenness on the part of the figure who is being supported by the three hands or stories in which he is being attacked from behind.

III. General Discussion   This picture, more than any of the others, is likely to produce anxiety due to the suggestive depiction of invisible forces attacking the figure. Thus, it is important to note how the subject handles his own anxiety as well as how the story character deals with his situation. Does he see himself as the victim of circumstance in which he is completely helpless? If so, how does he eventually resolve these feelings of helplessness? Is the helplessness a momentary phenomenon, or is it an ongoing personality trait? If the character is seen as the recipient of hard luck, then specifically what situation does the subject perceive as comprising hard luck? Exaggerated aggressiveness or attitudes toward addiction are also sometimes expressed with this picture.

PICTURE 18GF

I. Description of card   A woman has her hands around the throat of another woman. In the background is a flight of stairs.

II. Frequent Plots   Aggressive mother-daughter interactions or sibling relationships are often disclosed in response to this picture.

III. General Discussion   The manner in which the subject handles aggressive, hostile relationships with other women is the primary type of information this picture elicits. Particular note should be given to the types of events that trigger this aggressiveness and the manner in which the conflict is or is not resolved. Does the character submit passively, withdraw from the relationship, plot revenge, or negotiate change? Feelings of inferiority, jealousy, and response to being dominated are also often described. Although the representation of aggressiveness in the picture is quite explicit, subjects will occasionally attempt to deny or avoid this aggressiveness by creating a story in which one figure is attempting to help the other up the stairs. This may point to general denial and repression of hostility on the part of the subject.

PICTURE 19

I. Description of card   A surreal picture depicting clouds and a home covered with snow.

II. Frequent Plots   Stories are highly varied due to the unstructured and ambiguous nature of the stimuli.

III. General Discussion   Since the picture is one of the more unstructured cards, the subject's ability to integrate disparate visual stimuli is tested. For certain subjects, the ambiguous nature of this picture can create anxiety and insecurity, which provide the examiner with a way to observe how the subject handles his or her anxiety within the context of the story. Often, stories are produced dealing with impersonal aggression from such forces as nature or the supernatural.

PICTURE 20

I. Description of card   A hazy picture during the night of a man leaning against a lamp post.

II. Frequent Plots   Stories range from the benign theme of a late evening date, to a more sinister one, perhaps involving a gangster who is in imminent danger.

III. General Discussion   The picture often elicits information regarding a subject's attitudes toward loneliness, darkness, and uncertainty. Fears may be expressed explicitly through gangster stories, and, as with 18BM, the method of handling these fears and the examinee's response to physical danger should be noted.

Children's Apperception Test (CAT)

The following descriptions of, and typical responses to, pictures on the CAT are adapted from Bellak (1986, p. 245-247).

PICTURE 1

I. Bellak's Description   Chicks seated around a table on which is a large bowl of food. Off to one side is a large chicken, dimly outlined.

II. Discussion   Stories typically revolve around concerns about eating or sibling rivalry. The sibling rivalry may center on who is the best behaved, what the consequences of this behavior are, and which one gets more to eat. To obtain useful information on this card, it is particularly important to decide which character the subject identifies with. Food may be seen as a reward for "good" behavior, or conversely, it can be withheld as punishment for "bad" behavior.

PICTURE 2

I. Bellak's Description   One bear is pulling a rope on one side, while another bear and a baby bear pull on the other side.

II. Discussion   Of particular importance in interpreting this picture is whether the bear who is helping the baby bear is seen as a male (father figure) or a female (mother figure). The struggle that is depicted can either be seen as a playful game of tug-of-war or a struggle involving a high degree of seriousness and aggression. For example, the loser(s) may end up falling off the edge of the rock and into a pool of dangerous animals. In the most recent revision of the CAT, the large bears were made equal in size to avoid having the largest bear (previously depicted on the right) identified as the father.

PICTURE 3

I. Bellak's Description   A lion, with pipe and cane, sits in a chair; in the lower right corner, a little mouse appears in a hole.

II. Discussion   Since the lion is pictured with the characteristic symbols of authority (pipe and cane), this picture elicits attitudes and feelings toward father figures. It is important to note whether this figure is seen as benevolent and protecting or as dangerous and threatening. Sometimes, the subject will defensively attempt to minimize the threat of the lion by reducing him to a helpless cripple who needs a cane just to move around.

Most children notice the mouse in the hole and blend it into their stories. Since the mouse and the lion are frequently seen in adversarial roles, it is important to note how the threatening presence of the lion is handled. Is the mouse completely under the control of the lion, and does it adapt by being submissive and placating? On the other hand, the mouse may be described as clever and manipulating in order to trick and outsmart the lion. Some subjects will switch their identification back and forth between the lion and the mouse, suggesting some role confusion. This may be particularly true of enmeshed families or families in which the father is unable to set limits effectively.

PICTURE 4

I. Bellak's Description   A kangaroo, with a bonnet on her head, is carrying a basket with a milk bottle. In her pouch is a baby kangaroo with a balloon; on a bicycle, there is a larger kangaroo child.

II. Discussion   As in picture 1, this card elicits themes of sibling rivalry and occasionally themes revolving around a wish for regression, as demonstrated when the subject identifies with the baby kangaroo in the pouch. A regressive theme is particularly strong when a subject, who is in reality the oldest or middle child, identifies with the kangaroo in the pouch. On the other hand, a child who is actually the youngest may identify with the oldest kangaroo, thereby suggesting a strong need for autonomy and independence. On occasion, a theme of flight from danger may be introduced.

PICTURE 5

I. Bellak's Description   A darkened room contains a large bed in the background and a crib in the foreground in which there are two baby bears.

II. Discussion   Stories relating to attitudes and feelings about what occurs when parents are in bed are frequent responses to this card. They may involve such aspects as curiosity, conjecture, confusion, rejection, anger, and envy on the part of the children. Descriptions of the two children in the foreground may also center on themes of sexual manipulation and mutual exploration.

PICTURE 6

I. Bellak's Description   A darkened cave shows two dimly outlined bear figures in the background and a baby bear lying in the foreground.

II. Discussion   This is similar to picture 5 in that both cards elicit stories of parental bedtime activity. However, this picture tends to enlarge upon and extend themes that have only begun to develop in picture 5. Stories may also revolve around feelings of jealousy of the perceived intimacy between parents or may reflect possible feelings about masturbation on the part of the baby bear in the foreground.

PICTURE 7

I. Bellak's Description   A tiger with bared fangs and claws leaps at a monkey that is also leaping through the air.

II. Discussion   The subject will often discuss his or her fears of aggression and his or her characteristic manner of dealing with it. At times, the anxiety produced by this picture may result in an unwillingness to respond to it at all. On the other hand, the subject's defenses may be either effective enough, or perhaps unrealistic enough, for him or her to transform the picture into a harmless story.

PICTURE 8

I. Bellak's Description   Two adult monkeys are sitting on a sofa drinking from tea cups. One adult monkey in the foreground is sitting on a hassock talking to a baby monkey.

II. Discussion   The subject often discusses his or her relative position and characteristic roles within the family. The description of the dominant monkey in the foreground as either a mother or a father figure should be noted as a possible indication of who has more control in the family. It is also significant to note how the dominant monkey is described. Is it threatening and controlling or helpful and supportive?

PICTURE 9

I. Bellak's Description   A darkened room is seen through an open door from a lighted room. In the darkened one, there is a child's bed in which a rabbit sits up looking through the door.

II. Discussion   Typically, responses revolve around a subject's fears of darkness, possible desertion by parents, and curiosity about what is occurring in the next room.

PICTURE 10

I. Bellak's Description   A baby dog is lying across the knees of an adult dog; both figures have a minimum of expressive features. The figures are set in the foreground of a bathroom.

II. Discussion   A child's attitudes and feelings about misbehavior and its resulting punishments are usually discussed in response to this card. In particular, his or her conceptions of right and wrong are often revealed. This picture is a good indicator of the child's degree of impulse control and his or her attitude toward authority figures when their role involves setting limits.

SCORING PROCEDURES

Since the original publication of the TAT Manual in 1943, a number of alternate methods of scoring and interpretation have been developed by such individuals as Rapaport, Gill, and Schafer (1946); Wyatt (1947); Bellak (1954); Henry (1956); Arnold (1962); and Thomas and Dudek (1985). Whenever a large number of different theories are put forth to explain a particular phenomenon, it is usually a strong indication that none of them is fully adequate and that they all have significant shortcomings. This is true of the many alternate interpretation methods for the TAT. Difficulty arises primarily due to the type of information under investigation. Fantasy productions involve extremely rich and diverse information that is difficult to place into precise and specific categories. Even the selection of which categories to use is open to question. For example, Murray prefers a listing and weighting of the primary needs and press expressed in the stories, whereas Arnold (1962) emphasizes a restatement of the essential theme of the story on an interpretive level in order to highlight the basic meaning or moral of the story. Once the examiner has decided which method to use and evaluated the stories according to this method, the examiner is able to infer qualities of the subject's personality. Whether this final inference is valid and accurate is open to question and depends on a number of variables, including the skill and experience of the examiner, comparison with themes derived from other test data, and whether the state of the subject at the time of examination is representative of his or her usual orientation to the world.

For the purposes of this book, Murray's method of interpretation will be described because it is a relatively concise and clear approach, and has a more extensive history and familiarity within the field. However, all of the different approaches deserve consideration since each has unique advantages and an examiner may find an approach other than Murray's to be more helpful in providing interpretive information.

Although Murray's approach involves a certain degree of quantification, it is basically qualitative, focusing on specific story content. The goal is not so much to achieve a diagnosis of the subject, but to obtain a description of how the subject confronts and deals with basic universal life situations. To accomplish this, Murray suggests five categories of analysis:

1. The hero/heroine
2. Motives, trends, and feelings of the hero/heroine (needs)
3. Forces of the hero/heroine's environment (press)
4. Themes and outcomes
5. Interests and sentiments

These steps in scoring will be described in more detail. Although scoring and interpretation are discussed separately here, in actual practice it is difficult to distinguish between the two. Scoring, in its widest sense, is also interpretation. The section designated Interpretation serves primarily as a summary for arranging data as well as for providing suggestions in making generalizations about the subject's personality. This system can be used equally well with the TAT or with such derivatives as Bellak's Children's Apperception Test. Summary sheets (Figures 10-2 and 10-3) are provided at the end of the descriptions as aids in totaling and comparing the different needs and press.

The Hero/Heroine

The initial task of the examiner is to determine which story character is the focal figure. Presumably, the subject has identified with this figure and is therefore likely to project personal needs, attitudes, and feelings onto him or her. The hero/heroine can be described as the central character around which the story events revolve.

However, the subject might identify with more than one character. This may become evident from continual references or attribution of needs to a secondary figure. In this case, the weighting of the hero or heroine's needs should only be half those of the primary hero/heroine. If, on the other hand, there is no clear identification but rather an objective description of each character in turn, the needs and press of each character should be given equal weighting.

Motives, Trends, and Feelings of the Hero/Heroine (Needs)

The recognition and quantification of the hero or heroine's needs is the next category to be considered. However, Murray gives some latitude to the examiner in determining which set of variables is most appropriate: the selection of these variables depends on what the examiner wants to know about the subject. Although Murray clearly emphasizes his concept of needs, the examiner may wish to approach a description of the hero/heroine from additional conceptual frameworks.

Murray suggests a five-point scale, with 1 representing the "slightest suggestion" of a need and 5 indicating "the intense form" or "a repeated occurrence of a milder form." For example, a response to card 1 (a boy playing a violin) may include a description of the boy "practicing relentlessly in the hopes of someday living up to his expectations of being a famous concert violinist." This would clearly receive a rating of 5 for need for achievement. In contrast to this, an achievement rating of 1 might occur in a story in which "he hoped someday he would be able to enjoy playing the violin, but he was presently preoccupied with finding out how he could go out and play with his friends."

Another consideration, other than intensity, in rating the needs within a story is the relative importance or centrality of the need to the story. In the example in which the boy is primarily concerned with associating with his friends, the low score in need for achievement is given not only because it is low in intensity, but also because the story, at least the segment that is given, concerns itself more with the expression of the need for affiliation, which might have a score of 4 or 5 in this case. Another story might involve a man who extensively criticizes himself but compensates by working hard and trying to control other people. In this case, the most central need would be the need for abasement (5) with secondary needs being the need for achievement and the need for dominance (3 or 4). Even though the subject may choose to spend more time elaborating or discussing these latter needs, the underlying and central need would still be for abasement.

In some cases, more than one story is told for a particular card, or there might be a story within a story—for example, when a character elaborates on a dream the hero/heroine has had. In this situation, some of the ratings may total more than 5, in which case the examiner should scale down the overall totals to keep them within the five-point range.

To summarize, the examiner should consider the number of times a need is mentioned, and of equal importance, he or she should look at its relative intensity and the degree to which it is central to the story. The same procedure should be used when scoring press (forces of the hero/heroine's environment).

When all the stories are rated on the five-point scale, the overall strengths of the subject's needs (and press) for all the stories can be totaled. Their total values can then be compared with one another and rank ordered to determine their relative strength for the subject. The examiner can also determine their average strength at each occurrence by dividing the total values (ratings) by the number of times each need occurs. The different needs and inner states are given in Figure 10–2. In a similar manner, press is summarized later in Figure 10–3.

The following material includes descriptions of each of Murray's needs, which can be used for reference when deciding which story fragments represent specific needs. Inner states, which should be scored in the same manner as needs, are also discussed. Needs are designated by a small n before the specific name of each need. The definitions of needs and inner states have been adapted from Sanford's (1939) unpublished manual, which appears in Stein's (1981) book on the Thematic Apperception Test. The following list and definitions can be used as an aid in identifying which needs and inner states are illustrated in a subject's stories.

A. *Needs motivated by desire for Power, Property, Prestige, Knowledge, or Creative Achievement*
  1. *n Achievement*   To work toward a goal with energy, persistence, and singleness of purpose. To set high standards for oneself and work independently toward realizing these standards. To overcome obstacles or master and manipulate objects, situations,

	CARD NUMBER																				
	1	2	3	4	5	6	7	8	9	10	11	12	13	14	15	16	17	18	19	20	Total
n Achievement																					
n Acquisition																					
n Aggression																					
n Construction																					
n Counteraction																					
n Dominance																					
n Exposition																					
n Recognition																					
n Understanding																					
n Affiliation																					
n Deference																					
n Nurturance																					
n Sex																					
n Succorance																					
n Autonomy																					
n Change, Travel, Adventure																					
n Excitance, Dissipation																					
n Playmirth																					
n Abasement																					
n Blame Avoidance																					
n Cognizance																					
n Harm Avoidance																					
n Passivity																					
n Rejection																					
n Retention																					
n Sentience																					
Conflict																					
Emotional Change																					
Elation																					
Dejection																					
Distrust																					
Jealousy																					
Irreality																					
Ego Ideal, Pride																					
Superego																					
Miscellaneous																					

Figure 10–2.   TAT summary sheet for needs and inner states

or people. To accomplish or work persistently at a difficult task. To be ambitious, competitive, aspiring.*

After practicing every day for weeks, he finally feels that he is sufficiently skilled to play his first concert performance. His performance is a tremendous success and is the beginning of a brilliant career.

2. *n Acquisition*

a. *Social*   To work for money, material possessions, or valuable objects. A desire for economic mobility. To bargain or gamble. Greed or acquisitiveness.

She worked hard over a period of many years so she could eventually purchase a vacation home on the beach.

b. *Asocial*   To steal, cheat, rob, forage, or swindle. Greed, which, in order to accomplish its goal, causes harm to others or involves breaking some ethical principle or law. The desired goal may be money, an object, or even a person (e.g., during a kidnapping).

As a young man, he would break into neighbors' homes to steal guns, money, or any other valuables he could find.

3. *n Aggression*

a. *Emotional, Verbal*   To have a verbal fight or argument with another person. To become angry at, ridicule, blame, criticize, or curse. This may be expressed publicly by a speech or in writing.

In the middle of the conversation, she jumped up angrily and shouted her defiance at her political opponent.

b. *Physical, Social*   To kill or defend oneself in self-defense. To avenge an attack that was unwarranted and unprovoked. To defend one's country, for example, during war or to become physically aggressive while upholding the law. Activity that is revolutionary may be on the threshold between (b) social and (c) asocial.

After the thief had stolen the little old lady's purse, a bystander jumped on the offender and held him down until the police came.

c. *Physical, Asocial*   Aggression against some legal or moral standard or expressed without being provoked, such as in criminal activity. To fight legal authorities or authority figures (parents, police, employer, school principal). To initiate a brawl, turn traitor, or express sadistic behavior.

Once his victim was chained to the floor, he began his relentless program of torture and unnatural acts.

d. *Destruction*   To attack or maim. To destroy, smash, vandalize, or burn.

When the police were at a safe distance, the young hooligans approached their object of destruction only after having built up an incredible amount of ramming speed.

4. *n Construction*   To organize, build, create, or place something in a new order.

She eventually returns to the farm and repairs the fences and barn, and organizes the machinery in preparation for next year's planting.

* From Stein, M. *The thematic apperception test: An introductory manual for its clinical use with adults* (2nd Ed.), 1981. Courtesy of Charles C. Thomas, Publisher, Springfield, Illinois.

5. *n Counteraction*   To make up for a previous failure or disappointment. To over-compensate for a weakness or to have a determination to overcome. N Counteraction depends on a response to a previous failure or humiliation. To repress fear or keep one's self-respect. To be resolute, determined, indomitable, dauntless, dogged, or adventurous as a reaction to an earlier difficult situation.

   His stuttering had embarrassed him so strongly that he began practicing every day to speak clearly, with strength and dignity.

6. *n Dominance*   To control, influence, or direct one's human environment. This may involve being forceful, persuasive, assertive, masterful, decisive, or authoritative. To prevail upon, sway, lead, judge, set standards, induce, restrain, prohibit, manage, or govern.

   The hypnotic induction proceeded until the subject was completely under the hypnotist's control.

7. *n Exposition*   To relate information in an instructive or informative manner. To explain, lecture, interpret, instruct, teach. Merely telling something to another person in a casual or routine manner is not sufficient to score n Exposition. It is commonly fused with n Dominance, n Recognition, or n Achievement.

   Her elaboration on the intricacies of the space program kept her students writing page after page of notes.

8. *n Recognition*   To seek praise, prestige, appreciation, or attention. Making oneself conspicuous; dramatizing or performing. To boast or brag. The examiner should ask him- or herself* whether the hero/heroine's main motive is getting something done, in which case it would be scored as n Achievement, or actually being noticed.

   After singing a few more songs and throwing down two or more shots of whiskey, he began dancing on tables as the audience stared in disbelief.

9. *n Understanding*   Striving for knowledge and wisdom. To attempt to understand the relationship between one object or event and another. Discussion and argumentation with the goal directed toward increasing knowledge. Attempting to make thought correspond with fact. To analyze events and generalize.

   The boy was carefully considering everything his music instructor had told him in an attempt to conceptualize how his violin worked.

B. *Needs Motivated by Affection, Admiration, Sympathy, Love, and Dependence*
   1. *n Affiliation*
      a. *Associative*   To establish friendly relations. This may be focal, in which case the need is directed toward affectionate feelings for specific people. It may also be diffuse, in which case the feeling is directed toward all sorts of people, such as groups or organizations.

         As they saw more of one another, their friendship grew progressively stronger. After the church services, he usually felt a stronger bond with all members of her community.

      b. *Emotional*   Feelings of strong attachment, closeness, affection, or respect toward another person. This may include getting married, remaining faithful, or falling in love.

         Although the strength of their marriage was tested once again, the difficulty only brought them closer than they had ever been before.

* Stein's (1981) definitions of needs and press have been edited to insure nonsexist language.

2. *n Deference*
   a. *Compliance*   Quick to agree or cooperate. To obey the wishes or suggestions of another person. A willingness to please or follow another's leadership. It may be necessary at times to distinguish n Deference from n Abasement, in which there is compliance but it is unwilling.

   Since he had been requested sincerely to help, Jim agreed to help with the work until it was completed.

   b. *Respect*   To give praise to or express admiration toward. Hero worship or the acknowledgment of merit or talent. Dedication to a cause.

   Awe for his virtuosity was continually supported each time the master gave another performance.

3. *n Nurturance*   To give sympathy to or gratify the needs of another. To help, feed, support, console, protect, or comfort those who are in need. Kindness, consideration, protection. To encourage and further the welfare of those who are helpless. This may include being liberal with time, energy, or money as a means of helping others. Giving freedom, condoning, or being lenient.

   The man helped the lost child to find her parents and provided her with food until they came.

4. *n Sex*   To have or attempt to have a sexual relationship. To make sexual advances toward or seduce. Enjoying the company of members of the opposite sex, being fond of mixed parties and dancing. To fall in love. This may commonly be fused with n Affiliation (emotional) or, if not fused, should be distinguished from n Affiliation (emotional).

   After cleverly slipping him an aphrodisiac while he was in the presence of a small amount of kryptonite, Lois Lane was able to steal his virginity.

5. *n Succorance*   A tendency to cry, plead, ask for help, aid, protection, or love. Being dependent, helpless, and perhaps capitalizing on one's mishaps. To crave affection or tenderness and accept favors without hesitation. To have a close and devoted protector or supporter. Seeking to be nursed, supported, sustained, advised, guided, indulged, forgiven, or consoled. Someone with an n Nurturance satisfies the hero/heroine's succorance, although intranurturance may also be evident in an individual who derives some enjoyment as a result of his or her grief or seeks consolation through drugs, alcohol, or food.

   All the other kittens in the litter had been eaten by a Doberman pinscher so the girl took home the one survivor and slowly nursed it back to health.

C. *Needs Motivated by a Desire for Freedom, Change, Excitement, and Play*
   1. *n Autonomy*
      a. *Freedom*   To escape, shake off restraint, or become independent. To be unattached or unrestrained. To avoid all encumbering alliances or terminate a confining relationship. To wander, drop out, leave school, break off a relationship. To fight or argue for liberty in a positive way. Determination to remain independent.

      Finally, after arguments and much confusion, he decided that he needed more time to be alone, so he ended the relationship.

      b. *Resistance*   To refuse to comply with the demands of another. Negativism and defiance. Resistance toward coercion. To be "stubborn as a mule," to be obstinate, to disobey one's parents, or to present revolutionary ideas. Typically, a revolutionary will be scored on n Autonomy (a-c).

      All the prisoners went on a hunger strike to protest their living conditions.

c. *Asocial*   To express behavior that is not allowed and is punishable. Behavior that is disorderly, unruly, and counter to moral or social standards. Lying, cheating, whoring, stealing, drinking. Crimes other than stealing since stealing would be classified under n Acquisition.

> Then, as soon as the substitute teacher turned her back, the entire class assailed her with spitballs.

2. *n Change, Travel, Adventure*   To feel a sense of restlessness and a need to experience new lands or novel situations. To dream of exploring and having novel adventures. This need is commonly fused with n Autonomy.

> After returning from her travels and settling down for a short while, she again caught the wanderlust, her feet began itching, and she began planning a trip to the South Seas.

3. *n Excitance, Dissipation*   To act in a way that creates emotional excitement. This may involve travel (n Change), gambling (n Acquisition), involvement with drugs or alcohol (n Nurturance), or recklessly meeting danger. What distinguishes n Excitance, Dissipation from such needs as n Change or n Acquisition is its emphasis on emotional excitement, although these needs are frequently fused.

> While in the police department, she volunteered to work on the "wrong side of the tracks" hoping that there would be more action.

4. *n Play*   To act for "fun" and without a purpose other than amusement. To laugh, make jokes, play games, be jolly, merry, and easygoing. This may include sports, dancing, drinking, clowning, or make-believe activity. Meeting situations in a lighthearted and jovial manner. However, in those cases in which the game is taken seriously, such as in athletic competition, a score is given for n Achievement rather than n Play.

> These girls are playing hide-and-seek and soon the one behind the tree is going out to look for her sister, who is looking for a hiding place.

D. *Miscellaneous Needs*

1. *n Abasement*   To submit passively to an external force. To accept injury, blame, criticism, punishment, or to feel guilt or inferiority. To adopt an attitude that is passive, humble, meek, servile. Resignation or shame. To endure ordeals without attempting to counteract. Common fusions are with n Succorance, n Deference, or n Sex as in the case of masochism.

> After they were caught red-handed in the act, they were sent to a reform school where they willingly submitted to numerous restrictions.

2. *n Blame Avoidance*   To act in such a way as to avoid blame or rejection. To fear reproach; to inhibit one's asocial impulses. To avoid blame or punishment by refraining from misbehavior. To confess, apologize, atone, or repent in order to avoid more blame. This may involve being conventional, remorseful, apologetic, dutiful, or conscientious.

> After lashing out in anger, he begged her forgiveness and explained that it would never happen again.

3. *n Cognizance*   To express curiosity, search, investigate, explore, or act as a detective. To watch or gaze intently. Voyeurism. To ask questions, satisfy one's curiosity, look, listen, inspect. To read and seek knowledge. Common fusions occur with n Understanding, n Change (travel, etc.) or n Achievement.

> After opening the door and carefully observing every action they performed, she took another step forward to get an even better look.

4. *n Harm Avoidance*   To avoid physical pain, withdraw, flee, or conceal oneself from persons or objects who are attempting to inflict injury. This includes "startle" and "fear" reactions to such things as loud noises, loss of support, or the sudden appearance of strangers. To escape from a dangerous situation. To take precautionary measures. To be fearful, anxious, timid, cautious, wary, prudent, vigilant. To run away when chased by a dangerous animal or enemy. However, if the hero/heroine purposefully places him- or herself in a situation of danger, even if he or she takes precautionary measures to avoid being killed or injured, this should not be scored as n Harm Avoidance but rather as n Excitance, Dissipation.

> The settlers immediately began to build a fort in order to protect themselves from roving bands of savages.

5. *n Passivity*   To seek or enjoy quiet, rest, tranquility, peacefulness. To feel tired, apathetic, lazy. To need quiet contemplation, meditation, or reflection.

> After traveling to foreign lands, the monk longed for the quiet and solitude of his monastery.

6. *n Rejection*   To snub, ignore, or exclude others. To remain aloof and indifferent, or be discriminating in accepting others. To exclude, abandon, expel, or criticize. To demand a high standard of ability, intelligence, wit, or imagination. To reject a suitor, break with a friend, or withhold love. This is commonly fused with n Passivity or n Aggression. N Rejection may also become directed inward, thus becoming fused with n Abasement, perhaps resulting in feelings of depression or suicidal ideation.

> The head of the committee scorned every attempt that Tim made to become a member of the club, and, as a result, his application had already been turned down three times.

7. *n Retention*   To hold on to something, refuse to lend; to be possessive, miserly, and unwilling to give time, energy, and affection to others. To hoard or collect objects, or another person, with possessive love.

> This dragon up at the top has a huge treasure he's protecting, and if any travelers pass by, he takes their money and spends the rest of the time devising how he will arrange it inside his cave.

8. *n Sentience*   To seek and enjoy sensuous impressions. To have delicate, sensitive perceptions. To perceive and comment upon the sensuous quality of objects. To remark upon the atmosphere, temperature, colors in the room, pictures, various sounds, tastes, or odors. A genuine delight in one or more of the arts. May be fused with n Sex (erotic sentience), n Construction (enjoying composition or creativity), or n Recognition (performing in public).

> As soon as the feast was laid out on the table, the guests sat down to indulge in the culinary delights.

The following list describes the most frequently encountered inner states. These can each be scored in the same way as needs:

1. *Conflict*   A state in which two inner forces are pulling against one another; uncertainty, indecision. This may also include the conflict created by two opposing needs.

2. *Emotional Change*   To show an alteration in mood or attitude toward something or someone. To be labile, inconsistent, moody, or unstable.

3. *Elation*   Happiness, joyful enthusiasm, optimism, excitement, a positive outlook.

4. *Dejection*   Disappointment, discouragement, sadness, depression, melancholy, or despair.

5. *Distrust*   To have no confidence in; to be suspicious of; to be skeptical of. Refusing to accept other people's ideas, suggestions, or advice due to distrust. This may often be associated with n Rejection or n Autonomy.

6. *Jealousy*   To be afraid that a loved person will prefer or love another person. Envy. Requiring complete loyalty or faithfulness. Jealousy toward more favored or successful rivals.

7. *Irreality*   Visions or hallucinations. Reveries about the future or daydreams about the past. Entering into a hypnotic or dream state. An altered state of consciousness. However, this would not include mythological creatures (dragon, sorceress, unicorn, etc.) when the story takes place in a mythological setting, unless there was also an accompanying altered state existing within the hero/heroine.

8. *Ego Ideal, Pride*   Having a high opinion of one's own self-worth. To keep one's self-respect or to dream of a great future in which one will accomplish all one's goals. This may involve n Counteraction, n Achievement, n Autonomy (defiance), or n Aggression.

9. *Superego*   To be controlled by a conscience that demands a high moral standard. The hero/heroine, for example, might be extremely honest, dependable, and courageous, and express a high degree of integrity. This could be combined with n Achievement (working for a socially approved ideal), n Blame Avoidance (not succumbing to temptation), or n Abasement (confessing one's sins or experiencing guilt feelings).

10. *Miscellaneous*   The first nine items represent some of the more common inner states but cannot describe all the possibilities. Additional inner states can be identified and listed separately.

Forces of the Hero/Heroine's Environment (Press)

The examiner, in addition to noting the needs occurring within the hero/heroine, should also observe the type of environment in which the hero/heroine lives and functions. The recommended rating for these environmental forces, or press, is on a five-point scale. As with the rating for the hero/heroine's needs, the scale for press uses a 5 to designate the highest possible mark for any press on a story and a 1 to indicate the slightest reference to that press. The criteria for the relative strength of a press are based on intensity, duration, frequency, and general significance in the plot. After each story is rated on the basis of the occurrence and strength of its press, the scores can be totaled and compared to gain an overall picture of how the subject sees his or her world. The following definitions of press are derived from Sanford's (1939) unpublished manual and appear in print in Stein's (1981) book on the Thematic Apperception Test. A summary sheet (Figure 10–3) is provided as an aid in totaling and comparing the different press.

Basic trends and themes can be isolated by taking note of the subject's press. For example, are people seen as friendly or unfriendly? What attributes are given to older men as opposed to younger ones, or older women versus younger ones? Are members of the same age and sex seen as basically threatening or primarily helpful and cooperative? Is the world one in which there is a marked absence of beneficial press, or are personal needs provided for?

	CARD NUMBER																				
	1	2	3	4	5	6	7	8	9	10	11	12	13	14	15	16	17	18	19	20	Total
p Acquisition																					
p Retention																					
p Lack																					
p Loss																					
p Rejection																					
p Uncongenial Environment																					
p Dominance																					
p Imposed Task, Duty, Training																					
p Aggression																					
p Affliction																					
p Death of Hero																					
p Physical Danger																					
p Physical Injury																					
p Affiliation																					
p Deference																					
p Nurturance																					
p Sex																					
p Succorance																					
p Birth of Offspring																					
p Claustrum																					
p Cognizance																					
p Example																					
p Exposition																					
p Luck																					

Figure 10–3. TAT summary sheet for press

Although the following list of press and the scores that can be achieved by using them provide a certain amount of useful information, the examiner is encouraged to consider the unique and specific significance these have for the subject. For example, if a subject's highest press rating is for p Dominance, how does he or she characteristically cope with this press? Is it through rebellion, submission, impulsive acting out, or withdrawal and fantasy? In particular, does the subject see him- or herself as helplessly controlled by the forces of fate, or does he or she effectively control his or her environment and significantly affect the outcome of the stories? Thus, although the totals of the press scores are useful figures in themselves, it is also up to the examiner to broaden the significance of these totals by integrating their meaning into the overall story content and context. The following list can be used as an aid in identifying which press are present in a subject's stories.

A. *Press of Deprivation*

1. *p Acquisition*   A person wants to dispossess the hero/heroine of money or property, to rob or swindle him or her. For example, a competitor in business threatens the hero heroine's financial security.*

After developing false evidence against him, they hoped that his property would be turned over to themselves.

2. *p Retention*   A person retains something the hero/heroine wants; refuses to lend or give something to the hero/heroine; is stingy, miserly, or possessive.

She had been asking to borrow her father's tools, but her father said firmly that since she had not returned them in a timely manner before, she could not use them again.

B. *Press Descriptive of an Empty, Alien, or Rejecting Environment*

1. *p Lack*

a. *Things, Opportunities, Friends*   Few desirable objects are in the environment, few opportunities for enjoyment or advancement, or no jobs. The hero/heroine is poor and the family destitute, or the hero/heroine lacks status, influence, and/or friends.

Even though the government was clearly in the wrong, every attempt he made was frustrated by the bureaucrats' keeping a closed mind.

b. *Human Support*   The hero/heroine is miserable, solitary, helpless, and in need of assistance and support, encouragement, protection, food, medical care, or parental love and guidance. The hero/heroine has no father or no mother. The situation is insecure and perilous, or the hero/heroine is homesick. There are few nurturant people in the hero/heroine's environment. Commonly, fusions occur with p Loss, p Rejection, and n Succorance.

He's sitting on the outside of his cabin and it's the first day of summer camp. He misses his mother and father, and realizes that no one in the camp really wants to make friends with him.

2. *p Loss*   This is the same as for p Lack, except in this case the hero/heroine actually loses something or someone, such as money, job, friend, or opportunity. This may include the loss of a loved one by departure, misfortune, or death. Another example is the loss of property through bankruptcy, misfortune, swindling, or robbery. If the hero/heroine loses something and also experiences a sense of loss over an extended period of time, then a score on p Lack should also be given.

With one pronouncement of the judge, the family's entire holdings were turned over to the government.

3. *p Rejection*   A person rejects, scorns, loses respect for, repudiates, turns away from, or leaves the hero/heroine.

The older man has fallen in love with this woman, and she's explaining that she does not feel attracted to him in the least.

4. *p Uncongenial Environment*

a. *Alien Objects*   The people in the hero/heroine's environment are not to his or her liking; there is no mutual sympathy or understanding. He or she finds no one in

---

* From Stein, M. *The thematic apperception test: An introductory manual for its clinical use with adults* (2nd ed.), 1981. Courtesy of Charles C. Thomas, Publisher, Springfield, Illinois.

accord with his or her interests. There are people around him or her, but they dislike, reject, distrust, accuse, or disapprove of him or her. This refers to the hero/heroine's general human environment and not to one or two specific people within his or her environment. For example, this may be used to describe an overall feeling within an organization or community that rejects or is out of sympathy with the hero/heroine.

> Even though she had stood up for her beliefs, wherever she went within the village people gave her suspicious looks and avoided talking to her.

b. *Physical Surroundings*   The hero/heroine is dissatisfied with his or her physical environment and hates the farm, the city, the sea, or the island on which he or she is marooned. The environment is distrustful, ugly, sordid, dreary, barren (p Lack), noisy, or dangerous.

> He has worked in the graveyard for two years now, and he still hasn't gotten used to the sight of the cold, bleak gravestones.

c. *Monotony*   The hero/heroine must submit to a dull routine; work is drudgery. There is a great "sameness" in his or her life, causing boredom.

> Every day he worked steadily in the oppressive sameness of the coal mine and still he could not clearly see a way to end the routine work.

C. *Press of Coercion and Restraint*

1. *p Dominance*

a. *Coercion*   Someone tries to force the hero/heroine to do something. He or she is exposed to commands, orders, or strong arguments from a parent or authority.

> This guy has given him an offer he can't refuse, if you know what I mean, and so he has no other choice.

b. *Restraint*   Someone tries to prevent the hero/heroine from doing something. He or she is exposed to checks, prohibitions, or restraints.

> He tried many times to cross the border, but each time the border patrol apprehended him and sent him back to his own country.

c. *Inducement*   Someone tries to get the hero/heroine to do something, or to not do something, by pleading or by gentle persuasion, encouragement, clever strategy, or seduction. In this category, no threats of force are used.

> When she heard what had happened, she begged him to stay, appealing to his sense of peace until finally he agreed not to leave.

2. *p Imposed Task, Duty, Training*   The hero/heroine is given something to do: he or she must practice on the violin, study for an examination, accomplish something to keep his or her job, or win a reward. If the agent who imposes the task is named, then a score is also given to p Dominance (coercion).

> When he received his draft papers, he knew that he would have to go defend his country.

D. *Press Descriptive of a Hostile Aggressive Environment*

1. *p Aggression*

a. *Emotional, Verbal*   Someone gets angry at the hero/heroine or hates him or her. He or she is cursed, criticized, belittled, reproved, reprimanded, or ridiculed. Someone slanders the hero/heroine behind his or her back.

> They're having a big argument now, and he's yelling and calling her some pretty bad names that I would hate to even admit are in my vocabulary.

b. *Physical, Social*   The hero/heroine is in the wrong and is an aggressor or a criminal. Another person defends him- or herself, retaliates, pursues, imprisons, or perhaps kills the hero/heroine. The state, the police, a parent, or some other legitimate authority punishes the hero/heroine for misconduct.

> Finally they have enough clues to track her down, and then, in the dead of night, the police surround her house and prepare to take her into custody.

c. *Physical, Asocial*   A criminal or a gang assaults, injures, or kills the hero/heroine. Another person starts a fight and the hero/heroine defends him- or herself.

> Then, they took him out back to have him try on a pair of cement shoes before giving him a swimming lesson.

d. *Destruction*   Something belonging to the hero/heroine is damaged or destroyed.

> After stealing her car, they drove it off a cliff, where it was smashed to bits.

E. *Press of Danger, Injury, Death*

1. *p Affliction*

   a. *Physical*   The hero/heroine has a physical handicap such as a hunchback, or a chronic ailment. He or she is taken ill during the course of the story.

   > The cough started as a short, infrequent hacking and later developed into a serious case of pneumonia.

   b. *Mental*   The hero/heroine suffers from neurotic or psychotic symptoms. He or she is subject to hallucinations or obsessions, experiences premonitions of insanity, or is justifiably considered very strange.

   > Every day she would manicure her front lawn with scissors, and finally she completely went to pieces when a dog "dirtied" her garden.

2. *p Death of Hero/Heroine*   This is weighted according to the stress placed on the event. The hero/heroine may die from physical or mental illness (p Affliction), from physical injury, from p Aggression, or may commit suicide [n Abasement (intra-aggression)].

   > He eventually died a grisly death when the dragon ate him.

3. *p Physical Danger*

   a. *Active*   The hero/heroine is exposed to physical danger from nonhuman forms. He or she is attacked by animals, caught in a storm at sea, hit by a train, or struck by lightning. He or she is exposed to a tremendous bombardment. The danger may be as small as a threat, or it may actually injure or kill the hero/heroine.

   > The meteor shower assaulted them from all sides so that the captain and his party just barely escaped with their lives.

   b. *Insupport*   The hero/heroine is exposed to the danger of falling or drowning. His or her car overturns, his or her ship is wrecked, he or she is caught on the narrow ledge of a steep mountain, the ground is insecure.

   > As she was climbing, step by step, across the suspension bridge, all of a sudden two of the boards directly under her broke free.

4. *p Physical Injury*   The hero/heroine is hurt by a human aggressor (p Aggression); by a cave-in, collision, or fall (p Physical Danger); or by a wild animal. The hero/heroine is mutilated or disfigured.

   > The assassin opened fire and wounded him in the arm.

F. *Press of Friendliness, Sympathy, Respect, Dependence, Love*
   1. *p Affiliation*
      a. *Associative*   The hero/heroine has one or more friends or sociable companions; he or she is a member of a congenial group.
         The men lay next to one another letting the warmth of the day and the comfort of their friendship settle into their thoughts.
      b. *Emotional*   A person such as a parent, sibling, relative, or erotic object is devoted to the hero/heroine. The hero/heroine has a love affair that is reciprocated, or the hero/heroine gets married.
         The story ends where they fall in love again and end up getting married.
   2. *p Deference*
      a. *Compliance*   An individual or a group willingly follows the leadership or requests of the hero/heroine. A person is anxious to please him or her, to cooperate, or to obey. The obedience may be passive.
         At his command the entire battalion began to prepare for the next leg of their journey.
      b. *Respect*   The hero/heroine is admired by an individual or group. His or her talents or merits are appreciated; he or she is rewarded or publicly applauded.
         With each deft stroke of his violin, the audience became driven into a fervor of awe.
   3. *p Nurturance*   Someone nourishes, encourages, protects, or cares for the hero/heroine. He or she receives sympathy, consolation, pity.
      Finally, somebody found her in a corner of the store, gave her something to eat, and helped find her parents.
   4. *p Sex*   Another person is in love with the hero/heroine, or his or her affections are engaged by a seductress/seducer. The hero/heroine gets married.
      She moved softly under the candlelight and became a virtual Aphrodite to him.
   5. *p Succorance*   Someone seeks aid, protection, or sympathy from the hero/heroine. There is a helpless, miserable, pitiful object to whom the hero/heroine reacts. Someone is rescued by the hero/heroine.
      The pathetic and whimpering puppy soon got Julie to take it home with her and nurse it back to health.

G. *Miscellaneous Press*
   1. *p Birth of Offspring*   A child is born to the hero/heroine, or a woman is going to have a baby. The amount of weight given to this press depends on the relative importance of the birth to the overall story.
      All the relatives and neighbors came to see the new baby.
   2. *p Claustrum*   The hero/heroine finds him- or herself in a confining space, such as a solitary hideout, house, deep valley, or cave. The hero/heroine might be locked in his or her room, imprisoned, trapped in a cave-in, or confined in a space such as a house, vault, or tunnel. The hero/heroine seeks to enter, tries to break out of, or is forcibly expelled from, such a place.
      Just when he thought he was going to drown, he was swallowed by a whale and became safely protected by its insides.
   3. *p Cognizance*   Someone is curious about the hero/heroine and his or her doings; the hero/heroine is watched. Someone peers or probes into his or her affairs, asks questions.

I don't know exactly why anyone would be so interested, but every time this woman walked into the room, there was an eye peering at her through this knothole.

4. *p Example*
   a. *Good Influence*   A person, group, or case (social ideal, philosophical) influences the hero/heroine in a constructive way. A talented person serves as an example.
      Every time he heard his instructor play in a concert, he was inspired to practice even harder.
   b. *Bad Influence*   The hero/heroine is led into crime by his or her associates; the level of the hero/heroine's conduct or his or her ideals is lowered by following the suggestions or inducements of an untrustworthy or irresponsible person.
      When Mel showed him how much money he could make by selling drugs, he soon developed his own connections and networks for distribution.

5. *p Exposition*   Someone tells, explains, interprets, or teaches the hero/heroine something.
      After three more classes, the theories of Marx, which had previously been so clouded in mystery, were clearly explained and seemed to make sense.

6. *p Luck*
   a. *Good, Gratuity*   The hero/heroine is unusually privileged; he or she has everything he or she wants (status, wealth, friends). The hero/heroine is suddenly benefited by some unusual or unpredicted chance occurrence, or by some extraordinary opportunity that does not result from his or her own efforts. Although the hero/heroine may be deserving of the good fortune, he or she did not work directly for it. A benefactor is attracted by the hero/heroine's promise, and his or her ambitions are aided by another person, which would also involve p Nurturance.
      Then, while walking down this dusty country road, she found a 50-year-old two-dollar bill.
   b. *Bad*   Fortune is against the hero/heroine. He or she is underprivileged from the start, must endure an extraordinary series of misfortunes, or is suddenly confronted by a chance occurrence that serves to hinder or frustrate his or her efforts. However, the coercion from such sources as parents or enemies is not considered bad luck. In determining whether to score this press, the examiner should question the extent to which fate, chance, or destiny played a part in the character's life.
      It seemed as if wherever he drilled a well, Don never discovered oil despite his considerable expertise.

Themes and Outcomes

Once the examiner has determined who the hero/heroine of the story is and what needs and press occur within the protocol, the next step is to put these together in a meaningful way. It is certainly helpful to know that, for example, a subject's hero/heroine exhibits anxiety and passivity. It is also helpful to know that the environment may be seen as threatening and surrounded by domineering forces. However, this distinction is somewhat artificial since a hero/heroine and his or her environment are continually interacting to form certain outcomes as a result of these dynamics. Murray (1943) states that "the interaction of a hero/heroine's need (or fusion of needs) and an environmental press (or fusion of press) together with the outcome (success or failure of the hero/heroine) constitutes a simple thema" (p.13). A complex thema is composed of "combinations of simple thema, interlocked or forming a sequence" (p.13).

Murray gives relatively vague instructions on how to score, categorize, or interpret outcomes or thema. The following thematic concerns, adapted and expanded from Arnold (1962), can serve as a broader guideline for eliciting the basic themes that concern the subject. Arnold (1949) has also classified specific themes that are most likely to occur around different cards; parent-child themes (Cards 1,2,3,6,7), heterosexual situations (Cards 2,3, 4,6,7,8,9,13,17,18), same-sex themes (Cards 5,9), and single person themes (Cards 11,12, 14,15,16).

Achievement Success or Failure, Happiness/Unhappiness, or Active Effort as Opposed to Lack of It   In assessing the first area of thematic concern, the examiner might ask him- or herself the following questions: Does the hero/heroine succeed or fail in his or her attempts? If he or she does fail, under what circumstances does this occur? Is the hero/ heroine's path to success difficult or easy? What obstacles does he or she confront? Does the subject end up being happy or dissatisfied and sad? Of particular importance is the degree to which the hero/heroine influences the outcome of the story or the extent to which he or she is the passive recipient of fate. Is he or she generally active or passive?

Right and Wrong   The theme of dealing with right and wrong may emerge in stories in which the ethical significance of an action and the resulting consequences to the hero/ heroine are the primary focus of the story. Does the hero/heroine demonstrate adequate impulse control? If he or she acts out, is this behavior punished or does he or she avoid getting caught? Does he or she feel guilty about this behavior, and is this guilt realistic or the result of an overly oppressive conscience? Are his or her moral values based on simple fears of getting caught, or does he or she have a higher, internal set of ethical beliefs? Does he or she confess, atone, or reform? How much does the hero/heroine criticize him- or herself?

Human Relationships   Human relationships include actions or attitudes toward others or others' attitudes toward the central character. What issues or preoccupations are the heroes/ heroines concerned with? What types of activities do they spend the most time engaged in? How do they see other people: as domineering, threatening, affectionate, helpful, push-overs, boring, etc? What major assets or deficits do the heroes/heroines have, especially in their ability to deal effectively with interpersonal difficulties?

Reaction to Adversity   The manner in which the hero/heroine deals with life stresses and problems is indicative of his or her reaction to adversity. With what major dilemmas and conflicts does the hero/heroine deal? Do these conflicts center around rivalry, love, deprivation, coercion, punishment, war, etc? Is his or her approach characterized by withdrawal, manipulation, acting out, helplessness, or assertion?

Interests and Sentiments   The final category to be considered involves noting the characteristic interests that the subject attributes to the hero/heroine. These may include such areas as artistic appreciation, travel, athletic activities, creativity, or academic endeavors. Of particular importance are positive or negative feelings toward older women (mother figures), older men (father figures), and same-sex or opposite-sex persons of the hero/ heroine's age.

INTERPRETATION

Several points need to be made regarding Murray's scoring and interpretation system. Perhaps the most important is that scoring and interpretation cannot actually be differentiated from one another. The procedures considered here are a guide for arranging and summarizing previously obtained information rather than amassing additional data. Also, any of the numerous scoring and interpretation methods can be used, each of which will provide somewhat different perspectives and information on the TAT stories. Murray's approach, although it requires some quantification on the five-point scale for needs and press, is primarily qualitative. It is also oriented more toward content than toward the formal or stylistic attributes of the stories. Thus, Murray's approach, with its emphasis on content and qualitative aspects, is merely one method and is not intended to be all-inclusive.

Once the stories have been analyzed and scored for needs and press, they can be tabulated on the summary sheets that have been provided in Figures 10–2 and 10–3. From these sheets, a list of unusually high and unusually low needs and press can be determined. These can then be compared with a list of the prevalent themata, outcomes, and interests that have been analyzed according to Murray's procedure. Additional data may include historical facts about the subject and numerous behavioral observations.

Such information can be addressed from the perspective of two assumptions about the TAT. The first is that the attributes of the hero/heroine (needs, emotional states, and sentiments) represent characteristics of the subject's own personality. These may represent things the subject has done, things he or she has wanted or perhaps has felt tempted to do, core attributes of his or her personality of which he or she may be unconscious, feelings and wishes he or she is experiencing at the time of the test administration, or anticipations of his or her future behavior (Murray, 1943).

The second basic assumption is that the press described in the stories represent a combination of the subject's actual environment and, more important, the manner in which he or she interprets that environment. These may include situations that the subject has actually encountered, ones that he or she dreams or fantasizes encountering out of hope or fear, momentary situations during the time of examination, or situations he or she expects to encounter (Murray, 1943). In other words, the press encountered in the TAT represent the subject's worldview.

The variables of needs, inner states, and press should then be combined with the type of outcomes, thema, and interests to make generalizations about, and descriptions of, the subject. These conclusions, according to Murray (1943, p.14), are to be regarded as good "leads" or working hypotheses to be verified by other methods, rather than as proven facts. Dana (1982) urges that interpretation of the TAT be accompanied by an adequate commitment to the often extensive amount of time required. It is also useful to consider feedback from clients and input from more experienced clinicians.

Murray offers a number of additional considerations regarding the conclusions to be reached by the TAT. He states that approximately 30% of the stories are likely to be impersonal renditions or clichés of previously heard information and, due to their impersonal nature, cannot be used to infer the underlying determinants of personality. Yet another consideration is that even though, for the most part, high, moderate, or low scores on the stories correspond to high, moderate, and low characteristics within the subject, this is not always the case. For example, Murray (1938) found a negative correlation (-.33 to -.74) between n Sex on the TAT and n Sex expressed in overt behavior. Of final and particular note are the subject's current life situation and his or her emotional state at the time of examination. One of the more important variables that can affect the emotional state of the subject, and therefore the test results, is the particular interaction between the subject and the examiner. A sensitive and accurate interpretation can be obtained only if the examiner takes into account the existence and possible influence of all these variables.

RECOMMENDED READING

Arnold, M.B. (1962). *Story Sequence Analysis: A New Method of Measuring and Predicting Achievement*. New York: Columbia University Press.

Bellak, L. (1986). *The TAT, CAT and SAT in clinical use* (4th ed.). New York: Grune & Stratton.

Semeonoff, B. (1976). *Projective techniques*. New York: John Wiley & Sons, Inc.

Stein, M. (1981). *The Thematic Apperception Test: An introductory manual for its clinical use with adults* (2nd ed.). Springfield, IL.: Charles C. Thomas.

Chapter 11

PROJECTIVE DRAWINGS

Attempting to understand individuals based on the interpretations they make of their world has a long, often honored history. Sections of the Hindu *Upanishads* discuss the significance of three different interpretations offered by three different people about a statement made by a spiritual teacher. Utterances made by Greek oracles were likewise open to a number of interpretations that varied depending on the personal needs and expectations of the listener. Similarly, interpretations of works of art have generally been considered to state something about the artist as well as his or her subject. As Hammer (1958) states, "when an artist paints a portrait, he paints two, himself and the sitter" (p. 8). Although intuitive methods of interpreting drawings have a long history, extending back many centuries, a more empirically based approach has only been popular within the past 30 or 40 years.

Interpretation of drawings (and projective testing in general), draws heavily on psychoanalytic theory. One of the central assumptions of this procedure is that many important aspects of personality are not available to conscious self-report and thus questionnaires and inventories are of limited value. To obtain an accurate view of a person's inner world, it is necessary to somehow circumvent unconscious defenses and conscious resistances. From a psychoanalytic perspective, then, an indirect approach, such as through projective drawings, is essential. Through symbolical creation, an individual depicts important themes, dynamics, and attitudes. Psychoanalytic theory further assumes it is not only possible for this symbolical expression to occur, but a person's perceptions and responses to his or her world are actually determined by inner qualities and forces. These idiosyncratic expressions of inner dynamics are most likely to occur when a person is requested to interpret unstructured stimuli, such as might occur when the person draws something on a blank sheet of paper. This projection of inner aspects is most likely to involve anxiety provoking images, feelings, thoughts, and memories. By externalizing onto the outside world, the person creates distance between him- or herself and the anxiety-provoking images, thereby temporarily reducing anxiety. An understanding of these projections can potentially reveal a person's inner predispositions, conflicts, and dynamics.

Projective drawings are expressive techniques in that they suggest aspects of the person while he or she is performing some sort of activity. Other examples of expressive projective techniques are interpreting role-plays, drama, children's play, or understanding the latent meaning behind jokes. There are an extremely varied number of approaches for using expressive projective techniques in general as well as projective drawings themselves. Some clinicians request the subject to simply draw a picture of a person, while others might have the subject also draw a person of the opposite sex, a house, tree, to tell a story about his or her drawing, or to use colored pencils or crayons.

Despite criticisms of their psychometric qualities, projective drawings have proved to be highly popular. This was especially true during the 1950s and 1960s, when psychoanalytic theory dominated. In 1961, Sundberg reported that projective drawings represented the second most popular test used in hospitals, clinics, and counseling centers. During the 1970s and especially the 1980s, their use declined due to poor reviews regarding their validity, decreased belief in psychoanalytic theory, greater emphasis on situational determiners of behavior, and questions regarding their cost-effectiveness. Despite this, projective drawings are still ranked as among the ten most frequently used tests (Lubin et al., 1984, 1985; Piotrowski, 1984) and fully 83% of school psychologists reported that they frequently or always use them (Prout, 1983).

HISTORY AND DEVELOPMENT

The first formal development of a projective drawing technique was Goodenough's (1926) *Draw-A-Man Test*. She used it solely to estimate a child's cognitive abilities as reflected in the quality of the drawing. She assumed that the accuracy and number of details contained indicates the child's level of intellectual maturity. Points were given for the inclusion of different body parts, quality of lines, and connections. Although it has been used for children from the ages of 3-0 to 15-11, it has been found to be most accurate for ages 3-0 to 10-0. In 1963, Harris (1963) revised the *Draw-A-Man* by adding two new forms, a more detailed scoring system, and a much wider standardization. He suggested not only administering the draw-a-man portion, but also included drawings of a woman and a drawing of the self. The new, extended point system included 73 scoring items for the drawing of the man (compared with Goodenough's 51), 71 items for drawings of the woman, and a 12-point quality scale, with 1 representing the lowest quality and 12 the highest. No scoring system was provided for the drawing of the self. The test was standardized on 2,975 boys and girls from age 5 to 15, with 75 children in each age group. To date, the Goodenough-Harris version has been the most psychometrically sound form of interpreting projective drawings.

Machover's (1949) *Draw-A-Person* (DAP) expanded projective drawings beyond the area of cognitive assessment and into the interpretation of personality. She developed a number of hypotheses based on clinical observation and intuitive judgments. For example, she speculated that the size of the drawings relates to level of self-esteem and that placement on the page reflects the subject's mood and social orientation. During the administration phase, clients are given a blank sheet of paper and simply told to "draw a picture of a person." When they have completed the first drawing, they are given a new sheet of paper and requested to "draw a person of the opposite sex." An inquiry phase is often recommended in which the subject answers specific questions about the persons in the drawings—such as what their mood is, their interests, or what makes them angry. Koppitz (1968, 1984) extended the developmental and personality aspects of human figure drawings by creating objective scoring systems for developmental level and emotional indicators.

Concurrent with Machover's early work, Buck (1948) developed the *House-Tree-Person* (HTP). He theorized that, in addition to the significance attributed to human figure drawings, people similarly attach meaning to houses and trees. Jolles (1952, 1971) further expanded the HTP by recommending three different administrations. First, the client is requested to make pencil (achromatic) drawings, then to answer questions regarding his or her drawings, and, finally, make another series of drawings using crayons (chromatic). One variation of the above is to have the client draw the house, tree, and person all on one sheet of paper, whereas another is to draw the house, tree, and person separately on three sheets of paper. Some examiners also have the subject draw a person of the same sex and of the opposite sex (the HTPP). The Kinetic House-Tree-Person is a more recent variation in which the subject is requested to make the person in the drawing "doing something" (Burns, 1987).

To assess interpersonal relationships, several variations of projective drawings have involved the client depicting groups of significant people in his or her environment. For example, Hulse (1951) has developed the *Draw-A-Family* (DAF) in which subjects draw a picture of their whole family. He recommended interpreting the drawings both globally (mood, overall quality) as well as descriptively (relative size of figures, proximity to one another, line pressure, shading). Very few validity studies were performed on the DAF, although Wright and McIntyre (1982) have developed an objective scoring system that is a useful and reliable indicator of depression. One criticism of the DAF is that it produces stiff and static figures and, as a result, is of limited usefulness in assessing the more fluid, ongoing aspects of family relations. To counter this, some clinicians recommend the *Kinetic Family Drawing* (KFD; Burns, 1980; Burns & Kaufman, 1970) in which clients are requested to draw their whole family "doing something." The resulting drawings are assumed to be better than the DAF at revealing a person's perceptions and attitudes toward his or her ongoing family dynamics. The KFD has been used in the evaluation of therapy for abused children, diabetics, children with perceptual-motor delay, family relationships, and making cross-cultural comparisons. In a somewhat similar vein, the *Kinetic-School-Drawing* (KSD; Knoff & Prout, 1985; Prout & Phillips, 1974) requests a child to draw a picture in which he or she is doing something in school. It is designed to complement the KFD (Knoff & Prout, 1985) and provide information regarding the self, teacher, peers, and, when used with the KFD, to understand how the school and home environment interact. A qualitative analysis of the drawing is usually recommended (Scarbaugh, 1982), although quantitative ratings have been found to correlate with school achievement (Prout & Celmer, 1984).

Currently, the most frequently used version of projective drawings is the Draw-A-Person (DAP) as originally developed by Machover (1949) but greatly expanded by Hammer (1958), Handler (1985), Urban (1963), and Koppitz (1968, 1984). Within clinical settings, formal quantitative scoring systems for depression, impulsiveness, or maturational development are rarely used. Clinicians are far more likely to use intuitive judgments based on clinical experience and assumed isomorphy between the characteristics of the drawing and the client's outside environment. However, few of these interpretations are based on validated research. Given the lack of any unified administration, scoring, or interpretation as well as the complexity, diversity, and richness of the drawings themselves, it is unlikely that this intuitive approach will change significantly in the near future.

RELIABILITY AND VALIDITY

Establishing the reliability and validity of projective drawings is extremely difficult given the fluctuating conditions between one administration and the next, underlying, often difficult-to-prove (or disprove) assumptions behind the procedure; and the frequent richness and complexity of the productions. Several rigorous analyses of the psychometric properties of projective drawings have generally failed to demonstrate that the drawings are valid indicators of personality. However, other results have been more encouraging and provided at least partial support for some of the hypotheses. The greatest success has been achieved when projective drawings are used as a rough measure of intellectual maturation; moderate success has been achieved in making global ratings (level of adjustment, impulsiveness, anxiety); but little success has been recorded in assessing specific aspects of personality or making clear diagnoses.

A number of specific difficulties have characterized reliability studies on projective tests. Typically there is wide variation between one drawing and the next, particularly regarding content. A child might draw a picture of a cowboy during one administration, and an astronaut the next time. Although it is easy to subject global ratings of such areas as overall drawing quality to test-retest or interrater reliability, the specific contents can be expected to show wide variation. As would then be expected, test-retest reliabilities based on quantitative scorings using the Harris (1963) DAP guidelines have found moderate reliabilities of contents (Mdn r = .74), whereas test-retest reliabilities of contents have been low. Interrater reliabilities have been much better, with a median of .90 for the drawing of the man and .94 for the woman drawing (Scott, 1981). Further studies on interrater reliability on adult DAPs have likewise been respectable. In general, interrater reliabilities of structural/formal, content, and global ratings have usually been greater than .80 (Kahill, 1984).

Whereas some success has been achieved in establishing adequate reliability, attempts to demonstrate adequate validity have been more problematic. The greatest success has been achieved by using quantitative scoring specifications, such as those provided by Harris (1963). Accurate discriminations have been made in determining the ages of different children from the ages of 5 to 12, moderate to low correlations have been found between DAP scores and intelligence (.49), and poor correlations have been found with academic achievement (Scott, 1981). Thus, when quantitative scorings (number of details, overall quality) are made of children's (5 to 12 years) drawings, the DAP does seem to be a useful nonverbal screening device of cognitive ability. This is especially true for children in the lower ranges of intelligence (Scott, 1981).

Global ratings based on multiple signs or overall impressions (bizarreness, quality) have produced mixed results. For example, distinctions among diagnostic groups have not been successful when ratings were used of the drawing's bizarreness (Cauthen, Sandman, Kilpatrick, & Deabler, 1969), body disturbance (Carlson, Tucker, Harrow, & Quinlan, 1971) or Koppitz's emotional indicators (Rubin, Ragins, Schacter, & Wimberly, 1979). In contrast, overall DAP scores have correlated with such areas as scores on a self-concept scale (Ottenbacher, 1981), a modified Halstead-Reitan organicity scale (McLachlan & Head, 1974), and the presence of homosexuality (Janzen & Coe, 1975).

The most controversial area of projective drawings has been their use for the assessment of specific personality characteristics. The original basis for interpreting the drawings was developed from clinical experience combined with psychoanalytic theory. For example, Machover (1949) hypothesized that drawing the opposite-sex figure indicated possible homosexuality or at least confusion regarding sexual identity. In contrast, most empirical research has failed to support this interpretation. No differences have been found in the proportion of opposite-sex drawings made first by lesbians (Hassell & Smith, 1975; Janzen & Coe, 1975), homosexuals of both sexes (Roback, Langevin, & Zajac, 1974), or scores on the MMPI Mf scale (Gravitz, 1969), Bem Sex-Role Inventory (Paludi, 1978), or Wellesley Sex Role Orientation Scale (Teglasi, 1980). Another hypothesis by Hammer (1954, 1958) states that persons who placed their drawings on the left side of the page were more likely to be impulsive. However, no relationship was found for persons who emphasized left-sided placement and Pd (psychopathic deviance) scores on the MMPI (Dudley, Craig, Mason, & Hirsch, 1976) or between delinquent and nondelinquent adolescents (Montague & Prytula, 1975).

The early reviews of research rarely supported the validity of projective drawings in personality assessment (Suinn & Oskamp, 1969; Swenson, 1957). Klopfer & Taulbee (1976) lamented the expenditure of so much energy on research that had produced so few encouraging results. They suggested that projective drawings be considered not so much a formal test but rather a way to increase understanding of the client based on client/clinician interaction related to the drawing.

A more recent review of adult human-figure drawings by Kahill (1984) found varying levels of support for different aspects of projective drawing interpretations. In keeping with previous reviews, most of the hypotheses derived from specific aspects of drawings (eyes, ears, line pressure, etc.) were either not supported or were mixed. Global ratings of the overall drawing were somewhat more successful in discriminating level of adjustment. In particular, ratings of overall quality were related to levels of adjustment (Maloney & Glasser, 1982). In fact, ratings of overall quality have accounted for most of the variance in global ratings in general (Lewinsohn, 1965; Shaffer, Duszynski, & Thomas, 1984). However, this may be confounded by artistic ability and training, which have rarely been controlled in the studies. Kahill (1984) concludes by suggesting that:

> ...rather than making futile attempts to turn itself into a scientific instrument, figure drawings should more properly take its place as a rich and potentially valuable clinical tool that can provide working hypotheses and a springboard for discussion with the patient. (p. 288)

ASSETS AND LIMITATIONS

One difficulty in evaluating projective drawings is that most published studies were conducted either by enthusiastic psychoanalytically oriented clinicians or by highly critical, empirically based reviewers. The clinicians often provide verification for their findings by providing anecdotes and clinical experience, or by selectively presenting primarily supportive research. In contrast, empirically oriented reviewers have seriously criticized projective drawings, particularly when the interpretations are based on specific signs (ears, hair, edging, etc.). However, these reviewers have rarely been appreciative of the assumptions, procedures, and flexibility inherent in a holistic and interactive psychoanalytic approach. It is the exception when a reader is provided with a balanced perspective that combines consensually supported empirical research with an appreciation of working with unconscious processes.

An added difficulty is that many of the interpretive hypotheses have either not been fully investigated or, for the investigations that have been done, have been flawed. In particular, many early studies did not consider the importance of base rates in evaluating the significance of interpretations. For example, if the group studied was comprised of persons in psychotherapy, and their drawings were said to indicate low self-esteem or high levels of anxiety, then there would be a high chance of being correct simply because a relatively large proportion of persons in psychotherapy experience these difficulties. Base rates have also not been included for the presence of specific characteristics of drawings, such as the frequency of enlarged heads, persons drawn without clothes, or the inclusion of guns or knives. Furthermore, few studies have taken into account a number of factors that can considerably influence drawings. These include a person's artistic skill, the testing situation, intelligence, previous experience with similar situations, characteristics of the examiner, and test-taking attitudes.

Whereas some proponents have suggested that projective drawings are relatively culture free (Hammer, 1985; Oakland & Dowling, 1983), others have challenged this assumption. For example, Sundberg and Ballinger (1968) have noted the differences in content that are likely to occur in the drawings of Nepalese as compared with American children. Similarly, drawings of children from tropical regions might be likely to include more outdoor settings, a greater number of palm (as opposed to pine) trees, fewer chimneys, and possibly less clothes. Thus, interpretations need to take these types of influences into account. Other features of drawings do seem to be universal, such as the observation that the number of details increases with age.

One major criticism of projective drawings is the frequent subjectivity involved in their interpretation. This happens primarily when interpretations are made from intuitive judgments based on assumed isomorphy between the drawings and the person or his or her world (i.e., shrunken figure equals a shrunken ego). Subjectivity is doubled in that not only does the client subjectively project portions of him- or herself into the drawing, but the interpreter might project him- or herself into his or her interpretations. For example, Hammer (1968) has noted that interpretations of clients have been related to characteristics of the interpreters themselves (e.g., more hostile clinicians produced a greater number of "hostile indicators" in the drawings).

Chapman and Chapman (1971) suggested that reliance on incorrect but repeatedly used interpretations may be due to what they refer to as "illusory correlation." They demonstrated this by providing college undergraduates with human figure drawings accompanied by specific interpretive statements. They were thus clearly taught the "correct" interpretations. They were then given a list of six personality statements and requested to list the drawing characteristic associated with the statements. Despite the previous instruction, students listed aspects of the drawings based not on their previous learning, but on invalid yet intuitively derived associations (i.e., suspiciousness being reflected by overworking the eyes). Perhaps the most disturbing aspect of the study was that the intuitive interpretations from the students corresponded closely with impressionistic interpretations by trained clinicians. This illusory correlation has been found even when subjects were asked to guard against it (Waller & Keeley, 1978) and is stronger when attempting to process large amounts of information (Lueger & Petzel, 1979). This, combined with poor research results, suggests that clinical lore may be based more on common sense than validated hypotheses. In fact, interpreters may even ignore research data in favor of intuitively appealing interpretations that are unsupported or even contradicted by empirical literature.

A number of additional, more specific limitations have also been directed toward the projective use of drawings. No agreed-upon interpretation or scoring systems exist and there is a wide number of variations on administration. Furthermore, norms are either nonexistent or, where norms have been provided, typically poorly developed. In many cases, the catalogues used for interpretation are arranged in a way that allows them to be mistaken as test manuals with empirically established interpretations. The misinformed reader might thus make incorrect interpretations based on these seductively listed interpretive hypotheses. This problem is further compounded in that some of the manuals have been reprinted without taking into account much relevant research. Thus, many "interpretations" are still included, even though they quite clearly have been found to be invalid. The above factors are all likely to significantly alter both the drawings themselves, as well as the interpretations resulting from them.

Given the largely unencouraging empirical research, explanations need to be provided for the continued popularity of projective drawings. Proponents stress that the drawings are simple, easy procedures that can be administered quickly, require few materials, and are found to be enjoyable by most participants. In addition, the drawings can often provide a large amount of information relating to a person's self-concept, ego ideal, perceptions of persons of the opposite sex, level of adjustment, impulsiveness, anxiety, contact with reality, and conflict areas. Since responses are supposed to depend on a person's inner organizing abilities, the drawings theoretically provide an index of the nature and quality of these organizational processes. Furthermore, projective drawings can be used with children from a wide age range. Since drawings are nonverbal, they can be used with clients who have poor verbal skills, such as the intellectually disabled, non-English speaking clients, persons with reading/learning difficulties, or those who are withdrawn, evasive, or defensive. Administration can be done either individually or in groups. Not only can the results from projective drawings be easily integrated into psychological reports, but they can be used to indicate change as a result of psychotherapy.

In terms of the practical, day-to-day types of concerns encountered by clinicians, the above-mentioned assets of projective drawings are significant. However, each clinician who plans to use projective drawings should consider whether these assets are sufficient to counter the difficulties related to their psychometric properties. Clinicians who want a clear, valid, foolproof means of assessing personality will be disappointed. In contrast, practitioners comfortable with a more intuitive, metaphorical, tentative, and interactive approach for generating hypotheses and facilitating interaction will find projective drawings to be a useful tool.

ADMINISTRATION

Regardless of the different variations in administration, instructions are kept to a minimum. This helps to maintain the ambiguity of the situation, thereby increasing the likelihood that significant aspects of personality will be projected onto the drawings. Clients should be seated in a comfortable position, with sufficient room to freely move their arms while completing the drawings. They are provided with a single sheet of $8\frac{1}{2}$ x 11-inch sheet of paper and, if an achromatic drawing is desired, are given a sharp #2 pencil with an eraser. If chromatic drawings are desired, clients should be provided with crayons, colored pencils, or different-colored felt-tip pens. If the DAP is given, they would simply be requested to "Draw a picture of a person." Once the first drawing is completed, subjects are given another $8\frac{1}{2}$ x 11-inch, unlined sheet of paper and requested to "Draw me a person of the opposite sex." If the "self" version is also administered, they would be requested to "Draw me a picture of yourself." Some administrators suggest that no other instructions be given, whereas others recommend that the person also be told to take his or her time and do as good a job as possible. Administrations other than the DAP would require similar instructions. For example, one variation of the HTP recommends that the client be requested to "Draw me a picture that includes a house, a tree, and a person," or kinetic drawings would simply request them to "Draw a picture of your family (or persons in school) doing something." Once the drawing has been completed, the clinician should note the client's name, age, and date, and should number the drawings according to the order in which they were drawn.

Sometimes, clients complain that they are poor artists. This might be countered with the observation that most people's artistic ability stops when they are about 10 years of age so that most people are not particularly good artists. Furthermore it might be stressed that this is not a test of artistic ability but that they should still do the best they can. Occasionally, clients will request specific guidelines, such as how big to make the person, what sex they should be, or what the person in the drawing should be doing. The examiner should simply state that it is up to them. If they draw a stick figure, they should be given a new sheet of paper and requested to draw a more complete person. Some examiners recommend that, if subjects draw only the top half or quarter of a person, they should also be given a new sheet of paper and be requested to draw a complete person.

One option is to include an inquiry phase, in which the client might be requested to tell a story about the person in the drawing. This story can then be used to aid future interpretations. More specific questions might be asked, such as having subjects indicate what the person in the drawing is thinking or feeling, what makes him or her happy/sad, or what his or her interests are. A semistructured list of questions for the HTP is included in Appendix Q. If only the DAP is administered, the examiner might only select and ask the questions relevant to the person drawing(s). Some examiners might want clients to associate to and interpret the significance of their drawings. The clients themselves are thereby being used as consultants to help with the interpretations. This latter procedure is likely to be most successful for clients with a good level of insight and who are fairly appreciative of unconscious processes.

During the administration, the examiner should note any relevant behaviors. These might include clients' level of confidence or hesitancy, whether the procedure increases their anxiety, their degree of playfulness, impulsiveness, conscientiousness, or the presence of excessive erasures.

The most appropriate variation on administration will depend on the purpose of assessment as well as the personal preference of the clinician. In general, the most research and therefore the most strategies available for interpretation can be found with human-figure drawings. However, if a clinician would like to obtain information about family, school, or work, then variations such as the Kinetic Family Drawing or Kinetic School Drawing might be administered. Different authors argue the relative usefulness of different variations. For example, Burns (1987) has argued for and provided examples of the advantages of the Kinetic House-Tree-Person over the regular House-Tree-Person. Similarly, Sarrell & Berman (1981) have emphasized that the Draw-A-Person is good at uncovering attitudes toward the person's sexuality and body image.

GENERAL INTERPRETIVE CONSIDERATIONS

Interpretation of projective drawings varies on a continuum ranging from objective scoring to an intuitive, impressionistic analysis. Objective scoring is based primarily on specific details or patterns of details that occur in the drawings. These might include scoring for such factors as cognitive maturity, impulsiveness, neurological deficit, or overall level of adjustment. However, it is frequent in clinical practice to take a more flexible, impressionistic approach that might begin with considering the overall feel of the drawing, proceeding to standard interpretations of specific signs, and integrating the hypotheses derived from these steps within the context of information obtained from other sources.

Some clinicians prefer to base their interpretations on interactions with their clients in which both the client and the therapist confer to establish the individual meaning of the drawings. In this more interactive approach, the drawings can be used as a tool for focusing on the inner experience of the client in order to either expand the depth of assessment or accomplish therapeutic goals, such as resolving difficulties, uncovering unconscious patterns, or facilitating catharsis.

Interpretation by means of quantitative scoring provides clear results that can be empirically supported. In contrast, more impressionistic approaches often produce questionable results due to various types of clinician bias (illusory correlation, primacy/recency effects, etc.) combined with the generally poor psychometric properties of the test itself.

The advantage of an impressionistic approach lies in its flexibility, potentially allowing the clinician to discover unique aspects of the person that might be missed by an objective approach, and enabling the development of a deeper level of rapport between the client and clinician. However, the accuracy of this approach varies tremendously based on the individual skill of the clinician and/or various conditions surrounding test administration and interpretation.

The Body Image Hypothesis

The most central assumption behind projective interpretation of human-figure drawings is that they represent the artist or at least some aspect of the artist. All other interpretations (head size, nudity, sex of first-drawn figure, etc.) revolve around this central assumption. Some of the numerous studies made to test this hypothesis have been supportive. For example, a moderate relationship was found between human-figure drawings by adolescent males and judges' ratings of the boys' physical characteristics (Van Dyne & Carskadon, 1978). Similarly, obese subjects drew larger figures than persons with normal weight (Bailey, Shinedling, & Payne, 1970) and schizophrenics who had undergone training in movement and creative expression had increased scores using the Goodenough-Harris criteria (Rosenthal & Beutal, 1981). Similarly, subgroups of females who would be expected to have extra concern with their bodies have been found to reflect these concerns in their human-figure drawings. These subgroups included pubertal girls who were found to give more explicit representation to breasts (Reirdan & Koff, 1980), and pregnant women who were more likely to draw breasts and nude and/or distorted figures (Tolor & Digrazia, 1977).

The results of both the research on the body image hypothesis and the drawings themselves should be interpreted cautiously, since the projection of the self onto the drawings is likely to be complicated and multifaceted. Clients might even draw a figure that is opposite to their actual self if they "decided" to portray an unrealistic ego ideal. Central to the problem is the difficulty in determining what constitutes a "true" view of a person's body image:

> Is it a photograph, or a verbal self-description, or is the body image a function of the interaction between a person's physical appearance and his self-concept? Or is it something else, or some combination of something else? The question is, of course, unanswerable. (Swenson, 1968, p. 23)

Thus, the projection of the self should not be defined in narrow terms. It might be subjects' actual self, their ideal self, their feared self, or might represent their perception of other people in their environment.

Age Considerations

Some reviewers have concluded that the primary factor involved in children's drawings is cognitive maturity (see the Goodenough-Harris formal scoring criteria) and that personality or emotional states are relatively minor. In contrast, others believe that, since children have fewer defenses than adults, they are more likely to create drawings that are strong, direct, and clear expressions of their emotional states. Regardless of which position is correct, it is essential to understand the expected versus unusual features of the drawings produced by persons from different age groups. For example, it's normal for 5-year-olds not to draw feet, hair, or necks, which means their absence should not be considered clinically significant.

Koppitz (1968) summarized the items that are expected in between 86 to 100% of the drawings of children from age 5 to 12 (see Table 11–1). For example, Table 11–1 shows that it is normal for 86 to 100% of 5-year-olds to include a head, eyes, nose, mouth, etc. Only

Table 11–1. Expected and exceptional items on human figure drawings of boys and girls age 5 to 12

	Age 5		Age 6		Age 7		Age 8		Age 9		Age 10		Age 11 & 12	
	Boys	Girls	Boys	Girls	Boys	Girls	Boys	Girls	Boys	Girls	Boys	Girls	Boys	Girls
N	128	128	131	133	134	125	138	130	134	134	109	108	157	167
Expected Items														
Head	X	X	X	X	X	X	X	X	X	X	X	X	X	X
Eyes	X	X	X	X	X	X	X	X	X	X	X	X	X	X
Nose	X	X	X	X	X	X	X	X	X	X	X	X	X	X
Mouth	X	X	X	X	X	X	X	X	X	X	X	X	X	X
Body	X	X	X	X	X	X	X	X	X	X	X	X	X	X
Legs	X	X	X	X	X	X	X	X	X	X	X	X	X	X
Arms	X	X	X	X	X	X	X	X	X	X	X	X	X	X
Feet		X	X	X	X	X	X	X	X	X	X	X	X	X
Arms 2 dimension					X		X	X	X	X	X	X	X	X
Legs 2 dimension									X	X	X	X	X	X
Hair				X		X	X	X	X	X	X	X	X	X
Neck										X	X	X	X	X
Arm down											X	X	X	X
Arms at shoulder														
2 clothing items											X		X	X
Exceptional Items														
Knee	X	X	X	X	X	X	X	X	X	X	X	X	X	X
Profile	X	X	X	X	X	X	X	X	X	X		X		
Elbow	X	X	X	X	X	X	X	X	X	X		X		
Two lips	X	X	X	X	X	X	X	X						
Nostrils	X	X	X	X	X		X		X		X			
Proportions	X	X	X	X	X		X		X					
Arms at shoulder	X	X	X	X										
4 clothing items	X	X	X	X										
Feet 2 dimension	X													
Five fingers	X													
Pupils	X													

Note: E. Koppitz, *Psychological Evaluation of Children's Human Figure Drawings.* New York: Grune & Stratton, Inc., 1968. Reproduced by permission.

15% of the population fail to include these features and, when omitted, may suggest that the person is mentally immature. In contrast, Table 11–1 also includes unusual or "exceptional items" that are included by only 15% of the population. For example, a 5-year-old who includes such features as a knee, elbow, or two lips might be indicating either superior mental ability or perhaps some special concern with the area of the body that has been depicted. Thus, the table can be used to determine which features of a child's drawings are normal versus unusual for children of different ages. The more formal Goodenough-Harris scoring system used to determine a child's cognitive maturity can supplement Table 11–1 and is summarized in the section on objective scoring.

Although most change and variety occurs in the drawings of young children, some patterns have also emerged in the drawings of adolescents and the elderly. Adolescence is frequently a time of experimentation and exaggerated behaviors, which are often reflected in their drawings. For example, Saarni and Azara (1977) found it was fairly typical for adolescent males to have more extreme expressions of gender identity (huge muscles, dominant expressions), more hostile-aggressive features, and greater bizarreness. In contrast, drawings by female adolescents were more likely to have features suggesting insecurity-lability and to be more ambiguous and childlike. Thus, interpretations should take these features into account so that the drawings of adolescents are interpreted differently than the drawings of adults that contain these features. There is also some suggestion that the elderly are more likely to make relatively fragmented, incongruous, absurd, and primitive drawings (Gilbert & Hall, 1966).

The Healthy Drawing

Clinical psychology and psychiatry frequently show a bias toward focusing on problem areas. Frequently, little attention is paid to the person's strengths, resources, and areas of positive growth. This bias is clearly seen in the psychoanalytic interpretation of projective material. Most interpretive guides to projective drawings generally make a passing reference to the importance of adjustment and then quickly proceed into a long list of features suggesting pathology. Often, the implied assumption is that, if no pathological features are identified, then the drawing is probably from a healthy, well-adjusted person. Morena (1981) has reviewed the literature relating to healthy drawings and summarized different features found in drawings that suggest positive self-esteem, confidence, security, well-functioning interpersonal relations, openness to self and environment, clarity regarding sexual orientation, and ability to organize one's self and one's life effectively. The specifics of these areas are listed below, but the underlying factor can be considered to be the overall quality of the drawing. This is supported by the different scoring systems that have been used to assess drawings, which primarily identify the drawing quality (or lack of it) as the single common factor (Shaffer, Duszynski, & Thomas, 1984).

Self-esteem   Self-esteem might be indicated by moderate size (not excessively large or small), and by the figure being in a solid, open, well-balanced position. The line quality would be definite and firm, and all essential features of the person present (legs, arms, head, torso, etc.).

Security and Self-confidence   The figure(s) is grounded, placed in the center of the page, potentially capable of movement (not frozen or rigid), and the line quality is firm (not overly dark or light).

Openness   The person can potentially interact with the environment, the posture is open, and in the House-Tree-Person the house is accessible (pathway leading up to it, presence of doors and windows).

Positive Personal Relationships In drawings of groups (i.e., Draw-A-Family), the figures are moderately close and there is potential for interaction.

Stability and Orderliness The picture looks complete. There are no unfinished aspects or important missing details; the parts are integrated and complementary.

Sexual Identification The figures have clearly defined male or female features, all essential details are included, and the sizes are correct relative to the other persons and to the picture as a whole.

Interpretive Procedure

The following four steps are recommended as a sequence to follow when interpreting projective drawings. These steps combine options for both objective scoring and a more impressionistic approach. Individual clinicians may wish to vary their reliance on objective or impressionistic strategies based on personal preference (need for empirically valid interpretations, comfort with metaphorical approaches) or on the needs defined by the context of the assessment itself (as a prelude to therapy, high validity demanded by a legal assessment, relative richness of the drawings, time constraints).

1. Objective scoring Clinicians can score for one or more of the objective scoring systems included in the following section (cognitive maturity, impulsivity, adjustment, neurological deficit). This will both provide relatively valid interpretations as well as alert the clinician to specific, relevant details in the drawing. This approach is also in keeping with the conclusions of virtually all objective reviewers of projective drawings who have recommended global ratings and objective scoring as the preferred method of interpretation.

2. Overall impression Once a specific scoring has been calculated, the clinician can then step back from the drawing and consider it as a whole (Handler, 1985; Morena, 1981). Clinicians might ask themselves what the overall mood, general message, or feel is of the drawing. What does it convey about the client's view of the world, self-concept, attitude toward his or her body, perception of the opposite sex, or receptivity in interpersonal relationships? This is a highly intuitive process in which clinicians attempt to place themselves in the position of the client to see the client's world from the perspective suggested by the drawing(s). Any initial impressions/insights can be noted and considered in greater detail later.

Accuracy using this approach has been found to be related to persons who were high in empathy, intuition, flexibility, and creativity, and who were sensitive to interpersonal relations (Burley & Handler, 1970). This is emphasized by Hammer (1968) who states that " ... in the hands of some students, projective drawings are an exquisitely sensitive tool" but for others who use a stilted, rigid approach, the interpretations are "like disconnected phones" (p. 385). In addition to personality characteristics, knowledge relevant to this phase includes dream interpretation, mythology, psychoanalytic theory, art appreciation, and mechanisms of the unconscious—such as condensation, displacement, and substitution.

3. Consideration of specific details Once a global consideration has been made, clinicians can make a rational analysis of the different details in the drawing, as outlined in the section on Interpretation of Specific Details. This might include the meaning associated with unusual aspects of features, such as the size of the drawing, detailing, line quality, or breast emphasis. However, this detailed analysis should be made cautiously since very few individual signs have received clear empirical support.

Even the strongest proponents of projective drawings stress that one of the worst violations of working with drawings is to make rigid, single-sign interpretations. For example, Handler (1985) advises that clinicians should not ask *what* a specific sign means but rather what it *could* mean.

4. Integration   The final step is to take information derived from steps 1 through 3 and integrate it into a wider context derived from interview data, personal records, and other test results. For example, if the person scored high on Oas' (1984) measures of impulsiveness, did he or she also score high on measures of impulsiveness on the MMPI (primarily scales 4 and 9)? Likewise, do measures of neurological deficit found on the human-figure drawings correspond with the person's history and/or neurological indicators on the Bender? The final phase, then, is one of reality testing, which is intended to increase the incremental validity of assessment data.

INTERPRETATION OF SPECIFIC SIGNS

The hypotheses included in this section are those that, based on the three major reviews of the literature (Kahill, 1984; Roback, 1968; Swenson, 1968), have produced at least some support. Research between 1984 and 1989 has also been consulted. The criteria for inclusion is that at the very least, an equal number of studies have supported the hypothesis compared with those that failed to find support. In addition to the mere number of supportive versus nonsupportive studies, the quality and relevance of the studies was also taken into account. Those hypotheses that were clearly not supported are listed toward the end of the sections.

Before attempting interpretations of specific details, clinicians should observe a number of cautions. Most of the research has produced conflicting results for even the best of these signs. Swenson (1968) explains the widely varying results as consistent with the moderate to low reliabilities associated with both the occurrence of these signs (test-retest reliability) as well as low agreement found when scoring them (interrater reliability). From a practical perspective, this means any interpretation should be made tentatively. In particular, Handler's (1985) advice to ask what a specific sign *could* mean rather than what it *does* mean should be heeded. Interpreters should also keep in mind the possibility that a sign may take on specific meaning for a client and thereby lead to an idiosyncratic interpretation for that person, even though the sign may not be sufficiently supported in any normative sense. Clinicians who are comfortable with a more interactive, metaphorical approach might find the interpretation of specific signs to be a rich source of information about the client. At the same time, clinicians should be aware of the limitations and possible errors associated with clinical judgment (see Chapter 1). A final caution is that the vast majority of the research on specific interpretive signs has been done on adults and adolescents. Thus, the use of personality assessment for children's drawings should be approached with extreme caution. This is especially true since the drawings of children may relate more to cognitive ability than personality (Swenson, 1968). Even when aspects of children's drawings do relate to personality, it would be difficult to separate this from the effects of cognitive ability.

Interpretation of Structure and Form

Size   Machover (1949) hypothesized that the relative size of the drawing is related to a person's level of self-esteem and energy. Extremely small, miniaturized drawings reflect low self-concept, depression, and lack of energy. Moderately large drawings suggest higher levels of energy and self-esteem. If the drawing is extremely large, this suggests compensatory inflation, which is consistent with persons having energy levels characteristic of manics or persons with delusions of grandeur. If a male draws a much larger female figure than a male figure, Machover (1949) further hypothesized that the person may be dominated by his mother, a mother-type figure, and/or may have difficulties with sexual identity. The empirical research has produced inconsistent results but there has been moderate support for the view that size reflects varying levels of self-esteem, mood, and relative degree of self-inflation.

Detailing   Hammer (1954), Handler (1985), and Machover (1949) have all suggested that inclusion of an excessive number of details is consistent with persons who handle anxiety by becoming more obsessive. Thus, the number of details has been used as not only a rough index of anxiety, but also the style by which the person attempts to deal with his or her anxiety. In contrast, a noteworthy lack of detail suggests withdrawal and a reduction of energy. A low number of details may also be consistent with persons who are mentally deficient, hesitant, or merely bored with the task.

Line Characteristics   The line used to draw the figure can be conceptualized as the wall between the person's environment and his or her body (Machover, 1949). It can thus reflect the person's degree of insulation, vulnerability, or sensitivity to outside forces. Thick, heavily reinforced lines might be attempts to protect the self from anxiety-provoking forces and faint, sketchy, thin lines might conversely represent insecurity and anxiety.

Shading   Machover (1949) and Hammer (1954, 1958) have hypothesized that shading represents anxiety. The specific area that is shaded is likely to suggest concern regarding that area. Thus, a person who is self-conscious regarding facial complexion might provide a high amount of shading on the face, or a person with concern regarding his or her breasts might similarly include more shading in this area. However, this interpretation should be made cautiously since the lack of shading to specific areas does not then mean there is no anxiety regarding those areas. Shading might also represent adaptation and adjustment in the drawings of persons who are merely trying to increase the quality of their drawing by emphasizing its three-dimensional aspect.

Distortion   Distortion in drawings occurs when the overall drawing itself or specific details in the drawing are drawn in poor proportion, are disconnected, or are placed in inappropriate locations on the body. Hammer (1958) hypothesized that mild distortions reflect low self-concept, anxiety, and poor adjustment, whereas excessive distortions are characteristic of persons who had experienced a severe emotional upheaval. This has been found to be one of the most strongly supported hypotheses by all reviewers.

Chromatic Drawings   Some variations on administration suggest that, in addition to pencil drawings, the person is requested to draw a person in color by using crayons or felt-tip pens. Hammer (1969) suggested that the use of colors would be more likely to reveal emotionally charged and primitive aspects of the person, particularly if he or she is under stress or pressure. Although this has been supported by two studies, it has so far not been fully researched.

Hypotheses not Supported   A number of traditional personality hypotheses related to the structure and form of drawings have clearly not been supported. These include placement on the page, stance, perspective the person in the drawing is viewed from, number of erasures, omission, degree of symmetry, and presence of transparencies.

Interpretation of Content

Sex of First-Drawn Figure   The body image hypothesis states that not only do artists identify with the figure they have drawn, but this identification is likely to be strongest for the drawing they have chosen to draw first. Based on this hypothesis, Machover (1949) and Hammer (1954) have further suggested that persons with clear gender identity will make the first drawing the same sex as themselves and persons with sexual identity confusion will more often draw a member of the opposite sex. Later researchers and theorists have indicated that this relationship is more complex. For example, Handler (1985) has suggested that, although gender confusion is a possibility, drawing the same-sex person first might also indicate a strong attachment/dependence to a person of the opposite sex, greater awareness/interest in persons of the opposite sex, or a poor self-concept.

Over the past 40 years, the hypotheses that clients with sexual identity confusion will draw the opposite-sex person first has been tested by over 25 studies. The general consensus is that only weak support has been established. For example, in an early review, Brown and Tolor (1957) reported that 85% to 95% of the normal, college male population drew the same sex first as opposed to 75% to 92% of homosexuals. Although the percentage was slightly lower for homosexuals, the overlap between the two groups was sufficiently high to indicate that an unacceptably high rate of inaccuracies would occur if this is used to discriminate the two groups. Kahill (1984) reports that most recent studies investigating the more general distinction of sex-role identification or sex-role conflict have likewise not found significant relationships. The hypothesis is further complicated in that children quite frequently draw the opposite sex first, then this frequency gradually decreases in teenagers, and by college age, individuals draw opposite-sex persons first in percentages that approximate those reported above by Hammer and Kaplan (1964). There was also a general trend in normal college females to draw the opposite sex first 52% of the time. This suggests that any interpretations of females or children should be made with the knowledge that drawings in which the opposite sex is drawn first occur quite frequently within these groups. The above discussion is provided since sex of the first-drawn figure is one of the classic interpretive signs in human-figure drawings. However, the weak support for this sign clearly indicates that interpretations based on it should be considered with caution, flexibility, and even skepticism.

Mouth and Teeth   Intuitively, it might be conjectured that the manner in which subjects depict a figure's mouth reveals their attitudes toward processing things from the world or how they express themselves verbally. Specifically, Machover (1949) hypothesized that emphasis on the mouth suggests either an immature personality with oral characteristics, or verbal aggression. Although an emphasis on the mouth has not been found to be related to immature, oral characteristics, there is some indication that the presence of both teeth along with a slash representing the mouth suggests verbal (but not physical) aggression (see Kahill, 1984).

Breasts   Breast emphasis was theorized to occur in the drawings of emotionally and psychosexually immature males (Machover, 1949). However, breast emphasis in male drawings has been found in both normal and disturbed persons, so pathology should be inferred cautiously. In drawings by females, breast emphasis has been found to occur more frequently in drawings by pubescent girls (Rierdan & Koff, 1980) and pregnant women (Tolor & Digrazia, 1977).

Nudity/Clothing   Hammer (1954) hypothesized that underclothed drawings indicate "body narcissism" and possibly a person who is self-absorbed to the point of being schizoid. On a more global level, it might be a general sign of maladjustment particularly related to sexual difficulties. Although it has received some support, this interpretation is complicated in that either nudity or lack of clothing is sometimes found in the drawings of normals and frequently occurs in the drawings of artists. Specific populations who would be expected to have bodily concerns have likewise been found to draw a high proportion of nude figures. This includes 58% of the DAPs from pregnant women, 60% of those who have recently given birth, and 60% of those with gynecological problems (Tolor & Digrazia, 1973).

Hypotheses not Supported   The majority of the hypotheses relating to contents of human-figure drawings have clearly not been given support. This is partially due to the idio-syncratic meanings associated with many of the contents as well as the low reliabilities of these signs. Interpretations related to specific contents that have not been supported include those related to the head, head size, face, facial expressions, hair, facial features (eyes, ears, lips, nose), neck, contact features (arms, hands, legs, feet, toes, legs), trunk, shoulders, anatomy indicators (internal glands, genitals), hips/buttocks, waistline, and clothing details (buttons, earrings, heels, belt).

INTERPRETATION THROUGH OBJECTIVE SCORING

The following four representative scoring systems for cognitive maturity, maladjustment, impulsiveness, and neurological deficit have been selected because they are relatively psychometrically sound, relatively easily scored, and represent clearly different types of information. Each scoring system is intended to be used on drawings derived from the standard instructions to the DAP (see Administration section).

Cognitive Maturity

The Goodenough-Harris (Harris, 1963) system for scoring provides an adequate method for screening children to determine their level of cognitive maturity. The authors assumed that the skills needed for making a drawing require the child to make relevant discriminations related to that object. Children must not only accurately perceive the object, but also must organize their response into a systematic, meaningful pattern. The degree of complexity of their response (the drawing) can serve as an index of the complexity of their ability to form concepts. Complexity is measured by the number of relevant details included in the drawings. The previous summary of the Goodenough-Harris method indicated that reliability was good (test-retest = .74, interrater = .90 and .94), the standardization sample was sufficiently large (although age levels should have been divided into six-month intervals rather than full-year levels), and validity was adequate. In particular, the scale has been able to accurately discriminate between children of different ages (5 to 12). It has also been found to have low to moderate correlations with intelligence (.50), but could not predict academic performance (see Scott, 1981). Despite the moderate correlation with intelligence, the scale should not be used as a substitute for a formal intelligence test but is rather most appropriate as a rapid screening device.

Administration should follow the standard procedures described in the Administration section of this chapter. In addition, Harris (1963) recommends that the person also be requested to draw a picture of "the self." He believes this can potentially provide information on the emergence of the self-concept and is possibly a more valid projective device than the more vague drawing of "a person." No guidelines are provided for an objective scoring of the self drawing. Scoring for the two drawings of "the persons" are based on the number of details present. Each detail is scored as either a pass (1) if the detail is present, or fail (0) if it is absent. Scoring for the male drawing includes a total of 73 possible items, while the female drawing includes a possible 71 items. Clinicians are encouraged to familiarize themselves with the exact specifications included in the scoring manual provided by Harris (1963, pp. 242-292). Once these have been learned, they can refer to the "short scoring guides" that summarize the scoring details and are included in Tables 11–2 and 11–3. A child's relative standing can be determined by comparing their raw scores to the means and standard deviations presented for the "Man Scale" in Appendix R and the "Woman Scale" in Appendix S. In addition, Harris (1963) provides conversions from raw

Table 11–2.   Short Scoring Guide*—Man Point Scale

1. Head present	26. Detail of fingers correct	53. Proportion: legs
2. Neck present	27. Opposition of thumb shown	54. Proportion: limbs in two dimensions
3. Neck, two dimensions	28. Hands present	55. Clothing I
4. Eyes present	29. Wrist or ankle shown	56. Clothing II
5. Eye detail: brow or lashes	30. Arms present	57. Clothing III
6. Eye detail: pupil	31. Shoulders I	58. Clothing IV
7. Eye detail: proportion	32. Shoulders II	59. Clothing V
8. Eye detail: glance	33. Arms at side or engaged in activity	60. Profile I
9. Nose present	34. Elbow joint shown	61. Profile II
10. Nose, two dimensions	35. Legs present	62. Full face
11. Mouth present	36. Hip I (crotch)	63. Motor coordination: lines
12. Lips, two dimensions	37. Hip II	64. Motor coordination: junctures
13. Both nose and lips in two dimensions	38. Knee joint shown	65. Superior motor coordination
14. Both chin and forehead shown	39. Feet I: any indication	66. Directed lines and form: head outline
15. Projection of chin shown; chin clearly differentiated from lower lip	40. Feet II proportion	67. Directed lines and form: trunk outline
	41. Feet III heel	68. Directed lines and form: arms and legs
	42. Feet IV perspective	69. Directed lines and form: facial features
16. Line of jaw indicated	43. Feet V detail	70. "Sketching" technique
17. Bridge of nose	44. Attachment of arms and legs I	71. "Modeling" technique
18. Hair I	45. Attachment of arms and legs II	72. Arm movement
19. Hair II	46. Trunk present	73. Leg movement
20. Hair III	47. Trunk in proportion, two dimensions	
21. Hair IV	48. Proportion: head I	
22. Ears present	49. Proportion: head II	
23. Ears present: proportion and position	50. Proportion: face	
24. Fingers present	51. Proportion: arms I	
25. Correct number of fingers shown	52. Proportion: arms II	

*For use only after the scoring requirements have been mastered.

Note: Harris, D.B. *Children's Drawings as Measures of Intellectual Maturity*, 1963, p. 275. Reprinted by permission of Harcourt, Brace, & Jovanovich.

Table 11–3.   Short Scoring Guide*—Woman Point Scale

1. Head present	29. Correct number of fingers shown	53. Garb complete, without incongruities
2. Neck present	30. Detail of fingers correct	54. Garb a definite "type"
3. Neck, two dimensions	31. Opposition of thumb shown	55. Trunk present
4. Eyes present	32. Hands present	56. Trunk in proportion, two dimensions
5. Eye detail: brow or lashes	33. Legs present	57. Head-trunk proportionate
6. Eye detail: pupil	34. Hip	58. Head: proportion
7. Eye detail: proportion	35. Feet I: any indication	59. Limbs: proportion
8. Cheeks	36. Feet II: proportion	60. Arms in proportion to trunk
9. Nose present	37. Feet III: detail	61. Location of waist
10. Nose, two dimensions	38. Shoe I: "feminine"	62. Dress area
11. Bridge of nose	39. Shoe II: style	63. Motor coordination: junctures
12. Nostrils shown	40. Placement of feet appropriate to figure	64. Motor coordination: lines
13. Mouth present	41. Attachment of arms and legs I	65. Superior motor coordination
14. Lips, two dimensions	42. Attachment of arms and legs II	66. Directed lines and form: head outline
15. "Cosmetic lips"	43. Clothing indicated	67. Directed lines and form: breast
16. Both nose and lips in two dimensions	44. Sleeve I	68. Directed lines and form: hip contour
17. Both chin and forehead shown	45. Sleeve II	69. Directed lines and form: arms taper
18. Line of jaw indicated	46. Neckline I	70. Directed lines and form: calf of leg
19. Hair I	47. Neckline II: collar	71. Directed lines and form: facial features
20. Hair II	48. Waist I	
21. Hair III	49. Waist II	
22. Hair IV	50. Skirt "modeled" to indicate pleats or draping	
23. Necklace or earrings	51. No transparencies in the figure	
24. Arms present	52. Garb feminine	
25. Shoulders		
26. Arms at side (or engaged in activity or behind back)		
27. Elbow joint shown		
28. Fingers present		

*For use only after the scoring requirements have been mastered.
Note: From Harris, D.B. *Children's Drawings as Measures of Intellectual Maturity*, 1963, p. 292.
Reprinted by permission of Harcourt, Brace, & Jovanovich.

scores into standard scores with a mean of 100 and standard deviation of 15 (see pp. 294-301 in Harris, 1963). He also recommends estimating for drawing quality using a ranking from 1 (least mature) to 12 (most mature).

Adjustment

Several researchers have noted that global ratings are the major area in which the DAP has been found to have adequate reliability and validity. This is congruent with reviewers of the DAP, such as Roback (1968) who has stated that the most probable clear future for the DAP is as a "rough screening device (to determine) 'gross level of maladjustment'" (p. 17). Several studies have included overall ratings based on global subjective impressions (bizarreness, creativity, quality), number of details present, or quantitative scoring of one or more characteristics of the drawing. Comparisons of these different scoring systems indicate that most of the variance can be accounted for by the general factor of drawing quality (Shaffer, Duszynski, & Thomas, 1984).

Maloney and Glasser (1982) reviewed the literature on DAP signs that indicate maladjustment and developed a list of nine, easily scored characteristics that they found were most able to discriminate between persons with difficulties. These are listed, along with scoring criteria, in Table 11–4. All the indicators except Transparency and Vertical Imbalance were able to discriminate between normals and different patient groups. The most accurate discriminators were Head Simplification and Body Simplification, followed by Overall Quality, Sexual Differentiation, and Distortion (indicators 5, 6, 7, 9, 3). Overall interrater reliabilities ranged from .78 to .30 with the lowest levels being for vertical imbalance (.39) and sexual elaboration (.30). Discriminations between normals and psychiatric patients were most accurately made using Head Simplification, Body Simplification, Distortion, and Low Overall Quality (indicators 5, 6, 3, 7). These indicators occurred either rarely or not at all in the drawings of normals. Head Simplification, Body Simplification, Sexual Differentiation, and Sexual Elaboration (indicators 5, 6, 8, 9) occurred more frequently in the drawings of psychiatric psychotic patients than in those for psychiatric nonpsychotics (few or no indicators). Mentally retarded persons had the highest number of indicators (except 9; Sexual Elaboration) of any of the groups except psychiatric psychotics.

Table 11–4. DAP indicators for maladjustment

1. Omissions: Significant details of the drawing not included (no feet, legs, arms, etc.).

2. Transparency: Body parts can be seen through arms, legs, clothes, etc. or internal organs (heart, stomach, etc.) can be seen inside the body.

3. Distortion: Parts of the person are clearly drawn out of proportion (huge or elongated arms, tiny head, etc.), relevant portions of the body are not connected, body parts are connected to the wrong areas.

4. Vertical Imbalance of Stance: Person is clearly tilted to one side.

5. Head Simplification: Head is overly simple, primitive, or basic (similar or the same as a stick figure).

6. Body Simplification: (as in number 5).

7. Poor Overall Quality: The overall quality of the drawing as a whole, same as artistic quality, accuracy of depiction, related to number of details. The rating is impressionistic and rated on a scale from 1 (poor) to 9 (excellent).

8. Sexual Differentiation: Clarity to which the person resembles either a male or a female. Likewise rated on a scale from 1 (undifferentiated) to 9 (clearly differentiated).

9. Sexual Elaboration: Amount of details related to sex (breasts, penises, excessive makeup, etc.).

Adapted from Maloney and Glasser (1982)

The above data strongly suggests an increase in psychopathology associated with a greater number of the indicators summarized by Maloney and Glasser (1982). However, specific meanings associated with these signs is less clear. They might indicate overall maladjustment, be related to cognitive maturity/sophistication, a general but nonspecific disturbance, or, quite possibly, with anxiety since the first six indicators were derived from Handler's (1967) 21 anxiety indicators. Clinicians are best advised to use the nine indicators as a global screening device for the presence of maladjustment and determine the specific meaning of any maladjustment based on other test and/or interview data.

Impulsiveness

Impulsiveness is a disorder of attention involving behavior that is typically inappropriate to the situation and occurs with little self-reflection or awareness. In contrast, the previous indicators for maladjustment are more clearly identified with anxiety. Anxiety and impulsiveness are generally different constructs and are likely to have different expressions on the DAP. Probably, a moderate level of anxiety serves to place controls on impulsiveness so that one might even expect a negative correlation between anxiety and impulsiveness.

Various impulsive versus nonimpulsive (reflective) measures have been identified on the DAP. The most recent, extensive, and successful formulation was developed by Oas (1984). The study was unusual for DAP research in that it controlled for drawing ability, I.Q., age, drugs, organicity, and motivation. Using his scoring system (see Table 11–5), it was possible to accurately discriminate adolescents who were independently rated as impulsive from those independently rated as nonimpulsive. The impulsive adolescents had higher total DAP indicators (M = 3.4, SD = 1.5) than nonimpulsives (M = 1.4, SD = 1.0). Likewise, impulsive adolescents in school had a significantly higher number of indicators (M = 4.2, SD = 1.3) than nonimpulsive school adolescents (M = 1.6, SD = 1.1). The best discriminators for identifying impulsive from nonimpulsive adolescents (ages 12 to 18) were completion time, aggressive content, overall drawing quality, discontinuity (difficulty connecting lines), general omission of important details, specific omissions, poor proportion, and inadequately drawn shoulders. Using discriminant function analysis for the 13 different impulsive and 13 nonimpulsive indicators, 93% of hospitalized impulsives and 97% of school impulsives were correctly identified.

Oas (1984) also listed DAP indicators that were more characteristic of reflective (nonimpulsive) adolescents. The best discriminators were aspects of the drawings that required a delay of impulses and conscientiousness. These included detailing, a longer completion time, sketching, emphasis on the eyes, mouth details, and shading (see Table 11–5 and Appendix T). However, specific details should not be considered separately but rather placed into the overall context of the total number of impulsive versus nonimpulsive indicators. For clinical purposes, a cutoff of three impulsive indicators and five nonimpulsive indicators can be used.

Neurological Deficit

A number of drawing tests have been developed for the assessment of brain damage. These tests are based on the observation that brain damage interferes with the complex integration of spatial, perceptual, and motor responses required to accurately reproduce drawings. Specifically, right hemisphere lesions have been associated with clients who have difficulty maintaining the overall gestalt of the drawing. This results in distortions in the perspective or proper proportion of the drawing. For most persons, left hemisphere lesions will also

Table 11–5.   DAP indicators of impulsivity and nonimpulsivity

Impulsive:	Nonimpulsive:
1. completion time*	1. symmetry
2. aggression*	2. detailing**
3. overall quality*	3. completion time**
4. discontinuity*	4. placement
5. omissions*	5. sketching**
6. specific omissions*	6. erasures
7. proportion*	7. size
8. size increase	8. gender identification
9. neck	9. eye emphasis**
10. stance	10. right side
11. shoulders	11. perspective
12. poor planning	12. mouth detail**
13. left side	13. shading**

 * best discriminators for identifying impulsiveness
** best discriminators for identifying nonimpulsiveness
Adapted from Oas (1984)

result in drawing difficulties because the left hemisphere provides directions or commands to the right hand to correctly reproduce the design. Thus, drawings from persons with left hemisphere lesions are likely to get the overall proportion correct, but might omit significant details (Lezak, 1983). The most popular drawing (constructional) test is the Bender, but other developments include drawings of bicycles (Lezak, 1983), Memory for Designs (Graham & Kendall, 1960), Benton Visual Retention Test (Benton, 1974), and reproducing a square, clock, key and Greek cross on the Halstead Reitan aphasia screening test (Wheeler & Reitan, 1962). It would be logical to assume that similar efforts had been conducted to identify organic indicators on the DAP. Unfortunately, little work has ben reported in this area.

Some guidelines have been suggested by McLachlan and Head (1974), who reviewed the literature and developed a list of 15 possible indicators for organicity. Only five of these indicators were found to have significant correlations with an outside criterion measure (Halstead Reitan Neuropsychological Test Battery's Impairment Index). The resulting "Projective Impairment Rating Scale" (see Table 11–6) is scored on a three-point scale with ratings given for an indicator not being present (0), present on one drawing (1), or present on both drawings (2). The scale scores thus range from 0 to 10. Interjudge reliabilities for total score and each of the five indicators was high (.79 to .95) as was split half reliability (.89). Validity was low for each of the individual indicators (.31 to .37), but a moderate correlation was found between the summed scores and Reitan's Impairment Index (.50). A cutoff score of between 7 and 8 was recommended for identifying neurological deficit. Although the above findings are modest, these indicators might serve as a brief screening device for identifying organicity. However, the same cautions that apply to the Bender are likely to be at least as relevant when using the DAP for identifying organicity. These include insensitivity to subtle levels of impairment, overlap with emotional indicators, and difficulty identifying left hemisphere dysfunction (see assets and limitations for the Bender).

Table 11–6.   DAP Indicators of organicity and correlations with validity measures

Indicator:	Correlations with Impairment Index:
1. Figure off balance.	.37
2. Major detail missing (On head: eyes, nose, mouth, ears or hair; Body: arm, leg, or torso; Extremities: foot, hand, or fingers— do not score as missing if hands drawn behind back; score if figure runs off page).	.31
3. Gross body distortions (Other than head and extremities, e.g. square-shaped or pear-shaped bodies, lack of symmetry, legs smaller than arms, discrepancy between sizes of arms and legs, arms unequal, distended belly).	.46
4. Weak synthesis (Poor integration of arms, legs, head, neck with torso, arm "stuck on," dislocated at wrong place. Limb or body displaced).	.37
5. Poor motor control (Line destruction: bending a straight line more than one-quarter inch, dashed or dotted line, jagged lines, etc.).	.35
Sum of Projective Impairment Index	.50

Adapted from McLachlan & Head (1974).

THE HOUSE-TREE-PERSON TEST

The House-Tree-Person test (HTP) was originally developed by Buck (1948) and Buck and Hammer (1969) who reasoned that, in addition to human-figure drawings, drawings of houses and trees were also likely to be associated with relevant aspects of the person. Houses, trees, and persons all are familiar objects, are likely to be accepted objects for drawing, and will produce a greater number of associations than most other, more neutral objects. The HTP potentially has advantages over the DAP in that, not only does it include human-figure drawings, but the greater variety of objects drawn is likely to produce a greater number of areas for interpretation. If the house, tree, and person are all drawn on one sheet of paper as recommended by Burns and Kaufman (1970, 1972) and Burns (1987), then the picture often results in an integrated, interactional story.

The earlier developers tended to rely heavily on traditional Freudian theory, as is represented by the following discussion of chimneys by Handler (1985):

> ...if a subject suffers from psychosexual conflicts, the chimney—by virtue of its structural design and its protrusion from the body of the house—is susceptible to receive the projection of the subject's inner feelings about his phallus. (p. 137)

However, Burns (1987), as well as many other practitioners, have emphasized a more humanistic and/or Jungian approach.

The disadvantage of the HTP (and other drawing techniques included later in this chapter) is that it tends to lack the extensive research base associated with the more traditional DAP. As such, the HTP is even less of a standardized, empirically based test than the DAP. The HTP (and Draw-A-Family, Kinetic-Family-Drawing, etc.) tends to appeal to, and be used more extensively by, clinicians attracted to intuitive, interactive, and metaphorical approaches. In many ways, it is similar to dream interpretation in that it relies heavily on the client's and/or therapist's association to the drawings. Often, the meaning is derived primarily from interactively engaging the client. As such, a large number of art therapists tend to use this and related techniques for assessment and as a prelude to and technique for therapy.

The administration of the HTP tends to be similar to the DAP, except the person is requested to draw a house, a tree, and a person on separate sheets of paper. Typically, the order of drawings is given in the above sequence since the house and the tree are believed to be easier and less threatening to draw than a person. Some clinicians prefer to have the client draw "a person" for the first human figure and a second one that is requested to be "a person of the opposite sex." If two opposite-sex human-figure drawings are provided, clinicians can potentially score and interpret them in the same way they would a DAP. The sheet of paper on which the house is to be drawn should be given to the client with the longer side horizontal, whereas the pages intended for the tree and person(s) should be presented with the longer side vertical. The client should also be requested to draw as good a picture as possible. Whereas the first set of drawings is done with a pencil, some clinicians prefer to have the sequence repeated with a chromatic version in which clients make their drawings using crayons or felt-tip pens.

An efficient variation recommended by Burns and Kaufman (1970, 1972) is to have the person draw all three objects on the same sheet of paper. Burns (1987) has later included a kinetic version (Kinetic House-Tree-Person or KHTP) using the following set of instructions: "Draw a house, a tree and a whole person on this piece of paper with some kind of action. Try to draw a whole person, not a cartoon or stick person" (p. 5). This version is time efficient and often produces an energetic, integrated story. Unfortunately, there is usually less detail included on the individual objects derived from the HTP (or HTP variations) so the procedures and database used for scoring and interpreting the DAP cannot be employed.

Signs of Adjustment on the HTP

Just as there are signs of health on the DAP, there are somewhat similar signs on the HTP, which have been conceptualized and listed by Burns (1987). The house would be depicted as a place of happiness and contain signs of warmth and openness (pathway to the door, accessible appearances of doors and windows). It should also have a sense of wholeness and integration and contain the presence of homelike objects (pets, toys, flowers). The tree would be depicted as full, whole, and harmonious and would appear to move upward and outward, The branches would also be expected to look nourished and healthy and be continuous rather than broken. Most of the healthy characteristics from the DAP also apply to the person(s) drawn on the HTP in that all essential details should be included, they should be grounded, and the person would be expected to be open, moderately symmetrical, and accepting. If the house, tree, and person are all drawn on the same page, a healthy person would be expected to integrate the three objects into a coherent interaction. The objects would be neither too separate and distant nor overly enmeshed and colliding into one another. Their size and placement, while expressing individual differences between one client and the next, would be appropriate.

General Interpretative Considerations

One theoretical approach to interpreting the HTP is to consider the house, tree, and the person as representing different aspects of the self. The house represents the part of the self that is concerned with the body (the "house" one lives in) as well as nurturance, stability, and a sense of belonging. The tree is more concerned with a person's sense of growth, vitality, and development. The relative size and quality of these two figures can reveal attitudes and feelings toward these aspects of the client. The person depicted in the drawing is a more direct representation of the self, but the relative size and proximity of the person (if all three objects are drawn on one page) in relationship to the house and the tree can reveal how different aspects of the self relate to one another. For example, if different objects are touching, it may suggest the client is having difficulty separating or untangling different aspects of his or her life.

A similar view maintains that the house represents the client's mother whereas the tree represents his or her father. The placement of the person (self), then, might be able to indicate how close the client feels to one or both parents. The person might be distant from both parents, caught in the middle (pulled, mediating, supporting), or might be closer to one than the other. If the client's parents are experiencing conflict or are separated/divorced, then the house and the tree might be drawn on separate sides of the paper. If one "parent" is significantly larger than the other, this might reflect greater power and dominance on the part of the larger one.

Burns (1987) suggests that the order in which the objects are drawn reflects the relative degree of importance of the object (aspect of the person, parent). Drawing the tree first indicates clients who are primarily concerned with growth, development, or issues of life and death. The meaning can be made more clear by considering the details of the tree itself. Is it harmonious, balanced, and healthy or is it dead and decaying? If the house is drawn first, their primary concern will most likely be with a sense of belonging, nurturance, or concern with the body and its needs. Again, the way in which the house is drawn will provide more specific information on this aspect of the person. Is the house depicted as a nurturing and open place, is it a prison, is it dominating, or is it primarily a place to symbolize success and power? Likewise, the drawing of the person provides more direct information about clients. Is their depiction hidden or open, do they need to demonstrate success and power, what is their degree of concern with the body and its needs? If the person is both drawn first and is depicted as quite large relative to the other objects, this might suggest preoccupation with the self, which is consistent with a person who is self-absorbed perhaps to the point of narcissism or hedonism. If someone other than the artist is drawn, it might suggest extreme interest in or even obsession with the person depicted. This might suggest intense love, hate, hero worship, or perhaps unfinished grieving for a deceased family member.

The meaning of the structure and form (line pressure, shading, detailing, etc.) of the HTP/KHTP is similar to interpretations for the DAP. However, interpretations should be made with more caution since the greater number of drawings and the greater complexity of the task (when all objects are drawn on the same page) may result in some differences.

Interpretation of Content

The following summary of content features contains classic interpretations available in the literature. The material on HTP person drawings refers the reader back to the previous discussion of the DAP, whereas the more specific material on the house and tree is derived from the work of Bolander (1977), Buck (1948, 1966), Burns (1987), Jolles (1971), and Hammer (1954, 1958, 1985). Other authors are cited in the text as their research is discussed. Most of this material is based on clinical experience and theories of the unconscious, so it should not be considered empirically validated. Rather, the material is included here in an attempt to provide clinicians with useful leads they can pursue further through interactions with their clients as well as by integrating these leads within the context of interview data and other test results. Client/therapist interaction with the drawing might begin with an open-ended question, such as asking the person what is occurring in the picture. More specific questions are included in Appendix Q.

House   The symbolism of the house has been subject to several different interpretations. It might be perceived as a symbol of the self in which different portions of the house represent different aspects of the self (the roof as fantasy life or windows and doors as interpersonal accessibility). It might also represent the body. In addition, the home is usually the place where nurturing and a sense of security occur, so it might suggest attitudes toward these qualities as well as attitudes toward home life in general. Since many of these qualities are traditionally expressed by a person's mother, the house might also express the attitude toward his or her actual mother or, more generally, toward "mothering." The first and most general approach toward interpreting the house is to note the general mood, level of warmth, or accessibility of the house. Is it humble and simple or large and ostentatious. Is it covered with numerous details or is it sparse and empty? If details are included, what do they contribute to the general feel of the house? Is the house accessible or closed? Does it dominate the picture or is it small and placed to one corner of the page? An extremely small house suggests rejection of the home life, whereas an extremely large and dominating house might reflect a view of the home as overly restrictive and controlling.

Once the general feel of the house is determined, the clinician can focus on more specific details. The **roof** (and the attic within) is often considered to represent either someone's fantasy life or intellectual side. An extremely large roof suggests persons who are highly withdrawn and extremely involved with their inner world of fantasy. If windows are drawn in the roof, they might tend to view their environment through the world of their fantasy images. The absence of a roof suggests a highly constricted, concrete orientation. For example, mentally retarded persons often place a single line to represent the roof.

The **walls** represent the person's relative degree of ego strength. Crumbling or disintegrating walls might reflect the disintegration of personality, exaggerated reinforcement of the walls might suggest a fear of disintegration in which added protection is needed to provide protection, and transparent walls (although frequent in young children) might indicate poor reality testing.

The **door** and **windows** are the portions of the house that relate to the outside world. Small, bolted up, barred windows or doors suggest that the person might be shy, withdrawn, and inaccessible or possibly suspicious or even hostile. This is further exaggerated if the doors and windows are entirely missing. An open door and/or many windows suggests strong needs for contact with others. However, if the indicators of openness are overdone, the person might be highly dependent. Very large windows, especially on the bedroom or bathroom, suggest exhibitionism. The absence of windows on the HTP, in combination with several other features—including enlarged heads, absence of feet, and extremely geometric figures—have frequently been found in the drawings of abused children (Blain, Bergner, Lewis, & Goodstein, 1981).

A **chimney** can relate either to a person's availability and warmth, or to the degree of power and masculinity he or she feels. A missing chimney suggests passivity or a lack of psychological warmth in the person's home life. Whereas normal amounts of smoke accentuate warmth in the home, an excessive amount of smoke suggests inner tension, pent-up aggression, emotional turbulence, and conflict. However, interpretations of chimneys need to take into consideration biasing factors, such as geography (e.g., tropics) and season (summer versus winter).

In addition to the house itself, many clients also include a number of accessories to the house, the most frequent of which is a **pathway**. Pathways that are wide and lead directly to the door suggest the client is accessible, open, and direct. In contrast, the absence of pathways indicates the client may be closed, distant, and removed. Pathways that are long and winding may reflect someone who is initially aloof but who can later warm up and become accessible. If the pathway is extremely wide, the client might initially express a superficial sense of friendliness but later become aloof and distant. The presence of **fences** suggests defensiveness. If many irrelevant **details** are included, the client might be indicating strong needs to exercise a high degree of structure over his or her environment, perhaps due to an inner sense of insecurity.

Tree   Initially, a general impression of the tree can be obtained by noting its overall feel and tone. Based on this, an idea can be obtained regarding the relationship the person has with his or her environment. How full, balanced, harmonious, open, and integrated does the tree look? If the tree is withered by the environment, it might reflect a person who has been broken by external stress. A tree with no branches suggests the person has little contact with people. The age of the tree can also provide a general index of the psychological age the person feels.

In addition to the general impression derived from the tree, clinicians can also look at its specific features. As the center and most vital part of the tree, the **trunk** can be seen as representing degree of inner strength, self-esteem, and intactness of personality. The use of faint, sketchy lines to represent the trunk indicates a sense of vulnerability, passivity, and insecurity. These same concerns might also be represented by shading on the trunk or lines that are heavily reinforced (defensiveness) or perforated. Scars or knotholes suggest traumatic experiences, and the age the trauma occurred can often be determined by the relative height of the scar or knothole (i.e., a knothole half way up the trunk drawn by a ten-year-old suggests the trauma occurred at age five). Very thin trunks suggest a precarious level of adjustment. If the **bark** on the trunk is heavily drawn, it suggests anxiety; bark that is extremely carefully drawn might reflect a rigid, compulsive personality. If the tree or tree trunk is **split down the middle**, a severe disintegration of the personality is suggested.

The branches and root structure typically symbolize different aspects of the person. The **branches** function as a means by which the tree extends itself out into and relates to its environment. They reflect a person's growth and degree of perceived resources. If the branches are moving upwards, the person might be ambitious and "reaching" for opportunities, whereas downward (weeping willow) branches suggest low levels of energy. Branches that are cut represent a sense of being traumatized, and dead branches indicate feelings of emptiness and hopelessness. Tiny branches suggest that the person experiences difficulty getting attention from his or her environment, and small new branches might represent either new personal growth or psychological immaturity. If a **tree house** is drawn in the branches, the person might be expressing a need to escape from a threatening environment.

In contrast to the branches, the **roots** reflect the degree to which someone is settled and secure. The roots refer to the person's hold on reality but also reflect the person's relationship to past issues. If a person is having a difficult time "getting a grip on life" the roots might be either small and ineffective or the drawing might compensate by being piercing and talon-like. Dead roots indicate emptiness and anxiety consistent with obsessive compulsives, especially if there is excessive detailing in other areas.

Person   If the client is instructed to draw objects on separate sheets of paper, then the task and resulting production is quite similar to the DAP. As a result, similar interpretive principles can be used, including objective scoring and interpretation of content. However, some caution should be exercised in that the human-figure drawings come after the drawings of the house and tree, and the resulting fatigue might cause slight changes in the content and style of the drawings (e.g., less detail, lighter line pressure). If the administration is used in which all three objects are drawn on the same page, the human figure is likely to be significantly smaller than a regular DAP. Differences would be even further accentuated if the client/artist is requested to draw the person "doing something" (KHTP). As a result, interpretations of the human figure should be made with even greater caution. The preferred approach would then be to focus on the theme(s) expressed in the drawing and placement of the different objects/persons, and to engage the client in associating with the drawing.

FAMILY DRAWINGS: THE DRAW-A-FAMILY AND KINETIC FAMILY DRAWING TESTS

Whereas the DAP and, to a lesser extent, the HTP/KHTP focus on individual dynamics, many persons involved in assessment and therapy have been interested in understanding the structure of and relationships within families. As with previously discussed drawing techniques, family drawings provide a less threatening means of revealing this information than direct questioning. This is particularly true for children and adolescents, who usually have greater difficulties than adults in articulating how they feel about relationships. Family drawings were originally suggested by Appel (1931) and Wolff (1942) but later were more fully developed as the Draw-A-Family Test (DAF) by Hulse (1951) and Harris (1963). The technique gained considerable popularity in the 1960s and 1970s with the increased development and use of family therapy.

Administration involves giving the person a paper, pencil, and eraser and requesting him or her to "draw a picture of your family" (Harris, 1963). After the individual has completed the drawing, he or she is requested to identify the different persons in the drawings. These are labeled, along with the artist/client's name and the date the drawing was made.

Interpretation follows similar procedures as for the HTP. Initially, a holistic appraisal of the drawing is made by noting such features as its mood or tone. This is followed by assessing the meaning behind the size and placement of the figures. Usually, this assessment provides information about he way in which the person fits in with the family. Emotional closeness is reflected by the relative physical proximity on the page. A father whom no one can get close to might be placed in the corner, away from the other family members. A client who feels rejected might also place him- or herself quite far apart from other family members or on the back of the page or even might omit him- or herself entirely. The larger figures and those drawn first are likely to be perceived by the client as more important and powerful than figures drawn smaller or last. As with the DAP, structure and formal properties of the drawing might indicate such features as anxiety, hesitancy, or confidence. For example, a family member who invokes anxiety in the artist/client might have a greater amount of shading added to him or her.

A more recent and quite popular variation of the DAF is Burns and Kaufman's (1970, 1972) Kinetic-Family-Drawing (KFD). The authors have criticized the DAF as producing fairly rigid, low energy, noninteractive drawings and attempted to correct this by requesting that the client draw his or her family "doing something." These instructions are usually supplemented by asking the client to include him- or herself in the drawing. After completing the drawing, the client is requested to describe it and/or to tell a story about it. This aids the interpreter by clarifying the interactions, characters, and underlying message of the drawing.

As in the DAF, the interpreter should note the order in which each figure is drawn as well as the size, placement, and any indicators of anxiety (shading, line pressure, erasures). Unlike the DAF, it is important to note the type of activity the family is involved with. A passive activity, such as watching television might reflect that the family has a low level of energy and that family members rarely communicate. Placing the parents at opposite ends of the table during the depiction of eating might indicate that the parents are perceived as being emotionally distant. To facilitate KFD interpretation, Burns and Kaufman (1972) provide scoring through means of an Analysis Grid, which focuses on the different placement of the figures. The following interpretive hypotheses are derived primarily from the implications of different dimensions of the grid. Sometimes, different figures in the drawings are depicted in a **precarious position**, which suggests that the client feels a sense of inner tension in or toward the person. Placing a person in the **corner,** or in the **back,** or **omitting** the person altogether suggests the artist/client perceives the person as emotionally distant from the family or perhaps the artist/client has a wish to make this the case (as in intense sibling rivalry). If an individual in the drawing is **elevated,** the client perceives the person to be in a position of dominance, power, or status in the family. **Extended arms** suggest that the figure is controlling (and characteristically controls) his or her environment. If a person is **doing something different**, this individual might be different (exceptional, rejected, eccentric) in real life. **Fire** or **light** might represent positive feelings between persons. In contrast, placing a **wall** or **barrier** between people suggests interpersonal distance. Feelings of insecurity and anxiety might be represented by **heavy, dark clouds,** and **underlining** might serve to compensate for a sense of instability.

Five different objective scoring systems have been devised for use with the DAF or KFD. Each of these has produced varying degrees of success related to interscorer reliability, concurrent validity, and sensitivity to changes in the client's clinical condition. For example, Wright and McIntyre (1982) developed a scale comprised of 15 items, including such variables as poor organization, small figures, self drawn small relative to other figures, separation of self from others, lack of detail, poor sexual differentiation, low energy expressed by self and family, and a large amount of empty space. The presence of these (and other) items accurately discriminated between depressed and normals and also demonstrated sensitivity to improvement. Interscorer reliabilities have been in the range of .87, but test-retest reliabilities have been low, partially due to the greater degree of change found in children. Some authors have found that a greater degree of isolation of self in the drawings has been able to discriminate children with difficulties (Raskin & Bloom, 1979; Sayed & Leaverton, 1974), whereas, McGregor (1979) did not find that the KFD was able to make useful discriminations between normal and clinical populations.

MISCELLANEOUS PROCEDURES

The most frequently used projective drawings are the DAP, HTP/KHTP, and DAF/KFD. However, other noteworthy procedures include additional kinetic techniques, drawings produced by groups, and spontaneous drawings. Following Burns and Kaufman's (1970, 1972) initial emphasis that the persons in the drawings "do something," similar techniques have been used for different settings—including school, business, politics, and religion. The most fully developed is Prout and Phillip's (1974) Kinetic School Drawing (KSD) in which the person is requested to draw people at school "doing something." Scoring and interpretation is similar to the KFD in that such elements are considered as whether clients include or exclude themselves from the drawing, the distance between themselves and the teacher, types of interactions, and number of peers that are included. Although interpretations are mainly based on clinical impression, correlations have been found between elements in the drawings considered favorable to school and academic achievement (Prout & Celmer, 1984). Knoff and Prout (1985) emphasize that the KSD can be effectively complemented by the KFD and have attempted to integrate both these methods of data collection in their Kinetic Drawing System (Knoff & Prout, 1985).

Other projective drawing variations have been developed for use with groups. Members of the group might be requested to make their own drawings in the presence of each other or all might participate, as a group, in the creation of a single drawing. One possibility is to provide felt-tip pens and a large piece of paper in the center of the group, request members to draw designs, and every few minutes rotate the page. Kwiatkowska (1978) has emphasized family drawings and suggests that each family member work on his or her own drawing. However, there is opportunity to interact since the easels are arranged in a circle, with each member seated inside the circle so that he or she can easily observe what the other family members are doing. Observations and later interpretations can be made of both the group interaction while the drawings were being created as well as interpretations of the drawings themselves. Some groups or families make clear, smooth decisions while others develop conflict while members try to control what the others do. Group members might also become quite territorial about their drawing or portion of the drawing and defend it from encroachment by others. Typically, the method of interaction within the drawing session highlights typical patterns that occur outside the session.

Another technique is to have clients draw a picture of an island, with the suggestion that they include all the things they might need if they were to live on that island. The objects they choose to include and the manner in which each object is depicted can help to identify dominant themes and values in client's lives. More free-form options are to draw how they are feeling or to draw how they perceive a specific situation—such as birth, death, conflict, or happiness. The most unstructured approach is to observe spontaneous drawings.

Any of the above techniques can use many of the approaches for interpretation described for the more formal methods (DAP, HTP, etc.). Interpreters might look at the feel, tone, mood, or quality of the drawing and should consider the significance of the line quality, size of the figures, their relative placement to one another, themes, or contents. Such interpretations might vary in terms of the amount of interaction between the artist/client and interpreter, and might be influenced by the theoretical orientation of the interpreter.

RECOMMENDED READING

Burns, R. C. (1987). *Kinetic-House-Tree-Person Drawings (KHTP)*. New York: Brunner/Mazel.

Burns, R. C., & Kaufman, S. H. (1972). *Actions, styles, and symbols in Kinetic Family Drawings (KFD)*. New York: Brunner/Mazel.

Handler, L. (1985). The clinical use of the Draw-A-Person Test (DAP). In C. S. Newmark (Ed.) *Major psychological assessment instruments*. Newton, MA: Allyn & Bacon.

Kahill, S. (1984). Human figure drawings in adults: An update of the empirical evidence, 1962-1982. *Canadian Psychology, 25*, 269-292.

Oster, G., & Gould, P. (1987). *Using drawings in assessment and therapy*. New York: Brunner/Mazel.

Chapter 12

THE PSYCHOLOGICAL REPORT

The psychological report is the end product of assessment. It represents the clinician's efforts to integrate the assessment data into a functional whole so that the information can be of service to the client in solving problems and making decisions. Even the best tests will be useless unless the data from them is explained in a manner that is relevant and clear, and meets the needs of the client. This requires clinicians to not merely give test results, but to also interact with their data in a way that will make their conclusions useful in meeting the client's needs and helping to solve problems.

An evaluation can be written in several possible ways. The manner of presentation used depends on the purpose for which the report is intended as well as on the individual style and orientation of the clinician. The format provided in this chapter is merely a suggested outline that follows common and traditional guidelines. It includes techniques for elaborating on such essential areas as the referral question, behavioral observations, relevant history, impressions (interpretations), and recommendations. This format is especially appropriate for evaluations that are problem oriented and that offer specific prescriptions for change. Additional alternatives for organizing the report are to use a letter format, give only the summary and recommendations, focus on a specific problem, summarize the results test by test, or provide client descriptions around a particular theory of personality. The sample evaluations vary somewhat from the suggested format, although they usually still include the essential categories of information that will be discussed in this chapter.

One general style to be avoided is sometimes referred to as a "shotgun" report. This provides a wide variety of often fragmented descriptions in the hope that some useful information can be found within. The shotgun approach is usually vague, stereotyped, and overinclusive. The recommendations for treatment are often neither specific nor practical. The most frequent cause of a shotgun report is a referral question that is too general, vague, and therefore poorly understood. In contrast is the "case-focused" report, which centers on the specific problems outlined by the referring person. This reveals unique aspects of the client and provides specific accurate descriptions, rather than portraying stereotyped descriptions that may also be overly "theory linked" or overly "test linked." Furthermore, the recommendations for treatment are both specific and practical. The general approach of the "case-focused" report is not so much *what* is to be known, but rather *why* different types of information are important for the purposes of the report.

The creation of a case-focused report involves understanding and applying several basic principles. First, the report should use action-oriented language rather than metapsychological abstractions. This means the client's ongoing behaviors and likely personality processes should be described in relation to different situations. Harty (1986) indicates that the use of "action-language" clearly links the person with specific behaviors, forces reports to address specific therapeutic issues, and conveys a better understanding of the client's active role in the testing situation. Second, the recommendations in a case-focused report need to directly relate to what specifically can be done for this client within his or her particular environment. They may apply to such areas as occupational choice, psychotherapy, institutional programs, or additional testing. However, in certain types of referrals, especially clients self-referred for psychotherapy, an important goal may be to help them increase their level of personal insight. In these cases, a wider description of the client—that includes a number of different topics—might be more appropriate than the narrower, problem-solving approach. Also, there should be a focus on that which differentiates one person from another. This means avoiding discussions of what is average about the client, and emphasizing instead what stands out and is unique to this individual. Further, there is a current trend, consistent with the case-focused approach, toward deemphasizing diagnosis and etiology. There is rather an emphasis on current descriptions of the person that are tied to specific behaviors. In certain cases, especially within a medical setting, the clinician may still need to provide diagnoses in addition to behaviorally oriented descriptions. The final consideration is that a case-focused report should be written with an awareness of the point of view of the intended readers. This includes taking into consideration their level of expertise, their theoretical or professional orientation, the decisions they are facing, and the possible interpretations they are likely to make of the information.

GENERAL GUIDELINES

Style

The style or "flavor" of a report will be influenced primarily by the training and orientation of the examiner. The clinician can choose from three general report-writing approaches: literary, clinical, and scientific (Tallent, 1976). Each style has unique strengths, and all have a number of liabilities. The literary approach uses everyday language, is creative, and often dramatic. Although it can effectively capture a reader's attention and provide colorful descriptions, it is often imprecise and prone to exaggeration.

The clinical approach focuses on the pathological dimensions of a person. It describes the client's abnormal features, defenses, dynamics involved in maladjustment, and typical reactions to stress. The strength of the clinical approach is that it provides information about areas in need of change and alerts a potential counselor to difficulties that are likely to be encountered during the course of treatment. However, such a report tends to be one-sided in that it may omit important strengths of the person. The result is likely to be more a description of a "patient" rather than a person. Such a "maladjustment bias" is a frequent difficulty in clinical psychology and results in a distorted, unrealistic view of the client. Although most clinical reports should describe a person's problem areas, these problem areas should be given appropriate emphasis within the context of the client's relevant strengths and resources.

The scientific approach to report writing emphasizes normative comparisons, tends to be more academic, and to a lesser extent, relates to the nature of a client's pathology. The scientific style differs from the other two approaches chiefly in its reference to concepts, theories, and data. It looks at and describes test findings in an objective, factual manner. Thus, there might be frequent references to test data, normative comparisons, probability statements, and cutoff scores to be used for decision making. A scientific approach is likely to discuss the person by addressing different, often isolated, segments of personality. Thus, such areas as a client's cognitive, perceptual, and motivational abilities may be described as discrete and often unrelated functions. Although the scientific approach is objective and factual, it has been criticized for violating the unity of personality. Many readers, particularly those from other disciplines (Sandy, 1986; Tallent & Reiss, 1959b), do not respect or empathize with scientific evaluations and perceive them as cold, distant, and overly objective. Purely data-oriented evaluations can potentially do the profession a disservice by reinforcing the view that an assessment is like a laboratory test rather than a professional consultation with a clinician. Furthermore, a focus on factual data may not address the practical decisions the client and referral source are facing.

In actual practice, it is unusual to find a pure example of a literary, clinical, or scientific report. Clinicians will generally draw from all three approaches but will typically emphasize one. An important part of effective report writing is the ability to evaluate the assets and limitations of each style, and to maintain a flexible orientation toward appropriately combining them. In any one report, there may be a need to use creative literary descriptions, elaborate on different pathological dimensions, or provide necessary scientific information. Again, the key is to avoid the pitfalls associated with specializing in any one of these styles and to emphasize instead their relative strengths.

Ownby (1987) stresses that the most important style to use in report writing is what he refers to as a "professional style." This is characterized by short words that are of common usage and that have precise meanings. Grammatically, writers should use a variety of sentence constructions and lengths in order to maintain the reader's interest. The paragraphs should be short and should focus on a single concept. Similar concepts should be located close to one another in the report. Whereas Hollis and Donna (1979) urge writers to use short words, short sentences, and short paragraphs, the *Publication Manual of the American Psychological Association* (1983) recommends varying the lengths of sentences and paragraphs. The result should be a report that combines accuracy, clarity, integration, and readability.

Type of Reports

Clinicians generally prefer to orient their reports around specific hypotheses or different relevant domains, or adhere to interpreting the data test by test. The hypothesis-oriented model focuses heavily on answering specific questions asked by the referral source. The report tends to be highly focused and avoids any extraneous material. For example, if a referral source asks whether person X is brain-damaged, then all the interpretations based on the test data are directed toward answering whether this hypothesis is supported.

A domain-oriented report discusses the client in relation to specific topics—such as cognitive abilities, interpersonal relationships, or sexuality. This approach is comprehensive, indicates the client's strengths and weaknesses, and typically gives the reader a good feel for the person as a whole. The referral question is still answered but is addressed by responding to specific domains relating to the referral question. Reports written by addressing functional domains tend to be preferred and better comprehended by readers (Weiner, 1985). The weakness of domain-oriented reports lies in the potential to provide too much information, thus overloading the reader.

Occasionally, a report will be organized by presenting the results of each test, one at a time (WAIS-R, Bender, MMPI, etc.). This approach clarifies where the data came from and enables the reader to more clearly understand how the clinician made his or her inferences. This advantage is offset by some significant disadvantages. The emphasis on tests can distract the reader and tends to reduce the client from a person to a series of test numbers. It also encourages the belief that an examiner is a technician who merely administers tests rather than a clinician who uses multiple sources of information to answer referral questions and help people solve problems they are facing.

Topics

There is an extremely wide range of topics or domains that clinicians may decide to discuss in their reports. These topics serve as conceptual tools that enable report writers to give form and direction to the information they are trying to communicate. Possible topics include intellectual functioning, conflicts, interpersonal relationships, suicidal potential, defenses, behavior under stress, impulsiveness, or sexuality. Often, an adequate case-focused report can be developed by describing just a few of these topics. For example, a highly focused report may elaborate on one or two significant areas of functioning, whereas a more general evaluation may discuss seven or eight relevant topics. Table 12–1 is a representative list of possible topics that may be considered for inclusion in an evaluation. This list is by no means complete, but can provide a general guide or present a wide range of possible topics from which a report writer can choose.

Deciding What to Include

The general purpose of a psychological evaluation is to provide information that will be most helpful in meeting the needs of the client. Within this context, the clinician must strike a balance between providing too much information and providing too little, and between being too cold and being too dramatic. As a general rule, information should only be included if it serves to increase the understanding of the client. For example, descriptions of a client's appearance should be oriented toward such areas as his or her level of self-esteem or anxiety. Such information as the types of clothing he or she is wearing or color of his or her eyes or hair are generally not relevant. Likewise, an elaboration of family dynamics should be helpful in understanding such areas as a child's current behavioral problems or lack of academic motivation.

The basic guidelines for deciding what to include in a report relate to the needs of the referral setting, background of the readers, purpose of testing, relative usefulness of the information, and whether the information describes unique characteristics of the person. Once these general guidelines have been taken into account, the next step is to focus on and organize the information derived from the tests. For example, if a general review of aspects of personality is the purpose of the report, then a clinician can look at each test to determine what information it can provide. Ownby (1987) recommends using a worksheet with the domain or topic for consideration in the left column, a review of relevant data in the next, followed by a list of possible constructs, diagnoses or conclusions, and, finally, recommendations. This enables the clinician to extract relevant data from the mass of assessment data and to organize conclusions and recommendations in preparation for report writing. An example of a portion of such a worksheet is included in Figure 12–1.

A further general rule is that information should focus on the client's unique method of psychological functioning. A reader is concerned not so much with how the client is similar to the average person as in what ways he or she is different. A common error in psychological reports is the inclusion of generalized statements that are so vague they could apply to the majority of the population. Several researchers (Snyder, 1974; Sundberg, 1955; Ulrich, Stachnik, & Stainton, 1963) have studied the frequency, manner, and types of vague, generalized statements that individuals are likely to unconditionally accept as applying to themselves even though these statements were randomly selected. For example, Sundberg (1955) administered a "personality" test to a group of students and gave them all identical "interpretations" based on universal or stereotyped personality descriptions comprised of 13 statements, such as:

1. You have a great need for other people to like and admire you.
2. You have a tendency to be critical of yourself.
3. You have a great deal of unused capacity you have not turned to your advantage.
4. While you have some personality weaknesses, you are generally able to compensate for them.
5. At times you have serious doubts as to whether you have made the right decision or done the right thing.

Table 12–1.   Examples of general personality topics around which a case presentation may be conceptualized

Achievement	Intellectual controls
Aggressiveness	Intellectual level
Antisocial tendencies	Interests
Anxieties	Interpersonal relations
Aptitudes	Interpersonal skills
Attitudes	Life-style
Aversions	Molar surface behavior
Awareness	Needs
Background factors	Outlook
Behavioral problems	Perception of environment
Biological factors	Perception of self
Cognitive functioning	Personal consequences of behavior
Cognitive skills	Placement prospects
Cognitive style	Psychopathology
Competency	Rehabilitation needs
Cognitive factors	Rehabilitation prospects
Conflicts	Sentiments
Content of consciousness	Sex
Defenses	Sex identity
Deficits	Sex role
Developmental factors	Significant others
Diagnostic considerations	Situational factors
Drives, dynamics	Social consequences of behavior
Emotional cathexes	Social role
Emotional controls	Social stimulus value
Emotivity	Social structure
Fixations	Special assets
Flexibility	Subjective feeling states
Frustrations	Symptoms
Goals	Treatment prospects
Hostility	Value system
Identity	Vocational topics

Note: From Norman Tallent, *Psychological Report Writing*, (3rd ed.) © 1988, p. 120. Reprinted by permission of Prentice-Hall, Inc. Englewood Cliffs, N.J.

Topic	Data	Constructs	Conclusions	Recommendations
Appropriateness for therapy	Distractable	Possible anxiety	Mild manic state and significant use of denial	1. Weekly individual psychotherapy: focus on insight regarding decisions; supportive, mild confrontation
	High MMPI scale 9	Low sequencing ability		
	Poor judgment in history	Mildly inflated ideation		
	Low Digit Span & Digit Symbol	Irritable		2. Possible referral for medication
		Use of denial		
	Changes topic during discussion of difficult areas			

Figure 12–1. Worksheet for organizing a topic for a psychological report

Virtually all students used in the study reported that the evaluation statements were accurate descriptions of themselves. Other studies suggest that, not only were students unable to discriminate between fictitious and genuine feedback (Dies, 1972), but they may even prefer generalized fictitious results, particularly if they are framed within a positive context (Merrens & Richards, 1970; Mosher, 1965). This uncritical acceptance of test interpretations might be even further encouraged when objectively appearing, computer-generated interpretations are used (O'Dell, 1972; Groth-Marnat & Schumaker, 1989). Klopfer (1960) has referred to this uncritical acceptance of universally valid statements as the "Barnum effect," in reference to Phineas Barnum's saying, "There is a fool born every minute." Although "universal statements" may add to the "subjective" validity of the report when read by the client, such statements should be avoided in favor of stressing the person's essential uniqueness.

Once the data, conclusions, and recommendations have been outlined, the next step is to decide on the manner in which to present them. This involves clear communication about the relative degree of emphasis of the results, type of report, proper use of terminology, and the extent to which the raw data will be discussed.

Emphasis

Careful consideration should be given to the appropriate emphasis of conclusions. This is particularly important when indicating the relative intensity of a client's behavior. General summaries may be given, such as "this client's level of depression is characteristic of inpatient populations," or the relative intensity of certain aspects of a client's disorder may be more specifically discussed. To continue with the example of depression, a clinician may discuss the client's cognitive self-criticisms, degree of slowed behavior, or suicidal potential. In addition to discussing and giving the appropriate degree of emphasis to a client's pathology, his or her psychological strengths need to be compared with his or her relative weaknesses. Furthermore, the report should not discuss areas of minor relevance unless they somehow relate to the purpose of the evaluation. To achieve proper emphasis, the examiner and the referral source must clarify and agree on the purpose of the evaluation. Only after this has been accomplished can the examiner decide whether certain information should be elaborated in-depth, briefly mentioned, or deleted.

When clinicians present their conclusions, it is essential that they indicate their relative degree of certainty. Is a specific conclusion based on an objective fact, or is the clinician merely presenting a speculation? For example, the statement "John scored in the dull normal range of intelligence" is an objective fact. However, even in this case, examiners may want to give the standard error of measurement in order to provide an estimate of the probable range of scores. If only mild supporting data is available or if clinicians are presenting a speculation, then phrases such as "it appears . . .," "tends to . . .," or "probably . . ." should be used. This is especially important when clinicians are attempting to predict a person's behavior, because the predicted behavior has not yet been observed. It may be useful for clinicians to indicate that their predictions cannot be found directly in the tests themselves, but rather represent inferences that have been made based on the test data. There should be a clear distinction between what the client did, and what he or she anticipates doing. If a statement made in a report is a speculation, then it should be clearly indicated that the statement has only a moderate or small degree of certainty. Whenever a speculation is included, it should be relevant to the referral question.

Improper emphasis can reflect an incorrect interpretation by the examiner, and this misinterpretation is then passed down to the reader. Clinicians sometimes arrive at incorrect conclusions because their personal bias results in selective perception of the data. Thus, clinicians can develop an overly narrow focus in which potentially relevant data is overlooked. Personal bias may result from such factors as a restrictive theoretical orientation, incorrect subjective feelings regarding the client, or an overemphasis on pathology. Inaccurate conclusions can also result from attempts to please the referral source or from interpretations based on insufficient data. The reader may also be likely to misinterpret the conclusions if the report is generally overspeculative or if speculations are not specified as such but, rather, are disguised as assertions. If speculations are overly assertive, this may not only lead the reader to develop incorrect conclusions, but the report may also become overly authoritative and dogmatic, perhaps leading readers to become irritated and skeptical.

Misinterpretations can also result from vague and ambiguously worded sentences that place incorrect or misleading emphasis on a client's behavior. A statement such as "the client lacks social skills" is technically incorrect because the client must have some social skills, although these skills may be inadequate. A more correct description would be to state that the client's social skills are "poorly developed" or "below average." Likewise, a statement such as "the client uses socially inappropriate behavior" is subject to a myriad of interpretations. This could be rephrased to include more behaviorally oriented descriptions, such as "frequently interrupts" or "would often pursue irrelevant tangents."

Responsibility for a report's conclusions clearly rests on the clinician. This responsibility should not and cannot be transferred to the tests themselves. To take this a step further, decisions made about a person should never be in the hands of tests, which may even have questionable validity in certain contexts. Rather, conclusions and decisions regarding people should always be in the hands of responsible persons. Thus, the style of emphasizing results should reflect this. Phrases such as "test results indicate . . ." may give the impression that the examiner is trying to hide behind and transfer responsibility for his or her statements onto the tests. Not only is this not where the responsibility should be, but the reader may develop a lack of confidence in the clinician. If clinicians feel uncertain about a particular area, then they should either be clear about this uncertainty or, if they cannot personally stand by the results, they should exclude the results from the report.

Use of Raw Data

When writing the impressions and interpretation section, a report writer should generally avoid adhering too closely to the raw data. However, for certain purposes, it may be useful to include raw data or even to describe the tests themselves. Test descriptions allow untrained persons to know specific behaviors the client engaged in rather than merely the final inferences. For, example, a report may include a description such as "Mr. A had an average level of recall for short-term visual information, as indicated by his being able to accurately recall and reproduce five out of a possible nine geometric designs that he had previously worked with for five minutes." This sentence provides a more behaviorally referenced description than one like "Mr. A had an average level of recall as measured on the Bender memory." Thus, a test description is apt to give the reader a more in-depth, precise, and familiar reference regarding the subject's abilities. In addition to the test descriptions themselves, test responses can serve to make the description behavior specific and to balance high-level abstractions with concrete responses. For example, a clinician might discuss a client's impulsiveness and include illustrative items on the MMPI, such as:

38. During one period when I was a child I engaged in petty thievery. (True)

205. At times it has been impossible for me to keep from stealing or shoplifting. (True)

In discussing the same issue, a clinician could also include a portion of a TAT story that illustrates a similar point:

> ...so he took the violin and, without even thinking about it, threw it into the fire and ran outside.

However, it is crucial to stress that the purpose of providing raw data and behavioral descriptions is to enrich and illustrate the topic and not to enable the reader to follow the clinician's line of reasoning or document the inferences that have been made. In developing inferences, clinicians must draw upon a wide variety of data. They cannot possibly discuss all the patterns, configurations, and relationships they used to come to their conclusions. Any attempt to do so would necessarily be overly detailed, cumbersome, and incomplete. Statements such as, "In considering the pattern of elevated scales 4 and 9 on the MMPI, it is safe to conclude . . ." are unnecessary and rarely contribute to a report's overall usefulness. In certain types of reports, such as those for legal purposes, it might be helpful to include some raw data. However, the purpose for doing this is not so much to repeat the thinking process of the clinician but more to substantiate that the inferences are data based, to provide a point of reference for discussing the results, and to indicate what assessment procedures were used.

Terminology

Several arguments have been made in determining whether to use technical or nontechnical language in psychological reports. It might be argued that technical terminology is precise and economical, increases the credibility of the writer, and can communicate concepts that are impossible to convey through nontechnical language. However, a number of potential difficulties are often encountered with the use of technical language. One of the more frequent problems involves the varying backgrounds and levels of sophistication of the persons reading the report. The most frequent readers of reports include teachers, administrators, judges, attorneys, psychiatrists, and social workers, most of whom do not have the necessary background to interpret technical terminology accurately. Even psychologists with different theoretical persuasions may be apt to misinterpret some of the terms. Take, for example the differing uses of "ego" by Freud, Jung, and Erikson. Also, the term "anxiety" might have several different categories of use. Although technical words can undoubtedly be precise, their precision is only helpful within a particular context and with a reader who has the proper background. Generally, reports are rated as more effective when the material is described in clear, basic language (Berry, 1975; Sandy, 1986; Weiner, 1987). Even among readers who have the proper background to understand technical terms, many prefer a more straightforward presentation (Tallent & Reiss, 1959c). Technical terms also run the danger of becoming nominalisms in which, by merely naming the phenomenon, persons develop an illusory sense of understanding more than is actually the case. For example, terms like "immature" or "sadistic" cover a great deal of information because they are so general, but they say nothing about what the person is like when he or she is behaving in these maladaptive ways. They also do not adequately differentiate one person from the next and are frequently ambiguous. Furthermore, technical terms are often used inappropriately—for example, when a person who is sensitive and cautious in interpersonal relationships is labeled "paranoid," or when "compulsive" is used to describe someone who is merely careful, conscientious, and effective in dealing with details.

Klopfer (1960) provides an excellent and still relevant rationale for using basic English rather than technical terminology. First, and perhaps most important, the use of basic

English allows the examiner, through his or her report, to communicate with and affect a wide audience. This is particularly important since the number and variety of persons who read reports is much greater now than twenty or thirty years ago. Furthermore, basic English is more specific and descriptive of an individual's uniqueness, whereas technical terms tend to deal with generalities. Terms such as "sadomasochistic" and "hostile" do not provide essential information about whether the person is assaultive or suicidal. Finally, the use of basic English generally indicates that the examiner has more in-depth comprehension of the information he or she is dealing with and can communicate this comprehension in a precise, concrete manner. Klopfer (1960) stresses that any description found in a psychological report should be comprehensible to any literate person of at least average intelligence. The first four are his examples of translating technical concepts into basic English (Klopfer, 1960):

> "Hostility towards the father figure" becomes "the patient is so fearful and suspicious of people in positions of authority that he automatically assumes an aggressive attitude towards them, being sure that swift retaliations will follow. He doesn't give such people an opportunity to demonstrate their real characteristics since he assumes they are all alike."
>
> "The patient projects extensively" becomes "the patient has a tendency to attribute to other people feelings and ideas originating within himself regardless of how these other people might feel."
>
> "The defenses the patient uses are..." becomes "the methods characteristically employed by the patient for reducing anxiety are..."
>
> "Empathy" becomes "the patient can understand and sympathize with the feelings of others, since she finds it relatively easy to put herself in their place."
>
> "The client is hostile and resistant" may be changed to include a behavioral description; "when the client entered the room she stated, 'My Dad said I had to come and that's the only reason I'm here'" or "later on in the testing she made several comments such as 'This is a stupid question.'" (pp. 58-60)

The general principle involved in the above examples is to translate high-level abstract terms into basic English that provides concrete behavioral descriptions.

Ownby (1987) recommends combining any conclusion or generalization with specific behaviors or test observations. Recommendations should also be directly linked with the relevant behaviors/generalizations, either in the same place or in the recommendations section. For example, instead of saying a client is "depressed," a writer might state that "the client's behavior which included self-criticism and occasional crying suggested he was depressed." Linking generalizations with clear concrete descriptions tends to create reports that are perceived to be relatively credible and persuasive (Ownby, 1986a). If this process is followed, descriptions will be less subject to misinterpretation, less ambiguous, and more likely to convey the unique personality of the client. Although abstract technical terms can be important components of a psychological report, they should be used sparingly and only when clearly appropriate. This particularly means carefully considering the background of the persons who will be reading the report. Sandy (1986) even recommends having the clinician collaborate with the relevant recipients of the report so that the final report is descriptive rather than interpretive and the readers are not passive recipients of the "higher" wisdom of the psychologist.

Content Overload

There are no specific rules to follow in determining how much information to include in a report. A general guideline is to estimate how much information a reader can realistically be expected to assimilate. If too many details are given, the information may begin to become poorly defined and vague and, therefore, lack impact or usefulness. When clinicians are confronted with a great variety of data from which to choose, they should not attempt to include it all. A statement such as "The client's relative strengths are in abstract reasoning, general fund of knowledge, short-term memory, attention span, and mathematical computation" is likely to overload the reader with too many details. The clinician should instead focus on and discuss only those areas that are most relevant to the purpose of the report.

Feedback

During the earlier days of psychological assessment, examiners often kept the results of psychological assessments carefully concealed from the client. There was often an underlying belief that the results were too complex and mysterious for the client to adequately understand. In contrast, current practices are to provide the client with clear, direct, and accurate feedback regarding the results of an evaluation. Brodsky (1972) has even recommended that clients should have complete and open access to all files.

The change toward providing feedback to clients has been motivated by several factors. First, regulations have supported a growing list of consumer rights, including the right to various types of information. Second, it might be perceived as a violation if the client did not receive feedback regarding the results of testing after he or she had been subjected to several hours of assessment. Even the most secure of clients might easily feel uncomfortable knowing a report with highly personal information might be circulated and used by persons in power to make decisions regarding the client's future. Such practices could understandably result in suspicion and irritation on the part of the public. Finally, examiners cannot safely assume that the original referral source will provide feedback to the client. Even if the referral source does provide feedback, there is no guarantee that the information will be provided in an appropriate manner. Thus, the responsibility for providing feedback will ultimately be on the clinician.

The extent to which a clinician providing feedback will allow the client to actually read all or portions of the report will vary. The rationale for allowing the client to actually read the report is that doing so enables the client to experience the product of assessment in a direct manner. It also enables a clinician to explain any areas that are unclear. A significant difficulty is that the client might misinterpret various portions of the report, especially I.Q. scores and diagnosis. For this reason, most clinicians paraphrase and elaborate upon selected portions of the report. This increases the likelihood that clients will readily understand the most important material and will not be overloaded with too much content.

The likelihood of providing effective feedback can be enhanced by following several guidelines. Clinicians must first select the most essential information to be conveyed to the client. To a large extent, this will involve clinical judgment. Important considerations in this selection process include the client's ego strength, intelligence, life situation, stability, and receptiveness to different types of material. Typically, three to four general and well-developed areas will represent an optimum amount of information. The information that is provided should be carefully integrated into the overall context of the person's life. This integration might be enhanced by providing concrete behavioral examples, reflecting on aspects of the client's behavior, referring to relevant aspects of the client's history, or paraphrasing and expanding on a client's self-descriptions. A useful technique is to have the client evaluate the relevance and accuracy of the information. The client might also be requested to give his or her own examples of the trait or pattern of behavior described in the report. Such a collaboration with the client helps the clinician to determine how well the client has understood the feedback. Underlying any feedback should be an attempt to provide the information in a clear, intelligible manner. Commonplace language should be used instead of psychological jargon. It is also important to take into account the client's level of intelligence, education, vocabulary, and level of psychological sophistication. Importantly, feedback should not only be a neutral conveyance of data but should also be a clinical intervention. The information should provide the client with new perspectives and options, and should aid in the client's own problem solving.

FORMAT FOR A PSYCHOLOGICAL REPORT

Even though no single, agreed-upon format exists, every report should include both an integration of old information as well as a new and unique perspective on the person. Old information should include identifying information (name, birthdate, etc.), reason for referral, and relevant history. New information should include assessment results, impressions, summary/conclusions, and recommendations. A suggested outline is as follows:

Name:
Date of Birth:
Date of Examination:
I.   Referral Question
II.   Evaluation Procedures
III. Behavioral Observations
IV.   Relevant History
V.   Test Results
VI.   Impressions and Interpretation
VII. Recommendations

Referral Question

The purpose of describing the referral question is to provide a brief description of the client and a statement of the general reason for conducting the evaluation. In particular, this should include a brief description of the nature of the problem. If this section is adequately completed, it should give an initial focus to the report by orienting the reader to what will follow and to the types of issues that will be addressed. A necessary prerequisite is that the clinician has developed an adequate clarification of the referral question. The purpose of testing should be stated in a precise and problem-oriented manner. Thus, phrases such as "the client was referred for a psychological evaluation" or "as a requirement for a class project" are inadequate in that they lack focus and precision. It is helpful to include both the specific purpose of the evaluation and the decisions facing the referral source. Whenever possible, the reason for referral should be discussed directly with the referring person, and it may sometimes be necessary or useful to discuss the rationale for testing the client. Examples of general reasons for referral include:

1. Intellectual evaluation: routine, retarded, gifted
2. Differential diagnosis, such as the relative presence of psychological (functional) difficulties and organic impairment

3. Assessment of the nature and extent of brain damage
4. Evaluation as a component of and to provide recommendations for vocational counseling
5. Evaluation of appropriateness for, and possible difficulties encountered in, psychotherapy
6. Personal insight regarding difficulties with interpersonal relationships
7. Evaluation as an aid in client placement

These represent general referral questions that, in actual situations, would still require further clarification especially regarding the decisions facing the referral source. The key should be to find out what the referring person really wants from the report. This may require reading beneath the surface of the referral questions and articulating possible hidden agendas and placing the referral question into a wider context than the presenting problem. An effective referral question should accurately describe the client's and the referral source's current problems. In the report itself, the question(s) should then be answered in the summary of the report, and the recommendations should be relevant to the client's problem.

Evaluation Procedures

The report section that deals with evaluation procedures simply lists the tests used and does not include the test results. Usually, full test names are included along with their abbreviations. Later in the report the abbreviations can be used, but the initial inclusion of the entire name provides a reference for readers who may not be familiar with test abbreviations. For legal evaluations or other occasions in which precise details of administration are important, it is important to include the date on which different tests were administered and the length of time required to complete each one. It may also be important to include whether a clinical interview or mental status examination was given and, if so, the amount of time required for the examination.

Behavioral Observations

A description of the client's behaviors can provide insight into his or her problem and may be a significant source of data to confirm, modify, or question the test-related interpretations. Descriptions should be tied to specific behaviors and should not represent a clinician's inferences. For example, instead of making the inference that the client was "depressed," it is preferable to state that "her speech was slow and she frequently made self-critical statements such as 'I knew I couldn't get that one right.'"

Relevant behavioral observations made during the interview include physical appearance, behavior toward the task and examiner, and degree of cooperativeness. A description of the client's physical appearance should focus on any unusual features relating to facial expressions, clothes, body type, mannerisms, and movements. It is especially important to note any contradictions—for example, a 14-year-old boy who acts more like a 25-year-old or a person who appears dirty and disheveled but has an excellent vocabulary and high level of verbal fluency. The behaviors the client expresses toward the test material and the examiner often provide a significant source of information. These may include behaviors that reflect the person's level of affect, manifest anxiety, presence of depression, or degree of hostility. The client's role may be as an active participant or generally passive and submissive; he or she may be very much concerned with his or her performance or relatively indifferent. The client's method of problem solving is often a crucial area to note, and may range from careful and methodical to impulsive and disorganized. It is also important to pay attention to any unusual verbalizations that the client makes about the test material. One factor involved in assessing the validity of the test results is the level of cooperation expressed by the client. This is especially important for intelligence and ability tests, since a necessary prerequisite is that the client be alert and attentive, and put forth his or her best effort. It may also be important to note events prior to testing, such as situational crises, previous night's sleep, or use of medication. If there are situational factors that may modify or bring into question the test's validity, they should be noted with statements like, "The test results should be viewed with caution since . . ." or "The degree of maladjustment indicated on the test scores may represent an exaggeration of the client's usual level of functioning due to conditions surrounding the test administration." Often, the most important way to determine test validity in relationship to the client is through a careful look at the client's behaviors relating to the tests and his or her life situation prior to testing.

Sattler (1988) has developed a "behavior and attitude checklist" comprised of ten major categories that can be rated on a seven-point scale (see Figure 12–2). The examiner may wish to use this checklist as a tool to help focus on areas that might be significant to mention or discuss. It is important to emphasize that other crucial behaviors may occur that are not covered in the checklist and that still require discussion.

Behavioral observations should usually be kept concise, specific, and relevant. If a description does not serve to develop some insight about the person or demonstrate his or her uniqueness, then it should not be included. Thus, if a behavior is normal or average, it will usually not be important to discuss other than to briefly mention that the person had, for example, an average level of cooperation, alertness, or anxiety. The focus, then, should be on those client behaviors that create a unique impression. The relative length of this section will vary from a few brief sentences to considerably longer depending on the amount of relevant information the clinician has noticed. The relative importance of this section in relationship to the overall report will likewise be extremely varied. Sometimes, this section can be almost as important as the test results, whereas at other times it might consist of a few minor observations.

Clinicians who prefer behavioral assessment procedures might wish to emphasize the behavioral observation section by providing more in-depth descriptions of relevant antecedents. Also, consequent events surrounding the problem behavior itself might be evaluated in relationship to their onset, duration, frequency, and intensity. Specific strategies of behavioral assessment include narrative descriptions, interval recording, event recording, ratings recordings, and self-report inventories (see Chapter 4).

Relevant History

The writeup of a client's history should include aspects of the person's background that are relevant to the problem the person is confronting and to the interpretation of the test results. The history, along with the referral question, should also serve to place the problem and the test results into the proper context. In accomplishing these goals, the clinician does not need to include a long, involved chronology with a large number of details, but rather should be as succinct as possible. In selecting which areas to include and which to exclude, a clinician must continually evaluate these areas in relationship to the overall purpose of the report. It is difficult to specify precise rules since each individual will be different. Furthermore, each clinician may have his or her own personal and theoretical orientation, which will alter the

Behavior and Attitude Checklist

Client's name: ———————————   Examiner: ———————————

Age: ———————————   Date of report: ———————————

Test(s) administered: ———————————   Date of examination: ———————————

IQ: ———————————   Grade: ———————————

Instructions: Place an X on the appropriate line for each scale.

I. *Attitude toward examiner and test situation:*

   1. cooperative   __:__:__:__:__:__:__ uncooperative

   2. passive   __:__:__:__:__:__:__ aggressive

   3. tense   __:__:__:__:__:__:__ relaxed

   4. gives up easily   __:__:__:__:__:__:__ does not give up easily

II. *Attitude toward self:*

   5. confident   __:__:__:__:__:__:__ not confident

   6. critical of own work   __:__:__:__:__:__:__ accepting of own work

III. *Work habits:*

   7. fast   __:__:__:__:__:__:__ slow

   8. deliberate   __:__:__:__:__:__:__ impulsive

   9. thinks aloud   __:__:__:__:__:__:__ thinks silently

   10. careless   __:__:__:__:__:__:__ neat

IV. *Behavior:*

   11. calm   __:__:__:__:__:__:__ hyperactive

V. *Reaction to failure:*

   12. aware of failure   __:__:__:__:__:__:__ unaware of failure

   13. works harder after failure   __:__:__:__:__:__:__ gives up easily after failure

   14. calm after failure   __:__:__:__:__:__:__ agitated after failure

   15. apologetic after failure   __:__:__:__:__:__:__ not apologetic after failure

VI. *Reaction to praise:*

   16. accepts praise gracefully   __:__:__:__:__:__:__ accepts praise awkwardly

   17. works harder after praise   __:__:__:__:__:__:__ retreats after praise

VII. *Speech and language:*

   18. speech poor   __:__:__:__:__:__:__ speech good

   19. articulate language   __:__:__:__:__:__:__ inarticulate language

   20. responses direct   __:__:__:__:__:__:__ responses vague

   21. converses spontaneously   __:__:__:__:__:__:__ only speaks when spoken to

   22. bizarre language   __:__:__:__:__:__:__ reality-oriented language

VIII. *Visual-motor:*

   23. reaction time slow   __:__:__:__:__:__:__ reaction time fast

   24. trial-and-error   __:__:__:__:__:__:__ careful and systematic

   25. skillful movements   __:__:__:__:__:__:__ awkward movements

IX. *Motor:*

   26. defective motor coordination   __:__:__:__:__:__:__ good motor coordination

X. *Overall test results:*

   27. reliable   __:__:__:__:__:__:__ unreliable

   28. valid   __:__:__:__:__:__:__ invalid

Figure 12–2. Behavior and Attitude Checklist

Source: Reprinted with permission of the publisher and author, from J.M. Sattler, *Assessment of Children* (3rd ed.), 1988, p. 92. © Jerome M. Sattler, Publisher.

types of information he or she feels are significant. Whereas one clinician may primarily describe interpersonal relationships, another may focus on intrapsychic variables, birth order, early childhood events, or details about the client's present situation and environment. The key is to maintain a flexible orientation so that the interviewer will be aware of the most significant elements in the client's life. In general, the end product should include a good history of the problem, along with such areas as important life events, family dynamics, work history, personal interests, daily activities, and past and present interpersonal relationships (see Table 3–1).

Usually, a history will begin with a brief summary of the client's general background, including age, sex, family constellation, education, health, and a restatement of the problem. The first sentence might read something like, "Mary Smith is a 48-year-old, white, divorced female, with a high school education, who presents complaints of nervous tension, insomnia, and depression." This can be followed by sections describing family background, personal history, history of the problem, and current life situation.

The extent to which a clinician decides to pursue and discuss a client's family background is subject to a great degree of variability. Often, a brief description of the client's parents is warranted; this may include whether they are separated/divorced and alive/deceased, and their socioeconomic level, occupation, cultural background, and health status. Sometimes, it is important to include information about the emotional and medical backgrounds of parents and close relatives, since certain disorders occur with greater frequency in some families than in the overall population. A description of the general atmosphere of the family is often helpful, including the client's characteristic feelings toward family members and his or her perceptions of their relationships with each other. Descriptions of common family activities and whether the family was from an urban or a rural environment might also be included. If one or both parents died while the client was young, the clinician can still discuss the sort of speculations the client has regarding his or her parent(s) and who the significant persons for the client were as he or she was growing up.

The client's personal history can include information from infancy, early childhood, adolescence, and adulthood. Each stage has typical areas to investigate and problems to be aware of. The information from infancy will usually either represent vague recollections or be secondhand information derived from parents or relatives. Thus, it may be subject to a great deal of exaggeration and fabrication. If possible, it may be helpful to have details verified by additional sources, such as through direct questioning of parents or examination of medical records. The degree of contact with parents, toilet training, family atmosphere, and developmental milestones can all be important areas to discuss. Since physical and psychological difficulties often are related and occur simultaneously, a medical history is sometimes helpful. The most significant tasks during childhood are the development of peer relationships and adjustment to school. What was the quality of clients' early friendships? How much time did they spend with others? Were there any fights or rebellious acting out? Were they basically loners or did they have a large number of friends? Did they join clubs and have group activities, hobbies, or extracurricular interests? In the academic area, it may be of interest to note their usual grades, best or worst subjects, and whether they skipped or repeated grades. Furthermore, what was their relationship with their parents, and did their parents restrict their activities or were they relatively free? During adolescent years, clients typically face further academic, psychological, and social adjustments to high school. Of particular importance are their reactions to puberty and early heterosexual relationships. Did they have difficulties with sex role identity, abuse drugs or alcohol, or rebel against authority figures? The adult years center around occupational adjustment and establishing marital and family relationships. During early adulthood, what were clients' feelings and aspirations regarding marriage? What were their career goals? Did they effectively establish independence from parents? As adulthood progressed, were there any significant changes in the quality of their close relationships, employment, or expression of sexuality? What activities did they engage in during their leisure time? With advancing age, clients face challenges relating to their declining abilities, limitations, and developing a meaningful view of their lives.

Although the personal history can help place the problem in its proper context and explain certain causative factors, it is usually essential to spend some time focusing directly on the problem itself. Of particular importance are the initial onset and the nature of the symptoms. From the time when the client first noticed these symptoms, have there been any changes in their frequency, intensity, or nature? Furthermore, were there any previous attempts at treatment, and if so, what was the outcome? In some reports, the history of the problem will be the longest and most important part of the history section.

The family and personal histories usually reveal information relating to the predisposing cause of a client's difficulties, whereas the history of the problem often provides an elaboration of the precipitating and reinforcing causes. To complete this picture, the clinician also has to develop a sense of the factors that are currently reinforcing the problem. This requires information relating to the client's life situation. Significant areas may be the client's life stresses, including changes that he or she is confronting. Also, what are the nature of and resources provided by his or her family and work relationships? Finally, it is important to understand the alternatives and decisions that the client is facing.

Sometimes, an evaluation needs to assess the possible presence and nature of organic impairment. In many of these cases, the history is of even greater significance than test results and often the most valuable information a psychologist can provide to a referring medical practitioner is a thorough history. Thus, the history needs to be complete and must address a number of areas that are not ordinarily covered in personality evaluations. Several interview aids have been developed to help ensure that most relevant areas are covered. These include the Adult Neuropsychological Questionnaire (Mendez, 1978) and the Neuropsychological Status Examination (Schinka, 1983). If the person reports having had a head injury, it is important to note the length of time the client was unconscious (if at all), whether he or she actually remembers getting hit, the last memory before the injury and the first thing he or she clearly remembers following the injury. In all neuropsychological assessments, a crucial area is to establish the person's premorbid level of functioning. This may mean obtaining information on his or her grade point average in high school or college, sending for any relevant records (i.e. previous I.Q. results), previous highest level of employment, and personal interests such as hobbies. Often it may be necessary to verify the client's previous level of functioning from outside sources, such as from parents or employers. One difficulty with determining the probable cause of brain impairment lies in attempting to rule out other possible causes, such as exposure to toxic substances, strokes, high fevers, or other episodes of head trauma. Areas of current functioning that need to be addressed might include memory problems, word-finding difficulties, weakness on one side of the body, alterations in gait, loss of consciousness, and unusual sensations. Previous assessments with CT/NMR scans, EEGs, or neurological exams would also be important to obtain. Even though these medical records might be able to identify the site and size of a lesion, it is still the work of the psychologist to describe what the person is doing as a result of these lesions. It might also be important to obtain current or past information regarding drug intake, especially recent alterations in prescriptions since these might effect psychological functioning. Although the above topics are by no means exhaustive, they do represent some of the more important areas to consider when taking a history related to possible neuropsychological deficit.

A typical neuropsychological assessment includes some of the tests discussed in earlier chapters (WAIS-R/WISC-R, MMPI, Bender) as well as tests or test batteries designed specifically for the evaluation of organic impairment, such as the Halstead Reitan Neuropsychological Test Battery, Luria-Nebraska Neuropsychological Battery, or the Benton Visual Retention Test. The interview data and test results from a psychologist should ideally be combined with and complement medical records, such as CT scans and neurological exams.

The quantity of such information may seem immense. However, the above history format is intended only as a general guideline. At times, it may be appropriate to ignore many of the areas mentioned above and focus on others. In condensing the client's history into the report, it is important to avoid superfluous material and continually question whether the information obtained is relevant to the general purpose of the report. Furthermore, it is typically not useful to include material that is already in the possession of the referral source. This may be perceived as needless duplication and could result in the history section becoming needlessly long.

Test Results

For certain reports, it may not be necessary to list test scores. However, they should always be included in legal reports or when professionals who are knowledgeable about testing will be reading the report. Intelligence test scores are traditionally listed first and, for the Wechsler scales, should include Verbal I.Q., Performance I.Q., and Full Scale I.Q., along with the subtests and their scaled scores. This is often followed by Bender results, which may simply be summarized by a statement like: "Empirically not in the organic range, although there were difficulties organizing the designs and frequent erasures." MMPI results are often listed with the validity scales given first, followed by scales ordered from highest to lowest. They can also be listed in the order in which they appear on the profile sheet. Any MMPI results should always be referred to by their T scores and not the raw scores. Whereas it is fairly straightforward to list the objective and intelligence test scores, it is considerably more difficult to adequately describe the scores on projective tests. The Rorschach summary sheet can be included, but the results from projective drawings and the TAT are usually omitted. Should a clinician wish to summarize projective drawings, a brief statement is usually sufficient, such as: "Projective drawings were miniaturized and immature, with the inclusion of two transparencies." Likewise, TAT "scores" can be summarized by a brief statement of the strongest needs and press, and a mention of the most common themes encountered in the stories.

Impressions and Interpretations

The main findings of the tests must be presented in the form of integrated hypotheses. This section can be considered to be the main body of the report. The areas discussed and the style of presentation will vary according to the personal orientation of the clinician, the purpose of testing, the individual being tested, and the types of tests administered. One format that should be encouraged is to discuss the material by different topics rather than test by test. This provides a more coherent, integrated presentation of the information. Klopfer (1960) recommends using a grid with the topics for consideration in the left column (derived from Table 12–1) and the tests administered in the top row. This enables the clinician to list the essential findings in the appropriate box where the topic and the test intersect. When actually writing the Impressions and Interpretations section of the report, the clinician can then review all findings within a particular topic and summarize them on the report. An example of such a grid is given in Figure 12–3. The list of tests is dependent on which tests the examiner administered, but the topics can be chosen and arranged according to which areas the clinician would like to focus on.

All inferences made in the Impressions and Interpretations section should be based on an integration of the test data, behavioral observations, relevant history, and additional available data. The conclusions and discussion may relate to such areas as the client's overt behavior, self-concept, family background, intellectual abilities, emotional difficulties, medical disorders, school problems, or interpersonal conflicts. A client's intellectual abilities often provide a general frame of reference for a variety of personality variables. For this reason, a discussion of the client's intellectual abilities usually occurs first. Although this should include a general estimate of the person's intelligence as indicated by I.Q. scores, it is also important to provide a discussion of more specific abilities. This discussion may include an analysis of such areas as memory, problem solving, abstract reasoning, concentration, and fund of information. If the report is to be read by persons who are familiar with test theory, it may be sufficient to include I.Q. scores without an explanation of their normative significance. In most reports, it is helpful to include the I.Q. scores as well as the percentile ranking (see Appendix C) and general intellectual classification (high average, superior, etc., see Table 5–1). Some examiners may even prefer to omit the actual I.Q. scores in favor of including only percentile rank and general classification. This can be useful in cases where persons reading the report might be likely to misunderstand or misinterpret unexplained I.Q. scores. Once a general estimate of intelligence has been made, it should, whenever possible, be followed by a discussion of the client's intellectual strengths and weaknesses. This may involve elaborating on the meaning of the difference between Verbal I.Q. and Performance I.Q. or a discussion of subtest scatter. In addition, it can be useful to compare the client's potential level of functioning with his or her actual performance. If there is a wide discrepancy between these two, then reasons for this discrepancy should be offered. For example, the client may be underachieving due to anxiety, low motivation, emotional interference, or perceptual processing difficulties.

Topics	Tests Administered				
	WAIS	Bender	House-Tree-Person	MMPI	TAT
Intellectual aspects					
Interpersonal relations					
Emotional controls					
Basic conflict areas					
Defenses					
Hostility					
Personal resources					

Figure 12–3. Sample grid of personality characteristics by tests administered
Note: Modified from Klopfer, W.G., *The Psychological Report: Use and Communication of Psychological Findings.* New York: Grune & Stratton, 1960, p. 36. Reprinted by permission.

Whereas a discussion of intellectual abilities is relatively clear and straightforward, the next sections are frequently more difficult to select. There is an extremely wide number of possibilities to choose from, many of which have been listed in Table 12–1. If the referral question is clearly focused on a specific problem, then it may only be necessary to elaborate on two or three topics. A referral question that is general may require a wider approach in which six or more areas are discussed.

Some of the more common and important topics are the client's level of psychopathology, dependency, hostility, sexuality, interpersonal relationships, diagnosis, and behavioral predictions. A client's level of psychopathology refers to the relative severity of the disturbances he or she is experiencing. It is important to distinguish whether the results are characteristic of normals, outpatients, or inpatients, and whether the difficulties are long term or a reaction to current life stresses. Does the client use behaviors that are adaptive or those that are maladaptive and self-defeating? Within the area of ideation, are there persistent thoughts, delusions, hallucinations, loose associations, blocking of ideas, perseveration, or illogical thoughts? It may also be important to assess the adequacy of the client's judgments and relative degree of insight. Can the person effectively make plans, understand the impact he or she has on others, and judge the appropriateness of his or her behavior? To assess the likelihood of successful therapy, it is especially important to assess the client's level of insight. This includes assessing the person's ability to think psychologically, awareness of his or her own changing feelings, understanding of the behaviors of others, and ability to conceptualize and discuss relevant insights.

Usually, a client's greatest conflicts will center on difficulties with dependency, hostility, and sexuality. In discussing a client's dependency, it is important to discuss the strength of these needs, the typical roles played with others, and present or past significant relationships. In what ways does the client defend him- or herself against, or cope with, feelings of dependency? This evaluation may include a discussion of defense mechanisms, thoughts, behaviors, feelings, or somatic responses as they relate to dependency. The relative intensity of a client's hostility is also important. Is the expression of hostility indirect, or is it direct in the form of either verbal criticisms or actual assaultive behavior? If the expression of hostility is covert, it may be the result of such factors as fear of loss of love, retaliation, or guilt. When the client does feel anger, what are his or her characteristic defenses against these feelings? For example, some clients might express opposite behaviors, with overly exaggerated concern for others, or they might direct the anger inward by developing physical aches and pains that serve as self-punishment for having aggressive impulses. They may also adapt through such means as extreme suspiciousness of others, created by denying their hostility and attributing it to others. A discussion of a client's sexuality usually involves noting the relative intensity of his or her urges and the degree of anxiety associated with the expression of those urges. Does the client inhibit his or her sexuality due to a belief that it is dirty, experience anxiety over possible consequences, or associate it with aggressiveness? Defenses against sexual urges may be handled in ways similar to hostility, such as by performing the opposite behavior through extreme religiosity or celibacy, or by denying the feelings and attributing them instead to others. On the other hand, clients may impulsively act out their sexual urges and become promiscuous, at least in part out of a need to obtain self-affirmation through sexual contact. Clinicians may want to discuss the dynamics involved in any unusual sexual practices.

Discussing clients' characteristic patterns and roles in interpersonal relationships can also be extremely useful. These can often be discussed in relationship to the dimensions of submissiveness/dominance and love/hate, or the extent to which they orient themselves around the need to be included, control others, or seek affection. Is their style of communicating typically guarded or is it open and self-disclosing to the extent that they can discuss such areas as painful feelings and fears? Can they deal with the specifics of a situation or are they usually vague and general? Do they usually appear assertive and direct, or passive and indirect? Finally, it is often important to determine the extent to which they are perceptive about interpersonal relationships and their typical approaches toward resolving conflict.

It may also be appropriate to include descriptions of vocational goals and aptitudes. This is becoming increasingly important in educational reports, especially for students with special educational needs, such as those who are handicapped (Levinson, 1987). Many of the tests covered in this text can help in assessing a person's strengths and weaknesses, but a clinician may also need to include further assessment devices, such as the Strong-Campbell or Kuder Occupational Interest Survey.

Determining whether to include a diagnosis has been an area of some controversy. Some clinicians feel that labels should be avoided since they may result in self-fulfilling prophecies, be overly reductionistic, and allow clients to avoid responsibility for their own behavior. Other objections to diagnosis stem from researchers who feel that many of the terms are not scientifically valid (Rosenhan, 1973; Ziskin & Faust, 1988) or from psychiatrists who feel that it should be primarily their role to provide diagnoses (Tallent & Reiss, 1959c). If a clinician does decide to give a diagnosis, he or she must first have a clear operational knowledge of the diagnostic terms. He or she should also include the client's premorbid level of adjustment, and the severity and frequency of the disturbance. Instruments such as the Structured Clinical Interview for the DSM-III (SCID; Spitzer et al., 1983) or Diagnostic Interview Schedule (Robins et al., 1985; Wittchen, Semlar, & Von Zerssen, 1985) might help to increase the reliability of diagnosis. It is also important to include the possible causes of the disorder. A discussion of causes should not be simplistic and one-dimensional but rather should appreciate the complexity of causative factors. Thus, causes may be described from the perspective of primary, predisposing, precipitating, and reinforcing factors. Clinicians may also discuss the relative significance of biological, psychological, and sociocultural variables.

A frequent consideration is whether the client's difficulties will continue or, if currently absent, recur. If the client's future prospects are poor, then a statement of the rationale for this conclusion should be given. For example, if a clinician predicts that the response to treatment will be poor, then he or she should explain that this is due to such factors as a strong need to appear hypernormal, poor insight, and a high level of defensiveness. Likewise, favorable predictions should include a summary of the client's assets and resources, such as psychological mindedness, motivation to change, and social supports. If difficulties are likely to be encountered during the course of treatment, then the nature and intensity of these difficulties should be discussed. The prediction of suicidal potential, assaultive behavior, child abuse, or criminal behavior is essential in certain types of reports. Often the tests themselves are not useful in predicting these behaviors. For example, one of the best ways of predicting suicidal potential is to evaluate the client's past history, current environment, personal resources, and degree of suicide intent (Pallis, Gibbons, & Pierce, 1984). However, research indicates that many predictions of behavior, such as dangerousness, are quite poor (Hall, 1984; Ziskin & Faust, 1988). This is especially true for long-term predictions. Clinicians should thus exercise appropriate caution in making predictions and not exceed the bounds of reasonable certainty.

A summary paragraph should follow the discussion of main impressions and interpretations. The purpose of the summary is to restate succinctly the primary findings and conclusions. This requires that the clinician select only the most important issues and that he or she be careful not to overwhelm the reader with needless details. If the summary is included at the end of the section on impressions and interpretation, there is no need to summarize the entire report but only the major interpretations. However, some clinicians prefer to include a separate summary and recommendations section at the end of the entire report. In this case, the section should summarize the entire report and include the recommendations. Either location is acceptable; the choice can be based on the clinician's personal preference and the needs of the report as suggested by the referral question(s) and background of the readers.

Recommendations

The ultimate practical purpose of the report is contained in the recommendations since they suggest what steps clients can take in order to solve their problems. Such recommendations should be clear, practical, and obtainable, and should relate directly to the purpose of the report. The best reports are those that help the referral source and/or the client to solve the problems they are facing (Pryzwansky & Hanania, 1986). To achieve this report-writing goal, the clinician must clearly understand the nature of the problem, the best alternatives for remediation, and the resources available in the community. The practical implication is that writers can improve their reports by becoming as familiar as possible with the uses to which their reports will be applied. An effective report must answer the referral question and also have decisional value. Once these factors have been carefully considered, recommendations can be developed.

Reports are typically rated most useful when their recommendations are highly specific rather than general (Brandt & Giebink, 1968; White, Nielsen, & Prus, 1984). Thus, a recommendation that states "the client should begin psychotherapy" is not as useful as a statement of the need for "individual therapy focusing on the following areas: increased assertiveness, relaxation techniques for reducing anxiety, and increased awareness of the self-defeating patterns he creates in relationships." Likewise, a recommendation for "special education" can be improved by expanding it to "special education two hours a day, emphasizing exercises in auditory sequencing and increasing immediate recall for verbally relevant information." However, caution should be exercised when providing specific recommendations to some professionals since many psychiatrists feel that developing treatment recommendations is primarily their responsibility (Tallent & Reiss, 1959a). Once the report, with its recommendations, has been submitted, continued contact should be made with the readers(s) to make sure the report has not been filed and forgotten. Even the best report will not be functional unless the recommendations are practical, obtainable, and actually put into action.

SAMPLE REPORTS

The sample reports in this section are from the more common settings in which clinicians work and consult. The dimensions in which the reports vary are:
- Format
- Extent to which history rather than test data is emphasized
- Types of tests used
- Degree to which they include a variety of descriptions rather than being case focused with a relatively limited range of topics

Within each setting, specific questions have been presented along with decisions that must be made related to the client. The different reports illustrate how the clinician has integrated the test data, client's history, and behavioral observations in order to handle these questions. The reports were selected to illustrate a wide diversity in format, length, type of setting, referral question, and type of tests used.

The first report was developed for a psychiatric setting and was intended to be read by professional mental health personnel. For this reason, there is some use of technical language and a focus on developing a detailed, traditional DSM-III-R diagnosis. What is noteworthy in the handling of the test data is that the bulk of the discussion relating to test interpretation revolves around projective test findings (Rorschach, TAT, projective drawing). Furthermore, much of the projective data is used in a qualitative, content-oriented manner. This was achieved by providing actual verbatim responses, which give a more colorful and rich portrayal of the client's thought processes than could be achieved through quantitative scores. For example, some of the TAT stories are written out to illustrate attitudes toward the client's parents and how the client perceives and attempts to cope with his inner sense of "evilness."

The evaluation written for a legal context approaches the client from a variety of angles. It tries to fit the presenting problem into material derived from behavioral observations during the interview; discusses his reaction to the charges, family relationships, and interests; and reviews relevant aspects of test data. This noteworthy diversity of approaches also helps to develop a complete picture of the person. The psychological test results represent just one source of data; the structure of the report has some additional features. Initially, there is a personal letter format directed to the referral source. When a report is being directed to one primary referral person, an opening letter tends to make the report more personal, thereby enhancing the likelihood of good rapport between the clinician and the referring person. The section summarizing the report is placed at the end and given considerable emphasis. This section integrates information not only from psychological tests, but also from other sources. Furthermore, the recommendations are included in, and closely tied to, the summary.

The third sample is from an educational context and is the most case-focused of all the reports. It mainly discusses the intellectual strengths and weaknesses of the client, and connects these in a general way with her social development. For the most part, the report avoids a discussion of personality dynamics because these were not requested by the referral source. Furthermore, her history indicated that the client's level of interpersonal adjustment was good. The most important part of the report is the recommendations. These are given the most discussion, and are as specific and concrete as possible. Once the client's cognitive weaknesses are documented in the section on interpretation and impressions, the main thing her parents and teachers need to know is what specific measures can be taken to work with these weaknesses.

The final evaluation develops a far more global personality description than any of the other reports. In contrast to the previous educational evaluation, the decisions and issues facing the client are not as specific and concrete. Instead, an understanding of the client's general dynamics, including intellectual abilities, interpersonal relationships, impulse control, specific presenting problem, and potential for benefiting from psychotherapy, is the major concern. Thus, the client may benefit from a knowledge of the information included in the report perhaps even more than his probation officer or attorney. It is intended to be used as an aid in the psychotherapeutic process as much as it is a tool in decision making. As such, the recommendations are de-emphasized in favor of a more qualitative understanding of the client's personality.

THE PSYCHIATRIC SETTING*

NAME: Robert
DATE OF BIRTH: 2/5/74
DATES OF EVALUATION: 3/14/88

IDENTIFYING INFORMATION:
Robert M. is a 14-year-old high school student admitted to the psychiatric unit at Monte Hospital on March 10, 1988 for his second psychiatric hospitalization. He was referred for an interview and psychological testing by Harold Smith, M.D. to estimate his intelligence, differential diagnosis, behavioral dynamics, and potential for adjustment.

PRESENTING PROBLEM:
Robert stated that he was in the hospital "for family problems." (What kind?) "Just not getting along. Not being able to work out at home." He said these problems started two years ago when "my mom put me into a private school, and I got kicked out" for "doing wrong things. Inappropriateness." Reportedly, on March 9, 1988, Robert consumed a large quantity of alcohol, became acutely intoxicated and was agitated, belligerent, combative, tearful, and yelled obscenities. His family took him to Monte hospital where tests revealed a blood alcohol level of .24 without indication of other drugs. Seemingly he consumed this near lethal dose of alcohol in response to his hatred and fear of his parents.

BACKGROUND INFORMATION:
The following information was obtained from Robert, who was a restless and dubious historian, from his hospital chart, and from a March 12, 1988 telephone conversation with Dr. Smith.

Robert was born and reared in San Francisco County and his biological parents remain married. The father, approximately age 40, is a career Air Force person with a rank unknown to Robert. He said the father teaches machine maintenance and attends college. He described the father as "a mean, violent, cruel person." (How does he show this?) "He used to hit me." (What would cause him to do that?) "Sometimes when I did something wrong." (Like what?) "Anything, any little thing, sometimes." He said he was hit with objects such as "a belt, sticks, spoons, forks, knives. Any object a lot of time." He said the most significant injuries he suffered during such beatings were "large blood blisters on my hand." He said he never suffered an injury that required medical attention but that he did ask his father's permission to remain out of school to conceal the marks from his peers. He said the father refused the request.

Robert's mother is approximately age 35 and a business secretary. Asked to describe her, he said, "I don't know. I guess she's mean. That's what I think. Is it my opinion?" (Yes. Mean in what way?) "Verbal abuse, yelling, screaming." (What causes her to do this?) "Anything, like my father. Frustration." (How does she react when your father hits you?) "She doesn't do anything. She lets him."

Robert is the oldest of three siblings with a brother, age 13, and a sister, age 10. Both siblings live in the home and attend school. "My brother's a little strange. Very silly and inappropriate for his age." He said the brother shows these characteristics when he "runs around naked, talks real strange like he's on an acid trip when he's not." He said the brother excels in school and has never received counselling or psychotherapy. Regarding the sister, "She's fine."

*Submitted by Thomas MacSpeiden, Ph.D.

Medically, Robert believes he experienced an uneventful gestation and delivery. Regarding unusual illnesses or accidents, he said that at age 10 or 11 he broke either his wrist or his thumb during horse play with friends and that the break healed without limitation. He said that at a later age he could not recall he broke his finger and wrist in horse play and that he had broken such bones approximately four or five times. He said that otherwise his health has been good.

Asked about unusual events in his life before starting school, Robert said, "I can't remember that far back." He said he enrolled at Rutledge Elementary School at the usual age where he remained in regular classes through the sixth grade. He earned primarily "C's," and related to his peers "well." He said he also related to his teachers "well." He said he had no behavioral problems in elementary school and that his life was uneventful.

For the seventh grade Robert was placed in a Roman Catholic school "because during the sixth grade they felt I was failing, not doing my work, taking too much leisure time." He said he remained at the Catholic school until the last month of the school year when he was expelled because of frequent misbehavior. Initially he said he could not remember what act led to the expulsion but later said, "I lit a firecracker in class." (In your opinion, why did you do that?) "Rebelling." (Against?) "Parents. It was also for fun." (Why were you rebelling against them?) "'Cause I didn't want to go to that school. I wanted to go to public school." (Why?) "Because I had gone to a public school for six years, and all my friends were going there."

Robert said he remained home without attending school until the following fall, September 1986, when he enrolled in the eighth grade at Franklin Junior High School to remain in regular classes until entering Monte Hospital. In the eighth grade his marks were "failing, no, below standard." (Why were they so low?) "Because I had started using alcohol, drugs. I don't know. I don't know if that's the reason." (Why did you start using drugs?) "I don't know that, the reason why." He said he was introduced to alcohol and other drugs by his age peers. He estimated that he was intoxicated approximately 30 times during the eighth grade, usually at home with friends while his parents were out. The only street drug used was marijuana. He said his parents did not know about his substance misuse but complained about his grades. "They wanted me to bring them up, but I started failing even more." He said otherwise there were no unusual events during the eighth grade.

Last September Robert enrolled in the ninth grade. Then, "I started hanging out with more friends that drank and more drugs," but he misused only alcohol and marijuana. He said he was intoxicated "a few times a week" and misused marijuana "maybe four or five times a week." He said that otherwise his life was uneventful until he entered Monte Hospital for the first time during Christmas vacation because "I was dead drunk." He said he remained hospitalized three days, until "the doctor thought I should be discharged." A week later, he returned to Monte Hospital for his current hospitalization.

Asked about his future plans in life, Robert said, "I haven't made any. I want to live with my grandparents, but they're not going to let me." He said his mother and his treating psychiatrist were against this plan because "they think I'm running away from my problems."

PSYCHOLOGICAL IMPRESSIONS:
Robert was seen on the Delta unit at Monte Hospital on March 12, 1988. He presented himself looking his stated age and adequately nourished as a pubescent male with somewhat dishevelled dark blond hair parted approximately on the right side, a fair facial complexion with mild acne and dressed in a white T-shirt, a blue and white plaid long-sleeved shirt in poor repair and new appearing Levi's. A cross-shaped earring dangled from

his left ear. At the beginning of the interview and multiple times thereafter, Robert asked when the evaluation would end. At one point, this examiner asked what Robert would do after the evaluation was completed, and Robert said he would go to his room to lie down because he was tired. He had a depressed facial expression, but was physically agitated and demonstrated considerable motor overflow although he remained continuously seated in his chair. During the intelligence testing he seemed to exert effort until a task became difficult whereupon he became disheartened and reduced effort. During the projective testing he was brief and hurried to complete the tasks. There were no indications of delusions or hallucinations, and he was oriented in all three spheres. His hygiene was adequate. He was alert, and both recent and remote memory appeared intact.

Robert was administered the Wechsler Intelligence Scale for Children-Revised (WISC-R), Rorschach, Thematic Apperception Test (TAT), Bender Visual Motor Gestalt Test (Bender) and Draw-A-Family Test.

On the WISC-R Robert obtained a Verbal IQ of 91, a Performance IQ of 84 and a Full Scale IQ of 86. His Verbal scaled scores ranged from 7 to 10 without significant deviation from the Verbal mean. Similarly, his Performance scaled scores ranged from 6 to 10. The seven-point discrepancy between the Verbal and Performance IQ scores approached significance and is consistent with a diagnosis of depression. Verbally he functioned at the 27th percentile and in the average range. In terms of perceptual motor performance he functioned at the 14th percentile and in the low average range. Overall he functioned intellectually at the 18th percentile and in the low average range. His performance is probably a conservative reflection of his intellectual capacity which may be as high as the high average range.

The structure of Robert's personality was difficult to estimate from his limited 14 Rorschach responses but appears nonpsychotic. Because of his limited responses his ratios and percentages should be interpreted with caution. Clearly, he uses repression and denial excessively in an attempt to exclude unacceptable impulses and fantasies from consciousness (F = 92%). Nonetheless Robert has difficulty seeing those things in the environment seen by most persons (Populars = 1) and at times gravely distorts his perceptions (X + % = 65%). These distortions are not frequent and are most likely to occur when he is emotionally stimulated. Because of his rigid defense posture, he currently has few energies available (M + C = 2.0). He attempts to enhance control by denying emotional stimuli (Sum C = 0), and generally when expressing emotion has adequate control (FC:CF+C = 1:0). Because of his rigidity, his aspirations exceed his ability to perform (W:M = 7:0), and there was no indication of whether he prefers to accomplish more in fantasy or more in action (EB = 1:1). Because of his excessive repression and denial his depression is not obvious since he does not easily respond to emotional material (Afr = .60). For his age his interests are somewhat narrow and immature (A = 64%).

The content of Robert's personality projected in his Rorschach responses is a perception of himself as confused and disorganized, much as he projected in his first response to Card I: "A star. A messed up star. Someone drew it wrong." As noted in his Rorschach scores, he attempts to deny emotional stimuli to enhance control, a mechanism typified in his rejection of Cards VIII and IX, the first of three highly chromatic and therefore affectively stimulating cards. When presented with Card VIII, he responded in approximately two seconds, "I see nothing in this. I don't see anything." His response to Card IX was similar. On Card X he used the whole of the blot as "an insect," a response that had negative form level. Curiously, he saw on each of the first five Rorschach cards the percept of "insect." Such perseveration is often found among neurologically damaged persons although it appears more likely in Robert's case a product of anxiety which limited his ability to structure the amorphous blot material much beyond an unspecified insect.

The content of Robert's personality projected in his TAT responses is a painful perception of himself as evil, a perception that may have resulted in part from his already overly punitive superego receiving further stimulation while he was enrolled in a parochial school for the seventh grade. This content was suggested by his cryptic response to Card 2, a man plowing with a horse in the background, a pregnant woman standing to one side near a tree, and a girl in the foreground holding books:

> Past, going, gone to a church school. Present, leaving home. Future, death. (Death in what way?) Starvation.

Robert views his internal anger and violence as undeniable indicators of his evilness, an evilness from which he can escape by drowning it along with himself in alcohol. Vivid were his responses to Cards 8BM, a primitive surgical scene with a boy standing in the foreground and a gun to one side; and 13MF, a bare-breasted woman lying on a bed and a man standing with one hand to his forehead:

> 8BM   Past, Vietnam war. Present, remembering. Future, death of a heart attack. (What was he remembering?) The people being cut up in the Vietnam war.
>
> 13MF   Past, alcoholic. Present, wife died. Future, death from alcohol. (Why did the wife die?) Kidney disease.

Alternatively he conceptualizes continuing to live with the evil within him without death, as projected in his response to Card 15, a figure standing among tombstones:

> Past, possessed with evil. Present, trying to destroy the evil. Future, living with evil. (What was the evil?) The devil.

He believes that were he to continue living with his evil he would represent a danger to other persons. This content was typified in his response to Card 7BM, a younger and older man in conversation:

> Past, jail. Present, courtroom. Future, jail. (Why was he in jail?) Murder.

Robert believes that in the past he was unwanted by a significant other. This awareness instilled in him the belief he was lacking in some way. When someone now offers him acceptance, he rejects it although he hopes he will be able to accept it at some point in the future.

On the Bender, all figures were completed with relative accuracy, and there were no indications of a neurological dysfunction affecting Robert's perceptual motor control. There were several indicators of impulsivity including overlapping, poor planning, and poor overall quality (see Figure 12–4).

Asked to draw a picture of his family, Robert drew from left to right persons he later labeled orally as "Dad," "Sister," and "Mom." Above these three and along the upper margin of the page from left to right he drew "Me" and "Brother" (see Figure 12–5). The drawing projects Robert's perception of him and his brother as separate from the parents and sister, much as he indicated during the interview when he said, "My brother's a little strange;" and clearly he views himself as somewhat strange. Not surprisingly, he perceives the father as powerful and the mother as significantly weaker than the father.

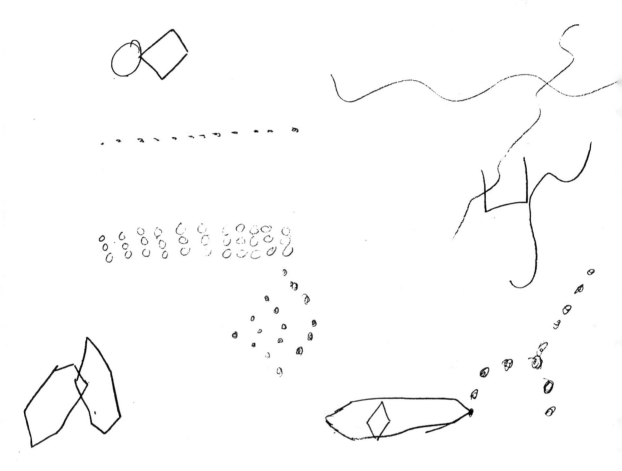

Figure 12–4.   Case: Robert.   Age: 14

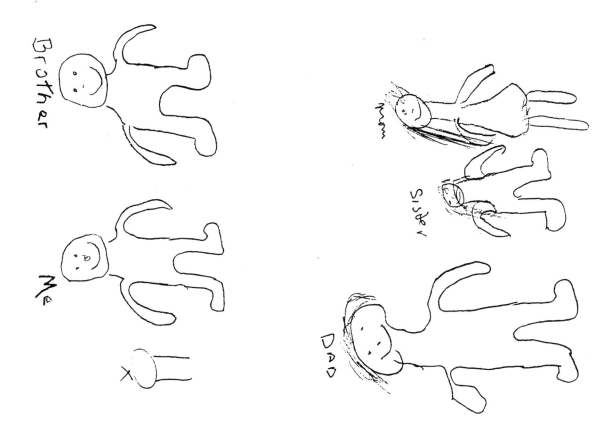

Figure 12–5.   Case: Robert. Age: 14

SUMMARY:
Robert functions intellectually in the low average range although his endowment may be in the high average range and currently reduced by his mental condition. He does not suffer from a neurological dysfunction affecting his perceptual motor control. His personality structure is nonpsychotic but exceedingly rigid and characterized by repression and denial such that he fails to see those things in the environment seen by most persons and has few energies available. He attempts to enhance control by denying emotional stimuli and generally can maintain control when responding emotionally. When highly stimulated emotionally, however, he gravely distorts his perceptions. With his rigid defense structure, he has few energies available to gratify his aspirations but is capable of concealing overt indications of depression such as tearfulness and significant withdrawal. When he is consuming disinhibiting chemicals such as alcohol, his behavioral and emotional expressions are far less controlled.

Robert has at least a vague awareness he is "messed up." It is probable he was highly critical of himself prior to enrollment in the Roman Catholic school. There he may have been overly scrupulous when interpreting moral teachings and his already punitive superego became self-destructive. He may have felt most guilty about the commandment to honor parental figures. He came to view himself as anathema. He believes his alternatives are to continue living with the believed devil inside him with the probability he will eventually murder someone or alternately to end his life to escape the internal evil and avoid harming others. Not unexpectedly, death is frightening to him and presently he flirts with self-destruction by poisoning himself with alcohol.

DIAGNOSTIC IMPRESSIONS [DSM-III-R]

AXIS	I	300.40	Dysthymia, Secondary Type, Early Onset
		303.90	Alcohol Dependence, Moderate
		305.20	Cannabis Abuse
AXIS	II	V71.09	No Developmental or Personality Disorder Diagnosed
AXIS	III		No Physical Condition or Disorder Diagnosed
AXIS	IV		Psychosocial Stressors: Perception of himself as intrinsically evil and unlovable, believed rejection by parents, effects of drug misuse, failure to adjust socially and psychiatric hospitalization. Severity: 4–Severe [Admixture of acute events and enduring circumstances]
AXIS	V		Global Assessment of Functioning [GAF]: Current GAF: 35 Highest GAF past year: 50

RECOMMENDATIONS:
A more complete social history would be useful in determining the major factors contributing to Robert's strong negative self-image. Although it is unlikely the father is as abusive as Robert describes him, some series of events have led Robert to view the father as unaccepting and unacceptable. A combination of family psychotherapy on a weekly basis and continuing individual psychotherapy with Robert are the treatments of choice. Initially, Robert will find individual treatment threatening and consequently may gain more in the family sessions. As he progresses in treatment he will profit more from the individual sessions. Without treatment, he is a significant danger to himself and could end his life in suicide.

THE LEGAL CONTEXT

Dear Mr. Hamlin,

I would like to thank you for your kind referral of Mr. Jones. As you know, he is a 27-year-old white, unmarried male with a 10th grade education who has been charged with assault and inflicting grievous bodily injury. I interviewed Mr. Jones on December 12 and 15, 1986 and administered the Wechsler Adult Intelligence Scale-Revised (WAIS-R), Bender, Bender Memory, Minnesota Multiphasic Personality Inventory (MMPI), Draw-A-Person, Incomplete Sentences, and Rorschach. He was dressed casually, appeared somewhat nervous, and he was slow to respond.

My understanding is that you would like me to evaluate Mr. Jones in order to develop a greater understanding of his recent legal difficulties. I further understand that, in the past, there have been other similar charges and you would like to have a description of what psychological factors might have been involved. In addition, you would like to have an estimate of his intelligence, possible presence of brain impairment, level of alcohol-related difficulties, and recommendations for counseling.

CURRENT SITUATION:
Mr. Jones lives with his parents and several younger brothers and sisters. He is the third in a family of seven. His father works as a packer for a pharmaceutical company and his mother is a waitress. Mr. Jones is employed as a meat packer at a nearby factory. He dislikes the work because he feels it is boring and would prefer to work outside. However, he is committed to continuing his employment at the factory until he finds other work that is more satisfactory. He has few friends and is apparently somewhat of a loner. Although he has had a relationship with a woman when he was between the ages of 20 and 24, he is not, and has not for some time, been involved with anyone else. He expresses some bitterness over the ending of this relationship since her family felt he was not "good enough." His primary activities are watching videos, fishing, and occasionally socializing. He stated that he is currently not drinking at all because his doctor and his attorney told him not to. Mr. Jones describes his life as being routine and meaningless, yet he has a difficult time conceptualizing what things he could do to improve his life or change himself.

BACKGROUND:
Mr. Jones was born in and lived in Smallport all his life with the exception of several months in two small, nearby cities. He was an extremely limited historian regarding his early years, stating that he was unable to recall any memories prior to the age of 13. He was also unable to conceptualize or describe his relationship with his parents or their relationship with one another. When pushed for specifics he simply but nondefensively stated "they're alright." It was as if he drew a blank when he either tried to describe family relationships or childhood experiences. In school he stated that "I wasn't much good at anything," and described his favorite subjects as motor mechanics, woodworking, and sheet metal work. Occasionally he was referred to the principal for creating problems.

Mr. Jones' prior convictions include a previous assault (1981) and willful damage, resisting arrest, and escape (1983). In describing the cause of previous fights he stated that when someone teased him "I go off me head" and elaborated that "I can't stop meself from doing it." During these situations in which he loses control, he reported that he often doesn't even know who it is he's attacking. The loss of control usually lasts for several minutes and is almost always associated with drinking. When questioned why he feels he is so "touchy," he stated that there are two types of people, those who "take it" and "those that don't" and that he was one of those that didn't take it. He expressed a desire to change and when asked how, he stated that he should develop patience.

On April 5, 1985 he was in an automobile accident in which his "head went through the windshield." There was apparently no loss of consciousness and few post-traumatic sequalae other than a headache for approximately 24 hours. Shortly after the accident he began drinking excessively, sometimes as much as 6 to 7 bottles of wine a day. This apparently resulted in physiological dependence for which he was treated by Dr. Welby. His drinking was characterized by a loss of control, preoccupation with drinking, morning drinking, and blackouts. He has never been to an A.A. meeting nor has he received other forms of psychological counseling. Although not currently drinking, he states that if he were to have 2 to 3 beers he would be unable to stop until completely intoxicated.

REACTION TO THE CHARGES:
Mr. Jones appears genuinely remorseful regarding the incident he has been charged for and wishes he could somehow undo the damage he has caused. He feels both empathy and concern. However, he maintains that it was the other person's fault since the other person called him a "gutless wonder" in front of the whole bar. In fact, his overall perception of his fights and his life in general is that he is a victim and really has little control over what happens to himself. However, for the few brief moments when he is assaulting someone, it's as if he gains some sort of brief sense of power and control over his life. Most of the time he responds to life in a relatively passive, conforming manner.

TEST RESULTS:

WAIS-R: Full Scale I.Q.   = 74
        Verbal I.Q.   = 83
        Performance I.Q. = 65

Information	6	Digit Symbol	6
Comprehension	7	Picture Completion	3
Arithmetic	7	Block Design	4
Similarities	6	Picture Arrangement	5
Digit Span	10	Object Assembly	5
Vocabulary	8		

MMPI:				
	L	42	5	58
	F	68	6	45
	K	44	7	60
	1	52	8	50
	2	80	9	32
	3	60	0	75
	4	74		

Bender: Empirically not in the organic range (although dashes rather than dots, minor distortion of designs, difficulty making smooth curves; see Figure 12–6)

Bender Memory: 4 designs recalled

Draw-A-Person: Absence of pupils, large heads (see Figures 12–7 and 12–8)

Rorschach: (data available on request)

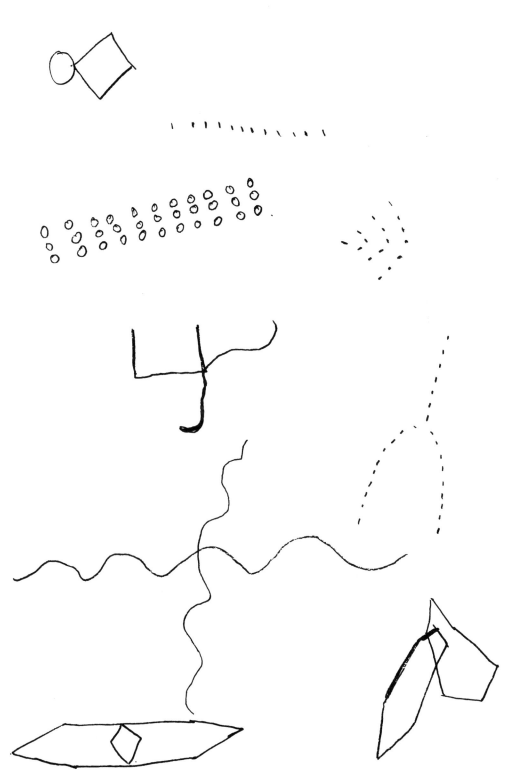

Figure 12–6.   Case: Mr. Jones. Age: 27

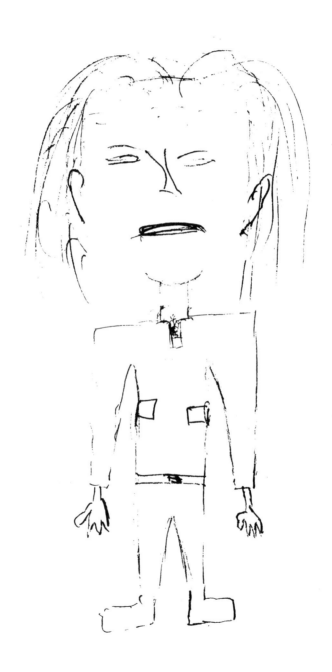

Figure 12–7.   Case: Mr. Jones.   Age: 27

Figure 12–8.   Case: Mr. Jones. Age: 27

INTERPRETATION AND IMPRESSIONS:

Mr. Jones obtained a Full Scale I.Q. of 74, Verbal I.Q. of 83, and Performance I.Q. of 65. Overall this places him in the 4th percentile when compared with his age-related peers. Relative mental strengths were in short-term memory for numbers and visual material in which he scored in the average range. In contrast, relative weaknesses were in problem-solving for visual tasks and distinguishing relevant from irrelevant details in his environment. In other words, he frequently has difficulty accurately perceiving relevant aspects of what is occurring around him. Furthermore, his perceptions are fairly rigid since he experiences difficulty sorting out his world and flexibly coming up with different possibilities. These difficulties or rigidities in perception are likely to be exaggerated either under stress or after consuming alcohol. Thus, when someone provokes him, he is fairly bound by the external situation and has difficulty developing an inner sense of directedness to free himself from outer events.

A general review of Mr. Jones' personality indicates a man who is usually cooperative and concerned with his behavior but who also has periods of impulsiveness and is highly self-critical. However, he is not by any means psychotic. His thoughts are coherent, he has the ability to form adequate relationships with others, and perceives his world without any exaggerated distortions. He typically feels a marked sense of distance between himself and his world. His level of depression is particularly noteworthy and I believe he is a mild to moderate suicide risk. In fact, he has made several previous suicide gestures and stated that he wouldn't want to live anywhere where there was a gun. The following sample of responses to several questions on the MMPI are noteworthy:

I certainly feel useless at times. (True)
I cry easily. (True)
I usually feel that life is worthwhile. (False)
Sometimes I feel I must injure myself. (True)

In dealing with his emotional world, he attempts to gain some control over it by ignoring most feelings he has. He accomplishes this by observing the most obvious features of his environment but blocks out or denies many of his emotions or relevant emotion-laden memories. For example, he was unable to give any description of his relationship with his family nor could he come up with any childhood memories prior to the age of 13. However, when he does experience emotions they are likely to overwhelm him such as during episodes of either crying or anger.

In understanding his aggressiveness, it is important to stress that he would by no means plot or anticipate retaliation against somebody. He lacks the inner directedness this would require and does not have a brooding sense of suspicion. Furthermore, he feels remorse and concern for those he has hurt. What does trigger off his aggressiveness is a combination of alcohol and being "swept away" by the controlling events in his world. In these conditions guilt does occur but usually too late to control his behavior. This is further complicated by the fact that his usual style is to block out his emotions so that, when they do occur, they overwhelm him. Thus he is typically unaware of his underlying sense of hostility unless actually acting out these feelings.

In the past, alcohol has significantly complicated Mr. Jones' life and, at time, he has apparently consumed large quantities. Several of the important warning signs for alcoholism are present including blackouts, morning drinking, and a loss of control. He currently states that if he were to have 2 or 3 beers he would have to continue drinking more and more until fully intoxicated. Given his level of depression, I would say that an important motivation for his drinking is as a form of "self-medication." Without some form of intervention his potential for future alcohol-related problems is moderately high.

Neuropsychologically, Mr. Jones demonstrates some "soft" neurological signs of mild brain impairment. Specifically, he has difficulty pronouncing certain words, a poor ability to reproduce designs, and his general spatial abilities were significantly lower than his verbal skills. In fact, given Mr. Jones' educational and occupational background, one would expect that his verbal abilities should be lower than his performance abilities and yet the opposite is true. One possibility for these impairments was injury from the automobile accident on April 5, 1985. However, the history surrounding the injury and the very limited number of post-traumatic sequalae argue against this. It is more likely that some form of earlier head injury or an accumulation of injuries might have caused these deficits. I would speculate that there would be some mild dysfunction in the right parietal and left temporal regions as a result of static lesions to these areas. However, the focus of the testing was not to assess brain impairment so that the above must necessarily be speculative in nature.

SUMMARY AND RECOMMENDATIONS:

Mr. Jones was a cooperative but somewhat isolated 27-year-old white male who, at the time of evaluation, was depressed and, in the past, has experienced alcohol-related difficulties. Although stating that he lost control of himself during the incident for which he was referred, he is by no means psychotic and understands the reasons and implications for his behavior. He does not have a criminal mentality. In other words he feels guilt regarding his behavior, concern for his victims, and is unlikely to make any long-term plans to either harm another person, or commit some premeditated criminal act. Rather, he is not by any means inner directed but experiences himself as controlled by external events. This is further complicated and exaggerated by alcohol and the fact that he attempts to block out uncomfortable emotions to the extent that when his environment triggers them, they are overwhelming. In addition, there is a mild to moderate suicide risk, definite potential for future alcohol-related problems, and some soft neurological signs suggesting a mild level of brain impairment.

The key to working with Mr. Jones would be to focus on teaching him to be more inner directed and to structure his environment, or at least his perception of his environment, in such a way as to not trigger his aggression. Effective counseling must include clear limits, a change in environment, warm support, and continual contact. In particular, Mr Jones would require concrete suggestions since his capacity for insight-oriented counseling is quite limited. He should enter the type of counseling that focuses on building his self-esteem and developing clear alternatives on how he might improve his life. If given probation, this should be accompanied by the requirement that he attend A.A. meetings and receive supportive counseling. He is currently experiencing a sufficient amount of psychological turmoil so that he is motivated to change. However, without some sort of intervention, there is a high risk of increasing alcohol-related problems and further, probably debilitating, levels of depression. Some long-term legal leverage over his future behavior should be maintained for supervision and monitoring of progress.

THE EDUCATIONAL SETTING

NAME: M.K.
DATE OF BIRTH: February 8, 1972
DATE OF EXAMINATION: May 12, 1981
EXAMINED BY: G. G-M.

REFERRAL QUESTION:
M. was referred by her mother for a psychological evaluation to assess her current level of functioning. An evaluation had become of particular importance since a decision was imminent regarding continued placement in her special education class as opposed to mainstreaming. Furthermore, the last psychological evaluation that had been performed on M. was over two years ago, and Mrs. K. requested a follow-up evaluation to assess possible improvement, stability, or deterioration in M.'s cognitive abilities.

EVALUATION PROCEDURES:
M. was administered the Wechsler Intelligence Scale for Children-Revised (WISC-R), the Bender Visual Motor Gestalt Test (Bender), and the House-Tree-Person Test (H-T-P).

BEHAVIORAL OBSERVATIONS:
M. appeared neatly dressed, and was cooperative and friendly throughout the testing procedure. When confronted with more difficult tasks, she would at times discontinue trying to perform as best as she could. However, for the most part, she gave the tasks her best efforts, and the test results appear to be an accurate assessment of her current level of functioning.

RELEVANT HISTORY:
M. is a right-handed female, 9 years and 3 months of age, with a history of delayed development resulting from a hypothyroid condition that was diagnosed and treated when she was 5 years old. She is currently living with her natural parents, and her older sister Susan (17) also lives with the family.

Mrs. K. reported that during her pregnancy with M., she was consistently under a doctor's care. There were no unusual features at birth, and she stated that M.'s early developmental milestones were normal. Between the ages of 2 and 4, Mr. and Mrs. K. noticed a gradual but progressive slowness in M.'s behavior. During the end of her fourth year, this pattern became more pronounced, and she was referred to a physician who diagnosed and treated her.

Her parents have responded to her condition with conscientiousness and support. She was assessed at the Speech, Hearing, and Neurosensory Center and treated for a period of six months. She has been enrolled in a special education class in school following a psychological evaluation performed by Dr. Lewis of the Los Angeles Union School District on August 15, 1979. He diagnosed her as being educable mentally retarded and summarized his report by stating that M. is "functioning with apparent developmental delays in many areas. She has significant cognitive difficulties along with severe academic deficiencies. Her ability to participate in a regular education program is extremely limited at this time" (p.3). She was placed in a learning handicapped program including speech therapy and a special education class. An important aspect of her overall program with regard to her interpersonal development was that all her social activities took place with a regular first-grade class. Her interpersonal adjustment in these activities has been described by her mother as good. Her mother reported that in most areas she has seen a great deal of improvement over the past year. M.'s parents are currently concerned with the most suitable academic and social placement for her, as well as what assets and limitations she may have for the future.

TEST RESULTS:

WISC-R: Full Scale I.Q. = 70
                 Verbal I.Q. = 73
         Performance I.Q. = 71

Subscale Scores		Subscale Scores	
Information	5	Picture Arrangement	1
Comprehension	7	Picture Completion	10
Digit Span	3	Block Design	5
Arithmetic	3	Object Assembly	7
Similarities	8		
Vocabulary	8		

BENDER: Impaired; lack of closure, distortions, difficulty making dots, rotations, perseverations (see Figure 12–9).

BENDER MEMORY: Two designs recalled.

HOUSE-TREE-PERSON: Disorganized, immature (see house, Figure 12–10).

INTERPRETATION AND IMPRESSIONS:

M. scored in the borderline range of intelligence on the WISC-R with a Full Scale I.Q. of 70, a Performance I.Q. of 71, and a Verbal I.Q. of 73, which places her in the second percentile when compared to her age-related peers. These scores are roughly equivalent to those taken by Dr. Lewis on August 9, 1979. Relative strengths were in the areas of ability to distinguish relevant from irrelevant details in her environment (10, within normal range), ability to conceptualize the similarity between one object or event and another (8), and vocabulary (8). Relative but pronounced weaknesses were in tasks requiring sequencing and a sustained attention span. This suggests that her overall social and verbal skills are nearly within normal limits, whereas her academic abilities, particularly in reading, writing, and arithmetic, are moderately impaired.

M.'s performance on the Bender was clearly in the impaired range and characterized by difficulties with closure, distortions of the designs, producing dashes instead of dots, rotations, and perseverations. This suggests that she is definitely lagging in her visual-motor abilities when compared with her age-related peers and may have a difficult time organizing the spatial information in her environment. Drawings of her house, tree, and person, although of appropriate size and good line pressure, were likewise disorganized and generally more like someone 6 years of age rather than 9.

In summary, M.'s performance is consistent with generalized impairment to both cerebral hemispheres. Her relative strengths are that she has normal abilities in noticing the relevant details in her environment, as well as good comprehension and vocabulary. In other words, she has made a good adjustment in learning how to deal with her environment, which reflects the impact that speech therapy and her special education program have had on her. Weaknesses, on the other hand, are in the academic areas, particularly attention, mathematical computation, sequencing, and visual organization. In these areas her abilities have stayed the same during the past two years. Although she has progressed academically, she has done so at a rate consistent with a child having an I.Q. of 70.

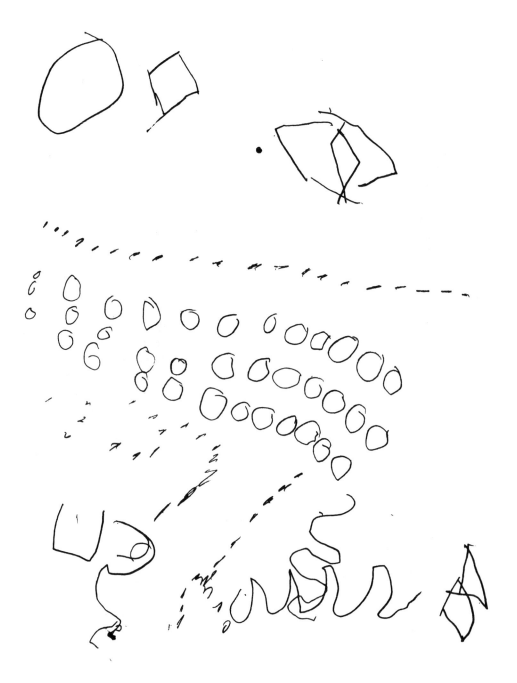

Figure 12–9.   Case: M.K.   Age: 9 years, 3 months

Figure 12–10.   Case: M.K.   Age: 9 years, 3 months

RECOMMENDATIONS:
1. Continued placement in special education classes emphasizing sequencing, math, memory training, visual organization, and sustained attention.
2. Social activities should be designed to increase or maintain social contacts with age-related peers in the normal school program. This is particularly important since M.'s social-verbal skills are close to normal, and contact with children in the normal school program would provide her with normal role models. On the other hand, her academic abilities are certainly well below most children, and placement in a normal program would be likely to create turmoil and a sense of inferiority.
3. Home tutoring emphasizing drill and repetition is recommended, in addition to what the school provides.
4. M. should have follow-up psychological assessment every 12 to 24 months since, as she gets older, the precision of measurements increases, and continual evaluations of her level of progress or stability can be made to aid in further academic or interpersonal recommendations.

THE PSYCHOLOGICAL CLINIC

NAME: B.C.
DATE OF BIRTH: March 12, 1948
DATE OF EXAMINATION: November 10, 1982
EXAMINER: G. G-M.

REFERRAL QUESTION:
Mr. C. was referred for a psychological evaluation in connection with his being arrested on two counts of exhibitionism. The specific questions that it was hoped the evaluation would answer related to whether the client could benefit from psychotherapy, important personality dynamics relevant to therapy, and possible difficulties likely to be encountered between the client and the therapist.

EVALUATION PROCEDURES:
On November 10, 1982, I interviewed Mr. C. and administered the following tests: Wechsler Adult Intelligence Scale-Revised (WAIS-R), Bender Visual Motor Gestalt Test (Bender), Draw-A-Person Test (DAP), Thematic Apperception Test (TAT), and the Minnesota Multiphasic Personality Inventory (MMPI).

BEHAVIORAL OBSERVATIONS:
Mr. C. appeared for both interviews casually dressed in jeans and a t-shirt. He had a moustache and long hair tied back in a ponytail. His eye contact was good, and his speech, although sometimes hesitant, was clear and soft. He was articulate and friendly; he expressed concern over his past behavior; and his overall style of speaking was engaging. There were no indications of delusions or hallucinations, and he was oriented in all three spheres. When approaching the tasks presented to him, he was cooperative and his problem solving style was usually adequate although sometimes slightly disorganized. Based on the above observations and the MMPI validity scales, the test results appear to be an accurate assessment of his current level of functioning.

RELEVANT HISTORY:

Mr. C. is a 34-year-old, white, unmarried male with a university education who was apprehended on two counts of exhibitionism. He was born and raised in Riverside, California, where his father was a plumber. An important incident relating to his birth and early childhood was that he was raised by his grandparents but, until the age of 15, was led to believe that his grandparents were his parents. To this day, he still refers to, and thinks of, his grandmother as his mother. He is the youngest of three children, having two older sisters—Carol (50, actually his biological mother) and Susan (47).

Mr. C.'s "parents" (actually grandparents) were somewhat distant from each other, and he describes his "mother" as extremely "introverted and passive." He states that she "tried to stamp out every expression of assertiveness in me" and usually "controlled me by making me feel guilty." There was also a great deal of closeness between the two of them, in contrast to his "father" whom he describes as somewhat distant. He states that in school he was a loner, but the few friends he did have were fairly close. His grades were good, and his performance in English and art was excellent. He did not date until his last year of high school and, throughout his early school years, felt shy and awkward around females.

Upon graduating from high school, he identified with counter-culture groups and used drugs to a moderate extent. His college attendance was inconsistent, although he did complete a master's degree in drama and has credit toward a masters in fine arts. Despite his university education he is currently working, and has in the past worked, in construction, never actually utilizing his educational background. His relationships with females have usually been short; the longest lasted for two years, and he lived with this woman for 1 1/2 years. As he describes it, his main difficulty is that he can be with a woman for a while, but several times a month he will have a feeling of being "extremely distant and I can't come out of my shell." He describes this as an intense sense of helplessness, passivity, and feeling "jagged." This is also accompanied by sexual impotence, which he indicated had become an increasing problem for him over the past four years.

Mr. C. reports that his first episode of exhibitionism occurred approximately eight years ago, but the episodes have been increasing in frequency over the past three years. He stated that prior to three years ago, he would exhibit himself only three or four times per year. During the past two to three years, this has increased to four to five times per month. His usual procedure is to pick up a female who is hitchhiking and, after a few minutes, open up his pants. Although most of the time he reports having an erection, he stated that he does not masturbate. He correlates an increase in his exhibitionism with a corresponding increase in feelings of helplessness and passivity, both in regard to his life and in terms of any relationship he is involved in at the time. After these episodes, he does feel guilt over his behavior and his need to exhibit temporarily subsides. However, he compares the excitement or "rush" he experiences to the feeling a drug addict must have. Eventually, his need for the "rush" increases to the extent that "I find myself doing it again."

During the past four months, Mr. C. has been arrested on two counts of exhibitionism. As a result, he is spending weekends in jail so as not to jeopardize his job as a construction worker. His case will be reevaluated in three weeks, and his probation officer is considering making counseling a requirement.

TEST RESULTS:

WAIS-R: Full Scale I.Q.   = 132
           Verbal I.Q.   = 142
           Performance I.Q. = 114

	Subscale Scores		Subscale Scores
Information	15	Picture Completion	11
Digit Span	15	Picture Arrangement	9
Vocabulary	15	Block Design	13
Arithmetic	17	Object Assembly	17
Comprehension	16	Digit Symbol	10
Similarities	17		

MMPI:

L	46	5	78
F	55	6	60
K	63	7	34
1	68	8	64
2	72	9	78
3	71	0	64
4	76		

BENDER: (see Figure 12–11)

DRAW-A-PERSON: (see Figures 12–12 and 12–13)

INTERPRETATION AND IMPRESSIONS:

Mr. C. obtained a Full Scale I.Q. of 132, a Verbal I.Q. of 142, and a Performance I.Q. of 114, thereby placing him in the 98th percentile when compared with his age-related peers. Relative cognitive strengths were in his overall verbal abilities, especially in mathematical computation and the ability to perceive the similarity between one event or object and another. Although his verbal ability to comprehend social interactions is excellent, a noteworthy weakness is his relatively poor ability to understand nonverbal social interactions. This is combined with a second relative weakness: learning rote tasks requiring visual-motor sequencing. In fact, overall, he appears to have some mild difficulties in organizing and sequencing his perceptions.

Within interpersonal relationships, Mr. C. is likely to experience a moderate level of distance and alienation. However, he also has a sufficient degree of verbal skills and psychological sophistication to begin to work with these feelings. Perhaps his major concern in relationships is the manner in which he deals with anger and dependency. What anger he does experience is likely to be both denied and turned inward in the form of self-criticism. In order to defend himself from the depression that would, and sometimes does, result from this self-criticism, he speeds up his level of activity in an attempt to distract himself from any unpleasant feelings. Another important area in relationships involves significant conflicts regarding strong dependency needs and a sense of being controlled and dominated by females. For example, after a long pause on card 2 of the TAT, he gave the following story fragment:

> "Big Mama's looking around. Mother looks like she's overseeing [long pause]. It's a family. The kids are going to school and mother's supervising. No, she's seeing the husband off to work."

The way he resolves this sense of dominance by females is through distracting himself by speeding up his level of activity, by impulsive acting out, or by emotional and/or physical withdrawal.

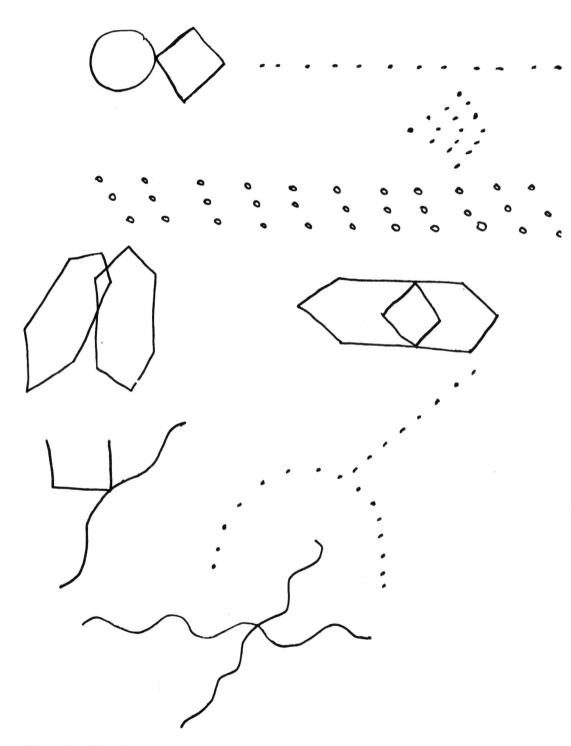

Figure 12–11.   Case: B.C.   Age: 34 years

Figure 12–12.   Case: B.C.   Age: 34 years,   "Fu Manchu Man" (first drawing)

Figure 12–13.   Case: B.C.   Age: 34 years,   "Dairy Queen Mama" (second drawing)

A significant area of concern is his difficulty in adequately controlling his impulses. In some ways he is overcontrolled in that he is prone to self-criticism and prefers to deny or withdraw from conflict. However, in other ways he is undercontrolled. He experiences a sense of underlying anger and alienation, and also has the energy to act on these feelings. Many of his thoughts and feelings are characterized by antisocial themes. For example, when asked what he would do if he found an addressed envelope with a stamp on it, he initially said, "I would probably soak the stamp off." The following MMPI critical items indicated authority conflicts and family discord:

59: I have often had to take orders from someone who did not know as much as I
      did. (True)

294: I have never been in trouble with the law. (False)

212: My people treat me more like a child than a grownup. (True)

Furthermore, he has a need for excitement, which, given his usually somewhat passive personality, is not likely to be met in overt ways but rather in indirect, impulsive ones. There are some indications that he can adequately control his impulses by being self-critical, withdrawing from conflict, and denying anger. In contrast, his underlying sense of anger, occasionally high energy level, antisocial thoughts, and need for excitement suggest that his pattern of acting out may be somewhat resistant to change.

Mr. C.'s exhibitionism can be perceived as serving the following important functions:

1. It serves as a means of exerting control over his environment. It is significant in that as he feels progressively more passive, distant, and helpless in relationships, his need to exhibit himself increases. The increase in control he achieves through exhibiting, although temporary, reduces his feeling that he is being dominated and controlled by females.

2. Since most direct feelings of anger are denied, exhibitionism serves as an indirect expression of anger. He will then be likely to rationalize his exhibitionism and perceive it as not in fact hostile through ignoring the effects it has on others.

3. Finally, it provides a feeling of excitement.

Mr. C. definitely has the intellectual capability to benefit from therapy and to develop significant insights into his behavior. However, numerous difficulties would likely be encountered when working with him. First, he would have difficulty focusing on any one topic for any length of time and would tend to go off on irrelevant tangents. Second, his anger either would be denied or, in contrast, might be directed indiscriminately at the therapist. Third, his approach to therapy might be manipulative in that he would superficially comply with the rules and make it look "as if" he were attempting to change. He might also attempt to bend the rules and push the limits to see how much he could get away with. Finally, he would be likely to continually rationalize his behavior, denying the effects that it has on others. Even though he might say the "right thing" in therapy to make it look as if he was clearly seeing the consequences, on a deeper, more permanent level, this might still be denied. This is not intended to indicate that he should not enter therapy, but rather that any person working with him would need to confront and deal with these problems.

In summary, Mr. C. is a bright, articulate man who appears, at the present time, to be genuinely remorseful regarding his episodes of exhibitionism. Interpersonally he experiences moderate levels of alienation and has significant conflicts relating to dependency, a sense of being dominated by females, and denied anger. Although his verbal social judgment is good, his ability to control his impulses is sometimes deficient. He does maintain a usually adequate level of control through self-criticism, withdrawal from conflict, and denial of anger. His episodes of exhibitionism serve to increase his experience of control, provide an indirect expression of his underlying anger, and create a sense of excitement. Mr. C. would be likely to benefit from therapy if clear limits were set regarding attendance and payment of fees, and if the therapist was willing to actively work with his distractive maneuvers, underlying anger, testing of limits, and denial of the negative effects he has on others.

RECOMMENDATIONS
1. Individual therapy once a week is recommended, emphasizing a confrontive approach and behavioral techniques, directed toward changing Mr. C.'s episodes of exhibitionism. Therapy should also focus on his relationships with females and creating skills for developing a sense of more overt assertive control.
2. After three months, group therapy should be considered, to enable Mr. C. to more accurately understand the impact he has on others.
3. There should be close monitoring by, and follow-up contact between, his probation officer and his therapist.

RECOMMENDED READING

Klopfer, W. G. (1983). Writing psychological reports. In C. E. Walker (Ed.), *The handbook of clinical psychology: Theory research and practice*. Homewood, IL: Dow Jones-Irwin.

Ownby, R. L. (1987). *Psychological reports: A guide to report writing in professional psychology*. Brandon, VT: Clinical Psychology Publishing Co., Inc.

Tallent, N. (1988). *Psychological report writing* (3rd ed.). Englewood Cliffs, NJ: Prentice-Hall.

Appendix A

WISC-R reliabilities, standard error of measurements, and factor loadings*

WISC-R Scales and sub-scales	Reliability **	Standard error of measurement **	Factor loadings***			Proportion of variance accounted for by g (%)
			Verbal Comprehension	Perceptual Organization	Freedom from Distractibility	
FSIQ	.96	3.19				
VIQ	.94	3.60				
PIQ	.90	4.66				
I	.85	1.19	.63	.25	.41	58
DS	.78	1.44	.18	.12	.56	24
VB	.86	1.15	.72	.24	.33	80
ARITH	.77	1.38	.37	.20	.58	42
COMP	.77	1.39	.64	.30	.24	52
SIM	.81	1.34	.64	.34	.28	58
PC	.77	1.45	.35	.57	.11	37
PA	.73	1.59	.33	.41	.12	36
BD	.85	1.17	.27	.66	.28	53
OA	.70	1.70	.21	.65	.12	38
CODING	.72	1.63	.15	.20	.42	17
MAZES	.72	1.70	.12	.47	.22	20

*All data represents averages across the 11 different age groups used in the standardization sample.

**Reliabilities and standard error of measurements (SEM) adapted from Wechsler (1974); reliabilities were based on split half correlations except for Digit Span and Coding, which were based on test-retest correlations over a one-month interval; SEMs represent I.Q. ranges for the scales (FSIQ; VIQ, PIQ) and subscale scores for the subscales.

***Data on factor loadings adapted from Kaufman (1975).

Appendix B

WAIS-R reliabilities, standard error of measurements, and factor loadings*

WAIS-R Scales and sub-scales	Reliability **	Standard error of measurement **	Factor loadings***			Proportion of variance accounted for by g (%)
			Verbal Comprehension	Perceptual Organization	Freedom from Distractibility	
FSIQ	.97	2.53				
VIQ	.97	2.74				
PIQ	.93	4.14				
I	.89	.93	.75	.20	.30	67
DS	.83	1.23	.30	.22	.64	38
VB	.96	.61	.81	.26	.34	76
ARITH	.84	1.14	.44	.34	.55	58
COMP	.84	1.20	.71	.30	.27	61
SIM	.84	1.24	.67	.36	.27	62
PC	.81	1.25	.44	.56	.17	50
PA	.74	1.41	.42	.42	.23	45
BD	.87	.98	.27	.69	.33	53
OA	.68	1.54	.19	.73	.17	40
DSYMB	.82	1.27	.32	.38	.36	36

*All data represents averages across the nine standardization age groups; reliabilities are based on a one- to seven-week retesting.

**Reliabilities and standard error of measurements (SEM) adapted from Wechsler (1981); SEMs represent I.Q. ranges for the scales (FSIQ, VIQ, PIQ) and scaled score ranges for the subscales.

***Adapted from Sattler and Ryan (1988).

Appendix C

Percentile rankings for Wechsler deviation I.Q.s

I.Q.	Percentile Rank	I.Q.	Percentile Rank	I.Q.	Percentile Rank
155	99.99	118	88	81	10
154	99.98	117	87	80	9
153	99.98	116	86	79	8
152	99.97	115	84	78	7
151	99.97	114	82	77	6
150	99.96	113	81	76	5
149	99.95	112	79	75	5
148	99.93	111	77	74	4
147	99.91	110	75	73	4
146	99.89	109	73	72	3
145	99.87	108	70	71	3
144	99.83	107	68	70	2
143	99.79	106	66	69	2
142	99.74	105	63	68	2
141	99.69	104	61	67	1
140	99.62	103	58	66	1
139	99.53	102	55	65	1
138	99	101	53	64	1
137	99	100	50	63	1
136	99	99	47	62	1
135	99	98	45	61	.47
134	99	97	42	60	.38
133	99	96	39	59	.31
132	98	95	37	58	.26
131	98	94	34	57	.21
130	98	93	32	56	.17
129	97	92	30	55	.13
128	97	91	27	54	.11
127	96	90	27	53	.09
126	96	89	23	52	.07
125	95	88	21	51	.05
124	95	87	19	50	.04
123	94	86	18	49	.03
122	93	85	16	48	.03
121	92	84	14	47	.02
120	91	83	13	46	.02
119	90	82	12	45	.01

Appendix D

WISC-R Profile Sheet

Name _____ Date _____ Birth Date _____ Age _____ Grade _____ School _____

School District _____ Examiner _____ VERBAL I.Q. _____ PERFORMANCE I.Q. _____ FULL SCALE I.Q. _____

Verbal Scale: Ability to work with abstract verbal symbols; perceptual skills included (auditory).

	5	6	7	8	9	10	11	12	13	14	15	16	17	18	19	SUBTEST MEANINGS
Information	·	·	·	·	·	·	·	·	·	·	·	·	·	·	·	Remote memory; experience and education; cultural background
Similarities	·	·	·	·	·	·	·	·	·	·	·	·	·	·	·	Verbal concept formation; logical and abstract reasoning
Arithmetic	·	·	·	·	·	·	·	·	·	·	·	·	·	·	·	Concentration; numerical reasoning; school learning
Vocabulary	·	·	·	·	·	·	·	·	·	·	·	·	·	·	·	Educational background; general verbal intelligence; range of ideas
Comprehension	·	·	·	·	·	·	·	·	·	·	·	·	·	·	·	Practical knowledge and social judgment; common sense
Digit Span	·	·	·	·	·	·	·	·	·	·	·	·	·	·	·	Concentration; immediate auditory memory

Performance Scale: Ability to work in concrete situations; perceptual skills included (visual).

	5	6	7	8	9	10	11	12	13	14	15	16	17	18	19	SUBTEST MEANINGS
Picture Completion	·	·	·	·	·	·	·	·	·	·	·	·	·	·	·	Visual concentration; ability to visually differentiate essential information
Picture Arrangement	·	·	·	·	·	·	·	·	·	·	·	·	·	·	·	Planning ability and foresight; ability to assess nonverbal social interactions
Block Design	·	·	·	·	·	·	·	·	·	·	·	·	·	·	·	Visual-motor coordination; spatial problem solving; concentration
Object Assembly	·	·	·	·	·	·	·	·	·	·	·	·	·	·	·	Visual-motor organization; seeing relationships of parts to wholes
Coding	·	·	·	·	·	·	·	·	·	·	·	·	·	·	·	Visual-motor speed; ability to learn rote tasks
Mazes (optional)	·	·	·	·	·	·	·	·	·	·	·	·	·	·	·	Planning and foresight in following a visual pattern

Appendix E

WAIS-R Profile Sheet

Name _____ Date _____ Birth Date _____ Age _____ Grade _____ School _____

School District _____ Examiner _____ VERBAL I.Q. _____ PERFORMANCE I.Q. _____ FULL SCALE I.Q. _____

Verbal Scale: Ability to work with abstract verbal symbols; perceptual skills included (auditory).

	5	6	7	8	9	10	11	12	13	14	15	16	17	18	19	SUBTEST MEANINGS
Information	.	.	.	.	.	.	.	.	.	.	.	.	.	.	.	Remote memory; experience and education; cultural background
Digit Span	.	.	.	.	.	.	.	.	.	.	.	.	.	.	.	Concentration; immediate auditory memory
Vocabulary	.	.	.	.	.	.	.	.	.	.	.	.	.	.	.	Educational background; general verbal intelligence; range of ideas
Arithmetic	.	.	.	.	.	.	.	.	.	.	.	.	.	.	.	Concentration; numerical reasoning; school learning
Comprehension	.	.	.	.	.	.	.	.	.	.	.	.	.	.	.	Practical knowledge and social judgment; common sense
Similarities	.	.	.	.	.	.	.	.	.	.	.	.	.	.	.	Verbal concept formation; logical and abstract reasoning

Performance Scale: Ability to work in concrete situation; perceptual skills included (visual).

	5	6	7	8	9	10	11	12	13	14	15	16	17	18	19	SUBTEST MEANINGS
Picture Completion	.	.	.	.	.	.	.	.	.	.	.	.	.	.	.	Visual concentration; ability to visually differentiate essential information
Picture Arrangement	.	.	.	.	.	.	.	.	.	.	.	.	.	.	.	Planning ability and foresight; ability to assess nonverbal social interactions
Block Design	.	.	.	.	.	.	.	.	.	.	.	.	.	.	.	Visual-motor coordination; spatial problem solving; concentration
Object Assembly	.	.	.	.	.	.	.	.	.	.	.	.	.	.	.	Visual-motor organization; seeing relationships of parts to wholes
Digit Symbol	.	.	.	.	.	.	.	.	.	.	.	.	.	.	.	Visual-motor speed; ability to learn rote tasks

Appendix F

Interpretive Rationales, Implications of High and Low Scores, and Instructional Implications for Wechsler Scales and Factor Scores

Ability	Background factors	Possible implications of high scores	Possible implications of low scores	Instructional implications
Full Scale				
General intelligence Scholastic aptitude Academic aptitude Readiness to master a school curriculum	Natural endowment Richness of early environment Extent of schooling Cultural opportunities Interests Rate of motor activity Persistence Visual-motor organization Alertness	Good general intelligence Good scholastic aptitude Readiness to master a school curriculum	Poor general intelligence Poor scholastic aptitude Not ready to master school curriculum	Focus on language development activities Focus on visual learning activities Develop concept formation skills Reinforce persistence
Verbal Scale or Verbal Comprehension Factor				
Verbal comprehension Application of verbal skills and information to the solution of new problems Verbal ability Ability to process verbal information Ability to think with words	Natural endowment Richness of early environment Extent of schooling Cultural opportunities Interests	Good verbal comprehension Good scholastic aptitude Possession of knowledge of the cultural milieu Good concept formation Readiness to master school curriculum Achievement orientation	Poor verbal comprehension Poor scholastic aptitude Inadequate understanding of the cultural milieu Poor concept formation Bilingual background Foreign background Not ready to master school curriculum Poor achievement orientation	Stress language development activities Use verbal enrichment activities Focus on current events Use exercises involving concept formation

Ability	Background factors	Possible implications of high scores	Possible implications of low scores	Instructional implications
Performance Scale or Perceptual Organization Factor				
Perceptual organization Ability to think in terms of visual images and manipulate them with fluency, flexibility, and relative speed Ability to interpret or organize visually perceived material against a time limit Nonverbal ability Ability to form relatively abstract concepts and relationships without the use of words	Natural endowment Rate of motor activity Persistence Visual-motor organization Alertness	Good perceptual organization Good alertness to detail Good nonverbal reasoning ability Good persistence Good ability to work quickly and efficiently Good spatial ability	Poor perceptual organization Poor alertness to detail Poor nonverbal reasoning ability Limited persistence Poor ability to work quickly and efficiently Poor spatial ability	Focus on visual learning activities Focus on part-whole relationships Use spatial-visual tasks Encourage trial-and-error activities Reinforce persistence Focus on visual planning activities Improve scanning techniques
Freedom from Distractibility				
Ability to sustain attention Short-term memory Numerical ability Encoding ability Ability to use rehearsal strategies Ability to shift mental operations on symbolic material Ability to self-monitor	Natural endowment Ability to passively receive stimuli	Good ability to sustain attention Good short-term memory Good numerical ability Good encoding ability Good use of rehearsal strategies Good ability to shift mental operations on symbolic material Good ability to self-monitor	Difficulty in sustaining attention Distractibility Anxiety Short-term retention deficits Encoding difficulties Poor rehearsal strategies Difficulty in rapidly shifting mental operations on symbolic material Inadequate self-monitoring skills	Develop attention skills Develop concentration skills Focus on small, meaningful units of instruction

Appendix G

Suggested Remediation Activities for Combinations of Wechsler Subtests

Subtests	Ability	Activities
Information, Vocabulary, and Comprehension	General knowledge and verbal fluency	(1) Review basic concepts, such as days of the week, months, time, distances, and directions; (2) have children report major current events by referring to pictures and articles from magazines and newspapers; (3) teach similarities and differences of designs, topography, transportation, etc.; (4) have children make a scrapbook of pictures of animals, buildings, etc.; (5) introduce words, dictionary work, abstract words; (6) have children repeat simple stories; (7) have children explain how story characters are feeling and thinking.
Similarities and Vocabulary	Verbal conceptual	(1) Use show-and-tell games; (2) have children make a scrapbook of classifications, such as of animals, vehicles, and utensils; (3) have children match abstract concepts; (4) have children find commonality in dissimilar objects; (5) review basic concepts such as days of the week, months, time, directions, and distances.
Digit Span, Arithmetic, Picture Completion, and Picture Arrangement	Attention and concentration	(1) Have children arrange cards in a meaningful sequence; (2) have children learn telephone number, address, etc.; (3) use spelling word games; (4) use memory games; (5) have children learn days of week, months of year; (6) use mathematical word problems; (7) use dot-to-dot exercises; (8) have children describe details in pictures; (9) use tracing activities; (10) use Tinker Toys.
Block Design and Object Assembly	Spatial-visual	(1) Have children identify common objects and discuss details; (2) use guessing games involving description of a person, place, or thing; (3) have children match letters, shapes, numbers, etc.; (4) use jigsaw puzzles; (5) use block-building activities.
Coding, Digit Symbol, Block Design, Object Assembly, Animal House, and Mazes	Visual-motor	(1) Use paper-folding activities; (2) use finger-painting activities; (3) use dot-to-dot exercises; (4) use scissor-cutting exercises; (5) use sky-writing exercises; (6) have children string beads in patterns; (7) use pegboard designs; (8) use puzzles (large jigsaw pieces); (9) have children solve a maze; (10) have children follow a moving object with coordinated eye movements; (11) use tracing exercises (e.g., trace hand, geometric forms, and letters); (12) have children make large circles and lines on chalkboard; (13) have children copy from patterns; (14) have children draw from memory.

Source: Reprinted with permission of the publisher and author, from J.M. Sattler, *Assessment of Children* (3rd ed.), 1988, © Jerome M. Sattler, Publisher.

Appendix H*
The Bender Visual Motor Gestalt Test
Detailed Scoring Instructions and Examples

The 12 organic signs described in the following pages are Hutt and Briskin's "essential discriminators of intracranial damage" (1960). In general, the presence of any 5 of these errors is taken to indicate organic impairment. However, all of these errors can also be made by subjects who do not put forth their best efforts because of lack of interest in the task, hostility toward the examiner, impulsivity, or carelessness. At all times, the examiner must try to determine whether an error was made because of factors such as these or because of true perceptual-motor difficulties. Only in the latter case should an error be scored. The behavioral observations section and the sample scoring summary sheet in Figure BG-1 (at the end of this appendix) can help you make this judgment. Other factors that may produce distortions that are not true errors are a rough drawing surface or improperly presented stimulus card, a debilitating physical handicap, or an inadequate drawing instrument.

Furthermore, at times an individual with brain dysfunction may, through extraordinary effort, make fewer than 5 errors but take considerable time to draw the figures. The average time for nonorganic psychiatric patients to complete the Bender Gestalt is 6 minutes. You may wish to count it as an extra error if the subject takes more than 15 minutes to complete the task.

There are numerous types of errors or distortions possible in drawing these figures. However, with this scoring system you should focus only on the 12 specific distortions described here. All others are irrelevant to this scoring system. For example, bizarre or symbolic behavior such as drawing stars or figure eights for circles is usually indicative of psychosis rather than organicity.

Finally, in this system, errors should be scored rather conservatively or only when clear-cut deviations are observed. Frequently, an error must be *severe* or *persistent* if it is to be scored. If in doubt, it is best *not* to score an error. Beginning scorers always err in the direction of *overscoring*. This lowers diagnostic accuracy considerably.

The most efficient way to proceed is to utilize a sign-by-sign approach. For example, take the first sign, which is Rotation, and examine the entire protocol for any instances of rotation. Then move on to the second sign and examine the whole protocol for its presence and so on. Be careful not to put the individual in double jeopardy by scoring the same distortion as two different errors. Any figure may contain more than one distortion (e.g., the figure may be rotated and also demonstrate poor motor coordination), but each distortion may only be scored as 1 error. You are looking for the presence or absence of each of 12 signs. If the sign appears once or five times, it is still scored as only 1 error. The maximum number of errors is 12 (or 13 if you add a time penalty).

Below is the BGT protocol of a psychotic inpatient in an acute psychiatric treatment center. It is an error-free protocol, using this scoring system, and as such, it may serve as a model against which to compare the scoring criteria.

*From Lacks, P. *Bender Gestalt Screening for Brain Dysfunction*, pp. 83-110. Copyright © 1984 by John Wiley & Sons, Inc. Reprinted by permission of John Wiley & Sons, Inc.

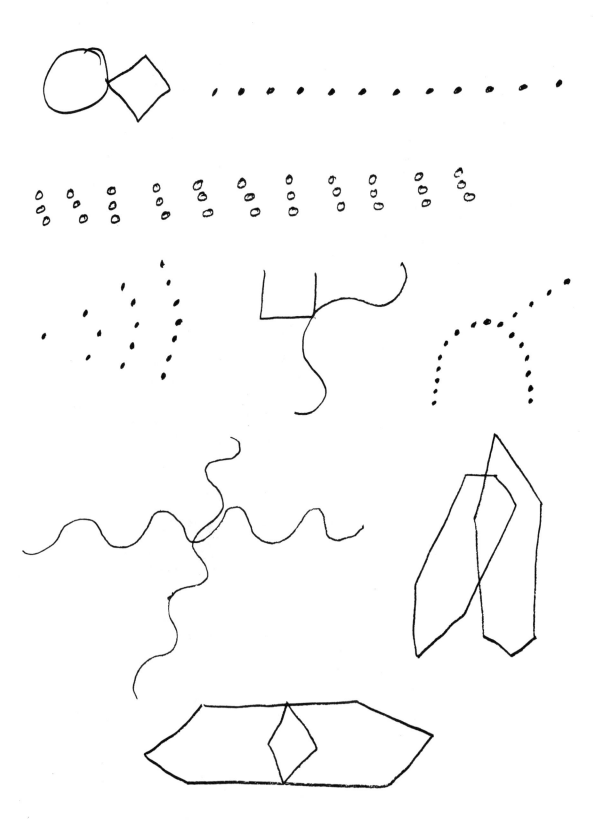

1. ROTATION   *Definition.* Score if there is a rotation of 80° to 180° (including mirror-imaging) of the major axis of the whole figure (not a part of the figure). Do not score if *S* shifts the position of the card or the paper and then draws the figure accurately.

Figures. Score for all figures.

90° rotations

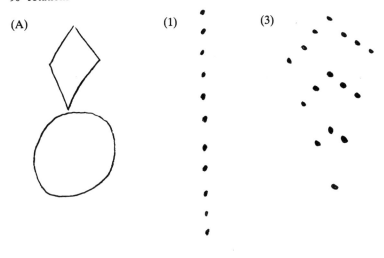

180° rotations

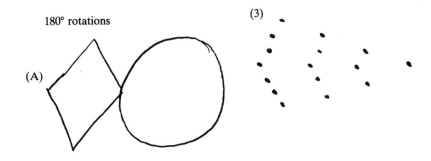

mirror-imaging

(2)

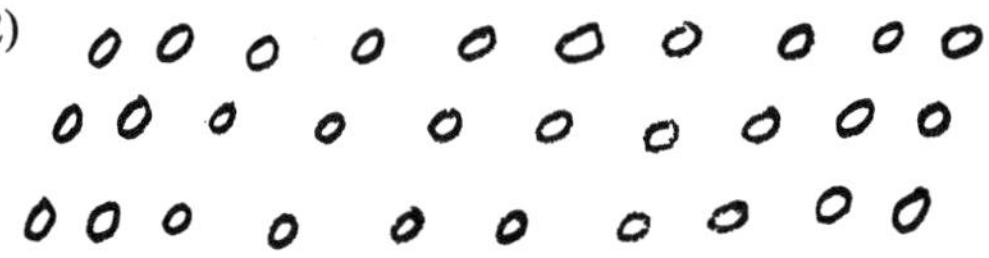

(5)

Do Not Score

(A)

(card was turned this way)

(3)

(approximately 45° rotation)

(5)

(only part of figure is rotated)

2. OVERLAPPING DIFFICULTY *Definition.* Difficulty in reproducing the portions of the figures that should overlap.

Figures. Score only for figures 6 and 7.

(7)    Omission of the portions of the figure which overlap

(7)    Simplification of figures only at the point of overlap

Marked sketching or reworking only at the point of overlap

(6) 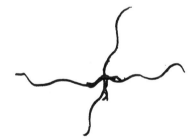   (7)

Distortion of the figure at the point of overlap

(7)

Figures overlap at the wrong place

(6)

(7)

Failure of figures to overlap

(6)   (7)

Do Not Score

(6)   (7)   (parts of figures more
                                  than ⅛ inch apart,
                                  score Simplification)

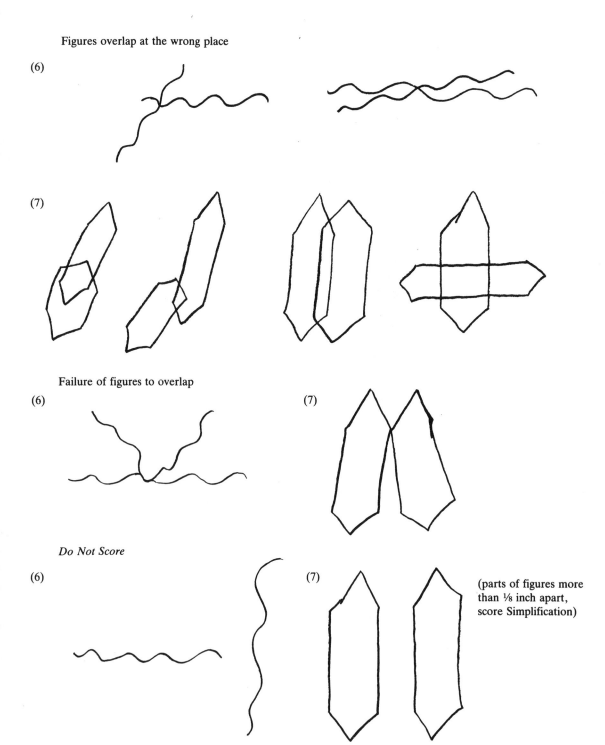

3. SIMPLIFICATION   *Definition.*   Score if the figure is drawn in a simplified or easier form that is not more primitive, from a maturational point of view, from the stimulus.

Figures.   Score for all figures.

Circles for dots on figure 1

Nonoverlapping parts

(6)   (7)

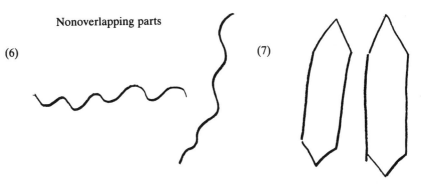

Joining parts of figures are more than ⅛ inch apart

(A)   (4)

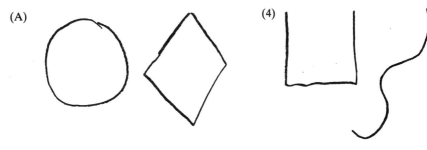

(5)   (8)

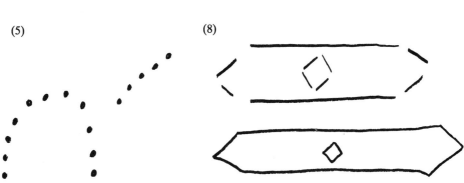

Very simplified drawing

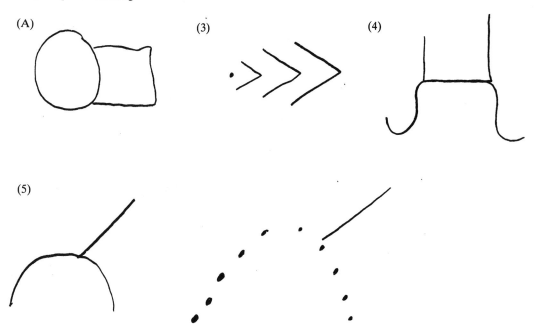

(A)   (3)   (4)

(5)

Do Not Score

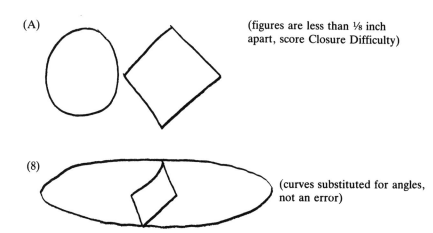

(A)   (figures are less than ⅛ inch apart, score Closure Difficulty)

(8)   (curves substituted for angles, not an error)

4. FRAGMENTATION   *Definition.*   Score if the figure is broken up into parts destroying the gestalt or if the figure is incomplete (unless *S* refuses to draw the entire figure).

Figures.   Score for all figures.

Figure broken into parts resulting in destruction of the gestalt

(1)

(2)

(one long row of 33 circles)

(2)

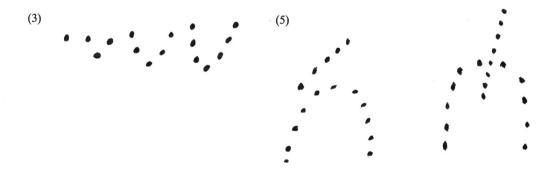

(2)   (random drawing of 33 circles with no recognition of the stimulus pattern)

(3)   (5)

(8)

Incomplete figure

(1)    (2)   (6 or fewer dots or columns of circles)

(2)    (2 instead of 3 rows of circles)

(4)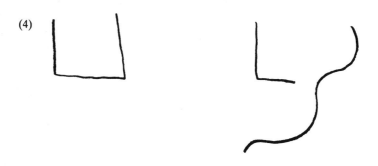

(5)

Do Not Score

(2) 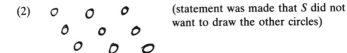   (statement was made that *S* did not want to draw the other circles)

5. RETROGRESSION   *Definition.*   Substitution of a more primitive gestalt form than the stimulus.

Figures.   Score for all figures except 4 and 6.

Loops for circles (if persistent)

(2)

Dashes for dots (if extreme and persistent)

(1)

(5)

Triangle for diamond or hexagon

(A)

(7)

Square for diamond

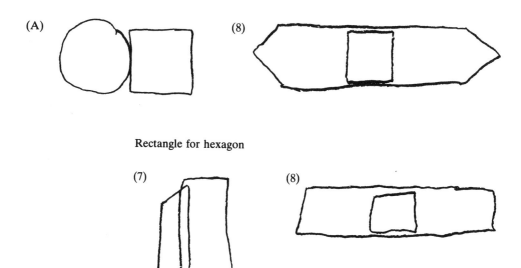

Rectangle for hexagon

Do Not Score

Do not score if curves are substituted for angles or angulation of bottom of hexagon on figure 7 is omitted.

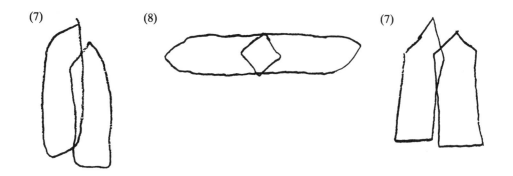

6. PERSEVERATION There are two kinds of Perseveration errors. If both occur, this error is still only scored once.

Type A *Definition.* Inappropriate substitution of the features of a preceding stimulus, such as replacing the circles of figure 2 with the dots of figure 1 (must have made dots, not circles on figure 1); replacing the dots of figures 3 and 5 with the circles of figure 2 (must have made circles on figure 2 and dots on 1).

Figures. Score only for figures 2, 3, and 5.

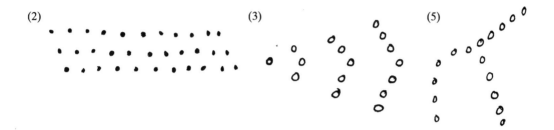

Type B *Definition.* Intradesign perseveration or continuing to draw a figure beyond the limits called for by the stimulus. For figure 1, 14 or more dots must be present; for figure 2, 13 or more columns of circles.

Figures. Score only for figures 1, 2, and 3.

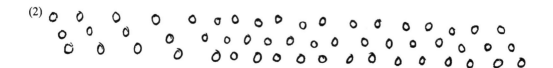

(2) 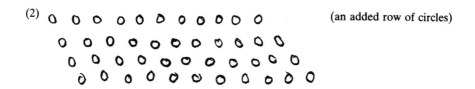   (an added row of circles)

(3)    (an added row of dots)

Do Not Score

(1) 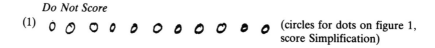   (circles for dots on figure 1, score Simplification)

(6)

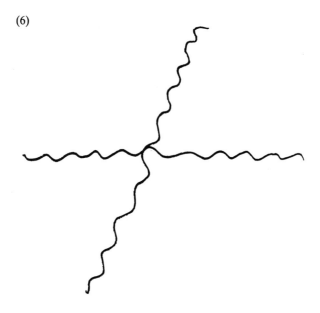

7. COLLISION OR COLLISION TENDENCY

Definition. One figure is drawn as touching or overlapping another figure (collision) or is drawn within ¼ inch or less of another figure but does not touch (collision tendency).

Figures. Score for all figures.

(5,6)

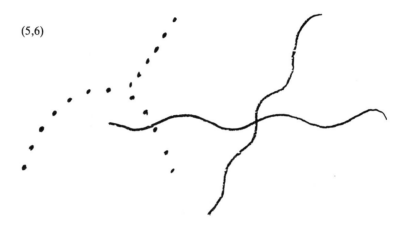

(4,5)

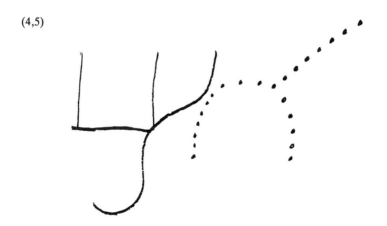

Do Not Score

(5,6)

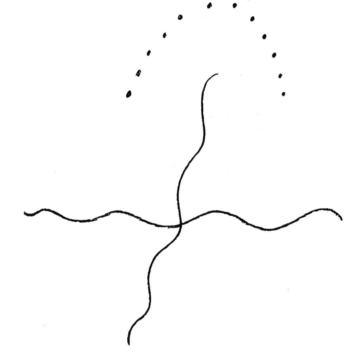

8. IMPOTENCE   *Definition.* Behavioral or verbal expressions of inability to draw a figure correctly (often accompanied by statements such as "I know this drawing is not right but I just can't make it right").

Figures. Score for all figures.

Repetitious drawings or numerous erasures of figures with similar inaccuracies

(A)

(4)

S realizes that an error has been made and tries to correct it unsuccessfully or expresses inability to correct it

(4)

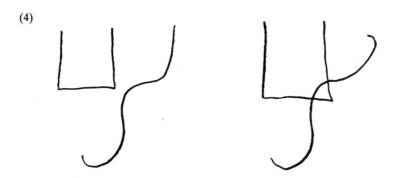

Do Not Score

(4)

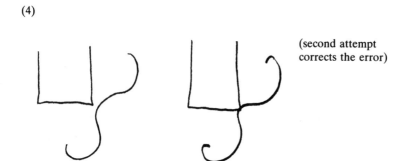

(second attempt corrects the error)

9. CLOSURE DIFFICULTY   *Definition.*   Difficulty in getting the joining parts of figures together or getting adjacent parts of a figure to touch. If figures are more than ⅛ inch apart at joining point, score Simplification.

Figures.   Score only for figures A, 4, 7, and 8.

Consistent but not significant joining problems on 2 out of these 3 figures

(A)

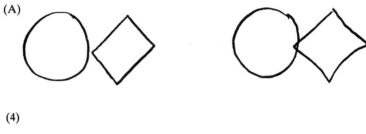

(4)

(8)

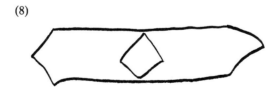

One *significant* problem with closing circles or figures or joining adjacent parts
of a figure

(A)

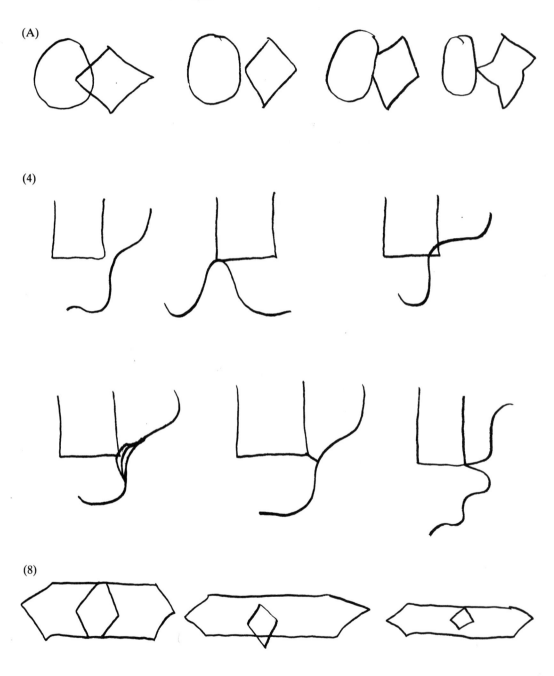

(4)

(8)

Marked and persistent gaps, overlap, redrawing, sketching, erasures, increased pressure at points where parts of the design join one another

(4)

(8)

Do Not Score

(A)

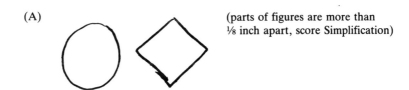

(parts of figures are more than
⅛ inch apart, score Simplification)

(8)

10. MOTOR INCOORDINATION

Definition.   Irregular (tremor-like) lines, especially with heavy pressure. Behavioral observations are important for scoring this error. Be sure *S* is drawing on a smooth surface.

Figures.   Score for all figures.

(1)

(8)

11. ANGULATION DIFFICULTY   *Definition.*   Severe difficulty in reproducing the angulation of figures.

Figures.   Score only for figures 2 and 3, but especially figure 2.

Failure to reproduce angulation of a figure

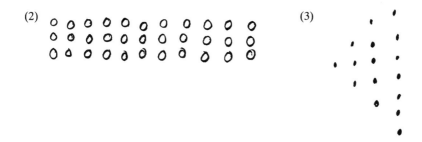

Angulation of the whole figure 45° to 80° rather than parts of a figure (but not by greater than 80°, which would be Rotation)

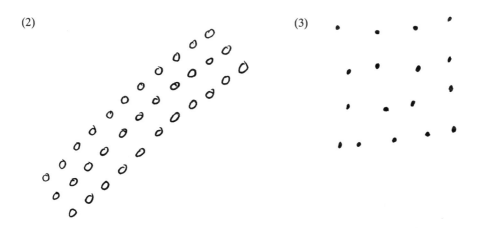

Variability of the angulation of more than half the rows of circles of figure 2

(2)

Do Not Score

(3)   •   (figure 3 should be scored leniently
                          because its angulation is especially
                          hard to reproduce)

(2)   (reversal of
                                                 angulation on
                                                 figure 2,
                                                 score Rotation)

12.   COHESION   *Definition.*   Isolated decrease or increase in size of figures. Score very conservatively. This error is most frequently overscored.

Figures.   Score for all figures.

Decrease in the size of *part* of a figure by more than ⅓ of the dimensions used in the rest of the figure

(A)

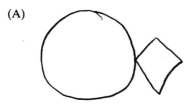

(4)

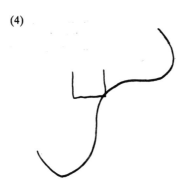

(7)

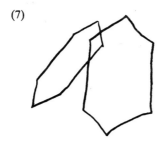

(8)

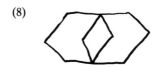

Increase or decrease in the size of a figure by ⅓ of the dimensions used in the *other drawings* (*not* compared to the size of the stimulus cards). Exclude parts of drawing that are larger due to Perseveration.

(5,6)

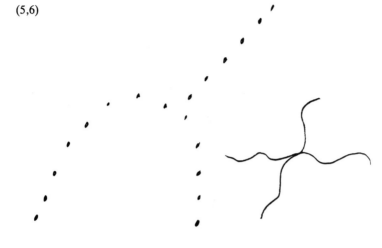

(7,8)

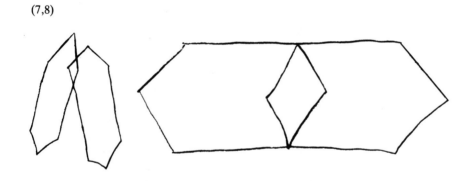

Bender Gestalt Test Scoring Summary

Name_____

Age_____   Sex_____

Education_____   Race_____

Occupation_____

Behavioral Observations:

_____ Evidence of fatigue
_____ Insufficient attention to stimulus
_____ Extremely rapid and careless execution
_____ Extreme care and deliberation
_____ Dissatisfaction expressed for poorly
      executed drawings or repeated unsuccessful
      attempts to correct errors.
_____ Poor motor coordination or hand tremor
_____ Rotation (on figures _____)
_____ Apparent difficulty seeing the figures
_____ Other comments _____

      Time _____

Scoring Checklist:

_____ 1. Rotation
_____ 2. Overlapping Difficulty
_____ 3. Simplification
_____ 4. Fragmentation
_____ 5. Retrogression
_____ 6. Perseveration
_____ 7. Collision or Collision Tendency
_____ 8. Impotence
_____ 9. Closure Difficulty
_____10. Motor Incoordination
_____11. Angulation Difficulty
_____12. Cohesion
_____ Time greater than 15 minutes

Total score _____

Test diagnosis _____

Appendix I

Summary and Scoring Sheet for Koppitz Developmental Scoring System

Design	Type of Error		Check if Present
A	1a	Distortion of Shape	_____
	1b	Disproportion	_____
	2	Rotation	_____
	3	Integration	_____
1	4	Circles for dots	_____
	5	Rotation	_____
	6	Perseveration	_____
2	7	Rotation	_____
	8	Row added, omitted	_____
	9	Perseveration	_____
3	10	Circles for dots	_____
	11	Rotation	_____
	12a	Shape test	_____
	12b	Lines for dots	_____
4	13	Rotation	_____
	14	Integration	_____
5	15	Circles for dots	_____
	16	Rotation	_____
	17a	Shape test	_____
	17b	Lines for dots	_____
6	18a	Angles in curves	_____
	18b	Straight line	_____
	19	Integration	_____
	20	Perseveration	_____
7	21a	Disproportion	_____
	21b	Incorrect angles	_____
	22	Rotation	_____
	23	Integration	_____
8	24	Incorrect angles	_____
	25	Rotation	_____

Appendix J

	Figure A	Figure 1	Figure 2	Figure 3	Figure 4	Figure 5	Figure 6	Figure 7	Figure 8
Adult	100%	25%	100%	100%	100%	100%	100%	100%	100%
11 yr	95%	95%	65%	60%	95%	90%	70%	75%	90%
10 yr	90%	90%	60%	60%	80%	80%	60%	60%	90%
9 yr	80%	75%	60%	70%	80%	70%	80%	65%	70%
8 yr	75%	75%	75%	60%	80%	65%	70%	65%	65%
7 yr	75%	75%	70%	60%	75%	65%	60%	65%	60%
6 yr	75%	75%	60%	80%	75%	60%	60%	60%	75%
5 yr	85%	85%	60%	80%	70%	60%	60%	60%	75%
4 yr	90%	85%	75%	80%	70%	60%	65%	60%	60%
3 yr		← Scribbling →							

Note: Maturational norms reproduced, with permission, from Clawson, A., *The Bender Visual Motor Gestalt Test for Children*, 1962, p. 143, Western Psychological Services. Bender designs reproduced, with permission, from Bender, L., *A Visual Motor Gestalt Test and Its Clinical Use*, 1938, American Orthopsychiatric Association and the Lauretta Bender estate.

Appendix K

Distribution of Bender Test Mean Scores and Standard Deviations

Age Group	1964 Normative Sample†			1974 Normative Sample‡		
	N	Mean	SD	N	Mean	SD
5–0 to 5–5	81	13.2	3.8	47	13.1	3.3
5–6 to 5–11	128	10.2	3.8	130	9.7	3.4
6–0 to 6–5	155	8.0	3.8	175	8.6	3.3
6–6 to 6–11	180	6.4	3.8	60	7.2	3.5
7–0 to 7–5	156	5.1	3.6	61	5.8	3.3
7–6 to 7–11	110	4.2	3.4	47	4.6	2.8
8–0 to 8–5	62	3.4	3.1	53	4.2	2.5
8–6 to 8–11	60	2.7	2.8	60	3.0	2.5
9–0 to 9–5	65	2.2	2.5	78	2.8	2.2
9–6 to 9–11	49	1.8	2.2	47	2.3	2.1
10–0 to 10–5	27	1.5	1.8	76	1.9	1.9
10–6 to 10–11	31	1.2	1.5	68	1.8	1.8
11–0 to 11–11				73	1.4	1.4

†N = 1104; socioeconomic cross section: 98% white, 2% nonwhite.
‡N = 975; socioeconomic cross section: 86% white, 8.5% black, 1% Oriental, 4.5% Mexican-American and Puerto Rican.

*Reprinted, by permission, from *The Bender Gestalt Test for Young Children, Vol. 2: Research and Applications 1963-1973,* by E.M. Koppitz, Grune & Stratton, 1975.

Appendix L

Directions for Hand Scoring the MMPI-2 Validity and Clinical Scales

1. Separate the scale 5 (Mf) scoring keys by sex to correspond with the gender of the person who has taken the test.

2. Items that have been either omitted or double marked should be crossed out with a colored pen, counted as cannot say (?) responses, and the raw score (total number) should be entered on the profile sheet indicated to the right of "? Raw Score."

3. The scoring keys for the validity and clinical scales are then placed over the "softcover answer sheet." The total number of marked items are counted to determine the raw scores for each of the scales. Items marked with a colored pen to designate they are cannot say (?) responses are ignored. The raw scores for each of the scales are entered in the designated sections on the profile sheet. Examiners should make sure that the gender indicated on the profile sheet matches the gender of the examinee.

4. Before plotting the profile, K corrections need to be added to the raw scores for Hs, Pd, Pt, Sc, and Ma. This is done by first calculating the appropriate fractions of K (.5K to Hs; .4K to Pd; 1K to Pt; 1K to Sc; and .2K to Ma). This can be easily done by using the box to the far left of the profile sheet designated as "Fractions of K." The raw score of K that was derived from scoring K can be located in the far left column of the "Fractions of K" box. The three numbers to the right of the raw score of K are the correct fractions of K. For example, if a raw score for K was 15, then .5K, .4K, and .2K would be 8, 6, and 3 respectively. The correct fractions of K can then be added to the raw scores for Hs, Pd, and Ma. Pt and Sc both have a full K correction added to them.

5. When K corrections have been added to Hs, Pd, Pt, Sc, and Ma, the raw scores can then be plotted on the profile sheet. This can be done by noting the lower scale labels (L, F, K, Hs+.5K, etc.) and finding the correct raw score on the profile sheet directly above them. These raw scores can then be marked with a dot, circle, or cross. When they have all been marked, a line can be made connecting the three validity scales and the 10 clinical scales. The T scores can be found by lining up the raw scores with the correct T scores on either the far right or the far left of the profile sheet (designated as "T or Tc"). For example, a raw score of 25 on Scale 1 (Hs) converts to a T score of 80.

Appendix M

Koss-Butcher Critical Items*

Acute Anxiety State

2(2).** I have a good appetite. (F)
3(3). I wake up fresh and rested most mornings. (F)
5(5). I am easily awakened by noise. (T)
10(9). I am about as able to work as I ever was. (F)
15(13). I work under a great deal of tension. (T)
28(29). I am bothered by an upset stomach several times a week. (T)
39(43). My sleep is fitful and disturbed. (T)
59(72). I am troubled by discomfort in the pit of my stomach every few days or oftener. (T)
140(152). Most nights I go to sleep without thoughts or ideas bothering me. (F)
172(186). I frequently notice my hand shakes when I try to do something. (T)
208(230). I hardly ever notice my heart pounding and I am seldom short of breath. (F)
218(238). I have periods of such great restlessness that I cannot sit long in a chair. (T)
223(242). I believe I am no more nervous than most others. (F).
301(337). I feel anxiety about something or someone almost all the time. (T)
444(506). I am a high strung person. (T)
463(543). Several times a week I feel as if something dreadful is about to happen. (T)
469(555). I sometimes feel that I am about to go to pieces. (T).

Threatened Assault

37(39). At times I feel like smashing things. (T)
85(97). At times I have a strong urge to do something harmful or shocking. (T)
134(145). At times I feel like picking a fist fight with someone. (T)
213(234). I get mad easily and get over it soon. (T)
389(381). I am often said to be hotheaded. (T)

Mental Confusion

24(27). Evil spirits possess me at times. (T)
31(328). I find it hard to keep my mind on a task or job. (T)
32(33). I have had very peculiar and strange experiences. (T)
72(50). My soul sometimes leaves my body. (T)
96(66). I see things or animals or people around me that others don't see. (T)
180(168). There is something wrong with my mind. (T)
198(184). I often hear voices without knowing where they come from. (T)
299(335). I cannot keep my mind on one thing. (T)
311(345). I often feel as if things are not real. (T)
316(349). I have strange and peculiar thoughts. (T)
325(356). I have more trouble concentrating than others seem to have. (T)

---

*Source for MMPI-2 numbers is Butcher, Dahlstrom, Graham, Tellegen, & Kaemmer (1989), and for MMPI numbers is Koss and Butcher (1973). Items are from *Minnesota Multiphasic Personality Inventory*, Copyright © the University of Minnesota 1942, 1943 (renewed 1970, 1989. Reproduced by permission of the publisher.
**Item numbers are according to the MMPI-2 with the numbers in parentheses indicating the numbers in the MMPI Group Form. All wording is according to the MMPI-2.
†MMPI-2 only.

Depressed Suicidal Ideation

9(318).	My daily life is full of things that keep me interested. (T)
38(41).	I have had periods of days, weeks, or months when I couldn't take care of things because I couldn't "get going." (T)
65(76).	Most of the time I feel blue. (T)
71(84).	These days I find it hard not to give up hope of amounting to something. (T)
75(88).	I usually feel that life is worthwhile. (F)
92(104).	I don't seem to care what happens to me. (T)
95(107).	I am happy most of the time. (F)
130(142).	I certainly feel useless at times. (T)
146(158).	I cry easily. (T)
215(236).	I brood a great deal. (T)
233(259).	I have difficulty starting to do things. (T)
273(301).	Life is a strain for me much of the time. (T)
303(339).	Most of the time I wish I were dead. (T)
306(252).	No one cares much what happens to you. (T)
388(379).	I very seldom have spells of the blues. (F)
411(418).	At times I think I am no good at all. (T)
454(526).	The future seems hopeless to me. (T)
485(418).	I often feel that I'm not as good as other people. (T)
506.†	I have recently considered killing myself. (T)
518.†	I have made lots of bad mistakes in my life. (T)
520.†	Lately I have though a lot about killing myself. (T)
524.†	No one knows it but I have tried to kill myself. (T)

Situational Stress Due to Alcoholism

125(137).	I believe that my home life is as pleasant as that of most people I know. (F)
264(215).	I have used alcohol excessively. (T)
487.†	I have enjoyed using marijuana. (T)
489.†	I have a drug or alcohol problem. (T)
502.†	I have some habits that are really harmful. (T)
511.†	Once a week or more I get high or drunk. (T)
518.†	I have made lots of bad mistakes in my life. (T)

Persecutory Ideas

17(16).	I am sure I get a raw deal from life. (T)
42(35).	If people had not had it in for me, I would have been much more successful. (T)
99(110).	Someone has it in for me. (T)
124(136).	I often wonder what hidden reason another person may have for doing something nice for me. (T)
138(121).	I believe I am being plotted against. (T)
144(123).	I believe I am being followed. (T)
145(157).	I feel that I have often been punished without cause. (T)
162(151).	Someone has been trying to poison me. (T)
216(197).	Someone has been trying to rob me. (T)
228(200).	There are persons who are trying to steal my thoughts and ideas. (T)
241(265).	It is safer to trust nobody. (T)
251(278).	I have often felt that strangers were looking at me critically. (T)
259(284).	I am sure I am being talked about. (T)
314(347).	I have no enemies who really wish to harm me. (F)
333(364).	People say insulting and vulgar things about me. (T)
361(293).	Someone has been trying to influence my mind. (T)

† Indicates MMPI-2 only.

Appendix N

Percentages for Rorschach Form Quality

**Mean Percentages (%) of +, *o, w,* and − Scorings
in the Protocols of Four Reference Groups.**

Scoring	Nonpsychiatric (*N* = 200)	Outpatient (*N* = 100)	Inpatient Nonschizophrenic (*N* = 70)	Inpatient Schizophrenic (*N* = 125)
+	26	31	16	21
o	58	47	65	37
w	12	14	15	24
−	4	8	4	19

*Reprinted, by permission, from Exner, J.E. *The Rorschach: A Comprehensive System,* New York: John Wiley & Sons, 1974, p. 248. Copyright 1974 by John Wiley & Sons, Inc.

Appendix O

Descriptive Statistics for 69 Rorschach Variables
for 600 Nonpatient Adults

Variable	Mean	SD	Mode	Min	Max	Freq	SK	KU
R	22.57	5.54	23	10	39	600	2.81	0.70
P	6.66	1.66	6	2	11	600	−0.62	−0.16
W	8.58	2.66	9	2	20	600	3.67	5.49
D	12.59	4.74	14	0	24	594	−1.85	−0.01
Dd	1.73	2.74	0	0	14	398	8.23	9.53
S	1.84	1.66	1	0	9	540	3.58	5.85
DQ+	6.90	2.25	6	2	14	600	0.77	−0.06
DQv/+	0.33	0.62	0	0	2	152	1.03	1.53
DQo	13.66	4.89	15	3	33	600	3.36	2.89
DQv	1.66	1.49	0	0	8	443	1.62	1.88
FQ+	0.87	0.85	0	0	4	351	0.37	−1.03
FQo	17.19	4.22	18	5	28	600	−1.18	0.44
FQu	2.94	2.12	3	0	12	557	3.92	5.75
FQ−	1.30	1.10	1	0	8	499	2.30	7.92
M	4.19	2.04	3	0	10	597	1.11	−0.41
M^a	2.82	1.60	2	0	8	586	0.50	−0.48
M^p	1.35	0.99	1	0	5	490	0.82	1.23
M−	0.09	0.45	0	0	4	38	3.43	72.97
FM	3.51	1.51	4	1	9	600	1.40	1.73
m	1.25	1.06	1	0	6	451	1.02	1.60
a (Active)	6.25	2.30	5	2	13	600	1.52	0.05
p (Passive)	2.70	1.69	3	0	9	548	1.26	0.85
FC	3.87	2.06	5	0	9	566	0.16	−0.55
CF	2.07	1.21	3	0	5	537	−0.02	−0.75
C+Cn	0.12	0.43	0	0	2	53	1.51	11.15
Wgt Sum C	4.23	1.82	3	0	8	597	−0.17	−0.94
FC'+C'F+C'	1.31	1.28	1	0	10	447	2.84	10.18
FT+TF+T	1.16	0.80	1	0	5	538	1.62	6.42
FV+VF+V	0.48	0.93	0	0	5	163	1.94	4.29
FY+YF+Y	0.98	1.60	0	0	10	280	4.28	8.65
Sum Shad'g	3.81	3.36	2	0	23	583	7.46	6.62
Fr+rF	0.12	0.46	0	0	4	47	2.29	29.07
(2)	8.44	2.65	8	1	17	600	0.11	0.78
FD	1.15	1.09	1	0	8	448	2.46	8.99
F	8.17	3.27	8	1	18	600	1.10	0.51

Variable	Mean	SD	Mode	Min	Max	Freq	SK	KU
Zf	11.22	2.96	11	5	23	600	3.10	3.02
Zd	0.84	3.11	+1	−8.5	9	600	0.28	0.69
EA	8.28	2.56	9	1.5	15	600	−0.56	−0.40
es	8.71	4.68	6	3	31	600	7.33	3.84
D Score	0.02	1.83	0	−10	3	600	−4.00	6.22
ADJ D	0.31	1.37	0	−6	4	600	−2.21	3.30
Afr	0.66	0.19	0.50	0.19	1.29	600	0.08	0.36
3r + (2)/R	0.39	0.11	0.32	0.03	0.84	600	0.01	2.91
Lambda	0.59	0.28	0.67	0.04	2.25	600	0.53	6.82
Blends	5.02	2.21	5	1	12	600	0.92	−0.13
Col-Sh B1	0.51	0.69	0	0	4	254	1.06	3.48
X + %	0.80	0.09	0.86	0.48	1.00	600	−0.11	2.04
F + %	0.76	0.17	1.00	0	1.00	600	−0.13	1.27
X − %	0.06	0.05	0.04	0	0.43	499	0.16	14.38
A %	0.45	0.10	0.42	0.15	0.92	600	0.09	2.60
Prim Cont	7.13	1.75	8	2	11	600	−1.15	0.22
Pure H	3.07	2.00	2	0	9	578	2.12	0.58
All H Cont	5.12	1.86	4	0	10	597	0.56	−0.27
S-Constell	2.07	2.11	0	0	9	433	2.31	0.43
SCZI	0.40	0.78	0	0	4	161	1.81	2.49
DEPI	0.95	1.08	0	0	4	322	0.95	−0.13
DV	0.36	1.20	0	0	4	101	2.79	11.43
DR	0.51	1.31	0	0	4	206	2.02	5.84
INCOM	0.54	0.79	0	0	5	258	1.90	8.45
FABCOM	0.18	0.56	0	0	4	70	2.20	17.64
ALOG	0.09	0.35	0	0	3	43	1.72	30.16
CONTAM	0.01	0.07	0	0	1	3	0.99	194.35
SUM6 SP SC	1.64	2.09	1	0	11	449	6.72	14.55
WSUM6 SP SC	3.96	1.76	2	0	23	449	5.34	8.13
AG	0.72	0.84	0	0	4	304	0.83	4.42
CONFAB	0.00	—	0	0	0	0	—	—
CP	0.01	0.11	0	0	1	7	0.98	80.45
MOR	0.70	0.94	0	0	6	283	1.67	4.80
PER	1.06	1.01	1	0	5	406	1.25	2.38
PSV	0.05	0.22	0	0	1	32	0.89	13.75

Note: From Exner, J. E., Jr. *The Rorschach: A Comprehensive System. Volume 1: Basic Foundations (2nd ed.)*, pp. 257-258. Copyright © 1986 by John E. Exner, Jr. Reprinted by permission of John Wiley & Sons, Inc.

Appendix P

Descriptive Statistics for 69 Rorschach Variables for 1580 Nonpatient Children and Adolescents, by Age

Age Variable	5 Mean	5 SD	6 Mean	6 SD	7 Mean	7 SD	8 Mean	8 SD	9 Mean	9 SD	10 Mean	10 SD
R	15.27	5.54	16.13	4.33	18.33	4.72	19.61	4.63	20.27	4.53	20.22	4.39
P	3.54	3.72	4.24	3.51	4.04	1.82	4.62	2.14	4.71	1.23	5.34	1.61
W	9.21	3.78	8.63	3.11	9.12	3.08	8.92	3.11	9.82	3.04	9.29	2.93
D	5.63	2.07	6.09	2.71	7.61	2.39	9.23	3.18	9.92	2.86	9.41	3.60
Dd	0.48	0.32	1.39	0.78	1.57	0.84	1.49	1.02	0.63	0.92	1.51	0.57
S	0.74	0.77	1.43	0.74	2.13	0.93	1.74	0.68	1.31	0.82	1.43	0.66
DQ+	2.61	1.74	2.64	1.87	3.90	1.77	4.08	2.33	4.92	1.62	5.43	2.41
DQv/+	0.69	0.84	1.33	1.54	1.12	1.04	2.03	1.14	1.17	0.86	0.84	0.88
DQo	7.18	3.64	7.85	3.73	9.73	3.62	10.63	3.64	11.56	3.36	11.97	3.94
DQv	4.84	2.34	4.31	2.53	4.03	2.53	3.89	1.96	3.62	2.09	2.03	0.98
FQ+	0	—	0.02	0.04	0.52	0.69	0.48	0.77	0.94	1.03	0.85	0.67
FQo	12.31	3.15	13.85	4.41	14.83	2.93	16.13	3.98	16.15	4.88	15.64	4.97
FQu	2.09	2.89	1.25	1.01	1.89	1.51	2.01	0.97	2.06	1.31	2.81	1.47
FQ−	0.71	0.81	1.03	0.71	1.18	0.73	0.99	0.68	1.06	0.56	0.91	1.01
M	0.83	0.60	1.43	0.57	1.72	0.64	1.93	0.83	1.74	0.83	2.03	1.12
Ma	0.69	0.77	1.13	0.67	1.38	0.58	1.23	0.86	1.11	0.62	1.45	0.89
Mp	0.24	0.64	0.30	0.41	0.44	0.37	0.71	0.41	0.63	0.57	0.57	0.63
M−	0.06	0.81	0.13	0.08	0.57	0.27	0.51	0.38	0.27	0.48	0.31	0.52
FM	2.84	1.23	2.94	1.58	3.64	1.78	3.44	1.81	3.64	1.69	3.09	0.92
m	0.16	0.13	0.28	0.51	0.31	0.28	0.59	0.44	0.33	0.20	0.19	0.23
a	2.64	1.30	3.31	1.39	3.92	1.62	3.82	1.19	3.44	1.51	3.92	1.39
p	1.14	0.69	1.27	0.74	1.37	0.56	2.08	0.88	2.08	0.66	1.38	0.61
FC	0.52	0.84	0.84	0.64	1.21	0.54	1.33	0.58	1.53	0.67	1.42	0.77
CF	1.91	0.65	2.62	1.36	2.64	1.29	2.72	1.22	2.04	0.77	2.08	0.74
C+Cn	0.92	0.70	0.74	0.58	0.61	0.33	0.41	0.33	0.39	0.59	0.38	0.19
Wgt Sum C	3.54	1.71	4.92	2.13	4.13	2.32	4.84	2.06	3.67	2.01	3.38	1.63
FC'+C'F+C'	0.56	0.47	0.62	0.54	0.78	0.63	0.73	0.63	0.56	0.51	0.62	0.52
FT+TF+T	0.81	0.44	0.97	0.58	0.82	0.49	0.93	0.40	0.89	0.72	0.91	0.34
FV+VF+V	0	—	0	—	0.01	0.07	0.01	0.06	0	—	0.13	0.09
FV+YF+Y	0.38	0.33	0.24	0.36	0.46	0.38	0.28	0.41	0.26	0.41	0.26	0.39
Sum Shad'g	1.64	1.09	1.74	0.86	1.83	0.84	1.74	0.89	1.64	0.77	1.82	0.78
Fr+rF	0.74	0.51	0.72	0.48	0.74	0.41	0.70	0.47	0.44	0.22	0.44	0.24
(2)	7.33	3.31	8.62	2.38	9.14	2.72	8.69	3.13	9.53	2.89	9.51	2.63
FD	0.02	0.02	0.18	0.23	0.32	0.24	0.61	0.29	0.47	0.27	0.68	0.37
F	8.18	2.91	7.72	3.58	8.73	2.53	9.11	2.68	8.84	3.14	9.03	2.90

Note: Adapted from Exner, J.E., Jr. *The Rorschach: A Comprehensive System. Volume 1: Basic Foundations (2nd ed.)*, pp. 262-285. Copyright © 1986 by John E. Exner, Jr. Reprinted by permission of John Wiley & Sons, Inc.

Age	5		6		7		8		9		10	
Variable	Mean	SD	Mean	SD	Mean	SD	Mean	SD	Mean	SD	Mean	SD
Zf	8.26	3.37	9.86	3.53	10.57	2.73	10.77	2.94	10.68	3.93	10.21	3.73
Zd	−1.14	2.61	−1.23	2.71	−0.94	2.41	−0.67	2.08	−0.07	2.77	−0.12	2.89
EA	3.96	1.89	4.99	2.01	4.98	2.89	5.23	2.50	5.39	2.55	5.67	2.48
es	5.03	2.11	5.14	2.34	5.78	2.03	5.89	2.39	5.73	2.48	5.32	2.71
D Score	−1.06	1.02	−0.44	1.83	−0.32	2.17	−0.68	2.16	−0.26	2.27	0.17	1.91
$ADJ\ D$	−1.01	0.78	−0.24	1.69	−0.19	2.60	−0.38	2.28	0.08	2.39	0.30	1.68
Afr	1.07	0.31	0.91	0.24	0.84	0.18	0.79	0.15	0.77	0.15	0.79	0.14
$3r+(2)/R$	0.61	0.15	0.60	0.13	0.61	0.14	0.56	0.13	0.52	0.10	0.51	0.10
Lambda	1.14	0.39	0.91	0.28	0.91	0.25	0.86	0.24	0.78	0.19	0.81	0.16
Blends	1.89	0.73	3.12	1.69	3.48	1.69	3.91	1.89	3.84	1.31	3.71	1.27
Col-Sh $B1$	0.37	0.21	0.41	0.48	0.51	0.48	0.47	0.22	0.83	0.64	0.91	0.78
$X+\%$	0.81	0.11	0.86	0.11	0.84	0.12	0.85	0.14	0.84	0.09	0.82	0.09
$F+\%$	0.83	0.12	0.89	0.09	0.86	0.11	0.85	0.16	0.84	0.11	0.83	0.11
$X-\%$	0.05	0.04	0.06	0.08	0.07	0.53	0.08	0.05	0.05	0.04	0.06	0.04
$A\%$	0.54	0.13	0.57	0.09	0.51	0.12	0.53	0.10	0.47	0.10	0.48	0.10
$Prim\ Cont$	4.23	2.13	5.06	2.18	6.03	2.11	5.89	2.18	6.07	2.94	5.94	2.69
$Pure\ H$	1.61	0.87	2.03	0.87	1.89	1.12	2.18	1.24	2.71	1.28	2.88	1.54
All H Cont	3.38	1.34	3.86	1.59	4.12	2.34	4.47	2.19	4.22	1.94	4.18	1.67
S-Constell	2.86	2.01	2.01	1.47	1.96	1.23	1.41	1.18	1.35	0.94	1.95	1.07
(Child)												
$SCZI$	0.73	0.84	0.89	1.23	1.01	0.80	0.89	0.78	1.38	0.78	1.23	1.31
$DEPI$	1.06	0.78	1.23	0.85	1.33	1.23	0.74	0.83	1.03	0.89	1.22	0.94
DV	1.03	1.21	1.32	0.78	1.42	0.73	0.68	0.51	1.02	0.89	0.51	0.54
DR	1.61	1.32	0.99	0.72	1.01	0.58	1.31	1.09	0.99	0.71	0.49	0.46
$INCOM$	1.14	0.68	1.69	0.93	1.12	0.59	0.84	0.61	0.93	0.57	0.81	0.57
$FABCOM$	0.64	0.29	0.73	0.44	0.79	0.52	1.03	0.72	0.81	0.73	0.77	0.43
$ALOG$	1.21	0.49	1.43	0.72	0.93	0.68	0.83	0.69	0.58	0.28	0.56	0.24
$CONTAM$	0.01	0.09	0	—	0.01	0.01	0	—	0	—	0	—
$SUM6\ SP\ SC$	5.84	2.76	6.07	2.35	5.27	2.81	4.46	2.05	4.23	2.31	3.58	1.68
$WSUM6\ SP\ SC$	13.72	5.02	14.41	5.96	13.36	5.39	10.64	4.90	9.76	3.87	7.33	2.73
AG	1.23	0.74	1.03	0.85	0.98	0.81	1.13	0.83	1.23	0.87	1.03	0.77
$CONFAB$	0.02	0.02	0.01	0.01	0.01	0.01	0.01	0.03	0.01	0.01	0	—
CP	0.03	0.12	0.14	0.12	0.01	0.03	0.02	0.03	0.01	0.01	0	—
MOR	1.46	0.86	1.08	1.02	1.24	0.62	1.05	0.62	1.17	0.93	1.20	0.83
PER	4.38	0.86	4.07	2.23	3.61	1.39	3.48	1.41	3.26	1.61	2.28	1.09
PSV	0.89	0.62	0.73	0.58	0.41	0.28	0.49	0.44	0.38	0.23	0.31	0.18

Age	11		12		13		14		15		16	
Variable	Mean	SD	Mean	SD	Mean	SD	Mean	SD	Mean	SD	Mean	SD
R	19.63	4.33	20.23	4.48	20.62	4.79	21.57	5.12	21.52	5.39	22.28	5.19
P	5.78	1.94	6.22	2.08	6.08	2.44	6.31	2.24	6.64	1.45	6.22	1.61
W	8.18	3.32	7.74	3.58	7.19	2.18	7.76	2.81	8.19	3.04	8.89	3.37
D	9.61	3.38	11.13	3.06	11.74	3.38	11.68	3.23	11.52	3.36	11.34	3.18
Dd	1.76	0.84	1.38	0.72	1.71	0.68	2.14	1.11	1.77	0.93	2.09	0.84
S	1.58	0.51	1.48	0.83	0.89	0.43	0.79	0.54	0.69	0.43	0.94	0.69
$DQ+$	5.12	2.30	5.79	2.64	5.41	2.16	5.91	2.27	5.71	1.94	6.33	2.14
$DQv/+$	1.27	1.83	0.97	0.96	0.86	0.57	0.83	0.72	0.74	0.69	0.76	0.66
DQo	11.71	3.54	11.37	4.02	12.68	4.02	13.54	3.66	13.13	3.43	13.75	3.91
DQv	1.52	0.73	2.10	0.77	1.67	0.91	1.33	0.73	1.94	0.87	1.44	0.85
$FQ+$	0.96	0.82	0.51	0.82	0.36	0.52	0.59	0.49	0.48	0.39	0.69	0.39
FQo	14.91	3.81	16.06	3.34	16.32	4.27	17.12	3.39	17.01	4.31	17.36	4.49
FQu	2.33	1.05	2.64	1.07	2.95	1.31	2.89	1.21	3.13	1.14	3.13	1.23
$FQ-$	1.40	0.82	1.01	0.79	0.99	0.67	1.01	0.83	0.90	0.83	1.01	0.61
M	2.64	1.28	2.70	1.02	3.13	1.19	2.92	1.19	2.81	1.19	3.23	1.09
M^a	1.78	0.91	1.89	0.95	2.04	0.88	1.88	0.93	1.93	0.96	2.12	0.92
M^p	0.86	0.71	0.81	0.72	1.09	0.49	1.04	0.71	0.88	0.98	1.11	0.58
$M-$	0.37	0.53	0.17	0.23	0.36	0.28	0.28	0.41	0.31	0.19	0.38	0.21
FM	3.09	0.84	3.22	1.08	3.64	1.52	3.24	0.91	3.34	1.33	3.43	1.31
m	0.23	0.39	0.34	0.28	0.42	0.18	0.21	0.34	0.43	0.29	0.33	0.24
a	4.04	1.14	4.31	1.93	4.84	1.62	4.12	1.79	4.12	1.28	4.67	1.09
p	1.92	0.58	1.89	0.71	2.28	0.89	2.23	0.84	2.37	0.68	2.26	0.79
FC	2.02	0.74	2.63	1.30	2.03	1.14	2.07	1.23	2.24	0.94	2.24	0.87
CF	2.14	0.88	2.49	1.72	2.33	1.19	2.42	1.28	1.93	0.78	2.02	0.84
$C+Cn$	0.43	0.39	0.22	0.10	0.41	0.36	0.21	0.34	0.19	0.23	0.13	0.14
Wgt Sum C	3.42	1.84	4.31	2.11	4.02	1.78	3.77	1.57	3.48	1.52	3.34	1.26
$FC'+C'F+C'$	0.71	0.67	0.73	0.53	0.62	0.67	0.48	0.31	0.54	0.47	0.71	0.52
$FT+TF+T$	0.91	0.54	1.01	0.54	0.93	0.68	0.81	0.51	0.93	0.63	1.01	0.73
$FV+VF+V$	0.01	0.03	0.34	0.42	0.42	0.29	0.34	0.27	0.32	0.28	0.24	0.18
$FY+YF+Y$	0.42	0.31	0.38	0.41	0.35	0.31	0.35	0.39	0.21	0.14	0.38	0.56
Sum Shad'g	2.04	0.86	2.24	0.91	2.14	1.03	1.73	0.58	1.81	0.91	2.08	0.86
$Fr+rF$	0.30	0.23	0.41	0.19	0.29	0.24	0.21	0.08	0.41	0.26	0.34	0.28
(2)	8.94	2.88	9.11	2.73	8.84	2.94	8.70	2.89	8.33	2.19	8.94	2.21
FD	0.81	0.37	0.61	0.38	0.84	0.38	0.87	0.62	1.02	0.74	0.68	0.44
F	9.22	3.39	9.33	3.09	8.73	3.13	9.37	2.51	9.52	2.78	10.13	3.39

Age	11		12		13		14		15		16	
Variable	Mean	SD	Mean	SD	Mean	SD	Mean	SD	Mean	SD	Mean	SD
Zf	9.92	3.12	10.26	3.09	9.48	1.89	9.13	2.61	10.37	2.93	11.87	3.14
Zd	0.02	2.84	0.29	2.61	−0.31	2.53	0.19	2.64	0.06	2.91	0.36	2.49
EA	6.23	2.89	7.01	3.11	7.15	3.28	6.69	2.91	6.29	2.63	6.57	2.38
es	5.43	2.60	5.92	2.75	6.74	2.80	5.18	3.01	5.58	2.76	5.85	3.03
D Score	0.23	1.06	0.49	1.57	0.14	1.07	0.41	0.93	0.19	1.02	0.22	1.41
ADJ D	0.31	1.01	0.58	1.49	0.38	1.02	0.49	0.83	0.28	0.87	0.41	1.27
Afr	0.75	0.17	0.71	0.15	0.73	0.15	0.72	0.09	0.70	0.17	0.72	0.11
$3r+(2)/R$	0.50	0.11	0.51	0.13	0.47	0.09	0.43	0.09	0.44	0.09	0.44	0.10
Lambda	0.88	0.21	0.85	0.18	0.73	0.12	0.77	0.17	0.79	0.11	0.83	0.14
Blends	3.44	1.23	3.42	1.33	3.92	1.41	3.37	1.12	3.81	1.53	4.18	1.78
Col-Sh B1	0.73	0.61	0.67	0.51	0.71	0.59	0.56	0.58	0.53	0.61	0.63	0.51
X+%	0.81	0.11	0.82	0.12	0.81	0.10	0.82	0.09	0.81	0.09	0.81	0.09
F+%	0.84	0.09	0.85	0.11	0.83	0.09	0.82	0.11	0.82	0.12	0.83	0.12
X–%	0.08	0.05	0.09	0.04	0.05	0.04	0.07	0.06	0.08	0.05	0.07	0.04
A%	0.46	0.13	0.48	0.14	0.43	0.08	0.47	0.08	0.42	0.09	0.45	0.11
Prim Cont	6.12	2.42	6.89	3.02	6.51	2.47	7.02	2.48	6.99	2.79	7.28	1.95
Pure H	3.26	1.19	2.68	1.14	2.38	1.24	2.78	0.99	2.41	0.93	2.71	1.57
All H Cont	4.51	2.08	4.27	1.81	4.43	1.74	4.72	1.93	4.73	1.89	4.80	1.64
S-Constell	2.07	1.48	1.69	1.02	1.93	1.71	2.18	1.06	1.91	2.07	3.16	1.86
(Adult)												
SCZI	1.12	0.98	0.89	0.67	0.78	0.51	0.48	0.67	0.54	0.49	0.62	0.48
DEPI	1.31	0.71	1.03	0.71	1.71	1.01	1.19	0.85	1.20	0.91	1.17	1.23
DV	0.59	0.37	0.47	0.29	0.54	0.40	0.56	0.38	0.28	0.14	0.21	0.26
DR	0.42	0.39	0.31	0.26	0.27	0.31	0.26	0.41	0.25	0.18	0.14	0.18
INCOM	0.92	0.68	0.79	0.34	0.92	0.42	0.81	0.57	0.62	0.38	0.63	0.34
FABCOM	0.68	0.49	0.34	0.12	0.39	0.23	0.49	0.32	0.41	0.25	0.31	0.34
ALOG	0.47	0.46	0.42	0.34	0.44	0.34	0.38	0.22	0.34	0.29	0.29	0.24
CONTAM	0	—	0	—	0	—	0	—	0	—	0	—
SUM6 SP SC	3.18	1.58	2.34	1.36	2.54	1.29	2.41	1.18	1.94	0.84	1.78	1.03
WSUM6 SP SC	6.90	2.03	6.31	2.24	6.13	2.57	5.71	2.38	4.84	1.79	4.36	1.71
AG	0.93	0.89	1.13	0.71	0.89	0.91	1.02	0.89	1.03	0.78	0.98	0.88
CONFAB	0	—	0.01	0.01	0	—	0	—	0	—	0	—
CP	0.14	0.17	0.01	0.01	0.01	0.01	0	—	0.01	0.02	0.01	0.04
MOR	1.22	0.89	1.07	0.73	1.02	0.89	0.95	0.71	1.05	0.81	1.08	0.89
PER	1.96	0.89	1.87	0.91	1.38	0.64	1.19	0.64	0.94	0.69	0.74	0.83
PSV	0.21	0.19	0.29	0.22	0.21	0.24	0.28	0.24	0.31	0.18	0.31	0.14

Appendix Q
Questions for the
House-Tree-Person Test

HOUSE

1. Is there anybody who lives in the house?
2. Does the person you drew live in the house?
3. How do the other people who live in the house feel about this person?
4. How does the person you drew feel about the house?
5. Do you think the house is strong or weak?
6. Do you think it would be difficult to get into the house?
7. What sort of activities occur in the house?
8. If the house were a person, how would it feel?
9. If there was a fire in the house, what do you think the person you drew would do?
10. What are the strongest and what are the weakest parts of the house?

TREE

1. What type of tree is this?
2. How does the person you drew feel about the tree?
3. What would the person like to use the tree for?
4. What are the weakest and strongest parts of the tree?
5. Is the tree flexible or rather rigid?
6. Would it be easy to climb the tree?
7. Are there any birds or other animals which live in the tree?
8. If the person you drew were to hurt the tree, how would he/she feel?
9. What do the people in the house think of the tree?
10. Do you think the tree is attractive or unattractive?

PERSON

1. Is the person you drew a male or a female?
2. How does he/she usually feel?
3. What things does this person most like to do?
4. What does he/she least like to do?
5. What are the best and worst qualities of the person?
6. What sort of things make this person angry?
7. What does he/she do when angry?
8. What sort of an animal does this person most remind you of?
9. What part of this person is the strongest and what is the weakest?
10. What do other people usually think of this person?

Appendix R

Smoothed Means and Standard Deviations for the Standardization Group, Man Scale

AGE	BOYS		GIRLS		COMBINED	
	MEAN	S.D.	MEAN	S.D.	MEAN	S.D.
5	15.8	5.01	17.4	5.27	16.6	5.29
6	18.4	5.71	20.0	5.94	19.2	5.95
7	22.5	6.82	23.5	6.91	23.0	6.92
8	25.9	7.77	27.6	7.91	20.8	7.88
9	30.7	8.95	31.8	8.68	31.3	8.83
10	34.5	9.84	36.3	9.35	35.4	9.65
11	37.6	10.85	40.2	9.78	38.9	10.42
12	40.3	11.01	43.0	10.32	41.6	10.77
13	42.0	10.67	44.2	9.89	43.4	10.34
14	44.7	10.51	45.1	9.57	44.9	10.05
15	45.1	10.60	45.2	9.01	45.2	9.83

From: Harris, D. B. *Children's Drawings as Measures of Intellectual Maturity*, 1963, p. 102.
Reprinted by permission of Hancourt, Brace, & Jovanovich.

Appendix S

Smoothed Means and Standard Deviations for the Standardization Group, Woman Scale

AGE	BOYS		GIRLS		COMBINED	
	MEAN	S.D.	MEAN	S.D.	MEAN	S.D.
5	16.0	5.43	19.3	6.04	17.6	6.01
6	18.8	6.41	22.8	7.08	20.8	7.07
7	23.3	7.17	27.0	7.88	25.2	7.78
8	27.6	7.93	31.3	8.73	29.5	8.57
9	32.1	8.37	35.3	8.80	33.7	8.71
10	35.0	9.15	39.7	9.39	37.3	9.60
11	37.3	9.53	43.3	9.41	40.3	9.96
12	39.8	9.61	45.8	9.58	42.8	10.08
13	42.0	9.61	47.4	9.37	44.7	9.88
14	44.1	9.41	48.2	8.97	46.1	9.43
15	44.4	9.31	48.2	8.48	46.3	9.10

From: Harris, D. B. *Children's Drawings as Measures of Intellectual Maturity*, 1963, p. 103. Reprinted by permission of Hancourt, Brace, & Jovanovich.

Appendix T

Scoring criteria for impulsive and nonimpulsive variables on the DAP (adapted from Oas, 1984). *

Impulsive Variables   The DAP impulsivity score for each subject is the total number of Impulsive variables scored. A variable is scored when it meets the scoring criteria listed under each individual for both male and female drawings. The maximum DAP-impulsivity score is 13.

1. *Completion time*   Completion time decreases with impulsivity. One point is scored if the total drawing time for each figure is less than five minutes (median completion time for adolescents is between five and ten minutes).

2. *Aggression*   Appearance of certain features suggesting acting out tendencies. One point is scored for the appearance of at least one of each of the following: teeth, knife, gun, bomb, stick fingers, blood, appearance of aggressive movement (striking, hitting, or kicking an object), or club.

3. *Overall quality*   The quality of the drawings is poor as defined by the Harris (1963) or Koppitz (1968) scoring system. Scores of less than 36 are scored one SD less than the group mean score of normal adolescent drawings according to Harris (1963) and Harris and Pinder (1974).

4. *Discontinuity*   Impulsives have difficulty connecting lines on drawings. One point is scored for overlapping lines that would normally be connected to give shape and form to at least two of the following parts: head, trunk, neck, arm, leg, foot.

5. *Omissions*   Impulsives leave out important aspects of the human figure such as head, arms, legs, etc. One point is scored for omission of at least one of the following missing body parts: head, trunk, neck, hand, arm, leg, foot, hair, all fingers. Not scored if hands behind back.

6. *Specific omissions*   Impulsives leave out the pupils, fingers, and nose. One point is scored for omission of either pupil or either eye, any finger or either hand, or nose.

7. *Proportion*   Impulsives are unconcerned with proportionality of drawing. One point is scored if at least one of the following items are drawn with either no proportion or out of proportion according to items in Harris (1963): Head (Item 48), Trunk (Item 47), Face (Item 50), Arms (Items 51, 52), Legs (Items 53).

8. *Size Increase*   Impulsives are expansive in their drawings. One point is scored for a figure drawn in excess of either six inches in height or three inches in width of trunk.

9. *Neck*   Impulsives tend to leave out or else draw the neck proportionately large. One point is scored if neck is omitted or one point is scored if neck is longer than 2/3 the length of the head.

10. *Stance*   Impulsive subjects draw figures with stances slanted or widened. One point is scored if legs are drawn 22.5 degrees or greater in distance from body midline.

11. *Shoulders*   Impulsives do not take the time to draw square shoulders. One point is scored if shoulders are improperly attached or not drawn squarely as defined by Harris (1963, p. 281).

*Permission to reproduce scoring guidelines granted by the author.

12 *Poor planning*   Impulsives do not plan their actions. One point is scored if any part of drawing is "cut off" by the side of the page it is drawn on or if any part of the figure is redrawn without erasure.

13. *Left side*   Impulsives tend to draw toward the left side of the page. One point is scored if midline of the figure is more than one inch to left of center of page.

Nonimpulsive Variables   The DAP nonimpulsivity score for each subject is the total number of nonimpulsive variables scored. A variable is scored when it meets the criteria listed under each individual for both the male and female drawings. The maximum DAP-impulsivity score is 13.

1. *Symmetry*   One point is scored if drawing has "a symmetrical quality" or appearance such that at least three of the following pairs of body parts are each drawn at the same angle and opposite position in space from the body midline: arms, legs, eyes, ears, feet.

2. *Detailing*   One point is scored for the presence of at least five of the following items: earrings, necklace, ring, bracelet, broach, shoe laces, hair styles, eyeglasses, pants, belt, shirt, dress, buttons, zipper, shoes, pockets, make-up, or socks.

3. *Completion time*   One point is scored if total drawing time for each figure is at least eight minutes.

4. *Placement*   One point is scored if at least 3/4 of drawing measured from top of head to bottom of feet is on the lower half of the page.

5. *Sketching*   One point is scored for sketching used to give form to any of the following body parts: arm, leg, trunk, head.

6. *Erasures*   One point is scored for complete erasure and subsequent redrawing of any of the following body parts: foot, leg, trunk, hand, arm, finger, head, facial features, hand held objects, other objects, or complete figure.

7. *Size*   One point is scored if drawing is less than four inches in length from head to foot or less than two inches in length in width of torso.

8. *Gender identity*   One point is scored if opposite sex of subject is drawn first.

9. *Eye emphasis*   One point is scored for presence of at least two of the following: glasses, eyebrows, eyelashes, large eyes, cornea detail, shaded eyes, pupils.

10. *Right side*   One point is scored if figure is drawn one inch or further to the right of the midline of the page.

11. *Perspective*   One point is scored for either a side-view or rear-view perspective of complete figure or head.

12. *Mouth detail*   One point is scored if mouth is drawn with both lips depicted in two dimensions (following guidelines provided by Harris, 1963, p. 249, item 12).

13. *Shading*   One point is scored for shading used to give form or color to at least two of the following body parts of clothing: foot, hand, trunk, arm, eye, mouth, leg, neck, shirt, pants, or dress.

References ─────────────────────────────────────

Abrams, E. (1955). Prediction of intelligence from certain Rorschach factors. *Journal of Clinical Psychology, 11*, 81-83.

Achenbach, T. M. (1978). The Child Behavior Profile: I. Boys aged 6-11. *Journal of Consulting and Clinical Psychology, 46*, 478-488.

Achenbach, T. M., & Edelbrock, C. S. (1979). The Child Behavior Profile: II. Boys aged 12-16 and girls 6-11 and 12-16. *Journal of Consulting and Clinical Psychology, 47*, 223-233.

Ackerman, P. T., Dykman, R. A., & Peters, J.E. (1976). Hierarchical Factor patterns on the WISC as related to area of learning deficit. *Perceptual and Motor Skills, 42*, 381-386.

Ackerman, P. T., Peters, J. R., & Dykman, R. A. (1971). Children with specific learning disabilities: Bender Gestalt Test findings and other signs. *Journal of Learning Disabilities, 4*, 437-446.

Acklin, M. W., & Bernat, E. (1987). Depression, alezythymia, and pain prone disorder: A Rorschach study. *Journal of Personality Assessment, 51*, 462-479.

Adams, H., Cooper, G., & Carrera, R. (1963). The Rorschach and the MMPI: A concurrent validity study. *Journal of Projective Techniques, 27*, 23-24.

Adams, R. L., Smigielski, J., & Jenkins, R. L. (1984). Developments of a Satz-Mogel short form of the WAIS-R. *Journal of Consulting and Clinical Psychology, 52*, 908.

Adcock, C.J. (1965). Thematic Apperception Test: A review. In O. K. Buros (Ed.), *The sixth mental measurements yearbook* (Vol. 1) (pp.533-535). Highland Park, NJ: Gryphon Press.

Affleck, D. C., & Mednick, S. A. (1959). The use of the Rorschach test in the prediction of the abrupt terminator in individual psychotherapy. *Journal of Consulting Psychology, 23*, 125-128.

Ahern, S., & Beatty, J. (1979). Pupillary responses vary during information-processing with scholastic aptitude test score. *Science, 205*, 1289-1292.

Akutagawa, D. A. (1956). A study in construct validity of the psychoanalytic concept of latent anxiety and a test of projection distance hypothesis. Unpublished doctoral dissertation. University of Pittsburgh.

Albert, N., & Beck, A. T. (1975). Incidence of depression in early adolescence: A preliminary study. *Journal of Youth and Adolescence, 4*, 301-307.

Albert, S., Fox, H. M., & Kahn, M. W. (1980). Faking psychosis on the Rorschach: Can expert judges detect malingering? *Journal of Personality Assessment, 44*, 115-119.

Alcock, T. (1963). *The Rorschach in practice*. Philadelphia: J.B. Lippincott.

Alker, H. A. (1978). Minnesota Multiphasic Personality Inventory: A review. In O. K. Buros (Ed.), *The eighth mental measurements yearbook* (Vol. 1) (pp.931-935). Highland Park, NJ: Gryphon Press.

Allen, R. M. (1953). *Introduction to the Rorschach technique.* New York: International Universities Press.

Allen, R. M. (1954). *Elements of Rorschach interpretation.* New York: Harper & Row.

Allison, J., & Blatt, S. J. (1964). The relationship of Rorschach whole responses to intelligence. *Journal of Projective Techniques, 28,* 255-260.

Allison, J., Blatt, S. J., & Zimet, C. N. (1968). *The interpretation of psychological tests.* (2nd ed.) New York: Harper & Row.

Allison, J., Blatt, S. J., & Zimet, C. N. (1988). *The interpretation of psychological tests* (2nd ed.). New York: Harper & Row.

Amabile, T. M. (1983). *The social psychology of creativity.* New York: Springer-Verlag.

American Association on Mental Deficiency (AAMD). (1973). *Manual on terminology and classification in mental retardation* (rev. ed.), H. J. Grossman (Ed.). Special publication series no. 2, 11+. Washington, DC: American Association on Mental Deficiency.

American Education Research Association, American Psychological Association, & National Council on Measurement in Education. (1985). *Standards for educational and psychological testing.* Washington, DC: American Psychological Association.

American Psychiatric Association. (1980). *Diagnostic and statistical manual of mental disorders* (3rd ed.). Washington, DC: American Psychiatric Association.

American Psychiatric Association. (1987). *Diagnostic and statistical manual of mental disorders* (3rd ed. rev.). Washington, DC: American Psychiatric Association.

American Psychological Association. (1967). *Casebook on ethical standards of psychologists.* Washington, DC: American Psychological Association.

American Psychological Association. (1981). *Ethical principals of psychologists.* Washington, DC: American Psychological Association.

American Psychological Association. (1983). *Publication manual of the American Psychological Association* (3rd ed.). Washington, DC: American Psychological Association.

American Psychological Association. (1985). *Standards for educational and psychological tests.* Washington, DC: American Psychological Association.

American Psychological Association. (1986). *Guidelines for computer-based test interpretations.* Washington, DC: American Psychological Association.

American Psychological Association. (1987). General guidelines for providers of psychological services. *American Psychologist, 42,* 7.

American Psychological Association. (1988). *Computer use in psychology.* Washington, DC: American Psychological Association.

Ames, L. B. (1959). Further check on the diagnostic validity of the Ames danger signals. *Journal of Projective Techniques, 23,* 291-298.

Ames, L. B., & Gillespie, C. (1973). Significance of Rorschach modified by responses to other projective tests. *Journal of Personality Assessment, 37,* 316-327.

Ames, L. B., Learned, J., Metraux, R., & Walker, R. N. (1952). *Child Rorschach responses.* New York: Hoeber.

Ames, L. B., Metraux, R. W., Rodell, J. L., & Walker, R. N. (1973). *Rorschach responses in old age* (rev. ed.). New York: Brunner/Mazel.

Ames, L. B., Metraux, R. W., Rodell, J. L., & Walker, R. N. (1974). *Child Rorschach responses: Developmental trends from two to ten years* (rev. ed.). New York: Brunner/Mazel.

Ames, L. B., Metraux, R. W., & Walker, R. N. (1971). *Adolescent Rorschach responses: Developmental trends from ten to sixteen years* (2nd ed.). New York: Brunner/Mazel.

Anastasi, A. (1967). Psychologists and psychological testing. *American Psychologist, 22,* 297-306.

Anastasi, A. (1982). *Psychological testing* (5th ed.). New York: Macmillan.

Anastasi, A. (1988). *Psychological testing* (6th ed.). New York: Macmillan.

Anderson, S., & Harthorn, B. H. (in press). The recognition, diagnosis, and treatment of mental disorders by primary care physicians. *Medical Care.*

Anderson, S., & Messick, S. (1974). Social competency in young children. *Developmental Psychology, 10,* 282-293.

Anderson, T. K., Cancelli, A. A., & Kratochwill, T. R. (1984). Self-reported assessment practices of school psychologists: Implications for training and practice. *Journal of School Psychology, 22,* 17-29.

Andert, J. N., Hustak, T., & Dinning, W. D. (1978). Bender-Gestalt reproduction times for retarded adults. *Journal of Clinical Psychology, 34,* 927-929.

Appel, K. E. (1931). Drawings by children as aids in personality studies. *American Journal of Orthopsychiatry, 1,* 129-144.

Appelbaum, A. S., & Tuma, J. M. (1982). The relationship of the WISC-R to academic achievement in a clinical population. *Journal of Clinical Psychology, 38,* 401-405.

Aram, D. M., & Ekelman, B. L. (1986). Cognitive profiles of children with early onset unilateral lesions. *Developmental Neuropsychology, 2,* 155-172.

Archer, R. P. (1984). Use of the MMPI with adolescents: A review of salient issues. *Clinical Psychology Review, 4,* 241-251.

Archer, R. P. (1987). *Using the MMPI with adolescents.* Hillsdale, NJ: Lawrence Erlbaum Associates, Inc.

Archer, R. P., & Gordon, R. (1988). MMPI and Rorschach indices of schizophrenic and depressive diagnosis among adolescent inpatients. *Journal of Personality Assessment, 52,* 276-287.

Archer, R. P., Gordon, R., Giannetti, R. A., & Singles, J. M. (1988). MMPI scale clinical correlates for adolescent inpatients. *Journal of Personality Assessment, 52,* 707-721.

Archer, R. P., Pancoast, D. L., & Klinefelter, D. (1989). A comparison of MMPI code types produced by traditional and recent adolescent norms. *Psychological Assessment, 1,* 23-29.

Armbuster, G. L., Miller, A. S., & Exner, J. E. (1974). Rorschach responses of parachute trainees at the beginning of training and shortly before their first jump. Workshop study No. 201 (unpublished), Rorschach Workshops.

Armstrong, R. G. (1965). A re-evaluation of copied and recalled Bender-Gestalt reproductions. *Journal of Projective Techniques and Personality Assessment, 29,* 134-139.

Armstrong, R. G., & Hauck, P. A. (1960). Correlates of the Bender-Gestalt scores in children. *Journal of Psychological Studies, 11*, 153-158.

Arnaud, S. (1959). A system for deriving quantitative Rorschach measures of certain psychological variables for group comparisons. *Journal of Projective Techniques, 23*, 311-400.

Arnold, M. B. (1949). A demonstration analysis of the TAT in a clinical setting. *Journal of Abnormal and Social Psychology, 44*, 97-111.

Arnold, M. B. (1962). *Story sequence analysis: A new method of measuring and predicting achievement.* New York: Columbia University Press.

Arrindell, W. A. (1980). Dimensional structure and psychopathology correlates of the Fear Survey Schedule (FSS-III) in a phobic population: A factorial definition of agoraphobia. *Behavior Research and Therapy, 18*, 229-242.

Arrindell, W. A., Emmelkamp, D. M. G., & van der Ende, J. (1984). Phobic dimensions: I. Reliability and generalizability across samples, gender, and nations. *Advances in Behavior Research and Therapy, 6*, 207-254.

Arvey, R. D., & Campion, J. E. (1982). The employment interview: A summary and review of recent research. *Personnel Psychology, 35*, 281-322.

Association for Measurement and Evaluation in Guidance. (1984). *Guide to microcomputer software in testing and assessment.* Washington, DC: American Association for Counseling and Development.

Atkinson, J. W., & Feather, N. T. (Eds.). (1966). *A theory of achievement motivation.* New York: John Wiley & Sons, Inc.

Ax, A. F. (1953). The physiological differentiation between fear and anger in humans. *Psychosomatic Medicine, 15*, 433-442.

Baer, J. S., Holt, C. S., & Lichtenstein, E. (1986). Self-efficacy and smoking re-examined: Construct validity and clinical utility. *Journal of Consulting and Clinical Psychology, 54*, 846-852.

Baer, J. S., & Lichtenstein, E. (1988). Classification and prediction of smoking relapse episodes: An exploration of individual differences. *Journal of Consulting and Clinical Psychology, 56*, 104-110.

Bailey, W. J., Shinedling, M. M., & Payne, I. R. (1970). Obese individuals' perception of body image. *Perceptual and Motor Skills, 31*, 617-618.

Baker, L. L., & Jessup, B. A. (1980). The psychophysiology of affective verbal and visual information processing in depression. *Cognitive Therapy and Research, 4*, 135-148.

Bakker, C., Bakker-Rabdau, M., & Breit, S. (1978). The measurement of assertiveness and aggressiveness. *Journal of Personality Assessment, 42*, 277-284.

Baldwin, M. V. (1950). A note regarding the suggested use of the Bender-Gestalt Test as a measure of school readiness. *Journal of Clinical Psychology, 6*, 412.

Bamgbose, O., Smith, G. T., Jesse, R. C., & Groth-Marnat, G. (1980). A survey of the current and future directions of professional psychology in acute general hospitals. *Clinical Psychologist, 33*, 24-25.

Bandura, A. (1977). Self-efficacy: Toward a unifying theory of behavioral change. *Psychological Review, 84*, 191-215.

Bandura, A. (1986). *Social foundations of thought and action: A social cognitive theory.* Englewood Cliffs, NJ: Prentice Hall.

Bannatyne, A. (1974). Diagnosis—a note on recategorization of the WISC scaled scores. *Journal of Learning Disabilities, 7,* 272-273.

Barber, T. X., & Silver, M. J. (1968). Fact, fiction and the experimenter bias effect. *Psychological Bulletin Monograph Supplement, 70,* 1-29.

Barkly, R. A. (1981). Learning disabilities. In E. Mash & L. Terdel (Eds.), *Behavioral assessment of childhood disorders* (pp. 441-482). New York: Guilford Press.

Baron, M., Asnis, L., & Gruen, R. (1981). The Schedule of Schizotypal Personalities (SSP): A diagnostic interview for schizotypal features. *Psychiatry Research, 4,* 213-228.

Barona, A., Reynolds, C., & Chastain, R. (1984). A demographically based index of premorbid intelligence for the WAIS-R. *Journal of Consulting and Clinical Psychology, 26,* 74-75.

Barrios, B. A., & Hartman, D. P. (1988). Fears and anxieties in children. In E. J. Mash & L. G. Terdel (Eds.), *Behavioral assessment of childhood disorders* (2nd ed.). New York: Guilford Press.

Barron, F. (1953). An ego-strength scale which predicts response to psychotherapy. *Journal of Consulting Psychology, 17,* 327-333.

Baucom, D. H. (1980). Independent CPI masculinity and femininity scales: Psychological correlates and a sex role typology. *Journal of Personality Assessment, 44,* 262-271.

Baucom, D. H. (1985). Review of the California Psychological Inventory. In J. V. Mitchel (Ed.), *The ninth mental measurements yearbook.* Highland Park, NJ: Gryphon Press.

Beck, A. T. (1967a). *The diagnosis and management of depression.* Philadelphia: University of Pennsylvania Press.

Beck, A. T. (1967b). *Depression: Clinical experimental and theoretical aspects.* New York: Harper & Row.

Beck, A. T., & Beck, R. W. (1972). Screening depressed patients in family practice: A rapid technique. *Postgraduate Medicine, 52,* 81-85.

Beck, A. T., Rial, W. Y., & Rickels, K. (1974). Short form of depression inventory: Cross-validation. *Psychological Reports, 34,* 1184-1186.

Beck, A. T., Rush, A. J., Shaw, B. F., & Emery, G. (1979). *Cognitive therapy of depression.* New York: Guilford Press.

Beck, A. T., Steer, R. A., & Garbin, M. (1988). Psychometric properties of the Beck Depression Inventory: Twenty-five years of evaluation. *Clinical Psychology Review, 8,* 77-100.

Beck, A. T., Ward, C. H., Mendelson, M., Mock, J., & Erbaugh, J. (1961). An inventory for measuring depression. *Archives of General Psychiatry, 4,* 561-571.

Beck, H. S. (1955). A study of the applicability of the H-T-P to children with respect to the drawn house. *Journal of Clinical Psychology, 11,* 60-63.

Beck, H. S. (1959). A comparison of convulsive organics, non-convulsive organics, and non-organic public school children. *American Journal of Mental Deficiency, 63,* 866-875.

Beck, J. G., & Heimberg, R. G. (1983). Self-report assessment of assertive behavior: A critical analysis. *Behavior Modification, 7,* 451-487.

Beck, S. J. (1937). *Introduction to the Rorschach method: A manual of personality study.* American Orthopsychiatric Association Monograph, 1.

Beck, S. J. (1945). *Rorschach's test: A variety of personality pictures.* (Vol. II). New York: Grune & Stratton.

Beck, S. J. (1951). The Rorschach test: A multi-dimensional test of personality. In H. H. Anderson & G. Anderson (Eds.), *An introduction to projective techniques.* Englewood Cliffs, NJ: Prentice-Hall.

Beck, S. J. (1960). *The Rorschach experiment.* New York: Grune & Stratton.

Beck, S. J. (1961). *Rorschach's test: Basic processes* (Vol. I). New York: Grune & Stratton.

Beck, S. J. (1968). Reality, Rorschach and perceptual theory. In A. I. Rabin (Ed.), *Projective techniques in personality assessment.* New York: Springer.

Beck, S. J., & Molish, H. B. (1967). *Rorschach's test. Vol. II: A variety of personality pictures* (2nd ed.). New York: Grune & Stratton.

Beck, S. J., Rabin, A. I., Thieson, W. C., Molish, H. B., & Thetford, W. N. (1950). The normal personality as projected in the Rorschach test. *Journal of Psychology, 30,* 241-298.

Beier, E. G. (1966). *The silent language of psychotherapy.* New York: Aldine.

Bellack, A. S., Hersen, M., & Turner, S. M. (1979). Relationship of roleplaying and knowledge of appropriate behavior to assertion in the natural environment. *Journal of Consulting and Clinical Psychology, 47,* 670-678.

Bellak, L. (1954). *The Thematic Apperception Test and the Children's Apperception Test in clinical use.* New York: Grune & Stratton.

Bellak, L. (1975). *The TAT, CAT, and SAT in clinical use* (3rd ed.). New York: Grune & Stratton.

Bellak, L. (1986). *The TAT, CAT, and SAT in clinical use.* (4th ed.). New York: Grune & Stratton.

Bellak, L., & Bellak, S. S. (1973). *Manual: Senior apperception test.* Larchmont, NY: C.P.S.

Bellak, L., & Hurvich, M. S. (1966). A human modification of the Children's Apperception Test (CAT-H). *Journal of Projective Techniques and Personality Assessment, 30,* 228-242.

Bem, D., & Funder, D. C. (1978). Predicting more of the people more of the time: Assessing the personality of situations. *Psychological Review, 85,* 485-501.

Bender, L. (1938). *A visual motor gestalt test and its clinical uses,* Research Monograms No. 3. New York: American Orthopsychiatric Association.

Bender, L. (1970). Use of the visual motor Gestalt test in the diagnosis of learning disabilities. *Journal of Special Education, 4,* 29-39.

Bennett, F., & Schubert, D. (1981). Use of local norms to improve configural reproducibility of an MMPI short form. *Journal of Personality Assessment, 45,* 33-39.

Ben-Porath, Y. S., & Butcher, J. (1989). The psychometric stability of rewritten MMPI items. *Journal of Personality Assessment, 53,* 645-653.

Ben-Porath, Y. S., Hostetler, K., Butcher, J. N., & Graham, J. R. (1989). New subscales for the MMPI-2 Social Introversion (Si) Scale. *Psychological Assessment, 1,* 169-174.

Ben-Porath, Y. S., Slutsky, W. S., & Butcher, J. N. (1989). A real-data simulation of computerized adaptive administration of the MMPI. *Psychological Assessment: A Journal of Consulting and Clinical Psychology, 1*, 18-22.

Benton, A. (1974). *The Revised Visual Retention Test* (4th ed.). New York: Psychological Corporation.

Bergin, A. E. (1971). The evaluation of therapeutic outcomes. In A. E. Bergin & S. L. Garfield (Eds.), *Handbook of psychotherapy and behavior change*. New York: John Wiley & Sons, Inc.

Bern, D. J., & Funder, D. C. (1978). Predicting more of the people more of the time: Assessing the personality of situations. *Psychological Review, 85*, 485-501.

Bernstein, L. (1956). The examiner as an inhibiting factor in clinical testing. *Journal of Consulting Psychology, 20*, 287-290.

Berry, K. K. (1975). Teacher impressions of psychological reports on children. *Journal of Pediatric Psychology, 3*, 11-14.

Beutler, L. E., Karacan, I., Anch, A. M., Salis, P., Scott, F. B., & Williams, R. (1975). MMPI and MIT discriminators of biogenic and psychogenic impotence. *Journal of Consulting and Clinical Psychology, 43*, 899-903.

Billingslea, F. Y. (1948). The Bender-Gestalt: An objective scoring method and validating data. *Journal of Clinical Psychology, 4*, 1-27.

Billingslea, F. Y. (1963). The Bender-Gestalt: A review and a perspective. *Psychological Bulletin, 60*, 233-251.

Binet, A., & Simon, T. (1908). Le développement de l'intelligence chez les enfants. *L'Anneé Psychologique, 14*, 1-94.

Binet, A., & Simon, T. (1916). *The development of intelligence in children* (E. S. Kit, Trans.). Baltimore: Williams & Wilkins.

Blaha, J., & Wallbrown, F. H. (1984). Hierarchical analyses of the WISC and WISC-R: Synthesis and clinical implications. *Journal of Clinical Psychology, 40*, 556-571.

Blain, G. H., Bergner, R. M., Lewis, M. L., & Goodstein, M. A. (1981). The use of objectively scorable House-Tree-Person indicators to establish child abuse. *Journal of Clinical Psychology, 37*, 667-673.

Blashfield, R. K., & Draguns, I. G. (1975). Evaluative criteria for psychiatric classification. *Journal of Abnormal Psychology, 85*, 140-148.

Blatt, S. J., & Allison, J. (1968). The intelligence test in personality assessment. In A.I. Rabin (Ed.), *Projective techniques in personality assessment*. New York: Springer.

Block, J. (1965). *The challenge of response sets: Unconfounding meaning, acquiescence, and social desirability in the MMPI*. New York: Appleton-Century-Crofts.

Block, J., & Bailey, D. Q. (1955). Q-sort item analysis of a number of MMPI scales. *Officer Education Research Laboratory, Technical Memorandum*. (OERL-TM-55-7).

Blum, G. S. (1950). *The Blacky pictures and manual*. New York: Psychological Corp.

Blum, G. S. (1962). A guide for research use of the Blacky pictures. *Journal of Projective Techniques, 26*, 3-29.

Blum, G. S. (1968). Assessment of psychodynamic variables by the Blacky Pictures. In P. McReynolds (Ed.), *Advances in psychological assessment* (Vol. I). Palo Alto: Science & Behavior Books.

Blum, L. H., Davidson, H. H., & Fieldsteel, N. D. (1975). *A Rorschach workbook*. New York: International Universities Press.

Boerger, A. R. (1975). *The utility of some alternative approaches to MMPI scale construction*. Doctoral dissertation, Kent State University.

Bolander, K. (1977). *Assessing personality through tree drawings*. New York: Basic Books.

Boll, T. J. (1974). Behavioral correlates of cerebral damage in children age 9-14. In R. M. Reitan & L. A. Davison (Eds.), *Clinical neuropsychology: Current status and application*. Washington, DC: V. H. Winston & Sons.

Boll, T. J. (1981). The Halstead-Reitan neuropsychological battery. In S. B. Filskov & T. J. Boll (Eds.), *Handbook of clinical neuropsychology*. New York: John Wiley & Sons, Inc.

Bonarius, H. (1984). Prediction or anticipation: Some implications of personal construct psychology for professional practice. *Jyvaskyla Studies in Education: Psychology and Social Research, 54*, 190-206.

Borkowski, J. G. (1985). Signs of intelligence: Strategy, generalization and metacognition. In S. R. Yussen (Ed.), *The growth of reflection in children*. (pp. 105-144). Orlando, FL: Academic Press.

Bornstein, P. H., Bridgewater, C. A., Hickey, J. S., & Sweeney, T. M. (1980). Characteristics and trends in behavioral assessment: An archival analysis. *Behavioral Assessment, 2*, 125-133.

Bornstein, R. A. (1983). Verbal I.Q.—Performance I.Q. discrepancies on the Wechsler Adult Intelligence Scale-Revised in patients with unilateral or bilateral cerebral dysfunction. *Journal of Consulting and Clinical Psychology, 51*, 779-789.

Bornstein, R. A., & Matarazzo, J. D. (1982). Wechsler VIQ versus PIQ differences in cerebral dysfunction: A literature review with emphasis on sex differences. *Journal of Clinical Neuropsychology, 4*, 319-334.

Bornstein, R. A., Suga, L., & Prifitera, A. (1987). Incidence of verbal I.Q.-Performance I.Q. discrepancies at various levels of education. *Journal of Clinical Psychology, 43*, 387-389.

Borus, J. F., Howes, M. J., Devins, N. P., & Rosenberg, R. (1988). Primary health care providers' recognition and diagnosis of mental disorders in their patients. *General Hospital Psychiatry, 10*, 317-321.

Bradway, K., Lion, E., & Corrigan, H. (1946). The use of the Rorschach in a psychiatric study of promiscuous girls. *Rorschach Research Exchange, 9*, 105-110.

Brandt, D. (1982). Comparison of various WISC-R summary scores for a psychiatric sample. *Journal of Clinical Psychology, 38*, 830-837.

Brandt, H., & Giebink, J. (1968). Concreteness and congruence in psychologists' reports to teachers. *Psychology in the Schools, 5*, 87-89.

Brar, H. S. (1970). Rorschach content responses of East Indian psychiatric patients. *Journal of Projective Techniques and Personality Assessment, 34*, 88-94.

Braun, P. R., & Reynolds, D. J. (1969). A factor analysis of a 100-item fear survey inventory. *Behavior Research and Therapy, 7*, 399-402.

Bravo, L. (1972). The conservation, stimulation, and development of superior mental ability. Paper presented to the California Association of School Psychologists.

Brayfield, A. H. (Ed.). (1965). Testing and public policy. *American Psychologist, 20,* 857-1005.

Breen, M. J. (1982). Comparison of educationally handicapped student's scores on the Revised Developmental Test of Visual-Motor Integration and Bender-Gestalt. *Perceptual and Motor Skills, 54,* 1227-1230.

Brennan, M., & Reichard, S. (1943). Use of the Rorschach test in predicting hypnotizability. *Bulletin of the Menninger Clinic, 7,* 183-187.

Brenner, O. C., & Bertsch, T. M. (1983). Do assertive people prefer merit pay? *Psychological Reports, 52,* 595-598.

Brewin, C. R. (1985). Depression and causal attributions: What is their relation? *Psychological Bulletin, 98,* 297-309.

Bricklin, H. (1984). *Bricklin Perceptual Scales.* Furlong, PA: Village Publishing Center.

Brodsky, S. L. (1972). Shared results and open files with the client. *Professional Psychology, 3,* 362-364.

Brooker, B. H., & Cyr, J. J. (1986). Tables for clinicians to use to convert WAIS-R short forms. *Journal of Clinical Psychology, 42,* 982-986.

Brooks, B. L., & Hosie, T. W. (1984). Assumptions and interpretations of the SOMPA in estimating learning potential. *Counselor Education and Supervision, 23,* 290-299.

Brown, D., & Tolor, A. (1957). Human figure drawings as indicators of sexual identification and inversion. *Perceptual and Motor Skills, 7,* 199-211.

Brown, F. (1953). An exploratory study of dynamic factors in the content of the Rorschach protocol. *Journal of Projective Techniques, 17,* 251-279.

Brown, F. G. (1965). The Bender-Gestalt and acting out. In L. E. Abt & S. L. Weissman (Eds.), *Acting Out: Theoretical and Clinical Aspects.* New York: Grune & Stratton.

Brown, F. G. (1979). The SOMPA: A system of measuring potential abilities. *School Psychology Digest, 8,* 37-46.

Brown, W. R., & McGuire, J. M. (1976). Current assessment practices. *Professional Psychology, 7,* 475-484.

Buck, J. N. (1948). The H-T-P technique, a qualitative and quantitative scoring manual. *Journal of Clinical Psychology, 4,* 317-396.

Buck, J. N. (1966). *The House-Tree-Person technique: Revised manual.* Beverly Hills, CA: Western Psychological Services.

Buck, J. N., & Hammer, E. F. (Eds.). (1969). *Advances in House-Tree-Person Techniques: Variations and applications.* Los Angeles: Western Psychological Services.

Buhler, C., & LeFever, D. (1947). A Rorschach study on the psychological characteristics of alcoholics. *Quarterly Journal of Studies on Alcoholism, 8,* 197-260.

Burke, H., & Marcus, R. (1977). MacAndrew MMPI Alcoholism Scale: Alcoholism and drug addiction. *Journal of Psychology, 96,* 141-148.

Burley, T., & Handler, L. (1970). *Creativity, empathy, and intuition in DAP interpretation.* Unpublished manuscript.

Burns, R. C. (1970). *Kinetic Family Drawings (KFD): An introduction to understanding children through kinetic drawings.* New York: Brunner/Mazel.

Burns, R. C. (1982). *Self-growth in families: Kinetic Family Drawings (K-F-D): Research and application.* New York: Brunner/Mazel.

Burns, R. C. (1987). *Kinetic-House-Tree-Person (K-H-T-P).* New York: Brunner/Mazel.

Burns, R. C., & Kaufman, S. H. (1972). *Action, styles, and symbols in Kinetic Family Drawings (K-F-D).* New York: Brunner/Mazel.

Buros, O. K. (Ed.). (1972a). *Personality tests and reviews.* Highland Park, NJ: Gryphon Press.

Buros, O. K. (Ed.). (1972b). *Seventh mental measurements yearbook.* Highland Park, NJ: Gryphon Press.

Buros, O. K. (Ed.). (1974). *Tests in print II.* Highland Park, NJ: Gryphon Press.

Buros, O. K. (Ed.). (1978). *Eighth mental measurements yearbook.* Highland Park, NJ: Gryphon Press.

Butcher, J. N. (1979). Use of the MMPI in personnel selection. In J. N. Butcher (Ed.), *New developments in the use of the MMPI.* Minneapolis: University of Minnesota Press.

Butcher, J. N. (1987). *Computerized psychological assessment: A practitioner's guide.* New York: Basic Books.

Butcher, J. N., Ball, B., & Ray, E. (1964). Effects of socioeconomic level on MMPI differences in Negro-white college students. *Journal of Consulting Psychology, 11,* 83-87.

Butcher, J. N., & Clark, L. A. (1979). Recent trends and application. In J. N. Butcher (Ed.), *New developments in the use of the MMPI.* Minneapolis: University of Minnesota Press.

Butcher, J. N., Dahlstrom, W. G., Graham, J. R., Tellegen, A., & Kaemmer, B. (1989). *Manual for administration and scoring: MMPI-2.* Minneapolis: University of Minnesota Press.

Butcher, J. N., Graham, J. R., Williams, C. L., & Ben-Porath, Y. S. (1989). *Development and use of the MMPI-2 content scales.* Minneapolis: University of Minnesota Press.

Butcher, J. N., Keller, S. K., & Bacon, S. F. (1985). Current developments and future directions in computerized personality assessment. *Journal of Consulting and Clinical Psychology, 53,* 803-815.

Butcher, J. N., Kendall, P. C., & Hoffman, N. (1980). MMPI short forms: CAUTION. *Journal of Consulting and Clinical Psychology, 48,* 275-278.

Butcher, J. N., & Owen, P. L. (1978). Objective personality inventories: Recent research and some contemporary issues. In B. B. Wolman (Ed.), *Clinical diagnosis of mental disorders: A handbook.* New York: Plenum.

Butcher, J. N., & Pancheri, P. (1976). *A handbook of cross-national MMPI research.* Minneapolis: University of Minnesota Press.

Butcher, J. N., & Pope, K. S. (1989). MMPI-2: A practical guide to psychometric, clinical, and ethical issues. Unpublished manuscript.

Byerly, E. C., & Carlson, W. A. (1982). Comparison among inpatients, outpatients, and normals on three self-report depression inventories. *Journal of Clinical Psychology, 38,* 797-804.

Byrne, D. (1964). Repression-sensitization as a dimension of personality. In B.A. Mohrer (Ed.), *Progress in experimental personality research* (Vol. 1). New York: Academic Press.

Byrne, D., Golightly, C., & Sheffield, J. (1965). The repression-sensitization scale as a measure of adjustment: Relationship with the CPI. *Journal of Consulting Psychology, 29*, 585-589.

Cacioppo, J. T., Glass, C. R., & Merluzzi, T. V. (1979). Self-statements and self-evaluations: A cognitive response analysis of heterosocial anxiety. *Cognitive Therapy and Research, 3*, 249-262.

Caldwell, A. B. (1988). *MMPI supplemental scale manual.* Los Angeles : Caldwell Report.

Caldwell-Colbert, A. T., & Robinson, W. L. (1984). Utilization and predicted trends of behavioral inventories. *Journal of Behavioral Assessment, 6*, 189-196.

Calvin, J. (1975). *A replicated study of the concurrent validity of the Harris subscales for the MMPI.* Unpublished doctoral dissertation, Kent State University, Kent, OH.

Campione, J. C., & Brown, A. L. (1978). Toward a theory of intelligence: Contributions from research with retarded children. *Intelligence, 2*, 279-304.

Canter, A. (1963). A background interference procedure for graphomotor tests in the study of deficit. *Perceptual and Motor Skills, 16*, 914.

Canter, A. (1966). A background interference procedure to increase sensitivity of the Bender-Gestalt Test to organic brain disorder. *Journal of Consulting Psychology, 30*, 91-97.

Canter, A. (1971). A comparison of the background interference procedure effect in schizophrenic, non-schizophrenic, and organic patients. *Journal of Clinical Psychology, 27*, 473-474.

Canter, A. (1976). *The Canter background interference procedure for the Bender-Gestalt Test: Manual for administration, scoring, and interpretation.* Nashville, TN: Counselor Recordings and Tests.

Carkhuff, R. R. (1969). *Helping and human relations. I: Selection and training. II: Practice and research.* New York: Holt, Rinehart & Winston.

Carlson, J. G. (1982). Some concepts of perceived control and their relationship to bodily self-control. *Journal of Biofeedback and Self-Regulation.*

Carlson, K., Tucker, G., Harrow, M., & Quinlan, D. (1971). Body image and mental illness. In I. Jakab (Ed.), *Psychiatry and art: Vol. 3 Conscious and unconscious expressive art.* Basel, Switzerland: Karger.

Carnes, G. D., & Bates, R. (1971). Rorschach anatomy response correlates in rehabilitation of failure subjects. *Journal of Personality Assessments, 35*, 527-537.

Carson, R. C., Butcher, J. N., & Coleman, J. C. (1988). *Abnormal Psychology and Modern Life* (8th ed.). Glenview, IL: Scott, Foresman & Co.

Cartwright, R. D. (1986). Affect and dream work from an information processing point of view. *Journal of Mind and Behavior, 7*, 411-428.

Caruso, K. R. (1988). *Manual for the Projective Storytelling Cards.* Sarasota, FL: Professional Resource Exchange.

Cass, W. A., & McReynolds, P. A. (1951). A contribution to Rorschach norms. *Journal of Consulting and Clinical Psychology, 15*, 178-183.

Cattell, R. B. (1963). Theory of fluid and crystalized intelligence: A critical experiment. *Journal of Educational Psychology, 54*, 1-22.

Cattell, R. B., Eber, H. W., & Tatsuoka, M. M. (1970). *Handbook for the Sixteen Personality Factor Questionnaire*. Champaign, IL: Institute for Personality and Abilities Testing.

Cauthen, N. R., Sandman, C. A., Kilpatrick, D. G., & Deabler, H. L. (1969). DAP correlates of Sc scores on the MMPI. *Journal of Projective and Personality Assessment, 33*, 262-264.

Cella, D. (1984). The modified WAIS-R: An extension and revision. *Journal of Clinical Psychology, 40*, 801-804.

Chambers, W. J., Puig-Antich, J., Hirsch, M., Paez, P., Ambrosini, P. J., Tabrizi, M. A., & Davies, M. (1985). The assessment of affective disorders in children and adolescents by semistructured interview: Test-retest reliability of the Schedule for Affective Disorders and Schizophrenia for School Age, Present Episode Version. *Archives of General Psychiatry, 42*, 696-702.

Chapman, L. J., & Chapman, J. P. (1967). Genesis of popular but erroneous psychodiagnostic observations. *Journal of Abnormal Psychology, 72*, 193-204.

Cheung, F. M. (Ed.). (1986). *The Chinese Minnesota Multiphasic Personality Inventory: Research and applications*. (Occasional paper No. 12). Hong Kong: Centre for Hong Kong Studies, The Chinese University of Hong Kong.

Cheung, F., & Song, W. (1989). A review on the clinical applications of the Chinese MMPI. *Psychological Assessment, 1*, 230-237.

Chusmir, L. H. (1985). Short-form scoring for McClelland's version of the TAT. *Perceptual and Motor Skills, 61*, 1047-1052.

Ciminero, A. R., Calhoun, K. S., & Adams, H. E. (Eds.). (1977). *Handbook of behavioral assessment*. New York: Wiley-Interscience.

Clark, C. G., & Miller, H. L. (1971). Validation of Gilberstadt and Duker's 8-6 profile type on a black sample. *Psychological Reports, 29*, 259-264.

Clawson, A. (1959). The Bender Visual Motor Gestalt Test as an index of emotional disturbance in children. *Journal of Projective Techniques, 23*, 198-206.

Clawson, A. (1962). *The Bender Visual Motor Gestalt for children: A manual*. Beverly Hills, CA: Western Psychological Services.

Cleveland, S. E. (1976). Reflections on the rise and fall of psychodiagnosis. *Professional Psychology, 7*, 309-318.

Clopton, J. R. (1978a). A note on the MMPI as a suicide predictor. *Journal of Consulting and Clinical Psychology, 46*, 335-336.

Clopton, J. R. (1978b). Alcoholism and the MMPI: A review. *Journal of Studies on Alcohol, 39*, 1540-1558.

Clopton, J. R., Weiner, R. H., & Davis, H. G. (1980). Use of the MMPI in identification of alcoholic psychiatric patients. *Journal of Consulting and Clinical Psychology, 48*, 416-417.

Coan, R. (1956). A factor analysis of Rorschach determinants. *Journal of Projective Techniques, 20*, 280-287.

Coche, E., & Sillitti, J. A. (1983). The Thematic Apperception Test as an outcome measure in psychotherapy. *Psychotherapy: Theory, Research, and Practice, 20*, 41-46.

Cohen, J. (1959). The factorial structure of the WISC at ages 7-6, 10-6, and 13-6. *Journal of Consulting Psychology, 23,* 285-299.

Coleman, J. C., Butcher, J. N., & Carson, R. C. (1980). *Abnormal psychology and modern life,* (6th ed.). Glenview, IL: Scott, Foresman & Co.

Collins, D. J. (1967). Psychological selection of drill sergeants: An exploratory attempt in a new program. *Military Medicine, 132,* 713-715.

Cone, J. D. (1977). The relevance of reliability and validity for behavioral assessment. *Behavior Therapy, 8,* 411-426.

Cone, J. D. (1978). The behavioral assessment grid (BAG): A conceptual framework and taxonomy. *Behavior Therapy, 9,* 882-888.

Conley, J. J. (1981). An MMPI typology of male alcoholics. *Journal of Personality Assessment, 45,* 40-43.

Conoley, J. C., & Kramer, J. J. (Eds.). (1989). *The tenth mental measurements yearbook.* Lincoln: University of Nebraska Press.

Cook, M. L., & Peterson, C. (1986). Depressive irrationality. *Cognitive Therapy and Research, 10,* 293-298.

Cooper, H. M., & Rosenthal, R. (1980). Statistical versus traditional procedures for summarizing research findings. *Psychological Bulletin, 87,* 442-449.

Cooper, J. O., Heron, T. B., & Heward, W. L. (1987). *Applied behavior analysis.* Columbus, OH: Merrill.

Cooper, W. H. (1981). Ubiquitous halo. *Psychological Bulletin, 90,* 218-244.

Costantino, G., & Malgady, R. G. (1983). Verbal fluency of Hispanic, Black and White children on TAT and TEMAS, a new thematic apperception test. *Hispanic Journal of Behavioral Sciences, 5,* 199-206.

Costantino, G., Malgady, R. G., Rogler, L. H., & Tsui, E. C. (1988). Discriminant analysis of clinical outpatients and public school children by TEMAS: A thematic apperception test for Hispanics and Blacks. *Journal of Personality Assessment, 52,* 670-678.

Costello, C. G. (1958). The Rorschach records of suicidal patients. *Journal of Projective Techniques, 22,* 272-275.

Costello, E. J., Edelbrock, C. S., & Costello, A. J. (1985). Validity of the NIMH Diagnostic Interview Schedule for Children: A comparison between psychiatric and pediatric referrals. *Journal of Abnormal and Child Psychology, 13,* 579-595.

Costello, E. J., Edelbrock, C. S., Duncan, M. K., & Kalas, R. (1984). *Testing of the NIMH Diagnostic Interview Schedule for Children (DISC) in a clinical population. Final report to the Center for Epidemiological Studies, National Institute for Mental Health.* Pittsburgh: University of Pittsburgh.

Costello, R. M., & Wicott, K. A. (1984). Impression management and testing for locus of control in an alcoholic sample. *International Journal of the Addictions, 19,* 45-56.

Cox, F. N., & Sarason, S. B. (1954). Test anxiety and Rorschach performance. *Journal of Abnormal and Social Psychology, 49,* 371-377.

Crenshaw, D. A., Bohn, S., Hoffman, M., Matheus, J. M., & Offenbach, S. G. (1968). The use of projective methods in research: 1947-1965. *Journal of Projective Techniques and Personality Assessment, 32*, 2-9.

Cronbach, L. J. (1978). Black Intelligence Test of Cultural Homogeneity: A review. In O. K. Buros (Ed.), *The eighth mental measurements yearbook* (Vol. 1). Highland Park, NJ: Gryphon Press.

Cross, D. T., & Burger, G. (1982). Ethnicity as a variable in responses to California Psychological Inventory items. *Journal of Personality Assessment, 46*, 155-158.

Crowne, D. P., & Marlowe, D. (1964). *The approval motive: Studies in evaluative dependence*. New York: John Wiley & Sons, Inc.

Crumpton, E. (1956). The influence of color on the Rorschach test. *Journal of Projective Techniques, 20*, 150-158.

Culkin, J., & Perrotto, R. S. (1985). Assertiveness factors and depression in a sample of college women. *Psychological Reports, 57*, 1015-1020.

Cunningham, T. R., & Thorp, R. G. (1981). The influence of settings on accuracy and reliability of behavioral observation. *Behavioral Assessment, 3*, 67-78.

Dahlstrom, W. G. (1969). Recurrent issues in the development of the MMPI. In J. N. Butcher (Ed.), *MMPI: Research developments and clinical applications*. New York: McGraw-Hill.

Dahlstrom, W. G. (1980). Altered versions of the MMPI. In W. G. Dahlstrom & L. Dahlstrom (Eds.), *Basic readings on the MMPI: A new selection on personality measurement*. (pp. 386-393). Minneapolis: University of Minnesota Press.

Dahlstrom, W. G., Lachar, D., & Dahlstrom, L. E. (1986). *MMPI patterns of American minorities*. Minneapolis: University of Minnesota Press.

Dahlstrom, W. G., & Welsh, G. S. (1960). *An MMPI handbook: A guide to use in clinical practice and research*. Minneapolis: University of Minnesota Press.

Dahlstrom, W. G., Welsh, G. S., & Dahlstrom, L. E. (1972). *An MMPI handbook (Vol. 1), Clinical Interpretation*. Minneapolis: University of Minnesota Press.

Dahlstrom, W. G., Welsh, G. S., & Dahlstrom, L. E. (1975). *An MMPI handbook, (Vol. 2), Research developments and applications*. Minneapolis: University of Minnesota Press.

Dana, R. H. (1955). Clinical diagnosis and objective TAT scoring. *Journal of Abnormal and Social Psychology, 50*, 19-24.

Dana, R. H. (1965). Review of the Rorschach. In O. K. Buros (Ed.), *Sixth mental measurements yearbook*. Highland Park, NJ: Gryphon.

Dana, R. H. (1968). Six constructs to define Rorschach M. *Journal of Projective Techniques and Personality Assessment, 32*, 138-145.

Dana, R. H. (1982). *A human science model for personality assessment with projective techniques*. Springfield, IL: Charles C. Thomas.

Dana, R. H. (1984). Personality assessment: Practice and teaching for the next decade. *Journal of Personality Assessment, 48*, 46-57.

Dana, R. H. (1985). Thematic Apperception Test (TAT). In C. S. Newmark (Ed.), *Major psychological assessment instruments*. Newton, MA: Allyn & Bacon.

Dana, R. H., & Cocking, R. R. (1968). Cue parameters, cue probabilities, and clinical judgment. *Journal of Clinical Psychology, 24*, 475-480.

Dana, R. H., Field, K., & Bolton, B. (1983). Variations of the Bender-Gestalt Test: Implications for training and practice. *Journal of Personality Assessment, 47*, 76-84.

Datel, W. E., Hall, F. D., & Rufe, C. P. (1965). Measurement of achievement motivation in army security agency foreign language candidates. *Educational and Psychological Measurement, 25*, 539-545.

Davis, W. E., Beck, S. J., & Ryan, T. A. (1973). Race-related and education related MMPI profile differences among hospitalized schizophrenics. *Journal of Clinical Psychology, 29*, 478-479.

Dawes, R. M., & Corrigan, B. (1974). Linear models in decision making. *Psychological Bulletin, 81*, 95-106.

Deabler, H. L. (1969). The H-T-P in group testing and as a screening device. In J. N. Buck & E. F. Hammer (Eds.), *Advances in the House-Tree-Person Technique: Variations and applications.* Los Angeles: Western Psychological Services.

Dean, R. S. (1982). Neuropsychological assessment. In T. Kratochwill (Ed.), *Advances in school psychology.* (Vol. 2). Hillsdale, NJ: Erlbaum.

Del Greco, L., Breitbach, L., & McCarthy, R. H. (1981). The Rathus Assertiveness Schedule modified for early adolescents. *Journal of Behavioral Assessment, 3*, 321-328.

Del Greco, L., Breitbach, L., Rumer, S., McCarthy, R. H., & Suissa, S. (1986). Further examination of the reliability of the Modified Rathus Assertiveness Schedule. *Adolescence, 21*, 483-485.

Delaney, R. C. (1982). Screening for organicity: The problem of subtle neuropsychological deficit and diagnosis. *Journal of Clinical Psychology, 38*, 843-846.

Delatte, J. G., & Hendrickson, N. J. (1982). Human figure drawing size as a measure of self-esteem. *Journal of Personality Assessment, 46*, 603-606.

Delay, J., Pichot, P., Lemperiere, T., & Mirouze, R. (1963). Classification of depressive states: Agreement between etiology and symptomatology: 2. Results of Beck's Questionnaire. *Encephale, 52*, 497-505.

Di Nardo, P. A., O'Brien, G. T., Barlow, D. H., Waddel, M. T., & Blanchard, E. B. (1983). Reliability of DSM-III anxiety disorder categories using a new structured interview. *Archives of General Psychiatry, 40*, 1070-1074.

Dibner, A. S., & Korn, E. J. (1969). Group administration of the Bender-Gestalt test to predict early school performance. *Journal of Clinical Psychology, 49*, 822-834.

Dicken, C. F. (1960). Simulated patterns on the California Psychological Inventory. *Journal of Counseling Psychology, 7*, 24-31.

DiClemente, C. (1986). Self-efficacy and the addictive behaviors. *Journal of Social and Clinical Psychology, 4*, 302-315.

Dies, R. R. (1972). Personal gullibility or pseudodiagnosis: A further test of the "fallacy of personal validation." *Journal of Clinical Psychology, 28*, 47-50.

Diller, L., Ben-Yishay, Y., Gertsman, L. J., Goodkin, R., Gordon, W., & Weinberg, J. (1976). *Studies in cognition and rehabilitation in hemiplegia* (Rehabilitation Monograph, No. 50). New York: New York University Medical Center, Institute of Rehabilitation Medicine.

Dimatteo, M. R., & Taranta, A. (1976). Nonverbal communication and physician-patient rapport: An empirical study. *Professional Psychology, 10,* 540-547.

Donahue, D., & Sattler, J. M. (1971). Personality variables affecting WAIS scores. *Journal of Consulting Psychology, 36,* 441.

Donnelly, E. F., & Murphy, D. L. (1974). Primary affective disorder: Bender-Gestalt sequence of placement as an indicator of impulse control. *Perceptual and Motor Skills, 38,* 1079-1082.

Dorken, H. A. (1954). A psychometric evaluation of 68 medical interns. *Journal of the Canadian Medical Association, 70,* 41-45.

Dougherty, T. W., Ebert, R. J., & Callender, J. C. (1986). Policy capturing in the employment interview. *Journal of Applied Psychology, 71,* 9-15.

Dove, A. (1968). Taking the Chitling Test. *Newsweek, 72,* 51-52.

Draguns, J. G., Haley, E. M., & Phillips, L. (1967). Studies of the Rorschach content: A review of the research literature. Part 1: Traditional content categories. *Journal of Projective Techniques and Personality Assessment, 31,* 3-32.

Drake, L. E. (1946). A social I.E. scale for the MMPI. *Journal of Applied Psychology, 30,* 51-54.

Dudek, S. Z. (1968). M and active energy system correlating Rorschach M with ease of creative expression. *Journal of Projective Techniques and Personality Assessment, 32,* 453-461.

Dudley, H. K., Craig, E. M., Mason, M., & Hirsch, S. M. (1976). Drawings of the opposite sex: Continued use of the Draw-A-Person test and young state hospital patients. *Journal of Adolescence, 5,* 201-219.

Duran, P., Pechoux, R., Escafit, M., & Davidow, P. (1949). Le contenu des réponses dans le test de Rorschach chez les schizophrènes. *Annual of Medical Psychologie, 107,* 198-200.

Durand, V. M., Blanchard, E. B., & Mindell, J. A. (1988). Training in projective testing: Survey of clinical training directors and internship directors. *Professional Psychology: Research and Practice, 19,* 236-238.

Edelbrock, C., Costello, A. J., Duncan, M. K., Kales, R., & Conover, N. C. (1985). Age differences in the reliability of the psychiatric interview of the child. *Child Development, 56,* 265-275.

Edell, W. S. (1987). Role of structure in disordered thinking in borderline and schizophrenic disorders. *Journal of Personality Assessment, 51,* 23-41.

Edwards, A. L. (1957). *The social desirability variables in personality assessment and research.* New York: Dryden Press.

Edwards, A. L. (1964). Social desirability and performance on the MMPI. *Psychometrika, 29,* 295-308.

Egeland, B. R. (1969). Examiner expectancy: Effects on the scoring of the WISC. *Psychology in the Schools, 6,* 313-315.

Eichler, R. M. (1951). Experimental stress and alleged Rorschach indices of anxiety. *Journal of Abnormal and Social Psychology, 46,* 169-177.

Eisdorfer, C. (1963). The WAIS performance of the aged: A retest evaluation. *Journal of Gerontology, 18,* 169-172.

Elashoff, J., & Snow, R. E. (Eds.). (1971). *Pygmalion revisited*. Worthington, OH: C.A. Jones.

Elion, V. H., & Megangee, E. I. (1975). Validity of the MMPI Pd scale among black males. *Journal of Consulting and Clinical Psychology, 43*, 166-172.

Elliot, L. L. (1960). WAF performance on the California Psychological Inventory. *Wright Air Development Division Technical Note 60-218*, Lackland AFB, Air Research and Development Command.

Elstein, A. A. (1965). Behavioral correlates of the Rorschach shading determinant. *Journal of Consulting Psychology, 29*, 231-236.

Embretson, S. (1986). Intelligence and its measurement: Extending contemporary theory to existing tests. In R. J. Sternberg (Ed.), *Advances in the psychology of human intelligence.* (Vol. 3). Hillsdale, NJ: Erlbaum.

Endicott, J., & Spitzer, R. L. (1978). A diagnostic interview: The schedule for affective disorders and schizophrenia. *Archives of General Psychiatry, 35*, 837-844.

Enelow, A. J., & Wexler, M. (1966). *Psychiatry in the practice of medicine.* New York: Oxford.

Engel, R., & Fay, W. H. (1972). Visual evoked responses at birth, verbal scores at three years, and I.Q. at four years. *Developmental Medicine and Child Neurology, 14*, 283-289.

Entwisle, D. R. (1972). To dispel fantasies about fantasy-based measures of achievement motivation. *Psychological Bulletin, 77*, 377-391.

Eppinger, M. G., Craig, P. L., Adams, R. L., & Parsons, O. A. (1987). The WAIS-R Index for estimating premorbid intelligence: Cross-validation and clinical utility. *Journal of Consulting and Clinical Psychology, 55*, 86-90.

Equal Employment Opportunity Commission (EEOC). (1970). Guidelines on employee selection procedures. *Federal Register, 35*, 12333-12336.

Erginel, A. (1972). On the test-retest reliability of the Rorschach. *Journal of Personality Assessment, 36*, 203-212.

Eron, L. D. (1950). A normative study of the Thematic Apperception Test. *Psychological Monographs, 64*, 315.

Exner, J. E. (1961). The influence of achromatic color in Cards IV and VI of the Rorschach. *Journal of Projective Techniques, 25*, 38-41.

Exner, J. E. (1969). *The Rorschach systems.* New York: Grune & Stratton.

Exner, J. E. (1974). *The Rorschach: A comprehensive system Vol. 1.* New York: John Wiley & Sons, Inc.

Exner, J. E. (1978). *The Rorschach: A comprehensive system: Vol. 2. Current research and advanced interpretations.* New York: John Wiley & Sons, Inc.

Exner, J. E. (1979). The effects of voluntary restraint on Rorschach retests. Workshops Study No. 258 (unpublished), Rorschach Workshops.

Exner, J. E. (1983). Rorschach assessment. In I. B. Weiner (Ed.), *Clinical methods in clinical psychology* (2nd ed.). New York: John Wiley & Sons, Inc.

Exner, J. E. (1984). *A computer program to assist in Rorschach interpretation.* (Revised). Bayville, NY: Rorschach Workshops.

Exner, J. E. (1986). *The Rorschach: A comprehensive system: Volume 1. Basic foundations* (2nd ed.). New York: John Wiley & Sons, Inc.

Exner, J. E. (1988). Problems with brief Rorschach protocols. *Journal of Personality Assessment, 52*, 640-647.

Exner, J. E., Armbuster, G. L., & Viglione, D. (1978). The temporal stability of some Rorschach features. *Journal of Personality Assessment, 42*, 474-482.

Exner, J. E., Armbuster, G. L., Walker, E. J., & Cooper, W. H. (1975). Anticipation of elective surgery as manifest in Rorschach records. Workshops Study No. 213 (unpublished), Rorschach Workshops.

Exner, J. E., & Bryant, E. L. (1974). Rorschach responses of subjects recently divorced or separated. Workshops Study No. 206 (unpublished), Rorschach Workshops.

Exner, J. E., & Exner, D. E. (1972). How clinicians use the Rorschach. *Journal of Personality Assessment, 36*, 403-408.

Exner, J. E., & Hillman, L. (1984). A comparison of content distributions for the records of 76 paranoid schizophrenics and 76 nonparanoid schizophrenics. Workshops Study No. 293 (unpublished), Rorschach Workshops.

Exner, J. E., & Kazaoka, K. (1978). Dependency gestures of 16 assertiveness trainees as related to Rorschach movement responses. Workshops Study No. 261 (unpublished), Rorschach Workshops.

Exner, J. E., Leura, A. V., & George, L. M. (1976). A replication of the Masling study using four groups of new examiners with two seating arrangements and ride evaluation. Workshops Study No. 256 (unpublished), Rorschach Workshops.

Exner, J. E., & Murillo, L. G. (1973). Effectiveness of regressive ECT with process schizophrenics. *Diseases of the Nervous System, 34*, 44-48.

Exner, J. E., & Murillo, L. G. (1977). A long-term follow up of schizophrenics treated with regressive ECT. *Diseases of the Nervous System, 38*, 162-168.

Exner, J. E., Murillo, L. G., & Sternklar, S. (1979). Anatomy and X-ray responses among patients with body delusions or body problems. Workshops Study No. 257 (unpublished), Rorschach Workshops.

Exner, J. E., Thomas, E. A., Cohen, J. B., Ridgeway, E. M., & Cooper, W. H. (1981). Stress indices in the Rorschachs of patients recovering from myocardial infarctions. Workshops Study No. 286 (unpublished), Rorschach Workshops.

Exner, J. E., Thomas, E. A., & Martin, L. S. (1980). Alterations in G. S. R. and cardiac and respiratory rates in Introversives and Extratensives during problem solving. Workshops Study No. 272 (unpublished), Rorschach Workshops.

Exner, J. E., Thomas, E. E., & Mason, B. (1985). Children's Rorschachs: Descriptions and prediction. *Journal of Personality Assessment, 49*, 13-20.

Exner, J. E., & Weiner, I. B. (1982). *The Rorschach: A comprehensive system: Vol. 3. Assessment of Children and Adolescents.* New York: John Wiley & Sons, Inc.

Exner, J. E., & Wylie, J. R. (1977). Some Rorschach data concerning suicide. *Journal of Personality Assessment, 41*, 339-348.

Exner, J. E., Wylie, J. R., Leura, A. V., & Parrill, T. (1977). Some psychological characteristics of prostitutes. *Journal of Personality Assessment, 41*, 474-485.

Exner, J. E., Zalis, T., & Schumacher, J. (1976). Rorschach protocols of chronic amphetamine users. Workshops Study No. 233 (unpublished), Rorschach Workshops.

Eysenck, H. J. (1976). Behavior therapy—dogma or applied science? In M. P. Feldman & A. Broadhurst (Eds.), *Theoretical and experimental bases of the behavior therapies.* New York: John Wiley & Sons, Inc.

Eysenck, H. J. (1985). Review of California Psychological Inventory. In J. V. Mitchell (Ed.), *The ninth mental measurements yearbook.* Highland Press, NJ: Gryphon Press.

Eysenck, H. J., & Barrett, P. (1985). Psychophysiology and measurement of intelligence. In C. R. Reynolds & V. L. Wilson (Eds.), *Methodological and statistical advances in the study of individual differences.* New York: Plenum Press.

Fauschingbauer, T. R., & Newmark, C. S. (1978). Short forms of the MMPI. Lexington, MA: Heath.

Feighner, J. P., Robins, E., Guze, S. B., Woodruff, R. A., Winokur, G., & Munoz, R. (1972). Diagnostic criteria for use in psychiatric research. *Archives of General Psychiatry, 26,* 57-63.

Feingold, A. (1983). The validity of the Information and Vocabulary Subtests of the WAIS for predicting college achievement. *Educational and Psychological Measurement, 43,* 1127-1131.

Feldman, S. E., & Sullivan, D. S. (1971). Factors mediating the efforts of enhanced rapport on children's performance. *Journal of Consulting and Clinical Psychology, 36,* 302.

Field, K., Bolton, B., & Dana, R. H. (1982). An evaluation of three Bender-Gestalt scoring systems as indicators of psychopathology. *Journal of Clinical Psychology, 38,* 838-842.

Filskov, S. B. (1978). The prediction of impairment from figure copying. Paper presented at the Southeastern Psychological Association Convention, Atlanta.

Finney, B. C. (1951). Rorschach test correlates of assaultive behavior. *Journal of Projective Techniques, 15,* 250-254.

Fischoff, D., Slovic, P., & Lichtenstein, S. (1977). Knowing with certainty: The appropriateness of extreme confidence. *Journal of Experimental Psychology: Human Perception and Performance, 3,* 552-564.

Fisher, S. (1951). The value of the Rorschach for detecting suicidal trends. *Journal of Projective Techniques, 15,* 250-254.

Fisher, S. (1962). Relationship of Rorschach human percepts to projective descriptions with self reference. *Journal of Projective Techniques, 26,* 231-233.

Flaherty, M. R., & Reutzel, G. (1965). Personality traits of high and low achievers in college. *Journal of Educational Research, 58,* 409-411.

Flaugher, R. L. (1978). The many definitions of test bias. *American Psychologist, 33,* 671-679.

Flaugher, R. L., & Schrader, W. B. (1978). *Eliminating differentially difficult items as an approach to test bias (RB-78-4).* Princeton, NJ: Educational Testing Service.

Follette, W., & Cummings, N. (1967). Psychiatric services and medical utilization in a prepaid health plan setting. *Medical Care, 5,* 25-35.

Folstein, M. F., et al. (1985). Brief report on the clinical reappraisal of the Diagnostic Interview Schedule carried out at the Johns Hopkins site of the Epidemiological Catchment Area Program of the NIMH. *Psychological Medicine, 15*, 809-814.

Foster, S. L., Bell-Dolan, D. J., & Burge, D. A. (1988). Behavioral observation. In A. S. Bellack & M. Hersen. (Eds.), *Behavioral assessment* (3rd ed.). New York: Pergamon.

Frederiksen, N. (1986). Toward a broader conception of human intelligence. *American Psychologist, 41*, 445-452.

French, C. C., & Beaumont, J. G. (1987). The reaction of psychiatric patients to computerized assessment. *British Journal of Clinical Psychology, 26*, 267-278.

Friedman, H. (1952). Perceptual regression in schizophrenia: An hypothesis suggested by the use of the Rorschach test. *Journal of Genetic Psychology, 81*, 63-98.

Friedman, H. S., & Booth-Kewley, S., (1987). The "Disease-prone personality": A meta-analytic view of the construct. *American Psychologist, 42*, 539-555.

Fuchs, D., & Fuchs, L. S. (1986). Test procedure bias: A meta-analysis of examiner familiarity effects. *Review of Educational Research, 56*, 243-262.

Fuller, G. B. (1969). *The Minnesota Percepto-Diagnostic Test* (rev. ed.). Brandon, VT: Clinical Psychology Publishing Co.

Fuller, G. B., & Chagnon, G. (1962). Factors influencing rotation in the Bender Gestalt performance of children. *Journal of Projective Techniques, 26*, 36-46.

Futch, E. J., & Lisman, S. A. (1977 - December). *Behavioral validation of an assertiveness scale: The incongruence of self-report behavior*. Paper presented at the annual meeting of the Association for Advancement of Behavior Therapy, Atlanta.

Galassi, J. P., & Galassi, M. D. (1979). Modification of heterosocial skills deficits. In A. S. Bellack & M. Hersen (Eds.), *Research and practice in social skills*. New York: Plenum.

Gambrill, E. D. (1977). *Behavior modification*. San Francisco: Jossey-Bass.

Gambrill, E. D., & Richey, C. A. (1975). An assertion inventory for use in assessment and research. *Behavior Therapy, 6*, 550-561.

Garb, H. N. (1984). The incremental validity of information used in personality assessment. *Clinical Psychology Review, 4*, 641-655.

Garb, H. N. (1989). Clinical judgment, clinical training, and professional experience. *Psychological Bulletin, 105*, 387-396.

Garcia, J. (1981). The logic and limits of mental aptitude testing. *American Psychologist, 36*, 1172-1180.

Gardner, H. (1983). *Frames of mind: The theory of multiple intelligences*. New York: Basic Books.

Gardner, R. W. (1951). Impulsivity as indicated by Rorschach test factors. *Journal of Consulting Psychology, 15*, 464-468.

Garron, D. C., & Chiefetz, D. I. (1965). Comment on Bender Gestalt discernment of organic pathology. *Psychological Bulletin, 63*, 197-200.

Gavales, D., & Millon, T. (1960). Comparison of reproduction and recall size deviations on the Bender Gestalt as measures of anxiety. *Journal of Clinical Psychology, 16*, 278-280.

Geer, J. H. (1965). The development of a scale to measure fear. *Behavior Research and Therapy, 3*, 45-53.

Geiselman, R. E., Woodward, J. A., & Beatty, J. (1982). Individual differences in verbal memory performance: A test of alternative information processing models. *Journal of Experimental Psychology: General, 111*, 109-134.

Gerstle, R. M., Geary, D. C., Himelstein, P., & Reller-Geary, L. (1988). Rorschach predictors of therapeutic outcome for inpatient treatment of children: A proactive study. *Journal of Clinical Psychology, 44*, 277-280.

Gilbert, J. (1969). *Clinical psychological tests in psychiatric and medical practice.* Springfield, IL: Charles C. Thomas.

Gilbert, J., & Hall, M. (1962). Changes with age in human figure drawings. *Journal of Gerontology, 17*, 397-404.

Gill, H. S. (1966). Delay of response and reaction to color on the Rorschach. *Journal of Projective Techniques and Personality Assessment, 30*, 545-552.

Gilmore, D. C., Beehr, T. A., & Love, K. G. (1986). Effects of applicant sex, applicant physical attractiveness, and type of job on interview decisions. *Journal of Occupational Psychology, 59*, 103-109.

Glass, C. R., Merluzzi, T. V., Biever, J. L., & Larsen, K. H. (1982). Cognitive assessment of social anxiety: Development and validation of a self-statement questionnaire. *Cognitive Therapy and Research, 6*, 37-55.

Glueck, S., & Glueck, E. (1950). *Unravelling juvenile delinquency.* New York: Common Wealth Fund.

Gocka, E. (1965). American Lake norms for 200 MMPI scales. Unpublished materials.

Goldberg, L. R. (1965). Diagnosticians versus diagnostic signs: The diagnosis of psychosis versus neurosis from the MMPI. *Psychological Monographs, 79*, No. 602.

Golden, C. J. (1979). *Clinical interpretation of objective psychological tests.* New York: Grune & Stratton.

Golden, C. J., Purisch, A. D., & Hammeke, T. A. (1985). *Luria-Nebraska Neuropsychological Battery: Forms I and II* (Manual). Los Angeles: Western Psychological Services.

Goldfried, M. R. (1982a). On the history of therapeutic integration. *Behavior Therapy, 13*, 572-593.

Goldfried, M. R. (1982b). *Behavioral assessment: An overview.* In A. S. Bellack, M. Hersen, & A. E. Kazdin (Eds.), *International handbook of behavior modification and therapy.* New York: Pergamon.

Goldfried, M. R. (1983). A behavior therapist looks at reapproachment. *Journal of Humanistic Psychology, 23*, 97-107.

Goldfried, M. R., Stricker, G., & Weiner, I. B. (1971). *Rorschach handbook of clinical and research application.* Englewood Cliffs, NJ: Prentice-Hall.

Goldman, R. D. (1960). Changes in Rorschach performance and clinical improvement in schizophrenia. *Journal of Consulting Psychology, 24*, 403-407.

Goldman, R. D., & Hartig, L. (1976). The WISC may not be a valid predictor of school performance for primary grade minority children. *American Journal of Mental Deficiency, 80*, 583-587.

Goldschmid, M. L. (1967). Prediction of college majors by personality tests. *Journal of Counseling Psychology, 14*, 302-308.

Goldstein, K., & Sheerer, M. (1941). Abstract and concrete behavior. An experimental study with special tests. *Psychological Monographs, 53*, 239.

Goodenough, F. (1926). *Measurement of intelligence by drawings.* New York: World Book.

Gordon, N. G., & Swart, E. C. (1973). A comparison of the Harris-Lingoes subscales between the original standardization population and an inpatient Veterans Administration hospital population. *Newsletter for Research in Mental Health and Behavioral Sciences, 15*, 28-31.

Gottlieb, A., & Parsons, O. (1960). A coaction compass evaluation of Rorschach determinants in brain damaged individuals. *Journal of Consulting Psychology, 24*, 54-60.

Gough, H. G. (1948). A new dimension of status. I. Development of a personality scale. *American Sociological Review, 13*, 401-409.

Gough, H. G. (1952). Identifying psychological femininity. *Educational and Psychological Measurement, 12*, 427-439.

Gough, H. G. (1957). *California Psychological Inventory Manual.* Palo Alto, CA: Consulting Psychologists Press.

Gough, H. G. (1964). Academic achievement in high school as predicted from the California Psychological Inventory. *Journal of Educational Psychology, 65*, 174-180.

Gough, H. G. (1965). Cross-cultural validation of a measure of asocial behavior. *Psychological Reports, 17*, 379-387.

Gough, H. G. (1966). Graduation from high school as predicted from the California Psychological Inventory. *Psychology in the Schools, 3*, 208-216.

Gough, H. G. (1968). An interpreter's syllabus for the California Psychological Inventory. In P. McReynolds (Ed.), *Advances in psychological assessment* (Vol. 1). Palo Alto, CA: Science and Behavior Books.

Gough, H. G. (1969). *Manual for the California Psychological Inventory* (rev. ed.). Palo Alto, CA: Consulting Psychologists Press.

Gough, H. G. (1975). *Manual for the California Psychological Inventory* (rev. ed.). Palo Alto, CA: Consulting Psychologists Press.

Gough, H. (1987). *California Psychological Inventory: Administrator's guide.* Palo Alto, CA: Consulting Psychologists Press.

Gough, H. G., Durflinger, G. W., & Hill, R. E., Jr. (1968). Predicting performance in student teaching from the California Psychological Inventory. *Journal of Educational Psychology, 52*, 119-127.

Gough, H. G., & Hall, W. B. (1964). Prediction of performance in medical school from the California Psychological Inventory. *Journal of Applied Psychology, 48*, 218-226.

Gough, H. G., & Kirk, B. A. (1970). Achievement in dental school as related to personality and aptitude variables. *Measurement and Evaluation in Guidance, 2*, 225-233.

Gough, H., & Lanning, K. (1986). Predicting grades in college from the California Psychological Inventory. *Educational and Psychological Measurement, 46*, 205-213.

Gough, H. G., Wenk, E. A., & Rozynko, V. V. (1965). Parole outcome as predicted from the CPI, the MMPI, and a Base Expectancy Table. *Journal of Abnormal Psychology, 70*, 432-441.

Gould, J. (1982). A psychometric investigation of the standard and short form Beck Depression Inventory. *Psychological Reports, 51*, 1167-1170.

Grace, W. C., & Sweeny, M. E. (1986). Comparison of the P>V sign on the WISC-R and WAIS-R in delinquent males. *Journal of Clinical Psychology, 42*, 173-176.

Graham, F. K., & Kendall, B. C. (1960). Memory-For-Designs Test: Revised general manual. *Perceptual and Motor Skills*, Monograph supplement no. 2-VIII, *11*, 147-188.

Graham, J. R. (1977). *The MMPI: A practical guide*. New York: Oxford University Press.

Graham, J. R. (1978). A review of some important MMPI special scales. In P. McReynolds (Ed.), *Advances in psychological assessment* (Vol. IV). San Francisco: Jossey-Bass.

Graham, J. R. (1987). *The MMPI: A practical guide* (2nd ed.). New York: Oxford University Press.

Graham, J. R., & Lilly, R. S. (1984). *Psychological Testing*. Englewood Cliffs, NJ: Prentice-Hall.

Graham, J. R., & McCord, G. (1985). Interpretation of moderately elevated MMPI scores for normal subjects. *Journal of Personality Assessment, 49*, 477-484.

Graham, J. R., Smith, R. L., & Schwartz, G. F. (1986). Stability of MMPI configurations for psychiatric inpatients. *Journal of Consulting and Clinical Psychology, 49*, 477-484.

Graham, P., & Rutter, M. (1968). The reliability and validity of the psychiatric assessment of the child: II. Interview with the parent. *British Journal of Psychiatry, 114*, 581-592.

Gravitz, M. A. (1968). The height of normal adult figure drawings. *Journal of Clinical Psychology, 24*, 75.

Gravitz, M. A. (1969). Direction of psychosexual interest and figure drawing choice. *Journal of Clinical Psychology, 25*, 311.

Grayson, H. M. (1951). *A Psychological Admissions Testing Program and Manual*. Los Angeles: Veterans Administration Center.

Green, B. F. (1978). In defense of measurement. *American Psychologist, 33*, 664-670.

Green, S. B., & Kelley, C. K. (1988). Racial bias in prediction with the MMPI for a juvenile delinquent population. *Journal of Personality Assessment, 52*, 263-275.

Greenbaum, R. S. (1955). A note on the use of the Word Association Test as an aid to interpreting the Bender-Gestalt. *Journal of Projective Techniques, 19*, 27-29.

Greene, R. L. (1980). *The MMPI: An interpretive manual*. New York: Grune & Stratton.

Greene, R. L. (1987). Ethnicity and MMPI performance: A review. *Journal of Consulting and Clinical Psychology, 55*, 497-512.

Greene, R. L. (Ed.). (1988). *The MMPI use with special populations*. San Diego : Grune & Stratton.

Greene, R. L. (1988). The relative efficiency of F-K and the obvious and subtle scales to detect overreporting of psychopathology on the MMPI. *Journal of Clinical Psychology, 44*, 152-159.

Greene, R. L. (1989). *The MMPI: An interpretive manual* (2nd ed.). New York : Grune & Stratton.

Gregory, R., & Morris, L. (1978). Adjective correlates for women on the CPI scales: A replication. *Journal of Personality Assessment, 42*, 258-264.

Gregory, R. J. (1987). *Adult intellectual assessment.* Boston: Allyn & Bacon.

Greif, E. B., & Hogan, R. (1973). The theory and measurement of empathy. *Journal of Counseling Psychology, 20,* 280-284.

Gresham, F. M. (1984). Behavioral interviews in school psychology: Issues in psychometric adequacy and research. *School Psychology Review, 13,* 17-25.

Griffin, M. L., & Flaherty, M. R. (1964). Correlation of CPI traits with academic achievement. *Educational and Psychological Measurement, 24,* 369-372.

Groff, M., & Hubble, L. (1981). Recategorized WISC-R scores of juvenile delinquents. *Journal of Learning Disabilities, 14,* 515-516.

Grossman, F. M. (1983). Percentage of WAIS-R standardization sample obtaining verbal-performance discrepancies. *Journal of Consulting and Clinical Psychology, 51,* 641-642.

Grossman, F. M., & Johnson, K. M. (1982). WISC-R Factor scores as predictors of WRAT performance: A multivariate analysis. *Psychology in the Schools, 19,* 465-468.

Groth-Marnat, G. (1985). Evaluating and using psychological testing software. *Human Resource Management Australia, 23,* 16-21.

Groth-Marnat, G. (1988). A survey of the current and future direction of professional psychology in acute general hospitals in Australia. *Australian Psychologist, 23,* 39-43.

Groth-Marnat, G., & Schumacher, J. (1989). Computer-based psychological testing. *American Journal of Orthopsychiatry, 59,* 257-263.

Guilford, J. P., & Zimmerman, W. S. (1956). *The Guilford-Zimmerman Temperament Survey.* Beverly Hills, CA: Sheridan Psychological Services.

Guilford, J. P. (1967). *The nature of human intelligence.* New York: McGraw-Hill.

Gulas, I., McClanahan, L. D., & Poetter, R. (1975). Phobic response factors from the Fear Survey Schedule. *Journal of Psychology, 90,* 19-25.

Gynther, M.D. (1978). The California Psychological Inventory: A review. In O. K. Buros (Ed.), *The eighth mental measurements yearbook* (Vol. I). Highland Park, NJ: Gryphon Press.

Gynther, M.D. (1979) Aging and personality. In J. N. Butcher (Ed.), *New developments in the use of the MMPI.* Minneapolis: University of Minnesota Press.

Gynther, M.D., & Green, S. B. (1980). Accuracy may make a difference, but does a difference make for accuracy?: A response to Pritchard and Rosenblatt. *Journal of Consulting and Clinical Psychology, 48,* 268-272.

Gynther, M.D., & Shimkuras, A. M. (1966). Age and MMPI performance. *Journal of Consulting Psychology, 30,* 118-121.

Haan, N. (1964). An investigation of the relationships of Rorschach scores, patterns and behaviors to coping and defense mechanisms. *Journal of Projective Techniques and Personality Assessment, 28,* 429-441.

Haas, A. P., Hendin, H., & Singer, P. (1987). Psychodynamic and structured interviewing: Issues of validity. *Comprehensive Psychiatry, 28,* 40-53.

Haddad, F. A. (1986). The performance of learning disabled children on the Kaufman Assessment Battery for Children and the Bender-Gestalt Test. *Psychology in the Schools, 23,* 342-345.

Hafner, A. J. (1958). Response time and Rorschach behavior. *Journal of Clinical Psychology*, *14*, 154-155.

Hain, J. D. (1964). The Bender Gestalt Test: A scoring method for identifying brain damage. *Journal of Consulting Psychology*, *28*, 34-40.

Hall, C. (Dec. 6, 1983). Psychiatrist's computer use stirs debate. *The Wall Street Journal*, 35, 39.

Hall, H. V. (1984). Predicting dangerousness for the courts. *American Journal of Forensic Psychiatry*, *5*, 77-96.

Hall, H. V., Catlin, E., Boissevain, A., & Westgate, J. (1984). Dangerous myths about predicting dangerousness. *American Journal of Forensic Psychology*, *2*, 173-193.

Halpern, F. (1940). Rorschach interpretation of the personality structure of schizophrenics who benefit from insulin therapy. *Psychiatric Quarterly*, *14*, 826-833.

Halpern, F. (1951). The Bender Visual Motor Gestalt Test. In H. H. Anderson & G. L. Anderson (Eds.), *An Introduction to Projective Techniques*. New York: Prentice-Hall.

Halpern, F. (1955). Rotation errors made by brain-injured and familial children on two visual motor tests. *American Journal of Mental Deficiency*, *59*, 485-489.

Halstead, W. C. (1961). Biological intelligence. In J. J. Jenkins & D. G. Paterson (Eds.), *Studies in Individual Differences* (pp.661-668). New York: Appleton-Century-Crofts.

Hammen, C. L. (1978). Depression, distortion, and life stress in college students. *Cognitive Therapy and Research*, *2*, 189-192.

Hammen, C. L., & Krantz, S. (1976). Effect of success and failure on depressive cognitions. *Journal of Abnormal Psychology*, *85*, 577-586.

Hammen, C. L., & Mayol, A. (1982). Depression and cognitive characteristics of stressful life-event types. *Journal of Abnormal Psychology*, *91*, 165-174.

Hammer, E. F. (1954). A comparison of H-T-P's of rapists and pedophiles. *Journal of Projective Techniques*, *18*, 346-354.

Hammer, E. F. (1958). *The clinical application of projective drawings*. Springfield, IL : Charles C. Thomas.

Hammer, E. F. (1960). The House-Tree-Person (H-T-P) drawings as a projective technique with children. In A. I. Rabin & R. Haworth (Eds.), *Projective techniques with children*. New York: Grune & Stratton.

Hammer, E. F. (1968). Projective drawings. In A. I. Rabin (Ed.), *Projective techniques in personality assessment* (pp.366-393). New York: Springer.

Hammer, E. F. (1969a). The use of the H-T-P in a criminal court: Predicting acting out. In J. N. Buck & E. F. Hammer (Eds.), *Advances in the House-Tree-Person technique: Variations and applications*. Los Angeles: Western Psychological Services.

Hammer, E. F. (1969b). Hierarchical organization of personality and the H-T-P, achromatic and chromatic. In J. N. Buck & E. F. Hammer (Eds.), *Advances in the House-Tree-Person technique: Variations and applications*. Los Angeles: Western Psychological Services.

Hammer, E. F. (1985). The House-Tree-Person Test. In C. S. Newmark (Ed.), *Major Psychological Assessment Instruments*. Newton, MA: Allyn & Bacon.

Hammer, M., & Kaplan, A. M. (1964). The reliability of size of children's drawings. *Journal of Clinical Psychology*, *20*, 121-122.

Handler, L. (1967). Anxiety indexes in the Draw-A-Person Test: A scoring manual. *Journal of Projective Techniques, 31,* 46-57.

Handler, L. (1985). The clinical use of the Draw-A-Person Test (DAP). In C. S. Newmark (Ed.), *Major Psychological Assessment Instruments.* Newton, MA: Allyn & Bacon.

Handler, L., & McIntosh, J. (1971). Predicting aggression and withdrawal in children with the Draw-A-Person and Bender-Gestalt. *Journal of Personality Assessment, 35,* 331-337.

Hansell, A. G., Lerner, H. D., Milden, R. S., & Ludolph, P. (1988). Single-sign Rorschach Suicide indicators: A validity study using a depressed inpatient population. *Journal of Personality Assessment, 52,* 658-669.

Hanson, R. K., Hunsley, J., & Parker, K. C. H. (1988). The relationship between WAIS subtest reliability, "g" loadings, and meta-analytically derived validity estimates. *Journal of Clinical Psychology, 44,* 557-562.

Hargrave, G. E., & Hiatt, D. (1987). Law enforcement selection with the interview, MMPI, and CPI: A study of reliability and validity. *Journal of Police Science and Administration, 15,* 110-117.

Hargrave, G. E., Hiatt, D., & Gaffney, T. W. (1986). A comparison of MMPI and CPI test profiles for traffic officers and deputy sheriffs. *Journal of Police Science and Administration, 14,* 250-258.

Harmon, M. H. (1980). The Barron Ego Strength Scale: A study of personality correlates among normals. *Journal of Clinical Psychology, 36,* 433-436.

Harper, R. G., Wiens, A. N., & Matarazzo, J. D. (1978). *Nonverbal communication: The state of the art.* New York: John Wiley & Sons, Inc.

Harris, D. B. (1963). *Children's drawings as measures of intellectual maturity.* New York: Harcourt, Brace, & World.

Harris, J. G. (1960). Validity: The search for a constant in a universe of variables. In M. Rickers-Ovsiankina (Ed.), *Rorschach psychology.* New York: John Wiley & Sons, Inc.

Harris, R., & Lingoes, J. (1968). *Subscales for the Minnesota Multiphasic Personality Inventory* (mimeographed materials). Department of Psychology, University of Michigan.

Harris, T. L., & Brown, N. W. (1979). Concurrent validity of the Rathus Assertiveness Schedule. *Educational and Psychological Measurement, 39,* 181-186.

Harrison, R. (1940). Studies in the use and validity of the Thematic Apperception Test with mentally disordered patients. II: A quantitative validity study. III. Validation by blind analysis. *Character and Personality, 9,* 122-133, 134-138.

Harrower, M. (1986). The Stress Tolerance Test. *Journal of Personality Assessment, 50,* 417-427.

Hart, K. J., & Ollendick, T. H. (1985). Prevalence of bulimia in working and university women. *American Journal of Psychiatry, 142,* 851-854.

Hartshorne, H., & May, M. A. (1928). *Studies in deceit.* New York: Macmillan.

Harty, M. K. (1986). Action language in the psychological test report. *Bulletin of the Menninger Clinic, 50,* 456-463.

Hase, H. D., & Goldberg, L. R. (1967). Comparative validity of different strategies of constructing personality inventory scales. *Psychological Bulletin, 67,* 231-248.

Hassell, J., & Smith, E. W. L. (1975). Female homosexuals' concept of self, men, and women. *Journal of Personality Assessment, 39,* 154-159.

Hathaway, S. R., & Mckinley, J. C. (1943). *Manual for the Minnesota Multiphasic Personality Inventory.* New York: Psychological Corporation.

Hathaway, S. R., & Monaches, E. D. (1963). *Adolescent personality and behavior: MMPI patterns of normal, delinquent, dropout, and other outcomes.* Minneapolis : University of Minnesota Press.

Hayes, S. C., Nelson, R. O., & Jarrett, R. B. (1987). The treatment utility of assessment: A functional approach to evaluating assessment quality. *American Psychologist, 42,* 963-974.

Haynes, J. P., & Howard, R. C. (1986). Stability of WISC-R scores in a juvenile forensic sample. *Journal of Clinical Psychology, 42,* 534-537.

Haynes, J. P., & Peltier, J. (1985). Patterns of practice with the TAT in juvenile forensic settings. *Journal of Personality Assessment, 49,* 26-29.

Haynes, S. N., & O'Brien, W. H. (1988). The gordian knot of DSM-III-R use: Integrating principles of behavior classification and complex causal models. *Behavioral Assessment, 10,* 95-106.

Haynes, S. N., & Wilson, C. C. (1979). *Behavioral assessment: Recent advances in methods, concepts and applications.* San Francisco: Jossey-Bass.

Heaton, R. K., Beade, L. E., & Johnson, K. L. (1978). Neuropsychological test results associated with psychiatric disorders in adults. *Psychological Bulletin, 85,* 141-162.

Hebb, D. O. (1972). *Textbook of psychology* (3rd ed.). Philadelphia: W.B. Saunders.

Hedlund, J. L., Sletten, I. W., Evenson, R. C., Altman, H., & Cho, D. W. (1977). Automated psychiatric information systems: A critical review of Missouri's Standard System of Psychiatry (SSOP). *Journal of Operational Psychiatry, 8,* 5-26.

Hedlund, J. L., Vieweg, B. W., & Cho, D. W. (1985). Mental health computing in the 1980's: II. Clinical applications. *Computers in Human Sciences I,* 97-131.

Heflinger, C. A., Cook, V. J., & Thackrey, M. (1987). Identification of mental retardation by the System of Multicultural Pluralistic Assessment: Nondiscriminatory or nonexistent? *Journal of School Psychology, 25,* 177-183.

Heilbrun, A. B. (1961). Male and female personality correlates of early termination in counseling. *Journal of Counseling Psychology, 8,* 31-36.

Heilbrun, A. B., Daniel, J. L., Goodstein, L. D., Stephenson, R. R., & Crites, J. O. (1962). The validity of two-scale pattern interpretation on the California Psychological Inventory. *Journal of Applied Psychology, 46,* 409-416.

Heimberg, R. G., Harrison, D. F., Goldberg, L. S., Desmarais, S., & Blue, S. (1979). The relationship of self-report and behavioral assertion in an offender population. *Journal of Behavior Therapy and Experimental Psychiatry, 10,* 283-286.

Hellkamp, D. T., & Hogan, M. E. (1985). Differentiation of organics from functional psychiatric patients across various I.Q. ranges using the Bender-Gestalt and Hutt scoring system. *Journal of Clinical Psychology, 41,* 259-264.

Helzer, J. E., & Robins, L. N. (1988). The Diagnostic Interview Schedule: Its development, evolution and use. *Social Psychiatry and Psychiatric Epidemiology, 23,* 6-16.

Helzer, J. E., Robins, L. N., Croughan, J. L., & Welner, A. (1981). Renard Diagnostic Interview: Its reliability and procedural validity with physicians and lay interviewers. *Archives of General Psychiatry, 38*, 393-398.

Helzer, J. E., Robins, L. N., McEvoy, L. F., Spitznagel, E. L., Stolzman, R. K., Farmer, A., & Brockington, I. F. (1985). A comparison of clinical and Diagnostic Interview Schedule diagnoses: Physician re-examination of lay-interviewed cases in the general population. *Archives of General Psychiatry, 42*, 657-666.

Henderson, M., & Furnham, A. (1983). Dimensions of assertiveness: Factor analysis of five assertion inventories. *Journal of Behavior Therapy and Experimental Psychiatry, 14*, 223-231.

Henderson, N. B., & Engel, R. (1974). Neonatal visual evoked potentials as predictors of psychoeducational tests at age seven. *Developmental Psychology, 10*, 269-276.

Henry, E. M., & Rotter, J. B. (1956). Situational influences on Rorschach responses. *Journal of Consulting Psychology, 20*, 457-462.

Henry, W. E. (1956). *The analysis of fantasy: The Thematic Apperception Test in the study of personality.* New York: John Wiley & Sons, Inc.

Herjanic, B., & Campbell, W. (1977). Differentiating psychiatrically disturbed children on the basis of a structured interview. *Journal of Abnormal Child Psychology, 51*, 127-134.

Herjanic, B., Herjanic, M., Brown, F., & Wheatt, T. (1975). Are children reliable reporters? *Journal of Abnormal Child Psychology, 3*, 41-48.

Hersen, M. (1988). Behavioral assessment and psychiatric diagnosis. *Behavioral Assessment, 10*, 107-121.

Hersen, M., & Bellack, A. S. (1976). *Behavioral assessment: A practical handbook.* New York: Pergamon Press.

Hersen, M., & Bellack, A. S. (1988). DSM-III and behavioral assessment. In A. S. Bellack and M. Hersen (Eds.), *Behavioral assessment: A practical handbook,* (3rd ed.). New York: Pergamon.

Hersen, M., & Greaves, S. T. (1971). Rorschach productivity as related to verbal performance. *Journal of Personality Assessment, 35*, 436-441.

Hersh, C. (1962). The cognitive functioning of the creative person: A developmental analysis. *Journal of Projective Techniques, 26*, 193-200.

Hertz, M. R. (1943). Personality patterns in adolescence as portrayed by the Rorschach ink blot method: IV. The "Erlebnistypus." *Journal of General Psychology, 29*, 3-45.

Hertz, M. R. (1960). The organization activity. In M. Rickers-Ovsiankina (Ed.), *Rorschach psychology.* New York: John Wiley & Sons, Inc.

Hertz, M. R. (1976). Detection of suicidal risks with the Rorschach. In M. Abt & S. L. Weissman (Eds.), *Acting out: Theoretical and clinical aspects.* (2nd ed.). New York: Aronson.

Hertz, M. R., & Paolino, A. (1960). Rorschach indices of perceptual and conceptual disorganization. *Journal of Projective Techniques, 24*, 310-388.

Higgins, R. L., Alonso, R. R., & Pendleton, M. G. (1979). The validity of roleplay assessments of assertiveness. *Behavior Therapy, 10*, 655-662.

Hill, A. H. (1967). Use of a structured autobiography in the construct validation of personality scales. *Journal of Consulting Psychology, 31,* 551-556.

Hill, R. E., Jr. (1960). Dichotomous prediction of student teaching excellence employing selected CPI scales. *Journal of Educational Research, 53,* 349-351.

Hirschenfang, S. A. (1960a). A comparison of Bender-Gestalt reproductions of right and left hemiplegic patients. *Journal of Clinical Psychology, 16,* 439.

Hirschenfang, S. A. (1960b). A comparison of WAIS scores of hemiplegic patients with and without aphasia. *Journal of Clinical Psychology, 16,* 351.

Hoffman, H., Loper, R. G., & Kammeier, M. L. (1974). Identifying future alcoholics with MMPI alcoholism scales. *Quarterly Journal of Studies on Alcohol, 35,* 490-498.

Hoffman, R. G., & Nelson, K. (1988). Cross-validation of six short forms of the WAIS-R in a healthy geriatric sample. *Journal of Clinical Psychology, 44,* 950-952.

Hogan, A. E., Quay, H. C., Vaughn, S., & Shapiro, S. K. (1989). Revised Behavior Problem checklist: Stability, prevalence, and incidence of behavior problems in kindergarten and first grade. *Psychological Assessment, 1,* 103-111.

Hogan, R. (1971). Personality characteristics of highly rated policemen. *Personnel Psychology, 24,* 679-686.

Hogan, R., & Kurtines, W. (1975). Personological correlates of police effectiveness. *Journal of Psychology, 92,* 289-295.

Hogan, R., & Nicholson, R. (1988). The meaning of personality test scores. *American Psychologist, 43,* 621-626.

Hoge, R. D., Andrews, D. A., Robinson, D., & Hollett, J. (1988). The construct validity of interview-based assessments in family counseling. *Journal of Clinical Psychology, 44,* 563-571.

Holliman, N. B., & Montross, J. (1984). The effects of depression upon responses to the California Psychological Inventory. *Journal of Clinical Psychology, 40,* 1373-1378.

Hollis, J. W., & Donna, P. A. (1979). *Psychological report writing: Theory and practice.* Muncie, IN: Accelerated Development Inc.

Hollon, S. D., & Kendall, P. C. (1980). Cognitive self-statements in depression: Development of an automatic thoughts questionnaire. *Cognitive Therapy and Research, 4,* 383-395.

Holmes, C. B., Dungan, D. S., & Medlin, W. J. (1984). Reassessment of inferring personality traits from Bender-Gestalt drawing styles. *Journal of Clinical Psychology, 40,* 1241-1243.

Holmes, C. B., & Stephens, C. L. (1984). Consistency of edging on the Bender-Gestalt, Memory for Designs, and Draw-A-Person Tests. *The Journal of Psychology, 117,* 269-271.

Holt, R. R. (1970). Yet another look at clinical and statistical prediction: Or is clinical psychology worthwhile? *American Psychologist, 25,* 337-349.

Holtzman, W. H. (1988). Beyond the Rorschach. *Journal of Personality Assessment, 52,* 578-609.

Holtzman, W. H., & Swartz, R. D. (1983). The Holtzman Inkblot Technique: A review of 25 years of research. *Zeitschrift für Differentielle und Diagnostische Psychologie, 4,* 241-259.

Holtzman, W. H., Thorpe, J. S., Swartz, R. D., & Herron, W. E. (1961). *Inkblot Perception and Personality.* Austin: University of Texas Press.

Honaker, L. M. (1988). The equivalency of computerized and conventional MMPI administration: A critical review. *Clinical Psychology Review, 8,* 561-577.

Horn, J. L. (1985). Remodeling old models of intelligence. In B. Wolman (Ed.), *Handbook of intelligence,* (pp. 267-300). New York: John Wiley & Sons, Inc.

Horowitz, M. J. (1985). *Report of the program on conscious and unconscious mental processes of the John D. and Catherine T. MacArthur Foundation.* U. C. San Francisco, California.

Houck, C. (1984). *Learning disabilities: Understanding concepts, characteristics, and issues.* Englewood Cliffs, NJ: Prentice-Hall.

Houts, P. L. (Ed.). (1977). *The myth of measurability.* New York: Hart Publishing.

Huesmann, L. R., Lefkowitz, M. M., & Eron, L. D. (1978). Sum of MMPI scales F, 4 and 9 as a measure of aggression. *Journal of Consulting and Clinical Psychology, 46,* 1071-1078.

Hulse, W. C. (1951). The emotionally disturbed child draws his family. *Quarterly Journal of Child Behavior, 3,* 152-174.

Hunsley, J., Hanson, R. K., & Parker, K. C. H. (1988). A summary of the reliability and stability of MMPI scales. *Journal of Clinical Psychology, 44,* 44-46.

Hurley, A. D., & Sovner, R. (1985). The use of the Thematic Apperception Test in mentally retarded persons. *Psychiatric Aspects of Mental Retardation Reviews, 4,* 9-12.

Hutt, M. L. (1953). Revised Bender Visual-Motor Gestalt Test. In A. Weider (Ed.), *Continuations towards medical psychology* (Vol. 2). New York: Ronald Press.

Hutt, M. L. (1968). The projective use of the Bender-Gestalt test. In A. I. Rabin (Ed.), *Projective techniques in personality assessment.* New York: Springer.

Hutt, M. L. (1969). *The Hutt adaptation of the Bender-Gestalt test* (2nd ed.). New York: Grune & Stratton.

Hutt, M. L. (1971). *The Hutt adaptation of the Bender-Gestalt Test* (3rd ed.). New York: Grune & Stratton.

Hutt, M. L. (1985). *The Hutt adaptation of the Bender-Gestalt Test* (4th ed.). New York: Grune & Stratton.

Hutt, M. L., & Briskin, G. J. (1960). *The clinical use of the revised Bender-Gestalt Test.* New York: Grune & Stratton.

Hutt, M. L., & Gibby, R. G. (1970). *An Atlas for the Hutt adaptation of the Bender-Gestalt Test.* New York: Grune & Stratton.

Insua, A. M., & Stella, M. (1986). Psychometric patterns on the Rorschach of healthy elderly persons and patients with suspected dementia. *Perceptual and Motor Skills, 63,* 931-936.

Ireland-Galman, M., Padilla, G., & Michael, W. (1980). The relationship between performance on the Mazes subtest of the Wechsler Intelligence Scale for Children-Revised (WISC-R) and speed of solving anagrams with simple and difficult arrangements of letter and order. *Educational and Psychological Measurement, 40,* 513-524.

Jacobs, J. C. (1971). Group administration of the Bender-Gestalt Test. *Psychology in the Schools, 8,* 345-346.

Jansky, J., & de Hirsch, K. (1972). *Preventing reading failure.* New York: Harper & Row.

Janzen, W. B., & Coe, W. C. (1975). Clinical and sign prediction: The Draw-A-Person and female homosexuality. *Journal of Clinical Psychology, 31,* 757-765.

Jarman, R. F., & Das, J. P. (1977). Simultaneous and successive synthesis and intelligence. *Intelligence, 1,* 151-169.

Jencks, S. F. (1985). Recognition of mental distress and diagnosis of mental disorder in primary care. *Journal of the American Medical Association, 253,* 1903.

Jensen, A. R. (1965). Review of the Rorschach. In O. K. Buros (Ed.), *The sixth mental measurements yearbook.* Highland Park, NJ: Gryphon Press.

Jensen, A. R. (1969). How much can we boost I.Q. and scholastic achievement? *Harvard Educational Review, 39,* 1-23.

Jensen, A. R. (1972). *Genetics and education.* New York: Harper & Row.

Jensen, A. R. (1984). The black-white difference on the K-ABC: Implications for future tests. *Journal of Special Education, 18,* 377-408.

Jensen, A. R., & Reynolds, C. R. (1982). Race, social class, and ability patterns on the WISC-R. *Personality and Individual Differences, 3,* 423-438.

Johnson, D. L., & Danley, W. (1981). Validity: Comparison of the WISC-R and SOMPA estimated learning potential scores. *Psychological Reports, 49,* 123-131.

Johnson, J. H. (1973). Bender-Gestalt constriction as an indicator of depression in psychiatric patients. *Journal of Personality Assessment, 37,* 53-55.

Johnson, J. W. (1977). Technology in mental health in the 21st century. In J. B. Sidowski & T. A. Williams (Eds.), *Technology in Mental Health Care Delivery Systems.* Norwood, NJ: Ablex.

Johnson, J. W. (1984). An overview of psychological testing. In M. D. Schwartz (Ed.), *Using computers in clinical practice.* New York: Haworth Press.

Johnson, J. W., & Mihal, W. L. (1973). The performance of blacks and whites in computerized versus manual testing environments. *American Psychologist, 28,* 694-699.

Johnson, J. W., & Williams, T. A. (1975). The use of on-line computer technology in a mental health admitting system. *American Psychologist, 30,* 388-390.

Johnson, J. W., & Williams, T. A. (1977). Using on-line computer technology to improve service response and decision-making effectiveness in a mental health admitting system. In J. B. Sidowski & T. A. Williams (Eds.), *Technology in mental health care delivery systems.* Norwood, NJ: Ablex.

Jolles, I. A. (1952). *A catalogue for the qualitative interpretation of the H-T-P.* Beverly Hills, CA: Western Psychological Services.

Jolles, I. A. (1969). The use of the H-T-P in a school setting. In J. N. Buck & E. F. Hammer (Eds.), *Advances in the House-Tree-Person Technique: Variations and Applications.* Beverly Hills, CA: Western Psychological Services.

Jolles, I. A. (1971). *A Catalogue for the Qualitative Interpretation of the H-T-P.* Beverly Hills, CA: Western Psychological Services.

Jones, M. C. (1924). The elimination of children's fears. *Journal of Experimental Psychology, 7,* 382-390.

Jones, R. G. (1969). A factored measure of Ellis's Irrational Belief System. *Dissertation Abstracts International, 29,* 4379B-4380B. (University Microfilms No. 69-64, 43).

Kagan, J., Moss, H. A., & Siegel, I. E. (1963). Psychological significance of styles of conceptualization. *Monographs of the Society for Research in Child Development, 28*, 73-124.

Kahill, S. (1984). Human figure drawings in adults: An update of the empirical evidence, 1967-1982. *Canadian Psychology, 25*, 269-290.

Kahn, M. (1984). The usefulness of the TAT blank card in clinical practice. *Psychotherapy in Private Practice, 2*, 43-50.

Kahn, M. W., Fox, H., & Rhode, R. (1988). Detecting faking on the Rorschach: Computer versus expert clinical judgment. *Journal of Personality Assessment, 52*, 516-523.

Kahn, R. L., & Cannell, C. F. (1961). *The dynamics of interviewing: Theory, technique, and cases.* New York: John Wiley & Sons, Inc.

Kahn, T. C., & Giffen, M. B. (1960). *Psychological techniques in diagnosis and evaluation.* New York: Pergamon.

Kaldegg, A. (1956). Psychological observations in a group of alcoholic patients with analysis of Rorschach, Wechsler-Bellevue and Bender-Gestalt test results. *Quarterly Journal of Studies of Alcohol, 17*, 608-628.

Kallingal, A. (1971). The prediction of grades for black and white students at Michigan State University. *Journal of Educational Measurement, 8*, 263-265.

Kallstedt, F. E. (1952). A Rorschach study of sixty-six adolescents. *Journal of Clinical Psychology, 8*, 129-132.

Kamin, L. J. (1974). *The science and politics of I.Q.* Hillsdale, NJ: Erlbaum.

Kanfer, F. H., & Grimm, L. G. (1977). Behavioral analysis: Selecting target behaviors in the interview. *Behavior Modification, 4*, 419-444.

Kanfer, F. H., & Saslow, G. (1969). Behavioral diagnosis. In C. M. Franks (Ed.), *Behavior therapy: Appraisal and status.* New York: McGraw-Hill.

Kaplan, R. M., & Sacuzzo, D. P. (1989). *Psychological testing: Principles, applications, and issues* (2nd ed.). Belmont: Wadsworth.

Karon, B. P. (1978). Projective tests are valid. *American Psychologist, 33*, 764-765.

Kaufman, A. S. (1975). Factor anlaysis of the WISC-R at eleven ages between 6 1/2 and 16 1/2 years. *Journal of Consulting and Clinical Psychology, 43*, 135-147.

Kaufman, A. S. (1976a). Verbal-performance I.Q. discrepancies on the WISC-R. *Journal of Consulting and Clinical Psychology, 44*, 739-744.

Kaufman, A. S. (1976b). A new approach to the interpretation of test scatter on the WISC-R. *Journal of Learning Disabilities, 9*, 160-168.

Kaufman, A. S. (1979). *Intelligent testing with the WISC-R.* New York: John Wiley & Sons, Inc.

Kaufman, A. S. (1983). Test review: WAIS-R. *Journal of Psychoeducational Assessment, 1*, 309-319.

Kaufman, A. S., & Kaufman, N. L. (1983). *K-ABC interpretive manual.* Circle Pines, MN: American Guidance Service.

Kaufman, A. S., McLean, J. E., & Reynolds, C. R. (1988). Sex, race, residence, region, and education differences on the 11 WAIS-R subtests. *Journal of Clinical Psychology, 44*, 231-248.

Kavale, K. A., & Forness, S. R. (1984). A meta-analysis of the validity of Wechsler Scale profiles and recategorizations: Patterns or parodies? *Learning Disability Quarterly, 7,* 136-156.

Kazdin, A. E. (1988). The diagnosis of childhood disorders: Assessment issues and strategies. *Behavioral Assessment, 10,* 67-94.

Kearney, P., Beatty, M. J., Plax, T. G., & McCroskey, J. C. (1984). Factor analysis of the Rathus Assertiveness Schedule and the Personal Report of Communication Apprehension—24: Replication and extension. *Psychological Reports, 54,* 851-854.

Keith, T. Z., Fehrmann, P. G., Harrison, P. L., & Pottebaum, S. M. (1987). The relation between adaptive behavior and intelligence: Testing alternative explanations. *Journal of School Psychology, 25,* 31-43.

Keller, J. (1955). The use of a Bender-Gestalt maturation level scoring system with mentally handicapped children. *American Journal of Orthopsychiatry, 25,* 563-573.

Kelly, D., Marguilies, H., & Barrera, S. (1941). The stability of the Rorschach method as demonstrated in electroconvulsive therapy cases. *Rorschach Research Exchange, 5,* 44-48.

Kelly, E. L., & Fiske, D. W. (1951). *The prediction of performance in clinical psychology.* Ann Arbor, MI: University of Michigan Press.

Kendall, P. C., & Hollon. (Eds.). (1981). *Assessment strategies for cognitive-behavioral interventions.* New York: Academic Press.

Keogh, B. K. (1968). The copying ability of young children. *New Research in Education, 11,* 43-47.

Keogh, B. K., & Smith, C. (1961). Group techniques and a proposed scoring system for the Bender-Gestalt Test with children. *Journal of Clinical Psychology, 17,* 172-175.

Kerns, L. L. (1986). Falsifications in the psychiatric history: A differential diagnosis. *Psychiatry, 49,* 13-17.

Keyser, D. J., & Sweetland, R. C. (Eds.). (1985). *Test critiques* (Vol. I). Kansas City: Test Corporation of America.

Keltikangas-Jarvinen, L. (1986). Concept of alexithymia: I. The prevalence of alexithymia in psychosomatic patients. *Psychotherapy and Psychosomatics, 44,* 132-138.

Kincel, R. L., & Murray, S. C. (1984). Kinesthesias in perception and the experience type: Dance and creative projection. *British Journal of Projective Psychology and Personality Study, 29,* 3-7.

Kipnis, D. (1968). Social immaturity, intellectual ability, and adjustive behavior in college. *Journal of Applied Psychology, 52,* 71-80.

Kirk, B. A., Cumming, R. W., & Hackett, H. H. (1963). Personal and vocational characteristics of dental students. *Personnel and Guidance Journal, 41,* 522-527.

Kitson, D. L., & Vance, H. B. (1982). Relationship of the Wechsler Intelligence Scale for Children-Revised and the Wide Range Achievement Test for a selected sample of young children. *Psychological Reports, 50,* 981-982.

Klassen, D., & O'Connor, W. A. (1989). Assessing the risk of violence in released mental patients: A cross-validation study. *Psychological Assessment, 1,* 75-81.

Klein, R. G. (1986). Questioning the usefulness of projective psychological tests for children. *Journal of Developmental and Behavioral Pediatrics, 7,* 378-382.

Kleinmuntz, B., & Szucko, J. J. (1984). Lie detection in ancient and modern times: A call for contemporary scientific study. *American Psychologist, 39*, 766-776.

Klinger, E. (1966). Fantasy need achievement as a motivational construct. *Psychological Bulletin, 66*, 291-308.

Klinger, E., Barta, S., & Mahoney, T. (1976). Motivation, mood, and mental events: Patterns and implications for adaptive processes. In G. Serban (Ed.), *Psychopathology of Human Adaptation*. New York: Plenum.

Klopfer, B. (1937). The present status of the theoretical development of the Rorschach method. *Rorschach Research Exchange, 1*, 142-147.

Klopfer, B. (1938). The shading response. *Rorschach Research Exchange, 2*, 76-79.

Klopfer, B., Ainsworth, M. D., Klopfer, W. G., & Holt, R. R. (1956). *Developments in the Rorschach technique* (Vol. 2). Yonkers, NY: World Book Company.

Klopfer, B., & Davidson, H. (1962). *The Rorschach Technique: An Introductory Manual*. New York: Harcourt.

Klopfer, B., & Kelly, D. (1942). *The Rorschach technique*. Yonkers, NY: World Book Company.

Klopfer, W. G. (1960). *The psychological report*. New York: Grune & Stratton.

Klopfer, W. G. (1983). Writing psychological reports. In C. E. Walker (Ed.), *The handbook of clinical psychology: Theory, research, and practice*. Homewood, IL: Dow Jones-Irwin.

Klopfer, W. G., & Taulbee, E. S. (1976). Projective tests. *Annual Review of Psychology, 27*, 543-567.

Knoff, H. M., & Prout, H. T. (1985). The Kinetic Drawing System: A review and integration of the kinetic family and school drawing techniques. *Psychology in the Schools, 22*, 50-59.

Kobler, F. (1983). The Rorschach test in clinical practice. *Interdisciplinaria, 4*, 131-139.

Kobler, F. J., & Stiel, A. (1953). The use of the Rorschach in involutional melancholia. *Journal of Consulting Psychology, 17*, 365-370.

Koch, C. (1952). *The tree test*. New York: Grune & Stratton.

Kolb, L. C. (1977). *Modern clinical psychiatry* (9th ed.). Philadelphia: W.B. Saunders.

Koppitz, E. M. (1958a). Relationships between the Bender-Gestalt Test and the Wechsler Intelligence Scale for Children. *Journal of Clinical Psychology, 14*, 413-416.

Koppitz, E. M. (1958b). The Bender-Gestalt Test and learning disturbance in young children. *Journal of Clinical Psychology, 14*, 292-295.

Koppitz, E. M. (1960a). Teacher's attitude and children's performance on the Bender-Gestalt Test and human figure drawings. *Journal of Clinical Psychology, 16*, 204-208.

Koppitz, E. M. (1960b). The Bender-Gestalt Test for children: A normative study. *Journal of Clinical Psychology, 16*, 432-435.

Koppitz, E. M. (1962a). Diagnosing brain damage in young children with the Bender-Gestalt Test. *Journal of Consulting Psychology, 26*, 541-546.

Koppitz, E. M. (1962b). *The Bender Gestalt Test with the Human Figure Drawing Test for young school children*. Columbus, OH: Department of Education.

Koppitz, E. M. (1963). *The Bender Gestalt Test for Young Children.* New York: Grune & Stratton.

Koppitz, E. M. (1965). Use of the Bender Gestalt Test in elementary school. *Skolepsykologi,* 2, 193-200.

Koppitz, E. M. (1968). *Psychological evaluation of children's human figure drawings.* Yorktown Heights, NY: The Psychological Corporation.

Koppitz, E. M. (1975). *The Bender Gestalt Test for Young Children: Vol. II. Research and Applications 1963-1973.* New York: Grune & Stratton.

Koppitz, E. M. (1984). *Psychological evaluation of human figure drawings by middle school pupils.* New York: Grune & Stratton.

Koppitz, E. M., Mardis, V., & Stephens, T. (1961). A note on screening school beginners with the Bender Gestalt Test. *Journal of Educational Psychology, 52,* 80-81.

Koss, M. P. (1979). MMPI item content: "recurring issues." In J. N. Butcher (Ed.), *New developments in the use of the MMPI.* Minneapolis: University of Minnesota Press.

Koss, M. P., & Butcher, J. N. (1973). A comparison of patient's self report with other sources of clinical information. *Journal of Personality Assessment, 7,* 225-236.

Koss, M. P., Butcher, J. N., & Hoffman, N. (1976). The MMPI critical items: How well do they work? *Journal of Consulting and Clinical Psychology, 44,* 921-928.

Kostlan, A. (1954). A method for the empirical study of psychodiagnosis. *Journal of Consulting Psychology, 18,* 83-88.

Kraiger, K., Hakel, M. D., & Cornelius, E. T. (1984). Exploring fantasies of TAT reliability. *Journal of Personality Assessment, 48,* 365-370.

Kratochwill, T. R. (1985). Selection of target behaviors in behavioral consultation. *Behavior Assessment, 7,* 49-61.

Krug, S. E. (1988). *Psychware sourcebook, 1987-1988.* Kansas City, MO: Test Corporation of America.

Krug, S. E. (1989). *Psychware sourcebook, 1988-1989.* Kansas City, MO: Test Corporation of America.

Kühn, R. (1963). Über die kritische Rorschach-Forschung und einige ihrer Ergebnisse. *Rorschachiana, 8,* 105-114.

Kunce, J. T., & Tamkin, A. S. (1981). Rorschach movement and color responses and MMPI social extraversion and thinking introversion personality types. *Journal of Personality Assessment, 45,* 5-10.

Kurtines, W. (1974). Autonomy: A concept reconsidered. *Journal of Personality Assessment, 38,* 243-246.

Kurtines, W., Hogan, R., & Weiss, D. (1975). Personality dynamics of heroin use. *Journal of Abnormal Psychology, 84,* 87-89.

Kurz, R. B. (1963). Relationship between time imagery and Rorschach human movement responses. *Journal of Consulting Psychology, 29,* 379-382.

Kwiatkowska, H. Y. (1978). *Family therapy and evaluation through art.* Springfield, IL: Charles C. Thomas.

Lachar, D., & Wrobel, T. A. (1979). Validation of clinician's hunches: Construction of a new MMPI critical item set. *Journal of Consulting and Clinical Psychology, 47,* 277-284.

Lacks, P. (1984). Bender-Gestalt screening for brain dysfunction. New York: John Wiley & Sons, Inc.

Lacks, P., & Newport, K. (1980). A comparison of scoring systems and level of scorer experience on the Bender-Gestalt test. *Journal of Personality Assessment, 44*, 351-357.

Lafer, B. (1989). Predicting performance and persistance in hospice volunteers. *Psychological Reports, 65*, 467-472.

Lanning, K. (1987). On the distinction between "faked" and "invalid" protocols: An analysis of the California Psychological Inventory. Unpublished manuscript, Institute of Personality and Research, University of California, Berkeley.

Lanyon, B. P., & Lanyon, R. I. (1980). *Incomplete Sentences Task: Manual.* Chicago: Stoelting.

Lanyon, R. I. (1984). Personality assessment. *Annual Review of Psychology, 35*, 667-701.

Lanyon, R. I., & Goodstein, L. D. (1982). *Personality Assessment* (2nd ed.). New York: John Wiley & Sons, Inc.

Lapouse, R., & Monk, M. A. (1958). An epidemiologic study of behavior characteristics of children. *American Journal of Public Health, 48*, 1134-1144.

Lapouse, R., & Monk, M. A. (1964). Behavior deviations in a representative sample of children: Variations by sex, age, race, social class, and family size. *American Journal of Orthopsychiatry, 34*, 436-446.

Larrabee, G. J. (1986). Another look at VIQ-PIQ scores and unilateral brain damage. *International Journal of Neuroscience, 29*, 141-148.

Laufer, W. S., Skoog, D. K., & Day, J. M. (1982). Personality and criminality: A review of the California Psychological Inventory. *Journal of Clinical Psychology, 38*, 562-573.

Lawrence, S. B. (1984). *Lawrence Psychological-Forensic Examination (Law-PSI).* San Bernadino, CA: Lawrence Psychological Center.

Lazarus, A. A. (1973). Multimodel behavior therapy: Treating the "BASIC ID". *The Journal of Nervous and Mental Diseases, 156*, 404-411.

Leary, T. (1957). *Interpersonal diagnosis of personality.* New York : Ronald Press.

Leavitt, F., & Garron, G. C. (1982). Rorschach and pain characteristics of patients with low back pain and "conversion V" MMPI profiles. *Journal of Personality Assessment, 46*, 18-25.

Leckliter, I. N., Matarazzo, J. D., Silverstein, A. B. (1986). A literature review of factor analytic studies of the WAIS-R. *Journal of Clinical Psychology, 42*, 332-342.

Lee, J. A., Moreno, K. E., & Sympson, J. B. (1986). The effects of mode of test administration on test performance. *Educational and Psychological Measurement, 46*, 467-473.

Lefkowitz, J., & Fraser, A. W. (1980). Assessment of achievment and power motivation of blacks and whites, using a black and white TAT with black and white administrators. *Journal of Applied Psychology, 65*, 685-696.

Leon, G. R., Gillum, B., Gillum, R., & Gouze, M. (1979). Personality stability and change over a 30-year period—middle age to old age. *Journal of Consulting and Clinical Psychology 47*, 517-524.

Leonard, C. V. (1973). Bender-Gestalt as an indicator of suicidal potential. *Psychological Reports, 32*, 665-666.

Lerner, E. A. (1972). *The projective use of the Bender-Gestalt Test.* Springfield, IL: Charles C. Thomas.

Lesiak, J. (1984). The Bender Visual Motor Gestalt Test: Implications for the diagnosis and prediction of reading achievement. *Journal of School Psychology, 22,* 391-405.

Lesser, G. S., Fifer, G., & Clark, D. H. (1965). Mental abilities of children from different social class and cultural groups. *Monographs of the Society for Research in Child Development, 30,* Serial No. 102.

LeUnes, A., Evans, M., Karnei, B., & Lowry, N. (1980). Psychological tests used in research with adolescents, 1969-1973. *Adolescence, 15,* 417-421.

Levi, J. (1951). Rorschach patterns predicting success or failure in rehabilitation of the physically handicapped. *Journal of Abnormal and Social Psychology, 46,* 240-244.

Levi, J. (1976). Acting out indicators on the Rorschach. In L. Abt & S. Weissman (Eds.), *Acting out* (2nd ed.). New York: Aronson.

Levine, D. (1981). Why and when to test: The social context of psychological testing. In A. I. Rabin (Ed.), *Assessment with projective techniques.* New York: Springer Publishing Co.

Levinson, E. M. (1987). Incorporating a vocational component into a school psychological evaluation: A case example. *Psychology in the Schools, 24,* 254-264.

Levitt, E. E. (1957). Results of psychotherapy with children: An evaluation. *Journal of Consulting Psychology, 21,* 189-196.

Levitt, E. E. (1963). Psychotherapy with children: A further evaluation. *Behavioral Research and Therapy, 1,* 45-51.

Levitt, E. E. (1980). *Primer on the Rorschach technique.* Springfield, IL: Charles C. Thomas.

Levitt, E. E., & Truumaa, A. (1972). *The Rorschach technique with children and adolescents: Applications and norms.* New York: Grune & Stratton.

Lewinsohn, P. M. (1965). Psychological correlates of overall quality of figure drawings. *Journal of Consulting Psychology, 29,* 504-512.

Lezak, M. (1983). *Neuropsychological assessment* (2nd ed.). New York: Oxford University Press.

Lichtenstein, S., & Fischoff, B. (1977). Do those who know more also know more about how much they know? *Organizational Behavior and Human Performance, 20,* 159-183.

Lick, J., Sushinsky, L., & Malow, R. (1977). Specificity of Fear Survey Schedule items and the prediction of avoidance behavior. *Behavior Modification, 1,* 195-203.

Light, B. H., & Amick, J. (1956). Rorschach responses of normal aged. *Journal of Projective Techniques, 20,* 185-195.

Lightfoot, S. L., & Oliver, J. M. (1985). The Beck Inventory: Psychometric properties in university students. *Journal of Personality Assessment, 49,* 434-436.

Lindgren, H. C., Moritsch, B., Thurlin, E. K., & Mich, G. (1986). Validity studies of three measures of achievement motivation. *Psychological Reports, 59,* 123-136.

Lindzey, G., & Herman, P. S. (1955). Thematic Apperception Test: A note on reliability and situational validity. *Journal of Projective Techniques, 19,* 36-42.

Lindzey, G., & Kalnins, D. (1958). Thematic Apperception Test: Some evidence bearing on the "hero assumption." *Journal of Abnormal and Social Psychology, 57,* 76-83.

Linton, H. B. (1954). Rorschach correlates of response to suggestion. *Journal of Abnormal and Social Psychology, 49,* 75-83.

Lipowski, Z. J. (1977). Psychosomatic medicine in the seventies: An overview. *American Journal of Psychiatry, 134,* 232-244.

Lipsitt, P. D., Lelos, D., & McGarry, A. L. (1971). Competency for trial: A screening instrument. *American Journal of Psychiatry, 128,* 137-141.

Lison, S., & Van der Spuy, H. I. J. (1977). *Cross-national MMPI research: Group personality in South Africa.* Unpublished manuscript, University of Capetown (mimeographed).

Little, K. B., & Shneidman, E. S. (1959). Congruencies among interpretations of psychological test and anamnestic data. *Psychological Monographs, 73,* (6, whole no. 476).

Loftus, E. P., & Loftus, G. R. (1980). On the permanence of stored information in the human brain. *American Psychologist, 35,* 409-420.

Loosli-Usteri, M. (1929). Le test de Rorschach applique aux différents groupes d'enfants de 10-13 ans. *Archives de Psychologie, 22,* 51-106.

Loughmiller, G. C., Ellison, R. L., Taylor, C. W., & Price, P. B. (1970). Predicting career performances of physicians using the autobiographical inventory approach. *Proceedings of the American Psychological Association, 5,* 153-154.

Lovell, V. R. (1967). The human use of personality tests: A dissenting view. *American Psychologist, 22,* 383-393.

Lowe, M. R. (1985). Psychometric evaluation of the Social Performance Survey Schedule. *Behavior Modification, 9,* 193-210.

Lubin, B., Larsen, R. M., & Matarazzo, J. D. (1984). Patterns of psychological test usage in the United States: 1935-1982. *American Psychologist, 39,* 451-454.

Lubin, B., Larsen, R. M., Matarazzo, J. D., & Seever, M. (1985). Psychological test usage patterns in five professional settings. *American Psychologist, 40,* 857-861.

Lubin, B., Larsen, R. M., Matarazzo, J. D., & Seever, M. (1986). Selected characteristics of psychologists and psychological assessment in five settings: 1959-1988. *Professional Psychology: Research and Practice, 17,* 155-157.

Lucas, R. W., Mullin, P. J., Luna, C. B., & McInroy, D. C. (1977). Psychiatrists and a computer as interrogators of patients with alcohol-related illnesses: A comparison. *British Journal of Psychiatry, 131,* 160-167.

Lueger, R. L., & Petzel, T. P. (1979). Illusory correlation in clinical judgement: Effects of amount of information to be processed. *Journal of Consulting and Clinical Psychology, 47,* 1120-1121.

Lukin, M. E., Down, E. T., Plake, B. S., & Kraft, R. G. (1985). Comparing computerized versus traditional psychological assessment. *Computers in Human Behavior, 1,* 49-58.

Lundy, A. (1985). The reliability of the Thematic Apperception Test. *Journal of Personality Assessment, 49,* 141-145.

Lundy, A. (1988). Instructional set and Thematic Apperception Test Validity. *Journal of Personality Assessment, 52,* 309-320.

Luria, A. R. (1973). *The working brain.* New York: Basic Books.

MacAndrews, C. (1965). The differentiation of male alcoholic outpatients from nonalcoholic psychiatric patients by means of the MMPI. *Quarterly Journal of Studies on Alcohol, 26*, 238-246.

Machover, K. (1949). *Personality projection in the drawings of the human figure*. Springfield, IL: Charles C. Thomas.

Maitra, A. K. (1983). Executive effectiveness: Characteristic thematic phantasy. *Managerial Psychology, 4*, 59-68.

Majumber, A. K., & Roy, A. B. (1962). Latent personality content of juvenile delinquents. *Journal of Psychological Research, 1*, 4-8.

Maloney, M. P., & Glasser, A. (1982). An evaluation of the clinical utility of the Draw-A-Person Test. *Journal of Clinical Psychology, 38*, 183-190.

Maloney, M. P., & Ward, M. P. (1976). *Psychological assessment: A conceptual approach*. New York: Oxford University Press.

Malpass, R. S., & Kravitz, J. (1969). Recognition for faces of own and other race. *Journal of Personality and Social Psychology, 13*, 330-334.

Mann, L. (1956). The relation of Rorschach indices of extratension and introversion to a measure of responsiveness to the immediate environment. *Journal of Consulting Psychology, 20*, 114-118.

Margolin, G., Hattem, D., John, R. S., & Yost, K. (1985). Perceptual agreement between spouses and outside observers when coding themselves and a stranger dyad. *Behavioral Assessment, 7*, 235-247.

Marks, I. M., & Mathews, A. M. (1979). Brief standard self-rating for phobic patients. *Behavior Research and Therapy, 17*, 263-267.

Marks, P. A., Seeman, W., & Haller, D. L. (1974). *The actuarial use of the MMPI with adolescents and adults*. Baltimore: Williams and Wilkins.

Marley, M. L. (1982). *Organic brain pathology and the Bender Gestalt Test: A differential diagnostic scoring system*. New York: Grune & Stratton.

Martin, J. D., Pfaadt, N. K., & MaKinister, J. G. (1983). Relationship of hostility and white space responses on the Rorschach. *Perceptual and Motor Skills, 57*, 739-742.

Matarazzo, J. D. (1965). The interview. In B. B. Wolman (Ed.), *Handbook of clinical psychology*. New York: McGraw-Hill.

Matarazzo, J. D. (1972). *Wechsler's measurement and appraisal of adult intelligence* (5th ed.). Baltimore: Williams and Wilkins.

Matarazzo, J. D. (1986). Computerized clinical psychological test interpretations: Unvalidated plus all mean and no sigma. *American Psychologist, 41*, 14-24.

Matarazzo, J. D., Daniel, M. H., Prifitera, A., & Herman, D. O. (1988). Inter-subtest scatter in the WAIS-R standardization sample. *Journal of Clinical Psychology, 44*, 940-950.

Matarazzo, J. D., & Herman, D. O. (1984). Base rate data for the WAIS-R: Test-retest stability and VIQ-PIQ differences. *Journal of Clinical Neuropsychology, 6*, 351-366.

Matarazzo, J. D., & Prifitera, A. (1989). Subtest scatter and premorbid intelligence: Lessons from the WAIS-R standardization sample. *Psychological Assessment, 1*, 186-191.

Mauger, P. A. (1972). The test-retest reliability of persons: An empirical investigation utilizing the MMPI and the personality research form. *Dissertation Abstracts International, 33,* 2816B.

May, A. E., Urquhart, A., & Tarran, J. (1969). Self-evaluation of depression in various diagnostic and therapeutic groups. *Archives of General Psychiatry, 21,* 191-194.

Mayman, M. (1959). Style, focus, language, and content of an ideal psychological test report. *Journal of Projective Techniques, 23,* 453-458.

McAllister, L. (1988). *A practical guide to CPI interpretation.* Palo Alto, CA: Consulting Psychologists Press.

McCarthy, D. A. (1972). *Manual for the McCarthy Scales for Children's Abilities.* New York: Psychological Corporation.

McClelland, D. C. (1961). *The achieving society.* Princeton, NJ: Van Nostrand.

McClelland, D. C. (1966). Longitudinal trends in the relation of thought to action. *Journal of Consulting Psychology, 30,* 479-483.

McClelland, D. C. (1971). *Assessing human motivation.* New York: General Learning Press.

McCormick, I. A. (1984). A simple version of the Rathus Assertiveness Schedule. *Behavioral Assessment, 7,* 95-99.

McCormick, T. T., & Brannigan, G. G. (1984). Bender-Gestalt signs as indicants of anxiety, withdrawal, and acting-out behaviors in adolescents. *Journal of Psychology, 118,* 71-74.

McCreary, C. P. (1976). Trait and type differences among male and female assaultive and nonassaultive offenders. *Journal of Personality Assessment, 40,* 617-621.

McFall, R. M., & Lillesand, D. V. (1971). Behavior rehearsal with modeling and coaching in assertive training. *Journal of Abnormal Psychology, 77,* 313-323.

McFarland, R. A. (1984). Effects of music upon emotional content of TAT stories. *Journal of Psychology, 116,* 227-234.

McFie, J. (1960). Psychological testing in clinical neurology. *Journal of Nervous and Mental Disease, 131,* 383-393.

McFie, J. (1969). The diagnostic significance of disorders of higher nervous activity syndromes related to frontal, temporal, parietal, and occipital lesions. In P. J. Vinken & G. W. Bruyn (Eds.), *Handbook of clinical neurology.* (Vol. 4). New York: American Elsevier Publishing.

McGregor, J. P. (1979). Kinetic Family Drawing Test: A validity study. *Dissertation Abstracts International, 40,* 927-928.

McIntosh, J. A., Belter, R. W., Saylor, C. F., Finch, A. J., & Edwards, G. L. (1988). The Bender-Gestalt with adolescents: Comparison of two scoring systems. *Journal of Clinical Psychology, 44,* 226-230.

McKay, M. F., & Neale, M. D. (1985). Predicting early school achievement in reading and handwriting using major "error" categories from the Bender-Gestalt Test for young children. *Perceptual and Motor Skills, 60,* 647-654.

McKnight, D. L., Nelson, R. O., Hayes, S. C., & Jarrett, R. B. (1984). Importance of treating individually-assessed response classes in the amelioration of depression. *Behavior Therapy, 15,* 315-335.

McLachlan, J. F. C., & Head, V. B. (1974). An impairment rating scale for human figure drawings. *Journal of Clinical Psychology, 30*, 405-407.

McNemar, Q. (1974). Correction to a correction. *Journal of Consulting and Clinical Psychology, 42*, 145-146.

McReynolds, P. (1989). Diagnosis and clinical assessment: Current status and major issues. *Annual Review of Psychology, 40*, 83-108.

Meehl, P. E. (1954). *Clinical versus statistical prediction: A theoretical analysis and a review of the evidence.* Minneapolis: University of Minnesota Press.

Meehl, P. E. (1965). Seer over sign: The first good example. *Journal of Experimental Research in Personality 1*, 27-32.

Meer, B. (1955). The relative difficulty of the Rorschach cards. *Journal of Projective Techniques, 9*, 43-59.

Megargee, E. I. (1964). *Undercontrol and overcontrol in assaultive and homicidal adolescents* (Doctoral dissertation, University of California, Berkley). University Microfilms, No.64-9923.

Megargee, E. I. (1965). Assault with intent to kill. *Trans-Action, 2*, 27-31.

Megargee, E. I. (1966a). Estimation of CPI scores from MMPI protocols. *Journal of Clinical Psychology, 22*, 456-458.

Megargee, E. I. (1966b). *Research in clinical assessment.* New York: Harper & Row.

Megargee, E. I. (1966c). The Edwards SD Scale: A measure of dissimulation or adjustment? *Journal of Consulting Psychology, 30*, 566.

Megargee, E. I. (1966d). Undercontrolled and overcontrolled personality types in extreme anti-social aggression. *Psychological Monographs, 80*, No. 611.

Megargee, E. I. (1972). *The California Psychological Inventory handbook.* San Francisco: Jossey-Bass.

Megargee, E. I., Cook, P. E., & Mendelsohn, G. A. (1967). Development and evaluation of an MMPI scale of assaultiveness in overcontrolled individuals. *Journal of Abnormal Psychology, 72*, 519-528.

Megargee, E. I., & Mendelsohn, G. A. (1962). A cross-validation of twelve MMPI indices of hostility and control. *Journal of Abnormal Psychology, 65*, 431-438.

Megargee, E. I., & Parker, G. V. (1968). An exploration of the equivalence of Murrayan needs as assessed by the Adjective Check List, the TAT, and the Edwards Personal Preference Schedule. *Journal of Clinical Psychology, 24*, 47-51.

Mehrabian, A. (1972). *Nonverbal communication.* Chicago: Aldine-Atherton

Meichenbaum, D. (1976). A cognitive behavior modification approach to assessment. In M. Hersen & A. S. Bellack (Eds.), *Behavioral Assessment.* New York: Pergamon Press.

Melzack, R. (1975). The McGill Pain Questionnaire: Major properties and scoring methods. *Pain, 1*, 277-299.

Mendez, F. (1978). *Adult Neuropsychological Questionnaire.* Odessa, FL: Psychological Assessment Resources.

Merbaum, M., & Hefetz, A. (1976). Some personality characteristics of soldiers exposed to extreme war stress. *Journal of Consulting and Clinical Psychology, 44*, 1-6.

Mercer, C. (1983). *Students with learning disabilities.* Columbus, Ohio: Charles E. Merrill.

Mercer, J. R. (1979). In defense of racially and culturally non-discriminatory assessment. *School Psychology Digest, 8,* 89-115.

Mercer, J. R., & Lewis, J. F. (1978). *System of multicultural pluralistic assessment.* San Antonio: The Psychological Corporation.

Mermelstein, J. J. (1983). The relationship between rotation on the Bender-Gestalt Test and ratings of patient disorientation. *Journal of Personality Assessment, 47,* 490-491.

Merrens, M. R., & Richards, W. S. (1970). Acceptance of generalized versus "bona fide" personality interpretation. *Psychological Reports, 27,* 691-694.

Messick, S. (1984). Assessment in context: Appraising student performance in relation to instructional quality. *Educational Research, 13,* 3-8.

Messick, S., & Jackson, D. N. (1961). Acquiescence and the factorial interpretation of the MMPI. *Psychological Bulletin, 58,* 299-304.

Michael, C. C., & Funabiki, D. (1985). Depression, distortion, and life stress: Extended findings. *Cognitive Therapy and Research, 9,* 659-666.

Miller, C., Knapp, S. C., & Daniels, C. W. (1968). MMPI study of Negro mental hygiene clinic patients. *Journal of Abnormal Psychology, 73,* 168-173.

Miller, I. W., III, & Norman, W. H. (1986). Persistance of depressive cognitions within a subgroup of depressed inpatients. *Cognitive Therapy and Research, 10,* 211-224.

Millon, T. (1985). The MCMI provides a good assessment of DSM-III disorders. The MCMI-II will prove even better. *Journal of Personality Assessment, 49,* 379-391.

Mills, C. J., & Bohannon, W. E. (1980). Personality characteristics of effective state police officers. *Journal of Applied Psychology, 65,* 680-684.

Milne, D. (1984). Improving the social validity and implementation of behavior therapy training for psychiatric nurses using a patient-centred learning format. *British Journal of Clinical Psychology, 23,* 313-314.

Mirza, L. (1977). Multiple administration of the MMPI with schizophrenics. Unpublished manuscript, Fountain House, Pakistan.

Mischel, W. (1968). *Personality and assessment.* New York: John Wiley & Sons, Inc.

Mishra, S. P., Ferguson, B. A., & King, P. V. (1985). Research with the Wechsler Digit Span subtest: Implications for assessment. *School Psychology Review, 14,* 37-47.

Mitchell, R. E., Grandy, T. G., & Lupo, J. V. (1986). Comparison of the WAIS and the WAIS-R in the upper ranges of I.Q. *Professional Psychology: Research and Practice, 17,* 82-83.

Mitchell, J. V. (Ed.), (1985). *The ninth mental measurements yearbook.* Highland Park, NJ: Gryphon Press.

Mittenberg, W., Hammeke, T. A., & Rao, S. M. (1989). Intrasubtest scatter on the WAIS-R as a pathognomonic sign of brain injury. *Psychological Assessment, 1,* 273-276.

Mizushima, K., & De Vos, G. (1967). An application of the California Psychological Inventory in a study of Japanese delinquency. *Journal of Clinical Psychology, 71,* 45-51.

Molish, H. B. (1967). Critique and problems of the Rorschach. A survey. In S. J. Beck & H. B. Molish (Eds.), *Rorschach's Test: Vol. 2 A variety of personality pictures* (2nd ed.). New York: Grune & Stratton.

Montague, D. J., & Prytula, R. E. (1975). Human figure drawing characteristics related to juvenile delinquents. *Perceptual and Motor Skills, 40,* 623-630.

Moreland, K. L. (1985). *Test-retest reliability of 80 MMPI scales.* Unpublished materials. (Available from NCS Professional Assessment Services, P. O. Box 1416, Minneapolis, MN, 55440).

Moreland, K. L. (1987). Computerized psychological assessment: What's available. In J. N. Butcher (Ed.), *Computerized psychological assessment: A practitioner's guide* (pp. 26-45). New York: Basic Books Inc.

Morena, D. (1981). The healthy drawing. In G. Groth-Marnat & D. Morena (Eds.), *Handbook of psychological assessment.* (Unpublished manuscript).

Morey, L. C., Blashfield, R. K., Webb, W. W., & Jewell, J. (1988). MMPI scales for DSM-III personality disorders: A preliminary validation study. *Journal of Clinical Psychology, 44,* 47-50.

Morgan, C. D., & Murray, H. A. (1935). A method for investigating fantasies. *AMA Archives of Neurology and Psychiatry, 34,* 389-406.

Morganstern, K. P. (1988). Behavioral interviewing. In A. S. Bellack & M. Hersen (Eds.), *Behavioral assessment: A practical handbook.* (3rd ed.). New York: Pergamon.

Morrison, R. L. (1988). Structured interviews and rating scales. In A. S. Bellack & M. Hersen (Eds.), *Behavioral assessment: A practical handbook.* (3rd ed.). New York: Pergamon.

Mosher, D. L. (1965). Approval motive and acceptance of personality-test interpretations which differ in favorability. *Psychological Reports, 17,* 395-402.

Mueller, H. H., Dash, V. N., Matheson, D. W., & Short, R. H. (1984). WISC-R subtest patterning of below average, average, and above average I.Q. children: A meta-analysis. *Alberta Journal of Educational Research, 30,* 68-85.

Mukerji, M. (1969). Rorschach indices of love, aggression, and happiness. *Journal of Projective Techniques and Personality Assessment, 33,* 526-529.

Mundy, J. (1972). The use of projective techniques with children. In B. B. Wolman (Ed.), *Manual of Child Psychopathology* (pp.791-819). New York: McGraw-Hill.

Munsinger, H. (1975). The adopted child's I.Q.: A critical review. *Psychological Bulletin, 82,* 623-659.

Munter, P. O. (1975). The medical model revisited: A humanistic reply. *Journal of Personality Assessment, 39,* 344.

Murillo, L. G., & Exner, J. E. (1973). The effects of regressive ECT with process schizophrenics. *American Journal of Psychiatry, 130,* 269-273.

Murray, E., & Roberts, F. (1956). The Bender-Gestalt Test in a patient passing through a brief manic-depressive cycle. *U.S. Armed Forces Medical Journal, 7,* 1206-1208.

Murray, H. A. (1938). *Explorations in personality.* New York: Oxford University Press.

Murray, H. A. (1943). *Thematic Apperception Test manual.* Cambridge, Mass: Harvard University Press.

Murstein, B. I. (1960). Factor analysis of the Rorschach. *Journal of Consulting Psychology, 24,* 262-275.

Murstein, B. I. (1963). *Theory and research in projective techniques (Emphasizing the TAT).* New York: John Wiley & Sons, Inc.

Murstein, B. L. (1972). Normative written TAT responses for a college sample. *Journal of Personality Assessment, 36*, 104-147.

Myers, P. I., & Hammill, D. D. (1982). *Learning disabilities: Basic concepts, assessment practices, and instructional strategies.* Austin: Pro-ed.

Naches, A. M. (1967). The Bender-Gestalt Test and acting out behavior in children. *Dissertation Abstracts, 28,* 2146.

Naglieri, J. A. (1980). A comparison of McCarthy General Cognitive Index and WISC-R I.Q. for educable mentally retarded, learning disabled, and normal children. *Psychological Reports, 47,* 591-596.

Naglieri, J. A., & Kaufman, A. S. (1983). How many factors underlie the WAIS-R? *Journal of Psychoeducational Assessment, 1,* 113-119.

Neale, M. D., & McKay, M. F. (1985). Scoring the Bender-Gestalt Test using the Koppitz Developmental System: Interrater reliability, item difficulty, and scoring implications. *Perceptual and Motor Skills, 60,* 627-636.

Nelson, R. E. (1977). Irrational beliefs in depression. *Journal of Consulting and Clinical Psychology, 45,* 1190-1191.

Nelson, R. E., & Maser, J. D. (1988). The DSM-III and depression: Potential contributions of behavioral assessment. *Behavioral assessment, 10,* 45-66.

Nevo, B. (1985). Face validity revisited. *Journal of Educational Measurement, 22,* 287-293.

Nevo, B., & Sfez, J. (1985). Examinee's feedback questionnaires. *Assessment and Evaluation in Higher Education, 10,* 236-249.

Newmark, C. S., & Thibodeau, J. R. (1979). Interpretive accuracy and empirical validity of abbreviated forms of the MMPI with hospitalized adolescents. In C. S. Newmark (Ed.) *MMPI: Clinical and research trends.* New York: Praeger.

Nicholi, A. M. (1978). History and mental status. In A. M. Nicholi (Ed.), *The Harvard guide to modern psychiatry.* Cambridge, MA: Harvard Press.

Nisbett, R. E., & Wilson, T. D. (1977). Telling more than we can know: Verbal reports on mental processes. *Psychological Review, 84,* 231-259.

Nobo, J., & Evans, R. G. (1986). The WAIS-R Picture Arrangement and Comprehension subtests as measures of social behavior characteristics. *Journal of Personality Assessment, 50,* 90-92.

Norman, R. D. (1966). A revised deterioration formula for the Wechsler Adult Intelligence Scale. *Journal of Clinical Psychology, 22,* 287-294.

Norton, J. C. (1978). The Trail Making Test and Bender Background Interference Procedure as screening devices. *Journal of Clinical Psychology, 34,* 916-922.

Norton, R., & Warnick, B. (1976). Assertiveness as a communication construct. *Human Communication Research, 3,* 62-66.

Nottingham, E. J., & Mattson, R. E. (1981). A validation study of the competency screening test. *Law and Human Behavior, 5,* 329-335.

Nunez, R. (1980). *Aplicacion del Inventario Multifasico de la Personalidad (MMPI) a la Psicopatologia* (2nd ed.). Mexico: El Manual Moderro.

O'Dell, J. P. (1972). Barnum explores the computer. *Journal of Consulting and Clinical Psychology, 38,* 270-273.

O'Leary, A. (1985). Self-efficacy and health. *Behavior Therapy and Research, 23,* 437-451.

Oakland, T. D. (1980). An evaluation of the ABIC, pluralistic norms, and estimated learning potential. *Journal of School Psychology, 18,* 3-11.

Oakland, T., & Dowling, L. (1983). The Draw-A-Person Test: Validity properties for non-biased assessment. *Learning Disabilities Quarterly, 6,* 526-534.

Oas, P. (1984). Validity of the Draw-A-Person and Bender Gestalt Tests as measures of impulsivity with adolescents. *Journal of Consulting and Clinical Psychology, 52,* 1011-1019.

Obrzut, J. E., & Cummings, J. A. (1983). The projective approach to personality assessment: An analysis of thematic picture techniques. *School Psychology Review, 12,* 414-420.

Office of Strategic Services Staff. (1948). *Assessment of men.* New York: Holt, Rinehart & Winston.

Office of Science and Technology. (1967). *Privacy and behavioral research.* Washington, DC: U.S. Government Printing Office.

Olbrisch, M. E. (1977). Psychotherapeutic interventions in physical health: Effectiveness and economic efficiency. *American Psychologist, 32,* 761-777.

Ollendick, T. H. (1978). *The Fear Survey Schedule for Children-Revised.* Unpublished manuscript, Indiana State University, Terre Haute, IN.

Ollendick, T. H. (1983). Reliability and validity of the revised fear survey schedule for children (FSSC-R). *Behavior Research and Therapy, 21,* 685-692.

Orne, M. T. (1962). On the social psychology of the psychological experiment: With particular reference to demand characteristics and their implications. *American Psychologist, 17,* 766-783.

Osato, S. S., Van Gorp, W. G., Kern, R. S., Satz, P., & Steinman, L. (1989). The Satz-Mogel Short form of the WAIS-R in an elderly, demented population. *Psychological Assessment, 1,* 339-341.

Oskamp, S. (1962). The relationship of clinical experience training methods to several criteria of clinical prediction. *Psychological Monographs, 76,* No. 547.

Oskamp, S. (1965). Overconfidence in case-study judgments. *Journal of Consulting Psychology, 29,* 261-265.

Oster, G. D., & Gould, P. (1987). *Using drawings in assessment and therapy.* New York: Brunner/Mazel.

Ottenbacher, K. (1981). An investigation of self concept and body image in the mentally retarded. *Journal of Clinical Psychology, 37,* 415-418.

Ownby, R. L. (1986). *A study of the expository process model (EPM) with clinical and counseling psychologists.* Manuscript submitted for publication.

Ownby, R. L. (1987). *Psychological reports: A guide to report writing in professional psychology.* Brandon, VT: Clinical Psychology Publishing Co., Inc.

Ownby, R. L., & Wallbrown, F. H. (1983). Evaluating school psychological reports, Part I: A procedure for systematic feedback. *Psychology in the Schools, 20,* 41-45.

Page, H. A. (1957). Studies in fantasy-daydreaming frequency and Rorschach scoring categories. *Journal of Consulting Psychology, 21,* 111-114.

Pallis, D. J., Gibbons, J. S., & Pierce, D. W. (1984). Estimating suicide risk among attempted suicides: II. Efficiency of predictive scales after the attempt. *British Journal of Psychiatry, 144,* 139-148.

Palmer, J. O. (1970). *The psychological assessment of children.* New York: John Wiley & Sons, Inc.

Paludi, M. A. (1978). Machover revisited: Impact of sex-role orientation on sex sequence on the Draw-A-Person Test. *Perceptual and Motor Skills, 47,* 713-714.

Pancoast, D. L., & Archer, R. P. (1988). MMPI adolescent norms: Patterns and trends across 4 decades. *Journal of Personality Assessment, 52,* 691-706.

Pardue, A. M. (1975). Bender-Gestalt test and background interference procedure in discernment of organic brain damage. *Perceptual and Motor Skills, 40,* 103-109.

Parker, K. (1983a). Factor analysis of the WAIS-R at nine age levels between 16 and 74 years. *Journal of Consulting and Clinical Psychology, 51,* 302-308.

Parker, K. (1983b). A meta-analysis of the reliability and validity of the Rorschach. *Journal of Personality Assessment, 47,* 227-231.

Parks, C. W. (1982). *A multi-dimensional view of the imagery construct: Issues of definition and assessment.* Unpublished manuscript.

Parks, C. W., & Hollon, S. D. (1988). Cognitive Assessment. In A. S. Bellack & M. Hersen (Eds.), *Behavioral assessment: A practical handbook.* (3rd ed.). New York: Pergamon.

Pascal, G. R., & Suttell, B. J. (1951). *The Bender Gestalt Test: Quantification and Validity for Adults.* New York: Grune & Stratton.

Patalano, F. (1986). Drug abusers and Card 3BM of the TAT. *Psychology: A Quarterly Journal of Human Behavior, 23,* 34-36.

Pauker, J. D. (1976). A quick-scoring system for the Bender-Gestalt: Interrater reliability and scoring validity. *Journal of Clinical Psychology, 32,* 86-89.

Payne, F. D., & Wiggins, J. S. (1972). MMPI profile types and the self-reports of psychiatric patients. *Journal of Abnormal Psychology, 79,* 1-8.

Perry, N. W., McCoy, J. G., Cunningham, W. R., Falgout, J. C., & Street, W. J. (1976). Multivariate visual evoked response correlates of intelligence. *Psychophysiology, 13,* 323-329.

Pfeifer, C., & Sedlacek, W. (1971). The validity of academic predictors for black and white students at a predominantly white university. *Journal of Educational Measurement, 8,* 253-261.

Phares, E. J., Stewart, L. M., & Foster, J. M. (1960). Instruction variation and Rorschach performance. *Journal of Projective Techniques, 24,* 28-31.

Phillips, L., & Smith, J. (1953). *Rorschach interpretation: Advanced technique.* New York: Grune & Stratton.

Piaget, J. (1950). *The psychology of intelligence.* New York: Harcourt, Brace & World.

Pickford, R. W. (1963). *Pickford Projective Pictures.* London: Tavistock.

Piedmont, R. L., Sokolove, R. L., & Fleming, M. Z. (1989a). On WAIS-R Difference Scores in a psychiatric population. *Psychological Assessment, 1,* 155-159.

Piedmont, R. L., Sokolove, R. L., & Fleming, M. Z. (1989b). An examination of some diagnostic strategies involving the Wechsler intelligence scales. *Psychological Assessment, 1,* 181-185.

Pilowsky, I., Spence, N., Cobb, J., & Katsikitis, M. (1984). The Illness Behavior Questionnaire as an aid in clinical assessment. *General Hospital Psychiatry, 6,* 123-130.

Piotrowski, C. (1984). The status of projective techniques: or, "Wishing won't make it go away." *Journal of Clinical Psychology, 40,* 1495-1502.

Piotrowski, C., & Keller, J. W. (1984). Psychodiagnostic testing in APA-approved clinical psychology programs. *Professional Psychology: Research and Practice, 15,* 450-456.

Piotrowski, C., & Keller, J. W. (in press). Psychological testing in outpatient mental health facilities: A national study. *Professional Psychology: Research and Practice.*

Piotrowski, C., Sherry, D., & Keller, J. W. (1985). Psychodiagnostic test usage: A survey of the Society for Personality Assessment. *Journal of Personality Assessment, 49,* 115-119.

Piotrowski, Z. A. (1937). The Rorschach ink-blot method in organic disturbances of the central nervous system. *Journal of Nervous and Mental Disorders, 86,* 525-537.

Piotrowski, Z. A. (1957). *Perceptanalysis.* New York: Macmillan.

Piotrowski, Z. A. (1960). The movement score. In M. Rickers-Ovsiankina (Ed.), *Rorschach psychology.* New York: John Wiley & Sons, Inc.

Piotrowski, Z. A. (1969a). A Piotrowski interpretation. In J. E. Exner (Ed.), *The Rorschach systems.* New York: Grune & Stratton.

Piotrowski, Z. A. (1969b). Long-term prognosis in schizophrenia based on Rorschach findings: the LTPTI. In D. V. Sira Sankar (Ed.), *Schizophrenia, current concepts and research* (pp.84-103). Hicksville, NY: PJD Publications.

Piotrowski, Z. A., & Bricklin, B. A. (1961). A second validation of a long-term prognostic index for schizophrenic patients. *Journal of Consulting Psychology, 25,* 123-128.

Piotrowski, Z. A., & Schreiber, M. (1952). Rorschach perceptanalytic measurement of personality changes during and after intensive psychoanalytically oriented psychotherapy. In G. Bychowski & J. L. Despert (Eds.), *Specialized techniques in psychotherapy.* New York: Basic Books.

Plenk, A. M., & Jones, J. (1967). An examination of the Bender-Gestalt performance of three and four year olds and its relationship to Koppitz scoring system. *Journal of Clinical Psychology, 23,* 367-370.

Polyson, J., Norris, D., & Ott, E. (1985). The recent decline in TAT research. *Professional Psychology: Research and Practice, 16,* 26-28.

Pope, B. (1979). *The mental health interview: Research and application.* New York: Pergamon Press.

Pope, B., & Scott, W. H. (1967). *Psychological diagnosis in clinical practice.* New York: Oxford University Press.

Porges, S. W., & Fox, N. A. (1986). Developmental psychophysiology. In M. G. H. Coles, E. Donchin, & S. W. Porges (Eds.), *Psychophysiology: Systems, processes and applications.* New York: Guilford.

Porter, E. H. (1950). *An introduction to therapeutic counseling.* Boston: Houghton-Mifflin.

Pritchard, D. A., & Rosenblatt, A. (1980). Reply to Gynther and Green. *Journal of Consulting and Clinical Psychology, 48,* 273-274.

Prokop, C. K. (1988). Chronic pain. In R. L. Greene (Ed.), *The MMPI: Use with specific populations.* San Diego: Grune & Stratton.

Prout, H. T., & Celmer, D. S. (1984). School drawings and academic achievement: A validity study of the Kinetic School Drawing technique. *Psychology in the Schools, 21*, 176-180.

Prout, H. T., & Phillips, D. D. (1974). A clinical note: The Kinetic School Drawing. *Psychology in the Schools, 11*, 303-306.

Pryzwansky, W. B., & Hanania, J. S. (1986). Applying problem-solving approaches to school psychological reports. *Journal of School Psychology, 24*, 133-141.

Pugh, G. (1985). The California Psychological Inventory and police selection. *Journal of Police Science and Administration, 13*, 172-177.

Puig-Antich, J., & Chambers, W. (1978). *The Schedule for Affective Disorders and Schizophrenia for School aged Children.* New York: New York State Psychiatric Institute.

Quay, H. C., & Peterson, D. R. (1987). *Manual for the Revised Behavior Problem Checklist.* Miami, FL: Authors (at University of Miami).

Query, W. T. (1966). CPI factors and success of seminary students. *Psychological Reports, 18*, 665-660.

Quillan, J., Besing, S., & Dinning, D. (1977). Standardization of the Rathus Assertiveness Schedule. *Journal of Clinical Psychology, 33*, 418-422.

Rabin, A. I. (1968). *Projective techniques in personality assessment: A modern introduction.* New York: Springer.

Rabin, A. I., & Beck, S. J. (1950). Genetic aspects of some Rorschach factors. *American Journal of Orthopsychiatry, 20*, 595-599.

Ramos, M. C., & Die, A. H. (1986). The WAIS-R Picture Arrangement subtest: What do scores indicate? *Journal of General Psychology, 113*, 251-261.

Rao, A. V., & Potash, H. M. (1985). Size factors on the Bender-Gestalt test and their relationship to trait anxiety and situationally induced anxiety. *Journal of Clinical Psychology, 41*, 834-838.

Rapaport, C., Gill, M., & Schafer, J. (1968). *Diagnostic psychological testing* (Vol. I). Chicago: Year Book Publishers.

Rapaport, C., Gill, M., & Schafer, J. (1946). *Diagnostic psychological testing* (Vol. 2). Chicago: Year Book Publishers.

Raskin, L. M., & Bloom, A. S. (1979). Kinetic Family Drawings by children with learning disabilities. *Journal of Pediatric Psychology, 4*, 247-251.

Rathus, S. A. (1972). An experimental investigation of assertive training in a group setting. *Journal of Behavior Therapy and Experimental Psychiatry, 3*, 81-86.

Rathus, S. A. (1973). A 30-item schedule for assessing assertive behavior. *Behavior Therapy, 4*, 398-406.

Rathus, S. A., & Nevid, J. S. (1977). Concurrent validity of the 30-item assertiveness schedule with a psychiatric population. *Behavior Therapy, 8*, 393-397.

Raven, J. (1983). The relationship between educational institutions and society with particular reference to the role of assessment. *International Review of Applied Psychology, 32*, 249-274.

Rawls, J. R., & Slack, G. K. (1968). Artists versus non-artists: Rorschach determinants and artistic creativity. *Journal of Projective Techniques and Personality Assessment, 32*, 233-237.

Raychaudhuri, M. (1971). Relation of creativity and sex to Rorschach M responses. *Journal of Personality Assessment, 35*, 27-36.

Redfering, D. L., & Collings, J. (1982). A comparison of the Koppitz and Hutt techniques of Bender Gestalt administration correlated with WISC-R performance scores. *Educational and Psychological Measurement, 42*, 41-47.

Reich, J. H., & Noyes, R. (1987). A comparison of DSM-III personality disorders in acutely ill panic and depressed patients. *Journal of Anxiety Disorders, 1*, 123-131.

Reich, W., Herjanic, B., Welner, Z., & Gandhy, P. R. (1982). Development of a structured psychiatric interview for children: Agreement on diagnosis comparing parent and child. *Journal of Abnormal Child Psychology, 10*, 325-326.

Reilly, T. P., Drudge, O. W., Rosen, J. C., Loew, D. E., & Fischer, M. (1985). Concurrent and predictive validity of the WISC-R, McCarthy Scales, Woodcock-Johnson, and academic achievement. *Psychology in the Schools, 22*, 380-382.

Reirdan, J., & Koff, E. (1980). Representation of the female body by early and late adolescent girls. *Journal of Youth and Adolescence, 9*, 339-346.

Reiss, S., Peterson, R. A., Gursky, D. M., & McNally, R. J. (1986). Anxiety sensitivity, anxiety frequency, and the prediction of fearfulness. *Behavior Research and Therapy, 24*, 1-8.

Reitan, R. M. (1955). Validity of the Rorschach test as a measure of the psychological effects of brain damage. *Archives of Neurology and Psychiatry, 73*, 445-451.

Reitan, R. M. (1974a). Methodological problems in clinical neuropsychology. In R. M. Reitan, & L. A. Davison, (Eds.), *Clinical neuropsychology: Current status and applications.* New York: John Wiley & Sons, Inc.

Reitan, R. M. (1974b). Psychological effects of cerebral lesions in children of early school age. In Reitan, R. M., & Davison, L. A. (Eds.), *Clinical neuropsychology: Current status and applications.* Washington, DC: V. H. Winston & Sons, pp.53-90.

Reitan, R. M., & Davison, L. A. (Eds.). (1974). *Clinical neuropsychology: Current status and applications.* New York: Halsted Press.

Reitan, R. M., & Wolfson, D. (1985). *The Halsted-Reitan Neuropsychological Battery: Theory and clinical interpretation.* Tucson, AZ: Tucson Neuropsychological Press.

Reschley, D. J. (1981). Psychological testing in educational classification and placement. *American Psychologist, 36*, 1094-1102.

Research and Education Association. (1981). *Handbook of psychiatric rating scales.* New York: Research and Education Association.

Retief, A. (1987). Thematic apperception testing across cultures: Tests of selection versus tests of inclusion. *South African Journal of Psychology, 17*, 47-55.

Reynolds, C. R. (1986). Wide Range Achievement Test (WRAT-R), 1984 edition. *Journal of Counseling and Development, 64*, 540-541.

Reynolds, C. R., & Gutkin, T. B. (1979). Predicting the premorbid intellectual status of children using demographic data. *Clinical Neuropsychology, 1*, 36-38.

Reynolds, C. R., & Hartlage, L. (1979). Comparison of WISC and WISC-R regression lines for academic prediction with black and white referred children. *Journal of Consulting and Clinical Psychology, 47*, 589-591.

Reynolds, W. M., & Sundberg, N. D. (1976). Recent research trends in testing. *Journal of Personality Assessment, 40*, 228-233.

Richter, R. H., & Winter, W. D. (1966). Holtzman ink-blot correlates of creative potential. *Journal of Projective Techniques and Personality Assessment, 30*, 62-67.

Rickers-Ovsiankina, M. A. (1977). *Rorschach psychology*. New York: Robert E. Krieger.

Ridgeway, E. M., & Exner, J. E. (1980). *Rorschach correlates of achievement needs in medical students under an arousal state*. Workshops Study No. 274 (unpublished), Rorschach Workshops.

Riessman, F., & Miller, S. M. (1958). Social class and projective tests. *Journal of Projective Techniques, 22*, 432-439.

Rissetti, F., Butcher, J. N., Agostini, J., Elgueta, M., Gaete, S., Marguilies, T., Morlans, I., & Ruiz, R. (1979). *Translation and adaptation of the MMPI in Chile: Use in a university student health service*. Papers given at the 14th Annual Symposium on the Recent Developments in the Use of the MMPI, St. Petersburg.

Riskind, J. H., Beck, A. T., Berchick, R. J., Brown, G., & Steer, R. A. (1987). Reliability of DSM-III diagnoses for major depression and generalized anxiety disorder using the Structured Clinical Interview for DSM-III. *Archives of General Psychiatry, 44*, 817-820.

Ritzler, B. A., & Alter, B. (1986). Rorschach teaching in APA-approved clinical graduate programs: Ten years later. *Journal of Personality Assessment, 50*, 44-49.

Ritzler, B. A., Sharkey, K. J., & Chudy, J. F. (1980). A comprehensive projective alternative to the TAT. *Journal of Personality Assessment, 44*, 358-362.

Roback, H. B. (1968). Human figure drawings: Their utility in the clinical psychologist's armamentarium for personality assessment. *Psychological Bulletin, 70*, 1-19.

Roback, H. B., Langevin, R., & Zajac, Y. (1974). Sex of free choice figure drawings by homosexual and heterosexual subjects. *Journal of Personality Assessment, 38*, 154-155.

Robiner, W. (1978). *An analysis of some of the variables influencing clinical use of the Bender-Gestalt*. Unpublished manuscript, Washington University in St. Louis.

Robins, L. N., Helzer, J. E., Croughan, J. L., & Ratcliff, K. S. (1981). National Institute of Mental Health Diagnostic Interview Schedule. *Archives of General Psychiatry, 38*, 381-389.

Robins, L. N., Helzer, J. E., Ratcliff, K. S., & Seyfried, W. (1982). Validity of the Diagnostic Interview Schedule, version II: DSM-III diagnoses. *Psychological Medicine, 12*, 855-870.

Rockland, L. H., & Pollin, W. (1965). Quantification of psychiatric mental status. *Archives of General Psychiatry, 12*, 23-28.

Rodgers, D. A. (1972). The MMPI: A review. In O. K. Buros (Ed.), *Seventh mental measurements yearbook* (Vol. 1). (pp.243-250) Highland Park, NJ: Gryphon Press.

Roe, A. (1952). Analysis of group Rorschachs of psychologists and anthropologists. *Journal of Projective Techniques, 16*, 212-242.

Rogers, C. R. (1961). A process conception of psychotherapy. In C. R. Rogers (Ed.), *On becoming a person*. Boston: Houghton Mifflin.

Rogers, R. (1984). *Rogers Criminal Responsibility Assessment Scales*. Odessa, FL: Psychological Assessment Resources.

Romancyzk, R. G., Kent, R. N., Diament, C., & O'Leary, K. D. (1973). Measuring the reliability of observational data: A reactive process. *Journal of Applied Behavior Analysis, 6*, 175-186.

Rorschach, H. (1921). *Psychodiagnostics*. (Hans Huber Verlag, Transl. 1942). Bern: Bircher.

Rosen, B. M., Bahn, A. K., & Kramer, M. (1964). Demographic and diagnostic characteristics of psychiatric clinic patients in the U.S.A., 1961. *American Journal of Orthopsychiatry, 34*, 455-468.

Rosenhan, D. L. (1973). On being sane in insane places. *Science, 179*, 250-257.

Rosenquist, C. M., & Megargee, E. I. (1969). *Delinquency in three cultures*. Austin: University of Texas Press.

Rosenthal, M. (1962). Some behavior correlated to the Rorschach experience-balance. *Journal of Projective Techniques, 26*, 442-446.

Rosenthal, M., & Beutell, N. J. (1981). Movement and body-image: A preliminary study. *Perceptual and Motor Skills, 53*, 758.

Rosenthal, R. (1966). *Experimenter effects in behavioral research*. New York: Appleton-Century-Crofts.

Rosenthal, R., & Fode, K. L. (1963). The effects of experimenter bias on the performance of the albino rat. *Behavioral Science, 8*, 183-189.

Rosenthal, R., & Jacobson, L. (1968). *Pygmalion in the Classroom*. New York: Holt, Rinehart and Winston.

Rosenzweig, S. (1976). *Manual for the Rosenzweig Picture-Frustration Study, Adolescent Form*. St. Louis : Author.

Rosenzweig, S. (1977). *Manual for the Children's Form of the Rosenzweig Picture-Frustration (P-F) Study*. St. Louis: Rana House.

Rosenzweig, S. (1978). *Adult Form Supplement to the Basic Manual of the Rosenzweig Picture Frustration (P-F) Study*. St. Louis: Rana House.

Ross, L. D. (1977). The intuitive psychologist and his shortcomings: Distortions in the attribution process. In L. Berkowitz (Ed.), *Advances in experimental social psychology*. (Vol. 10). New York: Academic Press.

Rossi, A., & Neuman, G. (1961). A comparative study of Rorschach norms: Medical students. *Journal of Projective Techniques, 25*, 334-338.

Rossini, E. D., & Kaspar, J. C. (1987). The validity of the Bender-Gestalt emotional indicators. *Journal of Personality Assessment, 51*, 254-261.

Roth, D. L., Hughes, C. W., Mankowski, P. G., & Crosson, B. (1984). Investigation of validity of WAIS-R short forms for patients suspected to have brain impairment. *Journal of Consulting and Clinical Psychology, 52*, 722-723.

Rotter, J. B., & Rafferty, J. E. (1950). *Manual: The Rotter Incomplete Sentences Blank*. New York: Psychological Corporation.

Royer, F. L., & Holland, T. R. (1975). Rotations of visual design in psychopathological groups. *Journal of Consulting and Clinical Psychology, 43*, 346-356.

Rubin, J. A., Ragins, N., Schacter, J., & Wimberly, F. (1979). Drawings by schizophrenics and non-schizophrenic mothers and their children. *Art Psychotherapy, 6*, 163-175.

Russell, E. W. (1972). Effect of acute lateralized brain damage on a factor analysis of the Wechsler-Bellevue intelligence test. *Proceedings of the 80th Annual Convention of the American Psychological Association, 7,* 421-422.

Russell, E. W. (1979). Three patterns of brain damage on the WAIS. *Journal of Clinical Psychology, 35,* 611-620.

Ryan, J. J. (1981). Clinical utility of a WISC-R short form. *Journal of Clinical Psychology, 37,* 389-391.

Ryan, J. J., Georgemiller, R. J., Geisser, M. E., & Randall, D. M. (1985). Test-retest stability of the WAIS-R in a clinical sample. *Journal of Clinical Psychology, 41,* 552-556.

Ryan, J. J., Georgemiller, R., & McKinney, B. (1984). Application of the four-subtest WAIS-R short form with an older clinical sample. *Journal of Clinical Psychology, 40,* 1033-1036.

Ryan, J. J., Nowak, T., & Geisser, M. E. (1987). On the comparability of the WAIS and WAIS-R: Review of the research and implications for clinical practice. *Journal of Psychoeducational Research, 5,* 15-30.

Ryan, J. J., & Rosenberg, S. J. (1983). Relationship between the WAIS-R and Wide Range Achievement Test in a sample of mixed patients. *Perceptual and Motor Skills, 56,* 623-626.

Saarni, C., & Azara, V. (1977). Developmental analyses of human figure drawings in adolescence, young adulthood, and middle age. *Journal of Personality Assessment, 41,* 31-38.

Sacuzzo, D. P., & Lewandowski, D. G. (1976). The WISC as a diagnostic tool. *Journal of Clinical Psychology, 32,* 115-124.

Salmon, R., Arnold, J. M., & Collyer, Y. M. (1972). What do the determinants determine: The internal validity of the Rorschach. *Journal of Personality Assessment, 36,* 33-38.

Sanchez, V., & Lewinsohn, P. M. (1980). Assertive behavior and depression. *Journal of Consulting and Clinical Psychology, 48,* 119-120.

Sandy, L. R. (1986). The descriptive-collaborative approach to psychological report writing. *Psychology in the Schools, 23,* 395-400.

Sanford, R. N. (1939). *Thematic Apperception Test-Directions for administration and scoring.* Cambridge, Mass: Harvard Psychological Clinic (mimeographed).

Sarrel, P., Sarrel, L., & Berman, S. (1981). Using the Draw-A-Person (DAP) Test in sex therapy. *Journal of Sex & Marital Therapy, 7,* 163-183.

Sattler, J. M. (1973a). Examiners scoring style, accuracy, ability, and culturally disadvantaged children. In L. Mann & D. Sabatino (Eds.), *The first review of special education* (Vol. 2). Philadelphia: J. S. E. Press.

Sattler, J. M. (1973b). Racial experimenter effects. In K. S. Miller & R. M. Dreger (Eds.), *Comparative studies of blacks and whites in the United States.* New York: Seminar Press.

Sattler, J. M. (1980). Learning disabled children do not have a perceptual organization deficit: Comments on Dean's WISC-R analysis. *Journal of Consulting and Clinical Psychology, 48,* 254-255.

Sattler, J. M. (1982). *Assessment of children's intelligence and special abilities* (2nd ed.). Boston: Allyn & Bacon.

Sattler, J. M. (1985). Review of the Hutt Adaptation of the Bender-Gestalt Test. In J. V. Mitchell (Ed.), *The ninth mental measurements yearbook*. (Vol. 1). Highland Park, NJ: Gryphon Press.

Sattler, J. M. (1988). *Assessment of children* (3rd ed.). San Diego: Sattler.

Sattler, J. M., & Gwynne, J. (1982). White examiners generally do not impede the intelligence test performance of black children: To debunk a myth. *Journal of Consulting and Clinical Psychology, 50*, 196-208.

Sattler, J. M., Hillix, W. A., & Neher, L. A. (1970). Halo effect in examiner scoring of intelligence test responses. *Journal of Consulting and Clinical Psychology, 34*, 172-176.

Sattler, J. M., & Winget, B. M. (1970). Intelligence testing procedures as affected by expectancy and I.Q. *Journal of Clinical Psychology, 26*, 446-448.

Satz, P., & Mogel, S. (1962). An abbreviation of the WAIS for clinical use. *Journal of Clinical Psychology, 18*, 77-79.

Saxe, L., Dougherty, D., & Cross, T. (1985). The validity of polygraph testing. *American Psychologist, 40*, 355-366.

Sayed, A. J., & Leaverton, D. R. (1974). Kinetic Family Drawings of children with diabetes. *Child Psychiatry and Human Development, 5*, 40-50.

Schactel, E. G. (1966). *Experimental foundations of Rorschach's test*. New York: Basic Books.

Schafer, R. (1954). *Psychoanalytic interpretation in Rorschach testing*. New York: Grune & Stratton.

Scherer, M. W., & Nakamura, C. Y. (1968). A fear survey schedule for children (FSS-FC): A factor analytic comparison with manifest anxiety. *Behavior Research and Therapy, 6*, 173-182.

Schinka, J. A.(1983). *Neuropsychological Status Examination*. Odessa, FL: Psychological Assessment Resources.

Schilder, P. (1953). *Medical psychology*. New York: International Universities Press.

Schmidt, H. O., & Fonda, C. P. (1954). Rorschach scores in the manic state. *Journal of Psychology, 38*, 427-437.

Schoor, D., Bower, G. H., & Kiernan, R. (1982). Stimulus variables in the block design task. *Journal of Consulting and Clinical Psychology, 50*, 479-487.

Schroth, M. L. (1987). Relationships between achievement-related motives, extrinsic conditions, and task performance. *Journal of Social Psychology, 127*, 39-48.

Schulman, I. (1953). *The relation between perception of movement on the Rorschach test and levels of conceptualization*. Doctoral dissertation, New York University.

Schultz, C. B., & Sherman, R. H. (1976). Social class, development, and differences in reinforcer effectiveness. *Review of Educational Research, 46*, 25-59.

Schut, B., Hutzell, R. R., Swint, E. B., & Gaston, C. D. (1980) CPI short form incorporating MMPI shared items: Construction, cross validation, and comparison. *Journal of Clinical Psychology, 36*, 940-944.

Schwartz, G. E. (1982). Testing the biopsychosocial model: The ultimate challenge facing behavioral medicine? *Journal of Consulting and Clinical Psychology, 50*, 1040-1053.

Schwartz, L., & Levitt, E. E. (1960). Short forms of the WISC for children in the educable, non-institutionalized mentally retarded. *Journal of Educational Psychology, 51,* 187-190.

Schwartz, S., & Wiedel, T. C. (1981). Incremental validity of the MMPI in neurological decision-making. *Journal of Personality Assessment, 45,* 424-426.

Scott, L. H. (1981). Measuring intelligence with the Goodenough-Harris Drawing Test. *Psychological Bulletin, 89,* 483-505.

Seamons, D. T., Howell, R. J., Carlisle, A. L., & Roe, A. V. (1981). Rorschach simulation of mental illness and normality by psychotic and nonpsychotic legal offenders. *Journal of Personality Assessment, 45,* 130-135.

Seeman, K., Yesarage, J., & Widrow, L. (1985). Correlations of self-directed violence in acute schizophrenics with clinical ratings and personality measures. *Journal of Nervous and Mental Diseases, 173,* 298-302.

Seligman, M. E. P., Abramson, L. Y., Semmel, A., & von Baeyer, C. (1979). Depressive attributional style. *Journal of Abnormal Psychology, 88,* 242-247.

Semeonoff, B. (1976). *Projective techniques.* New York: John Wiley & Sons, Inc.

Sewitch, T., & Kirsch, I. (1984). The cognitive content of anxiety: Naturalistic evidence for the predominance of threat-related thoughts. *Cognitive Therapy and Research, 8,* 49-58.

Shaffer, J. W., Duszynski, K. R., & Thomas, C. B. (1984). A comparison of three methods for scoring figure drawings. *Journal of Personality Assessment, 48,* 245-254.

Shalit, B. (1965). Effects of environmental stimulation on the M, FM, and in response to the Rorschach. *Journal of Projective Techniques and Personality Assessment, 29,* 228-231.

Shapiro, D. A. (1956). Color-response and perceptual passivity. *Journal of Projective Techniques, 20,* 52-69.

Shapiro, D. A. (1960). Perceptual understanding of color response. In M. Rickers-Ovsiankina (Ed.), *Rorschach psychology.* New York: John Wiley & Sons, Inc.

Shapiro, M. B., Field, J., & Post, F. (1981). An inquiry into the determinants of a differentiation between elderly "organic" and "non-organic" psychiatric patients on the Bender-Gestalt Test. *Journal of Mental Science, 103,* 364-374.

Shapiro, P. N., & Penrod, S. (1986). Meta-analysis of facial identification studies. *Psychological Bulletin, 100,* 139-156.

Sharkey, K. J., & Ritzler, B. A. (1985). Comparing diagnostic validity of the TAT and a new picture projective test. *Journal of Personality Assessment, 49,* 406-412.

Shatin, L. (1952). Psychoneurosis and psychosomatic reactions: A Rorschach contrast. *Journal of Consulting Psychology, 16,* 220-223.

Shaw, D. S., & Gynther, M. (1986). An attempt to obtain configural correlates for the California Psychological Inventory. *Psychological Reports, 59,* 675-678.

Sheehan, P. W., Ashton, R., & White, K. (1983). Assessment of mental imagery. In A. A. Sheikh (Ed.), *Imagery: Current theory, research, and application* (pp. 189-221). New York: John Wiley & Sons, Inc.

Sheppard, D., Smith, G. T., & Rosenbaum, G. (1988). Use of the MMPI subtypes in predicting completion of a residential alcoholism treatment program. *Journal of Consulting and Clinical Psychology, 4*, 590-596.

Sherman, M. A. (1952). A comparison of formal and content factors in the diagnostic testing of schizophrenia. *Genetic Psychology Monographs, 46*, 183-234.

Shneidman, E. S. (Ed.). (1951). *Thematic test analysis.* New York: Grune & Stratton.

Shorkey, C. L., Reyes, E., & Whiteman, V. L. (1977). Development of the rational behavior inventory: Initial validity and reliability. *Educational and Psychological Measurement, 37*, 527-534.

Siegler, R. S., & Richards, D. D. (1982). The development of intelligence. In R. J. Sternberg (Ed.), *Handbook of Intelligence.* (pp. 897-971). New York: Cambridge University Press.

Sigel, I. E. (1963). How intelligence tests limit understanding of intelligence. *Merrill-Palmer Quarterly, 9*, 39-56.

Silverstein, A. B. (1967). Validity of WISC short forms at three age levels. *California Mental Health Research Digest, 5*, 253-254.

Silverstein, A. B. (1982). Two- and four- subtest short forms of the Wechsler Adult Intelligence Scale-Revised. *Journal of Consulting and Clinical Psychology, 50*, 415-418.

Silverstein, A. B., & Mohan, P. J. (1962). Bender-Gestalt figure rotations in the mentally retarded. *Journal of Consulting Psychology, 26*, 386-388.

Simon, W. E. (1969). Expectancy effects in the scoring of vocabulary items: A study of scorer bias. *Journal of Educational Measurement, 6*, 159-164.

Singer, J. L. (1960). The experience type: Some behavioral correlates and theoretical implications. In M. Rickers-Ovsiankina (Ed.), *Rorschach psychology.* New York: John Wiley & Sons, Inc.

Sipps, G. J., Berry, G. W., & Lynch, E. M. (1987). WAIS-R and social intelligence: A test of established assumptions that uses the CPI. *Journal of Clinical Psychology, 43*, 499-504.

Skodol, A., Rosnick, L., Kellman, D., Oldham, J. M., & Hyler, S. E. (1988). Validating structured DSM-III-R personality disorder assessments with longitudinal data. *American Journal of Psychiatry, 145*, 1297-1299.

Skolnick, A. (1966). Motivational imagery and behavior over twenty years. *Journal of Consulting Psychology, 30*, 463-478.

Smith, C. E., & Keogh, B. K. (1962). The group Bender-Gestalt as a reading readiness screening instrument. *Perceptual and Motor Skills, 15*, 639-645.

Smith, C. P., & Graham, J. R. (1981). Behavioral correlates for the MMPI standard F scale and the modified F scale for black and white psychiatric patients. *Journal of Consulting and Clinical Psychology, 49*(3), 455-459.

Smith, N. M. (1981). The relationship between the Rorschach whole response and level of cognitive functioning. *Journal of Personality Assessment, 45*, 13-19.

Smith, R. E., & Sarason, I. G. (1975). Social anxiety and the evaluation of negative interpersonal feedback. *Journal of Consulting and Clinical Psychology, 43*, 429.

Snyder, C. R. (1974). Acceptance of personality interpretations as a function of assessment procedures. *Journal of Consulting and Clinical Psychology, 42*, 150.

Snyder, W. V. (1945). An investigation of the nature of nondirective psychotherapy. *Journal of General Psychology, 33*, 139-223.

Snyderman, M., & Rothman, S. (1987). Survey of expert opinion on intelligence and aptitude testing. *American Psychologist, 42*, 137-144.

Sommer, R., & Sommer, D. (1958). Assaultiveness and two types of Rorschach color responses. *Journal of Consulting Psychology, 22*, 57-62.

Southern, M. L., & Plant, W. T. (1968). Personality characteristics of very bright adults. *Journal of Social Psychology, 75*, 119-126.

Sparrow, S. S., Balla, D. A., & Cicchetti, D. V. (1984). *Vineland Adaptive Behavior Scales.* Circle Pines, MN: American Guidance Service.

Spearman, C. (1927). *The abilities of Man: Their nature and measurement.* New York: Macmillan.

Spiker, D. G., & Ehler, J. G. (1984). Structured psychiatric interviews for adults. In G. Goldstein & M. Hersen (Eds.), *Handbook of psychological assessment.* New York: Pergamon.

Spinks, P. M. (1980). An item and factor analysis of the FSS (III). *Personality and Individual Differences, 1*, 363-370.

Spirito, A., Faust, D., Myers, B., & Bechtel, D. (1988). Clinical utility of the MMPI in the evaluation of adolescent suicide attempters. *Journal of Personality Assessment, 52*, 204-211.

Spitz, H. H. (1986). Disparities in mentally retarded person's I.Q.'s derived from different intelligence tests. *American Journal of Mental Deficiency, 90*, 588-591.

Spitzer, R. L., & Endicott, J. (1971). An integrated group of forms for automated psychiatric case records: Progress report. *Archives of General Psychiatry, 24*, 540-547.

Spitzer, R. L., Endicott, J., & Cohen, J. (1974). Constraints on the validity of computer diagnosis. *Archives of General Psychiatry, 31*, 197-203.

Spitzer, R. L., Endicott, J., & Robins, E. (1978). Research diagnostic criteria: Rationale and reliability. *Archives of General Psychiatry, 35*, 773-782.

Spitzer, R. L., & Williams, J. B. W. (1983). *Instruction manual for the structured clinical interview for DSM-III (SCID).* New York: New York State Psychiatric Institute, Biometrics Research Department.

Spitzer, R. L., Williams, J. B. W., & Gibbon, M. (1987). *Structured clinical interview for DSM-III-R (SCID).* New York, NY: State Psychiatric Institute.

Spruill, J., & Beck, B. (1988). Comparison of the WAIS and the WAIS-R: Different results for different I.Q. groups. *Professional Psychology: Research and Practice, 19*, 31-34.

Staats, A. W. (1970). Intelligence, biology, or learning? Competing conceptions with social consequences. In H. C. Haywood (Ed.), *Social-cultural aspects of mental retardation: Proceedings of the Peabody-NIMH Conference.* New York: Appleton-Century-Crofts, pp.246-277.

Standage, K. (1986). Socialization scores in psychiatric patients and their implications for the diagnosis of personality disorders. *Canadian Journal of Psychiatry, 31*, 138-141.

Stangl, D., Pfohl, B., Zimmerman, M., Bowers, W., & Corenthal, C. (1985). A structured interview for the DSM-III personality disorders. *Archives of General Psychiatry, 42*, 591-596.

Steer, R. A., Beck, A. T., Brown, G., & Berchick, R. (1987). Self-reported depressive symptoms differentiating recurrent-episode major-depression from dysthymic disorders. *Journal of Clinical Psychology, 43*, 246-250.

Steer, R. A., Beck, A. T., & Garrison, B. (1986). Applications of the Beck Depression Inventory. In N. Sartorius & T. A. Ban (Eds.), *Assessment of depression.* (pp. 121-142). Geneva, Switzerland: World Health Organization.

Steichen, E. (1955). *Family of man.* New York: Simon & Schuster.

Stein, M. (1981). *The Thematic Apperception Test: An introductory manual for its clinical use with adults* (2nd ed.). Springfield, IL: Charles C. Thomas.

Steisel, I. M. (1952). The Rorschach test and suggestibility. *Journal of Abnormal and Social Psychology, 47*, 607-614.

Sternberg, D., & Levine, A. (1965). An indicator of suicidal ideation on the Bender Visual-Motor Gestalt Test. *Journal of Projective Techniques and Personality Assessment, 29*, 377-379.

Sternberg, R. J. (Ed.). (1982). *Handbook of human intelligence.* New York: Cambridge University Press.

Sternberg, R. J. (1985). *Beyond I.Q.: A triarchic theory of human intelligence.* New York: Cambridge University Press.

Stewart, L. H. (1962). Social and emotional adjustment during adolescence as related to the development of psychosomatic illness in adulthood. *Genetic Psychology Monographs, 65*, 175-215.

Stoloff, M. L., & Couch, J. V. (Eds.). (1988). *Computer use in psychology: A directory of software* (2nd ed.). Washington, DC: American Psychological Association.

Stormant, C. T., & Finney, B. C. (1953). Projection and behavior: A Rorschach study of assaultive mental hospital patients. *Journal of Projective Techniques, 17*, 349-360.

Stotsky, B. A. (1952). A comparison of remitting and non-remitting schizophrenics on psychological tests. *Journal of Abnormal and Social Psychology, 47*, 489-496.

Stroup, A., & Manderscheid, R. (1977). CPI and 16PF second-order factor congruence. *Journal of Clinical Psychology, 33*, 1023-1026.

Strub, R. L., & Black, F. W. (1977). *The mental status examination in neurology.* Philadelphia, PA: F. A. Davis.

Strupp, H. H. (1958). The psychotherapist's contribution to the treatment process. *Behavioral Science, 3*, 34-67.

Sturgis, E., & Gramling, S. (1988). Psychophysiological assessment. In A. S. Bellack & M. Hersen (Eds.), *Behavioral assessment: A practical handbook.* (3rd ed.). New York: Pergamon.

Suinn, R. M., & Oskamp, S. (1969). *The predictive validity of projective measures: A fifteen year evaluative review of research* (Chapter 8). Springfield, IL: Charles C. Thomas.

Sundberg, N. D. (1955). The acceptability of "fake" versus "bona fide" personality test interpretations. *Journal of Abnormal and Social Psychology, 50*, 145-147.

Sundberg, N. D. (1961). The practice of psychological testing in clinical services in the United States. *American Psychologist, 16,* 79-83.

Sundberg, N., & Ballinger, T. (1968). Nepalese children's cognitive development as revealed by drawings of man, woman, and self. *Child Development, 39,* 969-985.

Sutter, E. G., & Bishop, P. C. (1986). Further investigation of the correlations among the WISC-R, PIAT, and DAM. *Psychology in the Schools, 23,* 365-367.

Svanum, S., Levitt, E., & McAdoo, W. G. (1982). Differentiating male and female alcoholics from psychiatric outpatients: The MacAndrew and Rosenberg alcoholism scales. *Journal of Personality Assessment, 46,* 81-84.

Sweetland, R. C., & Keyser, D. J. (Eds.). (1983). *Tests: A comprehensive reference for assessment in psychology, education, and business.* Kansas City: Test Corporation of America.

Swensen, W. M., Pearson, J. S., & Osborne, D. (1973). *An MMPI source book: Basic item, scale, and pattern data on 50,000 medical patients.* Minneapolis: University of Minnesota Press.

Swenson, C. H. (1968). Empirical evaluations of human figure drawings: 1957-1966. *Psychological Bulletin, 70,* 20-44.

Swiercinsky, D. (1978). *Manual for the adult neuropsychological evaluation.* Springfield, IL: Charles C. Thomas.

Symmes, J., & Rapaport, J. (1972). Unexpected reading failure. *American Journal of Orthopsychiatry, 42,* 82-91.

Szasz, T. (1987). Justifying coercion through religion and psychiatry. *Journal of Humanistic Psychology, 27,* 158-174.

Taft, R. (1955). The ability to judge people. *Psychological Bulletin, 52,* 1-23.

Tallent, N. (1976). *Psychological report writing.* Englewood Cliffs, NJ: Prentice-Hall.

Tallent, N. (1988). *Psychological report writing* (3rd ed.). Englewood Cliffs, NJ: Prentice-Hall.

Tallent, N., & Reiss, W. J. (1959a). Multidisciplinary views on the preparation of written psychological reports: I. Spontaneous suggestions for content. *Journal of Clinical Psychology, 15,* 218-221.

Tallent, N., & Reiss, W. J. (1959b). Multidisciplinary views on the preparation of written psychological reports: II. Acceptability of certain common content variables and styles of expression. *Journal of Clinical Psychology, 15,* 273-274.

Tallent, N., & Reiss, W. J. (1959c). Multidisciplinary views on the preparation of written psychological reports: III. The trouble with psychological reports. *Journal of Clinical Psychology, 15,* 444-446.

Tanaka, J. S., & Huba, G. J. (1984). Confirmatory heirarchical factor analysis of psychological distress measures. *Journal of Personality and Social Psychology, 54,* 328-333.

Tanaka-Matsumi, J., & Kameoka, V. A. (1986). Reliabilities and concurrent validities of popular self-report measures of depression, anxiety, and social desirability. *Journal of Consulting and Clinical Psychology, 54,* 328-333.

Tasto, D. L. (1977). Self-report schedules and inventories. In A. R. Ciminero, K. S. Calhoun, & H. E. Adams (Eds.), *Handbook of behavioral assessment.* New York: John Wiley & Sons, Inc.

Taylor, M. A. (1981). *The neuropsychiatric mental status examination*. Jamaica, NY: Spectrum.

Taylor, R. L., Kauffman, D., & Partenio, I. (1984). The Koppitz developmental scoring system for the Bender-Gestalt: Is it developmental? *Psychology in the Schools, 21*, 425-428.

Taylor, R. L., Sternberg, L., & Partenio, I. (1986). Performance of urban and rural children on the SOMPA: Preliminary investigation. *Perceptual and Motor Skills, 63*, 1219-1223.

Teevan, R. C., Diffenderfer, D., & Greenfield, N. (1986). Need for achievement and sociometric status. *Psychological Reports, 58*, 446.

Teglasi, H. (1980). Acceptance of the traditional female role and sex of the first person drawn on the Draw-A-Person test. *Perceptual and Motor Skills, 51*, 267-271.

Temp, G. (1971). Test bias: Validity of the SAT for blacks and whites in thirteen integrated institutions. *Journal of Educational Measurement, 8*, 245-251.

Terman, L. M. (1916). *The measurement of intelligence*. Boston: Houghton Mifflin.

Terman, L. M., & Merril, M. A. (1960). *Stanford-Binet Intelligence Scale*. Boston: Houghton Mifflin.

Terman, L. M., & Miles, C. C. (1936). *Sex and personality: Studies in masculinity and femininity*. New York: McGraw-Hill.

Terrell, F., Taylor, J., & Terrell, S. L. (1978). Effects of types of social reinforcement on the intelligence test performance of lower-class black children. *Journal of Consulting and Clinical Psychology, 46*, 1538-1539.

Thiesen, J. W. (1952). A pattern analysis of structural characteristics of the Rorschach test in schizophrenia. *Journal of Consulting Psychology, 16*, 365-370.

Thomas, A. D., & Dudek, S. Z. (1985). Interpersonal affect in Thematic Apperception Test responses: A scoring system. *Journal of Personality Assessment, 49*, 30-36.

Thomas, C. B., & Duszynski, K. R. (1985). Are words of the Rorschach predictors of disease and death? The case of "whirling." *Psychosomatic Medicine, 47*, 201-211.

Thompson, G. M. (1948). MMPI correlates of movement responses on the Rorschach. *American Psychologist, 3*, 348-349.

Thompson, R. J. (1981). The diagnostic utility of Bannatyne's recategorized WISC-R scores with children referred to a developmental evaluation center. *Psychology in the Schools, 18*, 43-47.

Thorndike, R. L. (1959). The California Psychological Inventory: A review. In O. K. Buros (Ed.), *Fifth mental measurements yearbook*. Highland Park, NJ: Gryphon Press.

Thorndike, R. L. (1968). Review of Pygmalion in the classroom by R. Rosenthal & L. Jacobson. *American Educational Research Journal, 5*, 708-711.

Thurstone, L. L. (1938). Primary mental abilities. *Psychometric Monographs*, No. 1.

Thweatt, R. C., Obrzut, J. F., & Taylor, H. D. (1972). The development and validation of a soft-scoring system for the Bender Gestalt. *Psychology in the Schools, 9*, 170-174.

Thyer, B. A., Tomlin, P., Curtiss, G. C., Cameron, O. G., & Nesse, R. (1985). Diagnostic and gender differences in the expressed fears of anxious patients. *Journal of Behavior Therapy and Experimental Psychiatry, 16*, 111-115.

Todd, A. L., & Gynther, M. D. (1988). Have MMPI Mf scale correlates changed in the past 30 years? *Journal of Clinical Psychology, 44*, 505-510.

Todd, J., Coolidge, F., & Satz, P. (1977). The Wechsler Adult Intelligence Scale discrepancy index: A neuropsychological evaluation. *Journal of Consulting and Clinical Psychology, 45*, 450-454.

Tolor, A. A. (1956). A comparison of the Bender-Gestalt test and the digit-span test as measures of recall. *Journal of Consulting Psychology, 20*, 305-309.

Tolor, A., & Brannigan, G. C. (1980). *Research and clinical applications of the Bender Gestalt Test.* Springfield, IL: Charles C. Thomas.

Tolor, A., & Digrazia, P. V. (1977). The body image of pregnant women as reflected in their human figure drawings. *Journal of Clinical Psychology, 34*, 537-538.

Tolor, A., & Schulberg, H. C. (1963). *An evaluation of the Bender-Gestalt Test.* Springfield, IL: Charles C. Thomas.

Townsend, J. K. (1967). The relation between Rorschach signs of aggression and behavioral aggression in emotionally disturbed boys. *Journal of Projective Techniques and Personality Assessment, 31*, 13-21.

Truax, C. B., & Carkhuff, R. R. (1967). *Toward effective counseling and psychotherapy.* New York: Aldine.

Tsushima, W. T., & Onorato, V. A. (1982). Comparison of MMPI scores of white and Japanese-American medical patients. *Journal of Clinical and Consulting Psychology, 50*, 150-151.

Tucker, R. K., Weaver, R. L., Duran, R. L., Redden, E. M. (1983). Criterion-related validity of three measures of assertiveness. *Psychological Record, 33*, 361-370.

Tukey, J. W. (1977). *Exploratory data analysis.* Reading, MA: Addison-Wesley.

Turk, D., & Salovey, P. (1985). Cognitive structures, cognitive processes, and cognitive behavior modification. *Cognitive Therapy and Research, 9*, 19-33.

Ullman, L. P., & Krasner, L. A. (1965). *Case studies in behavior modification.* New York: Holt, Rinehart, & Winston.

Ulrich, L. P., & Trumbo, D. (1960). The selection interview since 1949. *Psychological Bulletin, 63*, 100-116.

Ulrich, R. E., Stachnik, T. J., & Stainton, N. R. (1963). Student acceptance of generalized personality interpretations. *Psychological Reports, 13*, 831-834.

Urban, W. H. (1963). *The Draw-A-Person Catalogue for Interpretive Analysis.* Los Angeles: Western Psychological Services.

Van Dyne, W. T., & Carsleadon, T. G. (1978). Relationships among three components of self-concept and same-sex and opposite-sex human figure drawings. *Journal of Clinical Psychology, 34*, 537-538.

Vance, B., Fuller, G. B., & Lester, M. L. (1986). A comparison of the Minnesota Perceptual Diagnostic Test Revised and the Bender-Gestalt. *Journal of Learning Disabilities, 19*, 211-214.

Vane, J. R. (1981). The Thematic Apperception Test: A review. *Social Psychology Review, 1*, 319-336.

Vane, J. R., & Guarnaccia, V. J. (1989). Personality theory and personality assessment measures: How helpful to the clinician? *Journal of Clinical Psychology, 45*, 5-19.

Veldman, D. J., & Kelly, S. J. (1965). Personality correlates of a composite criterion of teaching effectiveness. *Alberta Journal of Educational Research, 11*, 702-707.

Verma, S. K., Wig, N. N., & Shaw, D. K. (1962). Validity of Bender Gestalt Test in Indian psychiatric patients. *Indian Journal of Applied Psychology, 9*, 65-67.

Vernon, P. A. (Ed.). (1987). *Speed of information-processing and intelligence.* Norwood, NJ: Ablex.

Vernon, P. E. (1950). *The structure of human abilities.* London: Methuen.

Vernon, P. E. (1961). *The structure of human abilities* (2nd ed.). London: Methuen.

Vernon, P. E. (1964). *Personality assessment: A critical survey.* London: Methuen.

Vincent, K. R., Castillo, I., Hauser, R., Stuart, H. J., Zapata, J. A., Cohn, C. K., & O'Shanick, G. J. (1983). MMPI code types and DSM-III diagnosis. *Journal of Clinical Psychology, 39*, 829-842.

Vogt, A. T., & Heaton, R. L. (1977). Comparison of WAIS indices of cerebral dysfunction. *Perceptual and Motor Skills, 45*, 607-615.

Wade, T. C., & Baker, T. B. (1977). Opinions and use of psychological tests: A survey of clinical psychologists. *American Psychologist, 32*, 874-882.

Wade, T. C., Baker, T. B., & Hartman, D. P. (1979). Behavior therapist's self-reported views and practices. *The Behavior Therapist, 2*, 3-6.

Wagner, E. E. (1961). The interaction of aggressive movement responses and anatomy responses on the Rorschach in producing anxiety. *Journal of Projective Techniques, 25*, 212-215.

Wagner, E. E. (1971). Structural analysis: A theory of personality based on projective techniques. *Journal of Personality Assessment, 37*, 5-15.

Wagner, E. E. (1973). Diagnosis of conversion hysteria: An interpretation based on structural analysis. *Journal of Personality Assessment, 37*, 5-15.

Wagner, E. E., & Flamos, O. (1988). Optimized split-half reliability for the Bender Visual Motor Gestalt Test: Further evidence for the use of the maximization procedure. *Journal of Personality Assessment, 52*, 454-458.

Wagner, R. (1949). The employment interview: A critical review. *Personnel Psychology, 2*, 17-46.

Wakefield, J. F. (1986). Creativity and the TAT blank card. *Journal of Creative Behavior, 7*, 127-133.

Walker, N. W., & Myrick, C. C. (1985). Ethical considerations in the use of computers in psychological testing and assessment. *Journal of School Psychology, 23*, 51-57.

Waller, R. W., & Keeley, S. M. (1978). Effects of explanation and information feedback on the illusory correlation phenomenon. *Journal of Consulting and Clinical Psychology, 46*, 342-343.

Walters, G. D., Greene, R. L., Jeffrey, T. B., Kruzich, D. J., & Hastings, J. J. (1983). Racial variations on the MacAndrew Alcoholism Scale of the MMPI. *Journal of Consulting and Clinical Psychology, 51*, 947-948.

Watkins, C. E. (1986). Validity and usefulness of WAIS-R, WISC-R, and WPPSI short forms: A critical review. *Professional Psychology Research and Practice, 17*, 36-43.

Watkins, C. E., Edinger, J. D., & Shipley, R. H. (1986). Validity of a WAIS-R screening instrument (Satz-Moyd) for medical inpatients. *Rehabilitation Psychology, 31*, 103-109.

Watkins, J. T., & Rush, A. J. (1983). Cognitive response test. *Cognitive Therapy and Research, 7*, 425-435.

Watson, J. B., & Rayner, R. (1920). Conditioned emotional reactions. *Journal of Experimental Psychology, 3*, 1-14.

Watzlawick, P., Beavin, J. H., & Jackson, D. D. (1966). *Pragmatics of human communication.* New York: Norton.

Waugh, K. W., & Bush, W. J. (1971). *Diagnosing learning disorders.* Columbus, OH: Merrill.

Webb, J. T., McNamara, K. M., & Rodgers, D. A. (1981). *Configural interpretation of the MMPI and CPI.* Columbus, OH : Ohio Psychology Publishing.

Wechsler, D. (1949). *Manual for the Wechsler Intelligence Scale for Children.* New York: Psychological Corporation.

Wechsler, D. (1955). *Manual for the Wechsler Adult Intelligence Scale.* New York: Psychological Corporation.

Wechsler, D. (1958). *The measurement and appraisal of adult intelligence* (4th ed.). Baltimore: Williams and Wilkins.

Wechsler, D. (1967). *Manual for the Wechsler Preschool and Primary School of Intelligence.* New York: Psychological Corporation.

Wechsler, D. (1981). *Manual for the Wechsler Adult Intelligence Scale - Revised.* New York: Psychological Corporation.

Wedemeyer, B. (1954). Rorschach statistics on a group of 136 normal men. *Journal of Psychology, 37*, 51-58.

Weed, L. L. (1968). Medical records that guide and teach. *New England Journal of Medicine, 278*, 593-600.

Weinberg, R. A. (1989). Intelligence and I.Q.: Landmark issues and great debates. *American Psychologist, 44*, 98-104.

Weinberger, D. R. (1987). Implications of normal brain development for the pathogenesis of schizophrenia. *Archives of General Psychiatry, 44*, 660-669.

Weinberger, D. R., & Berman, K. F. (1988). Speculation on the meaning of cerebral metabolic hypofrontality in schizophrenia. *Schizophrenia Bulletin, 14*, 157-163.

Weiner, I. B. (1961). Cross-validation of a Rorschach checklist associated with suicidal tendencies. *Journal of Consulting Psychology, 25*, 312-315.

Weiner, I. B. (1966). *Psychodiagnosis in schizophrenia.* New York: John Wiley & Sons, Inc.

Weiner, I. B. (1977). Approaches to Rorschach validation. In M. A. Rickers-Ovsiankira (Ed.), *Rorschach Psychology.* Huntington, NY: Robert E. Krieger Publishing Co.

Weiner, I. B. (1986). Conceptual and empirical perspectives on the Rorschach assessment of psychopathology. *Journal of Personality Assessment, 50*, 472-479.

Weissman, A., & Beck, A. T. (1978, November). *Development and validation of the Dysfunctional Attitude Scale (DAS).* Paper presented at the 12th annual meeting of the Association for the Advancement of Behavior Therapy, Chicago.

Weller, R. A., et al. (1985). Agreement between two structured psychiatric diagnostic interviews: DIS and the PDI. *Comprehensive Psychiatry, 26*, 157-163.

Welsh, G. S. (1956). Factor dimensions A and R. In G. S. Welsh & W. G. Dahlstrom (Eds.), *Basic readings on the MMPI in psychology and medicine*. Minneapolis: University of Minnesota Press, pp.264-281.

Wenger, M. A. (1966). Studies of autonomic balance: A summary. *Psychophysiology, 2*, 173-186.

Wernick, R. (1955). The modern-style mind reader. *Life*, September 12, 95-108.

Wertheimer, M. (1923). Studies in the theory of Gestalt psychology. *Psychological Forsch, 41*, 301-350.

West, A., Martindale, C., Hines, D., & Roth, W. T. (1983). Marijuana-induced primary process content in the TAT. *Journal of Personality Assessment, 47*, 466-467.

Wheeler, L., & Reitan, R. M. (1962). Presence and laterality of brain damage predicted from responses to a short aphasia screening test. *Perceptual and Motor Skills, 15*, 783-799.

White, G. W., Nielsen, L., & Prus, J. S. (1984). Head start teacher and aide preferences for degree of specificity in written psychological recommendations. *Professional Psychology: Research and Practice, 15*, 785-790.

White, R. B., Jr., & McGraw, R. K. (1975). Note on the relationship between downward slant of Bender figures 1 and 2 and depression in adult psychiatric patients. *Perceptual and Motor Skills, 40*, 152.

White, R. W. (1941). An analysis of motivation in hypnosis. *Journal of General Psychology, 24*, 145-162.

Wickham, T. (1978). *WISC patterns in acting-out delinquents, poor readers, and normal controls*. Unpublished doctoral dissertation, United States International University.

Widiger, T. A., & Frances, A. (1987). Interviews and inventories for the measurement of personality disorders. *Clinical Psychology Review, 7*, 49-75.

Wiener, J. (1985). Teacher's comprehension of psychological reports. *Psychology in the Schools, 22*, 60-64.

Wiener-Levy, D., & Exner, J. E. (1981). The Rorschach Comprehensive System: An overview. In P. McReynolds (Ed.), *Advances in psychological assessment* (Vol. 5). San Francisco: Jossey-Bass.

Wiens, A. N. (1976). The assessment interview. In I. B. Weiner (Ed.), *Clinical methods in psychology*. New York: John Wiley & Sons, Inc.

Wiens, A. N. (1983). The assessment interview. In I. B. Weiner (Ed.), *Clinical methods in psychology*. New York: John Wiley & Sons, Inc.

Wiggins, J. S. (1966). Substantive dimensions of self-report in the MMPI item pool. *Psychological Monographs, 80*, No. 630.

Wiggins, J. S. (1971). *Content scales: Basic data for scoring and interpretation*. Unpublished materials.

Wiggins, J. S. (1973). *Personality and prediction: Principles of personality assessment*. Reading, MA: Addison-Wesley.

Wiggins, N., & Kohen, E. S. (1971). Man versus model of man revisited: The forecasting of graduate school success. *Journal of Personality and Social Psychology, 19*, 100-106.

Williams, A. F., McCourt, W. F., & Schneider, L. (1971). Personality self-descriptions of alcoholics and heavy drinkers. *Quarterly Journal of Studies on Alcohol, 32*, 310-317.

Williams, C. L., & Butcher, J. N. (1989a). An MMPI study of adolescents: I. Empirical validity of the standard scales. *Psychological Assessment, 1*, 251-259.

Williams, C. L., & Butcher, J. N. (1989b). An MMPI study of adolescents: II. verification and limitations of code type classifications. *Psychological Assessment, 1*, 260-265.

Williams, M., Little, M., Davis, K., & Haban, G. (1987). *Cognitive Behavior Rating Scale.* Odessa, FL: Psychological Assessment Resources.

Williams, M. H. (1954). The influence of variations in instructions on Rorschach reaction time. *Dissertation Abstracts, 14*, 2131.

Williams, R. L. (1974). Scientific racism, and I.Q.: The silent mugging of the black community. *Psychology Today, 7*, 32-41.

Williamson, D. A., Davis, C. J., & Prather, R. C. (1988). Assessment of health-related disorders. In A. S. Bellack & M. Hersen (Eds.), *Behavioral assessment: A practical handbook* (3rd ed.). New York: Pergamon.

Wilson, T. E., & Evans, I. M. (1983). The reliability of target behavior selection in behavioral assessment. *Behavioral Assessment, 5*, 33-54.

Wing, J. K., Cooper, J. E., & Sartorius, N. (1974). *Description and classification of psychiatric symptoms.* Cambridge, England: Cambridge University Press.

Wirt, R. D., Lachar, D., Klinedinst, J. K., & Seat, P. D. (1977). *Multidimensional description of child personality: A manual for the Personality Inventory for Children.* Los Angeles: Western Psychological Services.

Witmer, J. M., Bornstein, A. V., & Dunham, R. M. (1971). The effects of verbal approval and disapproval upon the performance of third and fourth grade children of four subtests of the Wechsler Intelligence Scale for Children. *Journal of School Psychology, 9*, 347-356.

Witt, J. C., & Elliott, S. N. (1983). Assessment in behavioral consultation: The initial interview. *School Psychology Review, 12*, 42-49.

Wittchen, H., Semler, G., & von Zerssen, D. (1985). A comparison of two diagnostic methods. *Archives of General Psychiatry, 42*, 667-684.

Wolff, W. (1942). Projective methods for personality analysis of expressive behavior in preschool children. *Character & Personality, 10*, 309-330.

Wolk, R., & Wolk, R. B. (1971). *Manual: Gerontological Apperception Test.* New York: Behavioral Publications.

Wolpe, J., & Lang, P. J. (1977). *Manual for the Fear Survey Schedule.* San Diego, California: EdITS.

Wolpe, J., & Lazarus, A. (1966). *Behavior therapy techniques.* New York: Pergamon.

Wolpe, J., & Lang, P. J. (1964). A fear survey schedule for use in behavior therapy. *Behavior Research and Therapy, 2*, 27-30.

Wong, M. R. (1984). MMPI scale five: Its meaning or lack thereof. *Journal of Personality Assessment, 48*, 279-284.

Woodruff, R. A., Goodwin, D. W., & Guze, S. B. (1974). *Psychiatric diagnosis.* New York: Oxford University Press.

Woody, R. W. (Ed.). (1980). *Encyclopedia of clinical assessment* (Vol. 1). San Francisco: Jossey-Bass Publishers.

Wright, D., & DeMers, S. T. (1982). Comparison of the relationship between two measures of visual-motor coordination and academic achievement. *Psychology in the Schools, 19*, 473-477.

Wright, J. H., & McIntyre, M. P. (1982). The family drawing depression scale. *Journal of Clinical Psychology, 38*, 853-861.

Wurtz, R. G., Sewell, T. E., & Manni, J. L. (1985). The relationship of estimated learning potential to performance on learning task and achievement. *Psychology in the Schools, 22*, 293-302.

Wyatt, F. (1947). The scoring and analysis of the Thematic Apperception Test. *Journal of Psychology, 24*, 319-330.

Wyndowe, J. (1987). The microcomputerized Diagnostic Interview Schedule: Clinical use in an out-patient setting. *Canadian Journal of Psychiatry, 32*, 93-99.

Yossef, S., Slutsky, W. S., & Butcher, J. N. (1989). A real-data simulation of computerized and adaptive administration of the MMPI. *Psychological Assessment, 1*, 18-22.

Yudin, L. W. (1966). An abbreviated form of the WISC for use with emotionally disturbed children. *Journal of Consulting Psychology, 30*, 272-275.

Zedeck, S., Tziner, A., & Middlestadt, S. E. (1983). Interviewer validity and reliability: An individual analysis approach. *Personnel Psychology, 36*, 355-370.

Zigler, E., & Farber, E. A. (1985). Commonalities between the intellectual extremes: Giftedness and mental retardation. In F. D. Horowitz & M. O'Brien (Eds.), *The gifted and talented: Developmental perspectives*. Washington, DC: American Psychological Association.

Ziskin, J., & Faust, D. (1988). *Coping with psychiatric and psychological testimony* (3rd ed.). Marina del Rey, CA: Law and Psychology Press.

Zolik, E. S. (1958). A comparison of the Bender-Gestalt reproduction of delinquents and non-delinquents. *Journal of Clinical Psychology, 14*, 24-24.

Zolliker, A. (1943). Schwangerschaftsdepression and Rorschach'scher formdeutversuch. *Schweiz Archeives Neurologie und Psychiatri, 53*, 62-78.

Author Index

A

Abrams, E., 299, 302
Abramson, L.Y., 98
Achenbach, T.M., 38
Ackerman, P.T., 148, 157, 168
Acklin, M.W., 282
Adams, H.E., 84
Adams, R.L., 152
Adcock, C.J., 327
AERA (American Education Research Association), 15
Affleck, D.C., 309
Ahern, S., 101, 116
Ainsworth, M.D., 300
Akutagawa, D.A., 104
Albert, N., 103
Albert, S., 282
Alcock, T., 303, 311, 314
Alessi, G.J., 95, 108
Allen, R.M., 304, 309
Allison, J., 135, 137, 300, 309, 314, 317
Allport, G., 106
Alonso, R.R., 87
Alter, B., 278
Altman, H., 69
Amabile, T.M., 150
American Association of Mental Deficiencies (AAMD), 149
American Psychological Association, 15, 47, 49, 50, 54, 397
Ames, L.B., 298, 299, 300, 303, 304, 306, 308, 314, 317
Amick, J., 307
Anastasi, A., 2, 8, 30, 127, 235, 329
Anderson, S., 85
Andert, J.N., 157, 170
Andrews, D.A., 61
Appel, K.E., 391
Appelbaum, A.S., 120
Aram, D.M., 144, 145

Archer, R.P., 186, 189, 210, 280
Armbuster, G.L., 304, 310, 317
Armstrong, R.G., 170
Arnold, J.M., 307
Arnold, M.B., 321, 327, 346, 361, 363
Arrindell, W.A., 104, 105
Arvey, R.D., 61, 62
Ashton, R., 99
Asnis, L., 75
Association for Measurement and Evaluation in Guidance, 53
Atkinson, J.W., 325
Ax, A.F., 101
Azara, V., 374

B

Baade, L.E., 162, 171
Bacon, S.F., 54
Baer, J.S., 99
Bahn, A.K., 59
Bailey, W.J., 228
Baker, L.L., 2, 88, 103
Bakker, C., 106
Bakker-Rabdau, M., 106
Balla, D.A., 38
Ballinger, T., 369
Bamgbose, O., 5, 34
Bandura, A., 20, 51, 97, 99
Bannatyne, A., 124, 131, 136, 143, 148
Barber, T.X., 42
Barkly, R.A., 148
Barlow, D.H., 75
Baron, M., 75
Barona, A., 147
Barrera, S., 301
Barrett, P., 117
Barrios, B.A., 89
Barron, F., 228
Barta, S., 97

F

G

Subject Index